PLA...
FOOTBALL
ANNUAL 1997-98

50th edition

EDITOR: GLENDA ROLLIN
EXECUTIVE EDITOR: JACK ROLLIN

HEADLINE

First published in 1997
by HEADLINE BOOK PUBLISHING

10 9 8 7 6 5 4 3 2 1

Cover photograph Left: David Beckham (Manchester United); right: Alan Shearer
(Newcastle United) (*Colorsport*) .

ISBN 0 7472 5644 6

Typeset by Wearset, Boldon, Tyne and Wear

Printed and bound in Great Britain by
Clays Ltd, St Ives plc

HEADLINE BOOK PUBLISHING
A division of Hodder Headline PLC
338 Euston Road
London NW1 3BH

European and International Football

Other Football

Information and Records

CONTENTS

EDITORIAL

England remain on course to qualify for the World Cup Finals in France next year, despite the hiccup against Italy. Expectations have been high for the success of the national team following the encouraging performances in Euro '96.

The promise shown in that tournament continued in the mini-tournament in France during the summer and although England suffered defeat against Brazil, they had already won the four-team competition. In achieving this overall victory, they did manage to overcome their arch rivals Italy to give themselves a possible psychological advantage when the two teams meet again in the World Cup this autumn.

If England fail to at least reach the semi-finals next year, there seems certain to be disappointment expressed, purely as a consequence of the heightened hopes generated during the past year.

There will be those who will quickly search for excuses and an area upon which to place the blame. One which is bound to be a source of discussion lies in the influx of foreign talent during the last couple of years. Many years ago, the Italians went through a similar experience. Failure to do well in the World Cup prompted the authorities there to ban the import of foreigners.

But that was before the European Community was established. It would be almost impossible to effect a similar ban today when free movement of labour between countries in the community is one of the cornerstones of the new regime.

But the impact on English football of leading foreign players has been remarkable. Last season, the Football Writers' Association elected Italian Gianfranco Zola as the Player of the Year with Brazilian Juninho the runner-up. Zola, of course, was Italy's marksman in their win over England. Interest in League football which has been steadily increasing overall during the last decade has been enhanced by the presence of world class players from abroad.

Premier League attendances in 1996–97 totalled 10,804,762 for an average of 28,434 compared with figures of 10,469,107 and 27,558 the previous season. The Football League also reported a healthy overall increase.

Paradoxically, as the restriction on foreigners has lessened, for British clubs competing in Europe, the maximum number of foreign players in the team is controlled. This is because footballing authorities are at variance with the dictates of the European Community.

While there remains the dilemma over imports, the growth of international competition, chiefly at club level, has put enormous pressures on the well-being of professional footballers.

Fifty years ago, the England national team could expect no more than six matches in a season, including three in the Home International Tournament. At club level, it was just as relatively straightforward. There was the normal League programme and just one Cup competition, the FA Cup. Nothing in Europe and the days of entering the World Cup had not arrived for us. There was no European Championship. Yet attendances in the post-war boom were double those of the present era.

Last season, the five English teams competing in Europe were given byes to the third round of the League Cup. Attendances decreased as a result. But UEFA also want to reduce the number of clubs in the top division of each country under their jurisdiction. Only there has to be a balance between playing fewer domestic matches and increasing those in Europe.

Cutting down the number of League games might benefit top clubs with heavy commitments, but would have a harmful effect on the majority of clubs. Yet UEFA's interests may not extend beyond the clubs who enter its own competitions. Otherwise why attempt to persuade countries that a maximum of 18 clubs is desirable?

In UEFA's summer bulletin one article seems to sum up the crowded situation.

"Some professional footballer somewhere, certainly has fond memories of the time in his life when the summer sun meant a long holiday period. Today, there is not much room in the agenda for holidays at the top level of the game. . . .".

STOP PRESS

Summer transfers included the following:-

Anders Andersson, Malmo to Blackburn Rovers; Lorenzo Amoruso, Fiorentina to Rangers; Celestine Babayaro, Anderlecht to Chelsea; Patrick Blondeau, Monaco to Sheffield Wednesday; Luis Boamorte, Sporting Lisbon to Arsenal; Eyal Berkovic, Southampton to West Ham United; Vassilis Borbokis, AEK Athens to Sheffield United; Chris Byrne, Macclesfield Town to Sunderland; Ian Bryson, Preston North End to Rochdale; Thierry Bonalair, Neuchatel Xamax to Nottingham Forest; Scott Booth, Aberdeen to Borussia Dortmund; David Connolly, Watford to Feyenoord; Lee Clark, Newcastle United to Sunderland; Neil Cox, Middlesbrough to Bolton Wanderers; Julian Darby, West Bromwich Albion to Preston North End; Martin Dahlin, Roma to Blackburn Rovers; Stefan Eranio, AC Milan to Derby County; Robbie Elliott, Newcastle U to Bolton W; Craig Fleming, Oldham Athletic to Norwich City; Gareth Farrelly, Aston Villa to Everton; Gilles Grimandi, Auxerre to Arsenal; Shay Given, Blackburn Rovers to Newcastle United; Scott Green, Bolton Wanderers to Wigan Athletic; Jimmy Floyd Hasselbaink, Boavista to Leeds United; Georgi Hristov, Partizan Belgrade to Barnsley; Jonathan Hunt, Birmingham City to Derby County; Barry Hayles, Stevenage Borough to Bristol Rovers; Mark Hottiger, Everton to Lausanne; Alf-Inge Haaland, Nottingham Forest to Leeds United; Richard Hughes, Atalanta to Arsenal; Ian Hathaway, Torquay United to Colchester United; Andrew Impey, Queens Park Rangers to West Ham United; Andy Johnson, Norwich City to Nottingham Forest; Lee Jones, Liverpool to Tranmere Rovers; Juninho, Middlesbrough to Atletico Madrid; George Koch, Fortuna Dusseldorf to Rangers; Ales Krizan, Branik Maribor to Barnsley; Temuri Ketsbaia, AEK Athens to Newcastle United; Kevin Kilbane, Preston North End to West Bromwich Albion; Oyvind Leonhardsen, Wimbledon to Liverpool; Bernard Lambourde, Bordeaux to Chelsea; Kyle Lightbourne, Walsall to Coventry City; Jason Lee, Nottingham Forest to Watford; Jamie Lawrence, Leicester City to Bradford City; Jim Leighton, Hibernian to Aberdeen; Kevin Miller, Watford to Crystal Palace; Paul Moody, Oxford United to Fulham; Colin Murdoch, Manchester United to Preston North End; Jim McInally, Dundee United to Dundee; Alberto Mendez-Rodriguez, Feucht to Arsenal; Scott Minto, Chelsea to Benfica; Paul Merson, Arsenal to Middlesbrough; Marco Negri, Perugia to Rangers; Antti Niemi, FC Copenhagen to Rangers; Eric Nevland, Viking Stavanger to Manchester United; Marc Overmars, Ajax to Arsenal; Emmanuel Petit, Auxerre to Arsenal; Sergio Porrini, Juventus to Rangers; Mark Patterson, Sheffield United to Burnley; Gary Parkinson, Burnley to Preston North End; Jason Perry, Cardiff City to Bristol Rovers; Gustavo Poyet, Zaragoza to Chelsea; Alan Rogers, Tranmere Rovers to Nottingham Forest; Bruno Riberio, Vitoria Setubal to Leeds United; David Robertson, Rangers to Leeds United; Matthew Rose, Arsenal to Queens Park Rangers; Teddy Sheringham, Tottenham Hotspur to Manchester United; Staale Stensaas, Rosenborg to Rangers; Mike Sheron, Stoke City to Queens Park Rangers; Trond Egil Soltvedt, Rosenborg to Coventry City; Robert Steiner, Norrkoping to Bradford City; Dean Smith, Hereford United to Leyton Orient; Aaron Skelton, Luton Town to Colchester United; Eric Tinkler, Cagliari to Barnsley; Andy Thompson, Wolverhampton Wanderers to Tranmere Rovers; David Terrier, Metz to West Ham United; Tony Vaughan, Ipswich Town to Manchester City; Patrick Valery, Bastia to Blackburn Rovers; Gerard Welkens, Veendam to Manchester City; Darren Wassall, Derby County to Birmingham City; Edwin Zoetebier, Volendam to Sunderland.

LEAGUE REVIEW AND CLUB SECTION

Manchester United retained the Premier League title to make it four successes in the five-year history of the new competition. However, after their 6-3 defeat at Southampton on 26 October, hopes of them holding on to their crown appeared unlikely. Only six days previously, they had crashed to a 5-0 defeat at Newcastle and no team having suffered defeats in which they conceded as many as six and five goals in a season had gone on to win the Championship. And this after beating Liverpool 1-0.

United dropped to as low as seventh in mid-November, but recovered the following month after a 5-0 win over Sunderland. This was comparatively early on in a sequence of sixteen matches without defeat, ending oddly enough, in a 2-1 defeat at Sunderland.

But when they were beaten 3-2 at home by Derby County on 5 April, the chasing pack which, by this time, consisted realistically of only three teams – Arsenal, Liverpool and Newcastle with outsiders Aston Villa a remote possibility – were given fresh hope. But while their rivals continually failed to take advantage of such an opportunity, United remained unbeaten to the end of the season, even though some of their performances may not have been as convincing as previously. In fact the title was handed to them when Liverpool lost 2-1 at Wimbledon on 6 May. Justice was perhaps done because only two matches previously, United had won convincingly 3-1 at Anfield.

Manchester United used 23 players in League games with the sprightly Ole Gunnar Solskjaer finishing as leading goalscorer on 18. He was by far the most impressive of United's five foreign newcomers but yet again, the vast resources of home grown talent available at Old Trafford were underlined when David Beckham established himself in the England team and was among a host of players to represent their various countries during the season. In addition to Beckham, Nicky Butt and Paul Scholes were also given their first international caps for England as was Philip Mulryne for Northern Ireland, even though he was not one of the players called upon to appear in Premier League games! In addition to him there were seventeen full internationals appearing in United colours.

Despite finishing second, it was a largely disappointing season for Newcastle, whose manager Kevin Keegan resigned early in the New Year to be replaced by Kenny Dalglish. He was able to make some improvements in what has been in recent years a shaky defence, but certainly needs a full season in which to turn things completely round.

Another new manager was at Arsenal in Arsene Wenger. They finished third on the same points as Newcastle and Liverpool, the team below them. Here again, there were opportunities in the season to put more pressure on Manchester United but they were unable to sustain any consistent challenge. Liverpool too, uncharacteristically showed signs of defensive weaknesses which did not help their cause at all.

Of the relegated teams, Nottingham Forest had known their fate well before the end of the season and the three points deducted by the Premier League from Middlesbrough's total because of their failure to fulfil a fixture with Blackburn due to a heavy injury and illness list weighed heavily and ultimately proved to be the difference between staying up and going down.

Coventry achieved their traditional last minute escape and Southampton improved noticeably in the last month, leaving newly promoted Sunderland with the third relegation place.

The outstanding team among the four English divisions was Bolton Wanderers from Division One. Only a last minute equaliser by Tranmere prevented them from a double century of 100 goals and 100 points. They were accompanied in automatic promotion by Barnsley, while Crystal Palace, who finished sixth in the table, took the successful play-off place. Down from Division One went Grimsby Town, Oldham Athletic and Southend United to be replaced by Bury, Stockport County and Crewe Alexandra, who had also finished sixth in Division Two.

Peterborough United, Shrewsbury Town, Rotherham United and Notts County were relegated from Division Two with Wigan Athletic, Fulham, Carlisle United and Northampton Town the fourth placed team moving up.

For the first time in five years, a Football League club was relegated with Hereford United being replaced by Macclesfield Town from the Vauxhall Conference.

FA Carling Premiership

			Home				Goals		Away				Goals			
		P	W	D	L	F	A	W	D	L	F	A	GD	Pts
1	Manchester U	38	12	5	2	38	17	9	7	3	38	27	+32	75
2	Newcastle U	38	13	3	3	54	20	6	8	5	19	20	+33	68
3	Arsenal	38	10	5	4	36	18	9	4	6	26	14	+30	68
4	Liverpool	38	10	6	3	38	19	9	5	5	24	18	+25	68
5	Aston Villa	38	11	5	3	27	13	6	5	8	20	21	+13	61
6	Chelsea	38	9	8	2	33	22	7	3	9	25	33	+3	59
7	Sheffield W	38	8	10	1	25	16	6	5	8	25	35	−1	57
8	Wimbledon	38	9	6	4	28	21	6	8	8	21	25	+3	56
9	Leicester C	38	7	5	7	22	26	5	6	8	24	28	−8	47
10	Tottenham H	38	8	4	7	19	17	5	3	11	25	34	−7	46
11	Leeds U	38	7	7	5	15	13	4	6	9	13	25	−10	46
12	Derby Co	38	8	6	5	25	22	3	7	9	20	36	−13	46
13	Blackburn R	38	8	4	7	28	23	1	11	7	14	20	−1	42
14	West Ham U	38	7	6	6	27	25	3	6	10	12	23	−9	42
15	Everton	38	7	4	8	24	22	3	8	8	20	35	−13	42
16	Southampton	38	6	7	6	32	24	4	4	11	18	32	−6	41
17	Coventry C	38	4	8	7	19	23	5	6	8	19	31	−16	41
18	Sunderland	38	7	6	6	20	18	3	4	12	15	35	−18	40
19	Middlesbrough	38	8	5	6	34	25	2	7	10	17	35	−9	39*
20	Nottingham F	38	3	9	7	15	27	3	7	9	16	32	−28	34

*Middlesbrough deducted 3 points

LEADING GOALSCORERS 1996-97

FA CARLING PREMIERSHIP

	League	FA Cup	Coca-Cola Cup	Other Cups	Total
Alan Shearer *(Newcastle U)*	25	1	1		28
Ian Wright *(Arsenal)*	23	0	5	2	30
Robbie Fowler *(Liverpool)*	18	1	5	7	31
Ole Gunnar Solskjaer *(Manchester U)*	18	0	0	1	19
Dwight Yorke *(Aston Villa)*	17	2	1	0	20
Fabrizio Ravanelli *(Middlesbrough)*	16	6	9	0	31
Les Ferdinand *(Newcastle U)*	16	1	0	4	21
Mike Evans *(Southampton)*	16	3	0	0	19
(All except 4 League goals for Plymouth Arg)					
Matthew Le Tissier *(Southampton)*	13	0	3	0	16
Dion Dublin *(Coventry C)*	13	0	0	0	13
Stan Collymore *(Liverpool)*	12	2	0	2	16
Juninho *(Middlesbrough)*	12	2	1	0	15
Dennis Bergkamp *(Arsenal)*	12	1	1	0	14
Dean Sturridge *(Derby Co)*	11	2	1	0	14
Steve Claridge *(Leicester C)*	11	1	2	0	14
Eric Cantona *(Manchester U)*	11	0	0	3	14
Chris Sutton *(Blackburn R)*	11	0	1	0	12
Efan Ekoku *(Wimbledon)*	11	0	1	0	12

Nationwide Football League Division 1

			Home			Goals			Away			Goals			
		P	W	D	L	F	A	W	D	L	F	A	Gls	Pts
1	Bolton W	46	18	4	1	60	20	10	10	3	40	33	100	98
2	Barnsley	46	14	4	5	43	19	8	10	5	33	36	76	80
3	Wolverhampton W	46	10	5	8	31	24	12	5	6	37	27	68	76
4	Ipswich T	46	13	7	3	44	23	7	9	7	24	27	68	74
5	Sheffield U	46	13	5	5	46	23	7	8	8	29	29	75	73
6	Crystal Palace	46	10	7	6	39	22	9	7	7	39	26	78	71
7	Portsmouth	46	12	4	7	32	24	8	4	11	27	29	59	68
8	Port Vale	46	9	9	5	36	28	8	7	8	27	27	58	67
9	QPR	46	10	5	8	33	25	8	7	8	31	35	64	66
10	Birmingham C	46	11	7	5	30	18	6	8	9	22	30	52	66
11	Tranmere R	46	10	9	4	42	27	7	5	11	21	29	63	65
12	Stoke C	46	15	3	5	34	22	3	7	13	17	35	51	64
13	Norwich C	46	9	10	4	28	18	8	2	13	35	50	63	63
14	Manchester C	46	12	4	7	34	25	5	6	12	25	35	59	61
15	Charlton Ath	46	11	4	8	36	28	5	3	15	16	38	52	59
16	WBA	46	7	7	9	37	33	7	8	8	31	39	68	57
17	Oxford U	46	14	3	6	44	26	2	6	15	20	42	64	57
18	Reading	46	13	7	3	37	24	2	5	16	21	43	58	57
19	Swindon T	46	11	6	6	36	27	4	3	16	16	44	52	54
20	Huddersfield T	46	10	7	6	32	27	4	6	13	12	20	41	48	54
21	Bradford C	46	8	5	8	29	32	2	7	14	18	40	47	48
22	Grimsby T	46	7	7	9	31	34	4	6	13	29	47	60	46
23	Oldham Ath	46	6	8	9	30	30	4	5	14	21	36	51	43
24	Southend U	46	8	7	9	32	32	1	6	16	10	54	42	39

NATIONWIDE DIVISION 1

	League	FA Cup	Coca-Cola Cup	Other Cups	Total
John McGinlay (Bolton W)	24	1	5	0	30
Steve Bull (Wolverhampton W)	23	0	0	0	23
Trevor Morley (Reading)	22	1	0	0	23
Nathan Blake (Bolton W)	19	2	3	0	24
Mike Sheron (Stoke C)	19	0	5	0	24
Clive Mendonca (Grimsby T)	19	0	1	0	20
Nigel Jemson (Oxford U)	18	0	5	0	23
John Aldridge (Tranmere R)	18	0	2	0	20
Tony Naylor (Port Vale)	17	0	3	0	20
John Spencer (QPR)	17	1	2	0	20
(Includes 2 Coca-Cola goals for Chelsea)					
Andy Payton (Huddersfield T)	17	0	2	0	19
Nigel Pepper (Bradford C)	17	1	1	0	19
(All except 5 League goals for York C)					
Neil Redfearn (Barnsley)	17	1	1	0	19
Bruce Dyer (Crystal Palace)	17	1	0	0	18
Darren Eadie (Norwich C)	17	0	0	0	17
Paul Devlin (Birmingham C)	16	2	1	0	19

Nationwide Football League Division 2

			Home			Goals		Away			Goals			
		P	W	D	L	F	A	W	D	L	F	A	Gls	Pts
1	Bury	46	18	5	0	39	7	6	7	10	23	31	62	84
2	Stockport Co	46	15	5	3	31	14	8	8	7	28	27	59	82
3	Luton T	46	13	7	3	38	14	8	8	7	33	31	71	78
4	Brentford	46	8	11	4	26	22	12	3	8	30	21	56	74
5	Bristol C	46	14	4	5	43	18	7	6	10	26	33	69	73
6	Crewe Alex	46	15	4	4	38	15	7	3	13	18	32	56	73
7	Blackpool	46	13	7	3	41	21	5	8	10	19	26	60	69
8	Wrexham	46	11	9	3	37	28	6	9	8	17	22	54	69
9	Burnley	46	14	3	6	48	27	5	8	10	23	28	71	68
10	Chesterfield	46	10	9	4	25	18	8	5	10	17	21	42	68
11	Gillingham	46	13	3	7	37	25	6	7	10	23	34	60	67
12	Walsall	46	12	8	3	35	21	7	2	14	19	32	54	67
13	Watford	46	10	8	5	24	14	6	11	6	21	24	45	67
14	Millwall	46	12	4	7	27	22	4	9	10	23	33	50	61
15	Preston NE	46	14	5	4	33	19	4	2	17	16	36	49	61
16	Bournemouth	46	8	9	6	24	20	7	6	10	19	25	43	60
17	Bristol R	46	13	4	6	34	22	2	7	14	13	28	47	56
18	Wycombe W	46	13	4	6	31	14	2	6	15	20	42	51	55
19	Plymouth Arg	46	7	11	5	19	18	5	7	11	28	40	47	54
20	York C	46	8	6	9	27	31	5	7	11	20	37	47	52
21	Peterborough U	46	7	7	9	38	34	4	7	12	17	39	55	47
22	Shrewsbury T	46	8	6	9	27	32	3	7	13	22	42	49	46
23	Rotherham U	46	4	7	12	17	29	3	7	13	22	41	39	35
24	Notts Co	46	4	9	10	20	25	3	5	15	13	34	33	35

DIVISION 2

	League	FA Cup	Coca-Cola Cup	Other Cups	Total
Tony Thorpe (Luton T)	28	1	2	0	31
Paul Barnes (Burnley)	24	1	0	0	25
Shaun Goater (Bristol C)	23	0	1	1	25
Carl Asaba (Brentford)	23	0	0	1	24
Iffy Onuora (Gillingham)	21	1	1	0	23
Kyle Lightbourne (Walsall)	20	4	1	0	25
Philip Clarkson (Blackpool)	18	2	1	0	21
(All except 5 League goals for Scunthorpe U)					
Ian Stevens (Shrewsbury T)	17	1	0	1	19
Dele Adebola (Crewe Alex)	16	1	1	0	18
Brett Angell (Stockport Co)	15	1	3	1	20
Tony Ellis (Blackpool)	15	0	3	2	20
David Reeves (Preston NE)	14	3	1	0	18
(Includes 3 League & 1 Coca-Cola goal for Carlisle U)					
Karl Connolly (Wrexham)	14	1	0	0	15
James Quinn (Blackpool)	13	1	3	0	17
Andy Cooke (Burnley)	13	0	1	0	14
Tommy Mooney (Watford)	13	0	0	0	13

Nationwide Football League Division 3

		P	W	D	L	F	A	W	D	L	F	A	Gls	Pts
			Home			Goals		Away			Goals			
1	Wigan Ath	46	17	3	3	53	21	9	6	8	31	30	84	87
2	Fulham	46	13	5	5	41	20	12	7	4	31	18	72	87
3	Carlisle U	46	16	3	4	41	21	8	9	6	26	23	67	84
4	Northampton T	46	14	4	5	43	17	6	8	9	24	27	67	72
5	Swansea C	46	13	4	5	37	20	8	3	12	25	38	62	71
6	Chester C	46	11	8	4	30	16	7	8	8	25	27	55	70
7	Cardiff C	46	11	4	8	30	23	9	5	9	26	31	56	69
8	Colchester U	46	11	9	3	36	23	6	8	9	26	28	62	68
9	Lincoln C	46	10	8	5	35	25	8	4	11	35	44	70	66
10	Cambridge U	46	11	5	7	30	27	7	6	10	23	32	53	65
11	Mansfield T	46	9	8	6	21	17	7	8	8	26	28	47	64
12	Scarborough	46	9	9	5	36	31	7	6	10	29	37	65	63
13	Scunthorpe U	46	11	3	9	36	33	7	6	10	23	29	59	63
14	Rochdale	46	10	6	7	34	24	4	10	9	24	34	58	58
15	Barnet	46	9	6	5	32	23	5	7	11	14	28	46	58
16	Leyton Orient	46	11	6	6	28	20	4	6	13	22	38	50	57
17	Hull C	46	9	8	6	29	26	4	10	9	15	24	44	57
18	Darlington	46	11	5	7	37	28	5	1	15	27	50	64	52
19	Doncaster R	46	9	7	7	29	23	5	3	15	23	43	52	52
20	Hartlepool U	46	8	6	9	33	32	6	3	14	20	34	53	51
21	Torquay U	46	9	4	10	24	24	4	7	12	22	38	46	50
22	Exeter C	46	6	9	8	25	30	6	3	14	23	43	48	48
23	Brighton & HA	46	12	6	5	41	27	1	4	18	12	43	53	47*
24	Hereford U	46	6	8	9	26	25	5	6	12	24	40	50	47

*Brighton & HA deducted 2 points
In the Nationwide Football League, goals scored determine League positions where clubs are level on points. If teams still cannot be separated, the team that has conceded fewer goals is placed higher.

DIVISION 3

	League	FA Cup	Coca-Cola Cup	Other Cups	Total
Graeme Jones (Wigan Ath)	31	0	1	1	33
Gareth Ainsworth (Lincoln C)	22	0	2	0	24
Mike Conroy (Fulham)	21	0	2	0	23
Colin Cramb (Doncaster R)	18	1	1	1	21
Phil Stant (Lincoln C)	18	0	0	0	18
(Includes 1 League goal for Bury, 2 for Northampton T)					
Darren Roberts (Darlington)	16	0	2	0	18
Adrian Foster (Hereford U)	16	0	1	0	17
Paul Baker (Hartlepool U)	15	5	3	0	23
(Includes 4 League, 3 Coca-Cola goals for Torquay U; 9 League & 5 FA Cup for Scunthorpe U)					
Craig Maskell (Brighton & HA)	14	1	0	1	16
Scott McGleish (Leyton Orient)	14	0	0	0	14
(Includes 7 League goals for Cambridge U)					
Duane Darby (Hull C)	13	6	0	1	20
Steve White (Cardiff C)	13	1	0	0	14
Ian Baird (Brighton & HA)	13	0	0	0	13
David Penney (Swansea C)	13	0	0	0	13
Andy Milner (Chester C)	12	2	0	0	14
Neil Grayson (Northampton T)	12	0	0	0	12

FA CARLING PREMIERSHIP

HOME TEAM	Arsenal	Aston Villa	Blackburn Rovers	Chelsea	Coventry City	Derby County	Everton	Leeds United	Leicester City	Liverpool
Arsenal	—	2-2	1-1	3-3	0-0	2-2	3-1	3-0	2-0	1-2
Aston Villa	2-2	—	1-0	0-2	2-1	2-0	3-1	2-0	1-3	1-0
Blackburn Rovers	0-2	0-2	—	1-1	4-0	1-2	1-1	0-1	2-4	3-0
Chelsea	0-3	1-1	1-1	—	2-0	3-1	2-2	0-0	2-1	1-0
Coventry City	1-1	1-2	0-0	3-1	—	1-2	0-0	2-1	0-0	0-1
Derby County	1-3	2-1	0-0	3-2	2-1	—	0-1	3-3	2-0	0-1
Everton	0-1	0-1	0-2	1-2	1-1	1-0	—	0-0	1-1	1-1
Leeds United	0-0	0-0	0-0	2-0	1-3	0-0	1-0	—	3-0	0-2
Leicester City	0-2	1-0	1-1	1-3	0-2	4-2	1-2	1-0	—	0-3
Liverpool	2-0	3-0	0-0	5-1	1-2	2-1	1-1	4-0	1-1	—
Manchester United	1-0	0-0	3-1	1-2	3-1	2-3	2-2	1-0	3-1	1-0
Middlesbrough	0-2	3-2	2-1	1-0	4-0	6-1	4-2	0-0	0-2	3-3
Newcastle United	1-2	4-3	2-1	3-1	4-0	3-1	4-1	3-0	4-3	1-1
Nottingham Forest	2-1	0-0	2-2	2-0	0-1	1-1	0-1	1-1	0-0	1-1
Sheffield Wednesday	0-0	2-1	1-1	0-2	0-0	0-0	2-1	2-2	2-1	1-1
Southampton	0-2	0-1	2-0	0-0	2-2	3-1	2-2	0-2	2-2	0-1
Sunderland	1-0	1-0	0-0	3-0	1-0	2-0	3-0	0-1	0-0	1-2
Tottenham Hotspur	0-0	1-0	2-1	1-2	1-2	1-1	0-0	1-1	1-2	0-2
West Ham United	1-2	0-2	2-1	3-2	1-1	1-1	2-2	0-2	1-0	1-2
Wimbledon	2-2	0-2	1-0	0-1	2-2	1-1	4-0	2-0	1-3	2-0

1996–97 RESULTS

	Manchester United	Middlesbrough	Newcastle United	Nottingham Forest	Sheffield Wednesday	Southampton	Sunderland	Tottenham Hotspur	West Ham United	Wimbledon
	1-2	2-0	0-1	2-0	4-1	3-1	2-0	3-1	2-0	0-1
	0-0	1-0	2-2	2-0	0-1	1-0	1-0	1-1	0-0	5-0
	2-3	0-0	1-0	1-1	4-1	2-1	1-0	0-2	2-1	3-1
	1-1	1-0	1-1	1-1	2-2	1-0	6-2	3-1	3-1	2-4
	0-2	3-0	2-1	0-3	0-0	1-1	2-2	1-2	1-3	1-1
	1-1	2-1	0-1	0-0	2-2	1-1	1-0	4-2	1-0	0-2
	0-2	1-2	2-0	2-0	2-0	7-1	1-3	1-0	2-1	1-3
	0-4	1-1	0-1	2-0	0-2	0-0	3-0	0-0	1-0	1-0
	2-2	1-3	2-0	2-2	1-0	2-1	1-1	1-1	0-1	1-0
	1-3	5-1	4-3	4-2	0-1	2-1	0-0	2-1	0-0	1-1
	—	3-3	0-0	4-1	2-0	2-1	5-0	2-0	2-0	2-1
	2-2	—	0-1	1-1	4-2	0-1	0-1	0-3	4-1	0-0
	5-0	3-1	—	5-0	1-2	0-1	1-1	7-1	1-1	2-0
	0-4	1-1	0-0	—	0-3	1-3	1-4	2-1	0-2	1-1
	1-1	3-1	1-1	2-0	—	1-1	2-1	2-1	0-0	3-1
	6-3	4-0	2-2	2-2	2-3	—	3-0	0-1	2-0	0-0
	2-1	2-2	1-2	1-1	1-1	0-1	—	0-4	0-0	1-3
	1-2	1-0	1-2	0-1	1-1	3-1	2-0	—	1-0	1-0
	2-2	0-0	0-0	0-1	5-1	2-1	2-0	4-3	—	0-2
	0-3	1-1	1-1	1-0	4-2	3-1	1-0	1-0	1-1	—

NATIONWIDE FOOTBALL LEAGUE

HOME TEAM	Barnsley	Birmingham City	Bolton Wanderers	Bradford City	Charlton Athletic	Crystal Palace	Grimsby Town	Huddersfield Town	Ipswich Town	Manchester City
Barnsley	—	0-1	2-2	2-0	4-0	0-0	1-3	3-1	1-2	2-0
Birmingham City	0-0	—	3-1	3-0	0-0	1-0	0-0	1-0	1-0	2-0
Bolton Wanderers	2-2	2-1	—	2-1	4-1	2-2	6-1	2-0	1-2	1-0
Bradford City	2-2	0-2	2-4	—	1-0	0-4	3-4	1-1	2-1	1-3
Charlton Athletic	2-2	2-1	3-3	0-2	—	2-1	1-3	2-1	1-1	1-1
Crystal Palace	1-1	0-1	1-1	3-1	1-0	—	3-0	1-1	0-0	3-1
Grimsby Town	2-3	1-2	1-2	1-1	2-0	2-1	—	2-2	2-1	1-1
Huddersfield Town	0-0	3-0	1-2	3-3	2-0	1-1	2-0	—	2-0	1-1
Ipswich Town	1-1	1-1	0-1	3-2	2-1	3-1	1-1	1-3	—	1-0
Manchester City	1-2	1-0	1-2	3-2	2-1	1-1	3-1	0-0	1-0	—
Norwich City	1-1	0-1	0-1	2-0	1-2	1-1	2-1	2-0	3-1	0-0
Oldham Athletic	0-1	2-2	0-0	1-2	1-1	0-1	0-3	1-2	3-3	2-1
Oxford United	5-1	0-0	0-0	2-0	0-2	1-4	3-2	1-0	3-1	1-4
Port Vale	1-3	3-0	1-1	1-1	2-0	0-2	1-1	0-0	2-2	0-2
Portsmouth	4-2	1-1	0-3	3-1	2-0	2-2	1-0	3-1	0-1	2-1
Queens Park Rangers	3-1	1-1	1-2	1-0	1-2	0-1	3-0	2-0	0-1	2-2
Reading	1-2	0-0	3-2	0-0	2-2	1-6	1-1	4-1	1-0	2-0
Sheffield United	0-1	4-4	1-1	3-0	3-0	3-0	3-1	3-1	1-3	2-0
Southend United	1-2	1-1	5-2	1-1	0-2	2-1	1-0	1-2	0-0	2-3
Stoke City	1-0	1-0	1-2	1-0	1-0	2-2	3-1	3-2	0-1	2-1
Swindon Town	3-0	3-1	2-2	1-1	1-0	0-2	3-3	6-0	0-4	2-0
Tranmere Rovers	1-1	1-0	2-2	3-0	4-0	1-3	3-2	1-1	3-0	1-1
West Bromwich Albion	1-2	2-0	2-2	0-0	1-2	1-0	2-0	1-1	0-0	1-3
Wolverhampton Wanderers	3-3	1-2	1-2	1-0	1-0	0-3	1-1	0-0	0-0	3-0

DIVISION 1 1996–97 RESULTS

	Norwich City	Oldham Athletic	Oxford United	Port Vale	Portsmouth	Queens Park Rangers	Reading	Sheffield United	Southend United	Stoke City	Swindon Town	Tranmere Rovers	West Bromwich Albion	Wolverhampton Wanderers
	3-1	2-0	0-0	1-0	3-2	1-3	3-0	2-0	3-0	3-0	1-1	3-0	2-0	1-3
	2-3	0-0	2-0	1-2	0-3	0-0	4-1	1-1	2-1	3-1	1-0	0-0	2-3	1-2
	3-1	3-1	4-0	4-2	2-0	2-1	2-1	2-2	3-1	1-1	7-0	1-0	1-0	3-0
	0-2	0-3	2-0	1-0	3-1	3-0	0-0	1-2	0-0	1-0	2-1	1-0	1-1	2-1
	4-4	1-0	2-0	1-3	2-1	2-1	1-0	0-0	2-0	1-2	2-0	3-1	1-1	0-0
	2-0	3-1	2-2	1-1	1-2	3-0	3-2	0-1	6-1	2-0	1-2	0-1	0-0	2-3
	1-4	0-3	0-2	1-1	0-1	2-0	2-0	2-4	4-0	1-1	2-1	0-0	1-1	1-3
	2-0	3-2	1-0	0-1	1-3	1-2	1-0	2-1	0-0	2-1	0-0	0-1	0-0	0-2
	2-0	4-0	2-1	2-1	1-1	2-0	5-2	3-1	1-1	1-1	3-2	0-2	5-0	0-1
	2-1	1-0	2-3	0-1	1-1	0-3	3-2	0-0	3-0	2-0	3-0	1-2	3-2	0-1
	—	2-0	1-1	1-1	1-0	1-1	1-1	1-1	0-0	2-0	2-0	1-1	2-4	1-3
	3-0	—	2-1	3-0	0-0	0-2	1-1	0-2	0-0	1-2	5-1	1-1	1-1	3-2
	0-1	3-1	—	0-2	2-0	2-3	2-1	4-1	5-0	4-1	2-0	2-1	1-0	1-1
	6-1	3-2	2-0	—	0-2	4-4	1-0	0-0	2-1	1-1	1-0	2-1	2-2	1-2
	0-1	1-0	2-1	1-1	—	1-2	1-0	1-1	1-0	1-0	0-1	1-3	4-0	0-1
	3-2	0-1	2-1	1-2	2-1	—	0-2	1-0	4-0	1-1	1-1	2-0	0-2	2-2
	2-1	2-0	2-0	0-1	0-0	2-1	—	1-0	3-2	2-2	2-0	2-0	2-2	2-1
	2-3	2-2	3-1	3-0	1-0	1-1	2-0	—	3-0	1-0	2-0	0-0	1-2	2-3
	1-1	1-1	2-2	0-0	2-1	0-1	2-1	3-2	—	2-1	1-3	1-1	2-3	1-1
	1-2	2-1	2-1	2-0	3-1	0-0	1-1	0-4	1-2	—	2-0	2-0	2-1	1-0
	0-3	1-0	1-0	1-1	0-1	1-1	3-1	2-1	0-0	1-0	—	2-1	2-3	1-2
	3-1	1-1	0-0	2-0	4-3	2-3	2-2	1-1	3-0	0-0	2-1	—	2-3	0-2
	5-1	1-1	3-3	1-1	0-2	4-1	3-2	1-2	4-0	0-2	1-2	1-2	—	2-4
	3-2	0-1	3-1	0-1	0-1	1-1	0-1	1-2	4-1	2-0	1-0	3-2	2-0	—

NATIONWIDE FOOTBALL LEAGUE

HOME TEAM	Blackpool	Bournemouth	Brentford	Bristol City	Bristol Rovers	Burnley	Bury	Chesterfield	Crewe Alexandra	Gillingham
Blackpool	—	1-1	1-0	1-0	3-2	1-3	2-0	0-1	1-2	2-0
Bournemouth	0-0	—	2-1	0-2	1-0	0-0	1-1	3-0	0-1	2-2
Brentford	1-1	1-0	—	0-0	0-0	0-3	0-2	1-0	0-2	2-0
Bristol City	0-1	0-1	1-2	—	1-1	2-1	1-0	2-0	3-0	0-1
Bristol Rovers	0-0	3-2	2-1	1-2	—	1-2	4-3	2-0	2-0	0-0
Burnley	2-0	1-0	1-2	2-3	2-2	—	3-1	0-0	2-0	5-1
Bury	1-0	2-1	1-1	4-0	2-1	1-0	—	1-0	1-0	3-0
Chesterfield	0-0	1-1	0-2	1-1	1-0	0-0	1-2	—	1-0	2-2
Crewe Alexandra	3-2	2-0	2-0	1-2	1-0	1-1	2-0	1-2	—	3-2
Gillingham	2-3	1-1	1-2	3-2	1-0	1-0	2-2	0-1	2-1	—
Luton Town	1-0	2-0	1-0	2-2	2-1	1-2	0-0	0-1	6-0	2-1
Millwall	2-1	0-1	0-0	0-2	2-0	2-1	1-0	2-1	2-0	0-2
Notts County	1-1	0-2	1-1	2-0	1-1	1-1	0-1	0-0	0-1	1-1
Peterborough United	0-0	3-1	0-1	3-1	1-2	3-2	1-2	1-1	2-2	0-1
Plymouth Argyle	0-1	0-0	1-4	0-0	0-1	0-0	2-0	0-3	1-0	2-0
Preston North End	3-0	0-1	1-0	0-2	0-0	1-1	3-1	0-1	2-1	1-0
Rotherham United	1-2	1-0	0-1	1-0		1-0	1-1	1-4	1-2	
Shrewsbury Town	1-3	1-1	0-3	1-0	2-0	2-1	1-1	2-0	0-1	1-2
Stockport County	1-0	0-1	1-2	1-1	1-0	1-0	2-1	1-0	1-0	2-1
Walsall	1-1	2-1	1-0	2-0	1-0	1-3	3-1	1-1	1-0	1-0
Watford	2-2	0-1	2-0	3-0	1-0	2-2	0-0	0-2	0-1	0-0
Wrexham	2-1	2-0	0-2	2-1	1-0	0-0	1-1	3-2	1-1	1-1
Wycombe Wanderers	1-0	1-1	0-1	2-0	2-0	5-0	0-1	1-0	2-0	1-1
York City	1-0	1-2	2-4	0-3	2-2	1-0	0-2	0-0	1-1	2-3

DIVISION 2 1996–97 RESULTS

Luton Town	Millwall	Notts County	Peterborough United	Plymouth Argyle	Preston North End	Rotherham United	Shrewsbury Town	Stockport County	Walsall	Watford	Wrexham	Wycombe Wanderers	York City
0-0	3-0	1-0	5-1	2-2	2-1	4-1	1-1	2-1	2-1	1-1	3-3	0-0	3-0
3-2	1-1	0-1	1-2	1-0	2-0	1-1	0-0	0-0	0-1	1-2	2-1	2-1	1-1
3-2	0-0	2-0	0-1	3-2	0-0	4-2	0-0	2-2	1-1	1-1	2-0	0-0	3-3
5-0	1-1	4-0	2-0	3-1	2-1	0-2	3-2	1-1	4-1	1-1	2-1	3-0	2-0
3-2	1-0	1-0	1-0	2-0	1-0	1-2	2-0	1-1	0-1	0-1	2-0	3-4	1-1
0-2	1-0	1-0	5-0	2-1	1-2	3-3	1-3	5-2	2-1	4-1	2-0	2-1	1-2
0-0	2-0	2-0	1-0	1-0	3-0	3-1	2-0	0-0	2-1	1-1	0-0	2-0	4-1
1-1	1-0	1-0	2-1	1-2	2-1	1-1	2-1	0-1	1-0	0-0	0-0	4-2	2-0
0-0	0-0	3-0	1-1	3-0	1-0	1-0	5-1	1-0	1-0	0-2	3-1	3-0	0-1
1-2	2-3	1-0	2-1	4-1	1-1	3-1	2-0	1-0	2-0	3-1	1-2	1-0	0-1
—	0-2	2-0	3-0	2-2	5-1	1-0	2-0	1-1	3-1	0-0	0-0	0-0	2-0
0-1	—	1-0	0-2	0-0	3-2	2-0	2-1	3-4	1-0	0-1	1-1	2-1	1-1
1-2	1-2	—	0-0	2-1	2-1	0-0	1-2	1-2	2-0	2-3	0-0	1-2	0-1
0-1	3-3	1-3	—	0-0	2-0	6-2	2-2	0-2	0-1	2-1	0-1	6-3	2-2
3-3	0-0	0-0	1-1	—	2-1	1-0	2-2	0-0	0-0	0-0	0-0	0-0	2-1
3-2	2-1	2-0	3-4	1-1	—	0-0	2-1	1-0	2-0	1-1	2-1	2-1	1-0
0-3	0-0	2-2	2-0	1-2	0-1	—	1-2	0-1	1-2	0-0	0-0	2-1	0-2
0-3	1-1	2-1	2-2	2-3	0-2	0-2	—	3-2	2-2	1-0	0-1	1-1	2-0
1-1	5-1	0-0	0-0	3-1	1-0	0-0	3-1	—	2-0	1-0	0-2	2-1	2-1
3-2	2-1	3-1	4-0	0-1	1-0	1-1	2-2	1-1	—	1-1	0-1	2-2	1-1
1-1	0-2	0-0	0-0	0-2	1-0	2-0	2-0	1-0	1-0	—	1-1	1-0	4-0
2-1	3-3	3-3	1-1	4-4	1-0	1-0	2-1	2-3	1-2	3-1	—	1-0	0-0
0-1	1-0	1-0	2-0	2-1	0-1	4-2	3-0	0-2	0-2	0-0	0-0	—	3-1
1-1	3-2	1-2	0-1	1-1	3-1	2-1	0-0	1-2	0-2	1-2	1-0	2-0	—

NATIONWIDE FOOTBALL LEAGUE

HOME TEAM	Barnet	Brighton & Hove Albion	Cambridge United	Cardiff City	Carlisle United	Chester City	Colchester United	Darlington	Doncaster Rovers	Exeter City
Barnet	—	3-0	2-1	3-1	0-0	1-2	2-4	0-0	3-0	3-0
Brighton & Hove Albion	1-0	—	1-2	2-0	1-3	2-1	1-1	2-3	1-0	1-0
Cambridge United	1-0	1-1	—	0-2	1-3	2-2	1-0	5-2	0-1	3-2
Cardiff City	1-2	1-0	0-0	—	2-0	1-0	1-2	2-0	0-2	2-1
Carlisle United	2-1	2-1	3-0	0-2	—	3-1	3-0	1-0	0-0	2-0
Chester City	1-0	2-1	1-1	0-1	1-1	—	1-2	2-1	6-0	2-1
Colchester United	1-0	2-0	2-2	1-1	1-1	0-0	—	0-3	2-2	1-0
Darlington	0-1	2-0	2-0	2-1	2-1	1-1	1-1	—	0-3	0-1
Doncaster Rovers	1-1	3-0	2-1	3-3	0-1	0-1	0-0	3-2	—	1-2
Exeter City	1-1	2-1	0-1	2-0	2-1	1-5	0-3	3-2	1-1	—
Fulham	2-0	2-0	3-0	1-4	1-0	1-1	3-1	6-0	3-1	1-1
Hartlepool United	4-0	2-3	0-2	2-3	1-2	2-0	1-0	1-2	2-4	1-1
Hereford United	1-1	1-1	0-1	1-1	2-3	1-2	1-0	1-1	1-0	1-2
Hull City	0-0	3-0	1-3	1-1	0-1	1-0	1-2	3-2	3-1	2-0
Leyton Orient	0-1	2-0	1-1	3-0	2-1	0-0	1-1	0-0	2-1	1-1
Lincoln City	1-0	2-1	1-1	2-0	1-1	0-0	3-2	2-0	3-2	2-3
Mansfield Town	0-0	1-1	1-0	1-3	0-0	0-2	1-1	2-1	2-0	0-1
Northampton Town	2-0	3-0	1-2	4-0	1-1	5-1	2-1	3-1	2-0	4-1
Rochdale	1-1	3-0	3-0	1-0	2-2	0-1	0-0	2-0	2-1	2-0
Scarborough	1-1	1-1	1-0	0-0	1-1	0-0	1-1	4-1	2-1	3-4
Scunthorpe United	1-2	1-0	3-2	0-1	0-0	0-2	2-1	3-2	1-2	4-1
Swansea City	3-0	1-0	3-1	0-1	0-1	2-1	1-1	1-1	2-0	3-1
Torquay United	1-2	2-1	0-1	2-0	1-2	0-0	0-2	1-1	1-0	2-0
Wigan Athletic	2-0	1-0	1-1	0-1	1-0	4-2	1-0	3-2	4-1	2-0

DIVISION 3 1996–97 RESULTS

Fulham	Hartlepool United	Hereford United	Hull City	Leyton Orient	Lincoln City	Mansfield Town	Northampton Town	Rochdale	Scarborough	Scunthorpe United	Swansea City	Torquay United	Wigan Athletic
2-2	1-0	2-3	1-0	0-0	1-0	1-1	1-1	3-2	1-3	1-1	0-1	0-0	1-1
0-0	5-0	0-1	3-0	4-4	1-3	1-1	2-1	3-0	3-2	1-1	3-2	2-2	1-0
0-1	1-0	0-1	1-0	2-0	1-3	2-1	0-0	2-2	2-1	0-2	2-1	2-1	1-1
1-2	2-0	2-0	2-0	0-0	1-3	1-2	2-2	2-1	1-1	0-0	1-3	2-0	0-2
1-2	1-0	2-3	0-0	1-0	1-0	1-1	2-1	3-2	1-0	3-2	4-1	5-1	0-3
1-1	0-0	1-3	0-0	0-1	4-1	1-0	2-1	0-0	1-0	1-0	2-0	0-0	1-1
2-1	0-2	1-1	1-1	2-1	7-1	1-0	1-0	1-5	1-3	1-1	3-1	2-0	3-1
0-2	1-2	1-0	1-0	1-1	5-2	2-4	3-1	1-1	1-1	2-0	4-1	2-3	3-1
0-0	2-1	1-0	0-0	2-1	1-3	0-0	1-2	3-0	1-2	1-1	0-1	2-1	2-0
0-1	2-0	1-1	0-0	3-2	3-3	0-0	0-1	0-0	2-2	0-1	1-2	1-1	0-1
—	1-0	1-0	2-0	1-1	1-2	1-2	0-1	1-1	4-0	2-1	2-1	1-2	1-1
2-1	—	2-1	1-1	3-1	2-1	2-2	0-2	1-2	1-0	0-1	1-1	1-1	1-1
0-0	0-1	—	0-1	2-0	1-1	1-1	1-2	3-0	2-2	3-2	0-1	1-1	3-1
0-3	1-0	1-1	—	3-1	2-1	1-1	1-1	1-0	0-2	0-2	1-1	2-0	1-1
0-2	2-0	2-1	1-1	—	2-3	2-1	2-1	2-1	0-1	0-1	1-0	1-0	1-2
2-0	2-1	3-3	0-1	1-1	—	0-0	1-1	0-2	1-1	2-0	4-0	1-2	1-3
0-0	1-0	3-1	1-0	2-2	1-1	—	1-1	1-0	2-0	0-0	1-2	2-0	0-1
0-1	3-0	1-0	2-1	0-1	1-1	3-0	—	2-2	1-0	1-0	1-2	1-1	0-1
1-2	1-3	0-0	1-2	1-0	2-0	0-1	1-1	—	3-3	1-2	2-3	2-1	3-1
0-2	2-4	1-1	3-2	2-1	0-2	2-1	1-1	2-2	—	3-2	0-1	3-1	3-1
1-4	2-1	5-1	2-2	1-2	2-0	0-2	2-1	2-2	0-2	—	1-0	1-0	2-3
1-2	2-2	4-0	0-0	1-0	1-2	3-2	1-0	2-1	1-2	1-1	—	2-0	2-1
3-1	0-1	2-1	1-1	0-0	2-1	1-2	1-2	0-1	1-0	1-2	2-0	—	0-3
1-1	2-2	4-1	1-2	5-1	1-0	2-0	2-1	0-1	7-1	3-0	3-2	3-2	—

Player	Ht	Wt	Birthplace	D.O.B.	Source
Adams Tony (D)	6 3	13 11	London	10 10 66	Apprentice
Anelka Nicolas (F)	6 0	12 00	Versailles	14 3 79	Paris St Germain.
Bartram Vince (G)	6 2	13 07	Birmingham	7 8 68	Bournemouth
Bergkamp Dennis (F)	6 0	12 05	Amsterdam	18 5 69	Internazionale
Black Michael (M)	5 8	11 08	Chigwell	6 10 76	Trainee
Bould Steve (D)	6 4	14 02	Stoke	16 11 62	Stoke C
Crowe Jason (M)	5 9	10 09	Sidcup	30 9 78	Trainee
Dixon Lee (D)	5 8	11 08	Manchester	17 3 64	Stoke C
Garde Remi (M)	5 9	11 07	L'Arbresle	3 4 66	Strasbourg
Gislason Valur (M)	6 1	11 12	Reykjavik	8 9 77	Fram
Harper Lee (G)	6 1	13 11	London	30 10 71	Sittingbourne
Helder Glenn (F)	5 11	11 07	Leiden	28 10 68	Vitesse
Hughes Stephen (M)	6 0	12 08	Wokingham	18 9 76	Trainee
Keown Martin (D)	6 1	12 04	Oxford	24 7 66	Everton
Kiwomya Chris (F)	5 9	10 07	Huddersfield	2 12 69	Ipswich T
Lukic John (G)	6 4	13 07	Chesterfield	11 12 60	Leeds U
Macdonald James (M)	6 0	12 05	Inverness	21 2 79	Trainee
Marshall Scott (D)	6 1	12 05	Edinburgh	1 5 73	Trainee
McGowan Gavin (M)	5 8	11 07	Blackheath	16 1 76	Trainee
Merson Paul (F)	6 0	13 02	London	20 3 68	Apprentice
Parlour Ray (M)	5 10	11 12	Romford	7 3 73	Trainee
Platt David (M)	5 10	11 12	Chadderton	10 6 66	Sampdoria
Rankin Isiah (F)	5 10	11 00	London	22 5 78	Trainee
Seaman David (G)	6 4	14 10	Rotherham	19 9 63	QPR
Selley Ian (M)	5 9	10 01	Chertsey	14 6 74	Trainee
Shaw Paul (F)	5 11	12 02	Burnham	4 9 73	Trainee
Taylor Ross (D)	5 10	11 12	Southend	14 1 77	Trainee
Upson Matthew (D)	6 1	11 05	Eye	18 4 79	Luton T
Vieira Patrick (M)	6 4	13 00	Dakar	23 6 76	AC Milan
Wicks Matthew (D)	6 2	13 05	Reading	8 9 78	Manchester U
Winterburn Nigel (D)	5 8	11 04	Coventry	11 12 63	Wimbledon
Wright Ian (F)	5 9	11 08	Woolwich	3 11 63	Crystal Palace

League Appearances: Adams, T. 27(1); Anelka, N. (4); Bergkamp, D. 28(1); Bould, S. 33; Dickov, P. (1); Dixon, L. 31(1); Garde, R. 7(4); Harper, L. 1; Hartson, J. 14(5); Helder, G. (2); Hillier, D. (2); Hughes, S. 9(5); Keown, M. 33; Linighan, A. 10(1); Lukic, J. 15; Marshall, S. 6(2); McGowan, G. 1; Merson, P. 32; Morrow, S. 5(9); Parlour, R. 17(13); Platt, D. 27(1); Rose, M. 1; Seaman, D. 22; Selley, I. (1); Shaw, P. 1(7); Vieira, P. 30(1); Winterburn, N. 38; Wright, I. 30(5)

League (62): Wright 23 (4 pens), Bergkamp 12 (3 pens), Merson 6, Platt 4, Adams 3, Hartson 3, Dixon 2, Parlour 2, Shaw 2, Vieira 2, Hughes 1, Keown 1, Linighan 1.

Coca-Cola Cup (8): Wright 5 (3 pens), Bergkamp 1, Merson 1, Platt 1.

FA Cup (3): Bergkamp 1, Hartson 1, Hughes 1.

Ground: Arsenal Stadium, Highbury, London N5 1BU. Telephone (0171) 704 4000.

Record attendance: 73,295 v Sunderland, Div 1, 9 March 1935. **Capacity:** 38,500.

Manager: Arsène Wenger.

Secretary: K. J. Friar.

Honours – Football League: Division 1 Champions – 1930–31, 1932–33, 1933–34, 1934–35, 1937–38, 1947–48, 1952–53, 1970–71, 1988–89, 1990–91. **FA Cup winners** 1929–30, 1935–36, 1949–50, 1970–71, 1978–79, 1992–93. **Football League Cup winners** 1986–87, 1992–93. **European Competitions: European Cup-Winners' Cup winners:** 1993–94. **Fairs Cup winners:** 1969–70.

Colours: Red shirts with white sleeves, white shorts, red and white stockings.

ASTON VILLA   FA PREMIERSHIP

Bosnich Mark (G)	6 1	14 07	Fairfield	13 1 72	Manchester U
Byfield Darren (F)	5 11	11 11	Birmingham	29 9 76	Trainee
Charles Gary (D)	5 9	11 03	London	13 4 70	Derby Co
Collins Lee (D)	6 1	12 06	Birmingham	10 9 77	Trainee
Collymore Stan (F)	6 3	14 10	Stone	22 1 71	Liverpool
Curcic Sasa (M)	5 9	11 00	Belgrade	14 2 72	Bolton W
Davis Neil (F)	5 10	11 07	Bloxwich	15 8 73	Redditch U
Draper Mark (F)	5 10	12 04	Long Eaton	11 11 70	Leicester C
Ehiogu Ugo (D)	6 2	14 10	London	3 11 72	WBA
Farrelly Gareth (M)	6 0	12 13	Dublin	28 8 75	Home Farm
Hazell Reuben (M)			Birmingham	24 4 79	Trainee
Hendrie Lee (F)	5 10	10 02	Birmingham	18 5 77	Trainee
Hines Leslie (M)	5 7	9 10	Germany	7 1 77	Trainee
Hughes David (D)	6 4	13 06	Wrexham	1 2 78	Trainee
Jaszczun Tommy (D)	5 10	10 10	Kettering	16 9 77	Trainee
Joachim Julian (F)	5 6	12 00	Peterborough	20 9 74	Leicester C
Kirby Alan (M)	5 7	10 06	Waterford	8 9 77	Trainee
Lee Alan (F)	6 2	13 09	Galway	21 8 78	Trainee
Lescott Aaron (M)	5 8	10 09	Birmingham	1 12 78	Trainee
Middleton Darren (F)	6 0	11 05	Lichfield	28 12 78	Trainee
Milosevic Savo (F)	6 1	13 08	Bijelina	2 9 73	Partizan Belgrade
Murray Scott (F)	5 9	10 12	Aberdeen	26 5 74	Fraserburgh
Nelson Fernando (D)	5 11	11 08	Lisbon	5 11 71	Sporting
Oakes Michael (G)	6 2	14 07	Northwich	30 10 73	Trainee
Petty Ben (M)	6 0	12 05	Solihull	22 3 77	Trainee
Rachel Adam (G)	5 11	12 08	Birmingham	10 12 76	Trainee
Scimeca Riccardo (D)	6 1	13 03	Leamington Spa	13 6 75	Trainee
Southgate Gareth (M)	6 0	12 03	Watford	3 9 70	Crystal Palace
Staunton Steve (D)	6 1	12 11	Drogheda	19 1 69	Liverpool
Taylor Ian (M)	6 1	12 00	Birmingham	4 6 68	Sheffield W
Townsend Andy (M)	5 11	13 06	Maidstone	27 7 63	Chelsea
Walker Richard (F)	6 0	12 00	Birmingham	8 11 77	Trainee
Wright Alan (D)	5 4	9 09	Ashton under Lyme	28 9 71	Blackburn R
Yorke Dwight (F)	5 10	12 03	Tobago	3 11 71	St Clair's

League Appearances: Bosnich, M. 20; Curcic, S. 17(5); Draper, M. 28(1); Ehiogu, U. 38; Farrelly, G. 1(2); Hendrie, L. (4); Hughes, D. 4(3); Joachim, J. 3(12); Johnson, T. 10(10); Milosevic, S. 29(1); Murray, S. Nelson, F. 33(1); Oakes, M. 18(2); Scimeca, R. 11(6); Southgate, G. 28; Staunton, S. 30; Taylor, I. 29(5); Tiler, C. 9(2); Townsend, A. 34; Wright, A. 38; Yorke, D. 37
League (47): Yorke 17 (1 pen), Milosevic 9, Johnson 4 (1 pen), Ehiogu 3, Joachim 3, Staunton 2, Taylor 2, Townsend 2, Southgate 1, Tiler 1, Wright 1, own goals 2.
Coca-Cola Cup (2): Taylor 1, Yorke 1 (pen).
FA Cup (4): Yorke 2, Curcic 1, Ehiogu 1.
Ground: Villa Park, Trinity Rd, Birmingham B6 6HE. Telephone (0121) 327 2299.
Record attendance: 76,588 v Derby Co, FA Cup 6th rd, 2 March 1946.
Capacity: 39,339.
Manager: Brian Little.
Secretary: Steven Stride.
Honours – Football League: Division 1 Champions – 1893–94, 1895–96, 1896–97, 1898–99, 1899–1900, 1909–10, 1980–81. Division 2 Champions – 1937–38, 1959–60. Division 3 Champions – 1971–72. **FA Cup:** Winners 1887, 1895, 1897, 1905, 1913, 1920, 1957. **Football League Cup:** Winners 1961, 1975, 1977, 1994, 1996. **European Competitions: European Cup winners:** 1981–82, **European Super Cup winners:** 1982–83.
Colours: Claret and blue shirts, white shorts, claret and blue hooped stockings.

Adams Kieran (M)	5 11	11 03	St Ives	20 10 77	Trainee
Brady Matthew (M)	5 11	11 01	London	27 10 77	Trainee
Campbell Jamie (M)	·6 2	13 00	Birmingham	21 10 72	Luton T
Devine Sean (F)	6 0	13 08	Lewisham	6 9 72	Omonia
Ford John (D)	6 0	12 12	Birmingham	12 4 68	Gillingham
Gale Shaun (D)	6 1	12 02	Reading	8 10 69	Portsmouth
Goodhind Warren (D)	5 11	11 02	Johannesburg	16 8 77	Trainee
Hardyman Paul (D)	5 7	12 03	Portsmouth	11 3 64	Wycombe W
Harrison Lee (G)	6 2	12 08	Billericay	12 9 71	Fulham
Hodges Lee (F)	6 0	12 00	Epping	4 9 73	Tottenham H
Howarth Lee (D)	6 3	13 09	Bolton	3 1 68	Mansfield T
McDonald David (D)	5 10	12 11	Dublin	2 1 71	Peterborough U
Mills Danny (M)	5 11	11 07	Sidcup	13 2 75	Charlton Ath
Primus Linvoy (D)	6 0	13 07	Stratford	14 9 73	Charlton Ath
Rattray Kevin (M)	5 11	11 02	London	6 10 68	Gillingham
Samuels Dean (F)	5 10	12 06	Hackney	29 3 73	Boreham Wood
Simpson Phil (M)	5 9	11 01	London	18 10 69	Stevenage Bor
Stockley Sam (D)	5 8	11 00	Tiverton	5 9 77	Southampton
Tomlinson Micky (M)	5 8	11 00	Lambeth	15 9 72	Leyton Orient
Wilson Paul (M)	5 10	11 02	London	29 9 64	Barking

League Appearances: Adams, K. 1(2); Brady, M. 1(6); Brazil, G. 15(4); Campbell, J. 36(7); Codner, R. 20(4); Constantinou, C. 1; Devine, S. 30(1); Dunwell, R. 1; Ford, J. 13; Gale, S. 40(3); Goodhind, W. 1(2); Hardyman, P. 13(3); Harrison, L. 21; Hodges, L. 28(3); Howarth, L. 37(1); McDonald, D. 10(8); Mills, D. 2(2); Ndah, J. 12(2); Pardew, A. 23(3); Patterson, G. 3; Primus, L. 46; Rattray, K. 9; Samuels, D. 13(4); Simpson, P. 29(3); Stockley, S. 21; Taylor, M. 25; Thompson, N. 1; Tomlinson, M. 19(11); Wilson, P. 37

League (46): Devine 11, Wilson 6 (5 pens), Campbell 4, Hodges 4, Ndah 4, Primus 3, Brazil 2, Gale 2, Hardyman 2, Simpson 2, Codner 1, Ford 1, Howarth 1, Samuels 1, Tomlinson 1, own goal 1.

Coca-Cola Cup (7): Simpson 2, Campbell 1, Codner 1, Devine 1, Tomlinson 1, Wilson 1.

FA Cup (8): Devine 4, Hodges 2, Campbell 1, Simpson 1.

Ground: Underhill Stadium, Barnet Lane, Barnet, Herts EN5 2BE. Telephone (0181) 441 6932.

Record attendance: 11,026 v Wycombe Wanderers. FA Amateur Cup 4th Round 1951–52. **Capacity:** 4057.

Manager: John Still.

Secretary: David Stanley.

Honours – FA Amateur Cup winners 1945–46. **GM Vauxhall Conference winners** 1990–91.

Colours: Amber and black striped shirts, black shorts, black stockings.

Appleby Matty (D)	5 7	11 04	Middlesbrough	16 4 72	Darlington
Beckett Duane (D)	5 8	10 11	Sheffield	31 1 78	Trainee
Beckett Luke (F)	5 11	11 02	Sheffield	25 11 76	Trainee
Bosancic Jovo (M)	5 11	12 04	Novi Sad	7 8 70	Uniao Madeira
Bullock Antony (G)	6 1	13 08	Warrington	18 2 72	Leek T
Bullock Martin (M)	5 4	10 09	Derby	5 3 75	Eastwood T
Davis Steve (D)	5 11	12 12	Birmingham	26 7 65	Burnley

De Zeeuw Arjan (D)	6 1	13 03	Castricum	16 4 70	Telstar
Eaden Nicky (D)	5 8	11 09	Sheffield	12 12 72	Trainee
Gregory Andrew (M)	5 8	10 09	Barnsley	8 10 76	Trainee
Hendrie John (F)	5 7	11 12	Lennoxtown	24 10 63	Middlesbrough
Hume Mark (D)	6 2	11 11	Barnsley	21 5 78	Trainee
Jackson Chris (F)	5 9	11 06	Barnsley	16 1 76	Trainee
Jones Dean (D)	6 1	12 03	Barnsley	12 10 77	Trainee
Jones Scott (D)	5 10	11 06	Sheffield	1 5 75	Trainee
Liddell Andrew (F)	5 6	10 09	Leeds	28 6 73	Trainee
Marcelle Clint (F)	5 4	10 00	Port of Spain	9 11 68	Felgueiras
McClare Sean (M)	5 9	10 13	Rotherham	12 1 78	Trainee
Morgan Chris (D)	5 10	11 11	Barnsley	13 2 78	Trainee
Moses Adrian (D)	5 10	12 08	Doncaster	4 5 75	School
Perry Jonathan (D)	6 0	11 11	Hamilton	22 11 76	Trainee
Prendergast Rory (F)	5 8	12 00	Pontefract	6 4 78	Rochdale
Redfearn Neil (M)	5 8	12 00	Dewsbury	20 6 65	Oldham Ath
Regis Dave (F)	6 0	13 08	Paddington	3 3 64	Southend U
Rose Karl (F)	5 8	10 08	Barnsley	12 10 78	
Sheridan Darren (D)	5 4	10 12	Manchester	8 12 67	Winsford U
Ten-Heuvel Laurens (F)	6 0	12 01	Duivendrecht	6 6 76	Den Bosch
Thompson Neil (D)	6 0	13 05	Beverley	2 10 63	Ipswich T
Van der Velden Carel (M)	5 11	13 08	Arnhem	3 8 72	Den Bosch
Watson David (G)	5 11	12 03	Barnsley	10 11 73	Trainee
Wilkinson Paul (F)	6 1	11 10	Louth	30 10 64	Middlesbrough

League Appearances: Appleby, M. 35; Bochenski, S. ; Bosancic, J. 17(8); Bullock, M. 7(21); Davis, S. 24; De Zeeuw, A. 43; Eaden, N. 46; Hendrie, J. 36; Hurst, G. (1); Jones, S. 12(6); Liddell, A. 25(13); Marcelle, C. 26(14); Moses, A. 25(3); Redfearn, N. 43; Regis, D. (4); Sheridan, D. 39(2); Shirtliff, P. 12(1); Ten-Heuvel, L. (3); Thompson, N. 24; Van der Velden, C. 1(1); Watson, D. 46; Wilkinson, P. 45
League (76): Redfearn 17 (6 pens), Hendrie 15, Wilkinson 9, Liddell 8, Marcelle 8, Thompson 5 (2 pens), Davis 3, Eaden 3, De Zeeuw 2, Moses 2, Sheridan 2, Bosancic 1, own goal 1.
Coca-Cola Cup (4): Wilkinson 2, Redfearn 1, own goal 1.
FA Cup (4): Bullock 1, Hendrie 1, Marcelle 1, Redfearn 1.
Ground: Oakwell Ground, Grove St, Barnsley S71 1ET. Telephone (01226) 211211.
Record attendance: 40,255 v Stoke C, FA Cup 5th rd, 15 February 1936. **Capacity:** 18,806.
Manager: Danny Wilson.
Secretary: Michael Spinks.
Honours – Football League: Division 3 (N) Champions – 1933–34, 1938–39, 1954–55. **FA Cup:** Winners 1912.
Colours: Red shirts, white shorts, red stockings.

BIRMINGHAM CITY DIV. 1

Ablett Gary (D)	6 0	11 04	Liverpool	19 11 65	Everton
Barnes Steve (D)	5 4	10 05	Wembley	5 1 76	Welling U
Bass Jonathan (D)	6 0	12 02	Weston-Super-Mare	1 1 76	Trainee
Bennett Ian (G)	6 0	12 10	Worksop	10 10 71	Peterborough U
Bowen Jason (M)	5 6	11 00	Merthyr	24 8 72	Swansea C
Brown Kenny (D)	5 8	11 06	Upminster	11 7 67	West Ham U
Bruce Steve (D)	6 0	12 06	Corbridge	31 12 60	Manchester U
Devlin Paul (F)	5 8	11 05	Birmingham	14 4 72	Notts Co
Dukes Lee (M)			Walsall	24 10 79	Trainee

23

Forster Nicky (F)	5 9	11 05	Caterham	8	9 73	Brentford
Francis Kevin (F)	6 7	15 08	Moseley	6	12 67	Stockport Co
Furlong Paul (F)	6 0	11 00	London	1	10 68	Chelsea
Grainger Martin (D)	5 10	11 07	Enfield	23	8 72	Brentford
Hatton Paul (M)	6 0	11 00	Kidderminster	2	11 78	Trainee
Hinton Craig (D)	5 11	11 00	Wolverhampton	26	11 77	Trainee
Holland Chris (M)	5 9	11 05	Whalley	11	9 75	Newcastle U
Horne Barry (M)	5 10	12 03	St Asaph	18	5 62	Everton
Hughes Bryan (M)	5 9	10 00	Liverpool	19	6 76	Wrexham
Hunt Jonathan (M)	5 10	11 00	London	2	11 71	Southend U
Johnson Michael (D)	5 11	11 00	Nottingham	4	7 73	Notts Co
Legg Andy (M)	6 0	12 10	Neath	28	7 66	Notts Co
Newell Mike (F)	6 0	13 00	Liverpool	27	1 65	Blackburn R
O'Connor Martin (M)	5 8	10 08	Walsall	10	12 67	Peterborough U
Otto Ricky (M)	5 10	11 00	Hackney	9	11 67	Southend U
Rea Simon (D)	6 1	13 00	Coventry	20	9 76	Trainee
Robinson Steve (M)	5 9	11 00	Nottingham	17	10 75	Trainee
Tait Paul (M)	6 1	10 07	Sutton Coldfield	31	7 71	Trainee

League Appearances: Ablett, G. 39(3); Barnett, D. 6; Bass, J. 11(2); Bennett, I. 40; Bowen, J. 19(6); Breen, G. 20(2); Brown, K. 11; Bruce, S. 30(2); Castle, S. 4(4); Cooke, T. 1(3); Devlin, P. 32(6); Donowa, L. (4); Edwards, A. 1(2); Finnan, S. 3; Forster, N. 4(3); Frain, J. 1; Francis, K. 4(15); Furlong, P. 37(6); Gabbiadini, M. (2); Grainger, M. 21(2); Holland, C. 28(4); Horne, B. 33; Hughes, B. 10(1); Hunt, J. 6(6); Jackson, M. 10; Johnson, M. 28(7); Legg, A. 22(11); Limpar, A. 3(1); Newell, M. 11(4); O'Connor, M. 24; Otto, R. 1(3); Poole, G. 9(1); Robinson, S. 6(3); Sutton, S. 6; Tait, P. 17(9); Wassall, D. 8
League (52): Devlin 16 (4 pens), Furlong 10 (1 pen), O'Connor 4 (1 pen), Legg 4, Bowen 3, Forster 3, Grainger 3, Hunt 2, Ablett 1, Breen 1, Francis 1, Newell 1, own goals 3.
Coca-Cola Cup (4): Newell 2, Devlin 1 (pen), Furlong 1.
FA Cup (6): Devlin 2 (1 pen), Francis 2, Bruce 1, Furlong 1.
Ground: St Andrews, Birmingham B9 4NH. Telephone (0121) 772 0101.
Record attendance: 66,844 v Everton, FA Cup 5th rd,11 February 1939. **Capacity:** 25,812.
Manager: Trevor Francis.
Secretary: Alan Jones BA, MBA
Honours – Football League: Division 2 Champions – 1892–93, 1920–21, 1947–48, 1954–55, 1994–95. **Football League Cup:** Winners 1963. **Leyland Daf Cup:** Winners 1991. **Auto Windscreens Shield:** Winners 1995.
Colours: Blue shirts, white shorts, blue/white stockings.

BLACKBURN ROVERS   FA PREMIERSHIP

Beattie James (F)	6 1	12 00	Lancaster	27	2 78	Trainee
Benson Mark (D)	5 5	10 05	Dublin	7	8 78	Trainee
Berg Henning (D)	6 0	12 04	Eidsvoll	1	9 68	Lillestrom
Bohinen Lars (M)	6 1	12 01	Vadso	8	9 69	Nottingham F
Brewer Ben (D)			Pontypool	6	10 78	Trainee
Broomes Marlon (D)	6 0	12 12	Birmingham	28	11 77	Trainee
Brown John (D)			Edinburgh	24	12 79	
Cassin Graham (F)	5 10	11 07	Dublin	24	3 78	Belvedere
Coleman Chris (D)	6 2	14 03	Swansea	10	6 70	Crystal Palace
Coughlan Graham (D)	6 2	13 04	Dublin	18	11 74	Bray Wanderers
Croft Gary (D)	5 9	11 08	Stafford	17	2 74	Grimsby T
Donis George (M)	6 0		Greece	29	10 69	Panathinaikos

Duff Damien (F)	5 10	9 07	Ballyboden	2 3 79	
Fenton Graham (F)	5 10	12 10	Wallsend	22 5 74	Aston Villa
Fitzpatrick Lee (M)			Manchester	31 10 78	Trainee
Flitcroft Garry (M)	6 0	12 09	Bolton	6 11 72	Manchester C
Flowers Tim (G)	6 3	14 04	Kenilworth	3 2 67	Southampton
Gallacher Kevin (F)	5 8	11 03	Clydebank	23 11 66	Coventry C
Gill Wayne (M)	5 10	11 04	Chorley	28 11 75	Trainee
Given Shay (G)	6 1	12 10	Lifford	20 4 76	Celtic
Gudmundsson Niklas (F)	5 11	12 01	Sweden	29 2 72	Halmstad
Hendry Colin (D)	6 1	12 07	Keith	7 12 65	Manchester C
Holmes Matt (F)	5 7	11 00	Luton	1 8 69	West Ham U
Johnson Damien (M)	5 9	10 00	Blackburn	18 11 78	Trainee
Kenna Jeff (D)	5 11	12 03	Dublin	28 8 70	Southampton
Le Saux Graeme (D)	5 10	12 02	Jersey	17 10 68	Chelsea
Marker Nicky (D)	6 0	13 00	Exeter	3 5 65	Plymouth Arg
McCallion Edward (D)			Derry	25 1 79	
McKinlay Billy (M)	5 8	11 04	Glasgow	22 4 69	Dundee U
Pearce Ian (D)	6 4	14 04	Bury St Edmunds	7 5 74	Chelsea
Pedersen Per (F)	5 11	13 05	Aalborg	30 3 69	Odense
Reed Adam (D)	6 0	11 00	Bishop Auckland	18 2 75	Darlington
Ripley Stuart (F)	6 0	13 00	Middlesbrough	20 11 67	Middlesbrough
Ryan Ciaran (D)			Dublin	3 9 79	Trainee
Sherwood Tim (M)	6 1	12 09	St Albans	2 2 69	Norwich C
Staton Luke (M)	5 7	9 10	Doncaster	10 3 79	Trainee
Stewart Gareth (G)			Preston	3 2 80	Trainee
Sutton Chris (F)	6 3	13 07	Nottingham	10 3 73	Norwich C
Thomas James (F)			Swansea	16 1 79	Trainee
Warhurst Paul (D)	6 0	11 04	Stockport	26 9 69	Sheffield W
Whealing Anthony (D)	5 9	10 02	Manchester	3 9 76	Trainee
Wilcox Jason (F)	6 0	11 00	Bolton	15 7 71	Trainee
Williams Anthony (G)				20 9 77	Trainee
Worrell David (D)	5 10	11 08	Dublin	12 1 78	Trainee

League Appearances: Beattie, J. 1; Berg, H. 36; Bohinen, L. 17(6); Coleman, C. 8; Croft, G. 4(1); Donis, G. 11(11); Duff, D. 1; Fenton, G. 5(8); Flitcroft, G. 27(1); Flowers, T. 36; Gallacher, K. 34; Given, S. 2; Gudmundsson, N. (2); Hendry, C. 35; Kenna, J. 37; Le Saux, G. 26; Marker, N. 5(2); McKinlay, B. 23(2); Pearce, I. 7(5); Pedersen, P. 6(5); Ripley, S. 5(8); Sherwood, T. 37; Sutton, C. 24(1); Warhurst, P. 5(6); Wilcox, J. 26(2).

League (42): Sutton 11 (1 pen), Gallacher 10, Flitcroft 3, Sherwood 3, Berg 2, Bohinen 2, Donis 2, Warhurst 2, Wilcox 2, Fenton 1, Hendry 1, Le Saux 1, McKinlay 1, Pedersen 1.

Coca-Cola Cup (4): Flitcroft 1, Gallacher 1, Sherwood 1, Sutton 1.

FA Cup (2): Bohinen 1, Sherwood 1.

Ground: Ewood Park, Blackburn BB2 4JF. Telephone (01254) 698888.

Record attendance: 61,783 v Bolton W, FA Cup 6th rd, 2 March, 1929. **Capacity:** 31,367.

Manager: Roy Hodgson.

Secretary: Tom Finn.

Honours – FA Premier League: Champions – 1994–95. Football League: Division 1 Champions – 1911–12, 1913–14. Division 2 Champions – 1938–39. Division 3 Champions – 1974–75. **FA Cup:** Winners 1884, 1885, 1886, 1890, 1891, 1928. **Full Members' Cup:** Winners 1986–87.

Colours: Blue and white halved shirts, white shorts, white stockings, blue trim.

BLACKPOOL   DIV. 2

Banks Steve (G)	6 0	13 02	Hillingdon	9	2 72	Gillingham
Bonner Mark (M)	5 10	11 00	Ormskirk	7	6 74	Trainee
Brabin Gary (M)	5 11	14 08	Liverpool	9	2 70	Bury
Bradshaw Darren (D)	5 11	11 04	Sheffield	19	3 67	Peterborough U
Bryan Marvin (D)	6 0	12 02	Paddington	2	8 75	QPR
Butler Tony (D)	6 2	12 00	Stockport	28	9 72	Gillingham
Clarkson Phil (M)	5 10	12 05	Hambleton	13	11 68	Scunthorpe U
Dixon Ben (D)	6 1	11 00	Lincoln	16	9 74	Lincoln C
Ellis Tony (F)	5 11	11 00	Salford	20	10 64	Preston NE
Linighan David (D)	6 2	12 06	Hartlepool	9	1 65	Ipswich T
Lydiate Jason (D)	5 11	12 03	Manchester	29	10 71	Bolton W
Malkin Chris (F)	6 3	12 09	Hoylake	4	6 67	Millwall
Mellon Micky (M)	5 9	11 03	Paisley	18	3 72	WBA
Ormerod Brett (F)	5 11	11 04	Blackburn	18	10 76	Accrington S
Philpott Lee (M)	5 9	11 08	Barnet	21	2 70	Leicester C
Preece Andy (F)	6 1	12 00	Evesham	27	3 67	Crystal Palace
Quinn James (F)	6 1	12 10	Coventry	15	12 74	Birmingham C
Russell Keith (M)	5 10	12 00	Aldridge	31	1 74	Hednesford T

League Appearances: Banks, S. 46; Barlow, A. 43(3); Bonner, M. 25(4); Brabin, G. 30(2); Bradshaw, D. 4(6); Brightwell, D. 1(1); Bryan, M. 34; Butler, T. 41(1); Carden, P. (1); Clarkson, P. 17; Darton, S. 8(7); Dixon, B. 3(8); Ellis, T. 41(4); Linighan, D. 42; Lydiate, J. 18(2); Malkin, C. 8(7); Mellon, M. 43; Onwere, U. 5(4); Ormerod, B. (4); Philpott, L. 20(6); Preece, A. 35(6); Quinn, J. 37(1); Russell, K. (1); Thorpe, L. 2(7); Woods, B. 3
League (60): Ellis 15, Quinn 13 (4 pens) Preece 10, Clarkson 5, Mellon 4, Malkin 3, Philpott 3, Brabin 2, Barlow 1, Bonner 1, Bryan 1, Darton 1, Linighan 1.
Coca-Cola Cup (7): Ellis 3, Quinn 3, Philpott 1.
FA Cup (1): Quinn 1 (pen).
Ground: Bloomfield Rd Ground, Blackpool FY1 6JJ. Telephone (01253) 404331.
Record attendance: 38,098 v Wolverhampton W, Division 1, 17 September 1955.
Capacity: 11,047.
Manager: Nigel Worthington.
Secretary: Carol Banks.
Honours – Football League: Division 2 Champions – 1929–30. **FA Cup:** Winners 1953. **Anglo-Italian Cup:** Winners 1971.
Colours: All tangerine.

BOLTON WANDERERS   FA PREMIERSHIP

Aljofree Hasney (D)	6 0	12 01	Manchester	11	7 78	Trainee
Bergsson Gudni (D)	6 1	12 03	Reykjavik	21	7 65	Tottenham H
Blake Nathan (F)	5 11	13 12	Cardiff	27	1 72	Sheffield U
Branagan Keith (G)	6 0	13 02	Fulham	10	7 66	Millwall
Coleman Simon (D)	6 0	10 08	Worksop	13	6 68	Sheffield W
Fairclough Chris (D)	5 11	11 02	Nottingham	12	4 64	Leeds U
Frandsen Per (M)	6 1	12 06	Copenhagen	6	2 70	FC Copenhagen
Green Scott (M)	5 10	12 05	Walsall	15	1 70	Derby Co
Johansen Michael (M)	5 6	10 05	Golstrup	22	7 72	FC Copenhagen
Lee David (M)	5 7	11 00	Whitefield	5	11 67	Southampton
McAnespie Steve (D)	5 9	10 07	Kilmarnock	1	2 72	Raith R
McGinlay John (F)	5 9	11 04	Inverness	8	4 64	Millwall
Paatelainen Mixu (F)	6 0	13 11	Helsinki	3	2 67	Aberdeen

Phillips Jimmy (D)	6 0	12 07	Bolton	8 2 66	Middlesbrough
Pollock Jamie (M)	5 10	14 00	Stockton	16 2 74	Osasuna
Sellars Scott (M)	5 7	9 10	Sheffield	27 11 65	Newcastle U
Sheridan John (M)	5 10	12 01	Stretford	1 10 64	Sheffield W
Small Bryan (D)	5 9	11 09	Birmingham	15 11 71	Aston Villa
Spooner Nicky (D)	5 10	11 09	Manchester	5 6 71	Trainee
Strong Greg (D)	6 2	11 12	Bolton	5 9 75	Wigan Ath
Taggart Gerry (D)	6 1	12 03	Belfast	18 10 70	Barnsley
Taylor Scott (F)	5 10	11 04	Chertsey	5 5 76	Millwall
Thompson Alan (M)	6 0	12 08	Newcastle	22 12 73	Newcastle U
Todd Andy (D)	5 10	10 11	Derby	21 9 74	Middlesbrough
Ward Gavin (G)	6 3	14 05	Sutton Coldfield	30 6 70	Bradford C
Whitehead Stuart (M)	5 11	12 04	Bromsgrove	17 7 76	Bromsgrove R
Xiourouppa Costas (F)			Dudley	11 9 79	Trainee

League Appearances: Bergsson, G. 30(3); Blake, N. 42; Branagan, K. 36; Burnett, W. (1); Fairclough, C. 46; Frandsen, P. 40(1); Green, S. 7(5); Johansen, M. 24(9); Lee, D. 13(12); McAnespie, S. 11(2); McGinlay, J. 43; Paatelainen, M. 3(7); Phillips, J. 36; Pollock, J. 18(2); Sellars, S. 40(2); Sheridan, J. 12(8); Small, B. 10(1); Taggart, G. 43; Taylor, S. 2(9); Thompson, A. 34; Todd, A. 6(9); Ward, G. 10(1)
League (100): McGinlay 24 (6 pens), Blake 19, Thompson 10, Fairclough 8, Sellars 8, Frandsen 5, Johansen 5, Pollock 4, Bergsson 3, Taggart 3, Lee 2, Paatelainen 2, Sheridan 2, Green 1, Taylor 1, own goals 3.
Coca-Cola Cup (11): McGinlay 5 (1 pen), Blake 3, Taggart 1, Taylor 1, Thompson 1.
FA Cup (9): Blake 2, Green 2, Pollock 2, McGinlay 1, Taylor 1, Thompson 1.
Ground: Burnden Park, Bolton BL3 2QR. Telephone Bolton (01204) 389200. Moving to new ground at Horwich.
Record attendance: 69,912 v Manchester C, FA Cup 5th rd, 18 February 1933.
Capacity: 20,500.
Manager: Colin Todd.
Secretary: Des McBain.
Honours – Football League: Division 1 Champions – 1996–97. Division 2 Champions – 1908–09, 1977–78. Division 3 Champions – 1972–73. **FA Cup winners** 1923, 1926, 1929, 1958. **Sherpa Van Trophy:** Winners 1989.
Colours: White shirts, navy blue shorts, blue stockings.

AFC BOURNEMOUTH   DIV. 2

Bailey John (M)	5 8	10 02	London	6 5 69	Enfield
Beardsmore Russell (M)	5 8	10 04	Wigan	28 9 68	Manchester U
Brissett Jason (M)	5 9	12 00	Redbridge	7 9 74	Peterborough U
Coll Owen (D)	6 0	11 07	Donegal	9 4 76	Tottenham H
Cotterell Leo (D)	5 9	10 00	Cambridge	2 9 74	Ipswich T
Cox Ian (M)	6 0	12 00	Croydon	25 3 71	Crystal Palace
Dean Michael (M)	5 9	11 10	Weymouth	9 3 78	Trainee
Fletcher Steve (F)	6 2	14 09	Hartlepool	26 6 72	Hartlepool U
Glass Jimmy (G)	6 1	13 04	Epsom	1 8 73	Crystal Palace
Holland Matthew (M)	5 9	11 12	Bury	11 4 74	West Ham U
Howe Eddie (D)	5 9	11 02	Amersham	29 11 77	Trainee
Murray Robert (D)	5 11	12 07	Hammersmith	31 10 74	Trainee
O'Neill Jon (F)	5 11	12 00	Glasgow	2 1 74	Celtic
Rawlinson Mark (M)	5 10	11 04	Bolton	9 6 75	Manchester U
Robinson Steve (F)	5 9	11 02	Lisburn	10 12 74	Tottenham H
Town David (F)	5 7	11 13	Bournemouth	9 12 76	Trainee
Vincent Jamie (D)	5 10	11 09	London	18 6 75	Crystal Palace

| Wells David (G) | 6 2 | 12 07 | Portsmouth | 29 12 77 | Trainee |
| Young Neil (D) | 5 9 | 12 00 | Harlow | 31 8 73 | Tottenham H |

League Appearances: Bailey, J. 40; Beardsmore, R. 37(1); Brissett, J. 16(9); Christie, I. 3(1); Coll, O. 16; Cotterill, S. 2(7); Cox, I. 44; Dean, M. 10(2); Ferdinand, R. 10; Fletcher, S. 33(2); Glass, J. 35; Gordon, D. 14(2); Hayter, J. (2); Holland, M. 45; Howe, E. 7(6); Marshall, A. 11; Morris, M. (1); Murray, R. 20(12); O'Brien, R. 1; O'Neill, J. 7(11); Omoyimni, E. 5(2); Rawlinson, M. 22(3); Robinson, S. 34(6); Town, D. 16(10); Vincent, J. 28(1); Watson, M. 6(9); Young, N. 44

League (43): Cox 8, Fletcher 7, Holland 7, Robinson 7 (2 pens), Brissett 4, Murray 2, Rawlinson 2, Town 2, Watson 2, Bailey 1, O'Neill 1.

Coca-Cola Cup (1): Fletcher 1.

FA Cup (0).

Ground: Dean Court Ground, Bournemouth BH7 7AF. Telephone (01202) 395381.

Record attendance: 28,799 v Manchester U, FA Cup 6th rd, 2 March 1957.

Capacity: 10,440.

Manager: Mel Machin.

Secretary: K. R. J. MacAlister.

Honours – Football League: Division 3 Champions – 1986–87. **Associate Members' Cup:** Winners 1984.

Colours: Red shirts with black stripe, white shorts, white stockings.

BRADFORD CITY   DIV. 1

Blake Robbie (F)	5 8	11 00	Middlesbrough	4 3 76	Darlington
Dreyer John (D)	6 1	13 02	Alnwick	11 6 63	Stoke C
Edinho(F)	5 8	12 12	Brazil	21 2 67	Guimaraes
Gould Jonathan (G)	6 1	12 07	Paddington	18 7 68	Bradford C
Jacobs Wayne (D)	5 8	11 02	Sheffield	3 2 69	Rotherham U
Jewell Paul (F)	5 8	12 01	Liverpool	28 9 64	Wigan Ath
Kiwomya Andy (F)	5 10	10 10	Huddersfield	1 10 67	Scunthorpe U
Kulcsar George (D)	6 1	13 08	Budapest	12 8 67	Antwerp
Liburd Richard (D)	5 10	10 12	Nottingham	26 9 73	Middlesbrough
Midgley Craig (F)	5 7	11 01	Bradford	24 5 76	Trainee
Mohan Nicky (D)	6 1	13 01	Middlesbrough	6 10 70	Leicester C
Murray Shaun (M)	5 7	10 10	Newcastle	7 2 70	Scarborough
O'Brien Andrew (D)	5 10	10 06	Harrogate	29 6 79	Trainee
Pepper Nigel (M)	5 10	11 13	Rotherham	25 4 68	York C
Sas Marco (D)	6 1	12 05	Vlaardingen	16 2 71	NAC Breda
Sundgot Ole (F)	6 1	11 04	Olsumd	21 3 72	Oldham Ath
Watson Gordon (F)	5 10	12 08	Sidcup	20 3 71	Southampton
Wilder Chris (D)	5 11	12 08	Stocksbridge	23 9 67	Notts Co
Youds Eddie (D)	6 1	13 03	Liverpool	3 5 70	Ipswich T

League Appearances: Blake, R. 3(2); Brightwell, D. 2; Cowans, G. 23(1); Davison, A. 10; Dreyer, J. 27(1); Duxbury, L. 33; Edinho. . 15; Gould, J. 9; Hamilton, D. 24(8); Huxford, R. 1(1); Jacobs, W. 37(2); Kiwomya, A. 20(7); Kulcsar, G. 9; Liburd, R. 33(3); Midgley, C. (1); Mitchell, G. 6; Mohan, N. 44; Moore, I. 6; Murray, S. 13(4); Newell, M. 7; Nixon, E. 12; O'Brien, A. 18(4); Oliveira, R. 2; Ormondroyd, I. (1); Pehrsson, M. 1; Pepper, N. 11; Pinto, S. 7(11); Regtop, E. 5(3); Roberts, B. 2; Sansam, C. (1); Sas, M. 31; Schwarzer, M. 13; Shutt, C. 10(12); Smithard, M. (1); Stallard, M. 13(9); Steiner, R. 14(1); Sundgot, O. 11(9); Vanhala, J. (1); Waddle, C. 25; Watson, G. 3; Wilder, C. 4(3); Wright, T. 2(9)

League (47): Sundgot 6, Edinho 5 (1 pen), Pepper 5, Waddle 5, Steiner 4, Duxbury

3, Jacobs 3, Sas 3 (1 pen), Shutt 3, O'Brien 2, Dreyer 1, Kiwomya 1, Liburd 1, Murray 1, Regtop 1 (pen), Stallard 1, Watson 1, Wright 1.
Coca-Cola Cup (1): Stallard 1.
FA Cup (5): Dreyer 3, Steiner 1, Waddle 1.
Ground: The Pulse Stadium at Valley Parade, Bradford BD8 7DY. Telephone (01274) 773355.
Record attendance: 39,146 v Burnley, FA Cup 4th rd, 11 March 1911. **Capacity:** 18,080.
Manager: Chris Kamara.
Secretary: Jon Pollard.
Honours – Football League: Division 2 Champions – 1907–08. Division 3 Champions – 1984–85. Division 3 (N) Champions – 1928–29. **FA Cup:** Winners 1911.
Colours: Claret and amber shirts, black shorts, black stockings.

BRENTFORD   DIV. 2

Anderson Ijah (D)	5 8	10 03	Hackney	30 12 75	Southend U
Asaba Carl (F)	6 1	13 07	London	28 1 73	Dulwich Hamlet
Ashby Barry (D)	6 1	13 08	London	21 11 70	Watford
Bates Jamie (D)	6 2	14 00	London	24 2 68	Trainee
Bent Marcus (F)	6 2	12 04	Hammersmith	19 5 78	Trainee
Canham Scott (M)	5 10	11 08	London	5 11 74	West Ham U
Dearden Kevin (G)	5 11	14 01	Luton	8 3 70	Tottenham H
Dennis Kevin (F)	5 10	12 00	Islington	14 12 76	Arsenal
Fernandes Tamer (G)	6 2	13 13	London	7 12 74	Trainee
Goddard-Crawley Richard (M)	6 3	14 00	Burnt Oak	31 3 78	Arsenal
Hurdle Gus (D)	6 0	11 04	London	14 10 73	Fulham
Hutchings Carl (M)	6 0	11 06	London	24 9 74	Trainee
McGhee David (F)	5 11	12 05	Sussex	19 6 76	Trainee
McPherson Malcolm (F)	6 1	12 00	Glasgow	19 12 74	West Ham U
Myall Stuart (M)	5 10	13 07	Eastbourne	12 11 74	Brighton & HA
Omigie Joe (F)	6 2	13 00	Hammersmith	13 6 72	Donna
Rapley Kevin (F)	5 9	10 08	Reading	21 9 77	Trainee
Smith Paul (M)	6 0	13 10	Lenham	18 9 71	Southend U
Statham Brian (D)	5 9	11 12	Zimbabwe	21 5 69	Tottenham H
Taylor Robert (F)	6 1	13 06	Norwich	30 4 71	Leyton Orient

League Appearances: Abrahams, P. 5(3); Anderson, I. 46; Asaba, C. 44; Ashby, B. 40; Bates, J. 37; Bent, M. 29(5); Canham, S. 13; Dearden, K. 44; Dennis, K. 9(3); Fernandes, T. 2; Forster, N. 25; Goddard-Crawley, R. (1); Harvey, L. 2(12); Hurdle, G. 28(3); Hutchings, C. 23(5); Janney, M. 1(1); McGhee, D. 44(1); McPherson, M. 2(1); Omigie, J. 7(6); Rapley, K. 1(1); Slade, S. 4; Smith, P. 46; Statham, B. 11(8); Taylor, R. 43
League (56): Asaba 23 (1 pen), Forster 10, Taylor 7, Bent 3, Abrahams 2, Bates 2, Hutchings 2, Anderson 1, Ashby 1, Canham 1, Janney 1, McGhee 1, Omigie 1, Smith 1.
Coca-Cola Cup (2): Forster 1, Taylor 1.
FA Cup (5): Taylor 2, Forster 1, McGhee 1, Smith 1.
Ground: Griffin Park, Braemar Rd, Brentford, Middlesex TW8 0NT. Telephone (0181) 847 2511.
Record attendance: 39,626 v Preston NE, FA Cup 6th rd, 5 March 1938. **Capacity:** 12,763.
Manager: David Webb.
Secretary: Polly Kates.

BRIGHTON & HOVE ALBION   DIV. 3

Allan Derek (D)	6 0	12 01	Irving	24 12 74	Southampton
Baird Ian (F)	6 0	12 00	Rotherham	1 4 64	Plymouth Arg
Hobson Gary (D)	6 2	13 04	North Ferriby	12 11 72	Hull C
Johnson Ross (D)	6 0	12 12	Brighton	2 1 76	Trainee
Maskell Craig (F)	5 10	11 10	Aldershot	10 4 68	Southampton
Mayo Kerry (M)	5 10	12 11	Cuckfield	21 9 77	Trainee
McDonald Paul (F)	5 6	10 00	Motherwell	20 4 68	Southampton
Minton Jeffrey (M)	5 6	11 00	Hackney	28 12 73	Tottenham H
Morris Mark (D)	6 2	14 00	Carshalton	26 9 62	Bournemouth
Mundee Denny (M)	5 10	13 00	Swindon	10 10 68	Brentford
Ormerod Mark (G)	6 0	12 11	Bournemouth	5 2 76	Trainee
Peake Jason (M)	5 10	13 00	Leicester	29 9 71	Rochdale
Reinelt Robbie (M)	5 11	11 11	Epping	11 3 74	Colchester U
Rust Nicky (G)	6 0	13 02	Ely	25 9 74	Arsenal
Smith Peter (D)	6 1	12 02	Stone	12 7 69	Alma Swanley
Storer Stuart (F)	5 11	12 12	Rugby	16 1 67	Exeter C
Tuck Stuart (D)	5 11	11 00	Brighton	1 10 74	Trainee

League Appearances: Adekola, D. 1; Allan, D. 31; Andrews, P. 1(6); Baird, I. 34(1); Fox, M. (2); Fox, S. 5(7); Hobson, G. 35(2); Humphrey, J. 11; Johnson, R. 21(8); Martin, D. 1; Maskell, C. 37; Mayo, K. 22(2); McDonald, P. 40(5); McGarrigle, K. 9(4); Minton, J. 22(3); Morris, M. 11(1); Mundee, D. 27(2); Neal, A. 8; Ormerod, M. 21; Parris, G. 17(1); Peake, J. 27(3); Reinelt, R. 7(5); Rust, N. 25; Smith, P. 26(4); Storer, S. 37(5); Tuck, S. 27; Warren, C. 3
League (53): Maskell 14, Baird 13, Storer 6, McDonald 4 (2 pens), Mundee 4 (3 pens), Minton 3, Reinelt 3, Andrews 1, Hobson 1, Morris 1, Parris 1, Peake 1, Smith 1.
Coca-Cola Cup (0).
FA Cup (1): Maskell 1.
Offices: Hanover House, 118 Queens Road, Brighton BN1 3XG. Telephone: (01634) 851584.
Record attendance: 36,747 v Fulham, Division 2, 27 December 1958. **Capacity:** 10,952.
Manager: Steve Gritt.
Secretary: Derek Allan.
Honours – Football League: Division 3 (S) Champions – 1957–58. Division 4 Champions – 1964–65.
Colours: Blue and white striped shirts, blue shorts, white stockings.

BRISTOL CITY   DIV. 2

Agostino Paul (F)	5 11	12 12	Woodville	9 6 75	Young Boys
Barclay Dominic (F)	5 10	11 07	Bristol	5 9 76	Trainee
Barnard Darren (D)	5 10	12 00	Rinteln	30 11 71	Chelsea
Bent Junior (F)	5 5	10 06	Huddersfield	1 3 70	Huddersfield T
Bokoto Mommainais (F)	5 11	11 13	France	20 10 74	Maria Aalter
Brennan Jim (M)	5 9	11 06	Toronto	8 5 77	Sora Lazio

Carey Louis (D)	5 10	11 05	Bristol	22 1 77	Trainee
Edwards Robert (D)	6 0	11 06	Kendal	1 7 73	Carlisle U
Goater Shaun (F)	6 1	11 10	Bermuda	25 2 70	Rotherham U
Goodridge Greg (F)	5 6	10 00	Barbados	10 2 75	QPR
Hewlett Matthew (M)	6 2	10 11	Bristol	25 2 76	Trainee
Langan Kevin (D)	6 1	11 05	Jersey	7 4 78	Trainee
Naylor Stuart (G)	6 4	12 02	Wetherby	6 12 62	WBA
Nugent Kevin (F)	6 1	13 03	Edmonton	10 4 69	Plymouth Arg
Owers Gary (M)	6 0	12 07	Newcastle	3 10 68	Sunderland
Paterson Scott (D)	5 11	12 00	Aberdeen	13 5 72	Liverpool
Phillips Steve (G)	6 1	11 10	Bath	6 5 78	Paulton R
Plummer Dwayne (F)	5 10	10 09	Bristol	12 10 76	Trainee
Seal David (F)	5 11	12 00	Penrith NSW	26 1 72	Aalst
Shail Mark (D)	6 1	13 03	Sweden	15 10 66	Yeovil T
Taylor Shaun (D)	6 1	13 00	Plymouth	26 2 63	Swindon T
Tinnion Brian (D)	6 1	13 00	Stanley	23 2 68	Bradford C
Welch Keith (G)	6 2	12 00	Bolton	3 10 68	Rochdale

League Appearances: Agostino, P. 34(10); Allen, P. 13(1); Barnard, D. 44; Bent, J. 17(5); Blackmore, C. 5; Brennan, J. 7(1); Carey, L. 40(2); Cundy, J. 6; Edwards, R. 31; Goater, S. 39(3); Goodridge, G. 19(9); Hewlett, M. 33(3); Kuhl, M. 22(9); McLeary, A. 1(2); Naylor, S. 35; Nugent, K. 19(17); Owers, G. 46; Partridge, S. (6); Paterson, S. 15(4); Plummer, D. (2); Seal, D. (12); Shail, M. 10(1); Taylor, S. 29; Tinnion, B. 30(2); Welch, K. 11
League (69): Goater 23 (1 pen), Barnard 11 (7 pens), Agostino 9, Goodridge 6, Nugent 6, Owers 4, Bent 3, Hewlett 2, Blackmore 1, Cundy 1, Taylor 1, Tinnion 1, own goal 1.
Coca-Cola Cup (5): Agostino 1, Barnard 1, Goater 1, Owers 1, Partridge 1.
FA Cup (11): Agostino 5, Hewlett 2, Kuhl 2, Goodridge 1, Nugent 1.
Ground: Ashton Gate, Bristol BS3 2EJ. Telephone (0117) 9630630.
Record attendance: 43,335 v Preston NE, FA Cup 5th rd, 16 February 1935.
Capacity: 21,479.
Manager: John Ward.
Secretary: Eddie Harrison.
Honours – Football League: Division 2 Champions – 1905–06. Division 3 (S) Champions – 1922–23, 1926–27, 1954–55. **Welsh Cup winners** 1934. **Anglo-Scottish Cup:** Winners 1977–78. **Freight Rover Trophy winners** 1985–86.
Colours: Red shirts, white shorts, red and white stockings.

BRISTOL ROVERS   DIV. 2

Alsop Julian (F)	6 4	13 00	Nuneaton	28 5 73	Halesowen T
Archer Lee (F)	5 6	9 06	Bristol	6 11 72	Trainee
Beadle Peter (F)	6 2	13 07	London	13 5 72	Watford
Bennett Frankie (F)	5 7	12 01	Birmingham	3 1 69	Southampton
Clark Billy (D)	6 0	12 03	Christchurch	19 5 67	Bournemouth
Collett Andy (G)	6 0	12 10	Middlesbrough	28 10 73	Middlesbrough
Cureton Jamie (F)	5 7	10 07	Bristol	28 8 75	Norwich C
French Jon (M)	5 10	10 10	Bristol	25 9 76	Trainee
Hayfield Matt (M)	5 10	11 07	Bristol	8 8 75	Trainee
Higgs Shane (G)	6 2	12 12	Oxford	13 5 77	Trainee
Holloway Ian (M)	5 7	10 10	Kingswood	12 3 63	QPR
Kite Phil (G)	6 2	15 04	Bristol	26 10 62	Bristol C
Lockwood Matthew (M)	5 9	10 12	Rochford	17 10 76	QPR
Low Josh (M)	6 0	11 12	Bristol	15 2 79	Trainee
Martin Lee (D)	6 0	12 08	Hyde	5 2 68	Celtic

Miller Paul (F)	6 0	11 07	Bisley	31 1 68	Wimbledon
Morgan Ryan (M)	6 1	12 07	Bristol	12 7 78	Trainee
Parmenter Steve (F)	5 9	11 00	Chelmsford	22 1 77	QPR
Power Graeme (D)	5 11	10 10	Northwick Park	7 3 77	QPR
Pritchard David (D)	5 7	11 04	Wolverhampton	27 5 72	WBA
Ramasut Tom (M)	5 10	11 00	Cardiff	30 8 77	Norwich C
Skinner Justin (M)	6 0	11 03	Hounslow	30 1 69	Fulham
Tillson Andy (D)	6 2	12 10	Huntingdon	30 6 66	QPR
White Tom (D)	5 11	12 02	Bristol	26 1 76	Trainee

League Appearances: Alsop, J. 10(6); Archer, L. 18(3); Beadle, P. 36(6); Bennett, F. 6(5); Browning, M. 24(2); Clapham, J. 4(1); Clark, B. 26(1); Collett, A. 44; Cureton, J. 33(5); French, J. 3(1); Gayle, B. 7; Gurney, A. 21(3); Harris, J. 5(1); Hayfield, M. 12(5); Higgs, S. 2; Holloway, I. 29(2); Lockwood, M. 36(3); Low, J. (3); Martin, L. 25; Miller, P. 22(3); Morgan, R. 1; Parmenter, S. 10(4); Power, G. 16; Pritchard, D. 26; Ramasut, T. 5(6); Skinner, J. 29(5); Tillson, A. 38; White, T. 18(3); Zabek, L. (1)
League (47): Beadle 12, Cureton 11, Alsop 3, Archer 2, Browning 2, Gurney 2, Harris 2, Miller 2, Parmenter 2, Skinner 2, Tillson 2, Bennett 1, Clark 1, Holloway 1, Lockwood 1, own goal 1.
Coca-Cola Cup (2): Archer 1, Gurney 1.
FA Cup (1): Parmenter 1.
Ground: The Memorial Ground, Filton Avenue, Horfield, Bristol BS7 0AQ.
Record attendance: 9464 v Liverpool, FA Cup 4th rd, 8 February 1992 (Twerton Park). 38,472 v Preston NE, FA Cup 4th rd, 30 January 1960 (Eastville). **Capacity:** 8475.
Manager: Ian Holloway.
Honours – Football League: Division 3 (S) Champions – 1952–53. Division 3 Champions – 1989–90.
Colours: Blue and white quartered shirts, white shorts, blue stockings.

BURNLEY   DIV. 2

Barnes Paul (M)	5 11	12 06	Leicester	16 11 67	Birmingham C
Beresford Marlon (G)	6 1	13 05	Lincoln	2 9 69	Sheffield W
Brass Chris (D)	5 9	12 06	Easington	24 7 75	Trainee
Carr-Lawton Colin (M)			South Shields	5 9 78	Trainee
Cooke Andy (F)	5 11	12 08	Stoke	20 1 74	Newtown
Duerden Ian (F)	5 10	12 07	Burnley	27 3 78	Trainee
Eastwood Philip (F)	5 10	12 02	Blackburn	6 4 78	Trainee
Eyres David (F)	5 9	11 10	Liverpool	26 2 64	Blackpool
Gleghorn Nigel (M)	6 0	13 07	Seaham	12 8 62	Stoke C
Harrison Gerry (M)	5 9	12 03	Lambeth	15 4 72	Huddersfield T
Helliwell Ian (F)	6 4	14 08	Rotherham	7 11 62	Stockport Co
Hoyland Jamie (D)	6 0	14 00	Sheffield	23 1 66	Sheffield U
Huxford Richard (D)	5 10	11 06	Scunthorpe	25 7 69	Bradford C
Little Glen (M)	6 3	13 00	Wimbledon	15 10 75	Glentoran
Matthew Damian (M)	5 11	10 10	Islington	23 9 70	Crystal Palace
Overson Vince (D)	6 2	14 13	Kettering	15 5 62	Stoke C
Parkinson Gary (D)	5 11	13 00	Thornaby	10 1 68	Bolton W
Smith Paul (F)	6 0	13 03	Easington	22 1 76	Trainee
Swan Peter (D)	6 3	15 09	Leeds	28 9 66	Plymouth Arg
Vinnicombe Chris (D)	5 8	10 12	Exeter	20 10 70	Rangers
Weller Paul (M)	5 8	11 02	Brighton	6 3 75	Trainee
West Gareth (D)	6 1	11 10	Oldham	1 8 78	Trainee
Winstanley Mark (D)	6 1	12 08	St Helens	21 1 68	Bolton W

League Appearances: Barnes, P. 39(1); Beresford, M. 40; Brass, C. 37(2); Cooke, A. 19(12); Eyres, D. 36; Gleghorn, N. 32(1); Guinan, S. (6); Harrison, G. 32(3); Heath, A. (2); Hodgson, D. 1; Hoyland, J. 24(1); Huxford, R. 2(7); Little, G. 5(4); Matthew, D. 29(3); Nogan, K. 30(1); Overson, V. 6(2); Parkinson, G. 43; Robinson, L. 3(5); Russell, W. 6; Smith, P. 30(7); Swan, P. 16(1); Thompson, S. 14(5); Vinnicombe, C. 6(2); Weller, P. 22(5); Winstanley, M. 34(1)
League (71): Barnes 24 (1 pen), Cooke 13 (1 pen), Nogan 10, Matthew 6, Gleghorn 4, Smith 4, Eyres 3 (1 pen), Swan 2, Weller 2, Hoyland 1, Parkinson 1, Thompson 1.
Coca-Cola Cup (7): Eyres 3, Nogan 2, Cooke 1, Matthew 1.
FA Cup (4): Barnes 1, Eyres 1, Gleghorn 1, Matthew 1.
Ground: Turf Moor, Burnley BB10 4BX. Telephone (01282) 700000.
Record attendance: 54,775 v Huddersfield T, FA Cup 3rd rd, 23 February 1924.
Capacity: 22,546.
Manager: Chris Waddle.
Secretary:
Honours – Football League: Division 1 Champions – 1920–21, 1959–60. Division 2 Champions – 1897–98, 1972–73. Division 3 Champions – 1981–82. Division 4 Champions – 1991–92. **FA Cup winners** 1913–14. **Anglo-Scottish Cup:** Winners 1978–79.
Colours: Claret and blue shirts, white shorts and stockings.

BURY   DIV. 1

Armstrong Gordon (M)	6 0	12 11	Newcastle	15 7 67	Sunderland
Bracey Lee (G)	6 1	13 07	Barking	11 9 68	Halifax T
Butler Paul (D)	6 2	13 00	Manchester	2 11 72	Rochdale
Crossland Mark (M)			Tameside	14 12 78	Lincoln C
Daws Nick (M)	5 11	13 03	Manchester	15 3 70	Altrincham
Hirst Matthew (F)	6 2	14 04	St Albans	14 11 77	Millwall
Hughes Ian (M)	5 10	12 08	Bangor	2 8 74	Trainee
Jepson Ronnie (F)	6 1	13 00	Audley	12 5 63	Huddersfield T
Johnrose Lenny (M)	5 10	12 04	Preston	29 11 69	Hartlepool U
Johnson David (F)	5 6	12 05	Jamaica	15 8 76	Manchester U
Kiely Dean (G)	6 0	12 13	Salford	10 10 70	York C
Lucketti Chris (D)	6 0	13 04	Littleborough	21 9 71	Halifax T
Matthews Rob (F)	6 0	13 00	Slough	14 10 70	York C
Pugh David (F)	5 10	13 02	Liverpool	19 9 64	Chester C
Randall Adrian (M)	5 11	12 04	Amesbury	10 11 68	York C
Rigby Tony (M)	5 7	12 12	Ormskirk	10 8 72	Barrow
West Dean (D)	5 10	12 02	Morley	5 12 72	Lincoln C
Woodward Andy (D)	6 0	13 06	Stockport	23 9 73	Crewe Alex

League Appearances: Armstrong, G. 16(16); Battersby, T. 9(2); Bimson, S. 1; Butler, P. 40(1); Carter, M. 28(12); Daws, N. 46; Hughes, I. 14(8); Jackson, M. 31; Jepson, R. 24(7); Johnrose, L. 43; Johnson, D. 34(10); Kiely, D. 46; Lucketti, C. 38; Matthews, R. 22(5); O'Kane, J. 11(2); Pugh, D. 16(2); Randall, A. 14(5); Reid, N. 6(1); Rigby, T. (15); Scott, A. 2(6); Stant, P. 3(5); West, D. 46; Woodward, A. 16(7)
League (62): Carter 12 (5 pens), Jepson 9, Johnson 8, Matthews 5, Johnrose 4, West 4, Jackson 3, O'Kane 3, Randall 3, Armstrong 2, Battersby 2, Butler 2, Daws 2, Pugh 2, Stant 1.
Coca-Cola Cup (3): Carter 1, Jackson 1, Pugh 1.
FA Cup (0).
Ground: Gigg Lane, Bury BL9 9HR. Telephone (0161) 764 4881.

Record attendance: 35,000 v Bolton W, FA Cup 3rd rd, 9 January 1960. **Capacity:** 11,841
Manager: Stan Ternent.
Assistant Secretary: J. Neville.
Honours – Football League: Division 2 Champions – 1894–95, 1996–97. Division 3 Champions – 1960–61. **FA Cup winners** 1900, 1903. **Auto Windscreens Shield winners** 1997.
Colours: White shirts, royal blue shorts, royal blue stockings.

CAMBRIDGE UNITED   DIV. 3

Name	Ht	Wt	Birthplace	Signed	Previous club
Ashbee Ian (D)	6 0	13 07	Birmingham	6 9 76	Derby Co
Barnwell-Edinboro Jamie (F)	5 10	11 05	Hull	26 12 75	Coventry C
Barrett Scott (G)	6 0	14 03	Ilkeston	2 4 63	Gillingham
Beall Billy (M)	5 7	10 06	Enfield	,4 12 77	Trainee
Benjamin Trevor (M)	6 2	13 06	Kettering	8 2 79	Trainee
Craddock Jody (D)	6 0	12 00	Redditch	25 7 75	Christchurch
Hayes Adie (M)	6 0	11 09	Norwich	22 5 78	Trainee
Hyde Micah (M)	5 9	11 07	Newham	10 11 74	Trainee
Joseph Marc (D)	6 1	12 09	Leicester	10 11 76	Trainee
Joseph Matt (D)	5 7	10 05	Bethnal Green	30 9 72	Gillingham
Kyd Michael (F)	5 11	12 07	Hackney	21 5 77	Trainee
Marshall Shaun (G)	6 1	12 12	Fakenham	3 10 78	Trainee
Preece David (M)	5 6	11 02	Bridgnorth	28 5 63	Derby Co
Raynor Paul (M)	5 11	13 03	Nottingham	29 4 66	Preston NE
Richards Tony (F)	5 10	13 06	Newham	17 9 73	Sudbury T
Taylor John (F)	6 3	14 03	Norwich	24 10 64	Luton T
Thompson David (D)	6 2	12 11	Ashington	20 11 68	Blackpool
Wanless Paul (M)	6 0	13 02	Banbury	14 12 73	Lincoln C
Wilde Adam (D)	5 10	11 08	Southampton	22 5 79	Trainee
Williamson Davey (D)	5 6	10 03	Hong Kong	15 12 75	Motherwell

League Appearances: Ashbee, I. 16(2); Barnwell-Edinboro, J. 35(5); Barrett, S. 45; Beall, B. 33(3); Benjamin, T. 1(6); Brazil, G. 1; Craddock, J. 41; Foster, C. 7; Granville, D. 37; Hay, D. (4); Hayes, A. 19(6); Hyde, M. 38; Joseph, M. 44; Joseph, M. 5(3); Kyd, M. 22(6); Marshall, S. 1; McGleish, S. 10; Pack, L. (1); Palmer, L. (1); Preece, D. 19(6); Raynor, P. 43(1); Richards, T. 14(9); San Miguel, X. (1); Taylor, J. 19(2); Thompson, D. 15(7); Turner, R. 2(5); Vowden, C. 5(1); Wanless, P. 27(3); Wilde, A. (1); Wilson, P. 7
League (53): Hyde 7 (2 pens), Kyd 7, McGleish 7, Barnwell-Edinboro 6, Raynor 4, Richards 4, Taylor 4, Wanless 3, Beall 2, Thompson 2, Benjamin 1, Brazil 1, Craddock 1, Turner 1, own goals 3.
Coca-Cola Cup (1): Thompson 1.
FA Cup (3): Barnwell-Edinboro 1, Beall 1, Kyd 1.
Ground: Abbey Stadium, Newmarket Rd, Cambridge CB5 8LN. Telephone (01223) 566500. **Capacity:** 9667
Record attendance; 14,000 v Chelsea, Friendly, 1 May 1970.
Manager: Roy McFarland.
Secretary: Steve Greenall.
Honours – Football League: Division 3 Champions – 1990–91. Division 4 Champions – 1976–77.
Colours: Amber & black shirts, black shorts, black & amber stockings.

Cross John (M)	5 9	13 00	Barking	6	4 76	QPR
Dale Carl (F)	5 9	11 11	Colwyn Bay	29	4 66	Chester C
Eckhardt Jeff (D)	6 0	11 07	Sheffield	7	10 65	Stockport Co
Elliott Tony (G)	6 1	13 07	Nuneaton	30	11 69	Carlisle U
Fowler Jason (M)	6 3	11 11	Bristol	20	8 74	Bristol C
Haworth Simon (F)	6 4	13 01	Cardiff	30	3 77	Trainee
Jarman Lee (D)	6 3	13 02	Cardiff	16	12 77	Trainee
Lloyd Kevin (D)	6 0	11 10	Llanidloes	26	9 70	Hereford U
Middleton Craig (M)	5 10	11 05	Nuneaton	10	9 70	Cambridge U
Partridge Scott (M)	5 9	10 09	Leicester	13	10 74	Bristol C
Perry Jason (D)	5 11	11 12	Caerphilly	2	4 70	Trainee
Philliskirk Tony (F)	6 1	13 00	Sunderland	10	2 65	Burnley
Stoker Gareth (M)	5 9	10 10	Bishop Auckland	22	2 73	Hereford U
White Steve (F)	5 11	12 08	Chipping Sodbury	2	1 59	Hereford U
Young Scott (M)	6 3	12 08	Tonypandy	14	1 76	Trainee

League Appearances: Baddeley, L. 4(5); Bennett, M. 5(9); Burton, D. 5; Coldicott, S. 6; Dale, C. 28(5); Davies, G. 6; Eckhardt, J. 34(1); Elliott, T. 36; Flack, S. 1; Fleming, H. 9(1); Fowler, J. 37; Gardner, J. 19(9); Haworth, S. 20(4); Jarman, L. 27(5); Lloyd, K. 27(4); McStay, R. 1; Michaels, J. (1); Middleton, C. 40(1); Mountain, P. 5; O'Halloran, K. 8; Partridge, S. 14(1); Perry, J. 35; Phillips, L. 2(1); Philliskirk, T. 27(6); Rodgerson, I. 15(6); Rollo, J. 3(7); Scott, A. 1(1); Stoker, G. 17; Ware, P. 5; White, S. 32(6); Williams, S. 5; Young, S. 32
League (56): White 13 (2 pens), Haworth 9, Dale 8 (1 pen), Eckhardt 5, Fowler 5, Middleton 4, Stoker 3, Burton 2, Davies 2, Bennett 1, Gardner 1, Lloyd 1, Philliskirk 1, Young 1.
Coca-Cola Cup (1): Dale 1.
FA Cup (2): Middleton 1, White 1.
Ground: Ninian Park, Cardiff CF1 8SX. Telephone Cardiff (01222) 398636.
Record attendance: 61,566, Wales v England, 14 October 1961. **Capacity:** 14,980.
Manager: Russell Osman.
Secretary: Ceri Whitehead.
Honours – Football League: Division 3 (S) Champions – 1946–47. **FA Cup winners** 1926–27 (only occasion the Cup has been won by a club outside England). **Welsh Cup winners** 21 times.
Colours: Blue shirts, white shorts, white stockings.

Archdeacon Owen (M)	5 9	11 01	Glasgow	4	3 66	Barnsley
Aspinall Warren (F)	5 9	12 08	Wigan	13	9 67	Bournemouth
Boertien Paul (D)	5 10	11 00	Haltwhistle	20	1 79	Trainee
Caig Tony (G)	6 0	13 04	Whitehaven	11	4 74	Trainee
Conway Paul (M)	6 1	12 12	London	17	4 70	Oldham Ath
Day Richard (G)	6 2	13 10	Chelmsford	25	1 79	Trainee
Delap Rory (M)	6 1	12 09	Coldfield	6	7 76	Trainee
Dixon George (G)	6 0	14 05	Whitehaven	24	10 78	Trainee
Dobie Scott (F)	6 1	11 12	Workington	10	10 78	Trainee
Hayward Steve (M)	5 11	12 01	Walsall	8	9 71	Derby Co
Hopper Tony (M)	5 11	12 02	Carlisle	31	5 76	Trainee
Jansen Matthew (F)	5 10	10 13	Carlisle	20	10 77	Trainee
Joyce Joe (D)	5 9	11 01	Consett	18	3 61	Scunthorpe U
McAlindon Gareth (F)	5 9	11 10	Hexham	6	4 77	Newcastle U

Peacock Lee (F)	6 0	13 01	Paisley	9 10 76	Trainee
Pounewatchy Stephane (D)	6 0	15 00	Paris	10 2 68	Gueugnon
Prokas Richard (M)	5 9	11 05	Penrith	22 1 76	Trainee
Sandwith Kevin (M)	5 11	12 05	Workington	30 4 78	Trainee
Smart Allan (F)	5 11	13 04	Perth	8 7 74	Preston NE
Stevens Ian (F)	5 11	12 04	Malta	21 10 66	Shrewsbury T
Taylor Lee (D)	6 0	12 13	Whitehaven	12 9 77	Trainee
Thorpe Jeff (M)	5 11	12 12	Whitehaven	17 11 72	Trainee
Varty Will (D)	6 0	12 06	Workington	1 10 76	Trainee
Walling Dean (D)	5 11	11 13	Leeds	17 4 69	Guiseley

League Appearances: Archdeacon, O. 46; Aspinall, W. 39(1); Bass, J. 3; Caig, T. 46; Conway, P. 22(3); Currie, D. 5(4); Delap, R. 25(7); Dobie, S. (2); Edmondson, D. 19(1); Freestone, C. 3(2); Hayward, S. 43; Heath, S. (1); Hopper, T. 13(7); Jansen, M. 4(15); Kerr, D. (1); McAlindon, G. 3(9); Peacock, L. 37(7); Pounewatchy, S. 42; Prokas, R. 10(3); Reeves, D. 8; Robinson, J. 6(1); Shirtliff, P. 5; Smart, A. 25(3); Thomas, R. 23(13); Thorpe, J. 2(3); Varty, W. 31(1); Walling, D. 46.
League (67): Smart 10, Conway 9, Peacock 9, Hayward 7, Archdeacon 6, Aspinall 5 (1 pen), Delap 4, Reeves 3, Walling 3, Freestone 2, McAlindon 2, Currie 1, Dobie 1, Edmondson 1, Hopper 1, Jansen 1, Pounewatchy 1, Prokas 1.
Coca-Cola Cup (6): Thomas 2, Archdeacon 1, Aspinall 1, Hayward 1, Reeves 1.
FA Cup (8): Archdeacon 2 (1 pen), Conway 1, Edmondson 1, McAlindon 1, Peacock 1, own goals 2.
Ground: Brunton Park, Carlisle CA1 1LL. Telephone (01228) 26237.
Record attendance: 27,500 v Birmingham C, FA Cup 3rd rd, 5 January 1957 and v Middlesbrough, FA Cup 5th rd, 7 February 1970. **Capacity:** 16,651.
Manager: Mervyn Day.
Secretary: A. Ritchie.
Honours – Football League: Division 3 Champions – 1964–65, 1994–95. **Auto Windscreens Shield winners:** 1997
Colours: Blue shirts, white shorts, white stockings.

CHARLTON ATHLETIC   DIV. 1

Allen Bradley (F)	5 7	10 07	Harold Wood	13 9 71	QPR
Balmer Stuart (D)	6 1	12 04	Falkirk	20 9 69	Celtic
Barness Anthony (D)	5 10	12 01	Lewisham	25 2 72	Chelsea
Brown Steve (D)	6 1	13 10	Brighton	13 5 72	Trainee
Chapple Phil (D)	6 2	12 07	Norwich	26 11 66	Cambridge U
Curbishley Alan (M)	5 10	11 07	Forest Gate	8 11 57	Brighton & HA
Emblen Paul (F)			Bromley	3 4 76	Tonbridge A
Jones Keith (M)	5 9	10 11	Dulwich	14 10 65	Southend U
Jones Steve (F)	5 11	12 00	Cambridge	17 3 70	West Ham U
Kearley Dean (D)			Greenwich	11 10 77	Trainee
Kinsella Mark (M)	5 9	11 05	Dublin	12 8 72	Colchester U
Leaburn Carl (F)	6 3	13 00	Lewisham	30 3 69	Apprentice
Lisbie Kevin (F)	5 9	11 00	Hackney	17 10 78	Trainee
Mortimer Paul (M)	5 11	11 03	Kensington	8 5 68	Crystal Palace
Newton Shaun (M)	5 8	11 00	Camberwell	20 8 75	Trainee
Nicholls Kevin (M)			Newham	2 1 79	Trainee
O'Connell Brendan (F)	5 9	12 01	London	12 11 66	Barnsley
Petterson Andy (G)	6 2	14 12	Fremantle	26 9 69	Luton T
Poole Gary (D)	6 0	11 00	Stratford	11 9 67	Birmingham C
Robinson John (M)	5 10	11 02	Bulawayo	29 8 71	Brighton & HA
Rufus Richard (D)	6 1	10 05	Lewisham	12 1 75	Trainee
Salmon Mike (G)	6 2	12 12	Leyland	14 7 64	Wrexham

Stuart Jamie (D)	5 10	11 00	Southwark	15 10 76	Trainee
Tindall Jason (F)			Stepney	15 11 77	Trainee
Whyte David (F)	5 8	10 07	Greenwich	20 4 71	Crystal Palace

League Appearances: Allen, B. 13(5); Balmer, S. 28(4); Barness, A. 45; Bright, M. 4(2); Brown, S. 22(5); Chapple, P. 25(1); Jones, K. 14(5); Jones, S. 2; Kinsella, M. 37; Leaburn, C. 40(4); Lee, J. 7(1); Lisbie, K. 4(21); Mortimer, P. 10(1); Newton, S. 39(4); Nicholls, K. 3(3); O'Connell, B. 33(5); Otto, R. 5(2); Petterson, A. 21; Poole, G. 14(2); Robinson, J. 41(1); Robson, M. 8(7); Rufus, R. 33(1); Salmon, M. 25; Scott, K. 4; Stuart, J. 10; Sturgess, P. 1(2); Whyte, D. 18(4)

League (52): Leaburn 8, Whyte 7, Kinsella 6, Allen 4, Lee 3, Newton 3, Robinson 3, Robson 3 (1 pen) Balmer 2, Barness 2, Bright 2, Chapple 2, O'Connell 2, Lisbie 1, Mortimer 1, Nicholls 1, Poole 1, Stuart 1.

Coca-Cola Cup (8): Allen 2, Robinson 2, Whyte 2, Leaburn 1, Newton 1.

FA Cup (2): Kinsella 1, Robson 1.

Ground: The Valley, Floyd Road, Charlton, London SE7 8BL. Telephone (0181) 333 4000.

Record attendance: 75,031 v Aston Villa, FA Cup 5th rd, 12 February 1938 (at The Valley). **Capacity:** 16,000.

Manager: Alan Curbishley.

Secretary: Chris Parkes.

Honours – Football League: Division 3 (S) Champions – 1928–29, 1934–35.

FA Cup winners 1947.

Colours: Red shirts, white shorts, red stockings.

CHELSEA   FA PREMIERSHIP

Burley Craig (M)	6 1	12 13	Ayr	24 9 71	Trainee
Clarke Steve (D)	5 10	12 05	Saltcoats	29 8 63	St Mirren
Clement Neil (D)	6 0	12 09	Reading	3 10 78	Trainee
Colgan Nick (G)	6 1	13 06	Eire	19 9 73	Drogheda
Di Matteo Roberto (M)	5 10	12 00	Sciaffusa	29 5 70	Lazio
Duberry Michael (D)	6 1	13 10	Enfield	14 10 75	Trainee
Granville Danny (D)	5 11	12 01	Islington	19 1 75	Cambridge U
Grodas Frode (G)			Sogndal	24 10 64	Lillestrom
Gullit Ruud (F)	6 3	13 12	Surinam	1 9 62	Sampdoria
Harley Jon (M)			Maidstone	26 9 79	Trainee
Hitchcock Kevin (G)	6 1	12 12	Custom House	5 10 62	Mansfield T
Hughes Mark (F)	5 10	13 01	Wrexham	1 11 63	Manchester U
Hughes Paul (M)	6 0	12 06	Hammersmith	19 4 76	Trainee
Johnsen Erland (D)	6 1	14 04	Fredrikstad	5 4 67	Bayern Munich
Kharine Dmitri (G)	6 2	13 09	Moscow	16 8 68	CSKA Moscow
Leboeuf Franck (D)	6 0	12 00	Paris	22 1 68	Strasbourg
Lee David (D)	6 3	14 11	Kingswood	26 11 69	Trainee
Minto Scott (D)	5 10	12 04	Cheshire	6 8 71	Charlton Ath
Morris Jody (M)	5 5	10 02	London	22 12 78	Trainee
Myers Andy (M)	5 10	12 11	Hounslow	3 11 73	Trainee
Newton Eddie (F)	6 0	12 08	Hammersmith	13 12 71	Trainee
Nicholls Mark (F)	5 10	10 01	Hillingdon	30 5 77	Trainee
Petrescu Dan (M)	5 10	11 07	Bucharest	22 12 67	Sheffield W
Rocastle David (F)	5 9	12 07	Lewisham	2 5 67	Manchester C
Sinclair Frank (D)	5 9	12 09	Lambeth	3 12 71	Trainee
Stein Mark (F)	5 6	11 07	S. Africa	29 1 66	Stoke C
Vialli Gianluca (F)	5 10	13 05	Cremona	9 7 64	Juventus
Wise Dennis (F)	5 6	10 10	Kensington	16 12 66	Wimbledon
Zola Gianfranco (F)	5 5	10 02	Oliena	5 7 66	Parma

League Appearances: Burley, C. 26(5); Clarke, S. 31; Clement, N. 1; Colgan, N. 1; Di Matteo, R. 33(1); Duberry, M. 13(2); Forrest, C. 2(1); Granville, D. 3(2); Grodas, F. 20(1); Gullit, R. 6(6); Hitchcock, K. 10(2); Hughes, M. 32(3); Hughes, P. 8(4); Johnsen, E. 14(4); Kharine, D. 5; Lebœuf, F. 26; Lee, D. 1; Minto, S. 24(1); Morris, J. 6(6); Myers, A. 15(3); Newton, E. 13(2); Nicholls, M. 3(5); Parker, P. 1(3); Petrescu, D. 34; Phelan, T. 1(2); Sheerin, J. (1); Sinclair, F. 17(3); Spencer, J. (4); Vialli, G. 23(5); Wise, D. 27(4); Zola, G. 22(1)
League (58): Vialli 9 (1 pen), Hughes M 8, Zola 8, Di Matteo 7, Lebœuf 6 (3 pens), Minto 4, Petrescu 3, Wise 3, Burley 2, Hughes P 2, Duberry 1, Gullit 1, Lee 1 (pen), Myers 1, Sinclair 1, own goal 1.
Coca-Cola Cup (6): Spencer 2, Hughes M 1, Minto 1, Morris 1, Petrescu 1.
FA Cup (17): Hughes M 5, Zola 4, Wise 3, Vialli 2, Burley 1, Di Matteo 1, Lebœuf 1 (pen).
Ground: Stamford Bridge, London SW6 1HS. Telephone (0171) 385 5545.
Record attendance: 82,905 v Arsenal, Division 1, 12 October 1935.
Capacity: 31,791 (up to 41,000).
Manager: Ruud Gullit.
Secretary: Yvonne Todd.
Honours – Football League: Division 1 Champions – 1954–55. **FA Cup winners** 1970, 1997. **Football League Cup winners** 1964–65. **Full Members' Cup winners** 1985–86. **Zenith Data Systems Cup winners** 1989–90. **European Cup-Winners' Cup winners** 1970–71.
Colours: Royal blue with white and amber shirts, royal blue and white shorts, white stockings.

CHESTER CITY   DIV. 3

Alsford Julian (D)	6 2	13 01	Poole	24 12 72	Watford
Brown Wayne (G)	6 0	11 12	Southampton	14 1 77	Weston-Super-Mare
Davidson Ross (D)	5 8	11 06	Chertsey	13 11 73	Sheffield U
Fisher Neil (M)	5 10	10 09	St Helens	7 11 70	Bolton W
Flitcroft David (M)	5 11	13 05	Bolton	14 1 74	Preston NE
Jenkins Iain (D)	5 9	11 10	Whiston	24 12 72	Everton
Jones Jon (F)	5 11	11 05	Wrexham	27 10 78	Trainee
McDonald Rod (F)	5 10	12 06	London	20 3 67	Partick T
Milner Andy (F)	6 0	11 00	Kendal	10 2 67	Rochdale
Murphy John (F)	6 1	14 00	Whiston	18 10 76	Trainee
Priest Chris (M)	5 10	10 10	Leigh	18 10 73	Everton
Ratcliffe Kevin (D)	6 1	13 06	Mancot	12 11 60	Derby Co
Reid Shaun (M)	5 8	12 10	Huyton	13 10 65	Bury
Richardson Nick (M)	6 1	12 06	Halifax	11 4 67	Bury
Rimmer Stuart (F)	5 7	11 00	Southport	12 10 64	Barnsley
Shelton Gary (M)	5 7	10 12	Nottingham	21 3 58	Bristol C
Sinclair Ronnie (G)	5 11	12 09	Stirling	19 11 64	Stoke C
Whelan Spencer (D)	6 2	11 00	Liverpool	17 9 71	Liverpool
Woods Mattie (D)	6 1	12 13	Gosport	9 9 76	Everton

League Appearances: Aiston, S. 14; Alsford, J. 43; Brown, G. (1); Brown, W. 2; Cutler, N. 5; Davidson, R. 40; Fisher, N. 19(10); Flitcroft, D. 30(2); Helliwell, I. 8(1); Jackson, P. 32; Jenkins, I. 39; Jones, J. 3(14); Knowles, C. 2; McDonald, R. 22; Milner, A. 38(8); Murphy, J. 4(7); Noteman, K. 30(5); Priest, C. 30(2); Reid, S. 27; Richardson, N. 9; Rimmer, S. 22(3); Rogers, D. 4(1); Shelton, G. 18(4); Sinclair, R. 37; Tallon, G. 1; Whelan, S. 18(7); Woods, M. 9(12)

League (55): Milner 12, Noteman 9 (2 pens), Flitcroft 6, McDonald 6, Rimmer 3, Shelton 3, Alsford 2, Davidson 2, Priest 2, Fisher 1, Helliwell 1, Jackson 1, Jones 1 (pen), Murphy 1, Reid 1 (pen), Whelan 1, Woods 1, own goals 2.
Coca-Cola Cup (1): Noteman 1.
FA Cup (4): Milner 2, Rimmer 2.
Ground: The Deva Stadium, Bumpers Lane, Chester CH1 4LT. Telephone (01244) 371376, 371809.
Record attendance: 20,500 v Chelsea, FA Cup 3rd rd (replay), 16 January, 1952 (at Sealand Road). **Capacity:** 6000.
Manager: Kevin Ratcliffe.
Secretary: Derek Barber JP, AMIPD.
Honours – Welsh Cup winners 1908, 1933, 1947. **Debenhams Cup:** Winners 1977.
Colours: Blue and white striped shirts, blue shorts, blue stockings.

CHESTERFIELD   DIV. 2

Beaumont Chris (M)	5 11	11 12	Sheffield	5 12 65	Stockport Co
Carr Darren (D)	6 2	13 07	Bristol	4 9 68	Crewe Alex
Curtis Tom (M)	5 8	10 08	Exeter	1 3 73	Derby Co
Dunn Iain (M)	5 10	10 07	Derwent	1 4 70	Huddersfield T
Dyche Sean (D)	6 0	11 07	Kettering	28 6 71	Nottingham F
Ebdon Marcus (M)	5 10	11 02	Pontypool	17 10 70	Peterborough U
Gaughan Steve (M)	6 0	12 04	Doncaster	14 4 70	Darlington
Hewitt Jamie (M)	5 10	10 08	Chesterfield	17 5 68	Doncaster R
Holland Paul (M)	5 11	12 10	Lincoln	8 7 73	Sheffield U
Howard Jonathan (F)	5 11	11 07	Sheffield	7 10 71	Rotherham U
Jules Mark (D)	5 7	10 09	Bradford	5 9 71	Scarborough
Leaning Andy (G)	6 2	13 00	York	18 5 63	Lincoln C
Lomas James (M)	5 11	10 09	Chesterfield	18 10 77	Trainee
Lormor Tony (F)	6 0	11 05	Ashington	29 10 70	Peterborough U
Mercer Billy (G)	6 1	11 00	Liverpool	22 5 69	Sheffield U
Morris Andy (F)	6 4	14 07	Sheffield	17 11 67	Rotherham U
Perkins Chris (M)	5 11	10 09	Nottingham	9 1 74	Mansfield T
Rogers Lee (D)	5 11	12 01	Doncaster	28 10 66	Doncaster R
Williams Mark (D)	6 0	12 04	Stalybridge	28 9 70	Shrewsbury T

League Appearances: Allison, N. (2); Beaumont, C. 29(4); Bowater, J. (1); Carr, D. 12; Curtis, T. 40; Davies, K. 28(6); Dunn, I. 10(1); Dyche, S. 36; Ebdon, M. 11(1); Gaughan, S. 14(4); Hanson, D. 3; Hewitt, J. 36(1); Holland, P. 24(1); Howard, J. 26(9); Jules, M. 41(1); Law, N. 4(3); Leaning, A. 9; Lomas, J. (2); Lormor, T. 25(11); Lund, G. 7(3); Mason, A. 1(1); Mercer, B. 35; Mitchell, A. 1(1); Morgan, P. 2; Morris, A. 19(8); Patterson, G. 7(2); Perkins, C. 26(4); Rogers, L. 14(3); Scott, A. 4(1); Williams, M. 42
League (42): Howard 9, Lormor 8 (1 pen), Morris 4, Curtis 3 (2 pens), Davies 3, Holland 3, Scott 3, Williams 3, Beaumont 1, Ebdon 1, Hanson 1, Hewitt 1, Law 1 (pen), own goal 1.
Coca-Cola Cup (2): Gaughan 1, Lormor 1 (pen).
FA Cup (13): Davies 4, Howard 2, Beaumont 1, Curtis 1 (pen), Dyche 1 (pen), Hewitt 1, Lormor 1, Morris 1, Williams 1.
Ground: Recreation Ground, Chesterfield S40 4SX. Telephone (01246) 209765.
Record attendance: 30,968 v Newcastle U, Division 2, 7 April 1939. **Capacity:** 8880.
Manager: John Duncan.
Secretary: Nicola Bellamy.
Honours – Football League: Division 3 (N) Champions – 1930–31, 1935–36. Division 4 Champions – 1969–70, 1984–85. **Anglo-Scottish Cup winners** 1980–81.
Colours: Blue shirts, white shorts, blue stockings.

Abrahams Paul (F)	5 11	11 02	Colchester	31 10 73	Brentford
Adcock Tony (F)	6 0	11 05	Bethnal Green	27 2 63	Luton T
Betts Simon (D)	5 7	11 00	Middlesbrough	3 3 73	Scarborough
Buckle Paul (M)	5 7	11 03	Welwyn	16 12 70	Wycombe W
Caldwell Garrett (G)	6 1	12 12	Princeton	6 11 73	
Cawley Peter (D)	6 4	15 07	London	15 9 65	Barnet
Duguid Karl (F)	5 11	11 05	Hitchin	21 3 78	Trainee
Dunne Joe (D)	5 9	11 08	Dublin	25 5 73	Gillingham
Emberson Carl (G)	6 1	12 00	Epsom	13 7 73	Millwall
Forbes Steve (M)	6 1	11 04	London	24 12 75	Millwall
Fry Chris (F)	5 10	10 07	Cardiff	23 10 69	Hereford U
Greene David (M)	6 4	14 04	Luton	26 10 73	Luton T
Gregory David (M)	5 10	12 00	Colchester	23 1 70	Peterborough U
Haydon Nicky (M)	5 10	11 07	Barking	10 8 78	Trainee
Lock Tony (F)	5 11	12 09	Harlow	3 9 76	Trainee
Locke Adam (M)	6 0	12 00	Croydon	20 8 70	Southend U
McCarthy Tony (D)	6 1	12 06	Dublin	9 11 69	Millwall
Sale Mark (F)	6 3	13 05	Burton-on-Trent	27 2 72	Mansfield T
Stamps Scott (D)	5 10	11 00	Edgbaston	20 3 75	Torquay U
Whitton Steve (M)	6 1	12 04	East Ham	4 12 60	Ipswich T
Wilkins Richard (M)	5 10	12 02	Streatham	28 5 65	Hereford U

League Appearances: Abrahams, P. 27(2); Adcock, T. 26(10); Barnes, D. 11; Betts, S. 10; Buckle, P. 24; Caldwell, G. 6; Cawley, P. 28; Duguid, K. 10(10); Dunne, J. 23(12); Emberson, C. 35; Forbes, S. 1; Fry, C. 31(11); Gibbs, P. 18(2); Greene, D. 44; Gregory, D. 32(6); Haydon, N. 1; Kelly, T. 2(1); Kinsella, M. 7; Lock, T. 1(5); Locke, A. 22(10); McCarthy, T. 34(1); Pitcher, G. 1; Reinelt, R. 8(13); Sale, M. 10; Stamps, S. 7(1); Taylor, J. 8; Vaughan, J. 5; Whitton, S. 36(3); Wilkins, R. 40
League (62): Adcock 11 (1 pen), Abrahams 7, Fry 6, Whitton 6, Locke 5, Taylor 5 (2 pens), Duguid 3 (1 pen), Reinelt 3, Sale 3, Greene 2, Kinsella 2, Wilkins 2, Betts 1 (pen), Cawley 1, Forbes 1, Gregory 1, Hayden 1, own goals 2.
Coca-Cola Cup (6): Reinelt 2, Adcock 1, Dunne 1, Fry 1, Kinsella 1.
FA Cup (1): Wilkins 1.
Ground: Layer Rd Ground, Colchester CO2 7JJ. Telephone (01206) 508800.
Record attendance: 19,072 v Reading, FA Cup 1st rd, 27 Nov, 1948. **Capacity:** 7190.
Manager: Steve Wignall.
Secretary: Mrs Marie Partner.
Honours – GM Vauxhall Conference winners 1991–92. **FA Trophy winners** 1991–92.
Colours: Blue and white striped shirts, white shorts, white stockings.

COVENTRY CITY FA PREMIERSHIP

Andrews John (D)			Cork	27 9 78	Trainee
Barnett Christopher (M)			Derby	20 12 78	Trainee
Blake Aslam (F)	5 11	11 12	Birmingham	19 10 79	Trainee
Boland Willie (M)	5 9	11 02	Ennis	6 8 75	Trainee
Borrows Brian (D)	5 10	11 12	Liverpool	20 12 60	Bolton W
Breen Gary (D)	6 3	11 12	London	12 12 73	Birmingham C
Burrows David (D)	5 10	11 08	Dudley	25 10 68	Everton
Christie Iyseden (F)	6 0	12 06	Coventry	14 11 76	Trainee
Daish Liam (D)	6 2	13 05	Portsmouth	23 9 68	Birmingham C

Name	Ht	Wt	Birthplace	Birthdate	Previous club
Dublin Dion (F)	6 2	12 04	Leicester	22 4 69	Manchester U
Ducros Andrew (F)	5 4	9 08	Evesham	16 9 77	Trainee
Eustace John (M)	5 10	11 12	Solihull	3 11 79	Trainee
Evtushok Alex (D)	6 2	12 10	Ukraine	11 1 70	Karpaty Lvov
Faulconbridge Craig (F)			Nuneaton	20 4 78	Trainee
Filan John (G)	5 11	13 02	Sydney	8 2 70	Cambridge U
Genaux Regis (D)	5 11	12 06	Belgium	31 8 73	Standard Liege
Goodwin Scott (D)	5 9	11 08	Hull	13 9 78	Trainee
Hall Marcus (D)	6 1	12 02	Coventry	24 3 76	Trainee
Huckerby Darren (F)	5 9	11 04	Nottingham	23 4 76	Newcastle U
Jess Eoin (F)	5 10	11 07	Aberdeen	13 12 70	Aberdeen
McAllister Gary (M)	5 10	10 11	Motherwell	25 12 64	Leeds U
Ndlovu Peter (F)	5 8	10 2	Zimbabwe	25 2 73	Highlanders
O'Neill Michael (F)	5 11	10 10	Portadown	5 7 69	Hibernian
Ogrizovic Steve (G)	6 5	15 00	Mansfield	12 9 57	Shrewsbury T
Prenderville Barry (D)	6 0	12 08	Dublin	16 10 76	Trainee
Quinn Barry (M)	6 0	12 02	Dublin	9 5 79	Trainee
Richardson Kevin (M)	5 7	11 07	Newcastle	4 12 62	Aston Villa
Salako John (F)	5 9	12 03	Nigeria	11 2 69	Crystal Palace
Shaw Richard (D)	5 9	12 08	Brentford	11 9 68	Crystal Palace
Shilton Sam (M)	5 10	11 06	Nottingham	21 7 78	Plymouth Arg
Strachan Gavin (M)	5 10	11 07	Aberdeen	23 12 78	Trainee
Strachan Gordon (M)	5 6	10 06	Edinburgh	9 2 57	Leeds U
Telfer Paul (M)	5 9	11 06	Edinburgh	21 10 71	Luton T
Whelan Noel (F)	6 2	12 03	Leeds	30 12 74	Leeds U
Williams Paul (D)	6 0	12 10	Burton	26 3 71	Derby Co
Willis Adam (M)	6 1	12 02	Nuneaton	21 9 76	Trainee

League Appearances: Boland, W. (1); Borrows, B. 16(7); Breen, G. 8(1); Burrows, D. 17(1); Daish, L. 20; Dublin, D. 33(1); Ducros, A. 1(4); Evtushok, A. 3; Filan, J. (1); Genaux, R. 3(1); Hall, M. 10(3); Huckerby, D. 21(4); Isaias, . (1); Jess, E. 19(8); McAllister, G. 38; Ndlovu, P. 10(10); O'Neill, M. 1; Ogrizovic, S. 38; Richardson, K. 25(3); Salako, J. 23(1); Shaw, R. 35; Strachan, G. 3(6); Telfer, P. 31(3); Whelan, N. 34(1); Williams, P. 29(3)
League (38): Dublin 13, McAllister 6 (3 pens), Whelan 6, Huckerby 5, Williams 2, Daish 1, Ndlovu 1, Salako 1, own goals 3.
Coca-Cola Cup (4): Telfer 2, Daish 1, McAllister 1.
FA Cup (7): Huckerby 2, Jess 2, Whelan 2, own goal 1.
Ground: Highfield Road Stadium, King Richard Street, Coventry CV2 4FW. Telephone (01203) 234000.
Record attendance: 51,455 v Wolverhampton W, Division 2, 29 April 1967.
Capacity: 23,662.
Manager: Gordon Strachan.
Secretary: Graham Hover.
Honours – Football League: Division 2 Champions – 1966–67. Division 3 Champions – 1963–64. Division 3 (S) Champions 1935–36. **FA Cup winners** 1986–87.
Colours: Sky blue and navy striped shirts, navy shorts and stockings.

CREWE ALEXANDRA   DIV. 1

Name	Ht	Wt	Birthplace	Birthdate	Previous club
Adebola Dele (F)	6 3	12 06	Lagos	23 6 75	Trainee
Anthrobus Steve (F)	6 3	12 13	Lewisham	10 11 68	Shrewsbury T
Bankole Ademola (G)			Nigeria	9 6 69	Leyton Orient
Charnock Phil (M)	5 10	11 03	Southport	14 2 75	Liverpool
Collins James (M)			Liverpool	28 5 78	Trainee

Cutler Neil (G)	6 4	13 04	Birmingham	3 9 76	WBA	
Garvey Steve (F)	5 9	10 09	Tameside	22 11 73	Trainee	
Gayle Mark (G)	6 2	12 03	Bromsgrove	21 10 69	Walsall	
Johnson Seth (D)			Birmingham	12 3 79	Trainee	
Kearton Jason (G)	6 1	11 10	Ipswich (Aus)	9 7 69	Everton	
Lightfoot Chris (M)	6 1	12 00	Warrington	1 4 70	Wigan Ath	
Little Colin (F)	5 10	11 00	Wythenshaw	4 11 72	Hyde U	
Macauley Steve (D)	6 1	12 00	Lytham	4 3 69	Fleetwood T	
Moralee Jamie (F)	5 11	11 00	Wandsworth	2 12 71	Watford	
Murphy Danny (M)	5 9	10 08	Chester	18 3 77	Trainee	
Norris Richard (M)			Birkenhead	5 1 78	Marine	
Pope Steven (D)	5 11	11 00	Mow Cop	8 9 76	Trainee	
Rivers Mark (F)	5 10	11 00	Crewe	26 11 75	Trainee	
Savage Rob (F)	6 0	10 01	Wrexham	18 10 74	Manchester U	
Smith Peter (F)			Rhuddlan	18 9 78	Trainee	
Smith Shaun (D)	5 10	11 00	Leeds	9 4 71	Halifax T	
Street Kevin (M)			Crewe	25 11 77	Trainee	
Tierney Francis (M)	5 10	11 00	Liverpool	10 9 75	Trainee	
Unsworth Lee (D)	5 11	11 02	Eccles	25 2 73	Ashton U	
Westwood Ashley (D)	6 0	11 03	Bridgnorth	31 8 76	Manchester U	
Whalley Gareth (M)	5 10	11 06	Manchester	19 12 73	Trainee	

League Appearances: Adebola, D. 27(5); Anthrobus, S. 10; Bankole, A. 3; Barr, B. 29(5); Billing, P. 9(6); Charnock, P. 24(8); Ellison, L. 3; Garvey, S. 9(7); Gayle, M. 4; Johnson, S. 8(3); Kearton, J. 30; Launders, B. 6(3); Lightfoot, C. 16(9); Little, C. 3(14); Macauley, S. 40(2); Mautone, S. 3; Moralee, J. 7; Murphy, D. 44(1); Rivers, M. 23(4); Savage, R. 41; Smith, P. (1); Smith, S. 34(4); Taylor, M. 6; Tierney, F. 18(14); Unsworth, L. 28(1); Westwood, A. 43(1); Whalley, G. 38
League (56): Adebola 16, Murphy 10, Rivers 6, Barr 5, Smith S 4 (1 pen), Tierney 3, Whalley 3, Ellison 2, Macauley 2, Westwood 2, Charnock 1, Johnson 1, Savage 1.
Coca-Cola Cup (1): Adebola 1.
FA Cup (10): Murphy 3, Adebola 1, Garvey 1, Lightfoot 1, Macauley 1, Smith S 1, Westwood 1, own goal 1.
Ground: Football Ground, Gresty Rd, Crewe CW2 6EB. Telephone (01270) 213014.
Record attendance: 20,000 v Tottenham H, FA Cup 4th rd, 30 January 1960.
Capacity: 6000.
Manager: Dario Gradi.
Secretary: Mrs Gill Palin.
Honours – Welsh Cup: Winners 1936, 1937.
Colours: Red shirts, red shorts, white stockings.

CRYSTAL PALACE   FA PREMIERSHIP

Andersen Leif (D)	6 4	13 00	Fredrikstad	19 4 71	Moss	
Boxall Danny (D)	5 8	10 05	Croydon	24 8 77	Trainee	
Burton Sagi (D)	6 2	13 06	Birmingham	25 11 77	Trainee	
Carlisle Wayne (M)	5 7	10 00	Lisburn	9 9 79	Trainee	
Davies Gareth (D)	6 1	12 00	Hereford	11 12 73	Hereford U	
Day Chris (G)	6 2	13 06	Whipps Cross	28 7 75	Tottenham H	
Dyer Bruce (F)	5 11	11 03	Ilford	13 4 75	Watford	
Edworthy Marc (D)	5 7	9 08	Barnstaple	24 12 72	Plymouth Arg	
Folan Anthony (F)	6 0	11 00	Lewisham	18 9 78	Trainee	
Freedman Dougie (F)	5 9	11 02	Glasgow	21 1 74	Barnet	
Ginty Rory (M)	5 9	11 00	Galway	23 1 77	Trainee	
Gordon Dean (D)	6 0	13 04	Thornton Heath	10 2 73	Trainee	

Graham Gareth (M)	5 7	10 07	Belfast	6 12 78	Trainee
Harris Jason (F)	6 1	11 10	Sutton	24 11 76	Trainee
Hibbert James (D)	5 11	11 07	Ashford	30 10 79	Trainee
Hopkin David (M)	5 9	10 03	Greenock	21 8 70	Chelsea
Houghton Ray (M)	5 7	10 10	Glasgow	9 1 62	Aston Villa
Kennedy Richard (M)	5 11	11 00	Waterford	28 8 78	Trainee
Linighan Andy (D)	6 4	13 10	Hartlepool	18 6 62	Arsenal
Martin Andrew (F)	6 0	11 01	Cardiff	28 2 80	Trainee
McKenzie Leon (F)	5 11	10 00	Croydon	17 5 78	Trainee
Morrison Clinton (F)	5 10	10 00	Tooting	14 5 79	Trainee
Mullins Hayden (M)	5 11	10 07	Reading	27 3 79	Trainee
Muscat Kevin (D)	5 11	11 07	Crawley	8 8 73	South Melbourne
Nash Carlo (G)	6 4	12 07	Bolton	13 9 73	Clitheroe
Ndah George (M)	6 1	11 04	Camberwell	23 12 74	Trainee
Ormshaw Gareth (G)	6 0	11 07	Durban	8 7 79	Ramblers
Pitcher Darren (M)	5 9	12 02	London	12 10 69	Charlton Ath
Quinn Robert (D)	5 11	11 02	Sidcup	8 11 76	Trainee
Roberts Andy (M)	5 10	13 00	Dartford	20 3 74	Millwall
Rodger Simon (M)	5 9	11 09	Shoreham	3 10 71	Trainee
Scully Tony (M)	5 7	11 05	Dublin	12 6 76	Trainee
Shipperley Neil (F)	6 1	13 11	Chatham	30 10 74	Southampton
Stevens David (F)	5 10	11 00	Ashford	29 4 79	Trainee
Thomson Steven (M)	5 7	10 00	Glasgow	23 1 78	Trainee
Tuttle David (D)	6 2	12 10	Reading	6 2 72	Sheffield U
Veart Carl (F)	5 10	11 05	Whyalla Adelaide	21 5 70	Sheffield U
Wordsworth Dean (F)			London	2 7 72	Bromley

League Appearances: Andersen, L. 7(7); Boxall, D. 4(2); Cyrus, A. 1; Davies, G. 5(1); Day, C. 24; Dyer, B. 39(4); Edworthy, M. 42(3); Freedman, D. 33(11); Gordon, D. 26(4); Harris, J. (2); Hopkin, D. 38(3); Houghton, R. 18(3); Linighan, A. 19; McKenzie, L. 4(17); Mimms, B. 1; Muscat, K. 42(2); Nash, C. 21; Ndah, G. 5(21); Pitcher, D. 3; Quinn, R. 17(4); Roberts, A. 45; Rodger, S. 9(2); Scully, T. (1); Shipperley, N. 29(3); Trollope, P. (9); Tuttle, D. 39; Veart, C. 35(4)
League (78): Dyer 17 (2 pens), Hopkin 13, Shipperley 12, Freedman 11, Veart 6, Gordon 3 (2 pens), Ndah 3, Linighan 2, McKenzie 2, Muscat 2, Roberts 2, Tuttle 2, Andersen 1, Houghton 1, Quinn 1.
Coca-Cola Cup (8): Hopkin 2, Veart 2, Edworthy 1, Freedman 1, Muscat 1, Quinn 1.
FA Cup (2): Dyer 1 (pen), Veart 1.
Ground: Selhurst Park, London SE25 6PU. Telephone (0181) 768 6000.
Record attendance: 51,482 v Burnley, Division 2, 11 May 1979. **Capacity:** 26,400.
Manager: Steve Coppell.
Club Secretary: Mike Hurst.
Honours – Football League: Division 1 – Champions 1993–94. Division 2 Champions – 1978–79. Division 3 (S) 1920–21. **Zenith Data Systems Cup winners 1991.**
Colours: Red and blue shirts, white shorts, white stockings.

DARLINGTON   DIV. 3

Atkinson Brian (M)	5 9	12 02	Darlington	19 1 71	Sunderland
Barnard Mark (D)	5 10	11 07	Sheffield	27 11 75	Rotherham U
Brumwell Phil (M)	5 8	11 00	Darlington	8 8 75	Sunderland
Brydon Lee (M)	5 11	11 00	Stockton	15 11 74	Liverpool
Crosby Andy (D)	6 2	13 07	Rotherham	3 3 73	Doncaster R
Devos Jason (D)			Ontario	2 1 74	Montreal Impact

Hope Richard (D)	6 2	12 06	Stockton	22 6 78	Blackburn R
Naylor Glenn (F)	5 11	11 00	York	11 8 72	York C
Oliver Michael (M)	5 10	12 04	Cleveland	2 8 75	Stockport Co
Roberts Darren (F)	6 0	12 04	Birmingham	12 10 69	Chesterfield
Shaw Simon (M)	5 11	11 02	Teeside	21 9 73	Trainee
Shutt Carl (F)	5 11	10 10	Sheffield	10 10 61	Bradford C
Twynham Gary (M)	5 11	12 07	Manchester	8 2 76	Manchester U

League Appearances: Atkinson, B. 25(5); Atkinson, J. 2(3); Barbara, D. 1(5); Barnard, M. 35(2); Blake. R. 28(2); Brumwell, P. 31(7); Brydon, L. 17(8); Byrne, W. 1(1); Carss, A. 20(9); Collins, M. (1); Crosby, A. 42; Devos, J. 7(1); Faulkner, D. 2(2); Gregan, S. 36; Hope, M. 1; Hope, R. 20; Hunt, D. (1); Innes, G. 1(14); Kelly, R. 13(10); Key, D. (3); Laws, B. 10; Lowe, K. 5(2); Lucas, D. 7; McClelland, J. 1; Moilanen, T. 16; Naylor, G. 30(7); Newell, P. 20; Oliver, M. 34(5); Painter, R. 2(4); Reed, A. 14; Roberts, D. 42(2); Robinson, P. (3); Shaw, S. 34(4); Shutt, C. 5(1); Speare, J. 3; Twynham, G. 21(8)
League (64): Roberts 16, Naylor 11 (1 pen), Blake 10 (2 pens), Oliver 9, Atkinson 4 (1 pen), Shaw 3, Twynham 3, Kelly 2, Shutt 2, Barbara 1, Brumwell 1, Crosby 1, own goal 1.
Coca-Cola Cup (4): Roberts 2, Blake 1, Painter 1.
FA Cup (4): Brumwell 1, Crosby 1, Naylor 1, Shaw 1.
Ground: Feethams Ground, Darlington DL1 5JB. Telephone (01325) 465097.
Record attendance: 21,023 v Bolton W, League Cup 3rd rd, 14 November 1960.
Capacity: 7046.
Manager: David Hodgson.
Secretary: K. J. Lavery.
Honours – Football League: Division 3 (N) Champions – 1924–25. Division 4 Champions – 1990–91.
Colours: Black and white.

DERBY COUNTY   FA PREMIERSHIP

Asanovic Aljosa (M)	6 1	11 12	Split	14 12 65	Hajduk Split
Boden Chris (D)	5 9	11 12	Wolverhampton	13 10 73	Aston Villa
Carbon Matt (D)	6 2	14 00	Nottingham	8 6 75	Lincoln C
Carsley Lee (D)	5 9	12 00	Birmingham	28 2 74	Trainee
Cooper Kevin (M)	5 7	10 07	Derby	8 2 75	Trainee
Dailly Christian (D)	6 0	12 06	Dundee	23 10 73	Dundee U
Elliott Steven (M)			Derby	29 10 78	Trainee
Flynn Sean (M)	5 8	12 00	Birmingham	13 3 68	Coventry C
Hoult Russell (G)	6 4	14 07	Ashby	22 11 72	Leicester C
Kozluk Robert (M)			Mansfield	5 8 77	Trainee
Laursen Jacob (D)	5 11	12 01	Vejle	6 10 71	Silkeborg
McDonald Jamie (M)			Luton	29 1 80	Trainee
Poom Mart (G)	6 5	13 05	Tallinn	3 2 72	Flora Tallinn
Powell Chris (M)	5 10	11 07	Lambeth	8 9 69	Southend U
Powell Darryl (M)	6 0	13 00	Lambeth	15 1 71	Portsmouth
Radzki Lee (M)			Mansfield	14 11 78	Trainee
Rowett Gary (D)	6 0	12 07	Bromsgrove	6 3 74	Everton
Simpson Paul (F)	5 8	11 11	Carlisle	26 7 66	Oxford U
Smith Craig (M)	6 1	13 07	Mansfield	2 8 76	Trainee
Solis Mauricio (M)	5 8	12 00	Costa Rica	13 12 72	Herediano
Stimac Igor (D)	6 2	13 00	Metkovic	6 9 67	Hajduk Split
Sturridge Dean (F)	5 8	12 06	Birmingham	27 7 73	Trainee
Sutton Wayne (D)	6 0	13 09	Derby	1 10 75	Trainee
Trollope Paul (M)	6 0	12 00	Swindon	3 6 72	Torquay U

Van der Laan Robin (M)	6 0	13 08	Schiedam	5 9 68	Port Vale
Wanchope Paulo (F)	6 4	12 05	Costa Rica	31 1 76	Herediano
Ward Ashley (F)	6 1	13 00	Manchester	24 11 70	Norwich C
Wilkinson Mark (M)			Coventry	16 3 79	Trainee
Willems Ron (F)	6 1	12 05	Epe	20 9 66	Grasshoppers
Wright Nick (F)	5 9	11 07	Derby	15 10 75	Trainee
Yates Dean (D)	6 1	12 08	Leicester	26 10 67	Notts Co

League Appearances: Asanovic, A. 34; Carbon, M. 6(4); Carsley, L. 15(9); Dailly, C. 31(5); Flynn, S. 10(7); Gabbiadini, M. 5(9); Hoult, R. 31(1); Laursen, J. 35(1); McGrath, P. 23(1); Parker, P. 4; Poom, M. 4; Powell, C. 35; Powell, D. 27(6); Rahmberg, M. 1; Rowett, G. 35; Simpson, P. 19(5); Solis, M. 2; Stimac, I. 21; Sturridge, D. 29(1); Taylor, M. 3; Trollope, P. 13(1); Van der Laan, R. 15(1); Wanchope, P. 2(3); Ward, A. 25(5); Willems, R. 7(9); Yates, D. 8(2)
League (45): Sturridge 11, Ward 8, Asanovic 6 (4 pens), Dailly 3, Rowett 2, Simpson 2, Van der Laan 2, Willems 2, Flynn 1, Laursen 1, Powell D 1, Stimac 1, Trollope 1, Wanchope 1, own goals 3.
Coca-Cola Cup (2): Simpson 1, Sturridge 1.
FA Cup (8): Van der Laan 3, Sturridge 2, Willems 2, Ward 1.
Ground: Pride Park Stadium, DE24 8XL. Telephone: (01332) 667503.
Record attendance: 41,826 v Tottenham H, Division 1, 20 September 1969.
Capacity: 30,000.
Manager: Jim Smith ACIS.
Secretary: Keith Pearson.
Honours – Football League: Division 1 Champions – 1971–72, 1974–75. Division 2 Champions – 1911–12, 1914–15, 1968–69, 1986–87. Division 3 (N) 1956–57. **FA Cup winners** 1945–46.
Colours: Black shirts, black shorts, white stockings.

DONCASTER ROVERS   DIV. 3

Clark Ian (M)	5 11	11 02	Stockton	23 10 74	Stockton
Cramb Colin (F)	6 0	13 00	Lanark	23 6 74	Hearts
Cunningham Harvey (D)			Manchester	11 9 68	Trafford Barons
Dixon Kerry (F)	6 1	13 10	Luton	24 7 61	Watford
Esdaille Darren (D)			Manchester	4 11 74	Hyde U
Gore Ian (D)	5 11	12 04	Whiston	10 1 68	Torquay U
Hawthorne Mark (M)			Sunderland	21 8 79	Trainee
Ireland Simon (M)	5 10	10 07	Barnstaple	23 11 71	Mansfield T
Larmour David (F)	5 9	11 00	Belfast	23 8 77	Liverpool
McDonald Martin (M)	6 0	11 07	Glasgow	4 12 73	Southport
Moore Darren (D)	6 2	15 00	Birmingham	22 4 74	Torquay U
Pemberton Martin (F)	5 11	10 04	Bradford	1 2 76	Oldham Ath
Pearce Stephen (F)	6 0	12 04	Sutton Coldfield	29 9 74	Wolverhampton W
Schofield Jon (M)	5 11	11 08	Barnsley	16 5 65	Lincoln C
Smith Mike (M)	5 10	11 05	Liverpool	28 9 73	Runcorn
Utley Darren (D)	6 0	11 07	Barnsley	28 9 77	Trainee
Warren Lee (M)	6 0	12 00	Manchester	28 2 69	Hull C
Williams Dean (G)	6 1	12 00	Lichfield	5 1 72	Brentford

League Appearances: Anderson, L. 6; Beirne, M. 1; Birch, P. 26(1); Bullimore, W. 4; Clark, I. 8(12); Coady, L. 1; Colcombe, S. 9(3); Cramb, C. 40(1); Cunningham, H. 11; Dixon, K. 13(3); Doling, S. 3(2); Donnelly, M. (2); Esdaille, D. 16(2); Fahy, A. (5); Gore, I. 35(1); Gray, A. 1; Ireland, S. 27; Larmour, D. 3(17); Lester, J. 5(6); Marquis, P. 3; McDonald, M. 33; Messer, G. (1); Mike, A. 5; Moore, D. 41; Murphy, J. 30(1); O'Connor, G. 18; Ohandjanian, D. (1); Pemberton, M. 9;

Piearce, S. 8(11); Robertson, P. 3(1); Ryan, T. 22(6); Schofield, J. 42; Smith, M. 12(6); Utley, D. 19(4); Walker, S. 1; Warren, L. 21(4); Weaver, S. 2; Wheeler, A. 1; Williams, D. 27
League (52): Cramb 18 (4 pens); Schofield 7 (1 pen), Moore 5, Dixon 3, Birch 2, Clark 2, Ireland 2, McDonald 2, Smith 2, Colcombe 1, Esdaille 1, Gore 1, Lester 1, Mike 1, Pemberton 1, Piearce 1, Utley 1, own goal 1.
Coca-Cola Cup (1): Cramb 1.
FA Cup (1): Cramb 1.
Ground: Belle Vue Ground, Doncaster DN4 5HT. Telephone (01302) 539441.
Record attendance: 37,149 v Hull C, Division 3 (N), 2 October 1948. **Capacity:** 8608.
Manager: Kerry Dixon.
Secretary: Mrs K. J. Oldale.
Honours – Football League: Division 3 (N) Champions – 1934–35, 1946–47, 1949–50. Division 4 Champions – 1965–66, 1968–69.
Colours: All red.

EVERTON   FA PREMIERSHIP

Allen Graham (D)	6 1	12 00	Bolton	8 4 77	Trainee
Ball Michael (D)			Liverpool	2 10 79	Trainee
Barmby Nick (F)	5 6	11 00	Hull	11 2 74	Middlesbrough
Barrett Earl (D)	5 10	11 02	Rochdale	28 4 67	Aston Villa
Bilic Slaven (D)	6 2	13 02	Split	11 9 68	West Ham U
Branch Michael (F)	5 9	11 00	Liverpool	18 10 78	Trainee
Cadamarteri Danny (F)			Bradford	12 10 79	Trainee
Dunne Richard (D)			Dublin	21 9 79	Trainee
Ferguson Duncan (F)	6 4	14 06	Stirling	27 12 71	Rangers
Gerrard Paul (G)	6 2	13 01	Heywood	22 1 73	Oldham Ath
Grant Tony (M)	5 10	10 02	Liverpool	14 11 74	Trainee
Hills John (D)	5 9	11 00	St Annes-on-Sea	21 4 78	Blackpool
Hinchcliffe Andy (D)	5 10	12 10	Manchester	5 2 69	Manchester C
Hottiger Marc (D)	5 9	11 00	Lausanne	7 11 67	Newcastle U
Jevons Phillip (M)			Liverpool	1 8 79	Trainee
McCann Gavin (M)	5 11	11 00	Blackpool	10 1 78	Trainee
O'Connor Jonathan (D)	6 0	11 00	Darlington	29 10 76	Trainee
O'Toole John (G)			Merseyside	23 2 79	Trainee
Parkinson Joe (M)	5 11	12 02	Eccles	11 6 71	Bournemouth
Phelan Terry (D)	5 8	10 00	Manchester	16 3 67	Chelsea
Short Craig (D)	6 0	11 04	Bridlington	25 6 68	Derby Co
Southall Neville (G)	6 1	12 02	Llandudno	16 9 58	Bury
Speed Gary (M)	5 11	10 12	Mancot	8 9 69	Leeds U
Stuart Graham (F)	5 8	11 06	Tooting	24 10 70	Chelsea
Thomsen Claus (M)	6 3	11 06	Aarhus	31 5 70	Ipswich T
Unsworth David (D)	6 0	13 00	Chorley	16 10 73	Trainee
Watson Dave (D)	5 11	11 12	Liverpool	20 11 61	Norwich C

League Appearances: Allen, G. (1); Ball, M.2(3); Barmby, N. 22(3); Barrett, E. 36; Branch, M. 13(12); Cadamarteri, D. (1); Dunne, R. 6(1); Ebbrell, J. 7; Ferguson, D. 31(2); Gerrard, P. 4(1); Grant, T. 11(7); Hills, J. 1(2); Hinchcliffe, A. 18; Hottiger, M. 4(4); Kanchelskis, A. 20; Limpar, A. 1(1); Parkinson, J. 28; Phelan, T. 15; Rideout, P. 4(6); Short, C. 19(4); Southall, N. 34; Speed, G. 37; Stuart, G. 29(6); Thomsen, C. 15(1); Unsworth, D. 32(2); Watson, D. 29
League (44): Ferguson 10, Speed 9, Stuart 5 (1 pen), Unsworth 5 (2 pens), Barmby 4, Kanchelskis 4, Branch 3, Short 2, Hinchcliffe 1, Watson 1.
Coca-Cola Cup (3): Kanchelskis 1, Rideout 1, Speed 1.

FA Cup (5): Barmby 1, Ferguson 1, Kanchelskis 1 (pen), Speed 1, own goal 1.
Ground: Goodison Park, Liverpool L4 4EL. Telephone (0151) 330 2200.
Record attendance: 78,299 v Liverpool, Division 1, 18 September 1948. **Capacity:** 40,200.
Manager: Howard Kendall.
Secretary: Michael J. Dunford.
Honours – Football League: Division 1 Champions – 1890–91, 1914–15, 1927–28, 1931–32, 1938–39, 1962–63, 1969–70, 1984–85, 1986–87. Division 2 Champions – 1930–31. **FA Cup:** Winners 1906, 1933, 1966, 1984, 1995. **European Competitions: European Cup-Winners' Cup winners:** 1984–85.
Colours: Blue shirts, white shorts, black/blue stockings.

EXETER CITY DIV. 3

Baddeley Lee (D)	6 1	12 07	Cardiff	12 7 74	Cardiff C
Bailey Danny (M)	5 8	12 11	Leyton	21 5 64	Reading
Bayes Ashley (G)	6 1	13 05	Lincoln	19 4 72	Torquay U
Birch Paul (M)	5 6	10 04	West Bromwich	20 11 62	Doncaster R
Blake Noel (D)	6 2	14 02	Jamaica	12 1 62	Dundee
Braithwaite Leon (F)	6 0	12 00	Hackney	17 12 72	Bishops Stortford
Flack Steve (F)	6 1	11 04	Cambridge	29 5 71	Cardiff C
Fox Peter (G)	5 11	13 10	Scunthorpe	5 7 57	Stoke C
Ghazghazi Sufyan (F)	5 7	11 00	Honiton	24 8 77	Trainee
Hare Matthew (D)	6 2	13 00	Barnstaple	26 12 76	Trainee
Hughes Darren (D)	5 11	13 01	Prescot	6 10 65	Northampton T
McConnell Barry (F)	5 11	10 03	Exeter	1 1 77	Trainee
Medlin Nicky (M)	5 7	10 01	Camborne	23 11 76	Trainee
Minett Jason (M)	5 9	10 04	Peterborough	12 8 71	Lincoln C
Rice Gary (D)	5 9	11 10	Zambia	29 9 75	Trainee
Richardson Jon (D)	6 1	12 05	Nottingham	29 8 75	Trainee
Rowbotham Darren (F)	5 10	12 13	Cardiff	22 10 66	Shrewsbury T

League Appearances: Baddeley, L. 8(3); Bailey, D. 32(3); Bayes, A. 41; Birch, P. 2; Blake, N. 46; Braithwaite, L. 26(12); Chamberlain, M. 22(4); Crowe, G. 10; Dailly, M. 8(9); Flack, S. 20(7); Fox, P. 5; Gayle, B. 10; Ghazghazi, S. 1(5); Hare, M. 16(9); Hodges, L. 16(1); Hughes, D. 33(3); McConnell, B. 20(14); McKeown, G. 3; Medlin, N. 7(4); Minett, J. 13; Myers, C. 31(2); Pears, R. 6(2); Rees, J. 7; Rice, G. 9(6); Richardson, J. 42(1); Richardson, N. 14; Rowbotham, D. 25; Sharpe, J. 19(2); Steele, T. 14(14)
League (48): Rowbotham 9 (1 pen), Blake 6, Braithwaite 5, Crowe 5, Flack 4, Chamberlain 3 (2 pens), Steele 3, Bailey 2, Myers 2, Hare 1, Hughes 1, Medlin 1, Pears 1, Richardson J 1, Sharpe 1, own goals 3.
Coca-Cola Cup (0).
FA Cup (3): Flack 1, Rowbotham 1, Sharpe 1.
Ground: St James Park, Exeter EX4 6PX. Telephone (01392) 254073.
Record attendance: 20,984 v Sunderland, FA Cup 6th rd (replay), 4 March 1931.
Capacity: 10,570.
Manager: Peter Fox.
Secretary: Margaret Bond.
Honours – Football League: Division 4 Champions – 1989–90. **Division 3 (S) Cup:** Winners 1934.
Colours: Red and white striped shirts, black shorts, red stockings.

FULHAM   DIV. 2

Angus Terry (D)	6 0	13 10	Coventry	14 1 66	Northampton T
Blake Mark (D)	6 0	12 06	Portsmouth	17 12 67	Shrewsbury T
Brooker Paul (F)	5 8	9 13	Hammersmith	25 11 76	Trainee
Carpenter Richard (M)	5 11	13 00	Sheppey	30 9 72	Gillingham
Conroy Mike (F)	5 11	13 03	Glasgow	31 12 65	Preston NE
Cullip Danny (D)	6 0	12 00	Bracknell	17 9 76	Oxford U
Cusack Nick (D)	6 0	12 08	Rotherham	24 12 65	Oxford U
Freeman Darren (F)	5 11	13 04	Brighton	22 8 73	Gillingham
Herrera Robbie (D)	5 6	10 07	Torbay	12 6 70	QPR
Lawrence Matthew (D)	6 1	12 12	Northampton	19 6 74	Wycombe W
McAree Rod (M)	5 7	10 10	Dungannon	10 8 74	Bristol C
Mison Michael (M)	6 3	14 00	London	8 11 75	Trainee
Morgan Simon (M)	5 10	12 05	Birmingham	5 9 66	Leicester C
Scott Rob (F)	6 1	12 02	Epsom	15 8 73	Sheffield U
Stewart Simon (D)	6 2	13 08	Leeds	1 11 73	Sheffield W
Thomas Martin (M)	5 8	12 06	Lyndhurst	12 9 73	Leyton Orient
Walton Mark (G)	6 4	15 00	Merthyr	1 6 69	Fakenham T
Watson Paul (D)	5 8	10 09	Hastings	4 1 75	Gillingham

League Appearances: Adams, M. 2(1); Angus, T. 28(4); Blake, M. 40(1); Brooker, P. (26); Carpenter, R. 34; Cockerill, G. 27(5); Conroy, M. 40(3); Cullip, D. 23(6); Cusack, N. 44(1); Davis, S. (1); Freeman, D. 32(7); Hartfield, C. 1(1); Herrera, R. 26; Lange, T. 18; Lawrence, M. 13(2); McAree, R. 5(4); Mison, M. 1(3); Morgan, S. 44; Parker, P. 3; Scott, R. 36(7); Soloman, J. 1(3); Stewart, D. 2(1); Thomas, M. 6(20); Walton, M. 28; Warren, C. 8(3); Watson, P. 44
League (72): Conroy 21, Freeman 9, Morgan 8, Scott 8, Blake 7 (7 pens), Carpenter 5, Watson 3, Brooker 2, Cusack 2, Angus 1, Cockerill 1, Cullip 1, Herrera 1, Lawrence 1, McAree 1, Warren 1, own goal 1.
Coca-Cola Cup (6): Conroy 2, Brooker 1, Morgan 1, Watson 1, own goal 1.
FA Cup (0).
Ground: Craven Cottage, Stevenage Rd, Fulham, London SW6 6HH. Telephone (0171) 736 6561.
Record attendance: 49,335 v Millwall, Division 2, 8 October 1938. **Capacity:** 14,969.
Manager: Micky Adams.
Secretary: Mrs Janice O'Doherty.
Honours – Football League: Division 2 Champions – 1948–49. Division 3 (S) Champions – 1931–32.
Colours: White shirts, red and black trim, black shorts, white stockings red and black trim.

GILLINGHAM   DIV. 2

Akinbiyi Ade (F)	6 0	12 07	Hackney	10 10 74	Norwich C
Bailey Dennis (F)	5 10	11 00	Lambeth	13 11 65	QPR
Bryant Matthew (D)	6 0	12 04	Bristol	21 9 70	Bristol C
Butler Steve (F)	6 1	12 07	Birmingham	27 1 62	Cambridge U
Butters Guy (D)	6 2	13 03	Hillingdon	30 10 69	Portsmouth
Chapman Ian (D)	5 8	11 12	Brighton	31 5 70	Brighton & HA
Fortune-West Leo (F)	6 4	13 00	Newham	9 4 71	Stevenage Bor
Green Richard (D)	6 0	13 01	Wolverhampton	22 11 67	Swindon T
Hessenthaler Andy (M)	5 7	10 04	Gravesend	17 8 65	Watford
Masters Neil (D)	5 10	14 05	Lisburn	25 5 72	Wolverhampton W
O'Connor Mark (M)	5 8	10 12	Rochdale	10 3 63	Bournemouth

48

Onuora Iffy (F)	6 0	12 07	Glasgow	28	7 67	Mansfield T
Pennock Adrian (D)	6 0	12 07	Ipswich	27	3 71	Bournemouth
Piper Len (M)	5 8	11 06	London	8	8 77	Wimbledon
Ratcliffe Simon (M)	6 0	12 10	Davyhulme	8	2 67	Brentford
Smith Neil (M)	5 8	11 12	London	30	9 71	Tottenham H
Stannard Jim (G)	6 2	16 00	London	6	10 62	Fulham
Thomas Glen (D)	6 0	13 02	Hackney	6	10 67	Barnet

League Appearances: Akinbiyi, A. 19; Armstrong, C. 10; Bailey, D. 16(14); Bryant, M. 38(1); Butler, S. 29(9); Butters, G. 30; Carpenter, R. 1; Chapman, I. 20(3); Ford, J. 2(2); Fortune-West, L. 7; Galloway, M. 6(3); Gould, J. 3; Green, R. 28(1); Harris, M. 19(2); Hessenthaler, A. 38; Humphrey, J. 9; Manuel, B. 3(8); Marshall, A. 5; Morris, M. 6; O'Connor, M. 18(4); Onuora, I. 37(3); Pennock, A. 26; Pinnock, J. 2; Piper, L. 4(15); Puttnam, D. 5(9); Ratcliffe, S. 43; Sambrook, A. (1); Smith, N. 42; Stannard, J. 38; Thomas, G. 4(6).
League (60): Onuora 21 (2 pens), Butler 9 (2 pens), Akinbiyi 7, Ratcliffe 6, Bailey 2, Fortune-West 2, Green 2, Hessenthaler 2, Pennock 2, Chapman 1, Galloway 1, Harris 1, Piper 1, Puttnam 1, Smith 1, own goal 1.
Coca-Cola Cup (8): Ratcliffe 2, Butler 1, Fortune-West 1, Onuora 1, Puttnam 1, Smith 1, own goal 1.
FA Cup (3): Butler 1, Hessenthaler 1, Onuora 1.
Ground: Priestfield Stadium, Gillingham ME7 4DD. Telephone (0134) 851854, 576828.
Record attendance: 23,002 v QPR, FA Cup 3rd rd 10 January 1948. **Capacity:** 10,600.
Manager: Tony Pulis.
Secretary: Mrs G. E. Poynter.
Honours – Football League: Division 4 Champions – 1963–64.
Colours: Blue shirts, blue shorts, white stockings.

GRIMSBY TOWN   DIV. 2

Black Kingsley (F)	5 8	12 03	Luton	22	6 68	Nottingham F
Clare Daryl (F)	5 9	12 00	Jersey	1	8 78	Trainee
Fickling Ashley (D)	5 10	11 08	Sheffield	15	11 72	Sheffield U
Gallimore Tony (D)	5 11	12 05	Crewe	21	2 72	Carlisle U
Handyside Peter (D)	6 1	13 07	Dumfries	31	7 74	Trainee
Jobling Kevin (D)	5 9	12 02	Sunderland	1	1 68	Leicester C
Lester Jack (F)	5 10	12 00	Sheffield	8	10 75	Trainee
Lever Mark (D)	6 3	13 06	Beverley	29	3 70	Trainee
Livingstone Steve (F)	6 1	13 07	Middlesbrough	8	9 68	Chelsea
Love Andrew (G)	6 2	13 10	Grimsby	28	3 79	Trainee
McDermott John (D)	5 7	10 13	Middlesbrough	3	2 69	Trainee
Mendonca Clive (F)	5 10	12 07	Islington	9	9 68	Sheffield U
Neil Jim (M)	5 8	11 13	Bury St Edmunds	28	2 76	Trainee
Oster John (F)	5 8	10 08	Boston	8	12 78	Trainee
Pearcey Jason (G)	6 1	14 00	Leamington Spa	23	7 71	Mansfield T
Rodger Graham (D)	6 2	13 08	Glasgow	1	4 67	Luton T
Smith Richard (D)	6 0	13 05	Lutterworth	3	10 70	Leicester C
Southall Nicky (M)	5 10	13 00	Middlesbrough	28	1 72	Hartlepool U
Widdrington Tommy (M)	5 8	11 01	Newcastle	1	10 71	Southampton
Wrack Darren (F)	5 9	12 00	Cleethorpes	5	5 76	Derby Co

League Appearances: Appleton, M. 10; Black, K. 19(5); Childs, G. 19(8); Fickling, A. 20(7); Forrester, J. 4(9); Gallimore, T. 36(6); Handyside, P. 8(1); Jobling, K. 24(4); Laws, B. 3; Lee, J. 2(5); Lester, J. 16(6); Lever, M. 20(1); Livingstone, S.

23(9); Love, A. 3; McDermott, J. 29; Mendonca, C. 45; Miller, A. 3; Neil, J. (1); Oster, J. 21(3); Pearcey, J. 40; Rodger, G. 27(1); Shakespeare, C. 23(3); Smith, R. 12(2); Southall, N. 23(11); Trollope, P. 6(1); Walker, J. (1); Webb, N. 3(1); Widdrington, T. 41(1); Woods, N. 21(3); Wrack, D. 5(7)
League (60): Mendonca 19 (5 pens), Livingstone 6, Lester 5, Southall 4, Widdrington 4, Appleton 3, Oster 3, Fickling 2, Lee 2, Rodger 2, Shakespeare 2, Childs 1, Forrester 1, Gallimore 1, Handyside 1, McDermott 1, Trollope 1, Woods 1, Wrack 1.
Coca-Cola Cup (1): Mendonca 1.
FA Cup (1): Oster 1.
Ground: Blundell Park, Cleethorpes, South Humberside DN35 7PY. Telephone (01472) 697111.
Capacity: 8870.
Record attendance: 31,651 v Wolverhampton W, FA Cup 5th rd, 20 February 1937.
Manager: Alan Buckley.
Secretary: Ian Fleming.
Honours – Football League: Division 2 Champions – 1900–01, 1933–34. Division 3 (N) Champions – 1925–26, 1955–56. Division 3 Champions – 1979–80. Division 4 Champions – 1971-72. **League Group Cup:** Winners 1981–82.
Colours: Black and white striped shirts, black shorts, white stockings.

HARTLEPOOL UNITED   DIV. 3

Allon Joe (F)	5 11	12 12	Gateshead	12 11 66	Lincoln C
Baker Paul (F)	6 0	13 00	Newcastle	5 1 63	Scunthorpe U
Beech Chris (M)	5 10	11 12	Blackpool	16 9 74	Blackpool
Cooper Mark (M)	5 10	12 03	Wakefield	18 12 68	Exeter C
Davies Glen (D)	6 1	13 09	Brighton	20 2 76	Burnley
Halliday Stephen (F)	5 10	12 11	Sunderland	3 5 76	Charlton Ath
Howard Steve (M)	6 1	14 06	Durham	10 5 76	Tow Law T
Ingram Denny (D)	5 10	12 03	Sunderland	27 6 76	Trainee
Knowles Darren (D)	5 6	11 01	Sheffield	8 10 70	Scarborough
Lee Graeme (D)	6 2	13 05	Middlesbrough	31 5 78	Trainee
Lucas Richard (M)	5 10	12 06	Sheffield	22 9 70	Scarborough
McDonald Chris (F)	6 2	13 00	Edinburgh	14 10 75	Arsenal
McGuckin Ian (D)	6 2	13 11	Middlesbrough	24 4 73	Trainee
Pears Steve (G)	6 0	14 00	Brandon	22 1 62	Liverpool
Tait Mick (D)	5 11	12 13	Wallsend	30 9 56	Darlington

League Appearances: Allon, J. 27(3); Baker, P. 6; Barron, M. 16; Beech, C. 42; Bradley, R. 12; Brown, M. 6; Clegg, D. 24(11); Cooper, M. 33; Cullen, J. 5(1); Davies, G. 30(2); Elliott, A. 2(2); Halliday, S. 28(3); Hislop, K. 23(4); Homer, C. (1); Horace, A. (1); Houchen, K. 2(3); Howard, S. 26(6); Ingram, D. 34(3); Irvine, S. 2(2); Knowles, D. 7; Lee, G. 23(1); Lucas, R. 7; McAuley, S. 38; McDonald, C. 9; McGuckin, I. 21(1); Mike, A. 7; O'Connor, P. 30; Pears, S. 16; Proctor, M. 6; Sunderland, J. 6(7); Tait, M. 16(3); Walton, P. 2(2); Winstanley, C. (1)
League (53): Allon 9, Cooper 9 (3 pens), Halliday 8, Howard 8, Beech 7, Baker 2, Clegg 2, Bradley 1, Brown 1, Davies 1, Ingram 1, Irvine 1, McAuley 1, Mike 1, Sunderland 1.
Coca-Cola Cup (4): Allon 2, Beech 1, Davies 1.
FA Cup (0).
Ground: The Victoria Ground, Clarence Road, Hartlepool TS24 8BZ. Telephone (01429) 272584.
Record attendance: 17,426 v Manchester U, FA Cup 3rd rd, 5 January 1957.
Capacity: 7229.
Manager: Mick Tait.

Secretary: Maureen Smith.
Honours – Nil.
Colours: Blue and white stripes.

HEREFORD UNITED   VAUXHALL CONFERENCE

Agana Tony (F)	5 11	12 05	London	2 10 63	Notts Co	
Cook Garry (M)	6 0	13 00	Northampton	31 3 78	Trainee	
Debont Andy (G)	6 0	15 07	Wolverhampton	7 2 74	Wolverhampton W	
Fishlock Murray (D)	5 8	10 09	Marlborough	23 9 73	Trowbridge T	
Foster Adrian (F)	5 10	12 01	Kidderminster	19 3 71	Gillingham	
Foster Ian (F)	5 7	10 07	Merseyside	11 11 76	Liverpool	
Hargreaves Chris (F)	5 11	12 07	Cleethorpes	12 5 72	WBA	
Mahon Gavin (M)	5 11	12 07	Birmingham	2 1 77	Wolverhampton W	
McGorry Brian (M)	5 10	12 07	Liverpool	16 4 70	Wycombe W	
Norton David (M)	5 10	11 10	Cannock	3 3 65	Northampton T	
Pitman Jamie (M)	5 8	10 12	Warminster	6 1 76	Swindon T	
Smith Dean (D)	6 0	13 00	West Bromwich	19 3 71	Walsall	
Warner Rob (D)	5 10	11 06	Stratford	20 4 77	Trainee	

League Appearances: Agana, T. 3(2); Bartlett, N. (3); Beeston, C. 9; Brough, J. 32(7); Cook, G. 17(3); Cross, J. 5; Debont, A. 27; Downing, K. 16; Ellison, L. (1); Fishlock, M. 29(1); Forsyth, M. 12; Foster, A. 42(1); Foster, I. 4(15); Hargreaves, C. 42(2); Hibbard, M. 5(2); Jordan, R. 1; Kottila, M. 11(2); Law, N. 14; Mahon, G. 10(1); Matthewson, T. 35; McGorry, B. 7; Norton, D. 45; O'Toole, G. 1; Pitman, J. 4(4); Preedy, P. 2(7); Sandeman, B. 7; Smith, D. 42; Stoker, G. 25(2); Sutton, W. 4; Townsend, Q. 6(1); Turner, M. 6; Warner, R. 16(5); Williams, J. 8(3); Wood, T. 19
League (50): Foster A 16, Smith 8 (3 pens), Hargreaves 4, Stoker 3, Williams 3, Agana 2, Beeston 2, Matthewson 2, Preedy 2, Brough 1, Cross 1, Fishlock 1, Hibbard 1, Kottila 1, McGorry 1, Mahon 1, own goal 1.
Coca-Cola Cup (4): Smith 2 (1 pen), Foster A 1, Norton 1.
FA Cup (0).
Ground: Edgar Street, Hereford HR4 9JU. Telephone (01432) 276666.
Record attendance: 18,114 v Sheffield W, FA Cup 3rd rd, 4 January 1958.
Capacity: 8843.
Manager: Graham Turner.
Secretary: Joan Fennessy.
Honours – Football League: Division 3 Champions – 1975–76. **Welsh Cup winners:** 1990.
Colours: White & black striped shirts, black shorts, white stockings.

HUDDERSFIELD TOWN   DIV. 1

Baldry Simon (F)	5 10	11 06	Huddersfield	12 2 76	Trainee	
Beresford David (M)	5 7	10 06	Middleton	11 11 76	Oldham Ath	
Browning Marcus (M)	6 1	13 00	Bristol	22 4 71	Bristol R	
Burnett Wayne (M)	5 10	12 00	Lambeth	4 9 71	Bolton W	
Collins Sam (D)	6 2	13 07	Pontefract	5 6 77	Trainee	
Cowan Tom (D)	5 8	11 10	Bellshill	28 8 69	Sheffield U	
Dalton Paul (M)	5 11	12 06	Middlesbrough	25 4 67	Plymouth Arg	
Dyson Jon (D)	6 1	12 09	Mirfield	18 12 71	School	
Edmondson Darren (D)	6 0	12 00	Coniston	4 11 71	Carlisle U	
Edwards Rob (F)	5 9	12 04	Manchester	23 2 70	Crewe Alex	
Facey Delroy (F)	6 0	13 00	Huddersfield	22 4 80	Trainee	

Francis Steve (G)	6 1	14 00	Billericay	29 5 64	Reading
Gray Kevin (D)	6 0	14 00	Sheffield	7 1 72	Mansfield T
Heary Thomas (M)	5 10	11 03	Dublin	14 2 79	Trainee
Illingworth Jeremy (M)	5 10	12 07	Huddersfield	20 5 77	Trainee
Jenkins Steve (D)	5 11	12 03	Merthyr	16 7 72	Swansea C
Kaye Peter (F)	5 8	11 06	Huddersfield	4 2 79	Trainee
Lawson Ian (F)	6 0	11 08	Huddersfield	4 11 77	Trainee
Makel Lee (M)	5 9	11 05	Sunderland	11 1 73	Blackburn R
Morrison Andy (D)	6 1	13 10	Inverness	30 7 70	Blackpool
Murphy Stephen (D)	5 11	12 00	Dublin	5 4 78	Belvedere
O'Connor Derek (G)	5 11	12 01	Dublin	9 3 78	Crumplin U
Payton Andy (F)	5 9	11 13	Burnley	23 10 67	Barnsley
Ryan Robbie (D)	5 10	12 00	Dublin	11 8 76	Belvedere
Sinnott Lee (D)	6 1	13 00	Pelsall	12 7 65	Bradford C
Stewart Marcus (F)	5 10	10 06	Bristol	7 11 72	Bristol R

League Appearances: Baldry, S. 2(5); Beresford, D. 6; Browning, M. 13; Bullock, D. 26(1); Burnett, W. 33(2); Collins, S. 10(6); Collins, S. 3(1); Cowan, T. 42; Crosby, G. 19(5); Dalton, P. 17(12); Davies, S. 3; Dunn, I. 1(4); Dyson, J. 18(5); Edmondson, D. 10; Edwards, R. 24(9); Facey, D. 1(2); Francis, S. 42; Glover, L. 11; Gray, K. 36(3); Heary, T. 2(3); Illingworth, J. 2(1); Jenkins, S. 33; Kaye, P. (1); Lawson, I. 8(10); Makel, L. 19; Morrison, A. 9(1); Norman, T. 4; Payton, A. 38; Reid, P. 20(2); Rowe, R. 1(6); Ryan, R. 2(3); Sinnott, L. 29(1); Stewart, M. 19(1); Tisdale, P. 1(1); Williams, M. 2
League (48): Payton 17, Stewart 7, Cowan 4, Dalton 4, Edwards 3, Lawson 3, Makel 3, Crosby 2, Beresford 1, Bullock 1, Gray 1, Morrison 1, own goal 1.
Coca-Cola Cup (9): Stewart 4, Payton 2, Collins 1, Cowan 1, Edwards 1.
FA Cup (2): Crosby 1, Edwards 1.
Ground: The Alfred McAlpine Stadium, Huddersfield HD1 6PX. Telephone (01484) 420335/6.
Record attendance: 67,037 v Arsenal, FA Cup 6th rd, 27 February 1932. **Capacity:** 19,600.
Manager: Brian Horton.
Secretary: Alan D. Sykes.
Honours – Football League: Division 1 Champions – 1923–24, 1924–25, 1925–26. Division 2 Champions – 1969–70. Division 4 Champions – 1969–70. **FA Cup winners** 1922.
Colours: Blue and white striped shirts, white shorts, white stockings.

HULL CITY   DIV. 3

Brien Tony (D)	6 0	13 02	Dublin	10 2 69	WBA
Brown Andrew (F)	6 3	13 10	Edinburgh	11 10 76	Leeds U
Darby Duane (F)	5 11	12 06	Birmingham	17 10 73	Doncaster R
Dewhurst Rob (D)	6 3	14 00	Keighley	10 9 71	Blackburn R
Doncel Antonio (D)	6 0	12 01	Lugo	31 1 67	Ferrol
Fewings Paul (F)	6 0	12 06	Hull	18 2 78	Trainee
Gordon Gavin (F)	6 1	12 00	Manchester	24 6 79	Trainee
Greaves Mark (D)	6 1	13 00	Hull	22 1 75	Brigg Town
Joyce Warren (M)	5 9	12 00	Oldham	20 1 65	Burnley
Lowthorpe Adam (D)	5 7	11 03	Hull	7 8 75	Trainee
Mann Neil (M)	5 10	12 01	Nottingham	19 11 72	Grantham T
Marks Jamie (D)	5 9	10 13	Belfast	18 3 77	Leeds U
Maxfield Scott (D)	5 10	11 05	Doncaster	13 7 76	Doncaster R
Peacock Richard (F)	5 10	11 05	Sheffield	29 10 72	Sheffield FC
Quigley Michael (M)	5 7	11 04	Manchester	2 10 70	Manchester C

Rioch Greg (D)	5 11	12 10	Sutton Coldfield	24 6 75	Peterborough U
Sharman Sam (M)	5 10	12 01	Hull	7 11 77	Sheffield W
Trevitt Simon (D)	5 11	12 09	Dewsbury	20 12 67	Huddersfield T
Wharton Paul (M)	5 4	10 00	Newcastle	26 6 77	Leeds U
Wilkinson Ian (M)	6 2	13 00	Ferriby	19 9 77	Trainee
Wilson Steve (G)	5 10	10 12	Hull	24 4 74	Trainee
Wright Ian (D)	6 1	13 04	Lichfield	10 3 72	Bristol R

League Appearances: Allison, N. 11; Brien, T. 29(3); Brown, A. 7(19); Carroll, R. 23; Darby, D. 40(1); Davison, A. 9; Dewhurst, R. 20(2); Dickinson, P. (1); Doncel, A. 22(4); Ellington, L. (2); Elliott, S. 3; Fewings, P. 3(9); Gilbert, K. 15(4); Gordon, G. 19(1); Greaves, M. 23(7); Joyce, W. 45; Lowthorpe, A. 13(1); Mann, N. 24(8); Marks, J. 7(3); Mason, A. 4(2); Maxfield, S. 10(7); Peacock, R. 34(6); Quigley, M. 23(6); Rioch, G. 38(1); Sansam, C. 2(1); Sharman, S. 2(2); Trevitt, S. 21(1); Turner, R. 5; Wharton, P. (1); Wilson, S. 14(1); Wright, I. 40
League (44): Darby 13, Joyce 5, Gordon 4, Peacock 4, Mason 3, Doncel 2, Greaves 2, Mann 2, Turner 2, Brien 1, Brown 1, Gilbert 1, Lowthorpe 1, Quigley 1, Rioch 1 (pen), Trevitt 1.
Coca-Cola Cup (4): Rioch 2 (1 pen), Gordon 1, Quigley 1.
FA Cup (9): Darby 6, Joyce 1, Mann 1, Peacock 1.
Ground: Boothferry Park, Hull HU4 6EU. Telephone (01482) 351119.
Record attendance: 55,019 v Manchester U, FA Cup 6th rd, 26 February 1949.
Capacity: 12,996.
Manager: Mark Hateley.
Secretary: M.W. Fish.
Honours – Football League: Division 3 (N) Champions – 1932–33, 1948–49. Division 3 Champions – 1965–66.
Colours: Amber shirts, black shorts, amber stockings.

IPSWICH TOWN   DIV. 1

Bell Leon (M)	5 8	11 00	Ipswich	23 9 77	Trainee
Brown Wayne (D)	6 0	12 06	Barking	20 8 77	Trainee
Cundy Jason (D)	6 1	13 13	Wimbledon	12 11 69	Tottenham H
Dyer Kieron (M)	5 7	9 07	Ipswich	29 12 78	Trainee
Forrest Craig (G)	6 5	14 00	Vancouver	20 9 67	Apprentice
Gaughan Kevin (D)	6 0	12 05	Glasgow	6 3 78	
Gregory Neil (F)	5 11	11 10	Zambia	7 10 72	Trainee
Mason Paul (M)	5 9	12 01	Liverpool	3 9 63	Aberdeen
Mathie Alex (F)	5 10	11 07	Bathgate	20 12 68	Newcastle U
Milton Simon (M)	5 10	11 05	Fulham	23 8 63	Bury St Edmunds
Mowbray Tony (D)	6 1	13 00	Saltburn	22 11 63	Celtic
Naylor Richard (F)	6 1	13 07	Leeds	28 2 77	Trainee
Niven Stuart (M)	5 11	12 08	Glasgow	24 12 78	Trainee
Petta Bobby (M)	5 7	11 03	Rotterdam	6 8 74	
Scowcroft James (F)	6 1	12 02	Bury St Edmunds	15 11 75	Trainee
Sedgley Steve (M)	6 1	13 13	Enfield	26 5 68	Tottenham H
Sonner Danny (M)	5 11	12 08	Wigan	9 1 72	Erzgebirge Aue
Stockwell Mick (M)	5 9	11 04	Chelmsford	14 2 65	Apprentice
Swailes Chris (D)	6 2	12 07	Gateshead	19 10 70	Doncaster R
Tanner Adam (M)	6 0	12 01	Maldon	25 10 73	Trainee
Taricco Mauricio (D)	5 8	11 05	Buenos Aires	10 3 73	Argentinos Juniors
Uhlenbeek Gus (M)	5 10	12 06	Paramaribo	20 8 70	TOPS SV
Vaughan Tony (D)	6 1	11 02	Manchester	11 10 75	Trainee
Williams Geraint (M)	5 7	12 06	Cwmpare	5 1 62	Derby Co
Wright Richard (G)	6 2	13 00	Ipswich	5 11 77	Trainee

League Appearances: Creaney, G. 6; Cundy, J. 13; Dyer, K. 2(11); Forrest, C. 6; Gregory, N. 10(7); Gudmundsson, N. 2(1); Howe, S. 2(1); Jean, E. (1); Marshall, I. 2; Mason, P. 41(2); Mathie, A. 11(1); Milton, S. 8(15); Mowbray, T. 8; Naylor, R. 19(8); Niven, S. 2; Petta, B. 1(5); Scowcroft, J. 40(1); Sedgley, S. 39; Sonner, D. 22(7); Stockwell, M. 42(1); Swailes, C. 23; Tanner, A. 10(6); Taricco, M. 41; Thomsen, C. 10(1); Uhlenbeek, G. 34(4); Vaughan, T. 27(5); Wark, J. 2; Williams, G. 43; Wright, R. 40

League (68): Mason 12, Scowcroft 9, Sedgley 7 (5 pens), Stockwell 7, Gregory 6, Mathie 4, Naylor 4, Tanner 4 (2 pens), Taricco 3, Cundy 2, Gudmundsson 2, Sonner 2, Vaughan 2, Creaney 1, Swailes 1, Williams 1, own goal 1.

Coca-Cola Cup (15): Mathie 5, Mason 3, Marshall 1, Milton 1, Naylor 1, Sedgley 1 (pen), Scowcroft 1, Sonner 1, Stockwell 1.

FA Cup (0).

Ground: Portman Road, Ipswich, Suffolk IP1 2DA. Telephone (01473) 400500.

Record attendance: 38,010 v Leeds U, FA Cup 6th rd, 8 March 1975. **Capacity:** 22,675.

Manager: George Burley.

Secretary: David C. Rose.

Honours – Football League: Division 1 Champions – 1961–62. Division 2 Champions – 1960–61, 1967–68, 1991–92. Division 3 (S) Champions – 1953–54, 1956–57. **FA Cup:** Winners 1977–78. **European Competitions: UEFA Cup winners:** 1980–81, 1982–83.

Colours: Blue shirts, white shorts, blue stockings.

LEEDS UNITED   FA PREMIERSHIP

Beeney Mark (G)	6 4	14 07	Pembury	30 12 67	Brighton & HA
Blunt Jason (M)	5 9	10 10	Penzance	16 8 77	Trainee
Bowyer Lee (M)	5 9	9 09	London	3 1 77	Charlton Ath
Boyle Wesley (M)			Portadown	30 3 79	Trainee
Brolin Tomas (M)			Hudiksvall	29 11 69	Parma
Butler John (D)			Dublin	28 10 79	Belvedere
Couzens Andy (D)	5 9	11 06	Shipley	4 6 75	Trainee
Deane Brian (F)	6 3	12 07	Leeds	7 2 68	Sheffield U
Donnelly Paul (M)			Dublin	31 8 79	Trainee
Dorigo Tony (D)	5 10	10 10	Melbourne	31 12 65	Chelsea
Ford Mark (M)	5 7	10 08	Pontefract	10 10 75	Trainee
Foster Martin (M)	5 5	9 10	Sheffield	29 10 77	Trainee
Gray Andy (M)	6 1	12 00	Harrogate	15 11 77	Trainee
Halle Gunnar (D)	5 11	11 00	Larvik	11 8 65	Oldham Ath
Harte Ian (D)	5 9		Drogheda	31 8 77	Trainee
Jackson Mark (D)	5 11		Barnsley	30 9 77	Trainee
Jobson Richard (D)	6 2	12 10	Hull	9 5 63	Oldham Ath
Kelly Gary (D)	5 8	13 03	Drogheda	9 7 74	Home Farm
Kewell Harry (M)	5 11		Australia	22 9 78	NSW Academy
Knarvik Tommy (M)			Bergen	1 11 79	Skjerjard
Laurent Pierre (M)	5 8	10 10	Tulle	13 12 70	Bastia
Lilley Derek (F)	5 10	12 07	Paisley	9 2 74	Morton
Lynch Damien (D)			Dublin	31 7 79	
Martyn Nigel (G)	6 1	14 07	St Austell	11 8 66	Crystal Palace
Matthews Lee (M)			Middlesbrough	16 1 79	Trainee
Maybury Alan (M)			Dublin	8 8 78	Trainee
McPhail Stephen (M)			London	9 12 79	Trainee
Molenaar Robert (D)	6 2	14 04	Holland	27 2 69	Volendam
Palmer Carlton (D)	6 2	12 04	Oldbury	5 12 65	Sheffield W
Quinn Andrew (M)			Halifax	1 9 79	

Name			Birthplace	Date	Previous club
Radebe Lucas (M)	6 1	11 09	Johannesburg	12 4 69	Kaiser Chiefs
Robinson Paul (G)			Beverley	15 10 79	Trainee
Rush Ian (F)	6 0	12 06	St Asaph	20 10 61	Liverpool
Sharpe Lee (F)	6 0	12 06	Halesowen	27 5 71	Manchester U
Shepherd Paul (F)			Leeds	17 11 77	Trainee
Wallace Rodney (F)	5 7	11 03	Lewisham	2 10 69	Southampton
Wetherall David (D)	6 2	13 12	Sheffield	14 3 71	Sheffield W
Woodgate Jonathan (D)			Leeds	22 1 80	Trainee
Wright Andrew (M)			Leeds	21 10 78	Trainee
Yeboah Tony (F)	5 11	13 13	Kumasi	6 6 66	Eintracht Frankfurt

League Appearances: Beeney, M. 1; Beesley, P. 11(1); Blunt, J. (1); Bowyer, L. 32; Boyle, W. (1); Couzens, A. 7(3); Deane, B. 27(1); Dorigo, T. 15(3); Ford, M. 15(1); Gray, A. 1(6); Halle, G. 20; Harte, I. 10(4); Hateley, M. 5(1); Jackson, M. 11(6); Jobson, R. 10; Kelly, G. 34(2); Kewell, H. (1); Laurent, P. 2(2); Lilley, D. 4(2); Martyn, N. 37; Molenaar, R. 12; Palmer, C. 26(2); Radebe, L. 28(4); Rush, I. 34(2); Sharpe, L. 26; Shepherd, P. 1; Tinkler, M. 1(2); Wallace, R. 17(5); Wetherall, D. 25(4); Yeboah, T. 6(1)

League (28): Deane 5, Sharpe 5, Bowyer 4, Rush 3, Wallace 3, Harte 2, Kelly 2, Couzens 1, Ford 1, Molenaar 1, own goal 1.

Coca-Cola Cup (5): Wallace 3, Harte 1, Sharpe 1.

FA Cup (6): Bowyer 2, Wallace 2, Deane 1, own goal 1.

Ground: Elland Road, Leeds LS11 0ES. Telephone (0113) 2716037.

Record attendance: 57,892 v Sunderland, FA Cup 5th rd (replay), 15 March 1967.

Capacity: 40,000.

Manager: George Graham.

Company Secretary: Nigel Pleasants.

Honours – Football League: Division 1 Champions – 1968–69, 1973–74, 1991–92. Division 2 Champions – 1923–24, 1963–64, 1989–90. **FA Cup:** Winners 1972. **Football League Cup:** Winners 1967–68. **European Competitions: European Fairs Cup winners:** 1967–68, 1970–71.

Colours: All white, yellow and blue trim.

LEICESTER CITY   FA PREMIERSHIP

Name			Birthplace	Date	Previous club
Campbell Stuart (M)	5 10	10 08	Corby	9 12 77	Trainee
Claridge Steve (F)	5 11	11 08	Portsmouth	10 4 66	Birmingham C
Elliott Matt (D)	6 3	14 10	Roehampton	1 11 68	Oxford U
Grayson Simon (D)	6 0	12 06	Ripon	16 12 69	Leeds U
Guppy Steve (M)	5 11	10 09	Winchester	29 3 69	Port Vale
Heskey Emile (M)	6 2	13 02	Leicester	11 1 78	Trainee
Izzet Muzzy (M)	5 10	10 12	Mile End	31 10 74	Chelsea
Kamark Pontus (D)	5 10	12 03	Sweden	5 4 69	IFK Gothenburg
Keller Kasey (G)	6 1	12 07	Washington	27 1 69	Millwall
Lawrence Jamie (M)	6 0	12 06	Balham	8 3 70	Doncaster R
Lennon Neil (D)	5 9	12 04	Lurgan	25 6 71	Crewe Alex
Lewis Neil (M)	5 8	10 05	Wolverhampton	28 6 74	Trainee
Marshall Ian (F)	6 1	12 12	Liverpool	20 3 66	Ipswich T
McMahon Sam (M)	5 10	11 06	Newark	10 2 76	Trainee
Parker Garry (M)	6 0	13 02	Oxford	7 9 65	Aston Villa
Prior Spencer (D)	6 3	12 12	Rochford	22 4 71	Norwich C
Robins Mark (F)	5 8	11 08	Ashton under Lyme	22 12 69	Norwich C
Skeldon Kevin (F)	5 11	11 03	Edinburgh	27 4 78	Trainee
Taylor Scott (M)	5 9	12 00	Portsmouth	28 11 70	Reading
Ullathorne Robert (M)	5 8	11 03	Wakefield	11 10 71	Osasuna
Walsh Steve (D)	6 3	14 06	Fulwood	3 11 64	Wigan Ath

Watts Julian (D)	6 3	12 01	Sheffield	17 3 71	Sheffield W
Wenlock Stephen (D)	5 7	11 01	Peterborough	11 3 78	Trainee
Whitlow Mike (D)	6 0	13 03	Northwich	13 1 68	Leeds U
Wilson Stuart (F)	5 8	9 12	Leicester	16 9 77	Trainee

League Appearances: Campbell, S. 4(6); Claridge, S. 29(3); Elliott, M. 16; Grayson, S. 36; Guppy, S. 12(1); Heskey, E. 35; Hill, C. 6(1); Izzet, M. 34(1); Kamark, P. 9(1); Keller, K. 31; Lawrence, J. 2(13); Lennon, N. 35; Lewis, N. 4(2); Marshall, I. 19(9); Parker, G. 22(9); Poole, K. 7; Prior, S. 33(1); Robins, M. 5(3); Rolling, F. 1; Taylor, S. 20(5); Walsh, S. 22; Watts, J. 22(4); Whitlow, M. 14(3); Wilson, S. (2)
League (46): Claridge 11, Heskey 10, Marshall 8, Elliott 4, Izzet 3, Parker 2 (2 pens), Walsh 2, Lennon 1, Robins 1, Watts 1, Wilson 1, own goals 2.
Coca-Cola Cup (12): Claridge 2, Grayson 2, Heskey 2, Lawrence 2, Izzet 1, Lennon 1, Parker 1 (pen), Robins 1.
FA Cup (6): Marshall 2, Claridge 1, Parker 1 (pen), Walsh 1, own goal 1.
Ground: City Stadium, Filbert St, Leicester LE2 7FL. Telephone (0116) 2915000.
Record attendance: 47,298 v Tottenham H, FA Cup 5th rd, 18 February 1928.
Capacity: 22,517.
Manager: Martin O'Neill.
Football Secretary: Ian Silvester.
Honours – Football League: Division 2 Champions – 1924–25, 1936–37, 1953–54, 1956–57, 1970–71, 1979–80. **Football League Cup:** Winners 1964, 1997.
Colours: Royal blue and white.

LEYTON ORIENT   DIV. 3

Arnott Andy (M)	6 0	12 02	Chatham	18 10 73	Gillingham
Ayorinde Sam (F)	6 0	12 07	Lagos	20 10 74	Sturm Graz
Baker Joe (F)	5 8	10 07	London	9 4 77	Charlton Ath
Channing Justin (D)	5 11	11 07	Reading	19 11 68	Bristol R
Griffiths Carl (F)	5 10	11 05	Oswestry	15 7 71	Peterborough U
Hanson Dave (F)	6 1	13 01	Huddersfield	19 11 68	Hednesford T
Howes Shaun (D)	5 10	11 07	Norwich	7 11 77	Cambridge U
Hyde Paul (G)	6 1	14 09	Hayes	7 4 63	Leicester C
Inglethorpe Alex (M)	5 11	11 04	Epsom	14 11 71	Watford
Ling Martin (M)	5 7	10 08	West Ham	15 7 66	Swindon T
McGleish Scott (F)	5 9	11 00	Camden Town	10 2 74	Peterborough U
Morrison Dave (M)	5 11	12 10	Waltham Forest	30 11 74	Peterborough U
Naylor Dominic (D)	5 9	12 01	Watford	12 8 70	Gillingham
Riches Steve (M)	6 2	12 06	Sydney	6 8 76	US Univ
Shearer Lee (D)	6 4	12 01	Rochford	23 10 77	Trainee
Warren Mark (D)	6 0	12 02	Hackney	12 11 74	Trainee
Weaver Luke (G)			Woolwich	26 6 79	Trainee
West Colin (F)	6 1	13 09	Wallsend	13 11 62	Swansea C
Winston Sam (F)			London	6 8 78	Norwich C

League Appearances: Ansah, A. (2); Arnott, A. 28(3); Atkin, P. 5; Ayorinde, S. 6(6); Baker, J. 15(5); Caldwell, P. 3; Castle, S. 4; Channing, J. 40; Chapman, D. 31(9); Clapham, J. 6; Fortune-West, L. 1(4); Garland, P. 13(8); Griffiths, C. 13; Hanson, D. 15(10); Heidenstrom, B. 3(1); Hendon, I. 28; Hodges, L. 3; Howes, S. 3(2); Hyde, P. 13; Inglethorpe, A. 10(6); Joseph, R. 15; Kelly, T. 6(3); Ling, M. 39(5); Martin, A. 16(1); Martin, D. 8; McCarthy, A. 3(1); McGleish, S. 28; Morrison, D. 8; Naylor, D. 44; Riches, S. 2(3); Sealey, L. 12; Shearer, L. 7(1); Shilton, P. 9; Timons, C. 6; Warren, M. 25(2); Weaver, L. 9; West, C. 22(1); Whyte, C. 1; Wilkins, R. 3; Winston, S. 3(8)

56

League (50): Inglethorpe 8, McGleish 7, Griffiths 6, Channing 5, Arnott 3, Hanson 3, Naylor 3 (2 pens), West 3, Ayorinde 2, Chapman 2, Timons 2, Castle 1, Hendon 1, Kelly 1, Ling 1, Warren 1, Winston 1.
Coca-Cola Cup (1): West 1.
FA Cup (3): Channing 1, West 1, Winson 1.
Ground: Leyton Stadium, Brisbane Road, Leyton, London E10 5NE. Telephone (0181) 539 2223.
Record attendance: 34,345 v West Ham U, FA Cup 4th rd, 25 January 1964.
Capacity: 13,842.
Manager: Tommy Taylor.
Secretary: David Burton.
Honours – Football League: Division 3 Champions – 1969–70. Division 3 (S) Champions – 1955–56.
Colours: White shirts with red V, black shorts.

LINCOLN CITY   DIV. 3

Ainsworth Gareth (F)	5 9	11 09	Blackburn	10	5 73	Preston NE
Alcide Colin (M)	6 2	13 11	Huddersfield	14	4 72	Emley
Austin Kevin (D)	6 1	14 00	Hackney	12	2 73	Leyton Orient
Barnett Jason (D)	5 9	10 10	Shrewsbury	21	4 76	Wolverhampton W
Bimson Stuart (D)	5 11	11 08	Liverpool	29	9 69	Bury
Bos Gijsbert (F)	6 5	13 07	Spakenburg	22	3 73	Ijsselmeervogels
Brown Grant (D)	6 0	11 12	Sunderland	19	11 69	Leicester C
Brown Steve (F)	6 0	11 06	Southend	6	12 73	Gillingham
Fleming Terry (M)	5 9	10 01	Marston Green	5	1 73	Preston NE
Holmes Steve (D)	6 2	13 00	Middlesbrough	13	1 71	Preston NE
Hone Mark (M)	6 1	12 00	Croydon	31	3 68	Southend U
Martin Jae (F)	5 11	11 00	London	5	2 76	Birmingham C
Richardson Barry (G)	6 1	12 01	Wallsend	5	8 69	Preston NE
Robertson John (D)	6 2	12 08	Liverpool	8	1 74	Wigan Ath
Stant Phil (F)	6 1	12 07	Bolton	13	10 62	Bury
Sterling Worrell (M)	5 7	10 01	Bethnal Green	8	6 65	Bristol R
Vaughan John (G)	5 10	13 01	Isleworth	26	6 64	Preston NE
Westley Shane (D)	6 2	13 01	Canterbury	16	6 65	Cambridge U
Whitney Jon (D)	5 11	13 08	Nantwich	23	12 70	Huddersfield T

League Appearances: Ainsworth, G. 46; Alcide, C. 38(4); Austin, K. 44; Barnett, J. 33(3); Bimson, S. 13(2); Bos, G. 18(5); Brown, G. 34; Brown, S. 9(6); Cort, C. 5(1); Dennis, T. 23(5); Fleming, T. 37; Foran, M. 1(1); Holmes, S. 27(1); Hone, M. 26(3); Martin, J. 29(5); Minett, J. 2(2); Richardson, B. 36; Robertson, J. 15(1); Stant, P. 22; Sterling, W. 15(6); Stones, C. (2); Taylor, J. 5; Vaughan, J. 10; Whitney, J. 18
League (70): Ainsworth 22 (3 pens), Stant 15, Alcide 7, Holmes 4, Martin 4, Brown S 3, Whitney 3, Dennis 2 (1 pen), Taylor 2, Austin 1, Bimson 1, Bos 1, Cort 1, Robertson 1, own goals 3.
Coca-Cola Cup (13): Bos 3, Ainsworth 2, Alcide 2, Holmes 2, Fleming 1, Hone 1, Martin 1, Whitney 1.
FA Cup (1): Bos 1.
Ground: Sincil Bank, Lincoln LN5 8LD. Telephone (01522) 880011.
Record attendance: 23,196 v Derby Co, League Cup 4th rd, 15 November 1967.
Capacity: 10,918.
Manager: John Beck.
Secretary: H. C. Sills.
Honours – Football League: Division 3 (N) Champions – 1931–32, 1947–48, 1951–52. Division 4 Champions – 1975–76.
Colours: Red and white striped shirts, white shorts, white stockings with red trim.

Name	Height	Weight	Birthplace	Birthdate	From
Babb Phil (D)	6 0	12 03	Lambeth	30 11 70	Coventry C
Barnes John (M)	5 11	12 07	Jamaica	7 11 63	Watford
Berger Patrik (M)	6 2	12 06	Prague	10 11 73	Borussia Dortmund
Bjornebye Stig Inge (D)	5 10	11 09	Norway	11 12 69	Rosenborg
Brazier Philip (D)			Liverpool	3 9 77	Trainee
Byrne Niall (F)			Dublin	3 9 79	Trainee
Carragher James (D)			Bootle	28 1 78	Trainee
Cassidy Jamie (M)	5 9	10 08	Liverpool	21 11 77	Trainee
Culshaw Thomas (M)	5 10	12 02	Liverpool	10 10 78	Trainee
Dalglish Paul (F)	5 9	10 00	Glasgow	18 2 77	Celtic
Fowler Robbie (F)	5 11	11 10	Liverpool	9 4 75	Trainee
Friars Sean (M)			Derry	15 5 79	Trainee
Harkness Steve (M)	5 10	11 02	Carlisle	27 8 71	Carlisle
James David (G)	6 5	14 02	Welwyn	1 8 70	Watford
Jones Lee (F)	5 8	10 08	Wrexham	29 5 73	Wrexham
Jones Rob (D)	5 8	11 00	Wrexham	5 11 71	Crewe Alex
Kennedy Mark (F)	5 11	11 00	Dublin	15 5 76	Millwall
Kvarme Bjorn (D)	6 1	12 04	Trondheim	17 7 72	Rosenborg
Matteo Dominic (D)	6 1	11 10	Dumfries	24 4 74	Trainee
McAteer Jason (M)	5 11	11 00	Birkenhead	18 6 71	Bolton W
McManaman Steve (F)	6 0	10 06	Liverpool	11 2 72	School
Nielsen Jorgen (G)			Nykobing	6 5 71	
Owen Michael (F)			Chester	14 12 79	Trainee
Redknapp Jamie (M)	6 0	12 10	Barton on Sea	25 6 73	Bournemouth
Rizzo Nicky (M)			Sydney	9 6 79	Sydney Olympic
Roberts Gareth (D)			Wrexham	6 2 78	Trainee
Ruddock Neil (D)	6 2	12 12	London	9 5 68	Tottenham H
Thomas Michael (M)	5 9	12 06	Lambeth	24 8 67	Arsenal
Thompson David (M)	5 7	10 00	Birkenhead	12 9 77	Trainee
Turkington Edmond (M)			Merseyside	15 5 78	Trainee
Warner Anthony (G)	6 4	13 09	Liverpool	11 5 74	School
Williams Daniel (M)			Wrexham	12 7 79	Trainee
Wright Mark (D)	6 2	13 03	Dorchester	1 8 63	Derby Co

League Appearances: Babb, P. 21(1); Barnes, J. 34(1); Berger, P. 13(10); Bjornebye, S. 38; Carragher, J. 1(1); Collymore, S. 25(5); Fowler, R. 32; Harkness, S. 5(2); James, D. 38; Jones, L. (2); Jones, R. 2; Kennedy, M. (5); Kvarme, B. 15; Matteo, D. 22(4); McAteer, J. 36(1); McManaman, S. 37; Owen, M. 1(1); Redknapp, J. 18(5); Ruddock, N. 15(2); Scales, J. 3; Thomas, M. 29(2); Thompson, D. (2); Wright, M. 33

League (62): Fowler 18, Collymore 12, McManaman 7, Berger 6, Barnes 4, Thomas 3, Bjornebye 2, Redknapp 2, Babb 1, Carragher 1, McAteer 1, Owen 1, Ruddock 1, own goals 3.

Coca-Cola Cup (10): Fowler 5 (1 pen), McManaman 2, Berger 1, Redknapp 1, Wright 1.

FA Cup (3): Collymore 2, Fowler 1.

Ground: Anfield Road, Liverpool L4 0TH. Telephone (0151) 263 2361.

Record attendance: 61,905 v Wolverhampton W, FA Cup 4th rd, 2 February 1952.

Capacity: 41,000.

Manager: Roy Evans.

Secretary: Bryce Morrison.

Honours – Football League: Division 1 – Champions 1900–01, 1905–06, 1921–22, 1922–23, 1946–47, 1963–64, 1965–66, 1972–73, 1975–76, 1976–77, 1978–79, 1979–80, 1981–82, 1982–83, 1983–84, 1985–86, 1987–88, 1989–90 (Liverpool have a record

number of 18 League Championship wins). Division 2 Champions – 1893–94, 1895–96, 1904–05, 1961–62. FA Cup: Winners 1965, 1974, 1986, 1989, 1992. **League Cup:** Winners 1981, 1982, 1983, 1984, 1995. Super Cup: Winners 1985–86. **European Competitions: European Cup winners:** 1976–77, 1977–78, 1980–81, 1983–84. **UEFA Cup winners:** 1972–73, 1975–76. **Super Cup winners:** 1977.
Colours: All red.

LUTON TOWN   DIV. 2

Abbey Nathan (G)	6 1	12 00	Islington	11 7 78	Trainee
Alexander Graham (M)	5 10	12 02	Coventry	10 10 71	Scunthorpe U
Davis Kelvin (G)	6 0	14 00	Bedford	29 9 76	Trainee
Davis Steve (D)	6 2	14 07	Hexham	30 10 68	Burnley
Douglas Stuart (F)	5 8	11 05	London	9 4 78	Trainee
Evers Sean (M)	5 9	9 11	Hitchin	10 10 77	Trainee
Feuer Ian (G)	6 7	15 06	Las Vegas	20 5 71	West Ham U
Fotiadis Andrew (F)	5 11	11 00	Hitchin	6 9 77	School
George Liam (F)			Luton	2 2 79	Trainee
Grant Kim (F)	5 10	10 12	Ghana	25 9 72	Charlton Ath
Hughes Ceri (M)	5 10	12 07	Pontypridd	26 2 71	Trainee
James Julian (D)	5 10	12 04	Tring	22 3 70	Trainee
Johnson Marvin (D)	6 1	13 06	Wembley	29 10 68	Apprentice
Kean Robert (M)			Luton	3 6 78	Trainee
Marshall Dwight (F)	5 7	11 02	Jamaica	3 10 65	Plymouth Arg
McLaren Paul (M)	6 1	13 04	High Wycombe	17 11 76	Trainee
Oldfield David (F)	6 0	13 04	Perth (Aus)	30 5 68	Leicester C
Patterson Darren (D)	6 1	12 10	Belfast	15 10 69	Crystal Palace
Showler Paul (M)	5 7	11 00	Doncaster	10 10 66	Bradford C
Sweeney Terry (F)			Paisley	26 1 79	Trainee
Thomas Mitchell (D)	6 2	13 00	Luton	2 10 64	West Ham U
Thorpe Tony (F)	5 9	12 04	Leicester	10 4 74	Leicester C
Waddock Gary (M)	5 10	12 05	Alperton	17 3 62	Bristol R
Willmott Chris (D)	6 2	11 05	Bedford	30 9 77	Trainee

League Appearances: Alexander, G. 44(1); Davis, S. 43(1); Douglas, S. 2(7); Evers, S. 1; Feuer, I. 46; Fotiadis, A. 9(8); Grant, K. 8(17); Guentchev, B. 15(12); Harvey, R. 1(1); Hughes, C. 36; James, J. 44; Johnson, M. 44; Kiwomya, A. 5; Linton, D. 3(4); Marshall, D. 9(15); McGowan, G. 2; McLaren, P. 13(11); Oldfield, D. 31(7); Patterson, D. 8(2); Showler, P. 21(2); Skelton, A. 2(1); Thomas, M. 42; Thorpe, T. 39(2); Upson, M. (1); Waddock, G. 38(1).
League (71): Thorpe 28 (7 pens), Davis S 8, Oldfield 6, Showler 6, Hughes 4, Marshall 4, Fotiadis 3, Thomas 3, Alexander 2, Grant 2, Waddock 2, Guentchev 1, James 1, Kiwomya 1.
Coca-Cola Cup (9): Grant 2, Oldfield 2, Thorpe 2 (1 pen), Hughes 1, James 1, own goal 1.
FA Cup (6): Marshall 3, Hughes 1, Johnson 1, Thorpe 1.
Ground: Kenilworth Road Stadium, 1 Maple Rd, Luton, Beds. LU4 8AW. Telephone (01582) 411622.
Record attendance: 30,069 v Blackpool, FA Cup 6th rd replay, 4 March 1959.
Capacity: 9975.
Manager: Lennie Lawrence.
Secretary: Cherry Newbery.
Honours – Football League: Division 2 Champions – 1981–82. Division 4 Champions – 1967–68. Division 3 (S) Champions – 1936–37. **Football League Cup winners** 1987–88.
Colours: White shirts with blue shoulder bar, blue shorts with white trim, blue stockings, with white, orange trim.

MACCLESFIELD TOWN DIV. 3

Name	Ht	Wt	Birthplace	Date	Club
Askey John (F)	6 0	12 01	Stoke	4 11 64	Port Vale
Bradshaw Mark (D)	5 9	10 03	Ashton	7 9 69	Stafford R
Byrne Chris (M)	5 9	10 02	Hulme	9 2 75	Droylsden
Davenport Peter (F)	5 10	11 06	Birkenhead	24 3 61	Stockport Co
Edey Cec (D)	6 1	12 04	Manchester	12 3 65	Witton A
Gardiner Mark (M)	5 10	12 07	Cirencester	25 12 66	Fredrikstad
Gee Danny (D)	5 11	12 05	Northwich	6 5 74	Barnton
Howarth Neil (D)	6 1	12 12	Bolton	15 11 71	Burnley
Levendis Andy (M)	5 8	11 06	Cheadle	4 1 78	Oldham Ath
Mitchell Neil (F)	5 6	11 12	Lytham	7 11 74	Blackpool
Oakes Andy (G)	6 1	11 02	Northwich	11 1 77	Barnton
Ohandjanian Dmis (F)	5 8	10 12	Manchester	1 5 78	Doncaster R
Peel Nathan (F)	6 1	13 03	Blackburn	17 5 72	Rotherham U
Payne Steve (D)	5 11	12 02	Castleford	1 8 75	Huddersfield T
Power Phil (F)	5 7	11 07	Salford	25 7 67	Stalybridge C
Price Ryan (G)	6 5	13 04	Govern	13 3 70	Birmingham C
Sorvel Neil (M)	5 10	11 04	Whiston	2 3 73	Crewe Alex
Tinson Darren (D)	5 10	12 12	Connah's Quay	15 11 69	Northwich V
Williams Carwyn (F)	5 9	11 10	Pwllheli	21 10 74	Northwich V
Wood Steve (M)	5 8	10 12	Oldham	23 6 63	Ashton U

Ground: The Moss Rose Ground, London Road, Macclesfield, Cheshire
SK11 7SP. Telephone: (01625) 264686.
Record attendance: 9008 v Winsford U, Cheshire Senior Cup 2nd rd, 4
February 1948. **Capacity:** 6028 (seated 1053, standing 4975).
Manager: Sammy McIlroy..
General Secretary: Colin Garlick.

MANCHESTER CITY DIV. 1

Name	Ht	Wt	Birthplace	Date	Club
Beagrie Peter (M)	5 8	12 00	Middlesbrough	28 11 65	Everton
Beesley Paul (D)	6 1	12 07	Liverpool	21 9 65	Leeds U
Brannan Ged (D)	6 0	12 05	Liverpool	15 1 72	Tranmere R
Brightwell Ian (M)	5 10	12 05	Lutterworth	9 4 68	Congleton T
Brisco Neil (M)	6 0	11 05	Wigan	26 1 78	Trainee
Brown Michael (G)	5 9	10 07	Stranraer	6 11 79	Trainee
Brown Michael R (M)	5 8	11 08	Hartlepool	25 1 77	Trainee
Callaghan Anthony (D)	5 7	10 00	Manchester	11 1 78	Trainee
Clough Nigel (M)	5 10	12 03	Sunderland	19 3 66	Liverpool
Creaney Gerry (F)	5 11	13 06	Coatbridge	13 4 70	Portsmouth
Crooks Lee (M)	5 11	12 01	Wakefield	14 1 78	Trainee
Dickov Paul (F)	5 5	11 09	Glasgow	1 11 72	Arsenal
Edghill Richard (D)	5 9	11 03	Oldham	23 9 74	Trainee
Fenton Anthony (D)	5 10	10 02	Preston	23 11 79	Trainee
Fenton Nicholas (D)	5 10	10 04	Preston	23 11 79	Trainee
Foster John (D)	5 11	13 02	Blackley	19 9 73	Trainee
Greenacre Chris (F)	5 11	12 08	Wakefield	23 12 77	Trainee
Heaney Neil (F)	5 9	11 07	Middlesbrough	3 11 71	Southampton
Hiley Scott (M)	5 9	11 05	Plymouth	27 9 68	Birmingham C
Horlock Kevin (M)	6 0	12 00	Plumstead	1 11 72	Swindon T
Ingram Rae (D)	5 11	12 08	Manchester	6 12 74	Trainee
Kavelashvili Mikhail (M)	5 11	12 01	Tbilisi	22 7 71	Spartak Vladikavkaz
Kelly Ray (F)	5 11	12 00	Athlone	29 12 76	Athlone T
Kernaghan Alan (D)	6 2	14 01	Otley	25 4 67	Middlesbrough
Kinkladze Georgiou (M)	5 8	10 09	Tbilisi	6 7 73	Dynamo Tbilisi
Margetson Martyn (G)	6 0	14 00	West Neath	8 9 71	Trainee
Mason Gary (M)	5 8	10 01	Edinburgh	15 10 79	Trainee

McGlinchey Brian (M)	5 7	10 02	Derry	26 10 77	Trainee
McGoldrick Eddie (M)	5 10	11 07	London	30 4 65	Arsenal
Morley David (D)			St Helens	25 9 77	Trainee
Morley Neil (M)	5 8	10 02	Warrington	16 11 78	Trainee
Phillips Martin (F)	5 9	10 03	Exeter	13 3 76	Exeter C
Rimmer Stephen (D)	6 3	13 02	Liverpool	23 5 79	Trainee
Rosler Uwe (F)	6 1	12 06	Attenburg	15 11 68	Dynamo Dresden
Rowlands Aled (F)	5 6	10 00	Bangor	9 6 78	Trainee
Summerbee Nicky (F)	5 11	12 08	Altrincham	26 8 71	Swindon T
Symons Kit (D)	6 1	13 07	Basingstoke	8 3 71	Portsmouth
Thomas Scott (M)	5 9	11 02	Bury	30 10 74	Trainee
Weaver Nick (G)	6 3	13 01	Sheffield	2 3 79	Mansfield T
Whitley Jeffrey (M)			Zambia	14 4 75	Trainee
Whitley Jim (M)	5 9	11 00	Zambia	14 4 75	Trainee
Wills David (F)	5 5	9 04	Ashton-u-Lyne	9 3 79	Trainee
Wright Tommy (G)	6 1	14 05	Belfast	29 8 63	Nottingham F

League Appearances: Atkinson, D. 7(1); Beagrie, P. (1); Beesley, P. 6; Brannan, G. 11; Brightwell, I. 36(1); Brown, M. 7(4); Clough, N. 18(5); Creaney, D. 1(4); Crooks, L. 8(7); Dibble, A. 12(1); Dickov, P. 25(4); Foster, J. 3; Frontzeck, M. 8(3); Greenacre, C. (4); Heaney, N. 10(5); Hiley, S. 2(1); Horlock, K. 18; Immel, E. 4; Ingram, R. 13(5); Kavelashvili, M. 6(18); Kernaghan, A. 9(1); Kinkladze, G. 39; Lomas, S. 35; Margetson, M. 17; McGoldrick, E. 33; Phillips, M. 1(3); Rodger, S. 8; Rosler, U. 43(1); Summerbee, N. 43(1); Symons, K. 44; Wassall, D. 14(1); Whitley, J. 12(11); Wright, T. 13
League (59): Rosler 15 (2 pens), Kinkladze 12 (6 pens), Dickov 5, Horlock 4, Summerbee 4, Lomas 3, Atkinson 2, Brightwell 2, Clough 2, Kavelashvili 2, Brannan 1, Creaney 1, Heaney 1, Rodger 1, Whitley 1, own goals 3.
Coca-Cola Cup (1): Rosler 1.
FA Cup (4): Summerbee 2, Heaney 1, Rosler 1.
Ground: Maine Road, Moss Side, Manchester M14 7WN. Telephone (0161) 224 5000.
Record attendance: 84,569 v Stoke C, FA Cup 6th rd, 3 March 1934 (British record for any game outside London or Glasgow). **Capacity:** 31,458.
Manager: Frank Clark.
General Secretary: J. B. Halford.
Honours – Football League: Division 1 Champions – 1936–37, 1967–68. Division 2 Champions – 1898–99, 1902–03, 1909–10, 1927–28, 1946–47, 1965–66. **FA Cup winners** 1904, 1934, 1956, 1969. **Football League Cup winners** 1970, 1976.
European Competitions: European Cup-Winners' Cup winners: 1969–70.
Colours: Light blue shirts, white shorts, navy stockings.

MANCHESTER UNITED   FA PREMIERSHIP

Appleton Michael (M)	5 9	12 04	Salford	4 12 75	Trainee
Beckham David (M)	6 0	11 12	Leytonstone	2 5 75	Trainee
Brebner Grant (M)	5 9	10 01	Edinburgh	6 12 77	Trainee
Brightwell Stuart (F)	5 6	10 11	Easington	31 1 79	Trainee
Brown David (F)	5 100	12 07	Bolton	2 10 78	Trainee
Brown Wesley (D)	6 1	13 02	Manchester	13 10 79	Trainee
Butt Nicky (M)	5 10	11 05	Manchester	21 1 75	Trainee
Cantona Eric (F)	6 2	14 01	Paris	24 5 66	Leeds U
Casper Chris (D)	6 0	12 01	Burnley	28 4 75	Trainee
Clegg Michael (D)	5 8	11 09	Tameside	3 7 77	Trainee
Cole Andy (F)	5 10	12 01	Nottingham	15 10 71	Newcastle U
Cooke Terry (F)	5 7	10 00	Marston Green	5 8 76	Trainee
Cruyff Jordi (F)	6 1	11 00	Amsterdam	9 2 74	Barcelona
Culkin Nick (G)	6 3	13 03	York	6 7 78	York C
Curtis John (D)	5 10	11 07	Nuneaton	3 9 78	Trainee
Davies Simon (M)	6 0	11 06	Middlewich	23 4 74	Trainee

Duncan Andrew (D)	6 0	13 05	Hexham	20 10 77	Trainee
Gibson Paul (G)	6 3	13 00	Sheffield	1 11 76	Trainee
Giggs Ryan (F)	5 11	10 12	Cardiff	29 11 73	School
Irwin Denis (D)	5 8	10 10	Cork	31 10 65	Oldham Ath
Johnsen Ronny (D)	6 3	13 01	Sandefjord	10 6 69	Besiktas
Keane Roy (M)	5 11	12 02	Cork	10 8 71	Nottingham F
Macken Jonathan (F)	5 11	12 04	Manchester	7 9 77	Trainee
May David (D)	6 0	13 03	Oldham	24 6 70	Blackburn R
McClair Brian (F)	5 10	12 12	Airdrie	8 12 63	Celtic
McGibbon Patrick (D)	6 2	13 10	Lurgan	6 9 73	Portadown
Mulryne Philip (M)	5 7	10 13	Belfast	1 1 78	Trainee
Murdock Colin (D)	6 3	12 13	Ballymena	2 7 75	Trainee
Mustoe Neil (F)	5 8	12 13	Gloucester	5 11 76	Trainee
Neville Gary (D)	5 11	12 04	Bury	18 2 75	Trainee
Neville Philip (D)	5 11	11 10	Bury	21 1 77	Trainee
Notman Alex (M)	5 7	11 05	Edinburgh	10 12 79	Trainee
O'Kane John (D)	5 10	11 11	Nottingham	15 11 74	Trainee
Pallister Gary (D)	6 4	15 00	Ramsgate	30 6 65	Middlesbrough
Pilkington Kevin (G)	6 1	13 01	Hitchin	8 3 74	Trainee
Poborsky Karel (M)	5 9	11 05	Jindinchuv-Hadec	30 3 72	Slavia Prague
Schmeichel Peter (G)	6 4	15 13	Gladsaxe	18 11 63	Brondby
Scholes Paul (F)	5 7	11 08	Salford	16 11 74	Trainee
Smith Tommy (M)	5 10	12 08	Northampton	25 11 77	Trainee
Solskjaer Ole Gunnar (F)	5 10	11 08	Kristiansund	26 2 73	Molde
Teather Paul (M)	6 0	11 05	Rotherham	26 12 77	Trainee
Thornley Ben (F)	5 9	11 08	Bury	21 4 75	Trainee
Tomlinson Graeme (F)	5 10	12 07	Watford	10 12 75	Bradford C
Twiss Michael (F)	5 11	12 08	Salford	26 12 77	Trainee
Van der Gouw Raimond (G)	6 3	13 07	Oldenzaal	24 3 63	Vitesse
Wallwork Ronnie (D)	5 10	12 12	Manchester	10 9 77	Trainee
Wellens Richard (M)	5 9	10 07	Manchester	26 3 80	Trainee
Wilson Mark (F)	6 0	12 02	Scunthorpe	9 2 79	Trainee

League Appearances: Beckham, D. 33(3); Butt, N. 24(2); Cantona, E. 36; Casper, C. (2); Clegg, M. 3(1); Cole, A. 10(10); Cruyff, J. 11(5); Giggs, R. 25(1); Irwin, D. 29(2); Johnsen, R. 26(5); Keane, R. 21; May, D. 28(1); McClair, B. 4(15); Neville, G. 30(1); Neville, P. 15(3); O'Kane, J. 1; Pallister, G. 27; Poborsky, K. 15(7); Schmeichel, P. 36; Scholes, P. 16(8); Solskjaer, O. 25(8); Thornley, B. 1(1); Van der Gouw, R. 2

League (76): Solskjaer 18, Cantona 11 (3 pens), Beckham 8, Cole 7, Butt 5, Cruyff 3, Giggs 3, May 3, Pallister 3, Poborsky 3, Scholes 3, Keane 2, Irwin 1, Neville G 1, own goals 5.

Coca-Cola Cup (2): Poborsky 1, Scholes 1.

FA Cup (3): Scholes 2, Beckham 1.

Ground: Old Trafford, Manchester M16 0RA. Telephone (0161) 872 1661.

Record attendance: 76,962 Wolverhampton W v Grimsby T, FA Cup semi-final. 25 March 1939. **Capacity:** 56,385

Manager: Alex Ferguson CBE.

Secretary: Kenneth Merrett.

Honours – FA Premier League: Champions – 1992–93, 1993–94, 1995–96, 1996–97.
Football League: Division 1 Champions – 1907–8, 1910–11, 1951–52, 1955–56, 1956–57, 1964–65, 1966–67. Division 2 Champions – 1935–36, 1974–75. **FA Cup** winners 1909, 1948, 1963, 1977, 1983, 1985, 1990, 1994, 1996. **Football League Cup** winners 1991–92. **European Competitions: European Cup winners:** 1967–68. **European Cup-Winners' Cup winners:** 1990–91. **European Fairs Cup winners:** 1964–65. **Super Cup winners:** 1991.

Colours: Red shirts, white shorts, black stockings.

MANSFIELD TOWN   DIV. 3

Bowling Ian (G)	6 3	14 03	Sheffield	27 7 65	Bradford C
Clarke Darrell (M)	5 10	10 03	Mansfield	16 12 77	Trainee
Doolan John (D)	6 1	13 01	Liverpool	7 5 74	Everton
Eustace Scott (D)	6 0	14 01	Leicester	13 6 75	Leicester C
Ford Tony (D)	5 9	13 02	Grimsby	14 5 59	Barrow
Hackett Warren (D)	6 0	13 00	Plaistow	16 12 71	Doncaster R
Hadley Stewart (F)	6 0	12 12	Dudley	30 12 72	Derby Co
Harper Steve (D)	5 10	11 06	Newcastle under Lyme	3 2 69	Doncaster R
Kerr David (M)	5 11	12 09	Dumfries	6 9 74	Manchester C
Parkin Steve (D)	5 6	11 01	Mansfield	7 11 65	WBA
Sedgemore Ben (M)	5 10	12 04	Wolverhampton	5 8 75	Peterborough U
Walker John (M)	5 6	10 04	Glasgow	12 12 73	Grimsby T
Watkiss Stuart (D)	6 1	13 00	Wolverhampton	8 5 66	Hereford U

League Appearances: Bowling, I. 46; Christie, I. 8; Clarke, D. 17(2); Clifford, M. 3; Cresswell, R. 5; Doolan, J. 41; Eustace, S. 41(1); Ford, T. 25(2); Hackett, W. 35(1); Hadley, S. 31(5); Harper, S. 37(3); Helliwell, I. 4(1); Holbrook, L. (1); Hurst, G. 5(1); Ireland, S. 5(1); Kerr, D. 9; Kilcline, B. 30(1); Martindale, G. 5; Robinson, I. 3(5); Sale, M. 12(6); Sedgemore, B. 37(2); Sherlock, P. 14(5); Walker, J. 33(3); Watkiss, S. 30(1); Williams, L. 3(3); Williams, R. 4(12); Wood, S. 23(8); Young, C. (1)

League (47): Doolan 6 (4 pens), Sale 5, Eustace 4, Hadley 4, Sedgemore 4, Kilcline 3, Walker 3 (1 pen), Wood 3, Clarke 2, Ford 2, Harper 2, Martindale 2, Cresswell 1, Hackett 1, Helliwell 1, Watkiss 1, own goals 3.
Coca-Cola Cup (0).
FA Cup (4): Doolan 1, Eustace 1, Ford 1, Wood 1.
Ground: Field Mill Ground, Quarry Lane, Mansfield NG18 5DA. Telephone (01623) 23567.
Record attendance: 24,467 v Nottingham F, FA Cup 3rd rd, 10 January 1953.
Capacity: 6905.
Manager: Steve Parkin.
Secretary: Christine Reynolds.
Honours – Football League: Division 3 Champions – 1976–77. Division 4 Champions – 1974–75. **Freight Rover Trophy winners** 1986–87.
Colours: Amber & blue striped shirts, amber shorts, blue stockings.

MIDDLESBROUGH   DIV. 1

Beck Mikkel (F)	6 2	12 09	Aarhus	12 5 73	Fortuna Cologne
Blackmore Clayton (M)	5 8	11 13	Neath	23 9 64	Manchester U
Campbell Andrew (F)			Middlesbrough	18 4 79	Trainee
Connor Paul (F)			Bishop Auckland	12 1 79	Trainee
Cox Neil (D)	6 0	13 07	Scunthorpe	8 10 71	Aston Villa
Cummins Michael (M)	6 0	11 12	Dublin	1 6 78	Trainee
Emerson (M)	6 0	14 05	Rio	12 4 72	Porto
Festa Gianluca (D)	6 0	13 06	Cagliari	15 3 69	Internazionale
Fleming Curtis (D)	5 10	12 08	Manchester	8 10 68	St Patrick's Ath
Freestone Chris (F)	5 10	12 01	Nottingham	4 9 71	Arnold T
Gavin Jason (D)			Dublin	14 3 80	Trainee
Harrison Craig (D)	6 0	11 13	Gateshead	10 11 77	Trainee
Hignett Craig (M)	5 9	11 03	Whiston	12 1 70	Crewe Alex
Juninho (F)	5 5	10 00	Sao Paulo	22 2 73	Sao Paulo
Kinder Vladimir (D)	5 10	13 00	Bratislava	9 3 69	Slovan Bratislava

Liddle Craig (D)	5 11	12 05	Chester-le-Street	21 10 71	Blyth Spartans
Moore Alan (M)	5 9	11 02	Dublin	25 11 74	Rivermount
Moreira Fabio (M)			Rio	14 3 72	Chaves
Mustoe Robbie (M)	5 10	11 10	Oxford	28 8 68	Oxford U
Ormerod Anthony (M)			Middlesbrough	31 3 79	Trainee
Pearson Nigel (D)	6 1	14 03	Nottingham	21 8 63	Sheffield W
Ravanelli Fabrizio (F)	6 1	13 04	Perugia	11 12 68	Juventus
Roberts Ben (G)	6 1	13 03	Bishop Auckland	22 6 75	Trainee
Robson Bryan (M)	5 9	12 05	Witton Gilbert	11 1 57	Manchester U
Schwarzer Mark (G)	6 5	13 08	Sydney	6 10 72	Bradford C
Stamp Philip (M)	5 10	13 05	Middlesbrough	12 12 75	Trainee
Summerbell Mark (M)	5 10	10 03	Durham	30 10 76	Trainee
Swalwell Andrew (M)			Middlesbrough	29 3 79	Trainee
Vickers Steve (D)	6 1	13 02	Bishop Auckland	13 10 67	Tranmere R
Walsh Gary (G)	6 3	14 11	Wigan	21 3 68	Manchester U
Whelan Phil (D)	6 4	14 07	Stockport	7 3 72	Ipswich T
White Alan (D)	6 0	13 04	Darlington	22 3 76	
White Darren (D)			Easington	13 1 79	Trainee
Whyte Derek (D)	5 11	12 13	Glasgow	31 8 68	Celtic

League Appearances: Barmby, N. 10; Beck, M. 22(3); Blackmore. C. 14(2); Branco 1(1); Campbell, A. (3); Cox, N. 29(2); Emerson 32; Festa, G. 13; Fjortoft, J. 2(3); Fleming, C. 30; Freestone, C. (3); Hignett, C. 19(3); Juninho 34(1); Kinder, V. 4(2); Liddle, C. 5; Miller, A. 10; Moore. A. 10(7); Morris, C. 3(1); Mustoe, R. 31; Pearson, N. 17(1); Ravanelli, F. 33; Roberts, B. 9(1); Robson, B. 1; Schwarzer, M. 7; Stamp, P. 15(9); Summerbell, M. (2); Vickers, S. 26(3); Walsh, G. 12; Whelan, P. 9; Whyte, D. 20(1).
League (51): Ravanelli 16 (3 pens), Juninho 12, Beck 5, Emerson 4 (1 pen), Hignett 4 (1 pen), Mustoe 3, Blackmore 2, Barmby 1, Festa 1, Kinder 1, Stamp 1, own goal 1.
Coca-Cola Cup (23): Ravanelli 9 (1 pen), Beck 4, Branco 2, Emerson 2, Fleming 1, Hignett 1, Juninho 1, Stamp 1, Vickers 1, Whyte 1.
FA Cup (18): Ravanelli 6, Beck 2, Hignett 2 (1 pen), Juninho 2, Cox 1, Emerson 1, Festa 1, Fjortoft 1, Stamp 1, own goal 1.
Ground: Cellnet Riverside Stadium, Middlesbrough, Cleveland TS3 6RS. Telephone (01642) 877700
Record attendance: 53,596 v Newcastle U, Division 1, 27 December 1949.
Capacity: 30,500.
Manager: Bryan Robson.
Secretary: Karen Nelson.
Honours – Football League: Division 1 Champions 1994–95. Division 2 Champions 1926–27, 1928–29, 1973–74. **Amateur Cup winners** 1895, 1898, **Anglo-Scottish Cup:** Winners 1975–76.
Colours: Red shirts, white shorts, red stockings.

MILLWALL   DIV. 2

Aris Steven (D)			London	27 4 78	
Bircham Marc (M)			Brent	11 5 78	Trainee
Bowry Bobby (M)	5 8	10 08	Croydon	19 5 71	Crystal Palace
Canoville Dean (M)			Perivale	30 11 78	Trainee
Carter Tim (G)	6 2	13 00	Bristol	5 10 67	Oxford U
Connor James (D)	6 0	13 00	Twickenham	22 8 74	Trainee
Crawford Steve (F)	5 10	10 07	Dunfermline	9 1 74	Raith R
Dair Jason (F)	5 11	10 08	Dunfermline	15 6 74	Raith R
Doyle Maurice (M)	5 8	10 07	Ellesmere Port	17 10 69	QPR

Edwards Daniel (M)			Greenwich	20 12 79	Trainee
Harle Mike (D)	6 0	12 06	Lewisham	31 10 72	Sittingbourne
Hartley Paul (M)	5 9	10 04	Baillieston	19 10 76	Hamilton A
Hockton Danny (F)			Barking	7 2 79	Trainee
Holsgrove Lee (D)			Halton	13 12 79	Trainee
Lavin Gerard (D)	5 10	11 00	Corby	5 2 74	Watford
Markey Brendan (F)			Dublin	19 5 76	Bohemians
McLeary Alan (D)	5 10	10 06	Lambeth	6 10 64	Bristol C
McRobert Lee (M)	5 9	10 12	Bromley	4 10 72	Sittingbourne
Neill Lucas (M)	6 1	12 00	Sydney	9 3 78	NSW Academy
Newman Ricky (M)	5 10	12 06	Guildford	5 8 70	Crystal Palace
Nurse David (G)	6 3	12 06	Kings Lynn	12 10 76	Manchester C
Pitwood Adam (F)			Crawley	24 1 80	School
Robertson Graham (F)	5 11	10 10	Edinburgh	2 11 76	Raith R
Roche Stephen			Dublin	2 10 78	Belvedere
Sadlier Richard (F)	6 2	12 10	Dublin	14 1 79	Belvedere
Savage Dave (M)	6 2	12 07	Dublin	30 7 73	Longford T
Stevens Keith (D)	6 0	12 12	Merton	21 6 64	Apprentice
Webber Damien (D)	6 4	14 00	Rustington	8 10 68	Bognor Regis T
Witter Tony (D)	6 2	13 02	London	12 8 65	QPR

League Appearances: Berry, G. 13(1); Bircham, M. 6; Bowry, B. 26(2); Bright, M. 3; Cadette, R. 7; Canoville, D. (2); Carter, T. 46; Crawford, S. 40(2); Dair, J. 21(3); Dolby, T. 15(6); Doyle, M. 19(9); Fitzgerald, S. 7; Harle, M. 12(9); Hartley, P. 35(9); Hockton, D. (2); Huckerby, D. 6; Iga, A. (1); Lavin, G. 7(2); Malkin, C. 7(2); McLeary, A. 15; McRobert, L. 3(1); Neill, L. 35(4); Newman, R. 39(2); Robertson, G. (1); Roche, S. 4(3); Rogan, A. 26(2); Sadlier, R. 7(3); Savage, D. 32(3); Sinclair, D. 6(2); Stevens, K. 6; Van Blerk, J. 2(2); Webber, D. 25(1); Wilkins, R. 3; Witter, T. 33

League (50): Crawford 11 (1 pen), Rogan 8 (3 pens), Hartley 4, Huckerby 3, Malkin 3, Neill 3, Newman 3, Savage 3, Dolby 2, Webber 2, Bowry 1, Bright 1, Cadette 1, Dair 1, Doyle 1, Harle 1, own goals 2.

Coca-Cola Cup (1): Malkin 1.

FA Cup (2): Crawford 1, Savage 1.

Ground: The Den, Zampa Road, Bermondsey SE16 3LN. Telephone (0171) 232 1222.

Record attendance: 20,093 v Arsenal, FA Cup 3rd rd, 10 January 1994. **Capacity:** 20,146.

Manager: Billy Bonds.

Secretary: Yvonne Haines.

Honours – Football League: Division 2 Champions – 1987–88. Division 3 (S) Champions – 1927–28, 1937–38. Division 4 Champions – 1961–62. **Football League Trophy winners** 1982–83.

Colours: Blue shirts, white shorts, blue stockings.

NEWCASTLE UNITED   FA PREMIERSHIP

Albert Philippe (D)	6 3	13 00	Bouillon	10 8 67	Anderlecht
Arnison Paul (M)	5 9	10 12	Hartlepool	18 9 77	Trainee
Asprilla Faustino (F)	5 9	11 03	Tulua	10 11 69	Parma
Barrett Paul (M)	5 9	10 11	Newcastle	13 4 78	Trainee
Barton Warren (D)	5 11	12 00	Stoke Newington	19 3 69	Wimbledon
Batty David (M)	5 8	12 00	Leeds	2 12 68	Blackburn R
Beardsley Peter (F)	5 8	11 07	Newcastle	18 1 61	Everton
Beresford John (M)	5 5	10 12	Sheffield	4 9 66	Portsmouth
Brayson Paul (F)	5 4	10 10	Newcastle	16 9 77	Trainee

Burghall Terence (F)	6 0	11 06	Liverpool	25	9 78	Liverpool
Clark Lee (M)	5 7	11 07	Wallsend	27	10 72	Trainee
Crawford Jimmy (M)	6 0	11 06	Chicago	1	5 73	Bohemians
Eatock David (F)	5 4	10 05	Wigan	11	11 76	Chorley
Elliott Robbie (D)	5 10	10 13	Gosforth	25	12 73	Trainee
Elliott Stuart (D)	5 8	11 05	London	27	8 77	Trainee
Ferdinand Les (F)	5 11	13 05	Acton	18	12 66	QPR
Gillespie Keith (F)	5 10	11 05	Larne	18	2 75	Manchester U
Ginola David (F)	5 11	11 10	Gassin	25	1 67	Paris St Germain
Hamilton Des (M)	5 10	12 13	Bradford	15	8 76	Bradford C
Harper Steve (G)	6 0	12 03	Easington	3	2 70	Seaham Red Star
Hislop Shaka (G)	6 4	14 04	Hackney	22	2 69	Reading
Howey Steve (M)	6 2	11 12	Sunderland	26	10 71	Trainee
Hughes Aaron (D)	6 0	11 02	Magherafelt	8	11 79	Trainee
Keen Peter (G)	6 0	11 09	Middlesbrough	16	11 76	Trainee
Lee Robert (F)	5 11	11 13	West Ham	1	2 66	Charlton Ath
Peacock Darren (D)	6 2	12 12	Bristol	3	2 68	QPR
Shearer Alan (F)	5 11	12 06	Newcastle	13	8 70	Blackburn R
Srnicek Pavel (G)	6 2	14 07	Ostrava	10	3 68	Banik Ostrava
Walker Kashka (M)	5 9	10 10	Toronto	10	11 78	Canada SA
Watson Steve (D)	6 0	12 07	North Shields	1	4 74	Trainee

League Appearances: Albert, P. 27; Asprilla, F. 17(7); Barton, W. 14(4); Batty, D. 32; Beardsley, P. 22(3); Beresford, J. 18(1); Clark, L. 9(16); Crawford, J. (2); Elliott, R. 29; Ferdinand, L. 30(1); Gillespie, K. 23(9); Ginola, D. 20(4); Hislop, S. 16; Howey, S. 8; Kitson, P. (3); Lee, R. 32(1); Peacock, D. 35; Shearer, A. 31; Srnicek, P. 22; Watson, S. 33(3)
League (73): Shearer 25 (3 pens), Ferdinand 16, Elliott 7, Beardsley 5 (2 pens), Lee 5, Asprilla 4, Albert 2, Clark 2, Barton 1, Batty 1, Gillespie 1, Ginola 1, Howey 1, Peacock 1, Watson 1.
Coca-Cola Cup (2): Beardsley 1 (pen), Shearer 1.
FA Cup (4): Clark 1, Ferdinand 1, Lee 1, Shearer 1.
Ground: St James' Park, Newcastle-upon-Tyne NE1 4ST. Telephone (0191) 201 8400.
Record attendance: 68,386 v Chelsea, Division 1, 3 Sept 1930. **Capacity:** 36,610.
Manager: Kenny Dalglish.
General Manager/Secretary: R. Cushing.
Honours – Football League: Division 1 – Champions 1904–05, 1906–07, 1908–09, 1926–27, 1992–93. Division 2 Champions – 1964–65. **FA Cup winners** 1910, 1924, 1932, 1951, 1952, 1955. **Texaco Cup winners** 1973–74, 1974–75. **European Competitions: European Fairs Cup winners:** 1968–69. **Anglo-Italian Cup winners:** 1973.
Colours: Black and white striped shirts, black shorts, black stockings.

NORTHAMPTON TOWN   DIV. 2

Beckford Jason (F)	5 9	14 03	Manchester	14	2 70	Millwall
Clarkson Ian (D)	5 10	12 03	Birmingham	4	12 70	Stoke C
Colkin Lee (D)	5 10	12 08	Nuneaton	15	7 74	Trainee
Frain John (D)	5 9	12 00	Birmingham	8	10 68	Birmingham C
Gayle John (F)	6 3	15 00	Bromsgrove	30	7 64	Stoke C
Gibb Ali (M)	5 9	11 07	Salisbury	17	2 76	Norwich C
Grayson Neil (F)	5 10	12 09	York	1	11 64	Chesterfield
Hunter Roy (M)	5 10	12 10	Cleveland	29	10 73	WBA
Lee Christian (F)	6 1	11 09	Aylesbury	8	10 76	Doncaster R
Martin Dave (M)	6 1	13 02	East Ham	25	4 63	Leyton Orient

Parrish Sean (M)	5 10	11 05	Wrexham	14 3 72	Doncaster R
Peer Dean (M)	6 2	12 02	Dudley	8 8 69	Walsall
Rennie David (D)	6 0	13 00	Edinburgh	29 8 64	Coventry C
Sampson Ian (D)	6 2	13 01	Wakefield	14 11 68	Sunderland
Turley Billy (G)	6 3	14 13	Wolverhampton	15 7 73	Evesham U
Warburton Ray (D)	6 0	13 00	Rotherham	7 10 67	York C
Warner Michael (M)	5 9	10 12	Harrogate	17 1 74	Tamworth
White Jason (F)	5 11	12 11	Meriden	19 10 71	Scarborough
Woodman Andy (G)	6 2	13 06	Denmark Hill	11 8 71	Exeter C

League Appearances: Burns, C. 6; Clarkson, I. 45; Colkin, L. 1(5); Cooper, M. 37(4); Frain, J. 13; Gayle, J. 9(4); Gibb, A. 6(12); Grayson, N. 32(8); Hunter, R. 26(10); Kirby, R. (1); Lee, C. 12(17); Lyne, N. 1; Maddison, L. 34; Martin, D. 10(2); O'Shea, D. 29(6); Parrish, S. 37(2); Peer, D. 7(14); Rennie, D. 42(1); Rush, M. 14; Sampson, I. 43; Smart, A. 1; Stant, P. 4(1); Thompson, G. (1); Turley, B. 1; Warburton, R. 35; Warner, M. 1(8); White, J. 15(17); Woodman, A. 45
League (67): Grayson 12, Cooper 10, Parrish 8, Lee 7, Hunter 6 (4 pens) Sampson 6, Warburton 4, Rush 3, Rennie 2, Stant 2 (1 pen) White 2, Gayle 1, Gibb 1, Peer 1, own goals 2.
Coca-Cola Cup (3): Lee 2, own goal 1.
FA Cup (0).
Ground: Sixfields, Upton Way, Northampton NN5 5QA. Telephone (01604) 757773.
Record attendance: 24,523 v Fulham, Division 1, 23 April 1966. **Capacity:** 7653.
Manager: Ian Atkins.
Secretary: Mrs Rebecca Kerr.
Honours – Football League: Division 3 Champions – 1962–63. Division 4 Champions – 1986–87.
Colours: Claret with white shirts, yellow panel, white shorts, claret stockings.

NORWICH CITY   DIV. 1

Adams Neil (M)	5 8	10 12	Stoke	23 11 65	Oldham Ath
Allen Alex (D)			Doncaster	10 2 80	Trainee
Bellamy Craig (M)	5 9	10 10	Cardiff	13 7 79	Trainee
Bradshaw Carl (D)	5 10	11 11	Sheffield	2 10 68	Sheffield U
Broughton Drewe (F)			Hitchin	25 10 78	Trainee
Brownrigg Andrew (D)	6 0	11 10	Sheffield	2 8 76	Hereford U
Carey Shaun (M)	5 9	10 10	Kettering	13 5 76	Trainee
Crook Ian (M)	5 8	10 08	Romford	18 1 63	Tottenham H
Eadie Darren (F)	5 8	11 00	Chippenham	10 6 75	Trainee
Fleck Robert (F)	5 8	11 09	Glasgow	11 8 65	Chelsea
Forbes Adrian (F)	5 8	11 04	London	23 1 79	Trainee
Gunn Bryan (G)	6 2	13 08	Thurso	22 12 63	Aberdeen
Hilton Damien (F)	6 2	12 06	Norwich	6 9 77	Trainee
Jackson Matt (D)	6 1	12 07	Leeds	19 10 71	Everton
Johnson Andy (M)	6 1	12 02	Bristol	2 5 74	Trainee
Llewellyn Chris (M)	5 11	11 06	Swansea	29 8 79	Trainee
Marshall Andy (G)	6 2	13 00	Bury	14 4 75	Trainee
Marshall Lee (D)	6 0	11 11	Islington	21 1 79	Enfield
Milligan Mike (M)	5 8	11 00	Manchester	20 2 67	Oldham Ath
Mills Danny (D)	6 0	11 11	Norwich	18 5 77	Trainee
Newman Rob (D)	6 2	13 00	Bradford-on-Avon	13 12 63	Bristol C
O'Neill Keith (M)	6 1	11 09	Dublin	16 2 76	Trainee
Polston John (D)	5 11	11 12	Walthamstow	10 6 68	Tottenham H
Scott Keith (F)	6 2	13 10	London	9 6 67	Stoke C

Scott Kevin (D)	6 2	14 03	Easington	17 12 66	Tottenham H
Shore Jamie (M)	5 9	10 09	Bristol	1 9 77	Trainee
Simpson Karl (D)	5 11	11 06	Newmarket	12 10 76	Trainee
Sutch Daryl (M)	6 0	11 13	Lowestoft	11 9 71	Trainee

League Appearances: Adams, N. 45; Akinbiyi, A. 3(9); Bellamy, C. (3); Bradshaw, C. 11(6); Broughton, D. 3(5); Carey, S. 8(6); Crook, I. 33(4); Eadie, D. 42; Fleck, R. 33(3); Forbes, A. 3(7); Gunn, B. 39; Jackson, M. 19; Johnson, A. 24(3); Marshall, A. 7; Milligan, M. 37; Mills, D. 27(5); Moore, N. 2; Newman, R. 44; O'Neill, K. 23(3); Ottosson, U. 4(3); Polston, J. 27(4); Rocastle, D. 11; Rush, M. (2); Scott, K. 5(8); Scott, K. 9; Simpson, K. 1(2); Sutch, D. 43(1); Wright, J. 3(1).
League (63): Eadie 17, Adams 13 (7 pens), O'Neill 6, Johnson 5, Fleck 4, Keith Scott 3, Sutch 3, Crook 2, Jackson 2, Polston 2, Broughton 1, Milligan 1, Newman 1, Ottosson 1, own goals 2.
Coca-Cola Cup (3): Adams 2 (1 pen), Johnson 1.
FA Cup (2): Adams 1 (pen), Polston 1.
Ground: Carrow Road, Norwich NR1 1JE. Telephone (01603) 760760.
Record attendance: 43,984 v Leicester C, FA Cup 6th rd, 30 March 1963. **Capacity:** 21,994.
Manager: Mike Walker.
Secretary: A. R. W. Neville.
Honours – Football League: Division 2 Champions – 1971–72, 1985–86. Division 3 (S) Champions – 1933–34. **Football League Cup:** Winners 1962, 1985.
Colours: Yellow shirts, green shorts, yellow stockings.

NOTTINGHAM FOREST   DIV. 1

Allen Chris (M)	5 11	12 04	Oxford	18 11 72	Oxford U
Anderson Dale (F)	5 11	11 12	Birmingham	10 11 79	Trainee
Archer Paul (M)	5 8	9 07	Leicester	25 4 78	Trainee
Armstrong Craig (M)	5 11	12 10	South Shields	23 5 75	Trainee
Bart-Williams Chris (M)	5 11	11 00	Freetown	16 6 74	Sheffield W
Blatherwick Steve (D)	6 1	15 00	Nottingham	20 9 73	Notts Co
Burns John (M)	5 10	11 00	Dublin	4 12 77	Belvedere
Campbell Kevin (F)	6 1	13 08	Lambeth	4 2 70	Arsenal
Chettle Steve (D)	6 1	13 01	Nottingham	27 9 68	Apprentice
Cooper Colin (D)	5 9	11 09	Sedgefield	28 2 67	Millwall
Cooper Richard (D)	5 9	11 00	Nottingham	27 9 79	Trainee
Cowling Lee (M)	5 9	10 03	Doncaster	22 9 77	Trainee
Cox Christopher (M)	5 7	10 01	Sunderland	17 9 79	Trainee
Crossley Mark (G)	6 0	16 00	Barnsley	16 6 69	Trainee
Dawson Andrew (M)	5 9	10 02	Northallerton	20 10 78	Trainee
Fettis Alan (G)	6 2	13 00	Belfast	1 2 71	Hull C
Finnigan John (M)	5 8	10 11	Wakefield	28 3 76	Trainee
Fitchett Scott (M)	5 8	9 06	Manchester	20 1 79	Trainee
Follett Richard (D)	5 9	10 02	Leamington Spa	29 8 79	Trainee
Freeman David (F)	5 10	10 13	Dublin	25 11 79	Cherry Orchard
Gemmill Scot (M)	5 11	11 06	Paisley	2 1 71	School
George Daniel (M)	6 1	12 01	Lincoln	22 10 78	Trainee
Goodlad Mark (G)	6 0	13 02	Barnsley	9 9 79	Trainee
Grim Robert (M)	5 11	11 08	London	10 9 78	Trainee
Guinan Stephen (F)	6 1	13 07	Birmingham	24 12 75	Trainee
Haaland Alf-Inge (D)	5 10	12 12	Stavanger	23 11 72	Bryne
Harewood Marlon (D)	6 1	10 00	Hampstead	25 8 79	Trainee
Henry David (G)	6 3	14 09	Belfast	12 11 77	
Hodgson Richard (M)	5 10	11 04	Sunderland	1 10 79	Trainee

Howe Stephen (M)	5 7	10 06	Annitsford	6 11 73	Trainee
Jerkan Nikola (D)	6 2	12 07	Sinj	8 12 64	Oviedo
Lee Jason (F)	6 3	13 03	Newham	9 5 71	Southend U
Lyttle Des (D)	5 8	12 13	Wolverhampton	26 9 71	Swansea C
Macari Jon (F)	5 9	11 04	Stoke	15 12 79	Trainee
McGregor Paul (F)	5 10	11 06	Liverpool	17 12 74	Trainee
Melton Stephen (M)	5 11	10 11	Lincoln	3 10 78	Trainee
Moore Ian (F)	5 11	12 02	Birkenhead	26 8 76	Tranmere R
Pearce Stuart (D)	5 10	12 12	Shepherds Bush	24 4 62	Coventry C
Phillips David (M)	5 9	12 05	Wegberg	29 7 63	Norwich C
Porteous Andrew (M)	5 11	10 11	Edinburgh	13 9 79	Trainee
Roy Bryan (M)	5 10	10 10	Amsterdam	12 2 70	Foggia
Saunders Dean (F)	5 8	10 06	Swansea	21 6 64	Galatasaray
Silenzi Andrea (F)	6 3	11 13	Rome	10 2 66	Torino
Smith Paul (M)	5 11	11 07	Hastings	25 1 76	Hastings T
Stone Steve (M)	5 8	12 05	Gateshead	20 8 71	Trainee
Thom Stuart (D)	6 2	11 12	Dewsbury	27 12 76	Trainee
Todd Andrew (M)	6 0	11 03	Nottingham	22 2 79	Trainee
Turner Barry (M)	5 9	10 01	Nottingham	1 12 78	Trainee
Van Hooijdonk Pierre (F)	6 4	13 13	Steenbergen	29 11 69	Celtic
Warner Vance (M)	6 0	13 02	Leeds	3 9 74	Trainee
Winters Kris (M)			Dundalk	28 8 79	Trainee
Woan Ian (M)	5 10	12 02	Wirral	14 12 67	Runcorn
Wood Scott (M)	5 10	11 11	Nottingham	16 11 79	Trainee

League Appearances: Allen, C. 16(8); Bart-Williams, C. 16; Blatherwick, S. 7; Campbell, K. 16(1); Chettle, S. 31(1); Clough, N. 10(3); Cooper, C. 36; Crossley, M. 33; Fettis, A. 4; Gemmill, S. 18(6); Guinan, S. (2); Haaland, A. 33(2); Howe, S. (1); Jerkan, N. 14; Lee, J. 5(8); Lyttle, D. 30(2); McGregor, P. (5); Moore, I. 1(4); O'Neil, B. 4(1); Pearce, S. 33; Phillips, D. 24(3); Roy, B. 8(12); Saunders, D. 33(1); Silenzi, A. 1(1); Stone, S. 5; Van Hooijdonk, P. 8; Warner, V. 2(1); Woan, I. 29(3); Wright, T. 1
League (31): Campbell 6, Haaland 6, Pearce 5 (2 pens), Roy 3, Saunders 3, Cooper 2, Bart-Williams 1, Clough 1, Lee 1, Lyttle 1, Van Hooijdonk 1, Woan 1.
Coca-Cola Cup (3): Cooper 1, Lee 1, Roy 1.
FA Cup (5): Saunders 2, Woan 2, Allen 1.
Ground: City Ground, Nottingham NG2 5FJ. Telephone (0115) 9526000.
Record attendance: 49,945 v Manchester U, Division 1, 28 October 1967. **Capacity:** 30,602.
Manager: Dave Bassett.
Secretary: Paul White.
Honours – Football League: Division 1 – Champions 1977–78. **Division 2** – Champions – 1906–07, 1921–22. **Division 3 (S)** Champions – 1950–51. **FA Cup:** Winners 1898, 1959. **Football League Cup:** Winners 1977–78, 1978–79, 1988–89, 1989–90. **Anglo-Scottish Cup:** Winners 1976–77. **Simod Cup:** Winners 1989. **Zenith Data Systems Cup:** Winners 1991–92. **European Competitions: European Cup** winners: 1978–79, 1979–80, 1980–81. **Super Cup** winners: 1979–80.
Colours: Red shirts, black shoulders, white shorts, red stockings.

NOTTS COUNTY   DIV. 3

Baraclough Ian (D)	6 1	12 02	Leicester	4 12 70	Mansfield T
Battersby Tony (F)	6 0	12 07	Doncaster	30 8 75	Sheffield U
Cunnington Shaun (M)	5 11	11 08	Bourne	4 1 66	WBA
Derry Shaun (D)	5 10	10 13	Nottingham	6 12 77	Trainee
Dudley Craig (F)	5 10	11 04	Ollerton	12 9 79	Trainee

Farrell Sean (F)	6 1	13 03	Watford	28	2 69	Peterborough U
Finnan Steve (F)	5 9	10 09	Chelmsford	20	4 76	Birmingham C
Galloway Mick (M)	5 11	11 05	Nottingham	13 10 74		Trainee
Hendon Ian (D)	5 11	11 05	Ilford	5 12 71		Leyton Orient
Hogg Graeme (D)	6 1	12 04	Aberdeen	17	6 64	Hearts
Jones Gary (F)	6 1	12 09	Huddersfield	6	4 69	Southend U
Kennedy Peter (F)	5 11	11 11	Lurgan	10	9 73	Portadown
Martindale Gary (F)	6 0	12 00	Liverpool	24	6 71	Peterborough U
Pollitt Michael (G)	6 4	14 00	Bolton	29	2 72	Darlington
Redmile Matthew (D)	6 46	12 11	Nottingham	12 11 76		Trainee
Richardson Ian (M)	5 10	11 01	Barking	22 10 70		Birmingham C
Robinson Phil (M)	5 10	11 07	Stafford	6	1 67	Chesterfield
Strodder Gary (D)	6 1	13 03	Cleckheaton	1	4 65	WBA
Ward Darren (G)	5 11	12 09	Worksop	11	5 74	Mansfield T
White Devon (F)	6 3	14 00	Nottingham	2	3 64	Watford

League Appearances: Agana, T. 17(6); Arkins, V. 13(2); Baraclough, I. 36(2); Battersby, T. 6(12); Cunnington, S. 6(2); Derry, S. 37(2); Diuk, W. (1); Dudley, C. 6(4); Farrell, S. 10(4); Finnan, S. 18(5); Gallagher, T. 1; Galloway, M. 4(1); Hendon, I. 12; Hogg, G. 35; Hunt, J. 5(4); Jones, G. 21(6); Kennedy, P. 20(2); Ludlam, C. 1; Martindale, G. 16(12); Mendez, G. 2(1); Mitchell, P. 1; Murphy, S. 16; Nogan, L. 6; Pollitt, M. 8; Redmile, M. 23; Regis, D. 7(3); Richardson, I. 16(3); Ridgway, I. 3(3); Robinson, P. 33(4); Rogers, P. (1); Simpson, M. 1; Strodder, G. 28; Walker, R. 13(3); Ward, D. 38; White, D. 7(2); Wilder, C. 37; Wilkes, T. 3
League (33): Martindale 6 (3 pens). Agana 3, Jones 3, Baraclough 2, Derry 2, Dudley 2, Redmile 2, Regis 2, Robinson 2, Strodder 2, Arkins 1, Battersby 1, Farrell 1, Richardson 1, own goals 3.
Coca-Cola Cup (1): Jones 1.
FA Cup (5): Agana 1, Arkins 1, Jones 1, Kennedy 1, Robinson 1.
Ground: County Ground, Meadow Lane, Nottingham NG2 3HJ. Telephone (0115) 952 9000.
Record attendance: 47,310 v York C, FA Cup 6th rd, 12 March 1955. **Capacity:** 20,300.
Manager: Sam Allardyce.
Secretary: Ian Moat.
Honours – Football League: Division 2 Champions – 1896–97, 1913–14, 1922–23. Division 3 (S) Champions – 1930–31, 1949–50. Division 4 Champions – 1970–71. **FA Cup:** Winners 1893–94. **Anglo-Italian Cup:** Winners 1995.
Colours: Black and white striped shirts, white shorts, black stockings.

OLDHAM ATHLETIC   DIV. 2

Allott Mark (F)	6 0	10 12	Manchester	16	3 78	Trainee
Barlow Stuart (F)	5 10	11 00	Liverpool	16	7 68	Everton
Duxbury Lee (D)	5 10	10 07	Keighley	7 10 69		Bradford C
Fleming Craig (D)	6 0	12 09	Calder	6 10 71		Halifax T
Garnett Shaun (D)	6 2	13 01	Wallasey	22 11 69		Swansea C
Graham Richard (D)	6 2	12 09	Dewsbury	28 11 74		Trainee
Hart Barrie (D)	6 1	11 09	Oldham	17	7 77	Trainee
Hodgson Doug (D)	6 3	13 05	Frankston	27	2 69	Sheffield U
Holt Andy (D)	6 1	11 11	Manchester	21	5 78	Trainee
Hughes Andy (M)	6 0	11 00	Manchester	2	1 78	Trainee
Innes Mark (D)			Bellshill	27	9 78	Trainee
Kelly Gary (G)	5 11	12 10	Fulwood	3	8 66	Bury
McCarthy Sean (F)	6 1	12 10	Bridgend	12	9 67	Bradford C
McNiven David (F)	5 10	10 06	Leeds	27	5 78	Trainee

McNiven Scott (D)	5 10	10 06	Leeds	27 5 78	Trainee
Murphy Gerard (M)			Manchester	19 12 78	Trainee
Orlygsson Toddy (M)	5 11	10 12	Odense	2 8 66	Stoke C
Ormondroyd Ian (F)	6 4	14 00	Bradford	22 9 64	Bradford C
Ramplin Jamie (M)			Manchester	14 10 79	Trainee
Redmond Steve (D)	6 0	11 02	Liverpool	2 11 67	Manchester C
Reid Paul (M)	5 10	10 12	Oldbury	19 1 68	Huddersfield T
Richardson Lee J (M)	5 11	10 06	Halifax	12 3 69	Aberdeen
Richardson Lloyd M (F)	6 0	11 02	Dewsbury	7 10 77	Trainee
Rickers Paul (M)	5 10	10 07	Leeds	9 5 75	Trainee
Ritchie Andy (F)	5 11	11 10	Manchester	28 11 60	Scarborough
Rush Matthew (F)	5 11	11 02	Dalston	6 8 71	Norwich C
Serrant Carl (D)	6 0	10 02	Bradford	12 9 75	Trainee
Swain Iain (M)			Glasgow	14 10 79	Trainee

League Appearances: Allott, M. (5); Banger, N. 16(7); Barlow, S. 26(9); Beresford, D. 24(9); Duxbury, L. 11(1); Fleming, C. 44; Foran, M. (1); Gannon, J. 1; Garnett, S. 22(1); Graham, R. 16(3); Halle, G. 18(2); Hallworth, J. 4; Henry, N. 21(1); Hodgson, D. 11(1); Holt, A. (1); Hughes, A. 7(1); Kelly, G. 42; McCarthy, S. 17(4); McNiven, D. 2(6); McNiven, S. 11(1); Morrow, J. 1(1); Orlygsson, T. 23(4); Ormondroyd, I. 26(4); Pemberton, M. 23; Redmond, S. 24; Reid, P. 9; Richardson, Lee J. 27(4); Richardson, Lloyd M. (1); Rickers, P. 45(1); Ritchie, A. 4(6); Rush, M. 6(2); Serrant, C. 34(6); Snodin, I. 14
League (51): Barlow 12, Ormondroyd 8, Banger 5, Lee Richardson 4 (3 pens), Rickers 4, Halle 3, McCarthy 3, Redmond 2, Rush 2, Allott 1, Duxbury 1, Garnett 1, Graham 1, Henry 1, Orlygsson 1 (pen), Reid 1, own goal 1.
Coca-Cola Cup (4): Banger 1, McCarthy 1, Redmond 1, Lee Richardson 1.
FA Cup (0).
Ground: Boundary Park, Oldham OL1 2PA. Telephone (0161) 624 4972.
Record attendance: 47,671 v Sheffield W, FA Cup 4th rd. 25 January 1930.
Capacity: 13,700.
Manager: Neil Warnock.
Secretary: Terry Cale.
Honours – Football League: Division 2 Champions – 1990–91, Division 3 (N) Champions – 1952–53. Division 3 Champions – 1973–74.
Colours: All blue with red and white trim.

OXFORD UNITED   DIV. 1

Aldridge Martin (F)	5 11	12 02	Northampton	6 12 74	Northampton T
Angel Mark (F)	5 10	11 10	Newcastle	23 8 75	Sunderland
Beauchamp Joey (M)	5 10	12 11	Oxford	13 3 71	Swindon T
Ford Bobby (M)	5 8	11 00	Bristol	22 9 74	Trainee
Ford Mike (D)	6 0	12 06	Bristol	9 2 66	Cardiff C
Gilchrist Phil (D)	6 0	13 12	Stockton	25 8 73	Hartlepool U
Gray Martin (M)	5 9	11 05	Stockton	17 8 71	Sunderland
Jackson Elliott (G)	6 2	14 06	Swindon	27 8 77	Trainee
Jemson Nigel (F)	5 11	13 03	Hutton	10 8 69	Notts Co
Lewis Mickey (M)	5 9	12 10	Birmingham	15 2 65	Derby Co
Marsh Simon (D)	5 11	11 04	Ealing	29 1 77	Trainee
Massey Stuart (M)	5 10	12 13	Crawley	17 11 64	Crystal Palace
Moody Paul (F)	6 3	14 08	Portsmouth	13 6 67	Southampton
Murphy Matt (F)	6 0	12 06	Northampton	20 8 71	Corby T
Powell Paul (D)	5 8	11 06	Wallingford	30 6 78	Trainee
Purse Darren (D)	6 2	12 10	London	14 2 77	Leyton Orient
Robinson Les (D)	5 8	12 10	Shirerook	1 3 67	Doncaster R

Smith David (M)	5 8	12 09	Liverpool	26 12 70	Norwich C
Stevens Mark (F)	6 5	12 07	Swindon	3 12 77	School
Weatherstone Simon (F)	5 9	11 11	Reading	26 1 80	Trainee
Whitehead Phil (G)	6 2	15 11	Halifax	17 12 69	Barnsley
Wilsterman Brian (D)	6 1	13 01	Surinam	19 11 66	Beerschot

League Appearances: Aldridge, M. 18(12); Angel, M. 15(9); Beauchamp, J. 36(9); Elliott, M. 26; Ford, B. 29(4); Ford, M. 42; Gabbiadini, M. 5; Gilchrist, P. 38; Gray, M. 41(2); Jackson, E. 3; Jemson, N. 44; Marsh, S. 6(2); Massey, S. 15(14); Moody, P. 19(19); Murphy, M. 5(25); Phillips, M. (1); Purse, D. 25(6); Robinson, L. 36(2); Rush, D. 4(11); Smith, D. 45; Weatherstone, S. (1); Whitehead, P. 43; Whyte, C. 10; Wilsterman, B. 1
League (64): Jemson 18 (4 pens), Aldridge 8, Beauchamp 7, Elliott 4, Ford M 4, Moody 4, Massey 3, Murphy 3, Angel 2, Gilchrist 2, Gray 2, Gabbiadini 1, Marsh 1, Purse 1, Rush 1, own goals 3.
Coca-Cola Cup (11): Jemson 5, Moody 2, Aldridge 1, Elliott 1, Ford M 1, Ford R 1.
FA Cup (0).
Ground: Manor Ground, Headington, Oxford OX3 7RS. Telephone (01865) 761503.
Record attendance: 22,750 v Preston NE, FA Cup 6th rd, 29 February 1964.
Capacity: 9572.
Manager: Denis Smith.
Secretary: Mick Brown.
Honours – Football League: Division 2 Champions – 1984–85. Division 3 Champions – 1967–68, 1983–84. **Football League Cup:** Winners 1985–86.
Colours: Gold shirts with blue sleeves, blue shorts, blue stockings.

PETERBOROUGH UNITED   DIV. 3

Bodley Mike (D)	6 1	13 01	Hayes	14 9 67	Southend U
Boothroyd Aidy (D)	5 9	11 07	Bradford	8 2 71	Mansfield T
Bullimore Wayne (M)	5 9	12 01	Mansfield	12 9 70	Bradford C
Carruthers Martin (F)	5 11	11 07	Nottingham	7 8 72	Stoke C
Castle Steve (M)	5 10	12 07	Ilford	17 5 66	Birmingham C
Clark Simon (D)	6 0	12 12	Boston	12 3 67	Stevenage Bor
Cleaver Christopher (F)	5 9	11 07	Hitchin	24 3 79	Trainee
De Souza Miguel (F)	5 11	13 08	Newham	11 2 70	Wycombe W
Drury Adam (D)	5 10	11 08	Cottenham	29 8 78	Trainee
Edwards Andy (D)	6 2	12 00	Epping	17 9 71	Birmingham C
Foran Mark (D)	6 3	13 04	Aldershot	30 10 73	Sheffield U
Grazioli Guiliano (F)	5 11	12 00	London	23 3 75	Wembley
Griemink Bart (G)	6 3	15 04	Holland	29 3 72	Birmingham C
Heald Greg (D)	6 2	13 01	London	26 9 71	Enfield
Houghton Scott (M)	5 6	12 01	Hitchin	22 10 71	Walsall
Inman Niall (F)	5 9	11 06	Wakefield	6 2 78	Trainee
Linton Des (D)	6 1	13 10	Birmingham	5 9 71	Luton T
Payne Derek (M)	5 6	10 08	Edgware	26 4 67	Watford
Rowe Zeke (M)	5 10	11 08	Stoke Newington	30 10 73	Chelsea
Sheffield Jon (G)	6 0	12 08	Bedworth	1 2 69	Cambridge U
Tyler Mark (G)	5 11	12 00	Norwich	2 4 77	Trainee
Willis Roger (M)	6 0	12 00	Islington	17 6 67	Southend U

League Appearances: Basham, M. 4(1); Billington, D. 2(3); Bodley, M. 31; Boothroyd, A. 24(2); Bullimore, W. 2(4); Carruthers, M. 13(1); Carter, D. 3(5); Charlery, K. 36(1); Clark, S. 30(4); Cleaver, C. 6(7); De Souza, M. 8; Donowa, L. 16(6); Drury, A. 5; Ebdon, M. 12(8); Edwards, A. 25; Etherington, M. 1; Farrell, S.

4(3); Foran, M. 2(2); Grazioli, G. (4); Griemink, B. 27; Griffiths, C. 2(10); Heald, G. 34(2); Houghton, S. 26(6); Huxford, R. 7; Inman, N. (3); Le Bihan, N. 2; Linton, D. 8; McGleish, S. (1); McKeever, M. 2(1); Morrison, D. 4(7); Neal, A. 4; O'Connor, M. 18; Otto, R. 15; Payne, D. 36; Ramage, C. 7; Regis, D. 4(3); Rowe, Z. 10(12); Sheffield, J. 16; Spearing, T. 11(2); Tyler, M. 3; Welsh, S. 6; Williams, M. 6; Willis, R. 34(6)
League (55): Houghton 8 (2 pens), Willis 6, Charlery 5, Carruthers 4, Otto 4, Clark 3, Farrell 3, O'Connor 3 (1 pen), Rowe 3, De Souza 2, Heald 2, Morrison 2, Payne 2, Boothroyd 1 (pen), Cleaver 1, Donowa 1, Drury 1, Ebdon 1, Griffiths 1, Regis 1, own goal 1.
Coca-Cola Cup (3): Charlery 1, Farrell 1, Griffiths 1.
FA Cup (11): Charlery 6, Carruthers 2, Grazioli 1, Griffiths 1, Houghton 1.
Ground: London Road Ground, Peterborough PE2 8AL. Telephone (01733) 63947.
Record attendance: 30,096 v Swansea T, FA Cup 5th rd, 20 February 1965.
Capacity: 15,500.
Manager: Barry Fry.
Secretary: Miss Caroline Hand.
Honours – Football League: Division 4 Champions – 1960–61, 1973–74.
Colours: Royal blue shirts, white shorts, white stockings.

PLYMOUTH ARGYLE   DIV. 2

Barlow Martin (M)	5 7	10 03	Barnstable	25	6 71	Trainee
Billy Chris (M)	5 11	11 08	Huddersfield	2	1 73	Huddersfield T
Collins Simon (M)	6 0	11 02	Pontefract	16	12 73	Huddersfield T
Corazzin Carlo (F)	5 9	12 05	Canada	25	12 71	Cambridge U
Curran Chris (D)	5 11	11 09	Birmingham	17	9 71	Torquay U
Dungey James (G)	5 9	11 08	Plymouth	7	2 78	Trainee
Heathcote Mike (D)	6 2	12 08	Durham	10	9 65	Cambridge U
Illman Neil (F)	5 7	10 07	Doncaster	29	4 75	Eastwood T
James Tony (D)	6 3	14 02	Sheffield	27	6 67	Hereford U
Littlejohn Adrian (F)	5 9	11 00	Wolverhampton	26	9 70	Sheffield U
Logan Richard (D)	6 0	13 03	Barnsley	24	5 69	Huddersfield T
Mauge Ron (M)	5 10	10 06	Islington	10	3 69	Bury
Patterson Mark (D)	5 10	11 05	Leeds	13	9 68	Derby Co
Saunders Mark (M)	5 10	11 06	Reading	23	7 71	Tiverton
Williams Paul (D)	5 10	11 00	Leicester	11	9 69	Coventry C
Wotton Paul (M)	5 11	11 07	Plymouth	17	8 77	Trainee

League Appearances: Barlow, M. 38(2); Billy, C. 44(1); Blackwell, K.. 4; Clayton, G. (1); Collins, S. 11(1); Corazzin, C. 22(8); Curran, C. 20(2); Dungey, J. 6; Evans, M. 33; Grobbelaar, B. 36; Heathcote, M. 41(1); Illman, N. 12(13); James, T. 34; Leadbitter, C. 17(2); Littlejohn, A. 33(4); Logan, R. 19(9); Mauge, R. 29(6); Patterson, M. 11(1); Perkins, S. 1(3); Phillips, L. (2); Rowbotham, J. 12(3); Saunders, M. 22(3); Simpson, M. 10(2); Williams, P. 46; Wotton, P. 5(4)
League (47): Evans 12 (2 pens), Littlejohn 6, Corazzin 5 (1 pen), Illman 4, Logan 4, Billy 3, Mauge 3, Saunders 3, Williams 2, Barlow 1, Collins 1, Heathcote 1, James 1, Wotton 1.
Coca-Cola Cup (0):
FA Cup (9): Evans 3 (1 pen), Littlejohn 2, Mauge 2, Billy 1, Corazzin 1.
Ground: Home Park, Plymouth, Devon PL2 3DQ. Telephone (01752) 562561.
Record attendance: 43,596 v Aston Villa, Division 2, 10 October 1936.
Capacity: 19,630.
Manager: Mick Jones.

Secretary: Roger Matthews.
Honours – Football League: Division 3 (S) Champions – 1929–30, 1951–52. Division 3 Champions – 1958–59.
Colours: Green and black striped shirts, black shorts, black stockings.

PORTSMOUTH   DIV. 1

Allen Martin (M)	5 11	12 06	Reading	14 8 65	West Ham U
Awford Andy (D)	5 9	11 09	Worcester	14 7 72	Worcester C
Bradbury Lee (F)	6 2	13 10	Oswestry	15 7 71	Cowes
Bundy Scott (F)	6 1	12 00	Southampton	20 10 77	Trainee
Burton Deon (F)	5 8	10 09	Ashford	25 10 76	Trainee
Carter Jimmy (M)	5 10	11 02	London	9 11 65	Arsenal
Cook Andy (M)	5 9	12 00	Romsey	10 8 69	Swansea C
Durnin John (F)	5 10	11 10	Bootle	18 8 65	Oxford U
Flahavan Aaron (G)	6 1	11 12	Southampton	- 15 12 75	Trainee
Hall Paul (F)	5 9	10 02	Manchester	3 7 72	Torquay U
Hawley Jon (D)	6 0	12 05	Lincoln	23 1 78	Trainee
Hillier David (M)	5 10	11 12	Blackheath	18 12 69	Arsenal
Hinshelwood Danny (D)	5 9	11 00	Bromley	4 12 75	Nottingham F
Igoe Sammy (M)	5 6	9 07	Spelthorne	30 9 75	Trainee
Knight Alan (G)	6 1	13 11	Balham	3 6 61	Apprentice
McLoughlin Alan (M)	5 8	10 10	Manchester	20 4 67	Southampton
Perrett Russell (D)	6 2	13 00	Barton-on-Sea	18 6 73	AFC Lymington
Pethick Robbie (M)	5 10	11 11	Tavistock	8 9 70	Weymouth
Russell Lee (D)	5 10	11 09	Southampton	3 9 69	Trainee
Simpson Fitzroy (M)	5 8	12 00	Trowbridge	26 2 70	Manchester C
Simpson Robert (D)	5 10	11 06	Luton	3 3 76	Tottenham H
Svensson Mathias (F)	6 0	12 04	Boras	24 9 74	Elfsborg
Thompson Mark (M)	6 2	11 07	Southampton	17 9 77	Trainee
Thomson Andy (D)	6 3	14 00	Swindon	28 3 74	Swindon T
Turner Andy (M)	5 10	11 02	Woolwich	23 5 75	Tottenham H
Walsh Paul (F)	5 8	10 04	Plumstead	1 10 62	Manchester C
Waterman David (D)	5 10	13 02	Guernsey	16 5 77	Trainee
Whitbread Adrian (D)	6 0	12 02	Epping	22 10 71	West Ham U

League Appearances: Allen, M. 3(1); Awford, A. 37(2); Bradbury, L. 38(4); Burton, D. 12(9); Butters, G. 7; Carter, J. 23(4); Cook, A. 6(2); Dobson, T. 4(2); Durnin, J. 16(18); Flahavan, A. 24; Hall, P. 36(6); Hillier, D. 21; Igoe, S. 22(18); Knight, A. 22; McLoughlin, A. 33(3); Perrett, R. 31(1); Pethick, R. 27(8); Rees, J. 1(2); Russell, L. 18(2); Simpson, F. 40(1); Svensson, M. 17(2); Thomson, A. 22(6); Turner, A. 22(2); Waterman, D. (4); Whitbread, A. 24
League (59): Bradbury 15, Hall 13, Svensson 6, McLoughlin 5 (4 pens), Simpson 4 (1 pen), Durnin 3 (1 pen), Hillier 2, Igoe 2, Russell 2, Turner 2, Burton 1, Carter 1, Perrett 1, Rees 1, Thomson 1.
Coca-Cola Cup (3): Burton 2, Carter 1.
FA Cup (9): Bradbury 2, Hall 2, McLoughlin 2, Burton 1, Hillier 1, Svensson 1.
Ground: Fratton Park, Frogmore Rd, Portsmouth PO4 8RA. Telephone (01705) 731204.
Record attendance: 51,385 v Derby Co, FA Cup 6th rd, 26 February 1949.
Capacity: 16,061.
Manager: Terry Fenwick.
Secretary: Paul Weld.
Honours – Football League: Division 1 Champions – 1948–49, 1949–50. Division 3 (S) Champions – 1923–24. Division 3 Champions – 1961–62, 1982–83. **FA Cup:** Winners 1939.
Colours: Blue shirts, white shorts, red stockings.

PORT VALE   DIV. 1

Name			Birthplace	Date	Previous club
Aspin Neil (D)	6 0	13 12	Gateshead	12 4 65	Leeds U
Bogie Ian (M)	5 9	11 10	Newcastle	6 12 67	Leyton Orient
Boswell Matthew (G)	6 2	13 08	Shrewsbury	19 8 77	
Corden Wayne (M)	5 10	11 03	Leek	1 11 75	Trainee
Eyre Richard (M)	5 11	11 06	Poynton	15 9 76	Trainee
Foyle Martin (F)	5 11	12 01	Salisbury	2 5 63	Oxford U
Glover Dean (D)	5 11	12 02	West Bromwich	29 12 63	Middlesbrough
Griffiths Gareth (D)	6 4	14 04	Winsford	10 4 70	Rhyl
Hill Andy (D)	6 0	13 08	Maltby	21 1 65	Manchester C
Holwyn Jermaine (D)	6 2	13 01	Amsterdam	16 4 73	Ajax
Koordes Rogier (M)	6 1	12 11	Holland	13 6 72	Telstar
McCarthy Jon (M)	5 10	11 04	Middlesbrough	18 8 70	York C
Mills Lee (F)	6 2	12 09	Mexborough	10 7 70	Derby Co
Musselwhite Paul (G)	6 2	14 04	Portsmouth	22 12 68	Scunthorpe U
Naylor Tony (F)	5 7	10 06	Manchester	29 3 67	Crewe Alex
O'Reilly Justin (F)	6 0	13 08	Derby	29 6 73	Gresley R
Porter Andy (M)	5 9	12 00	Holmes Chapel	17 9 68	Trainee
Stokes Dean (D)	5 8	11 02	Birmingham	23 5 70	Halesowen T
Talbot Stuart (M)	6 0	13 07	Birmingham	14 6 73	Moor Green
Tankard Allen (D)	5 10	12 10	Islington	21 5 69	Wigan Ath
Van Heusden Arjan (G)	6 2	13 12	Alphen	11 12 72	Noordwijk

League Appearances: Aspin, N. 32(1); Bogie, I. 28(3); Corden, W. 5(7); Foyle, M. 9(28); Glover, D. 40(2); Griffiths, G. 24(2); Guppy, S. 34; Hill, A. 36(2); Holwyn, J. 5(2); Jansson, J. 10(1); Koordes, R. 7(6); McCarthy, J. 45; Mills, L. 22(13); Musselwhite, P. 33; Naylor, T. 40(3); Porter, A. 44; Stokes, D. 8(2); Talbot, S. 25(9); Tankard, A. 37; Van Heusden, A. 13; Walker, R. 9(8)
League (58): Naylor 17, Mills 13, Guppy 6, McCarthy 4, Porter 4 (1 pen), Talbot 4, Foyle 3, Glover 2, Bogie 1, Hill 1, Jansson 1, Tankard 1, own goal 1.
Coca-Cola Cup (9): Naylor 3, McCarthy 2, Mills 2, Bogie 1, Foyle 1.
FA Cup (0).
Ground: Vale Park, Burslem, Stoke-on-Trent ST6 1AW. Telephone (01782) 814134.
Record attendance: 50,000 v Aston Villa, FA Cup 5th rd, 20 February 1960.
Capacity: 22,356
Manager: John Rudge.
Secretary: F. W. Lodey.
Honours – Football League: Division 3 (N) Champions – 1929–30, 1953–54. Division 4 Champions – 1958–59.
Colours: White shirts, black shorts, black and white stockings.

PRESTON NORTH END   DIV. 2

Name			Birthplace	Date	Previous club
Ashcroft Lee (F)	5 10	11 02	Preston	7 9 72	WBA
Atkinson Graeme (M)	5 8	11 05	Hull	11 11 71	Hull C
Barrick Dean (D)	5 8	12 00	Hemsworth	30 9 69	Cambridge U
Cartwright Lee (M)	5 9	11 00	Rossendale	19 9 72	Trainee
Davey Simon (M)	5 10	12 00	Swansea	1 10 70	Carlisle U
Gage Kevin (D)	5 10	12 12	Chiswick	21 4 64	Sheffield U
Gregan Sean (D)	6 1	13 09	Cleveland	29 3 74	Darlington
Holt Michael (F)	5 10	11 06	Burnley	28 7 77	Blackburn R
Jackson Michael (D)	5 11	13 10	Chester	4 12 73	Bury
Kidd Ryan (D)	6 1	13 03	Radcliffe	6 10 71	Port Vale

Kilbane Kevin (M)	6 0	13 00	Preston	1 2 77	Trainee	
Lucas David (G)	6 1	13 04	Preston	23 11 77		
McDonald Neil (D)	6 0	13 10	Wallsend	2 11 65	Bolton W	
McKenna Paul (M)	5 7	11 13	Chorley	20 10 77	Trainee	
Mimms Bobby (G)	6 4	14 04	York	12 10 63	Crystal Palace	
Moilanen Teuvo (G)	6 5	13 10	Oulu	12 12 73	Jaro	
Morgan Mark (M)			Belfast	23 10 78	Trainee	
Moyes David (D)	6 1	12 12	Glasgow	25 4 63	Hamilton A	
Nogan Kurt (F)	5 11	11 11	Cardiff	9 9 70	Burnley	
O'Hanlon Kelham (G)	6 1	13 12	Saltburn	16 5 62	Dundee U	
Rankine Mark (D)	5 10	11 01	Doncaster	30 9 69	Wolverhampton W	
Reeves David (F)	6 0	12 06	Birkenhead	19 11 67	Carlisle U	
Sparrow Paul (D)	6 0	11 00	London	24 3 75	Crystal Palace	
Squires Jamie (G)	6 2	13 03	Preston	15 11 75	Trainee	
Wilcox Russ (D)	6 0	12 12	Hemsworth	25 3 64	Doncaster R	
Wilkinson Steve (F)	5 11	11 11	Lincoln	1 9 68	Mansfield T	

League Appearances: Ashcroft, L. 26(1); Atkinson, G. 12(5); Barrick, D. 30(6); Beckford, D. (2); Bennett, G. 10(6); Brown, M. 5(1); Bryson, I. 32(9); Cartwright, L. 14; Davey, S. 30(7); Gage, K. 16; Gregan, S. 21; Holt, M. 8(11); Jackson, M. 7; Kay, J. 7; Kidd, R. 33(2); Kilbane, K. 32(4); Lucas, D. 2; McDonald, N. 12(10); McKenna, P. 4(1); Mimms, B. 27; Moilanen, T. 4; Moyes, D. 26; Nogan, K. 5(2); O'Hanlon, K. 13; Patterson, D. 2; Rankine, M. 19(4); Reeves, D. 33(1); Saville, A. 12; Sparrow, P. 6; Squires, J. 6(3); Stallard, M. 4; Teale, S. 5; Wilcox, R. 35; Wilkinson, S. 8(2)

League (49): Reeves 11, Ashcroft 8 (1 pen), Davey 6 (1 pen), Moyes 4, Bennett 3, Bryson 3, Holt 3, Wilkinson 3, Kilbane 2, Cartwright 1, Gregan 1, McKenna 1, Saville 1, Stallard 1, own goal 1.
Coca-Cola Cup (8): Wilkinson 4, Atkinson 1, Davey 1, Holt 1, McDonald 1.
FA Cup (6): Ashcroft 3 (1 pen), Reeves 3.
Ground: Deepdale, Preston PR1 6RU. Telephone (01772) 902020.
Record attendance: 42,684 v Arsenal, Division 1, 23 April 1938. **Capacity:** 15,295.
Manager: Gary Peters.
Secretary: Mrs Audrey Shaw.
Honours – Football League: Division 1 Champions – 1888–89 (first champions), 1889–90. Division 2 Champions – 1903–04, 1912–13, 1950–51. Division 3 Champions – 1970–71, 1995–96. **FA Cup winners** 1889, 1938.
Colours: White and navy shirts, navy shorts, navy stockings.

QUEENS PARK RANGERS   DIV. 1

Bardsley David (D)	5 10	11 07	Manchester	11 9 64	Oxford U	
Barker Simon (M)	5 9	11 07	Farnworth	4 11 64	Blackburn R	
Brazier Matthew (M)	5 8	11 06	Whipps Cross	2 7 76	Trainee	
Brevett Rufus (D)	5 8	11 04	Derby	24 9 69	Doncaster R	
Bruce Paul (F)	5 11	12 01	London	18 2 78	Trainee	
Challis Trevor (D)	5 8	11 00	Paddington	23 10 75	Trainee	
Charles Lee (F)	5 11	12 04	Hillingdon	20 8 71	Chertsey T	
Dichio Daniele (F)	6 3	12 03	Hammersmith	19 10 74	Trainee	
Gallen Kevin (F)	5 11	12 10	Hammersmith	21 9 75	Trainee	
Graham Mark (M)	5 7	10 12	Newry	24 10 74	Trainee	
Graham Richard (F)	5 7	10 00	Newry	5 8 79	Trainee	
Hart Paul (G)			London	16 11 78	Trainee	
Hurst Richard (G)	6 0	13 00	Hammersmith	23 12 76	Trainee	
Impey Andrew (M)	5 8	11 02	Hammersmith	13 9 71	Yeading	
Langley Richard (F)	5 10	11 04	London	27 12 79	Trainee	

Lopez Rik (F)			Northwick Park	25 12 79	Arsenal
Lusardi Mario (F)			Islington	27 9 79	Trainee
Maddix Danny (D)	5 11	11 07	Ashford	11 10 67	Tottenham H
Mahoney-Johnson Michael (F)	5 10	12 00	Paddington	6 11 76	Trainee
Morrow Steve (D)	6 0	11 03	Bangor	2 7 70	Arsenal
Murray Frazer (M)	5 8	10 06	Paisley	24 9 79	Trainee
Murray Paul (M)	5 8	10 05	Carlisle	31 8 76	Carlisle U
Owen Karl (D)	5 11	12 06	Coventry	12 10 79	Trainee
Peacock Gavin (M)	5 8	11 08	Eltham	18 11 67	Chelsea
Perry Mark (D)	5 10	11 03	Perivale	19 10 78	Trainee
Plummer Chris (D)	6 2	12 09	Isleworth	12 10 76	Trainee
Purser Wayne (F)	5 10	12 00	Basildon	13 4 80	Trainee
Quashie Nigel (M)	5 9	11 00	Nunhead	20 7 78	Trainee
Ready Karl (D)	6 1	13 03	Neath	14 8 72	Trainee
Roberts Tony (G)	6 0	13 11	Bangor	4 8 69	Trainee
Sinclair Trevor (F)	5 10	12 05	Dulwich	2 3 73	Blackpool
Slade Steve (F)	6 0	10 13	Hackney	6 10 75	Tottenham H
Sommer Jurgen (G)	6 5	15 12	New York	27 2 69	Luton T
Spencer John (F)	5 7	11 05	Glasgow	11 9 70	Chelsea
Whittle David (D)			Waterford	2 12 78	Trainee
Yates Steve (D)	5 10	12 02	Bristol	29 1 70	Bristol R

League Appearances: Barker, S. 38; Brazier, M. 22(5); Brevett, R. 44; Challis, T. 2; Charles, L. 6(6); Dichio, D. 31(6); Gallen, K. 2; Graham, M. 16(2); Hateley, M. 8(5); Impey, A. 26(6); Jackson, M. 7; Maddix, D. 18(7); Mahoney-Johnson, M. (2); McDermott, A. 6; McDonald, A. 38(1); Morrow, S. 5; Murray, P. 26(6); Peacock, G. 27; Perry, M. 2; Plummer, C. 4(1); Quashie, N. 9(4); Ready, K. 28(1); Roberts, T. 13; Sinclair, T. 39; Slade, S. 11(6); Sommer, J. 33; Spencer, J. 25; Wilkins, R. 4; Yates, S. 16
League (64): Spencer 17, Dichio 7, Murray 5, Peacock 5, Barker 4 (2 pens), Slade 4, Gallen 3, Sinclair 3, Brazier 2, Impey 2, McDermott 2, McDonald 2, Charles 1, Hateley 1, Morrow 1, Perry 1, Yates 1, own goals 3.
Coca-Cola Cup (3): Brazier 1, Dichio 1, Impey 1.
FA Cup (7): Hateley 2, Peacock 2, McDonald 1, Sinclair 1, Spencer 1.
Ground: South Africa Road, W12 7PA. Telephone (0181) 743 0262.
Record attendance: 35,353 v Leeds U, Division 1, 27 April 1974. **Capacity:** 19,148.
Manager: Stewart Houston.
Secretary: Sheila Marson.
Honours – Football League: Division 2 Champions – 1982–83. Division 3 (S) Champions – 1947–48. Division 3 Champions – 1966–67. **Football League Cup winners** 1966–67.
Colours: Blue and white hooped shirts, white shorts, white stockings.

READING   DIV. 1

Bernal Andy (D)	5 10	12 05	Canberra	16 7 66	Sydney Olympic
Bibbo Sal (G)	6 2	14 00	Basingstoke	24 8 74	Sheffield U
Bodin Paul (D)	6 0	12 06	Cardiff	13 9 64	Swindon T
Booty Martyn (D)	5 8	11 02	Kirby Muxloe	30 5 71	Crewe Alex
Caskey Darren (M)	5 8	11 09	Basildon	21 8 74	Tottenham H
Freeman Andy (F)	5 7	9 04	Reading	8 9 77	Crystal Palace
Glasgow Byron (M)	5 6	10 11	London	18 2 79	Trainee
Hammond Nicky (G)	6 0	11 13	Hornchurch	7 9 67	Plymouth Arg
Holsgrove Paul (F)	6 2	12 11	Wellington	26 8 69	Millwall
Hunter Barry (D)	6 3	13 02	Coleraine	18 11 68	Wrexham

Lambert James (F)	5 7	11 02	Henley	14	9 73	School
Lovell Stuart (M)	5 10	12 03	Sydney	9	1 72	Trainee
Mautone Steve (G)	6 2	13 03	Myrtleford	10	8 70	West Ham U
McPherson Keith (D)	5 10	12 00	Greenwich	11	9 63	Northampton T
Meaker Michael (M)	5 11	12 00	Greenford	18	8 71	QPR
Morley Trevor (F)	5 11	12 01	Nottingham	20	3 61	Brann
Nogan Lee (F)	5 8	11 01	Cardiff	21	5 69	Watford
Parkinson Phil (M)	6 0	12 09	Chorley	1	12 67	Bury
Roach Neville (F)	5 10	11 00	Reading	29	9 78	Trainee
Smith Ben (M)	5 9	11 09	Chelmsford	23	11 78	Arsenal
Swales Steve (D)	5 8	10 03	Whitby	26	12 73	Scarborough
Thorp Michael (D)	6 0	11 07	Wallington	5	12 75	Trainee
Wdowczyk Dariusz (D)	5 11	11 11	Warsaw	21	9 62	Celtic
Williams Martin (F)	5 9	11 12	Luton	12	7 73	Luton T

League Appearances: Bass, D. (2); Bernal, A. 41; Bibbo, S. 5; Blatherwick, S. 6(1); Bodin, P. 37; Booty, M. 14; Brown, K. 5; Caskey, D. 26(9); Gilkes, M. 27(5); Glasgow, B. 2(2); Gooding, M. 40(3); Hammond, N. 1; Holsgrove, P. 12(2); Hopkins, J. 17(1); Hunter, B. 26(1); Lambert, J. 20(11); Lovell. S. 17(9); Mautone, S. 15; McPherson, K. 39; Meaker, M. 15(10); Mikhailov, B. 8; Morley, T. 36(1); Nogan, L. 21(11); Parkinson, P. 15(9); Quinn, J. 10(14); Roach, N. 2(1); Smith, B. (1); Swales, S. 3; Wdowczyk, D. 8; Williams, M. 21(8); Wright, T. 17
League (58): Morley 22 (7 pens), Nogan 6, Lambert 5, Lovell 5, Quinn 3 (1 pen), Williams 3, Holsgrove 2, Hunter 2, McPherson 2, Bodin 1, Gilkes 1, Meaker 1, Parkinson 1, Roach 1, own goals 3.
Coca-Cola Cup (1): Quinn 1.
FA Cup (3): Caskey 1, Lambert 1, Morley 1 (pen).
Ground: Elm Park, Norfolk Road, Reading RG30 2EF. Telephone (01189) 507878.
Record attendance: 33,042 v Brentford, FA Cup 5th rd, 19 February 1927.
Capacity: 15,000.
Manager: Terry Bullivant.
Secretary: Ms Andrea Barker.
Honours – Football League: Division 2 Champions – 1993–94. Division 3 Champions – 1985–86. Division 3 (S) Champions – 1925–26. Division 4 Champions – 1978–79. **Simod Cup** winners 1987–88.
Colours: Royal blue and white hooped shirts, white shorts, white and blue stockings.

ROCHDALE   DIV. 3

Bailey Mark (M)	5 9	10 12	Stoke	12	8 76	Stoke C
Bayliss David (D)	6 0	11 01	Liverpool	8	6 76	Trainee
Farrell Andy (D)	5 11	12 00	Colchester	7	10 65	Wigan Ath
Fensome Andy (D)	5 8	11 09	Northampton	18	2 69	Preston NE
Gouck Andy (M)	5 10	12 12	Blackpool	8	6 72	Blackpool
Gray Ian (G)	6 2	13 00	Manchester	25	2 75	Oldham Ath
Hill Keith (D)	6 0	12 04	Bolton	17	5 69	Plymouth Arg
Johnson Alan (D)	6 0	14 00	Ince	19	2 71	Lincoln C
Leonard Mark (F)	6 1	13 02	St Helens	27	9 62	Wigan Ath
Painter Robbie (M)	5 10	12 02	Ince	26	1 71	Darlington
Robson Glen (F)	5 10	10 10	Sunderland	25	9 77	Murton
Russell Alex (M)	5 10	11 00	Crosby	17	3 73	Burscough
Stuart Mark (M)	5 9	11 09	Hammersmith	15	12 66	Huddersfield T
Whitehall Steve (F)	5 11	11 07	Bromborough	8	12 66	Southport

League Appearances: Bailey, M. 13(2); Bayliss, D. 22(2); Brown, M. 5; Cecere, M. 2(2); Deary, J. 37(1); Dowell, W. 6(1); Farrell, A. 37(3); Fensome, A. 38(2);

78

Formby, K. 12(4); Gouck, A. 22(6); Gray, I. 46; Hill, K. 43; Johnson, A. 46;
Lancaster, D. 1(5); Leonard, M. 39; Martin, D. (1); Painter, R. 21(6); Robson, G.
(3); Russell, A. 35(4); Stuart, M. 28(3); Taylor, J. (1); Thackeray, A. 17; Thompson,
D. 9(19); Whitehall, S. 27(8).
League (58): Russell 9, Whitehall 9 (3 pens), Painter 7, Stuart 7, Deary 5 (1 pen),
Johnson 4, Leonard 4, Gouck 3, Hill 3, Farrell 2, Cecere 1, Formby 1, Thompson 1,
own goals 2.
Coca-Cola Cup (2): Deary 1, Whitehall 1.
FA Cup (3): Deary 1, Johnson 1, Thackeray 1.
Ground: Spotland, Sandy Lane, Rochdale OL11 5DS. Telephone (01706) 44648.
Record attendance: 24,231 v Notts Co, FA Cup 2nd rd, 10 December 1949.
Capacity: 6448.
Manager: Graham Barrow.
Secretary: Mrs Karen Jagger.
Honours – Nil.
Colours: Blue shirts with jade trim, white shorts, blue stockings with jade and
white.

ROTHERHAM UNITED   DIV. 3

Bain Kevin (M)	5 11	12 05	Kirkcaldy	19 9 72	Dundee
Berry Trevor (M)	5 6	11 00	Haslemere	1 8 74	Aston Villa
Bowman Rob (D)	6 0	12 04	Durham	21 11 75	Leeds U
Breckin Ian (D)	5 11	11 07	Rotherham	24 2 75	Trainee
Davis Craig (G)	6 2	12 00	Rotherham	12 10 77	Trainee
Dillon Paul (D)	5 9	10 11	Limerick	22 10 78	Trainee
Druce Mark (F)	6 0	12 07	Oxford	3 3 74	Oxford U
Garner Darren (M)	5 9	12 07	Plymouth	10 12 71	Dorchester T
Glover Lee (F)	5 11	11 09	Kettering	24 4 70	Port Vale
Hayward Andy (M)	6 0	11 00	Barnsley	21 6 70	Frickley Ath
Hurst Paul (D)	5 4	9 00	Sheffield	25 9 74	Trainee
Jean Earl (F)			St Lucia	9 10 71	Ipswich T
McDougald Junior (F)	5 9	11 00	Big Spring	12 1 75	Brighton & HA
Monington Mark (D)	6 1	14 02	Bilsthorpe	21 10 70	Burnley
Roscoe Andy (D)	5 10	11 08	Liverpool	4 6 73	Bolton W

League Appearances: Bain, K. 10(2); Barnes, P. 2; Berry, T. 19(11); Blades, P. 9;
Bowman, R. 13; Bowyer, G. 10(1); Breckin, I. 42; Cherry, S. 20; Clarke, A. 1(1);
Crawford, J. 11; Dillon, P. 11(2); Dobbin, J. 17(2); Druce, M. 16(4); Farrelly, S. 7;
Garner, D. 30; Gayle, B. 19(1); Glover, L. 16(6); Goodwin, S. 7(1); Hayward, A.
32(2); Hurst, P. 25(5); James, M. (3); Jean, E. 7(11); Landon, R. 7(1); McDougald,
J. 14(4); McGlashan, J. 28(3); McKenzie, R. 6(5); Monington, M. 28; Pell, R. 2;
Pilkington, K. 17; Richardson, N. 10(4); Roscoe, A. 39(4); Sandeman, B. 20(1);
Slawson, S. 2(3); Smith, S. 9(2)
League (39): Jean 6, Berry 4, Druce 4, Hayward 4, Breckin 3, Goodwin 3 (2 pens),
Hurst 3, Bowyer 2, Garner 2, McDougald 2 (1 pen), Sandeman 2, Blades 1, Dillon
1, Glover 1, Richardson 1.
Coca-Cola Cup (0).
FA Cup (1): McGlashan 1.
Ground: Millmoor Ground, Rotherham S60 1HR. Telephone (01709) 512434.
Record attendance: 25,000 v Sheffield U, Division 2, 13 December 1952 and v
Sheffield W, Division 2, 26 January 1952. **Capacity:** 11,514.
Manager: Ronnie Moore.
Honours – Football League: Division 3 Champions – 1980–81. Division 3 (N)
Champions – 1950–51. Division 4 Champions – 1988–89. **Auto Windscreens Shield:**
Winners 1996
Colours: Red shirts, white shorts, red stockings.

SCARBOROUGH DIV. 3

Bazelya Eammon (M)	5 7	9 12	Birmingham	25 10 78	Trainee
Bennett Gary (D)	6 1	13 01	Manchester	4 12 61	Carlisle U
Bochenski Simon (F)	5 10	11 13	Worksop	6 12 75	Barnsley
Brodie Steve (F)	5 8	10 10	Sunderland	14 1 73	Sunderland
Kay John (D)	5 10	11 05	Sunderland	29 1 64	Preston NE
Martin Kevin (G)	6 0	12 08	Bromsgrove	22 6 76	Norwich C
McElhatton Mike (D)	6 1	13 00	Co. Kerry	16 4 75	Bournemouth
Mitchell Jamie (M)	5 7	10 01	Glasgow	6 11 76	Trainee
Rockett Jason (D)	5 11	11 05	London	26 9 69	Rotherham U
Russell Matthew (M)	5 11	11 05	Dewsbury	17 1 78	Trainee
Sutherland Colin (D)	6 0	11 05	Glasgow	15 3 75	Clydebank
Williams Gareth (F)	5 10	12 01	Isle of Wight	12 3 67	Northampton T
Worrall Ben (M)	5 6	9 11	Swindon	7 12 75	Swindon T

League Appearances: Bennett, G. 46; Bennett, T. 4(1); Bochenski, S. 5(14); Brodie, S. 23(1); Brooke, D. 28(6); Currie, D. 16; Daws, T. 4(2); Hanby, R. 1(3); Hicks, S. 36(2); Ironside, I. 39; Kay, J. 34; Knowles, D. 1(2); Lucas, R. 19(9); Martin, K. 3; McElhatton, M. 26(2); Midgley, C. 6; Mitchell, J. 23(20); Moilanen, T. 4; Mowbray, D. 2(1); Rigby, T. 5; Ritchie, A. 26(5); Rockett, J. 40; Russell, M. 1(4); Sunderland, J. (2); Sutherland, C. 17(4); Thompstone, I. 12(7); Wells, M. 22(8); Williams, A. 1; Williams, G. 45; Worrall, B. 6(9).
League (65): Williams G 10, Bennett G 9, Ritchie 9 (1 pen), Mitchell 7, Currie 6 (2 pens), Brodie 5, Rockett 5, Brooke 2, Midgley 2, Thompstone 2, Bennett T 1, Bochenski 1, Hicks 1, McElhatton 1, Rigby 1, Wells 1, Worrall 1, own goal 1.
Coca-Cola Cup (6): Bennett G 2, Ritchie 2, Daws 1, Williams G 1.
FA Cup (2): Kay 1, Ritchie 1.
Ground: The McCain Stadium, Seamer Road, Scarborough YO12 4HF. Telephone (01723) 735094.
Record attendance: 11,130 v Luton T, FA Cup 3rd rd, 8 January 1938.
Capacity: 6899.
Manager: Mick Wadsworth.
Secretary: Mrs Gillian Russell.
Honours — FA Trophy: Winners 1973, 1976, 1977. **GM Vauxhall Conference:** Winners 1987.
Colours: Red shirts, white shorts, red stockings.

SCUNTHORPE UNITED DIV. 3

Calvo-Garcia Alexander (M)	5 11	11 08	Ordizia	1 1 72	Eibar
Clarke Tim (G)	6 4	15 07	Stourbridge	19 9 68	York C
D'Auria David (M)	5 8	11 09	Swansea	26 3 70	Scarborough
Eyre John (F)	5 11	12 06	Humberside	9 10 74	Oldham Ath
Forrester Jamie (F)	5 6	10 04	Bradford	1 11 74	Grimsby T
Gavin Mark (M)	5 9	11 00	Bailleston	10 12 63	Exeter C
Hope Chris (D)	6 1	12 07	Sheffield	14 11 72	Nottingham F
Housham Steven (D)	5 10	12 07	Gainsborough T	24 2 76	Trainee
McAuley Sean (D)	5 11	11 13	Sheffield	23 6 72	Hartlepool U
Paterson Jamie (F)	5 3	10 02	Dumfries	26 4 73	Falkirk
Sertori Mark (M)	6 1	14 00	Manchester	1 9 67	Bury
Walker Justin (M)	5 10	12 12	Nottingham	6 9 75	Nottingham F
Walsh Michael (D)	5 11	12 09	Rotherham	5 8 77	Trainee

League Appearances: Baker, P. 21; Borland, J. (2); Bradley, R. 22; Calvo-Garcia, A. 7(6); Clarke, T. 15; Clarkson, P. 28; D'Auria, D. 39; Dunn, I. 3; Eyre, J. 41(1); Forrester, J. 10; Francis, J. 1(4); Gavin, M. 10(1); Hope, C. 46; Housham, S. 31(3); Jackson, K. (4); Jones, G. 9(2); Knill, A. 29; Laws, B. 2(2); Lucas, D. 6; McAuley, S. 9; McFarlane, A. 7(7); Moss, D. 4; Paterson, J. 11(18); Samways, M. 25; Sertori, M. 42; Turnbull, L. 11(3); Walker, J. 8(1); Walsh, M. 32(4); Wilson, P. (1); Wilson, P. 37
League (59): Clarkson 13, Baker 9, Eyre 8 (3 pens), Forrester 6, Jones 5, D'Auria 3, Hope 3, Housham 3, McFarlane 3, Bradley 1, Calvo-Garcia 1, Jackson 1, Sertori 1, Turnbull 1, Wilson 1.
Coca-Cola Cup (2): Clarkson 1, Moss 1.
FA Cup (8): Baker 5 (1 pen), Clarkson 2, D'Auria 1.
Ground: Glanford Park, Scunthorpe, South Humberside DN15 8TD. Telephone (01724) 848077.
Record attendance: Old Showground: 23,935 v Portsmouth, FA Cup 4th rd, 30 January 1954. Glanford Park: 8775 v Rotherham U, Division 4, 1 May 1989.
Capacity: 9183.
Manager: Brian Laws.
Secretary: A. D. Rowing.
Honours – Division 3 (N) Champions – 1957–58.
Colours: Sky blue with claret shirts, sky blue shorts, claret and white trim, sky blue stockings, claret and white trim.

SHEFFIELD UNITED   DIV. 1

Beard Mark (D)	5 10	11 04	Roehampton	8 10 74	Millwall
Bettney Chris (F)	5 10	10 10	Chesterfield	27 10 77	Trainee
Ebbrell John (M)	5 10	11 11	Bromborough	1 10 69	Everton
Fjortoft Jan-Aage (F)	6 3	14 03	Aaesund	10 1 67	Middlesbrough
Hawes Steve (M)	5 8	11 11	High Wycombe	17 7 78	Trainee
Henry Nick (M)	5 10	10 12	Liverpool	21 2 69	Oldham Ath
Heritage Paul (G)	6 2	12 11	Sheffield	17 4 79	Trainee
Hocking Matthew (D)	5 11	11 05	Boston	30 1 78	Trainee
Holdsworth David (D)	6 0	12 10	Walthamstow	8 11 68	Watford
Hutchison Don (M)	6 1	11 11	Gateshead	9 5 71	West Ham U
Katchuro Petr (F)	6 0	12 06	Minsk	2 8 72	Dynamo Minsk
Kelly Alan (G)	6 3	14 02	Preston	11 8 68	Preston NE
Nilsen Roger (D)	5 11	11 13	Tromso	8 8 69	Viking Stavanger
Patterson Mark (M)	5 8	11 12	Darwen	24 5 65	Bolton W
Quinn Wayne (M)	5 10	11 11	Truro	19 11 76	
Sandford Lee (D)	6 0	13 07	Basingstoke	22 4 68	Stoke C
Scott Andy (F)	6 1	11 09	Epsom	2 8 72	Sutton U
Short Chris (D)	5 10	12 03	Munster	9 5 70	Notts Co
Spackman Nigel (M)	6 1	13 03	Romsey	2 12 60	Chelsea
Taylor Gareth (F)	6 2	13 08	Weston-Super-Mare	25 2 73	Crystal Palace
Tiler Carl (D)	6 2	13 10	Sheffield	11 2 70	Aston Villa
Tracey Simon (G)	6 0	13 12	Woolwich	9 12 67	Wimbledon
Vonk Michael (D)	6 3	13 01	Alkmaar	28 10 68	Manchester C
Walker Andy (F)	5 8	11 05	Glasgow	6 4 65	Celtic
Ward Mitch (M)	5 9	11 07	Sheffield	11 6 71	Trainee
White David (M)	6 1	13 09	Manchester	30 10 67	Leeds U
Whitehouse Dane (M)	5 10	12 08	Sheffield	14 10 70	Trainee

League Appearances: Anthony, G. (2); Beard, M. 9(7); Bettney, C. (1); Ebbrell, J. 1; Fjortoft, J. 15(2); Hartfield, C. 1(1); Hawes, S. (2); Henry, N. 9; Hodgson, D. 12(1); Holdsworth, D. 37; Hutchison, D. 38(3); Katchuro, P. 28(12); Kelly, A. 39; Nilsen, R. 32(1); Parker, P. 7(3); Patterson, M. 34(1); Sandford, L. 25(5); Scott, A.

4(4); Short, C. 22(2); Simpson, P. 2(4); Spackman, N. 19(4); Starbuck, P. 1(1); Taylor, G. 26(8); Tiler, C. 6; Tracey, S. 7; Vonk, M. 17; Walker, A. 20(17); Ward, M. 34; White, D. 31(6); Whitehouse, D. 30

League (75): Katchuro 12, Taylor 12, Walker 12, Fjortoft 10, White 6, Whitehouse 6, Ward 4 (4 pens), Hutchison 3, Sandford 2, Vonk 2, Holdsworth 1, Patterson 1, Scott 1, Tiler 1, own goals 2.

Coca-Cola Cup (8): Vonk 2, Walker 2 (1 pen), Katchuro 1, Taylor 1, Ward 1, White 1.

FA Cup (0).

Ground: Bramall Lane Ground, Sheffield S2 4SU. Telephone (0114) 2215757

Record attendance: 68,287 v Leeds U, FA Cup 5th rd, 15 February 1936.

Capacity: 30,370.

Manager:

Secretary: D. Capper AFA.

Honours – Football League: Division 1 Champions – 1897–98. Division 2 Champions – 1952–53. Division 4 Champions – 1981–82. **FA Cup:** Winners 1899, 1902, 1915, 1925.

Colours: Red and white striped shirts, black shorts and black stockings with red trim.

SHEFFIELD WEDNESDAY $\qquad$ FA PREMIERSHIP

Agogo Manuel (M)			Accra	1 8 79	
Atherton Peter (D)	5 11	14 00	Wigan	6 4 70	Coventry C
Batty Mark (F)	5 9	10 12	Nottingham	30 1 79	Trainee
Billington David (D)			Oxford	15 10 80	Peterborough U
Blinker Regi (F)	5 8	11 07	Surinam	2 6 69	Feyenoord
Booth Andy (F)	6 1	13 00	Huddersfield	6 12 73	Huddersfield T
Briscoe Lee (F)	5 11	11 13	Pontefract	30 9 75	Trainee
Carbone Benito (F)	5 6	10 10	Bagnara Calabra	14 8 71	Internazionale
Clarke Matthew (G)	6 4	13 08	Sheffield	3 11 73	Rotherham U
Collins Wayne (M)	6 0	12 00	Manchester	4 3 69	Crewe Alex
Donaldson O'Neill (F)	5 11	12 02	Birmingham	24 11 69	Doncaster R
Haslam Steven (M)			Sheffield	6 9 79	Trainee
Hercock David (M)	5 7	11 12	Peterborough	17 4 77	Cambridge C
Hirst David (F)	6 0	14 00	Barnsley	7 12 67	Barnsley
Humphreys Richie (F)	5 11	14 06	Sheffield	30 11 77	Trainee
Hyde Graham (M)	5 8	12 06	Doncaster	10 11 70	Trainee
Jones Ryan (M)	6 3	14 00	Sheffield	23 7 73	Trainee
Kotylo Krystof (M)	5 10	11 02	Sheffield	28 9 77	School
McKeever Mark (F)			Derry	16 11 78	Peterborough U
Newsome Jon (D)	6 3	13 10	Sheffield	6 9 70	Norwich C
Nicol Steve (D)	5 10	12 06	Irvine	11 12 61	Notts Co
Nolan Ian (D)	5 11	12 00	Liverpool	9 7 70	Tranmere R
Oakes Scott (M)	5 11	11 11	Leicester	5 8 72	Luton T
Pembridge Mark (M)	5 7	12 03	Merthyr Tydfil	29 11 70	Derby Co
Platts Mark (F)	5 8	11 12	Sheffield	23 5 79	Trainee
Poric Adem (M)	5 10	12 06	London	22 4 73	St George's Budapest
Pressman Kevin (G)	6 1	14 13	Fareham	6 11 67	Apprentice
Smith Gavin (F)	5 10	10 10	Sheffield	24 9 77	Trainee
Stefanovic Dejan (D)	6 2	13 02	Yugoslavia	28 10 74	Red Star Belgrade
Trustfull Orlando (M)	5 11	13 00	Amsterdam	4 8 70	Feyenoord
Walker Des (D)	5 11	11 11	Hackney	26 11 65	Sampdoria
Weaver Simon (D)	6 1	10 08	Doncaster	20 12 77	Trainee
Whittingham Guy (F)	5 10	12 00	Evesham	10 11 64	Aston Villa

League Appearances: Atherton, P. 37; Blinker, R. 15(18); Booth, A. 32(3); Bright, M. (1); Briscoe, L. 5(1); Carbone, B. 24(1); Clarke, M. (1); Collins, W. 8(4); Donaldson, O. 2(3); Hirst, D. 20(5); Humphreys, R. 14(15); Hyde, G. 15(4); Newsome, J. 10; Nicol, S. 19(4); Nolan, I. 38; Oakes, S. 7(12); Pembridge, M. 33(1); Pressman, K. 38; Sheridan, J. (2); Stefanovic, D. 27(2); Trustfull, O. 9(10); Walker, D. 36; Whittingham, G. 29(4); Williams, M. (1)
League (50): Booth 10, Carbone 6 (1 pen), Hirst 6, Pembridge 6 (1 pen), Humphreys 3, Trustful 3, Whittingham 3, Atherton 2, Donaldson 2, Hyde 2, Stefanovic 2, Blinker 1, Collins 1, Newsome 1, Nolan 1, Oakes 1.
Coca-Cola Cup (1): Whittingham 1.
FA Cup (10): Booth 3, Humphreys 3, Hyde 1, Pembridge 1, Whittingham 1, own goal 1.
Ground: Hillsborough, Sheffield, S6 1SW. Telephone (0114) 2212121
Record attendance: 72,841 v Manchester C, FA Cup 5th rd, 17 February 1934.
Capacity: 39,859
Manager: David Pleat.
Secretary: Graham Mackrell FCCA.
Honours – Football League: Division 1 Champions – 1902–03, 1903–04, 1928–29, 1929–30. Division 2 Champions – 1899–1900, 1925–26, 1951–52, 1955–56, 1958–59.
FA Cup winners 1896, 1907, 1935. **Football League Cup winners** 1990–91.
Colours: Blue and white striped shirts, black shorts, black stockings.

SHREWSBURY TOWN   DIV. 3

Berkley Austin (F)	5 11	11 06	Dartford	28 1 73	Swindon T
Blamey Nathan (D)	5 11	11 00	Plymouth	10 6 77	Southampton
Brown Mickey (F)	5 9	11 12	Birmingham	8 2 68	Preston NE
Cope James (M)	6 1	11 01	Birmingham	4 10 77	Trainee
Currie Darren (M)	5 11	12 07	Hampstead	29 11 74	West Ham U
Dempsey Mark (D)	5 7	12 10	Dublin	10 12 72	Leyton Orient
Edwards Paul (G)	6 2	13 07	Liverpool	22 2 65	Crewe Alex
Evans Paul (M)	5 7	12 01	Oswestry	1 9 74	Trainee
Gall Benny (G)	6 1	13 11	Copenhagen	14 3 71	De Graafschap
Nielsen Thomas (D)	6 1	13 07	Aarhus	25 3 72	Fremad
Nwadike	6 0	12 07	Camberwell	9 8 78	Wolverhampton W
Chukwuemeka (D)					
Reed Ian (M)	5 8	10 13	Lichfield	4 9 75	Trainee
Scott Richard (M)	5 9	12 13	Dudley	29 9 74	Birmingham C
Seabury Kevin (D)	5 9	11 05	Shrewsbury	24 11 73	Trainee
Spink Dean (D)	5 11	14 00	Birmingham	22 1 67	Aston Villa
Taylor Lee (D)	5 11	12 00	Hammersmith	24 2 76	Faweh
Taylor Mark (M)	5 8	12 04	Birmingham	22 2 66	Sheffield W
Walton David (D)	6 2	14 07	Bedlingham	10 4 73	Sheffield U
Ward Nicholas (F)	5 9	11 09	Wrexham	30 11 77	Trainee
Whiston Peter (D)	6 0	12 02	Widnes	4 1 68	Southampton
Wray Shaun (F)	6 1	12 10	Dudley	14 3 78	Trainee

League Appearances: Anthrobus, S. 33; Bennett, F. 2(2); Bent, J. 6; Berkley, A. 20(4); Blamey, N. 6; Briscoe, A. (1); Brown, M. 17(2); Cope, J. 3; Currie, D. 25(12); Dempsey, M. 37(3); Edwards, P. 23; Evans, P. 42; Gall, B. 23; Nielsen, T. 19(3); Nwadike, C. 1(1); Reed, I. (3); Rowbotham, D. 11(3); Scott, R. 20(7); Seabury, K. 34(4); Spink, D. 39(2); Stevens, I. 41; Tate, C. (1); Taylor, L. 13(3); Taylor, M. 33(4); Walton, D. 23(1); Ward, N. 5(9); Whiston, P. 26(1); Wrack, D. 3(1); Wray, S. 1
League (49): Stevens 17, Anthrobus 6, Evans 6 (1 pen), Spink 4, Bennett 3, Currie 2, Brown 1, Nielsen 1, Rowbotham 1, Scott 1, Taylor M 1, Walton 1, Ward 1, Whiston 1, own goals 3.

Coca-Cola Cup (1): Rowbotham 1.
FA Cup (1): Stevens 1.
Ground: Gay Meadow, Shrewsbury SY2 6AB. Telephone (01743) 360111.
Record attendance: 18,917 v Walsall, Division 3, 26 April 1961. **Capacity:** 8000.
Manager: Jake King.
Secretary: M. J. Starkey.
Honours – Football League: Division 3 Champions – 1978–79, 1993–94. **Welsh Cup winners** 1891, 1938, 1977, 1979, 1984, 1985.
Colours: Blue shirts, white trim, blue shorts, blue stockings, white trim.

SOUTHAMPTON   FA PREMIERSHIP

Name			Birthplace			Previous club
Basham Steve (F)	5 10	11 07	Southampton	2 12 77	Trainee
Beasant Dave (G)	6 4	14 05	Willesden	20 3 59	Chelsea
Benali Francis (M)	5 9	11 00	Southampton	30 12 68	Apprentice
Berkovic Eyal (M)	5 7	10 00	Haifa	2 4 72	Maccabi Haifa
Charlton Simon (D)	5 8	11 09	Huddersfield	25 10 71	Huddersfield T
Davies Kevin (F)	6 0	13 05	Sheffield	26 3 77	Chesterfield
Dodd Jason (D)	5 10	12 04	Bath	2 11 70	Bath C
Dryden Richard (D)	5 11	13 11	Stroud	14 6 69	Bristol C
Evans Mike (F)	6 1	13 04	Plymouth	1 1 73	Plymouth Arg
Flahavan Darryl (G)	5 10	12 01	Southampton	28 11 78	Trainee
Hughes David (M)	5 10	11 07	St Albans	30 12 72	Trainee
Le Tissier Matthew (F)	6 0	14 00	Guernsey	14 10 68	Trainee
Lundekvam Claus (D)	6 3	13 03	Norway	22 2 73	Brann
Maddison Neil (M)	5 10	11 11	Darlington	2 10 69	Trainee
Magilton Jim (M)	6 0	14 00	Belfast	6 5 69	Oxford U
Monkou Ken (D)	6 3	14 06	Surinam	29 11 64	Chelsea
Moss Neil (G)	6 2	13 09	New Milton	10 5 75	Bournemouth
Neilson Alan (D)	5 11	13 01	Wegburg	26 9 72	Newcastle U
Oakley Matthew (M)	5 10	12 01	Peterborough	17 8 77	Trainee
Ostenstad Egil (F)	5 11	13 00	Haugesund	2 1 72	Viking
Piper David (D)	5 8	10 00	Bournemouth	31 10 77	Trainee
Robinson Matthew (M)	5 11	11 07	Exeter	23 12 74	Trainee
Slater Robbie (M)	5 10	13 03	Ormskirk	22 11 64	West Ham U
Spedding Duncan (M)	6 1	11 01	Camberley	7 9 77	Trainee
Taylor Maik (G)	6 3	14 02	Germany	4 9 71	Barnet
Van Gobbel Ulrich (D)	6 0	15 00	Surinam	16 1 71	Galatasaray
Venison Barry (M)	5 10	11 12	Consett	16 8 64	Galatasaray
Warren Christer (F)	5 10	11 12	Poole	10 10 74	Cheltenham T
Watkinson Russ (F)	6 0	12 00	Epsom	3 12 77	Woking
Williams Andrew (F)	5 10	10 10	Bristol	8 10 77	Trainee

League Appearances: Basham, S. 1(5); Beasant, D. 13(1); Benali, F. 14(4); Berkovic, E. 26(2); Charlton, S. 24(3); Dia, A. (1); Dodd, J. 23; Dryden, R. 28(1); Evans, M. 8(4); Heaney, N. 4(4); Hughes, D. 1(5); Le Tissier, M. 25(6); Lundekvam, C. 28(1); Maddison, N. 14(4); Magilton, J. 31(6); Monkou, K. 8(5); Moss, N. 3; Neilson, A. 24(5); Oakley, M. 23(5); Ostenstad, E. 29(1); Potter, G. 2(6); Robinson, M. 3(4); Shipperley, N. 9(1); Slater, R. 22(8); Taylor, M. 18; Van Gobbel, U. 24(1); Venison, B. 2; Warren, C. (1); Watkinson, R. (2); Watson, G. 7(8); Woods, C. 3.
League (50): Le Tissier 13 (5 pens), Ostenstad 9, Berkovic 4, Evans 4, Magilton 4 (2 pens), Oakley 3, Slater 2, Watson 2, Dodd 1, Dryden 1, Heaney 1, Maddison 1, Shipperley 1, Van Gobbel 1, own goals 3.
Coca-Cola Cup (18): Dryden 3, Le Tissier 3, Ostenstad 3, Watson 3, Berkovic 2, Magilton 2 (1 pen), Charlton 1, Van Gobbel 1.

FA Cup (1): Ostenstad 1.

Ground: The Dell, Milton Road, Southampton SO15 2XH. Telephone (01703) 220505.

Record attendance: 31,044 v Manchester U, Division 1, 8 October 1969. **Capacity:** 15,000.

Manager: Dave Jones

Secretary: Brian Truscott.

Honours – Football League: Division 3 (S) Champions – 1921–22. Division 3 Champions – 1959–60. **FA Cup:** Winners 1975–76.

Colours: Red and white striped shirts, black shorts, red and white hooped stockings.

SOUTHEND UNITED   DIV. 2

Boere Jeroen (F)	6 3	13 02	Arnheim	18 11 67	Crystal Palace
Byrne Paul (M)	5 11	13 00	Dublin	30 6 72	Celtic
Dublin Keith (D)	6 0	12 10	Wycombe	29 1 66	Watford
Gridelet Phil (M)	5 11	13 00	Edgware	30 4 67	Barnsley
Hails Julian (F)	5 10	11 02	Lincoln	20 11 67	Fulham
Harris Andrew (D)	5 10	11 11	Springs	26 2 77	Liverpool
Henriksen Tony (G)	6 3	13 09	Hammel	25 4 73	Randers Freja
Lapper Mike (D)	6 0	12 02	California	28 8 70	USSF
Marsh Mike (F)	5 8	11 00	Liverpool	21 7 69	Galatasaray
Nielsen John (M)			Aarhus	7 4 72	Ikast
Rammell Andy (F)	6 2	13 10	Nuneaton	10 2 67	Barnsley
Roche David (M)	6 0	13 02	Newcastle	13 12 70	Doncaster R
Roget Leo (D)	6 1	12 02	Ilford	1 8 77	Trainee
Royce Simon (G)	6 2	12 10	Forest Gate	9 9 71	Heybridge Swifts
Stimson Mark (D)	5 10	12 06	Plaistow	27 12 67	Portsmouth
Thomson Andy (F)	5 10	10 12	Motherwell	1 4 71	Queen of South
Williams Paul (F)	5 7	10 09	London	16 8 65	Charlton Ath

League Appearances: Boere, J. 27(9); Byrne, P. 23(9); Clarke, A. 7; Codner, R. 3(1); Dublin, K. 46; Dursun, P. (1); Gridelet, P. 34(7); Hails, J. 32(5); Hanlon, R. 1(1); Harris, A. 43(1); Jones, M. (1); Lapper, M. 23(5); Marsh, M. 35; McNally, M. 32(2); Nielsen, J. 17(7); Patterson, M. 4; Poric, A. 7; Rammell, A. 26(10); Roget, L. 25; Royce, S. 43; Sansome, P. 3; Selley, I. 3(1); Stimson, M. 7(2); Thomson, A. 14(3); Tilson, S. 27(1); Williams, P. 24(9)

League (42): Boere 9, Rammell 9, Williams 6, Marsh 5 (3 pens), Thomson 5, Nielsen 3, Byrne 1, Gridelet 1, Lapper 1, Tilson 1, own goal 1.

Coca-Cola Cup (2): Nielsen 1, Rammell 1.

FA Cup (0).

Ground: Roots Hall Football Ground, Victoria Avenue, Southend-on-Sea SS2 6NQ. Telephone (01702) 304050

Record attendance: 31,090 v Liverpool FA Cup 3rd rd, 10 January 1979. **Capacity:** 12,306

Manager:

Secretary: J. W. Adams.

Honours – Football League: Division 4 Champions – 1980–81.

Colours: Royal blue and yellow.

STOCKPORT COUNTY   DIV. 1

| Angell Brett (F) | 6 2 | 13 10 | Marlborough | 20 8 68 | Sunderland |
| Armstrong Alun (F) | 6 0 | 10 05 | Gateshead | 22 2 75 | Newcastle U |

Bennett Tom (D)	5 11	11 08	Falkirk	12 12 69	Wolverhampton W
Bound Matthew (D)	6 2	13 09	Trowbridge	9 11 72	Southampton
Cavaco Luis (F)	5 9	11 06	Portugal	1 3 72	Estoril
Charlery Ken (F)	6 0	12 00	Stepney	28 11 64	Peterborough U
Connelly Sean (D)	5 10	11 10	Sheffield	26 6 70	Hallam
Cowans Gordon (M)	5 7	9 07	Durham	27 10 58	Bradford C
Da Costa Nelson (D)	5 10	12 03	Angola	8 12 78	Belenenses
Dinning Tony (D)	5 11	12 00	Wallsend	12 4 75	Newcastle U
Durkan Kieron (M)	5 10	10 05	Chester	1 12 73	Wrexham
Edwards Neil (G)	5 8	11 02	Aberdare	5 12 70	Leeds U
Flynn Mike (D)	6 0	11 02	Oldham	23 2 69	Preston NE
Gannon Jim (D)	6 2	13 00	Southwark	7 9 68	Sheffield U
Jeffers John (F)	5 10	11 10	Liverpool	5 10 68	Port Vale
Jones Lea (D)	6 0	14 06	Southport	25 9 77	Trainee
Jones Paul (G)	6 3	14 00	Chirk	18 4 67	Wolverhampton W
Kiko Manuel (D)	5 10	12 05	Portugal	24 10 76	Belenenses
Landon Richard (F)	6 3	13 05	Worthing	22 3 70	Plymouth Arg
Marsden Chris (M)	6 0	10 12	Sheffield	3 1 69	Notts Co
Mutch Andy (F)	5 11	11 00	Liverpool	28 12 63	Swindon T
Nash Martin (F)	5 11	12 03	Regina	27 12 75	Vancouver
Searle Damon (D)	5 11	10 04	Cardiff	26 10 71	Cardiff C
Todd Lee (D)	5 5	10 03	Hartlepool	7 3 72	Hartlepool U

League Appearances: Angell, B. 30(4); Armstrong, A. 38(1); Bennett, T. 43; Bound, M. 4; Cavaco, L. 19(8); Charlery, K. 8(2); Connelly, S. 45; Cooper, K. 11(1); Cowans, G. 6(1); Dinning, T. 12(8); Durkan, K. 36(5); Flynn, M. 46; Gannon, J. 38(2); Jeffers, J. 25(9); Jones, P. 46; Kiko, M. (3); Landon, R. (2); Marsden, C. 34(1); Mike, A. (1); Mutch, A. 15(18); Nash, M. (3); Searle, D. 7(3); Todd, L. 39(2); Ware, P. 4(4)
League (59): Angell 15, Armstrong 9 (1 pen), Cavaco 5, Gannon 4, Mutch 4, Bennett 3, Cooper 3 (2 pens), Durkan 3, Jeffers 3, Dinning 2 (1 pen), Flynn 2, Marsden 2, own goals 4.
Coca-Cola Cup (20): Mutch 4, Angell 3, Armstrong 3, Bennett 2, Cavaco 2, Connelly 1, Flynn 1, Gannon 1, Ware 1, own goals 2.
FA Cup (8): Durkan 3, Angell 1, Armstrong 1, Flynn 1, Mutch 1, own goal 1.
Ground: Edgeley Park, Hardcastle Road, Stockport, Cheshire SK3 9DD. Telephone (0161) 286 8888.
Record attendance: 27,833 v Liverpool, FA Cup 5th rd, 11 February 1950.
Capacity: 12,500.
Manager: Gary Megson.
Secretary: Gary Glendenning BA (HONS) ACCA.
Honours – Football League: Division 3 (N) Champions – 1921–22, 1936–37. Division 4 Champions – 1966–67.
Colours: Royal blue shirts, white shorts, blue stockings.

STOKE CITY   DIV. 1

Birch Mark (D)	5 11	12 02	Stoke	5 1 77	Trainee
Cairns Kwesi (M)	5 5	10 00	Westminster	5 8 79	
Cartwright Jamie (M)	5 6	9 06	Lichfield	11 10 79	Trainee
Clarke Clive (D)	5 11	12 03	Dublin	14 1 80	Trainee
Crowe Dean (F)	5 5	11 03	Stockport	6 6 79	Trainee
Devlin Mark (M)	5 10	11 13	Irvine	18 1 73	Trainee
Forsyth Richard (M)	5 10	12 13	Dudley	3 10 70	Birmingham C
Godbold Jamie (F)	5 4	9 0	Great Yarmouth	10 1 80	Trainee
Griffin Andrew (D)	5 8	10 10	Wigan	17 3 79	Trainee

Heath Robert (M)	5 8	10 00	Stoke	31	8 78	
Kavanagh Graham (M)	5 10	12 06	Dublin	2	12 73	Middlesbrough
Keen Kevin (M)	5 7	10 09	Amersham	25	2 67	Wolverhampton W
Macari Mike (F)	5 7	11 05	Kilwinning	4	2 73	West Ham U
Macari Paul (F)	5 8	11 06	Manchester	23	8 76	Trainee
Mackenzie Neil (M)	6 2	12 05	Birmingham	15	4 76	
McMahon Gerry (F)	5 11	11 13	Belfast	29	12 73	Tottenham H
McNally Mark (D)	5 11	12 02	Bellshill	10	3 71	Southend U
Morgan Phil (G)	6 2	14 01	Stoke	18	12 74	Ipswich T
Muggleton Carl (G)	6 2	13 03	Leicester	13	9 68	Celtic
Nyamah Kofi (F)	5 10	11 07	Islington	20	6 75	Kettering T
O'Connor James (M)	5 7	10 04	Dublin	1	9 79	Trainee
Pickering Ally (D)	5 9	11 04	Manchester	22	6 67	Coventry C
Prudhoe Mark (G)	6 0	14 00	Washington	8	11 63	Darlington
Sheron Mike (F)	5 10	11 13	Liverpool	11	1 72	Norwich C
Sigurdsson Larus (D)	6 0	12 12	Akureyri	4	6 73	Thor
Stokoe Graham (M)	6 1	11 13	Newcastle	17	12 75	Birmingham C
Sturridge Simon (F)	5 6	11 05	Birmingham	9	12 69	Birmingham C
Taaffe Stephen (F)	5 5	9 0	Stoke	10	9 79	Trainee
Wallace Ray (D)	5 7	11 05	Lewisham	2	10 69	Leeds U
Whittle Justin (D)	6 1	12 13	Derby	18	3 71	Celtic
Woods Stephen (D)	5 11	11 13	Davenham	15	12 76	Trainee
Wooliscroft Ashley (D)	5 10	11 02	Stoke	28	12 79	Trainee

League Appearances: Beeston, C. 17(1); Carruthers, M. (1); Cranson, I. 6; Da Costa, H. 1(1); Devlin, M. 13(8); Dreyer, J. 12; Flynn, S. 5; Forsyth, R. 40; Gayle, J. 8(4); Griffin, A. 29(5); Kavanagh, G. 32(6); Keen, K. 5(11); Macari, M. 15(15); Mackenzie, N. 5(17); McMahon, G. 31(4); McNally, M. 3; Muggleton, C. 33; Nyamah, K. (7); Pickering, A. 39(1); Prudhoe, M. 13; Rodger, S. 5; Sheron, M. 41; Sigurdsson, L. 45; Stein, M. 11; Stokoe, G. (2); Sturridge, S. 5; Wallace, R. 45; Whittle, J. 35(2); Worthington, N. 12

League (51): Sheron 19 (2 pens), Forsyth 8, Kavanagh 4, Stein 4, McMahon 3, Macari 3, Wallace 2, Dreyer 1, Gayle 1, Griffin 1, Keen 1, MacKenzie 1, own goals 3.

Coca-Cola Cup (6): Sheron 5, Worthington 1.

FA Cup (0).

Ground: Victoria Ground, Stoke-on-Trent ST4 4EG. Telephone (01782) 413511.

Record attendance: 51,380 v Arsenal, Division 1, 29 March 1937. **Capacity:** 24,054.

Manager: Chic Bates.

Secretary: M. J. Potts.

Honours – Football League: Division 2 Champions – 1932–33, 1962–63, 1992–93. Division 3 (N) Champions – 1926–27. **Football League Cup:** Winners 1971–72. **Autoglass Trophy winners** 1992.

Colours: Red and white striped shirts, white shorts, white stockings.

SUNDERLAND   DIV. 1

Agnew Steve (M)	5 10	11 12	Shipley	9	11 65	Leicester C
Aiston Sam (F)	6 1	12 13	Newcastle	21	11 76	Newcastle U
Ball Kevin (D)	5 9	12 09	Hastings	12	11 64	Portsmouth
Beavers Paul (F)	6 3	13 05	Blackpool	2	10 78	Trainee
Bracewell Paul (M)	5 9	12 04	Stoke	19	7 62	Newcastle U
Bridges Michael (F)	6 1	11 02	Whitley Bay	5	8 78	Trainee
Conlon Paul (F)	5 9	11 08	Sunderland	5	1 78	Hartlepool U
Coton Tony (G)	6 2	16 02	Tamworth	19	5 61	Manchester U
Dickman Elliot (D)	5 9	9 08	Hexham	11	10 78	Trainee

Eriksson Jan (D)	6 0	13 03	Sundsvall	24 8 67	Helsingborg
Gray Michael (D)	5 8	10 12	Sunderland	3 8 74	Trainee
Hall Gareth (D)	5 11	13 04	Croydon	12 3 69	Chelsea
Heckingbottom Paul (D)	6 0	12 05	Barnsley	17 7 77	Manchester U
Heiselberg Kim (D)	5 11	11 07	Tarm	21 9 77	Esbjerg
Holloway Darren (D)	6 0	12 05	Bishop Auckland	3 10 77	Trainee
Howey Lee (F)	6 3	14 05	Sunderland	1 4 69	AC Hemptinne
Johnston Alan (F)	5 7	9 07	Glasgow	14 12 73	Rennes
Kelly David (F)	5 11	11 11	Birmingham	25 11 65	Wolverhampton W
Kubicki Dariusz (D)	5 11	12 02	Kozuchow	6 6 63	Aston Villa
Melville Andy (D)	6 0	13 10	Swansea	29 11 68	Oxford U
Mullin John (F)	6 1	12 05	Bury	11 8 75	Burnley
Naisbett Philip (F)	6 2	12 05	Easington	2 1 79	Trainee
Ord Richard (D)	6 2	12 12	Easington	3 3 69	Trainee
Perez Lionel (G)	6 0	14 02	Bagnols Ceze	24 4 67	Bordeaux
Quinn Niall (F)	6 5	15 03	Dublin	6 10 66	Manchester C
Rae Alex (M)	5 9	11 05	Glasgow	30 9 69	Millwall
Russell Craig (F)	5 10	12 08	Jarrow	4 2 74	Trainee
Scott Martin (M)	5 9	11 02	Sheffield	7 1 68	Bristol C
Smith Martin (F)	5 11	12 00	Sunderland	13 11 74	Trainee
Stewart Paul (M)	5 11	11 10	Manchester	7 10 64	Liverpool
Thirlwell Paul (M)	5 11	11 04	Newcastle	13 2 79	Trainee
Williams Darren (M)	5 11	11 02	Middlesbrough	28 4 77	York C

League Appearances: Agnew, S. 11(4); Aiston, S. (2); Ball, K. 32; Bracewell, P. 38; Bridges, M. 10(15); Coton, T. 10; Eriksson, J. 1; Gray, M. 31(3); Hall, G. 32; Howey, L. 9(3); Johnston, A. 4(2); Kelly, D. 23(1); Kubicki, D. 28(1); Melville, A. 30; Mullin, J. 9(1); Ord, R. 33; Perez, L. 38(1); Quinn, N. 8(4); Rae, A. 13(10); Russell, C. 10(19); Scott, M. 15; Smith, M. 6(5); Stewart, P. 20(4); Waddle, C. 7; Williams, D. 10(1)
League (35): Russell 4, Stewart 4 (1 pen), Ball 3, Bridges 3, Gray 3, Agnew 2 (1 pen), Melville 2, Ord 2, Quinn 2, Rae 2 (1 pen), Williams 2, Johnston 1, Mullin 1, Scott 1 (pen), Waddle 1, own goals 2.
Coca-Cola Cup (4): Ball 1, Quinn 1, Rae 1, Scott 1.
FA Cup (1): Gray 1.
Ground: Stadium Park, Sunderland, Tyne and Wear SR5 1BT. Telephone: (0191) 5515000.
Record attendance: 75,118 v Derby Co, FA Cup 6th rd replay, 8 March 1933 (at Roker Park). **Capacity:** 42,000.
Manager: Peter Reid.
Secretary: Mark Blackbourne.
Honours — Football League: Division 1 Champions – 1891–92, 1892–93, 1894–95, 1901–02, 1912–13, 1935–36, 1995–96. Division 2 Champions – 1975–76. Division 3 Champions – 1987–88. **FA Cup:** Winners 1937, 1973.
Colours: Red and white striped shirts, black shorts, black stockings, red turnover.

SWANSEA CITY   DIV. 3

Ampadu Kwame (M)	5 10	11 10	Bradford	20 12 70	WBA
Appleby Ritchie (F)	5 9	11 04	Middlesbrough	18 9 75	Ipswich T
Brown Linton (F)	5 10	12 07	Driffield	12 4 68	Hull C
Casey Ryan (F)	6 0	10 02	Coventry	3 1 79	Trainee
Chapple Shaun (M)	5 11	12 03	Swansea	14 2 73	Trainee
Clode Mark (D)	5 10	10 10	Plymouth	24 2 73	Plymouth Arg
Coates Jonathan (F)	5 8	10 04	Swansea	27 6 75	Trainee
Edwards Christian (M)	6 2	11 09	Caerphilly	23 11 75	Trainee

Freestone Roger (G)	6 3	14 06	Newport	19	8 68	Chelsea
Heggs Carl (F)	6 1	13 02	Leicester	11	10 70	WBA
Jenkins Lee (F)	5 9	10 00	Pontypool	28	6 79	Trainee
Jones Lee (G)	6 3	14 04	Pontypridd	9	8 70	Porth
Jones Steve (D)	5 10	12 02	Bristol	25	12 70	Cheltenham T
King Robert (D)	5 8	10 06	Merthyr	2	9 77	Trainee
Lacey Damien (M)	5 9	11 03	Bridgend	3	8 77	Trainee
McDonald Colin (F)	5 7	11 04	Edinburgh	10	4 74	Falkirk
Miles Ben (G)	6 1	11 07	Middlesex	13	4 76	Trainee
Molby Jan (M)	6 2	15 10	Kolding	4	7 63	Liverpool
Moreira Joao (D)	6 3	14 00	Oporto	30	6 70	Benfica
O'Leary Kristian (M)	6 0	13 04	Port Talbot	30	8 77	Trainee
Penney David (M)	5 10	12 00	Wakefield	17	8 64	Oxford U
Price Jason (M)	6 2	11 05	Aberdare	12	4 77	Aberaman Ath
Thomas David (F)	5 11	12 07	Caerphilly	26	9 75	Trainee
Torpey Steve (F)	6 3	14 03	Islington	18	12 70	Bradford C
Walker Keith (M)	6 0	13 03	Edinburgh	17	4 66	St Mirren

League Appearances: Ampadu, K. 25(4); Appleby, R. 8(3); Brayson, P. 11; Brown,
L. 13(8); Casey, R. 3(7); Chapple, S. 10(8); Clode, M. 16(2); Coates, J. 38(2);
Edwards, C. 36; Freestone, R. 45; Garnett, S. 6; Heggs, C. 5(10); Hills, J. 11; Jenkins,
L. 21(2); Jones, L. 1; Jones, S. 46; King, R. 2; Lacey, D. 9(1); McDonald, C. 3(7);
McGibbon, P. 1; Molby, J. 26(2); Moreira, J. 10; O'Leary, K. 9(3); Penney, D. 44;
Phillips, G. (1); Price, J. 1(1); Thomas, D. 31(5); Torpey, S. 37(2); Walker, K. 31;
Willer, T. 7
League (62): Penney 13 (6 pens), Thomas 9, Torpey 9, Molby 6 (3 pens), Brayson
5, Ampadu 4, Brown 3, Coates 3, Heggs 2, Jenkins 2, Appleby 1, Clode 1, Jones 1,
O'Leary 1, Walker 1, own goal 1.
Coca-Cola Cup (0).
FA Cup (1): Torpey 1.
Ground: Vetch Field, Swansea SA1 3SU. Telephone (01792) 474114.
Record attendance: 32,796 v Arsenal, FA Cup 4th rd, 17 February 1968. **Capacity:**
11,477.
Team Manager: Jan Molby.
Honours – Football League: Division 3 (S) Champions – 1924–25, 1948–49.
Autoglass Trophy: Winners 1994. **Welsh Cup:** Winners 9 times.
Colours: White shirts with black trim, white shorts, black stockings.

SWINDON TOWN   DIV. 1

Allison Wayne (F)	6 1	14 00	Huddersfield	16	10 68	Bristol C
Bullock Darren (M)	5 9	12 10	Worcester	12	2 69	Huddersfield T
Collins Lee (M)	5 8	10 08	Bellshill	3	2 74	Albion R
Cowe Steve (M)	5 6	10 10	Gloucester	29	9 74	Aston Villa
Culverhouse Ian (D)	5 10	11 02	Bishop's Stortford	22	9 64	Norwich C
Darras Frederic (D)	6 0	11 06	Calais	19	8 66	Bastia
Digby Fraser (G)	6 2	13 10	Sheffield	23	4 67	Manchester U
Drysdale Jason (D)	5 10	13 00	Bristol	17	11 70	Newcastle U
Elkins Gary (D)	5 9	13 00	Wallingford	4	5 66	Wimbledon
Finney Stephen (F)	5 11	13 00	Hexham	31	10 73	Manchester U
Gooden Ty (M)	5 8	12 02	Canvey Island	23	10 72	Wycombe W
Holcroft Peter (M)	5 9	11 05	Liverpool	3	1 76	Everton
King Phil (D)	5 11	12 09	Bristol	28	12 67	Aston Villa
Leitch Scott (D)	5 8	11 10	Motherwell	6	10 69	Hearts
Mildenhall Steve (G)	6 4	13 00	Swindon	13	5 78	Trainee
O'Sullivan Wayne (D)	5 8	10 09	Akrotiri	25	2 74	Trainee

89

Robinson Mark (D)	5 10	12 04	Rochdale	21 11 68	Newcastle U
Seagraves Mark (M)	6 0	13 12	Bootle	22 10 66	Bolton W
Smith Alex (D)	5 9	10 06	Liverpool	15 2 76	Everton
Talia Frank (G)	6 1	13 08	Melbourne	20 7 72	Blackburn R
Taylor Craig (M)			Plymouth	24 1 74	Dorchester T
Thorne Peter (F)	6 0	13 00	Manchester	21 6 73	Blackburn R
Walters Mark (M)	5 10	12 08	Birmingham	2 6 64	Southampton
Watson Kevin (M)	5 9	12 09	Hackney	3 1 74	Tottenham H

League Appearances: Allen, P. 5(5); Allison, W. 39(2); Anthony, G. 3; Broomes, M. 12; Bullock, D. 12(1); Collins, L. 3(1); Coughlan, G. 3; Cowe, S. 28(10); Culverhouse, I. 31; Darras, F. 30(5); Digby, F. 31; Drysdale, J. 13(1); Elkins, G. 19(4); Finney, S. 8(12); Gooden, T. 7(6); Holcroft, P. 2(1); Horlock, K. 28; Kerslake, D. 8; King, P. 5; Leitch, S. 36; McMahon, S. 2(1); Mildenhall, S. (1); O'Sullivan, W. 16(9); Pattimore, M. 1; Robinson, M. 43; Seagraves, M. 27(1); Smith, A. 13(5); Talia, F. 15; Taylor, S. 2; Thorne, P. 24(7); Walters, M. 24(3); Watson, K. 17(10)

League (52): Allison 11, Horlock 8, Thorne 8, Walters 7 (2 pens), Cowe 6, Finney 2, Allen 1, Broomes 1, Bullock 1, Elkins 1, Gooden 1, Robinson 1, Smith 1, Watson 1, own goals 2.

Coca-Cola Cup (7): Allison 2, Thorne 2, Leitch 1, O'Sullivan 1, Walters 1.

FA Cup (0).

Ground: County Ground, Swindon, Wiltshire SN1 2ED. Telephone (01793) 430430.

Record attendance: 32,000 v Arsenal, FA Cup 3rd rd, 15 January 1972. **Capacity:** 15,728.

Manager: Steve McMahon.

Secretary: Steve Jones.

Honours – Football League: Division 2 Champions – 1995–96. Division 4 Champions – 1985–86. **Football League Cup:** Winners 1968–69. **Anglo-Italian Cup:** Winners 1970.

Colours: All red.

TORQUAY UNITED   DIV. 3

Barrow Lee (D)	5 11	12 05	Worksworth	1 5 73	Scarborough
Gittens Jon (D)	6 0	12 07	Moseley	22 1 64	Portsmouth
Hodges Kevin (M)	5 8	11 03	Bridport	12 6 60	Plymouth Arg
Jack Rodney (F)	5 7	10 07	Kingston, Jamaica	28 9 72	Lambada
McCall Steve (M)	5 11	12 08	Carlisle	15 10 60	Plymouth Arg
McFarlane Andy (F)	6 3	12 06	Wolverhampton	30 11 66	Scunthorpe U
Nelson Garry (F)	5 10	11 13	Braintree	16 1 61	Charlton Ath
Oatway Charlie (M)	5 7	11 00	Hammersmith	28 11 73	Cardiff C
Preston Michael (M)	5 8	10 07	Plymouth	22 11 77	Trainee
Watson Alex (D)	6 1	11 09	Liverpool	15 4 68	Bournemouth

League Appearances: Adcock, P. (1); Baker, P. 10; Barrow, L. 45(1); Bedeau, A. 3(5); Chandler, D. 4; Crane, S. (2); Gittens, J. 33; Gregg, M. 1; Gregory, N. 5; Hancox, R. 6(5); Hapgood, L. (1); Hathaway, I. 21(14); Hawthorne, M. 25(9); Hinshelwood, D. 7(2); Hockley, W. (2); Hodges, K. (1); Howell, J. 2(2); Jack, R. 30(3); Laight, E. 6(4); McCall, S. 23(1); McFarlane, A. 19; Mitchell, P. 22(2); Ndah, J. 9(3); Nelson, G. 30(4); Newland, R. 11; Oatway, C. 39(2); Preston, M. (2); Stamps, S. 30; Thirlby, A. 1(2); Thomas, W. 1(11); Tucker, L. (1); Watson, A. 46; Wilmot, R. 34; Winter, S. 36(1); Wright, M. 7(2)

League (46): Jack 10, Nelson 8, Winter 6 (2 pens), Baker 4, Gittens 3, McFarlane 3, Stamps 3, Hawthorne 2, Bedeau 1, Hathaway 1, Laight 1, McCall 1, Ndah 1,

Oatway 1, Watson 1.
Coca-Cola Cup (3): Baker 3 (1 pen).
FA Cup (0).
Ground: Plainmoor Ground, Torquay, Devon TQ1 3PS. Telephone (01803) 328666.
Record attendance: 21,908 v Huddersfield T, FA Cup 4th rd, 29 January 1955.
Capacity: 6000.
Player-Manager: Kevin Hodges.
Secretary: M. Bateson.
Honours – Nil
Colours: Yellow and navy striped shirts, navy shorts, yellow stockings.

TOTTENHAM HOTSPUR — FA PREMIERSHIP

Allen Rory (F)	5 11	11 02	Beckenham	17 10 77	Trainee
Anderton Darren (F)	6 1	12 05	Southampton	3 3 72	Portsmouth
Arber Mark (D)	6 1	11 09	South Africa	9 10 77	Trainee
Armstrong Chris (F)	6 0	12 10	Newcastle	19 6 71	Crystal Palace
Austin Dean (D)	6 0	11 06	Hemel Hempstead	26 4 70	Southend U
Baardsen Espen (G)	6 5	13 03	San Rafael	7 12 77	San Francisco AB
Brady Garry (M)	5 10	10 95	Glasgow	7 9 76	Trainee
Brown Simon (G)	6 2	15 01	Chelmsford	3 12 76	Trainee
Bunn James (F)			Tottenham	12 1 78	Trainee
Calderwood Colin (D)	6 0	13 00	Glasgow	20 1 65	Swindon T
Campbell Sol (D)	6 21	14 04	Newham	18 9 74	Trainee
Carr Stephen (D)	5 9	12 04	Dublin	29 8 76	Trainee
Clapham Jamie (M)	5 9	10 11	Lincoln	7 12 75	Trainee
Clemence Stephen (M)	5 11	11 07	Liverpool	31 3 78	Trainee
Darcy Ross (D)	6 0	12 02	Balbriggan	21 3 78	Trainee
Davies Darren (M)	5 8	11 07	Port Talbot	13 8 78	Trainee
Dozzell Jason (M)	6 2	13 10	Ipswich	9 12 67	Ipswich T
Edinburgh Justin (D)	5 10	12 01	Basildon	18 12 69	Southend U
Fenn Neale (F)	5 10	12 08	Edmonton	18 1 77	Trainee
Fox Ruel (F)	5 6	10 05	Ipswich	14 1 68	Newcastle U
Gain Peter (M)	6 1	11 00	Hammersmith	11 11 76	Trainee
Gower Mark (M)			Edmonton	5 10 78	Trainee
Hill Danny (M)	5 9	11 12	Edmonton	1 10 74	Trainee
Howells David (M)	6 0	12 07	Guildford	15 12 67	Trainee
Iversen Steffen (F)	6 1	11 08	Oslo	10 11 76	Rosenborg
Mabbutt Gary (D)	5 10	13 01	Bristol	23 8 61	Bristol R
Maher Kevin (D)	6 0	12 05	Ilford	17 10 76	Trainee
Mahorn Paul (F)	5 10	13 01	Whipps Cross	13 8 73	Trainee
McVeigh Paul (F)	5 6	10 05	Belfast	6 12 77	Trainee
Nethercott Stuart (D)	6 1	14 00	Chadwell Heath	21 3 73	Trainee
Nielsen Allan (M)	5 8	11 02	Esbjerg	13 3 71	Brondby
Scales John (D)	6 2	13 05	Harrogate	4 7 66	Liverpool
Sheringham Teddy (F)	6 0	12 08	Highams Park	2 4 66	Nottingham F
Sinton Andy (M)	5 8	11 01	Newcastle	19 3 66	Sheffield W
Townley Leon (D)	6 2	13 03	Loughton	16 2 76	Trainee
Vega Ramon (D)	6 3	13 00	Olten	14 6 71	Cagliari
Walker Ian (G)	6 2	13 01	Watford	31 10 71	Trainee
Webb Simon (M)	5 11	12 03	Castle Bar	19 1 78	Trainee
Wilson Clive (D)	5 7	11 04	Manchester	13 11 61	QPR

League Appearances: Allen, R. 9(3); Anderton, D. 14(2); Armstrong, C. 12; Austin, D. 13(2); Baardsen. E. 1(1); Calderwood, C. 33(1); Campbell, S. 38; Carr,

S. 24(2); Clapham, J. (1); Dozzell, J. 10(7); Edinburgh, J. 21(3); Fenn, N. (4); Fox,
R. 19(6); Howells, D. 32; Iversen, S. 16; Mabbutt, G. 1; McVeigh, P. 2(1);
Nethercott, S. 2(7); Nielsen, A. 28(1); Rosenthal, R. 4(16); Scales, J. 10(2);
Sheringham, T. 29; Sinton, A. 32(1); Vega, R. 8; Walker, I. 37; Wilson, C. 23(3)
League (44): Sheringham 7, Iversen 6, Nielsen 6, Sinton 6, Armstrong 5 (1 pen),
Anderton 3, Allen 2, Dozzell 2, Howells 2, Fox 1, McVeigh 1, Rosenthal 1, Vega 1,
Wilson 1 (pen).
Coca-Cola Cup (7): Allen 2, Anderton 2, Armstrong 1, Campbell 1, Sheringham 1.
FA Cup (0).
Ground: 748 High Rd, Tottenham, London N17 0AP. Telephone (0181) 365 5000.
Record attendance: 75,038 v Sunderland, FA Cup 6th rd, 5 March 1938. **Capacity:**
33,208.
Manager: Gerry Francis.
Secretary: Peter Barnes.
Honours – Football League: Division 1 Champions – 1950–51, 1960–61. Division 2
Champions – 1919–20, 1949–50. **FA Cup:** Winners 1901 (as non-League club),
1921, 1961, 1962, 1967, 1981, 1982, 1991. **Football League Cup:** Winners 1970–71,
1972–73. **European Competitions:** European Cup-Winners' Cup winners: 1962–63.
UEFA Cup winners: 1971–72, 1983–84.
Colours: White shirts, navy blue shorts, white stockings.

TRANMERE ROVERS   DIV. 1

Aldridge John (F)	5 11	12 03	Liverpool	18 9 58	Real Sociedad
Branch Graham (F)	6 2	12 02	Liverpool	12 2 72	Heswall
Challinor Dave (D)	6 2	12 00	Chester	2 10 75	Bromborough Pool
Connolly Stuart (M)	5 8	10 09	Dublin	8 12 77	Stella Maris
Cook Paul (M)	5 11	11 00	Liverpool	22 6 67	Coventry C
Coyne Danny (G)	5 11	12 06	Prestatyn	27 8 73	Trainee
Irons Kenny (M)	5 10	11 02	Liverpool	4 11 70	Trainee
Jones Gary (F)	6 3	13 05	Chester	10 5 75	Trainee
Mahon Alan (M)	5 10	11 05	Dublin	4 4 78	Crumplin U
McGreal John (D)	5 11	10 12	Birkenhead	2 6 72	Trainee
McIntyre Kevin (M)			Liverpool	23 12 77	Trainee
Morgan Alan (D)	5 10	11 00	Aberystwyth	2 11 73	Trainee
Morrissey John (F)	5 8	11 09	Liverpool	8 3 65	Wolverhampton W
Nevin Pat (F)	5 6	11 09	Glasgow	6 9 63	Everton
Nixon Eric (G)	6 4	14 00	Manchester	4 10 62	Manchester C
O'Brien Liam (M)	6 1	11 10	Dublin	5 9 64	Newcastle U
Parkinson Andrew (M)			Liverpool	27 5 79	Liverpool
Rogers Alan (D)	5 10	11 08	Liverpool	3 1 77	Trainee
Simonsen Steve (G)	6 2	12 08	South Shields	3 4 79	Trainee
Stevens Gary (D)	5 11	11 02	Barrow	27 3 63	Rangers
Teale Shaun (D)	6 0	12 02	Southport	10 3 64	Aston Villa
Thomas Tony (D)	5 11	12 05	Liverpool	12 7 71	Trainee
Thorn Andy (D)	6 0	13 02	Carshalton	12 11 66	Hearts

League Appearances: Aldridge, J. 32(11); Bonetti, I. 9(4); Branch, G. 22(13);
Brannan, G. 31(3); Challinor, D. 4(1); Cook, P. 30(6); Coyne, D. 21; Higgins, D.
21(1); Irons, K. 34(7); Jones, G. 13(17); Jones, L. 8; Mahon, A. 14(11); McGreal, J.
24; Moore, I. 14(7); Morgan, A. (1); Morrissey, J. 21(10); Nevin, P. 10(11); Nixon,
E. 25; O'Brien, L. 41; Rogers, A. 28(3); Stevens, G. 31; Teale, S. 25; Thomas, T.
28(2); Thorn, A. 19; Woods, B. 1
League (63): Aldridge 18 (3 pens), Brannan 6, Jones G 6, Branch 5, Irons 5, Jones
L 5, Cook 3, Moore 3, Higgins 2, Mahon 2, Nevin 2, Bonetti 1, Morrissey 1,
O'Brien 1, Thorne 1, own goals 2.

Coca-Cola Cup (5): Aldridge 2 (1 pen), Bonetti 1, Branch 1, Morrissey 1.
FA Cup (0).
Ground: Prenton Park, Prenton Road West, Birkenhead L42 9PN. Telephone (0151) 608 4194.
Record attendance: 24,424 v Stoke C, FA Cup 4th rd, 5 February 1972.
Capacity: 16,789.
Manager: John Aldridge.
Secretary: Mick Horton.
Honours – Football League Division 3 (N) Champions – 1937–38. **Welsh Cup:** Winners 1935. **Leyland Daf Cup:** Winners 1990.
Colours: White shirts, blue shorts.

WALSALL   DIV. 2

Beckford Darren (F)	6 1	11 01	Manchester	12 5 67	Fulham
Blake Mark (M)	5 11	12 06	Nottingham	16 12 70	Leicester C
Butler Martin (F)	5 11	11 09	Dudley	15 9 74	Trainee
Evans Wayne (D)	5 10	12 07	Abermule	25 8 71	Welshpool
Hodge John (F)	5 7	11 03	Ormskirk	1 4 69	Swansea C
Keates Dean (M)	5 5	10 03	Walsall	30 6 78	Trainee
Keister John (M)	5 8	10 09	Manchester	11 11 70	Faweh FC
Lightbourne Kyle (F)	6 2	12 04	Bermuda	29 9 68	Scarborough
Marsh Chris (M)	5 10	13 02	Dudley	14 1 70	Trainee
Ntamark Charlie (M)	5 9	11 09	Paddington	22 7 64	Boreham Wood
Platt Clive (F)			Wolverhampton	27 10 77	Trainee
Ricketts Michael (F)			Birmingham	4 12 78	Trainee
Rogers Darren (D)	5 11	13 02	Birmingham	9 4 70	Birmingham C
Roper Ian (D)	6 3	14 00	Nuneaton	20 6 77	Trainee
Ryder Stuart (D)	6 0	12 08	Sutton Coldfield	6 11 73	Trainee
Smith Mark (G)	6 1	13 09	Birmingham	2 1 73	Crewe Alex
Thomas Wayne (M)	5 8	12 02	Walsall	28 8 78	Trainee
Viveash Adrian (D)	6 3	12 13	Swindon	30 9 69	Swindon T
Walker James (G)	5 11	13 03	Sutton-in-Ashfield	9 7 73	Notts Co
Watson Andy (D)	5 9	11 02	Huddersfield	1 4 67	Blackpool
Wilson Kevin (F)	5 8	11 03	Banbury	18 4 61	Notts Co

League Appearances: Beckford, D. 3(5); Blake, M. 35(3); Bradley, D. 21(5); Butler, M. 20(3); Daniel, R. 8(2); Donowa, L. 6; Evans, W. 27(1); Hodge, J. 32(5); Keates, D. 1(1); Keister, J. 30(6); Lightbourne, K. 45; Marsh, C. 28(2); Mountfield, D. 42; Ntamark, C. 36(2); Platt, C. (1); Ricketts, M. 2(9); Rogers, D. 1(1); Roper, I. 5(6); Ryder, S. (1); Thomas, W. 14(6); Viveash, A. 46; Walker, J. 36; Watson, A. 22(14); Wilson, K. 36(1); Wood, T. 10
League (54): Lightbourne 20, Viveash 9, Wilson 7 (2 pens), Watson 5, Blake 4, Hodge 4, Bradley 2, Butler 1, Donowa 1, Keates 1, Keister 1, Ntamark 1, Ricketts 1.
Coca-Cola Cup (1): Lightbourne 1.
FA Cup (7): Lightbourne 4, Wilson 2 (1 pen), Viveash 1.
Ground: Bescot Stadium, Bescot Cresent, Walsall WS1 4SA. Telephone (01922) 22791.
Record attendance: 10,628 B International, England v Switzerland, 20 May 1991.
Capacity: 9000.
Manager: Jan Sorensen.
Secretary/Commercial Manager: Roy Whalley.
Honours – Football League: Division 4 Champions – 1959–60.
Colours: Red and black chequered shirts, black shorts, white stockings.

Name			Birthplace	Date		From
Andrews Wayne (F)	5 9	11 04	Paddington	25 11 77		Trainee
Bazeley Darren (D)	5 10	11 02	Northampton	5 10 72		Trainee
Chamberlain Alec (G)	6 2	13 09	March	20 6 64		Sunderland
Connolly David (F)	5 8	10 09	Willesden	6 6 77		Trainee
Easton Clint (M)	5 11	10 04	Barking	1 10 77		Trainee
Flash Richard (M)	5 9	11 08	Birmingham	8 4 76		Wolverhampton W
Gibbs Nigel (D)	5 7	11 04	St Albans	20 11 65		Apprentice
Grieves Daniel (M)	5 9	10 07	Watford	21 9 78		Trainee
Johnson Andy (F)	5 9	12 01	Brighton	25 1 79		Trainee
Johnson Chris (M)	5 9	12 03	Brighton	25 1 79		Trainee
Johnson Richard (M)	5 10	11 13	Kurri Kurri	27 4 74		Trainee
Lowndes Nathan (F)	5 11	10 04	Salford	2 6 77		Leeds U
Ludden Dominic (D)	5 7	10 09	Basildon	30 3 74		Leyton Orient
Millen Keith (D)	6 2	12 04	Croydon	26 9 66		Brentford
Miller Kevin (G)	6 1	13 00	Falmouth	15 3 69		Birmingham C
Mooney Tommy (F)	5 11	12 06	Teesside North	11 8 71		Southend U
Noel-Williams Gifton (F)	6 1	14 06	Islington	21 1 80		Trainee
Page Robert (D)	6 0	12 05	Llwynpia	3 9 74		Trainee
Palmer Steve (M)	6 1	12 13	Brighton	31 3 68		Ipswich T
Phillips Kevin (F)	5 7	11 00	Hitchin	25 7 73		Baldock T
Pluck Colin (D)	6 0	12 10	London	6 9 78		Trainee
Ramage Craig (M)	5 9	11 08	Derby	30 3 70		Derby Co
Robinson Paul (D)	5 9	12 11	Watford	14 12 78		Trainee
Rooney Mark (D)	5 10	10 10	Lambeth	19 5 78		Trainee
Slater Stuart (M)	5 8	10 05	Sudbury	27 3 69		Leicester C
Talboys Steve (M)	5 11	11 10	Bristol	18 9 66		Wimbledon
Ward Darran (D)	6 3	12 10	Kenton	13 9 78		Trainee

League Appearances: Andrews, W. 16(9); Armstrong, C. 15; Bazeley, D. 38(3); Chamberlain, A. 4; Connolly, D. 12(1); Easton, C. 17; Flash, R. (1); Gibbs, N. 43(2); Johnson, C. 1; Johnson, R. 35(2); Lowndes, N. (3); Ludden, D. 18(2); Millen, K. 42; Miller, K. 42; Mooney, T. 33(4); Noel-Williams, G. 9(16); Page, R. 35(1); Palmer, S. 40(1); Penrice, G. 22(10); Phillips, K. 13(3); Porter, G. 6; Ramage, C. 10(1); Robinson, P. 8(4); Scott, K. 6; Slater, S. 13(3); Talboys, S. 2(1); Ward, D. 7; White, D. 19(3).

League (45): Mooney 13 (2 pens), Andrews 4, Phillips 4, Bazeley 3, Ramage 3, Connolly 2, Easton 2, Johnson R 2, Millen 2, Noel-Williams 2, Palmer 2, Scott 2, White 2, Easton 1, Gibbs 1, Penrice 1, Slater 1.

Coca-Cola Cup (2): Andrews 1, Porter 1.

FA Cup (9): Connolly 4, Bazeley 3, Noel-Williams 1, White 1.

Ground: Vicarage Road Stadium, Watford WD1 8ER. Telephone (01923) 496000.

Record attendance: 34,099 v Manchester U, FA Cup 4th rd (replay), 3 February 1969. **Capacity:** 22,000.

General Manager: Graham Taylor.

Secretary: John Alexander.

Honours – Football League: Division 3 Division 1 – 1968–69. Division 4 Champions – 1977–78.

Colours: Yellow shirts, red shorts, red stockings.

Name			Birthplace	Date		From
Burgess Daryl (D)	5 11	12 04	Birmingham	20 4 71		Trainee
Butler Peter (M)	5 9	11 02	Halifax	27 8 66		Notts Co

Coldicott Stacy (D)	5 8	11 04	Worcester	29 4 74	Trainee
Crichton Paul (G)	6 1	12 02	Pontefract	3 10 68	Grimsby T
Darby Julian (M)	6 0	11 04	Bolton	3 10 67	Coventry C
Donovan Kevin (F)	5 8	11 02	Halifax	17 12 71	Huddersfield T
Germaine Gary (G)	6 0	13 10	Birmingham	2 8 76	Trainee
Gilbert Dave (M)	5 4	10 08	Lincoln	22 6 63	Grimsby T
Groves Paul (M)	5 11	11 05	Derby	28 2 66	Grimsby T
Hamilton Ian (F)	5 9	11 03	Stevenage	14 12 67	Scunthorpe U
Hanmer Gary (D)			Shrewsbury	12 10 73	Newtown
Holmes Paul (D)	5 10	10 13	Wortley	18 2 68	Everton
Hunt Andy (F)	6 0	11 12	Thurrock	9 6 70	Newcastle U
Mardon Paul (D)	6 0	11 10	Bristol	14 9 69	Birmingham C
McDermott Andrew (D)	5 9	11 03	Sydney	24 3 77	QPR
Miller Alan (G)	6 3	14 08	Epping	29 3 70	Middlesbrough
Murphy Shaun (D)	6 1	12 00	Sydney	5 11 70	Notts Co
Nicholson Shane (D)	5 11	11 00	Newark	3 6 70	Derby Co
Peschisolido Paul (F)	5 7	10 06	Canada	25 5 71	Birmingham C
Potter Graham (M)	6 1	11 12	Solihull	20 5 75	Southampton
Raven Paul (D)	6 1	12 11	Salisbury	28 7 70	Doncaster R
Rodosthenous Michael (F)	5 11	11 02	Islington	25 8 76	Trainee
Smith David (M)	5 8	10 08	Gloucester	29 3 68	Birmingham C
Sneekes Richard (M)	5 11	12 03	Amsterdam	30 10 68	Bolton W
Spink Nigel (G)	6 2	14 06	Chelmsford	8 8 58	Aston Villa
Taylor Bob (F)	5 10	12 02	Horden	3 2 67	Bristol C

League Appearances: Agnew, P. 21(1); Ashcroft, L. 2(3); Bennett, D. (1); Burgess, D. 33; Butler, P. 12(5); Coldicott, S. 13(6); Crichton, P. 30; Cunnington, S. (4); Darby, J. 13(4); Donovan, K. 17(15); Gilbert, D. 11(7); Groves, P. 27(2); Hamilton, I. 39; Holmes, P. 37(1); Hunt, A. 42(3); Joseph, R. (2); Mardon, P. 11(3); McDermott, A. 6; Miller, A. 12; Murphy, S. 16(1); Nicholson, S. 16(2); Peschisolido, P. 30(7); Potter, G. 2(4); Raven, P. 33; Rodosthenous, M. (1); Smith, D. 21(3); Sneekes, R. 42(3); Spink, N. 4; Taylor, B. 16(16).
League (68): Hunt 15 (4 pens), Peschisolido 15, Taylor 10 (1 pen), Sneekes 8, Hamilton 5, Groves 4, Coldicott 3, Murphy 2, Smith 2, Burgess 1, Gilbert 1, Holmes 1, Raven 1.
Coca-Cola Cup (4): Donovan 1, Groves 1, Hamilton 1, Hunt 1.
FA Cup (0).
Ground: The Hawthorns, West Bromwich B71 4LF. Telephone (0121) 525 8888.
Record attendance: 64,815 v Arsenal, FA Cup 6th rd, 6 March 1937. **Capacity:** 25,296.
Manager: Ray Harford.
Secretary: Dr. John J. Evans BA, PHD. (Wales).
Honours – Football League: Division 1 Champions – 1919–20. Division 2 Champions – 1901–02, 1910–11. **FA Cup:** Winners 1888, 1892, 1931, 1954, 1968. **Football League Cup:** Winners 1965–66.
Colours: Navy blue and white striped shirts, white shorts, blue and white stockings.

WEST HAM UNITED   FA PREMIERSHIP

Bishop Ian (M)	5 9	10 12	Liverpool	29 5 65	Manchester C
Boogers Marco (M)	6 1	12 00	Dordrecht	12 1 67	Sparta
Breacker Tim (D)	5 11	13 00	Bicester	2 7 65	Luton T
Coyne Christopher (D)	6 1	13 10	Brisbane	20 12 78	Perth SC
Dicks Julian (D)	5 10	13 00	Bristol	8 8 68	Liverpool
Dowie Iain (F)	6 1	13 07	Hatfield	9 1 65	Crystal Palace
Ferdinand Rio (D)	6 2	12 00	Peckham	7 11 78	Trainee

Hall Richard (D)	6 2	13 11	Ipswich	14	3 72	Southampton
Hartson John (F)	6 1	14 06	Swansea	5	4 75	Arsenal
Hodges Lee (F)	5 5	10 02	Newham	2	3 78	Trainee
Hughes Michael (F)	5 6	10 08	Larne	2	8 71	Strasbourg
Kitson Paul (F)	5 11	10 12	Murton	9	1 71	Newcastle U
Lampard Frank (M)	6 0	11 12	Romford	20	6 78	Trainee
Lazaridis Stan (M)	5 9	12 00	Perth	16	8 72	West Adelaide
Lomas Steve (M)	6 0	11 09	Hanover	18	1 74	Manchester C
Mean Scott (M)	5 11	13 08	Crawley	13	12 73	Bournemouth
Miklosko Ludek (G)	6 5	14 00	Protesov	9	12 61	Banik Ostrava
Moncur John (M)	5 7	9 10	Stepney	22	9 66	Swindon T
Moore Jason (D)	5 8	11 04	Dover	16	2 79	Trainee
Omoyimni Emmanuel (M)	5 6	10 07	Nigeria	28	12 77	Trainee
Philson Graeme (D)	5 10	11 00	Ireland	24	3 75	Coleraine
Potts Steve (D)	5 7	10 11	Hartford (USA)	7	5 67	Apprentice
Rieper Marc (D)	6 3	13 10	Denmark	5	6 68	Brondby
Rowland Keith (M)	5 10	10 00	Portadown	1	9 71	Bournemouth
Sealey Les (G)	6 1	13 06	Bethnal Green	29	9 57	Leyton Orient
Williamson Danny (M)	5 10	11 06	West Ham	5	12 73	Trainee

League Appearances: Bilic, S. 35; Bishop, I. 26(3); Bowen, M. 15(2); Boylan, L. (1); Breacker, T. 22(4); Cottee, T. 2(1); Dicks, J. 31; Dowie, I. 18(5); Dumitrescu, I. 3(4); Ferdinand, R. 11(4); Futre, P. 4(5); Hall, R. 7; Hartson, J. 11; Hughes, M. 31(2); Jones, S. 5(3); Kitson, P. 14; Lampard, F. 3(10); Lazaridis, S. 13(9); Lomas, S. 7; Mautone, S. 1; Miklosko, L. 36; Moncur, J. 26(1); Newell, M. 6(1); Omoyimni, E. (1); Porfirio, H. 15(8); Potts, S. 17(3); Raducioiu, F. 6(5); Rieper, M. 26(2); Rowland, K. 11(4); Sealey, L. 1(1); Slater, R. 2(1); Williamson, D. 13(2)
League (39): Kitson 8, Dicks 6 (5 pens), Hartson 5, Hughes 3, Bilic 2, Ferdinand 2, Moncur 2, Porfirio 2, Raducioiu 2, Bishop 1, Bowen 1, Lazaridis 1, Rieper 1, Rowland 1, own goals 1.
Coca-Cola Cup (8): Dicks 2 (1 pen), Dowie 2, Bilic 1, Cottee 1, Porfirio 1, Raducioiu 1.
FA Cup (1): Porfirio 1.
Ground: Boleyn Ground, Green Street, Upton Park, London E13 9AZ. Telephone (0181) 548 2748.
Record attendance: 42,322 v Tottenham H, Division 1, 17 October 1970. **Capacity:** 25,985.
Manager: Harry Redknapp.
Secretary: Neil Harrison.
Honours – Football League: Division 2 Champions – 1957–58, 1980–81. **FA Cup:** Winners 1964, 1975, 1980. **European Competitions:** European Cup-Winners' Cup winners: 1964–65.
Colours: Claret shirts, white shorts, light blue and claret stockings.

WIGAN ATHLETIC   DIV. 2

Bishop Charlie (D)	5 9	13 07	Nottingham	16	2 68	Barnsley
Black Tony (F)	5 8	11 01	Barrow	15	7 69	Bamber Bridge
Butler Lee (G)	6 1	14 04	Sheffield	30	5 66	Barnsley
Carroll Roy (G)	6 2	11 09	Belfast	30	9 77	Hull C
Diaz Isidro (M)	5 7	9 04	Valencia	15	5 72	Balaguer
Farnworth Simon (G)	5 11	13 04	Chorley	28	10 63	Preston NE
Greenall Colin (D)	5 11	12 12	Billinge	30	12 63	Lincoln C
Johnson Gavin (D)	5 11	11 07	Eye	10	10 70	Luton T
Jones Graeme (F)	6 0	12 12	Gateshead	13	3 70	Doncaster R
Kilford Ian (M)	5 10	11 00	Bristol	6	10 73	Nottingham F

Lancashire Graham (F)	5 10	11 12	Blackpool	19 10 72	Preston NE
Lowe David (F)	5 10	11 04	Liverpool	30 8 65	Leicester C
Martinez Roberto (M)	5 11	11 12	Balaguer	13 7 73	Balaguer
Morgan Steve (D)	6 0	11 00	Oldham	19 9 68	Coventry C
Pender John (D)	6 0	13 09	Luton	19 11 63	Burnley
Rogers Paul (M)	6 0	11 13	Portsmouth	21 3 65	Notts Co
Saville Andy (F)	6 1	12 11	Hull	12 12 64	Preston NE
Sharp Kevin (M)	5 9	10 07	Ontario	19 9 74	Leeds U

League Appearances: Biggins, W. 20(13); Bishop, C. 20(1); Butler, J. 20(4); Butler, L. 46; Carragher, M. 12(6); Diaz, J. 26(13); Greenall, C. 46; Johnson, G. 37; Jones, G. 39(1); Kilford, I. 24(11); Kirby, R. 5(1); Lancashire, G. 15(9); Love, M. (3); Lowe, D. 31(11); Martinez, R. 38(5); McGibbon, P. 10; Morgan, S. 18(5); Pender, J. 27(2); Rogers, P. 18(2); Saville, A. 17(3); Seba, J. (1); Sharp, K. 30(5); Ward, M. 5; Whittaker, S. 2(1)
League (84): Jones 31 (3 pens), Lancashire 9, Kilford 8, Diaz 6, Lowe 6, Martinez 4, Saville 4, Biggins 3, Johnson 3, Rogers 3, Greenall 2, Sharp 2, McGibbon 1, Morgan 1, own goal 1.
Coca-Cola Cup (6): Lancashire 4, Greenall 1, Jones 1.
FA Cup (0).
Ground: Springfield Park, Wigan WN6 7BA. Telephone (01942) 244433.
Record attendance: 27,500 v Hereford U, FA Cup 2nd rd, 12 December 1953.
Capacity: 7466
Manager: John Deehan.
Secretary: Mrs Brenda Spencer.
Honours – Football League: Division 3 Champions – 1996–97. **Freight Rover Trophy:** Winners 1984–85.
Colours: Blue and green striped shirts, blue shorts, blue and white stockings.

WIMBLEDON   FA PREMIERSHIP

Ardley Neal (M)	5 11	11 09	Epsom	1 9 72	Trainee
Blackwell Dean (D)	6 1	12 10	Camden	5 12 69	Trainee
Castledine Stewart (M)	6 1	12 13	Wandsworth	22 1 73	Trainee
Clarke Andy (F)	5 10	11 07	Islington	22 7 67	Barnet
Cort Carl (F)	6 4	12 07	Southwark	1 11 77	Trainee
Cunningham Kenny (D)	5 11	11 02	Dublin	28 6 71	Millwall
Earle Robbie (F)	5 9	10 10	Newcastle under Lyme	27 1 65	Port Vale
Ekoku Efan (F)	6 1	12 00	Manchester	8 6 67	Norwich C
Euell Jason (F)	5 11	11 02	South London	6 2 77	Trainee
Fear Peter (D)	5 10	11 07	London	10 9 73	Trainee
Fitzgerald Scott (D)	6 0	12 02	London	13 8 69	Trainee
Francis Damien (M)	6 1	10 07	London	27 2 79	Trainee
Futcher Andy (D)	5 7	10 07	Enfield	10 2 78	Trainee
Gardner James (D)	5 11	10 06	Beckenham	26 10 78	Trainee
Gayle Marcus (M)	6 1	12 09	Hammersmith	27 9 70	Brentford
Goodman Jon (F)	6 0	12 03	Walthamstow	2 6 71	Millwall
Harford Mick (F)	6 3	14 05	Sunderland	12 2 59	Coventry C
Hawkins Peter (D)	6 0	11 04	Maidstone	18 9 78	Trainee
Heald Paul (G)	6 2	13 03	Wath-on-Dearne	20 9 68	Leyton Orient
Hinds Leigh (F)	5 8	10 07	Beckenham	17 8 78	Trainee
Hodges Danny (D)	6 0	12 07	Greenwich	14 9 76	Trainee
Holdsworth Dean (F)	5 11	11 13	Walthamstow	8 11 68	Brentford
Jennings Patrick (G)	5 9	11 00	Herts	24 9 79	
Jones Vinnie (M)	6 0	11 12	Watford	5 1 65	Chelsea
Jupp Duncan (D)	6 0	12 11	Guildford	25 1 75	Fulham

Kimble Alan (D)	5 10	12 04	Poole	6	8 66	Cambridge U
Leonhardsen Oyvind (M)	5 10	11 02	Norway	17	8 70	Rosenborg
McAllister Brian (D)	5 11	12 05	Glasgow	30	11 70	Trainee
Murphy Brendan (G)	5 11	11 12	Wexford	19	8 75	Bradford C
O'Connor Richard (F)	5 9	10 07	Wandsworth	30	8 78	Trainee
Odlum Gary (D)	5 11	11 04	Beckenham	19	10 78	Trainee
Pearce Andy (D)	6 4	14 11	Bradford-on-Avon	20	4 66	Sheffield W
Perry Chris (D)	5 8	10 08	London	26	4 73	Trainee
Reeves Alan (D)	6 0	12 00	Birkenhead	19	11 67	Rochdale
Renner Victor (F)	6 0	11 02	Sierra Leone	18	4 79	Trainee
Reynolds Paul (D)	6 1	11 04	Widnes	13	9 78	Trainee
Sullivan Neil (G)	6 0	12 01	Sutton	24	2 70	Trainee
Thatcher Ben (D)	5 11	12 07	Swindon	30	11 75	Millwall

League Appearances: Ardley, N. 33(1); Blackwell, D. 22(5); Castledine, S. 4(2); Clarke, A. 4(7); Cort, C. (1); Cunningham, K. 36; Earle, R. 32; Ekoku, E. 28(2); Euell, J. 4(3); Fear, P. 9(9); Gayle, M. 34(2); Goodman, J. 6(7); Harford, M. 3(10); Heald, P. 2; Holdsworth, D. 10(15); Jones, V. 29; Jupp, D. 6; Kimble, A. 28(3); Leonhardsen, O. 27; McAllister, B. 19(4); Perry, C. 37; Reeves, A. (2); Sullivan, N. 36; Thatcher, B. 9

League (49): Ekoku 11, Gayle 8, Earle 7, Holdsworth 5, Leonhardsen 5, Jones 3, Ardley 2, Euell 2, Castledine 1, Clarke 1, Goodman 1, Harford 1, Perry 1, own goal 1.

Coca-Cola Cup (9): Gayle 3, Holdsworth 2, Castledine 1, Ekoku 1, Fear 1, Leonhardsen 1.

FA Cup (9): Earle 4, Gayle 2, Holdsworth 2, Perry 1.

Ground: Selhurst Park, South Norwood, London SE25 6PY. Telephone (0181) 771 2233.

Record attendance: 30,115 v Manchester U, FA Premier League, 9 May 1993.

Capacity: 26,309.

Manager: Joe Kinnear.

Secretary: Steve Rooke.

Honours – Football League: Division 4 Champions – 1982–83. **FA Cup:** Winners 1987–88.

Colours: All navy blue with yellow trim.

WOLVERHAMPTON WANDERERS   DIV. 1

Atkins Mark (M)	6 0	13 01	Doncaster	14	8 68	Blackburn R
Bull Steve (F)	6 0	12 10	Tipton	28	3 65	WBA
Corica Steve (M)	5 8	10 10	Cairns	24	3 73	Leicester C
Crowe Glen (F)	5 10	12 13	Dublin	25	12 77	Trainee
Curle Keith (D)	6 1	12 12	Bristol	14	11 63	Manchester C
Daley Tony (M)	5 9	11 00	Birmingham	18	11 67	Aston Villa
Dixon Alan (M)			Dublin	9	10 79	Trainee
Emblen Neil (M)	6 0	13 03	Bromley	19	6 71	Millwall
Ferguson Darren (M)	5 8	12 02	Glasgow	9	2 72	Manchester U
Foley Dominic (F)	6 1	12 08	Cork	7	7 76	St James Gate
Froggatt Steve (M)	5 10	11 00	Lincoln	9	3 73	Aston Villa
Gilkes Michael (M)	5 8	11 02	Hackney	20	7 65	Reading
Goodman Don (F)	5 10	13 03	Leeds	9	5 66	Sunderland
Jones Mark (M)			Walsall	7	9 79	Trainee
Leadbeater Richard (F)	6 0	11 05	Dudley	21	10 77	Trainee
Osborn Simon (M)	5 8	11 03	New Addington	19	1 72	QPR
Richards Dean (D)	6 2	13 08	Bradford	9	6 74	Bradford C
Roberts Iwan (F)	6 3	14 04	Bangor	26	6 68	Leicester C

Robinson Carl (M)	5 10	11 11	Llandrindod Wells	13 10 76	Trainee
Smith James (D)	5 8	10 01	Birmingham	9 9 74	Trainee
Stowell Mike (G)	6 3	13 10	Portsmouth	19 4 65	Everton
Venus Mark (D)	6 0	12 09	Hartlepool	6 4 67	Leicester C
Westwood Chris (D)	6 0	12 02	Dudley	13 2 77	Trainee
Williams Adrian (D)	6 1	13 03	Reading	16 8 71	Reading
Wright Jermaine (M)	5 10	11 09	Greenwich	21 10 75	Millwall

League Appearances: Atkins, M. 44(1); Bull, S. 43; Corica, S. 33(3); Crowe, G. 5(1); Curle, K. 20(1); Dennison, R. 9(5); Dowe, J. 5(3); Emblen, N. 27(1); Ferguson, D. 10(6); Foley, D. (5); Froggatt, S. 27; Gilkes, M. 5; Goodman, D. 19(8); Law, B. 4(3); Leadbeater, R. (1); Osborn, S. 33(2); Pearce, D. 4; Richards, D. 19(2); Roberts, I. 24(9); Robinson, C. 1(1); Romano, S. 1(3); Smith, J. 36(2); Stowell, M. 46; Thomas, G. 15(7); Thompson, A. 26(6); Van der Laan, R. 7; Venus, M. 36(4); Williams, A. 6; Wright, J. (3); Young, E. 1
League (68): Bull 23, Roberts 12, Goodman 6, Osborn 5 (1 pen), Atkins 4, Ferguson 3, Thomas 3, Corica 2, Curle 2 (2 pens), Froggatt 2, Thompson 2 (2 pens), Dennison 1, Foley 1, Gilkes 1, Richards 1.
Coca-Cola Cup (1): Osborn 1.
FA Cup (1): Ferguson 1.
Ground: Molineux Grounds, Wolverhampton WV1 4QR. Telephone (01902) 655000.
Record attendance: 61,315 v Liverpool, FA Cup 5th rd, 11 February 1939.
Capacity: 28,525.
Team Manager: Mark McGhee.
Secretary: Richard Skirrow.
Honours – Football League: Division 1 Champions – 1953–54, 1957–58, 1958–59. Division 2 Champions – 1931–32, 1976–77. Division 3 (N) Champions – 1923–24. Division 3 Champions – 1988–89. Division 4 Champions – 1987–88. **FA Cup:** Winners 1893, 1908, 1949, 1960. **Football League Cup:** Winners 1973–74, 1979–80. **Sherpa Van Trophy winners** 1988.
Colours: Gold shirts, black shorts, gold stockings.

WREXHAM   DIV. 2

Bennett Gary (F)	5 11	12 00	Kirby	20 9 63	Preston NE
Brace Deryn (D)	5 7	10 12	Haverfordwest	15 3 75	Norwich C
Brammer David (M)	5 10	11 00	Bromborough	28 2 75	Trainee
Carey Brian (D)	6 3	13 12	Cork	31 5 68	Leicester C
Cartwright Mark (G)	6 2	13 06	Chester	13 1 73	York C
Chalk Martyn (F)	5 6	10 00	Swindon	30 8 69	Stockport Co
Connolly Karl (F)	5 9	11 00	Prescot	9 2 70	Napoli (Liverpool)
Cross Jonathan (M)	5 10	11 07	Wallasey	2 3 75	Trainee
Hardy Phil (D)	5 7	11 08	Chester	9 4 73	Trainee
Humes Tony (D)	6 0	12 00	Blyth	19 3 66	Ipswich T
Jones Barry (D)	5 11	11 12	Prescot	20 6 70	Liverpool
Marriott Andy (G)	6 1	12 08	Nottingham	11 10 70	Nottingham F
McGregor Mark (D)	5 11	11 05	Chester	16 2 77	Trainee
Morris Steve (F)	5 10	12 00	Liverpool	13 5 76	Liverpool
Owen Gareth (M)	5 7	12 00	Chester	21 10 71	Trainee
Phillips Wayne (M)	5 10	11 02	Bangor	15 12 70	Trainee
Ridler Dave (D)	6 1	12 02	Liverpool	12 3 76	Prescot T
Roberts Neil (F)	5 10	11 01	Wrexham	7 4 78	Trainee
Roberts Paul (F)	5 11	11 09	Bangor	29 7 77	Porthmadog
Russell Kevin (F)	5 9	10 12	Portsmouth	6 12 66	Notts Co
Skinner Craig (F)	5 10	11 00	Bury	21 10 70	Plymouth Arg

Wainwright Neil (F)	6 0	11 05	Warrington	4 11 77	Trainee
Ward Peter (F)	5 10	11 07	Durham	15 10 64	Stockport Co
Watkin Steve (F)	5 10	11 10	Wrexham	16 6 71	School
Williams Scott (D)	6 0	12 00	Bangor	7 8 74	Trainee

League Appearances: Bennett, G. 15; Brace, D. 26; Brammer, D. 17(4); Carey, B. 38; Cartwright, M. 3; Chalk, M. 34(9); Connolly, K. 27(3); Cross, J. 11(7); Hardy, P. 13; Hughes, B. 20(3); Humes, T. 34; Jones, B. 14(8); Jones, L. 2(4); Jones, P. 6; Marriott, A. 43; McGregor, M. 37(1); Morris, S. 10(7); Owen, G. 12(11); Phillips, W. 26; Ridler, D. 7(4); Roberts, P. (1); Russell, K. 37(4); Skinner, C. 21(6); Soloman, J. 2; Ward, P. 24; Watkin, S. 24(2); Williams, S. 3(1)
League (54): Connolly 14 (2 pens), Watkin 7 (1 pen), Bennett 5 (2 pens), Phillips 5, Humes 4, Morris 4, Skinner 4, Hughes 3, Cross 2, Brace 1, Brammer 1, Chalk 1 (pen), McGregor 1, Owen 1, Ward 1.
Coca-Cola Cup (1): Skinner 1.
FA Cup (17): Hughes 6, Russell 3, Watkin 3 (1 pen), Morris 2, Connolly 1, Humes 1, Ward 1.
Ground: Racecourse Ground, Mold Road, Wrexham LL11 2AH. Telephone (01978) 262129.
Record attendance: 34,445 v Manchester U, FA Cup 4th rd, 26 January 1957.
Capacity: 9200.
Manager: Brian Flynn.
Secretary: D. L. Rhodes.
Honours – Football League: Division 3 Champions – 1977–78. **Welsh Cup:** Winners 22 times.
Colours: Red shirts, white shorts, white stockings.

WYCOMBE WANDERERS   DIV. 2

Bell Mickey (D)	5 9	11 08	Newcastle	15 11 71	Northampton T
Brown Steve (D)	5 11	11 08	Northampton	6 7 66	Northampton T
Carroll Dave (F)	6 0	11 08	Paisley	20 9 66	Ruislip Manor
Cornforth John (M)	6 1	12 08	Whitley Bay	7 10 67	Birmingham C
Cousins Jason (D)	5 10	12 06	Hayes	14 10 70	Brentford
Forsyth Mike (D)	5 11	12 06	Liverpool	20 3 66	Notts Co
Harkin Maurice (F)			Derry	16 8 79	Trainee
Kavanagh Jason (D)	5 9	12 07	Birmingham	23 11 71	Derby Co
McCarthy Paul (D)	5 10	13 05	Cork	4 8 71	Brighton & HA
McGavin Steve (F)	5 8	12 03	North Walsham	24 1 69	Birmingham C
Parkin Brian (G)	6 4	14 07	Birkenhead	12 10 65	Bristol R
Read Paul (F)	5 11	12 06	Harlow	25 9 73	Arsenal
Ryan Keith (M)	5 11	12 07	Northampton	25 6 70	Berkhamsted T
Simpson Michael (M)	5 9	10 08	Derby	28 2 74	Notts Co
Stallard Mark (F)	5 11	12 12	Derby	24 10 74	Bradford C

League Appearances: Bell, M. 46; Brown, S. 28(6); Carroll, D. 42(1); Cheesewright, J. 18; Cornforth, J. 8(2); Cousins, J. 36(1); Crossley, M. 7(2); Davis, N. 13; De Souza, M. 29(4); Evans, T. 38(4); Farrell, D. 17(10); Forsyth, M. 22(1); Harkin, M. (4); Kavanagh, J. 27; Lawrence, M. 12(1); Mahoney-Johnson, M. 2(2); Markman, D. (2); McCarthy, P. 36(4); McGavin, S. 33(2); Parkin, B. 24; Patterson, G. 6(3); Read, P. 7(6); Scott, K. 9; Simpson, M. 16(4); Skiverton, T. 2(4); Stallard, M. 12; Taylor, M. 4; Wilkins, R. 1; Williams, J. 11(8)
League (51): Carroll 9 (4 pens), McGavin 9, Brown 5, De Souza 5, Read 4, Stallard 4, Scott 3, Bell 2, Evans 2, Forsyth 2, Mahoney-Johnson 2, Farrell 1, Lawrence 1, Simpson 1, Williams 1.
Coca-Cola Cup (4): Williams 2, Evans 1, McCarthy 1.

FA Cup (8): Williams 4, De Souza 2, Carroll 1, McGavin 1.
Ground: Adams Park, Hillbottom Road, Sands, High Wycombe HP12 4HJ.
Telephone (01494) 472100.
Record attendance: 9002 v West Ham U, FA Cup 3rd rd, 7 January 1995. **Capacity:**
10,000.
Manager: John Gregory
Secretary: John Reardon.
Honours – GM Vauxhall Conference winners: 1993. **FA Trophy winners:** 1991,
1993.
Colours: Light & dark blue striped shirts, light blue shorts, light blue stockings.

YORK CITY   DIV. 2

Atkinson Paddy (D)	5 9	11 06	Singapore	22 5 70	Workington
Barras Tony (D)	6 0	13 00	Stockton	29 3 71	Stockport Co
Bull Gary (F)	5 10	12 02	West Bromwich	12 6 66	Nottingham F
Bushell Steve (M)	5 9	11 05	Manchester	28 12 72	Trainee
Campbell Neil (F)	5 10	13 00	Middlesbrough	26 1 77	Trainee
Cresswell Richard (F)	5 11	11 07	Bridlington	20 9 77	Trainee
Greening Jonathan (F)	5 11	11 07	Scarborough	2 1 79	Trainee
Hall Wayne (D)	5 9	10 06	Rotherham	25 10 68	Darlington
Himsworth Gary (F)	5 7	9 10	Appleton	19 12 69	Darlington
Jordan Scott (M)	5 9	11 05	Newcastle	19 7 75	Trainee
McMillan Andy (D)	5 11	11 02	Bloemfontein	22 6 68	
Murty Graeme (M)	5 10	11 12	Middlesbrough	13 11 74	Trainee
Pouton Alan (M)	6 0	12 02	Newcastle	1 2 77	Oxford U
Reed Martin (F)	6 1	11 07	Scarborough	10 1 78	Trainee
Rowe Rodney (M)	5 8	12 00	Huddersfield	30 7 75	Huddersfield T
Rush David (F)	5 8	11 04	Sunderland	15 1 71	Oxford U
Sharples John (D)	6 0	11 03	Bury	26 1 73	Ayr U
Stephenson Paul (F)	5 9	12 05	Wallsend	2 1 68	Brentford
Tinkler Mark (M)	5 11	12 03	Bishop Auckland	24 10 74	Leeds U
Tolson Neil (F)	6 3	11 05	Wordley	25 10 73	Bradford C
Tutill Steve (D)	5 11	12 01	Derwent	1 10 69	Trainee
Warrington Andy (G)	6 3	12 11	Sheffield	10 6 76	Trainee

League Appearances: Atkin, P. 6(6); Atkinson, P. 13(1); Barras, T. 46; Bull, G.
33(8); Bushell, S. 26(5); Campbell, N. 5(6); Clarke, T. 17; Cresswell, R. 9(8);
Gilbert, D. 9; Greening, J. (5); Hall, W. 12(1); Harrison, T. (1); Himsworth, G.
32(1); Jordan, S. 7(3); McMillan, A. 46; Murty, G. 25(2); Naylor, G. (1); Pepper, N.
26(3); Pouton, A. 18(4); Prudhoe, M. 2; Randall, A. 13(3); Reed, M. 2; Rowe, R.
9(1); Rush, D. 1(1); Sharples, J. 28; Stephenson, P. 33(2); Tinkler, M. 9; Tolson, N.
39(1); Tutill, S. 13(2); Warrington, A. 27; Williams, D. (1)
League (47): Pepper 12 (7 pens), Tolson 12, Bushell 3, Rowe 3, Bull 2, Himsworth
2, Murty 2, Randall 2, Barras 1, Campbell 1, Gilbert 1, Jordan 1, Pouton 1,
Sharples 1, Stephenson 1, Tinkler 1, own goal 1.
Coca-Cola Cup (7): Tolson 3, Bull 1, Bushell 1, Murty 1, Pepper 1.
FA Cup (6): Tolson 2, Barras 1, Himsworth 1, Pepper 1, own goal 1.
Ground: Bootham Crescent, York YO3 7AQ. Telephone (01904) 624447.
Record attendance: 28,123 v Huddersfield T, FA Cup 6th rd, 5 March 1938.
Capacity: 9534.
Manager: Alan Little.
Secretary: Keith Usher.
Honours – Football League: Division 4 Champions – 1983–84.
Colours: Red shirts, blue shorts, red stockings.

LEAGUE POSITIONS: FA PREMIER from 1992–93 and DIVISION 1 1971–72 to 1991–92

	1995-96	1994-95	1993-94	1992-93	1991-92	1990-91	1989-90	1988-89	1987-88	1986-87	1985-86	1984-85	1983-84
Arsenal	5	12	4	10	4	1	4	1	6	4	7	7	6
Aston Villa	4	18	10	2	7	17	2	17	–	22	16	10	10
Birmingham C	–	–	–	–	–	–	–	–	–	–	–	–	20
Blackburn R	7	1	2	4	–	–	–	–	–	–	–	–	–
Blackpool	–	–	–	–	–	–	–	–	–	–	–	–	–
Bolton W	20	–	–	–	–	–	–	–	–	–	–	–	–
Brighton & HA	–	–	–	–	–	–	–	–	–	–	–	–	–
Bristol C	–	–	–	–	–	–	–	–	–	–	–	–	–
Burnley	–	–	–	–	–	–	–	–	–	–	–	–	–
Carlisle U	–	–	–	–	–	–	–	–	–	–	–	–	–
Charlton Ath	–	–	–	–	–	–	19	14	17	19	–	–	–
Chelsea	11	11	14	11	14	11	5	–	18	–	6	6	–
Coventry C	16	16	11	15	19	16	12	7	10	10	17	18	19
Crystal Palace	–	19	–	20	10	3	15	–	–	–	–	–	–
Derby Co	–	–	–	–	–	20	16	5	15	–	–	–	–
Everton	6	15	17	13	12	9	6	8	4	1	2	1	7
Huddersfield T	–	–	–	–	–	–	–	–	–	–	–	–	–
Ipswich T	–	22	19	16	–	–	–	–	–	–	20	17	12
Leeds U	13	5	5	17	1	4	–	–	–	–	–	–	–
Leicester C	–	21	–	–	–	–	–	–	–	20	19	15	15
Liverpool	3	4	8	6	6	2	1	2	1	2	1	2	1
Luton T	–	–	–	–	20	18	17	16	9	7	9	13	16
Manchester C	18	17	16	9	5	5	14	–	2	–	21	15	–
Manchester U	1	2	1	1	2	6	13	11	2	11	4	4	4
Middlesbrough	12	–	–	21	–	–	–	18	–	–	–	–	–
Millwall	–	–	–	–	–	20	10	–	–	–	–	–	–
Newcastle U	2	6	3	–	–	–	–	20	8	17	11	14	–
Norwich C	–	20	12	3	18	15	10	4	14	5	–	20	14
Nottingham F	9	3	–	22	8	8	9	3	3	8	8	9	3
Notts Co	–	–	–	–	21	–	–	–	–	–	–	–	21
Oldham Ath	–	–	21	19	17	–	–	–	–	–	–	–	–
Oxford U	–	–	–	–	–	–	–	–	21	18	18	–	–
Portsmouth	–	–	–	–	–	–	–	19	–	–	–	–	–
QPR	19	8	9	5	11	12	11	9	5	16	13	19	5
Sheffield U	–	–	20	14	9	13	–	–	–	–	–	–	–
Sheffield W	15	13	7	7	3	–	18	15	11	13	5	8	–
Southampton	17	10	18	18	16	14	7	13	12	12	14	5	2
Stoke C	–	–	–	–	–	–	–	–	–	–	–	–	–
Sunderland	–	–	–	–	–	19	–	–	–	–	–	21	13
Swansea C	–	–	–	–	–	–	–	–	–	–	–	–	–
Swindon T	–	–	22	–	–	–	–	–	–	–	–	–	–
Tottenham H	8	7	15	8	15	10	3	6	13	3	10	3	8
Watford	–	–	–	–	–	–	20	9	12	11	11	12	11
WBA	–	–	–	–	–	–	–	–	–	22	12	17	–
West Ham U	10	14	13	–	22	–	–	19	16	15	3	16	9
Wimbledon	14	9	6	12	13	7	8	12	7	6	–	–	–
Wolv'hampton W	–	–	–	–	–	–	–	–	–	–	–	–	22

1982-83	1981-82	1980-81	1979-80	1978-79	1977-78	1976-77	1975-76	1974-75	1973-74	1972-73	1971-72	
10	5	3	4	7	5	8	17	16	10	2	5	Arsenal
6	11	1	7	8	8	4	16	-	-	-	-	Aston Villa
17	16	13	-	21	11	13	19	17	19	10	-	Birmingham C
-	-	-	-	-	-	-	-	-	-	-	-	Blackburn R
-	-	-	-	-	-	-	-	-	-	-	22	Blackpool
-	-	-	22	17	-	-	-	-	-	-	-	Bolton W
22	13	19	16	-	-	-	-	-	-	-	-	Brighton & HA
-	-	-	20	13	17	18	-	-	-	-	-	Bristol C
-	-	-	-	-	-	-	21	10	6	-	-	Burnley
-	-	-	-	-	-	-	-	22	-	-	-	Carlisle U
-	-	-	-	-	-	-	-	-	-	-	-	Charlton Ath
-	-	-	-	-	-	-	-	21	17	12	7	Chelsea
19	14	16	15	10	7	19	14	14	16	19	18	Coventry C
-	-	22	13	-	-	-	-	-	-	21	20	Crystal Palace
-	-	-	21	19	12	15	4	1	3	7	1	Derby Co
7	8	15	19	4	3	9	11	4	7	17	15	Everton
-	-	-	-	-	-	-	-	-	-	-	22	Huddersfield T
9	2	2	3	6	18	3	6	3	4	4	13	Ipswich T
-	20	9	11	5	9	10	5	9	1	3	2	Leeds U
-	-	21	-	-	22	11	7	18	9	16	12	Leicester C
1	1	5	1	1	2	1	1	2	2	1	3	Liverpool
18	-	-	-	-	-	-	-	20	-	-	-	Luton T
20	10	12	17	15	4	2	8	8	14	11	4	Manchester C
3	3	8	2	9	10	6	3	-	21	18	8	Manchester U
-	22	14	9	12	14	12	13	7	-	-	-	Middlesbrough
-	-	-	-	-	-	-	-	-	-	-	-	Millwall
-	-	-	-	21	5	15	15	15	9	11	-	Newcastle U
14	-	20	12	16	13	16	10	-	22	20	-	Norwich C
5	12	7	5	2	1	-	-	-	-	-	21	Nottingham F
15	15	-	-	-	-	-	-	-	-	-	-	Notts Co
-	-	-	-	-	-	-	-	-	-	-	-	Oldham Ath
-	-	-	-	-	-	-	-	-	-	-	-	Oxford U
-	-	-	-	-	-	-	-	-	-	-	-	Portsmouth
-	-	-	-	20	19	14	2	11	8	-	-	QPR
-	-	-	-	-	-	22	6	13	14	10	-	Sheffield U
-	-	-	-	-	-	-	-	-	-	-	-	Sheffield W
12	7	6	8	14	-	-	-	20	13	19	-	Southampton
13	18	11	18	-	-	21	12	5	5	15	17	Stoke C
16	19	17	-	-	-	20	-	-	-	-	-	Sunderland
21	6	-	-	-	-	-	-	-	-	-	-	Swansea C
-	-	-	-	-	-	-	-	-	-	-	-	Swindon T
4	4	10	14	11	-	22	9	19	11	8	6	Tottenham H
2	-	-	-	-	-	-	-	-	-	-	-	Watford
11	17	4	10	3	6	7	-	-	-	22	16	WBA
8	9	-	-	-	20	17	18	13	18	6	14	West Ham U
-	-	-	-	-	-	-	-	-	-	-	-	Wimbledon
-	21	18	6	18	15	-	20	12	12	5	9	Wolv'hampton W

LEAGUE POSITIONS: DIVISION 1 from 1992–93 and DIVISION 2 1971–72 to 1991–92

	1995-96	1994-95	1993-94	1992-93	1991-92	1990-91	1989-90	1988-89	1987-88	1986-87	1985-86	1984-85	1983-84
Aston Villa	–	–	–	–	–	–	–	–	2	–	–	–	–
Barnsley	10	6	18	13	16	8	19	7	14	11	12	11	14
Birmingham C	15	–	22	19	–	–	–	23	19	19	–	2	–
Blackburn R	–	–	–	–	6	19	5	5	5	12	19	5	6
Blackpool	–	–	–	–	–	–	–	–	–	–	–	–	–
Bolton W	–	3	14	–	–	–	–	–	–	–	–	–	–
Bournemouth	–	–	–	–	–	–	22	12	17	–	–	–	–
Bradford C	–	–	–	–	–	–	23	14	4	10	13	–	–
Brentford	–	–	–	22	–	–	–	–	–	–	–	–	–
Brighton & HA	–	–	–	–	23	6	18	19	–	22	11	6	9
Bristol C	–	23	13	15	17	9	–	–	–	–	–	–	–
Bristol R	–	–	–	24	13	13	–	–	–	–	–	–	–
Burnley	–	22	–	–	–	–	–	–	–	–	–	–	–
Bury	–	–	–	–	–	–	–	–	–	–	–	–	–
Cambridge U	–	–	–	23	5	–	–	–	–	–	–	–	22
Cardiff C	–	–	–	–	–	–	–	–	–	–	–	21	15
Carlisle U	–	–	–	–	–	–	–	–	–	–	20	16	7
Charlton Ath	6	15	11	12	7	16	–	–	–	–	2	17	13
Chelsea	–	–	–	–	–	–	–	1	–	–	–	–	–
Crystal Palace	3	–	1	–	–	–	3	6	6	5	–	15	18
Derby Co	2	9	6	8	3	–	–	–	–	1	–	20	–
Fulham	–	–	–	–	–	–	–	–	–	–	22	9	11
Grimsby T	17	10	16	9	19	–	–	–	–	21	15	10	5
Hereford U	–	–	–	–	–	–	–	–	–	–	–	–	–
Huddersfield T	8	–	–	–	–	–	–	–	23	17	16	13	12
Hull C	–	–	–	–	24	14	21	15	14	6	–	–	–
Ipswich T	7	–	–	–	1	14	9	8	8	5	–	–	–
Leeds U	–	–	–	–	–	–	1	10	7	4	14	7	10
Leicester C	5	–	4	6	4	22	13	15	13	–	–	–	–
Leyton Orient	–	–	–	–	–	–	–	–	–	–	–	–	–
Luton T	24	16	20	20	–	–	–	–	–	–	–	–	–
Manchester C	–	–	–	–	–	–	–	2	9	–	–	3	4
Manchester U	–	–	–	–	–	–	–	–	–	–	–	–	–
Mansfield T	–	–	–	–	–	–	–	–	–	–	–	–	–
Middlesbrough	–	1	9	–	2	7	21	–	3	–	21	19	17
Millwall	22	12	3	7	15	5	–	1	16	9	–	–	–
Newcastle U	–	–	–	1	20	11	3	–	–	–	–	–	3
Norwich C	16	–	–	–	–	–	–	–	–	–	1	–	–
Nottingham F	–	–	2	–	–	–	–	–	–	–	–	–	–
Notts Co	–	24	7	17	–	4	–	–	–	–	–	20	–
Oldham Ath	18	14	–	–	–	1	8	16	10	3	8	14	19
Oxford U	–	–	23	14	21	10	17	17	–	–	–	1	–
Peterborough U	–	–	24	10	–	–	–	–	–	–	–	–	–
Plymouth Arg	–	–	–	–	22	18	16	18	16	7	–	–	–
Port Vale	12	17	–	–	24	15	11	–	–	–	–	–	–
Portsmouth	21	18	17	3	9	17	12	20	–	2	4	4	16
Preston NE	–	–	–	–	–	–	–	–	–	–	–	–	–
QPR	–	–	–	–	–	–	–	–	–	–	–	–	–

1982-83	1981-82	1980-81	1979-80	1978-79	1977-78	1976-77	1975-76	1974-75	1973-74	1972-73	1971-72	
–	–	–	–	–	–	–	–	2	14	3	–	Aston Villa
10	6	–	–	–	–	–	–	–	–	–	–	Barnsley
–	–	–	3	–	–	–	–	–	–	–	2	Birmingham C
11	10	4	–	22	5	12	15	–	–	–	–	Blackburn R
–	–	–	–	20	5	10	7	5	7	6	–	Blackpool
22	19	18	–	–	1	4	4	10	11	–	–	Bolton W
–	–	–	–	–	–	–	–	–	–	–	–	Bournemouth
–	–	–	–	–	–	–	–	–	–	–	–	Bradford C
–	–	–	–	–	–	–	–	–	–	–	–	Brentford
–	–	–	2	4	–	–	–	–	–	22	–	Brighton & HA
–	21	–	–	–	–	–	2	5	16	5	8	Bristol C
–	–	22	19	16	18	15	18	19	–	–	–	Bristol R
21	–	–	21	13	11	16	–	–	–	1	7	Burnley
–	–	–	–	–	–	–	–	–	–	–	–	Bury
12	14	13	8	12	–	–	–	–	–	–	–	Cambridge U
–	20	19	15	9	19	18	–	21	17	20	19	Cardiff C
14	–	–	–	–	–	20	19	–	3	18	10	Carlisle U
17	13	–	22	19	17	7	9	–	–	–	21	Charlton Ath
18	12	12	4	–	–	2	11	–	–	–	–	Chelsea
15	15	–	1	9	–	–	–	20	–	–	–	Crystal Palace
13	16	6	–	–	–	–	–	–	–	–	–	Derby Co
4	–	–	20	10	10	17	12	9	13	9	20	Fulham
19	17	7	–	–	–	–	–	–	–	–	–	Grimsby T
–	–	–	–	–	–	22	–	–	–	–	–	Hereford U
–	–	–	–	–	–	–	–	–	21	–	–	Huddersfield T
–	–	–	–	–	22	14	14	8	9	13	12	Hull C
–	–	–	–	–	–	–	–	–	–	–	–	Ipswich T
8	–	–	–	–	–	–	–	–	–	–	–	Leeds U
3	8	–	1	17	–	–	–	–	–	–	–	Leicester C
–	22	17	14	11	14	19	13	12	4	15	17	Leyton Orient
–	1	5	6	18	13	6	7	–	2	12	13	Luton T
–	–	–	–	–	–	–	–	–	–	–	–	Manchester C
–	–	–	–	–	–	–	1	–	–	–	–	Manchester U
–	–	–	–	21	–	–	–	–	–	–	–	Mansfield T
16	–	–	–	–	–	–	–	–	1	4	9	Middlesbrough
–	–	–	–	21	16	10	–	20	12	11	3	Millwall
5	9	11	9	8	–	–	–	–	–	–	–	Newcastle U
–	3	–	–	–	–	–	–	3	–	–	1	Norwich C
–	–	–	–	–	–	3	8	16	7	14	–	Nottingham F
–	–	2	17	6	15	8	5	14	10	–	–	Notts Co
7	11	15	11	14	8	13	17	18	–	–	–	Oldham Ath
–	–	–	–	–	–	–	20	11	18	8	15	Oxford U
–	–	–	–	–	–	–	–	–	–	–	–	Peterborough U
–	–	–	–	–	21	16	–	–	–	–	–	Plymouth Arg
–	–	–	–	–	–	–	–	–	–	–	–	Port Vale
–	–	–	–	–	–	–	22	17	15	17	16	Portsmouth
–	–	20	10	7	–	–	–	21	19	18	–	Preston NE
1	5	8	5	–	–	–	–	–	–	2	4	QPR

LEAGUE POSITIONS: DIVISION 1 from 1992–93 and DIVISION 2 1971–72 to 1991–92 (cont.)

	1995-96	1994-95	1993-94	1992-93	1991-92	1990-91	1989-90	1988-89	1987-88	1986-87	1985-86	1984-85	1983-84
Reading	19	2	–	–	–	–	–	–	22	13	–	–	–
Rotherham U	–	–	–	–	–	–	–	–	–	–	–	–	–
Sheffield U	9	8	–	–	–	–	2	–	21	9	7	18	–
Sheffield W	–	–	–	–	3	–	–	–	–	–	–	–	2
Shrewsbury T	–	–	–	–	–	–	–	22	18	18	17	8	8
Southampton	–	–	–	–	–	–	–	–	–	–	–	–	–
Southend U	14	13	15	18	12	–	–	–	–	–	–	–	–
Stoke C	4	11	10	–	–	–	24	13	11	8	10	–	–
Sunderland	1	20	12	21	8	–	6	11	–	20	18	–	–
Swansea C	–	–	–	–	–	–	–	–	–	–	–	–	21
Swindon T	–	21	–	5	8	21	4	6	12	–	–	–	–
Tottenham H	–	–	–	–	–	–	–	–	–	–	–	–	–
Tranmere R	13	5	5	4	14	–	–	–	–	–	–	–	–
Walsall	–	–	–	–	–	–	–	24	–	–	–	–	–
Watford	23	7	19	16	10	20	15	4	–	–	–	–	–
WBA	11	19	21	–	–	23	20	9	20	15	–	–	–
West Ham U	–	–	–	2	–	2	7	–	–	–	–	–	–
Wimbledon	–	–	–	–	–	–	–	–	–	–	3	12	–
Wolv'hampton W	20	4	8	11	12	10	–	–	–	–	22	–	–
Wrexham	–	–	–	–	–	–	–	–	–	–	–	–	–
York C	–	–	–	–	–	–	–	–	–	–	–	–	–

LEAGUE POSITIONS: DIVISION 2 from 1992–93 and DIVISION 3 1971–72 to 1991–92

	1995-96	1994-95	1993-94	1992-93	1991-92	1990-91	1989-90	1988-89	1987-88	1986-87	1985-86	1984-85	1983-84
Aldershot	–	–	–	–	–	–	–	24	20	–	–	–	–
Aston Villa	–	–	–	–	–	–	–	–	–	–	–	–	–
Barnet	–	–	24	–	–	–	–	–	–	–	–	–	–
Barnsley	–	–	–	–	–	–	–	–	–	–	–	–	–
Birmingham C	–	1	–	–	2	12	7	–	–	–	–	–	–
Blackburn R	–	–	–	–	–	–	–	–	–	–	–	–	–
Blackpool	3	12	20	18	–	4	23	19	10	9	12	–	–
Bolton W	–	–	–	2	13	4	6	10	–	21	18	17	10
Bournemouth	14	19	17	17	8	9	–	–	–	1	15	10	17
Bradford C	6	14	7	10	16	8	–	–	–	–	–	1	7
Brentford	15	2	16	–	1	6	13	7	12	11	10	13	20
Brighton & HA	23	16	14	9	–	–	–	–	2	–	–	–	–
Bristol C	13	–	–	–	–	–	2	11	5	6	9	5	–
Bristol R	10	4	8	–	–	–	1	5	8	19	16	6	5

1982-83	1981-82	1980-81	1979-80	1978-79	1977-78	1976-77	1975-76	1974-75	1973-74	1972-73	1971-72	Club
–	–	–	–	–	–	–	–	–	–	–	–	Reading
20	7	–	–	–	–	–	–	–	–	–	–	Rotherham U
–	–	–	–	20	12	11	–	–	–	–	–	Sheffield U
6	4	10	–	–	–	–	–	22	19	10	14	Sheffield W
9	18	14	13	–	–	–	–	–	–	–	–	Shrewsbury T
–	–	–	–	–	2	9	6	13	–	–	–	Southampton
–	–	–	–	–	–	–	–	–	–	–	–	Southend U
–	–	–	–	3	7	–	–	–	–	–	–	Stoke C
–	–	–	2	4	6	–	1	4	6	6	5	Sunderland
–	–	3	12	–	–	–	–	–	–	–	–	Swansea C
–	–	–	–	–	–	–	–	–	22	16	11	Swindon T
–	–	–	–	–	3	–	–	–	–	–	–	Tottenham H
–	–	–	–	–	–	–	–	–	–	–	–	Tranmere R
–	–	–	–	–	–	–	–	–	–	–	–	Walsall
–	2	9	18	–	–	–	–	–	–	–	22	Watford
–	–	–	–	–	–	–	3	6	8	–	–	WBA
–	–	1	7	5	–	–	–	–	–	–	–	West Ham U
–	–	–	–	–	–	–	–	–	–	–	–	Wimbledon
2	–	–	–	–	–	1	–	–	–	–	–	Wolv'hampton W
–	21	16	16	15	–	–	–	–	–	–	–	Wrexham
–	–	–	–	–	–	–	21	15	–	–	–	York C

1982-83	1981-82	1980-81	1979-80	1978-79	1977-78	1976-77	1975-76	1974-75	1973-74	1972-73	1971-72	Club
–	–	–	–	–	–	–	21	20	8	–	–	Aldershot
–	–	–	–	–	–	–	–	–	–	–	1	Aston Villa
–	–	–	–	–	–	–	–	–	–	–	–	Barnet
–	–	2	11	–	–	–	–	–	–	–	22	Barnsley
–	–	2	–	–	–	–	1	13	3	–	10	Birmingham C
–	–	23	18	12	–	–	–	–	–	–	–	Blackburn R
–	–	–	–	–	–	–	–	1	7	–	–	Blackpool
14	–	–	–	–	–	21	11	7	3	–	–	Bolton W
12	–	–	–	–	22	–	–	–	–	–	24	Bournemouth
–	–	–	–	–	–	–	–	–	–	–	–	Bradford C
9	8	9	19	10	–	–	–	–	22	–	2	Brentford
–	–	–	–	–	2	4	19	19	–	–	2	Brighton & HA
–	23	–	–	–	–	–	–	–	–	–	–	Bristol C
7	15	–	–	–	–	–	–	2	5	6	–	Bristol R

	1995-96	1994-95	1993-94	1992-93	1991-92	1990-91	1989-90	1988-89	1987-88	1986-87	1985-86	1984-85	1983-84
Burnley	17	–	6	13	–	–	–	–	–	–	–	21	12
Bury	–	–	–	–	21	7	5	13	14	16	20	–	–
Cambridge U	–	20	10	–	–	1	–	–	–	–	–	24	–
Cardiff C	–	22	19	–	–	–	21	16	–	–	22	–	–
Carlisle U	21	–	–	–	–	–	–	–	–	22	–	–	–
Charlton Ath	–	–	–	–	–	–	–	–	–	–	–	–	–
Chester C	–	23	–	24	18	19	16	8	15	15	–	–	–
Chesterfield	7	–	–	–	–	–	–	22	18	17	17	–	–
Colchester U	–	–	–	–	–	–	–	–	–	–	–	–	–
Crewe Alex	5	3	–	–	–	22	12	–	–	–	–	–	–
Crystal Palace	–	–	–	–	–	–	–	–	–	–	–	–	–
Darlington	–	–	–	–	24	–	–	–	–	22	13	–	–
Derby Co	–	–	–	–	–	–	–	–	–	–	3	7	–
Doncaster R	–	–	–	–	–	–	–	24	13	11	14	–	–
Exeter C	–	–	22	19	20	16	–	–	–	–	–	–	24
Fulham	–	–	21	12	9	21	20	4	9	18	–	–	–
Gillingham	–	–	–	–	–	–	–	23	13	5	5	4	8
Grimsby T	–	–	–	–	3	–	–	22	–	–	–	–	–
Halifax T	–	–	–	–	–	–	–	–	–	–	–	–	–
Hartlepool U	–	–	23	16	11	–	–	–	–	–	–	–	–
Hereford U	–	–	–	–	–	–	–	–	–	–	–	–	–
Huddersfield T	–	5	11	15	3	11	8	14	–	–	–	–	–
Hull C	24	8	9	20	14	–	–	–	–	–	–	3	4
Leyton Orient	–	24	18	7	10	13	14	–	–	–	–	22	11
Lincoln C	–	–	–	–	–	–	–	–	–	21	19	14	6
Luton T	–	–	–	–	–	–	–	–	–	–	–	–	–
Mansfield T	–	–	–	22	–	24	15	15	19	10	–	–	–
Middlesbrough	–	–	–	–	–	–	–	–	2	–	–	–	–
Millwall	–	–	–	–	–	–	–	–	–	–	–	2	9
Newport Co	–	–	–	–	–	–	–	–	–	23	19	18	13
Northampton T	–	–	–	–	–	–	22	20	6	–	–	–	–
Notts Co	4	–	–	–	–	3	9	4	7	8	–	–	–
Oldham Ath	–	–	–	–	–	–	–	–	–	–	–	–	–
Oxford U	2	7	–	–	–	–	–	–	–	–	–	–	1
Peterborough U	19	15	–	–	6	–	–	–	–	–	–	–	–
Plymouth Arg	–	21	3	14	–	–	–	–	–	–	2	15	19
Portsmouth	–	–	–	–	–	–	–	–	–	–	–	–	–
Port Vale	–	–	2	3	–	–	–	3	11	12	–	–	23
Preston NE	–	–	–	21	17	17	19	6	16	–	–	23	16
Reading	–	–	1	8	12	15	10	18	–	–	1	9	–
Rochdale	–	–	–	–	–	–	–	–	–	–	–	–	–
Rotherham U	16	17	15	11	–	23	9	–	21	14	14	12	18
Scunthorpe U	–	–	–	–	–	–	–	–	–	–	–	–	21
Sheffield U	–	–	–	–	–	–	–	2	–	–	–	–	3
Sheffield W	–	–	–	–	–	–	–	–	–	–	–	–	–
Shrewsbury T	18	18	–	–	22	18	11	–	–	–	–	–	–
Southend U	–	–	–	–	2	–	21	17	–	–	–	–	22
Southport	–	–	–	–	–	–	–	–	–	–	–	–	–

1982-83	1981-82	1980-81	1979-80	1978-79	1977-78	1976-77	1975-76	1974-75	1973-74	1972-73	1971-72	
–	–	–	–	–	–	–	–	–	–	–	–	Stockport Co
–	–	–	–	–	–	–	–	–	–	–	–	Stoke C
–	–	–	–	–	–	–	–	–	–	–	–	Sunderland
–	–	–	–	3	–	–	–	–	–	23	14	Swansea C
–	22	17	10	5	10	11	19	4	–	–	–	Swindon T
–	–	–	–	–	–	–	–	–	–	–	23	Torquay U
–	–	–	–	23	12	14	–	22	16	10	20	Tranmere R
10	20	20	–	22	6	15	7	8	15	17	9	Walsall
–	–	–	–	2	–	–	–	23	7	19	–	Watford
18	–	–	–	–	–	–	–	–	–	–	–	WBA
–	21	–	24	–	–	–	–	–	–	–	–	Wigan Ath
–	–	–	–	–	–	–	–	–	–	–	–	Wimbledon
–	–	–	–	–	–	–	–	–	–	–	–	Wolv'hampton W
22	–	–	–	–	1	5	6	13	4	12	16	Wrexham
–	–	–	–	–	–	–	–	–	–	–	–	Wycombe W
–	–	–	–	–	–	24	–	–	3	18	19	York C

1982-83	1981-82	1980-81	1979-80	1978-79	1977-78	1976-77	1975-76	1974-75	1973-74	1972-73	1971-72	
18	16	6	10	5	5	17	–	–	–	4	17	Aldershot
–	–	–	–	–	–	–	–	–	–	–	–	Barnet
–	–	–	–	4	7	6	12	15	13	14	–	Barnsley
–	–	–	–	–	–	–	–	–	–	–	22	Barrow
21	12	–	–	–	–	–	–	–	–	–	–	Blackpool
–	–	–	–	–	–	–	–	–	–	–	–	Bolton W
–	4	13	11	18	17	13	6	–	–	–	–	Bournemouth
–	2	14	5	15	–	4	17	10	8	16	–	Bradford C
–	–	–	–	4	15	18	8	19	–	–	3	Brentford
14	–	–	–	–	–	–	–	–	–	–	–	Bristol C
–	–	–	–	–	–	–	–	–	–	–	–	Burnley
5	9	12	–	–	–	–	–	–	4	12	9	Bury
–	–	–	–	–	–	1	13	6	–	3	10	Cambridge U
–	–	–	–	–	–	–	–	–	–	–	–	Cardiff C
–	–	–	–	–	–	–	–	–	–	–	–	Carlisle U
13	9	–	–	–	–	–	–	4	7	15	20	Chester C
–	–	–	–	–	–	–	–	–	–	–	–	Chesterfield

	1995-96	1994-95	1993-94	1992-93	1991-92	1990-91	1989-90	1988-89	1987-88	1986-87	1985-86	1984-85	1983-84
Colchester U	7	10	17	10	–	–	24	22	9	5	6	7	8
Crewe Alex	–	–	3	6	6	–	–	3	17	17	12	10	16
Darlington	5	20	21	15	–	1	–	24	13	–	–	3	14
Doncaster R	13	9	15	16	21	11	20	23	–	–	–	–	2
Exeter C	14	22	–	–	–	–	1	13	22	14	21	18	–
Fulham	17	8	–	–	–	–	–	–	–	–	–	–	–
Gillingham	2	19	16	21	11	15	14	–	–	–	–	–	–
Grimsby T	–	–	–	–	–	–	2	9	–	–	–	–	–
Halifax T	–	–	–	22	20	22	23	21	18	15	20	21	21
Hartlepool U	20	18	–	–	–	3	19	19	16	18	7	19	23
Hereford U	6	16	20	17	17	17	17	15	19	16	10	5	11
Huddersfield T	–	–	–	–	–	–	–	–	–	–	–	–	–
Hull C	–	–	–	–	–	–	–	–	–	–	–	–	–
Leyton Orient	21	–	–	–	–	–	6	8	7	5	–	–	–
Lincoln C	18	12	18	8	10	14	10	10	–	24	–	–	–
Maidstone U	–	–	–	–	18	19	5	–	–	–	–	–	–
Mansfield T	19	6	12	–	3	–	–	–	–	–	3	14	19
Newport Co	–	–	–	–	–	–	–	24	–	–	–	–	–
Northampton T	11	17	22	20	16	10	–	–	–	1	8	23	18
Peterborough U	–	–	–	–	4	9	17	7	10	17	11	7	–
Plymouth Arg	4	–	–	–	–	–	–	–	–	–	–	–	–
Portsmouth	–	–	–	–	–	–	–	–	–	–	–	–	–
Port Vale	–	–	–	–	–	–	–	–	–	–	4	12	–
Preston NE	1	–	5	5	–	–	–	–	–	2	23	–	–
Reading	–	–	–	–	–	–	–	–	–	–	–	–	3
Rochdale	15	15	9	11	8	12	12	18	21	21	18	17	22
Rotherham U	–	–	–	–	2	–	–	1	–	–	–	–	–
Scarborough	23	21	14	13	12	9	18	5	12	–	–	–	–
Scunthorpe U	12	7	11	14	5	8	11	4	4	8	15	9	–
Sheffield U	–	–	–	–	–	–	–	–	–	–	–	–	–
Shrewsbury T	–	–	1	9	–	–	–	–	–	–	–	–	–
Southend U	–	–	–	–	–	3	–	–	3	9	20	–	–
Southport	–	–	–	–	–	–	–	–	–	–	–	–	–
Stockport Co	–	–	–	–	2	4	20	20	19	11	22	12	–
Swansea C	–	–	–	–	–	–	–	6	12	–	–	–	–
Swindon T	–	–	–	–	–	–	–	–	–	–	1	8	17
Torquay U	24	13	6	19	–	7	15	14	5	23	24	24	9
Tranmere R	–	–	–	–	–	–	2	14	20	19	6	10	–
Walsall	–	2	10	5	15	16	–	–	–	–	–	–	–
Watford	–	–	–	–	–	–	–	–	–	–	–	–	–
Wigan Ath	10	14	19	–	–	–	–	–	–	–	–	–	–
Wimbledon	–	–	–	–	–	–	–	–	–	–	–	–	–
Wolv'hampton W	–	–	–	–	–	–	–	–	1	4	–	–	–
Workington	–	–	–	–	–	–	–	–	–	–	–	–	–
Wrexham	–	–	–	2	14	24	21	7	11	9	13	15	20
Wycombe W	–	–	4	–	–	–	–	–	–	–	–	–	–
York C	–	–	–	4	19	21	13	11	–	–	–	–	1

1982–83	1981–82	1980–81	1979–80	1978–79	1977–78	1976–77	1975–76	1974–75	1973–74	1972–73	1971–72	
6	6	–	–	–	–	3	–	–	3	22	11	Colchester U
23	24	18	23	24	15	12	16	18	21	21	24	Crewe Alex
17	3	8	22	21	19	11	20	21	20	24	19	Darlington
–	–	3	12	12	12	8	10	17	22	17	12	Doncaster R
–	–	–	–	–	–	2	7	9	10	8	15	Exeter C
–	–	–	–	–	–	–	–	–	–	–	–	Fulham
–	–	–	–	–	–	–	–	–	2	9	13	Gillingham
–	–	–	18	2	6	–	–	–	–	–	1	Grimsby T
11	19	23	18	23	20	21	–	–	–	–	–	Halifax T
22	14	9	19	13	21	22	14	13	11	20	18	Hartlepool U
24	10	22	21	14	–	–	–	–	–	2	–	Hereford U
–	–	–	1	9	11	9	5	–	–	–	–	Huddersfield T
2	8	–	–	–	–	–	–	–	–	–	–	Hull C
–	–	–	–	–	–	–	–	–	–	–	–	Leyton Orient
–	–	2	7	–	–	–	1	5	12	10	5	Lincoln C
–	–	–	–	–	–	–	–	–	–	–	–	Maidstone U
10	20	7	–	–	–	–	–	1	17	6	–	Mansfield T
–	–	–	3	8	16	19	22	12	9	5	14	Newport C
15	22	10	13	19	10	–	2	16	5	23	21	Northampton T
9	5	5	8	–	–	–	–	–	1	19	8	Peterborough U
–	–	–	–	–	–	–	–	–	–	–	–	Plymouth Arg
–	–	–	4	7	–	–	–	–	–	–	–	Portsmouth
3	7	19	20	16	–	–	–	–	–	–	–	Port Vale
–	–	–	–	–	–	–	–	–	–	–	–	Preston NE
–	–	–	–	1	8	–	3	7	6	7	16	Reading
20	21	15	24	20	24	18	15	19	–	–	–	Rochdale
–	–	–	–	–	–	–	–	3	15	–	–	Rotherham U
–	–	–	–	–	–	–	–	–	–	–	–	Scarborough
4	23	16	14	12	14	20	19	24	18	–	4	Scunthorpe U
–	1	–	–	–	–	–	–	–	–	–	–	Sheffield U
–	–	1	–	–	–	–	2	–	–	–	–	Shrewsbury T
–	–	–	–	2	10	–	–	–	–	–	2	Southend U
–	–	–	–	–	23	23	23	11	–	1	7	Southport
16	18	20	16	17	18	14	21	20	24	11	23	Stockport Co
–	–	–	–	3	5	11	22	14	–	–	–	Swansea C
8	–	–	–	–	–	–	–	–	–	–	–	Swindon T
12	15	17	9	11	9	16	9	14	16	18	–	Torquay U
19	11	21	15	–	–	–	4	–	–	–	–	Tranmere R
–	–	–	2	–	–	–	–	–	–	–	–	Walsall
–	–	–	–	–	1	7	8	–	–	–	–	Watford
–	3	11	6	6	–	–	–	–	–	–	–	Wigan Ath
1	–	4	–	3	13	–	–	–	–	–	–	Wimbledon
–	–	–	–	–	–	–	–	–	–	–	–	Wolv'hampton W
–	–	–	–	–	–	24	24	23	23	13	6	Workington
–	–	–	–	–	–	–	–	–	–	–	–	Wrexham
–	–	–	–	–	–	–	–	–	–	–	–	Wycombe W
7	17	24	17	10	22	–	–	–	–	–	–	York C

LEAGUE CHAMPIONSHIP HONOURS

FA PREMIER LEAGUE
Maximum points: 126

	First	Pts	Second	Pts	Third	Pts
	First	*Pts*	*Second*		*Third*	*Pts*
1992–93	Manchester U	84	Aston Villa	74	Norwich C	72
1993–94	Manchester U	92	Blackburn R	84	Newcastle U	77
1994–95	Blackburn R	89	Manchester U	88	Nottingham F	77

Maximum points: 114

1995–96	Manchester U	82	Newcastle U	78	Liverpool	71
1996–97	Manchester U	75	Newcastle U*	68	Arsenal*	68

DIVISION 1
Maximum points: 138

1992–93	Newcastle U	96	West Ham U*	88	Portsmouth††	88
1993–94	Crystal Palace	90	Nottingham F	83	Millwall††	74
1994–95	Middlesbrough	82	Reading††	79	Bolton W	77
1995–96	Sunderland	83	Derby Co	79	Crystal Palace††	75
1996–97	Bolton W	98	Barnsley	80	Wolverhampton W	76

DIVISION 2
Maximum points: 138

1992–93	Stoke C	93	Bolton W	90	Port Vale††	89
1993–94	Reading	89	Port Vale	88	Plymouth Arg††	85
1994–95	Birmingham C	89	Brentford††	85	Crewe Alex††	83
1995–96	Swindon T	92	Oxford U	83	Blackpool††	82
1996–97	Bury	84	Stockport Co	82	Luton T	78

DIVISION 3
Maximum points: 126

1992–93	Cardiff C	83	Wrexham	80	Barnet	79
1993–94	Shrewsbury T	79	Chester C	74	Crewe Alex	73
1994–95	Carlisle U	91	Walsall	83	Chesterfield	81

Maximum points: 138

1995–96	Preston NE	86	Gillingham	83	Bury	79
1996–97	Wigan Ath*	87	Fulham	87	Carlisle U	84

†† *Not promoted after play-offs.*

FOOTBALL LEAGUE
Maximum points: a 44; b 60

	First	Pts	Second	Pts	Third	Pts
1888–89a	Preston NE	40	Aston Villa	29	Wolverhampton W	28
1889–90a	Preston NE	33	Everton	31	Blackburn R	27
1890–91a	Everton	29	Preston NE	27	Notts Co	26
1891–92b	Sunderland	42	Preston NE	37	Bolton W	36

DIVISION 1 to 1991–92
Maximum points: a 44; b 52; c 60; d 68; e 76; f 84; g 126; h 120; k 114.

1892–93c	Sunderland	48	Preston NE	37	Everton	36
1893–94c	Aston Villa	44	Sunderland	38	Derby Co	36
1894–95c	Sunderland	47	Everton	42	Aston Villa	39
1895–96c	Aston Villa	45	Derby Co	41	Everton	39
1896–97c	Aston Villa	47	Sheffield U*	36	Derby Co	36
1897–98c	Sheffield U	42	Sunderland	37	Wolverhampton W*	35

	First	Pts	Second	Pts	Third	Pts
1914–15e	Derby Co	53	Preston NE	50	Barnsley	47
1919–20f	Tottenham H	70	Huddersfield T	64	Birmingham	56
1920–21f	Birmingham*	58	Cardiff C	58	Bristol C	51
1921–22f	Nottingham F	56	Stoke C*	52	Barnsley	52
1922–23f	Notts Co	53	West Ham U*	51	Leicester C	51
1923–24f	Leeds U	54	Bury*	51	Derby Co	51
1924–25f	Leicester C	59	Manchester U	57	Derby Co	55
1925–26f	Sheffield W	60	Derby Co	57	Chelsea	52
1926–27f	Middlesbrough	62	Portsmouth*	54	Manchester C	54
1927–28f	Manchester C	59	Leeds U	57	Chelsea	54
1928–29f	Middlesbrough	55	Grimsby T	53	Bradford PA*	48
1929–30f	Blackpool	58	Chelsea	55	Oldham Ath	53
1930–31f	Everton	61	WBA	54	Tottenham H	51
1931–32f	Wolverhampton W	56	Leeds U	54	Stoke C	52
1932–33f	Stoke C	56	Tottenham H	55	Fulham	50
1933–34f	Grimsby T	59	Preston NE	52	Bolton W*	51
1934–35f	Brentford	61	Bolton W*	56	West Ham U	56
1935–36f	Manchester U	56	Charlton Ath	55	Sheffield U*	52
1936–37f	Leicester C	56	Blackpool	55	Bury	52
1937–38f	Aston Villa	57	Manchester U*	53	Sheffield U	53
1938–39f	Blackburn R	55	Sheffield U	54	Sheffield W	53
1946–47f	Manchester C	62	Burnley	58	Birmingham C	55
1947–48f	Birmingham C	59	Newcastle U	56	Southampton	52
1948–49f	Fulham	57	WBA	56	Southampton	55
1949–50f	Tottenham H	61	Sheffield W*	52	Sheffield U*	52
1950–51f	Preston NE	57	Manchester C	52	Cardiff C	50
1951–52f	Sheffield W	53	Cardiff C*	51	Birmingham C	51
1952–53f	Sheffield U	60	Huddersfield T	58	Luton T	52
1953–54f	Leicester C*	56	Everton	56	Blackburn R	55
1954–55f	Birmingham C*	54	Luton T*	54	Rotherham U	54
1955–56f	Sheffield W	55	Leeds U	52	Liverpool*	48
1956–57f	Leicester C	61	Nottingham F	54	Liverpool	53
1957–58f	West Ham U	57	Blackburn R	56	Charlton Ath	55
1958–59f	Sheffield W	62	Fulham	60	Sheffield U*	53
1959–60f	Aston Villa	59	Cardiff C	58	Liverpool*	50
1960–61f	Ipswich T	59	Sheffield U	58	Liverpool	52
1961–62f	Liverpool	62	Leyton Orient	54	Sunderland	53
1962–63f	Stoke C	53	Chelsea*	52	Sunderland	52
1963–64f	Leeds U	63	Sunderland	61	Preston NE	56
1964–65f	Newcastle U	57	Northampton T	56	Bolton W	50
1965–66f	Manchester C	59	Southampton	54	Coventry C	53
1966–67f	Coventry C	59	Wolverhampton W	58	Carlisle U	52
1967–68f	Ipswich T	59	QPR*	58	Blackpool	58
1968–69f	Derby Co	63	Crystal Palace	56	Charlton Ath	50
1969–70f	Huddersfield T	60	Blackpool	53	Leicester C	51
1970–71f	Leicester C	59	Sheffield U	56	Cardiff C*	53
1971–72f	Norwich C	57	Birmingham C	56	Millwall	55
1972–73f	Burnley	62	QPR	61	Aston Villa	50
1973–74f	Middlesbrough	65	Luton T	50	Carlisle U	49
1974–75f	Manchester U	61	Aston Villa	58	Norwich C	53
1975–76f	Sunderland	56	Bristol C*	53	WBA	53
1976–77f	Wolverhampton W	57	Chelsea	55	Nottingham F	52
1977–78f	Bolton W	58	Southampton	57	Tottenham H*	56
1978–79f	Crystal Palace	57	Brighton & HA*	56	Stoke C	56
1979–80f	Leicester C	55	Sunderland	54	Birmingham C*	53

Won or placed on goal average/goal difference.
†† *Not promoted after play-offs.*

	First	Pts	Second	Pts	Third	Pts
1980–81f	West Ham U	66	Notts Co	53	Swansea C*	50
1981–82g	Luton T	88	Watford	80	Norwich C	71
1982–83g	QPR	85	Wolverhampton W	75	Leicester C	70
1983–84g	Chelsea*	88	Sheffield W	88	Newcastle U	80
1984–85g	Oxford U	84	Birmingham C	82	Manchester C	74
1985–86g	Norwich C	84	Charlton Ath	77	Wimbledon	76
1986–87g	Derby Co	84	Portsmouth	78	Oldham Ath††	75
1987–88h	Millwall	82	Aston Villa*	78	Middlesbrough	78
1988–89k	Chelsea	99	Manchester C	82	Crystal Palace	81
1989–90k	Leeds U*	85	Sheffield U	85	Newcastle U††	80
1990–91k	Oldham Ath	88	West Ham U	87	Sheffield W	82
1991–92k	Ipswich T	84	Middlesbrough	80	Derby Co	78

No official competition during 1915–19 and 1939–46; Regional Leagues operating.

DIVISION 3 to 1991–92
Maximum points: 92; 138 from 1981–82.

	First	Pts	Second	Pts	Third	Pts
1958–59	Plymouth Arg	62	Hull C	61	Brentford*	57
1959–60	Southampton	61	Norwich C	59	Shrewsbury T*	52
1960–61	Bury	68	Walsall	62	QPR	60
1961–62	Portsmouth	65	Grimsby T	62	Bournemouth*	59
1962–63	Northampton T	62	Swindon T	58	Port Vale	54
1963–64	Coventry C*	60	Crystal Palace	60	Watford	58
1964–65	Carlisle U	60	Bristol C*	59	Mansfield T	59
1965–66	Hull C	69	Millwall	65	QPR	57
1966–67	QPR	67	Middlesbrough	55	Watford	54
1967–68	Oxford U	57	Bury	56	Shrewsbury T	55
1968–69	Watford*	64	Swindon T	64	Luton T	61
1969–70	Orient	62	Luton T	60	Bristol R	56
1970–71	Preston NE	61	Fulham	60	Halifax T	56
1971–72	Aston Villa	70	Brighton & HA	65	Bournemouth*	62
1972–73	Bolton W	61	Notts Co	57	Blackburn R	55
1973–74	Oldham Ath	62	Bristol R*	61	York C	61
1974–75	Blackburn R	60	Plymouth Arg	59	Charlton Ath	55
1975–76	Hereford U	63	Cardiff C	57	Millwall	56
1976–77	Mansfield T	64	Brighton & HA	61	Crystal Palace*	59
1977–78	Wrexham	61	Cambridge U	58	Preston NE*	56
1978–79	Shrewsbury T	61	Watford*	60	Swansea C	60
1979–80	Grimsby T	62	Blackburn R	59	Sheffield W	58
1980–81	Rotherham U	61	Barnsley*	59	Charlton Ath	59
1981–82	Burnley*	80	Carlisle U	80	Fulham	78
1982–83	Portsmouth	91	Cardiff C	86	Huddersfield T	82
1983–84	Oxford U	95	Wimbledon	87	Sheffield U*	83
1984–85	Bradford C	94	Millwall	90	Hull C	87
1985–86	Reading	94	Plymouth Arg	87	Derby Co	84
1986–87	Bournemouth	97	Middlesbrough	94	Swindon T	87
1987–88	Sunderland	93	Brighton & HA	84	Walsall	82
1988–89	Wolverhampton W	92	Sheffield U*	84	Port Vale	84
1989–90	Bristol R	93	Bristol C	91	Notts Co	87
1990–91	Cambridge U	86	Southend U	85	Grimsby T*	83
1991–92	Brentford	82	Birmingham C	81	Huddersfield T	78

* Won or placed on goal average/goal difference.

DIVISION 4 (1958–1992)
Maximum points: 92; 138 from 1981–82.

	First	Pts	Second	Pts	Third	Pts
1958–59	Port Vale	64	Coventry C*	60	York C	60
1959–60	Walsall	65	Notts Co*	60	Torquay U	60
1960–61	Peterborough U	66	Crystal Palace	64	Northampton T*	60
1961–62†	Millwall	56	Colchester U	55	Wrexham	53
1962–63	Brentford	62	Oldham Ath*	59	Crewe Alex	59
1963–64	Gillingham*	60	Carlisle U	60	Workington	59
1964–65	Brighton & HA	63	Millwall*	62	York C	62
1965–66	Doncaster R*	59	Darlington	59	Torquay U	58
1966–67	Stockport Co	64	Southport*	59	Barrow	59
1967–68	Luton T	66	Barnsley	61	Hartlepools U	60
1968–69	Doncaster R	59	Halifax T	57	Rochdale*	56
1969–70	Chesterfield	64	Wrexham	61	Swansea C	60
1970–71	Notts Co	69	Bournemouth	60	Oldham Ath	59
1971–72	Grimsby T	63	Southend U	60	Brentford	59
1972–73	Southport	62	Hereford U	58	Cambridge U	57
1973–74	Peterborough U	65	Gillingham	62	Colchester U	60
1974–75	Mansfield T	68	Shrewsbury T	62	Rotherham U	59
1975–76	Lincoln C	74	Northampton T	68	Reading	60
1976–77	Cambridge U	65	Exeter C	62	Colchester U*	59
1977–78	Watford	71	Southend U	60	Swansea C*	56
1978–79	Reading	65	Grimsby T*	61	Wimbledon*	61
1979–80	Huddersfield T	66	Walsall	64	Newport Co	61
1980–81	Southend U	67	Lincoln C	65	Doncaster R	56
1981–82	Sheffield U	96	Bradford C*	91	Wigan Ath	91
1982–83	Wimbledon	98	Hull C	90	Port Vale	88
1983–84	York C	101	Doncaster R	85	Reading*	82
1984–85	Chesterfield	91	Blackpool	86	Darlington	85
1985–86	Swindon T	102	Chester C	84	Mansfield T	81
1986–87	Northampton T	99	Preston NE	90	Southend U	80
1987–88	Wolverhampton W	90	Cardiff C	85	Bolton W	78
1988–89	Rotherham U	82	Tranmere R	80	Crewe Alex	78
1989–90	Exeter C	89	Grimsby T	79	Southend U	75
1990–91	Darlington	83	Stockport Co*	82	Hartlepool U	82
1991–92†*	Burnley	83	Rotherham U*	77	Mansfield T	77

†*Maximum points:* 88 owing to Accrington Stanley's resignation. ††*Not promoted after play-offs.*
†**Maximum points:* 126 owing to Aldershot being expelled.

DIVISION 3—SOUTH (1920–1958)
Maximum points: a 84; b 92.

1920–21a	Crystal Palace	59	Southampton	54	QPR	53
1921–22a	Southampton*	61	Plymouth Arg	61	Portsmouth	53
1922–23a	Bristol C	59	Plymouth Arg*	53	Swansea T	53
1923–24a	Portsmouth	59	Plymouth Arg	55	Millwall	54
1924–25a	Swansea T	57	Plymouth Arg	56	Bristol C	53
1925–26a	Reading	57	Plymouth Arg	56	Millwall	53
1926–27a	Bristol C	62	Plymouth Arg	60	Millwall	56
1927–28a	Millwall	65	Northampton T	55	Plymouth Arg	53
1928–29a	Charlton Ath*	54	Crystal Palace	54	Northampton T*	52
1929–30a	Plymouth Arg	68	Brentford	61	QPR	51
1930–31a	Notts Co	59	Crystal Palace	51	Brentford	50
1931–32a	Fulham	57	Reading	55	Southend U	53
1932–33a	Brentford	62	Exeter C	58	Norwich C	57

119

	First	Pts	Second	Pts	Third	Pts
1933–34a	Norwich C	61	Coventry C*	54	Reading*	54
1934–35a	Charlton Ath	61	Reading	53	Coventry C	51
1935–36a	Coventry C	57	Luton T	56	Reading	54
1936–37a	Luton T	58	Notts Co	56	Brighton & HA	53
1937–38a	Millwall	56	Bristol C	55	QPR*	53
1938–39a	Newport Co	55	Crystal Palace	52	Brighton & HA	49
1939–46	Competition cancelled owing to war.					
1946–47a	Cardiff C	66	QPR	57	Bristol C	51
1947–48a	QPR	61	Bournemouth	57	Walsall	51
1948–49a	Swansea T	62	Reading	55	Bournemouth	52
1949–50a	Notts Co	58	Northampton T*	51	Southend U	51
1950–51b	Nottingham F	70	Norwich C	64	Reading*	57
1951–52b	Plymouth Arg	66	Reading*	61	Norwich C	61
1952–53b	Bristol R	64	Millwall*	62	Northampton T	62
1953–54b	Ipswich T	64	Brighton & HA	61	Bristol C	56
1954–55b	Bristol C	70	Leyton Orient	61	Southampton	59
1955–56b	Leyton Orient	67	Brighton & HA	65	Ipswich T	64
1956–57b	Ipswich T*	59	Torquay U	59	Colchester U	58
1957–58b	Brighton & HA	60	Brentford*	58	Plymouth Arg	58

* Won or placed on goal average.

DIVISION 3—NORTH (1921–1958)
Maximum points: a 76; b 84; c 80; d 92.

	First	Pts	Second	Pts	Third	Pts
1921–22a	Stockport Co	56	Darlington*	50	Grimsby T	50
1922–23a	Nelson	51	Bradford PA	47	Walsall	46
1923–24b	Wolverhampton W	63	Rochdale	62	Chesterfield	54
1924–25b	Darlington	58	Nelson*	53	New Brighton	53
1925–26b	Grimsby T	61	Bradford PA	60	Rochdale	59
1926–27b	Stoke C	63	Rochdale	58	Bradford PA	55
1927–28b	Bradford PA	63	Lincoln C	55	Stockport Co	54
1928–29g	Bradford C	63	Stockport Co	62	Wrexham	52
1929–30b	Port Vale	67	Stockport Co	63	Darlington*	50
1930–31b	Chesterfield	58	Lincoln C	57	Wrexham*	54
1931–32c	Lincoln C*	57	Gateshead	57	Chester	50
1932–33b	Hull C	59	Wrexham	57	Stockport Co	54
1933–34b	Barnsley	62	Chesterfield	61	Stockport Co	59
1934–35b	Doncaster R	57	Halifax T	55	Chester	54
1935–36b	Chesterfield	60	Chester*	55	Tranmere R	55
1936–37b	Stockport Co	60	Lincoln C	57	Chester	53
1937–38b	Tranmere R	56	Doncaster R	54	Hull C	53
1938–39b	Barnsley	67	Doncaster R	56	Bradford C	52
1939–46	Competition cancelled owing to war.					
1946–47b	Doncaster R	72	Rotherham U	60	Chester	56
1947–48b	Lincoln C	60	Rotherham U	59	Wrexham	50
1948–49b	Hull C	65	Rotherham U	62	Doncaster R	50
1949–50b	Doncaster R	55	Gateshead	53	Rochdale*	51
1950–51d	Rotherham U	71	Mansfield T	64	Carlisle U	62
1951–52d	Lincoln C	69	Grimsby T	66	Stockport Co	59
1952–53d	Oldham Ath	59	Port Vale	58	Wrexham	56
1953–54d	Port Vale	69	Barnsley	58	Scunthorpe U	57
1954–55d	Barnsley	65	Accrington S	61	Scunthorpe U*	58
1955–56d	Grimsby T	68	Derby Co	63	Accrington S	59
1956–57d	Derby Co	63	Hartlepools U	59	Accrington S*	58
1957–58d	Scunthorpe U	66	Accrington S	59	Bradford C	57

* Won or placed on goal average.

120

PROMOTED AFTER PLAY-OFFS
(Not accounted for in previous section)
1986–87   Aldershot to Division 3.
1987–88   Swansea C to Division 3.
1988–89   Leyton Orient to Division 3.
1989–90   Cambridge U to Division 3; Notts Co to Division 2; Sunderland to
          Division 1.
1990–91   Notts Co to Division 1; Tranmere R to Division 2; Torquay U to
          Division 3.
1991–92   Blackburn R to Premier League; Peterborough U to Division 1.
1992–93   Swindon T to Premier League; WBA to Division 1; York C to Division 2.
1993–94   Leicester C to Premier League; Burnley to Division 1; Wycombe W to
          Division 2.
1994–95   Huddersfield T to Division 1.
1995–96   Leicester C to Premier League; Bradford C to Division 1; Plymouth Arg
          to Division 2
1996–97   Crystal Palace to Premier League; Crewe Alex to Division 1; Northamp-
          ton T to Division 2

RELEGATED CLUBS

FA PREMIER LEAGUE TO DIVISION 1

1992–93 Crystal Palace, Middlesbrough, Nottingham F
1993–94 Sheffield U, Oldham Ath, Swindon T
1994–95 Crystal Palace, Norwich, Leicester C, Ipswich T
1995–96 Manchester C, QPR, Bolton W
1996–97 Sunderland, Middlesbrough, Nottingham F

DIVISION 1 TO DIVISION 2

1898–99 Bolton W and Sheffield W	1925–26 Manchester C and Notts Co
1899–1900 Burnley and Glossop	1926–27 Leeds U and WBA
1900–01 Preston NE and WBA	1927–28 Tottenham H and
1901–02 Small Heath and Manchester C	Middlesbrough
1902–03 Grimsby T and Bolton W	1928–29 Bury and Cardiff C
1903–04 Liverpool and WBA	1929–30 Burnley and Everton
1904–05 League extended. Bury and	1930–31 Leeds U and Manchester U
Notts Co, two bottom clubs in	1931–32 Grimsby T and West Ham U
First Division, re-elected.	1932–33 Bolton W and Blackpool
1905–06 Nottingham F and	1933–34 Newcastle U and Sheffield U
Wolverhampton W	1934–35 Leicester C and Tottenham H
1906–07 Derby Co and Stoke C	1935–36 Aston Villa and Blackburn R
1907–08 Bolton W and Birmingham C	1936–37 Manchester U and Sheffield W
1908–09 Manchester C and Leicester	1937–38 Manchester C and WBA
Fosse	1938–39 Birmingham C and Leicester C
1909–10 Bolton W and Chelsea	1946–47 Brentford and Leeds U
1910–11 Bristol C and Nottingham F	1947–48 Blackburn R and Grimsby T
1911–12 Preston NE and Bury	1948–49 Preston NE and Sheffield U
1912–13 Notts Co and Woolwich	1949–50 Manchester C and
Arsenal	Birmingham C
1913–14 Preston NE and Derby Co	1950–51 Sheffield W and Everton
1914–15 Tottenham H and Chelsea*	1951–52 Huddersfield T and Fulham
1919–20 Notts Co and Sheffield W	1952–53 Stoke C and Derby Co
1920–21 Derby Co and Bradford PA	1953–54 Middlesbrough and Liverpool
1921–22 Bradford C and Manchester U	1954–55 Leicester C and Sheffield W
1922–23 Stoke C and Oldham Ath	1955–56 Huddersfield T and Sheffield U
1923–24 Chelsea and Middlesbrough	1956–57 Charlton Ath and Cardiff C
1924–25 Preston NE and Nottingham F	1957–58 Sheffield W and Sunderland

1958–59	Portsmouth and Aston Villa
1959–60	Luton T and Leeds U
1960–61	Preston NE and Newcastle U
1961–62	Chelsea and Cardiff C
1962–63	Manchester C and Leyton Orient
1963–64	Bolton W and Ipswich T
1964–65	Wolverhampton W and Birmingham C
1965–66	Northampton T and Blackburn R
1966–67	Aston Villa and Blackpool
1967–68	Fulham and Sheffield U
1968–69	Leicester C and QPR
1969–70	Sunderland and Sheffield W
1970–71	Burnley and Blackpool
1971–72	Huddersfield T and Nottingham F
1972–73	Crystal Palace and WBA
1973–74	Southampton, Manchester U, Norwich C
1974–75	Luton T, Chelsea, Carlisle U
1975–76	Wolverhampton W, Burnley, Sheffield U
1976–77	Sunderland, Stoke C, Tottenham H
1977–78	West Ham U, Newcastle U, Leicester C
1978–79	QPR, Birmingham C, Chelsea
1979–80	Bristol C, Derby Co, Bolton W
1980–81	Norwich C, Leicester C, Crystal Palace

1981–82	Leeds U, Wolverhampton W, Middlesbrough
1982–83	Manchester C, Swansea C, Brighton & HA
1983–84	Birmingham C, Notts Co, Wolverhampton W
1984–85	Norwich C, Sunderland, Stoke C
1985–86	Ipswich T, Birmingham C, WBA
1986–87	Leicester C, Manchester C, Aston Villa
1987–88	Chelsea**, Portsmouth, Watford, Oxford U
1988–89	Middlesbrough, West Ham U, Newcastle U
1989–90	Sheffield W, Charlton Ath, Millwall
1990–91	Sunderland and Derby Co
1991–92	Luton T, Notts Co, West Ham U
1992–93	Brentford, Cambridge U, Bristol R
1993–94	Birmingham C, Oxford U, Peterborough U
1994–95	Swindon T, Burnley, Bristol C, Notts Co
1995–96	Millwall, Watford, Luton T
1996–97	Grimsby T, Oldham Ath, Southend U

**Relegated after play-offs.*
Subsequently re-elected to Division 1 when League was extended after the War.

DIVISION 2 TO DIVISION 3

1920–21	Stockport Co
1921–22	Bradford PA and Bristol C
1922–23	Rotherham Co and Wolverhampton W
1923–24	Nelson and Bristol C
1924–25	Crystal Palace and Coventry C
1925–26	Stoke C and Stockport Co
1926–27	Darlington and Bradford C
1927–28	Fulham and South Shields
1928–29	Port Vale and Clapton Orient
1929–30	Hull C and Notts Co
1930–31	Reading and Cardiff C
1931–32	Barnsley and Bristol C
1932–33	Chesterfield and Charlton Ath
1933–34	Millwall and Lincoln C
1934–35	Oldham Ath and Notts Co
1935–36	Port Vale and Hull C
1936–37	Doncaster R and Bradford C
1937–38	Barnsley and Stockport Co
1938–39	Norwich C and Tranmere R
1946–47	Swansea T and Newport Co
1947–48	Doncaster R and Millwall
1948–49	Nottingham F and Lincoln C
1949–50	Plymouth Arg and Bradford PA

1950–51	Grimsby T and Chesterfield
1951–52	Coventry C and QPR
1952–53	Southampton and Barnsley
1953–54	Brentford and Oldham Ath
1954–55	Ipswich T and Derby Co
1955–56	Plymouth Arg and Hull C
1956–57	Port Vale and Bury
1957–58	Doncaster R and Notts Co
1958–59	Barnsley and Grimsby T
1959–60	Bristol C and Hull C
1960–61	Lincoln C and Portsmouth
1961–62	Brighton & HA and Bristol R
1962–63	Walsall and Luton T
1963–64	Grimsby T and Scunthorpe U
1964–65	Swindon T and Swansea T
1965–66	Middlesbrough and Leyton Orient
1966–67	Northampton T and Bury
1967–68	Plymouth Arg and Rotherham U
1968–69	Fulham and Bury
1969–70	Preston NE and Aston Villa
1970–71	Blackburn R and Bolton W
1971–72	Charlton Ath and Watford

1972–73 Huddersfield T and Brighton & HA

1973–74 Crystal Palace, Preston NE, Swindon T

1974–75 Millwall, Cardiff C, Sheffield W

1975–76 Oxford U, York C, Portsmouth

1976–77 Carlisle U, Plymouth Arg, Hereford U

1977–78 Blackpool, Mansfield T, Hull C

1978–79 Sheffield U, Millwall, Blackburn R

1979–80 Fulham, Burnley, Charlton Ath

1980–81 Preston NE, Bristol C, Bristol R

1981–82 Cardiff C, Wrexham, Orient

1982–83 Rotherham U, Burnley, Bolton W

1983–84 Derby Co, Swansea C, Cambridge U

1984–85 Notts Co, Cardiff C, Wolverhampton W

1985–86 Carlisle U, Middlesbrough, Fulham

1986–87 Sunderland**, Grimsby T, Brighton & HA

1987–88 Huddersfield T, Reading, Sheffield U**

1988–89 Shrewsbury T, Birmingham C, Walsall

1989–90 Bournemouth, Bradford C, Stoke C

1990–91 WBA and Hull C

1991–92 Plymouth Arg, Brighton & HA, Port Vale

1992–93 Preston NE, Mansfield T, Wigan Ath, Chester C

1993–94 Fulham, Exeter C, Hartlepool U, Barnet

1994–95 Cambridge U, Plymouth Arg, Cardiff C, Chester C, Leyton Orient

1995–96 Carlisle U, Swansea C, Brighton & HA, Hull C

1996–97 Peterborough U, Shrewsbury T, Rotherham U, Notts Co

DIVISION 3 TO DIVISION 4

1958–59 Rochdale, Notts Co, Doncaster R, Stockport Co

1959–60 Accrington S, Wrexham, Mansfield T, York C

1960–61 Chesterfield, Colchester U, Bradford C, Tranmere R

1961–62 Newport Co, Brentford, Lincoln C, Torquay U

1962–63 Bradford PA, Brighton & HA, Carlisle U, Halifax T

1963–64 Millwall, Crewe Alex, Wrexham, Notts Co

1964–65 Luton T, Port Vale, Colchester U, Barnsley

1965–66 Southend U, Exeter C, Brentford, York C

1966–67 Doncaster R, Workington, Darlington, Swansea T

1967–68 Scunthorpe U, Colchester U, Grimsby T, Peterborough U (demoted)

1968–69 Oldham Ath, Crewe Alex, Hartlepool, Northampton T

1969–70 Bournemouth, Southport, Barrow, Stockport Co

1970–71 Reading, Bury, Doncaster R, Gillingham

1971–72 Mansfield T, Barnsley, Torquay U, Bradford C

1972–73 Rotherham U, Brentford, Swansea C, Scunthorpe U

1973–74 Cambridge U, Shrewsbury T, Southport, Rochdale

1974–75 Bournemouth, Tranmere R, Watford, Huddersfield T

1975–76 Aldershot, Colchester U, Southend U, Halifax T

1976–77 Reading, Northampton T, Grimsby T, York C

1977–78 Port Vale, Bradford C, Hereford U, Portsmouth

1978–79 Peterborough U, Walsall, Tranmere R, Lincoln C

1979–80 Bury, Southend U, Mansfield T, Wimbledon

1980–81 Sheffield U, Colchester U, Blackpool, Hull C

1981–82 Wimbledon, Swindon T, Bristol C, Chester

1982–83 Reading, Wrexham, Doncaster R, Chesterfield

1983–84 Scunthorpe U, Southend U, Port Vale, Exeter C

1984–85 Burnley, Orient, Preston NE, Cambridge U

1985–86 Lincoln C, Cardiff C, Wolverhampton W, Swansea C

1986–87 Bolton W**, Carlisle U, Darlington, Newport Co

1987–88 Doncaster R, York C, Grimsby T, Rotherham U**

1988–89 Southend U, Chesterfield, Gillingham, Aldershot

1989–90 Cardiff C, Northampton T, Blackpool, Walsall

1990–91 Crewe Alex, Rotherham U, Mansfield T

1991–92 Bury, Shrewsbury T, Torquay U, Darlington

** Relegated after play-offs.

LEAGUE TITLE WINS

FA PREMIER LEAGUE – Manchester U 4, Blackburn R 1.

LEAGUE DIVISION 1 – Liverpool 18, Arsenal 10, Everton 9, Manchester U 7, Aston Villa 7, Sunderland 7, Newcastle U 5, Sheffield W 4, Huddersfield T 3, Leeds U 3, Wolverhampton W 3, Blackburn R 2, Portsmouth 2, Preston NE 2, Burnley 2, Manchester C 2, Tottenham H 2, Derby Co 2, Bolton W 1, Chelsea 1, Sheffield U 1, WBA 1, Ipswich T 1, Nottingham F 1, Crystal Palace 1, Middlesbrough 1.

LEAGUE DIVISION 2 – Leicester C 6, Manchester C 6, Sheffield W 5, Birmingham C (one as Small Heath) 5, Derby Co 4, Liverpool 4, Ipswich T 3, Leeds U 3, Notts Co 3, Preston NE 3, Middlesbrough 3, Stoke C 3, Bury 2, Grimsby T 2, Norwich C 2, Nottingham F 2, Tottenham H 2, WBA 2, Aston Villa 2, Burnley 2, Chelsea 2, Manchester U 2, West Ham U 2, Wolverhampton W 2, Bolton W 2, Swindon T, Huddersfield T, Bristol C, Brentford, Bradford C, Everton, Fulham, Sheffield U, Newcastle U, Coventry C, Blackpool, Blackburn R, Sunderland, Crystal Palace, Luton T, QPR, Oxford U, Millwall, Oldham Ath, Reading 1 each.

LEAGUE DIVISION 3 – Portsmouth 2, Oxford U 2, Carlisle U 2, Preston NE 2, Shrewsbury T 2, Plymouth Arg, Southampton, Bury, Northampton T, Coventry C, Hull C, QPR, Watford, Leyton Orient, Aston Villa, Bolton W, Oldham Ath, Blackburn R, Hereford U, Mansfield T, Wrexham, Grimsby T, Rotherham U, Burnley, Bradford C, Bournemouth, Reading, Sunderland, Wolverhampton W, Bristol R, Cambridge U, Brentford, Cardiff C, Wigan Ath 1 each.

LEAGUE DIVISION 4 – Chesterfield 2, Doncaster R 2, Peterborough U 2, Port Vale, Walsall, Millwall, Brentford, Gillingham, Brighton, Stockport Co, Luton T, Notts Co, Grimsby T, Southport, Mansfield T, Lincoln C, Cambridge U, Watford, Reading, Huddersfield T, Southend U, Sheffield U, Wimbledon, York C, Swindon T, Northampton T, Wolverhampton W, Rotherham U, Exeter C, Darlington, Burnley 1 each.

To 1957–58

DIVISION 3 (South) – Bristol C 3; Charlton Ath, Ipswich T, Millwall, Notts Co, Plymouth Arg, Swansea T 2 each; Brentford, Bristol R, Cardiff C, Crystal Palace, Coventry C, Fulham, Leyton Orient, Luton T, Newport Co, Nottingham F, Norwich C, Portsmouth, QPR, Reading, Southampton, Brighton & HA 1 each.

DIVISION 3 (North) – Barnsley, Doncaster R, Lincoln C 3 each; Chesterfield, Grimsby T, Hull C, Port Vale, Stockport Co 2 each; Bradford PA, Bradford C, Darlington, Derby Co, Nelson, Oldham Ath, Rotherham U, Stoke C, Tranmere R, Wolverhampton W, Scunthorpe U 1 each.

LEAGUE ATTENDANCES 1996–97

FA CARLING PREMIERSHIP ATTENDANCES

	Average Gate			Season 1996/97	
	1995/96	1996/97	+/-%	Highest	Lowest
Arsenal	37,568	37,821	+0.7	38,264	33,461
Aston Villa	32,614	36,027	+10.5	39,339	26,726
Blackburn Rovers	27,714	24,947	-10.0	30,476	19,214
Chelsea	25,466	27,001	+6.0	29,056	22,762
Coventry City	18,507	19,625	+6.0	23,080	15,266
Derby County	14,327	17,889	+24.9	18,287	17,022
Everton	35,435	36,186	+2.1	40,177	30,368
Leeds United	32,578	32,109	-1.4	39,981	25,860
Leicester City	16,530	20,184	+22.1	21,134	17,562
Liverpool	39,553	39,777	+0.6	40,892	36,126
Manchester United	41,700	55,081	+32.1	55,314	54,178
Middlesbrough	29,283	29,848	+1.9	30,215	29,484
Newcastle United	36,507	36,466	-0.1	36,579	36,143
Nottingham Forest	25,916	24,587	-5.1	29,181	17,525
Sheffield Wednesday	24,877	25,693	+3.3	38,943	16,390
Southampton	14,820	15,099	+1.9	15,256	14,318
Sunderland	17,482	20,865	+19.4	22,512	18,581
Tottenham Hotspur	30,510	31,067	+1.8	33,040	22,943
West Ham United	22,340	23,242	+4.0	25,064	19,105
Wimbledon	13,246	15,156	+14.4	25,786	8,572

NATIONWIDE FOOTBALL LEAGUE: DIVISION ONE ATTENDANCES

	Average Gate			Season 1996/97	
	1995/96	1996/97	+/-%	Highest	Lowest
Barnsley	8,086	11,356	+40.4	18,605	6,307
Birmingham City	18,090	17,751	-1.9	25,157	13,189
Bolton Wanderers	18,822	15,826	-15.9	22,030	12,448
Bradford City	5,708	12,925	+126.4	17,609	9,249
Charlton Athletic	11,185	11,081	-0.9	14,816	8,487
Crystal Palace	15,248	16,085	+5.5	21,410	12,633
Grimsby Town	5,992	5,859	-2.2	9,041	3,927
Huddersfield Town	13,151	12,175	-7.4	18,358	9,578
Ipswich Town	12,604	11,953	-5.2	22,025	7,053
Manchester City	27,869	26,753	-4.0	30,729	23,079
Norwich City	14,581	14,719	+0.9	20,256	11,946
Oldham Athletic	6,634	7,045	+6.2	12,992	4,852
Oxford United	5,876	7,608	+29.5	9,221	6,334
Port Vale	8,227	7,385	-10.2	14,396	4,522
Portsmouth	9,406	8,857	-5.8	12,844	5,579
Queens Park Rangers	15,683	12,554	-20.0	17,376	7,776
Reading	8,918	9,160	+2.7	14,853	5,513
Sheffield United	12,901	16,638	+29.0	25,596	12,301
Southend United	5,898	5,072	-14.0	8,274	3,046
Stoke City	12,275	12,698	+3.4	21,735	7,444
Swindon Town	10,602	9,917	-6.5	14,792	7,452
Tranmere Rovers	7,861	8,127	+3.4	14,309	4,577
West Bromwich Albion	15,061	15,064	0.0	21,179	11,792
Wolverhampton Wanderers	24,786	24,763	-0.1	27,336	21,072

NATIONWIDE FOOTBALL LEAGUE: DIVISION TWO ATTENDANCES

	Average Gate		+/− %	Season 1996/97	
	1995/96	1996/97		Highest	Lowest
AFC Bournemouth	4,213	4,581	+8.7	8,201	2,747
Blackpool	5,818	4,987	−14.3	8,017	2,690
Brentford	4,768	5,832	+22.3	8,679	3,675
Bristol City	7,017	10,802	+53.9	18,642	7,028
Bristol Rovers	5,279	5,630	+6.6	8,078	4,123
Burnley	9,064	10,053	+10.9	16,186	7,903
Bury	3,262	4,502	+38.0	9,785	2,690
Chesterfield	4,884	4,639	−5.0	8,690	2,805
Crewe Alexandra	3,974	3,978	+0.1	4,858	3,125
Gillingham	7,198	6,021	−16.3	9,305	3,572
Luton Town	7,223	6,781	−6.1	9,623	4,978
Millwall	9,571	7,743	−19.1	9,371	5,702
Notts County	5,130	4,239	−17.4	6,879	2,423
Peterborough United	4,655	5,295	+13.7	9,499	2,975
Plymouth Argyle	7,120	6,495	−8.8	9,645	4,237
Preston North End	10,012	9,411	−6.0	14,626	7,004
Rotherham United	3,413	2,844	−16.7	4,562	1,797
Shrewsbury Town	3,348	3,177	−5.1	5,341	1,610
Stockport County	5,903	6,424	+8.8	9,187	3,446
Walsall	3,982	3,892	−2.3	6,306	2,659
Watford	9,457	8,894	−5.6	14,109	6,139
Wrexham	3,705	4,112	+11.0	6,864	2,002
Wycombe Wanderers	4,573	5,232	+14.4	8,438	3,438
York City	3,538	3,359	−5.1	5,958	2,136

NATIONWIDE FOOTBALL LEAGUE: DIVISION THREE ATTENDANCES

	Average Gate		+/− %	Season 1996/97	
	1995/96	1996/97		Highest	Lowest
Barnet	2,282	2,141	−6.2	3,316	1,194
Brighton & Hove Albion	5,448	5,844	+7.3	10,923	1,933
Cambridge United	2,767	3,363	+21.5	6,032	2,033
Cardiff City	3,420	3,594	+5.1	6,144	1,667
Carlisle United	5,704	5,440	−4.6	9,171	3,839
Chester City	2,674	2,263	−15.4	4,005	1,540
Colchester United	3,274	3,245	−0.9	5,920	1,842
Darlington	2,408	2,796	+16.1	4,662	1,563
Doncaster Rovers	2,090	2,091	0.0	3,274	1,030
Exeter City	3,442	3,014	−12.4	4,991	2,155
Fulham	4,191	6,644	+58.5	11,479	4,423
Hartlepool United	2,072	2,107	+1.7	3,799	1,120
Hereford United	2,973	2,931	−1.4	8,350	1,382
Hull City	3,803	3,413	−10.3	5,414	1,775
Leyton Orient	4,478	4,336	−3.3	7,946	2,419
Lincoln City	2,870	3,163	+10.2	6,495	2,033
Mansfield Town	2,415	2,282	−5.5	4,375	1,505
Northampton Town	4,831	4,823	−0.2	6,822	3,519
Rochdale	2,214	1,829	−17.4	3,320	1,074
Scarborough	1,714	2,455	+43.2	3,607	1,573
Scunthorpe United	2,434	2,606	+7.1	4,257	1,524
Swansea City	2,996	3,850	+28.5	7,353	2,227
Torquay United	2,454	2,380	−3.0	4,021	1,087
Wigan Athletic	2,856	3,899	+36.5	7,106	2,606

TRANSFERS 1996–97

JUNE 1996	From	To
10 Ablett, Gary I.	Everton	Birmingham City
3 Allen, Christopher A.	Oxford United	Nottingham Forest
19 Appleby, Matthew W.	Darlington	Barnsley
12 Archdeacon, Owen D.	Barnsley	Carlisle United
31 Austin, Kevin L.	Leyton Orient	Lincoln City
31 Baird, Ian J.	Plymouth Argyle	Brighton & Hove Albion
23 Beaumont, Christopher P.	Stockport County	Chesterfield
1 Bishop, Darren C.	Barnsley	Wigan Athletic
16 Black, Kingsley	Nottingham Forest	Grimsby Town
8 Booth, Andrew D.	Huddersfield Town	Sheffield Wednesday
5 Bowyer, Lee D.	Charlton Athletic	Leeds United
30 Brabin, Gary	Bury	Blackpool
22 Butler, Paul J.	Rochdale	Bury
30 Butler, Philip A.	Gillingham	Blackpool
9 Carey, Brian P.	Leicester City	Wrexham
10 Chamberlain, Alec F.R.	Sunderland	Watford
11 Clarke, Matthew J.	Rotherham United	Sheffield Wednesday
18 Coton, Anthony P.	Manchester United	Sunderland
4 Crawford, Stephen	Raith Rovers	Millwall
30 Cutler, Neil	West Bromwich Albion	Crewe Alexandra
4 Dair, Jason	Raith Rovers	Millwall combined
13 Davies, Martin L.	Cambridge United	Rushden & Diamonds
12 Dixon, Ben	Lincoln City	Blackpool
25 Dowell, Wayne A.	Burnley	Rochdale
4 Forsyth, Richard	Birmingham City	Stoke City
4 Freeman, Darren B.A.	Gillingham	Fulham
4 Furlong, Paul A.	Chelsea	Birmingham City
17 Goater, Leonardo S.	Rotherham United	Bristol City
8 Groves, Paul	Grimsby Town	West Bromwich Albion
19 Hall, Richard A.	Southampton	West Ham United
4 Hartley, Paul	Hamilton Academical	Millwall
19 Horne, Barry	Everton	Birmingham City
27 Houghton, Scott A.	Walsall	Peterborough United
12 Hunter, Barry V.	Wrexham	Reading
8 Izzet, Mustafa K.	Chelsea	Leicester City
26 Jemson, Nigel B.	Notts County	Oxford United
27 Jepson, Ronald F.	Huddersfield Town	Bury
8 Jones, Graeme A.	Doncaster Rovers	Wigan Athletic
25 Jones, Paul S.	Wolverhampton Wanderers	Stockport County
10 Joyce, Warren G.	Burnley	Hull City
31 Kerr, David W.	Manchester City	Mansfield Town
30 Martin, David	Gillingham	Leyton Orient
26 Martyn, Antony M.	Crystal Palace	Leeds United
23 Matthew, Damien	Crystal Palace	Burnley
26 McAllister, Gary	Leeds United	Coventry City
5 McCarthy, Paul J.	Brighton & Hove Albion	Wycombe Wanderers
30 McDougald, David E.J.	Brighton & Hove Albion	Rotherham United
4 Morrison, Andrew C.	Blackpool	Huddersfield Town
26 Nash, Carlo J.	Clitheroe	Crystal Palace
29 Newell, Michael C.	Blackburn Rovers	Birmingham City
26 O'Connell, Brendan	Barnsley	Charlton Athletic
12 O'Connor, Martin J.	Walsall	Peterborough United
26 O'Neill, Michael A.	Hibernian	Coventry City
4 Payton, Andrew P.	Barnsley	Huddersfield Town
26 Peake, Jason W.	Rochdale	Brighton & Hove Albion
24 Peschisolido, Paolo P.	Birmingham City	West Bromwich Albion
2 Piper, Leonard H.	Wimbledon	Gillingham
23 Potter, Graham S.	Stoke City	Southampton
23 Purse, Darren J.	Leyton Orient	Oxford United
15 Roberts, Iwan W.	Leicester City	Wolverhampton Wanderers
22 Sandford, Lee R.	Stoke City	Sheffield United
17 Sealey, Leslie J.	West Ham United	Leyton Orient
4 Sinclair, David	Raith Rovers	Millwall combined

12 Slade, Steven A.	Tottenham Hotspur	Queens Park Rangers
1 Speed, Gary A.	Leeds United	Everton
2 Stewart, Marcus P.	Bristol Rovers	Huddersfield Town
5 Thatcher, Ben D.	Millwall	Wimbledon
15 Tolson, Neil	Bradford City	York City
30 Watson, Paul D.	Gillingham	Fulham
11 Widdrington, Thomas	Southampton	Grimsby Town
3 Wilkins, Richard J.	Hereford United	Colchester United
3 Williams, Adrian	Reading	Wolverhampton Wanderers
19 Wrack, Darren	Derby County	Grimsby Town

TEMPORARY TRANSFERS

| 18 Mean, Scott | AFC Bournemouth | West Ham United |

AUGUST 1996

8 Barness, Anthony	Chelsea	Charlton Athletic
5 Bodley, Michael J.	Southend United	Peterborough United
8 Bryant, Matthew	Bristol City	Gillingham
2 Butler, Peter J.	Notts County	West Bromwich Albion
29 Canham, Scott W.	West Ham United	Brentford
9 Collins, Wayne A.	Crewe Alexandra	Sheffield Wednesday
15 Cousins, Robert P.	Bath City	Yeovil Town
23 Curcic, Sasa	Bolton Wanderers	Aston Villa
2 Curle, Keith	Manchester City	Wolverhampton Wanderers
9 Day, Christopher N.	Tottenham Hotspur	Crystal Palace
2 Debont, Andrew C.	Wolverhampton Wanderers	Hereford United
23 Dickov, Paul	Arsenal	Manchester City
6 Dryden, Richard A.	Bristol City	Southampton
22 Eckhardt, Jeffrey E.	Stockport County	Cardiff City
16 Ford, Jonathan S.	Bradford City	Gillingham
16 Gaughan, Steven E.	Darlington	Chesterfield
2 Gerrard, Paul W.	Oldham Athletic	Everton
19 Glover, Edward L.	Port Vale	Rotherham United
19 Goodridge, Gregory R.S.	Queens Park Rangers	Bristol City
12 Hargreaves, Christian	West Bromwich Albion	Hereford United
2 Hessenthaler, Andrew	Watford	Gillingham
13 James, Anthony C.	Hereford United	Plymouth Argyle
17 Keller, Kasey C.	Millwall	Leicester City
15 Kiely, Dean L.	York City	Bury
16 Leitch, Donald S.	Heart of Midlothian	Swindon Town
31 Marshall, Ian P.	Ipswich Town	Leicester City
7 Oakes, Scott J.	Luton Town	Sheffield Wednesday
16 Onuora, Ifem	Mansfield Town	Gillingham
15 Overson, Vincent D.	Stoke City	Burnley
2 Parrish, Sean	Doncaster Rovers	Northampton Town
15 Pickering, Albert G.	Coventry City	Stoke City
17 Prior, Spencer J.	Norwich City	Leicester City
17 Quinn, Niall J.	Manchester City	Sunderland
2 Robinson, Philip J.	Chesterfield	Notts County
14 Sharpe, Lee S.	Manchester United	Leeds United
19 Showler, Paul	Bradford City	Luton Town
30 Vincent, Jamie R.	Crystal Palace	AFC Bournemouth
16 Welsh, Stephen	Partick Thistle	Peterborough United

TEMPORARY TRANSFERS

19 Angell, Brett A.	Sunderland	Stockport County
27 Bass, David	Reading	Basingstoke Town
16 Bochenski, Simon	Barnsley	Scarborough
30 Coldicott, Stacy	West Bromwich Albion	Cardiff City
23 Cundy, Jason V.	Tottenham Hotspur	Bristol City
3 Cutler, Neil A.	Crewe Alexandra	Chester City
23 Dunwell, Richard K.	Barnet	Walton & Hersham
31 Evans, Thomas	Crystal Palace	Harrow Borough
30 Grant, Anthony J.	Preston North End	Glenavon
17 Harding, Paul	Cardiff City	Kettering Town
20 Hateley, Mark W.	Queens Park Rangers	Leeds United
20 Jackson, Matthew A.	Everton	Queens Park Rangers

128

27 Kelly, Gary A.	Bury	Oldham Athletic
30 Mahoney-Johnsen, Michael	Queens Park Rangers	Wycombe Wanderers
27 Martin, Jae A.	Birmingham City	Lincoln City
30 Miles, Benjamin D.	Swansea City	Slough Town
14 O'Hagan, Daniel A.	Plymouth Argyle	Weston-Super-Mare
30 Pack, Lenny J.	Cambridge United	Baldock Town
27 Roberts, Ben J.	Middlesbrough	Bradford City
30 Trollope, Paul J.	Derby County	Grimsby Town
1 Turpin, Simon A.	Crewe Alexandra	Sligo Rovers
30 Whittaker, Stuart	Bolton Wanderers	Wigan Athletic
21 Wigg, Nathan M.	Cardiff City	Merthyr Tydfill

SEPTEMBER 1996

6 Barnes, Paul L.	Birmingham City	Burnley
17 Burnett, Wayne	Bolton Wanderers	Huddersfield Town
26 Carpenter, Richard	Gillingham	Fulham
19 Elkins, Gary	Wimbledon	Swindon Town
13 Flack, Steven R.	Cardiff City	Exeter City
17 Garnett, Shaun M.	Swansea City	Oldham Athletic
17 Kelly, Gary A.	Bury	Oldham Athletic
27 Kinsella, Mark	Colchester United	Charlton Athletic
17 McMahon, Gerard J.	Tottenham Hotspur	Stoke City
13 Moss, David	Scunthorpe United	Partick Thistle
27 Naylor, Glenn	York City	Darlington
6 O'Hanlon, Kelham G.	Dundee United	Preston North End
20 Ormondroyd, Ian	Bradford City	Oldham Athletic
6 Parks, Anthony	Falkirk	Blackpool
17 Rankine, Simon M.	Wolverhampton Wanderers	Preston North End
13 Rattray, Kevin	Gillingham	Barnet
6 Robertson, Paul	Doncaster Rovers	Witton Albion
6 Sedgemore, Benjamin R.	Peterborough United	Mansfield Town
3 Slater, Robert D.	West Ham United	Southampton
6 Taylor, Shaun	Swindon Town	Bristol City
4 Turner, Andrew P.	Tottenham Hotspur	Portsmouth
5 Watson, Andrew A.	Blackpool	Walsall

TEMPORARY TRANSFERS

20 Adams, Kieren	Barnet	Hayes
5 Ashcroft, Lee	West Bromwich Albion	Preston North End
6 Barron, Michael J.	Middlesbrough	Hartlepool United
23 Boswell, Matthew H.	Port Vale	Hinckley Town
9 Brown, Kenneth J.	West Ham United	Reading
13 Brown, Michael A.	Preston North End	Rochdale
6 Bullimore, Wayne A.	Bradford City	Doncaster Rovers
6 Burnett, Wayne	Bolton Wanderers	Huddersfield Town
6 Byng, David	Doncaster Rovers	Ilkeston Town
30 Charnock, Philip A.	Liverpool	Crewe Alexandra
27 Crawford, James	Newcastle United	Rotherham United
9 Crichton, Paul A.	Grimsby Town	West Bromwich Albion
6 Cureton, Jamie	Norwich City	Bristol Rovers
26 Druce, Mark A.	Oxford United	Rotherham United
6 Dunn, Iain G.W.	Huddersfield Town	Scunthorpe United
27 Forsyth, Michael E.	Notts County	Hereford United
9 Griemink, Bart	Birmingham City	Barnsley
26 Hamill, Rory	Fulham	Glentoran
6 Helliwell, Ian	Burnley	Mansfield Town
13 Hodges, Lee L.	West Ham United	Exeter City
5 Holland, Christopher J.	Newcastle United	Birmingham City
6 Huckerby, Darren C.	Newcastle United	Millwall
13 Kavanagh, Graham A.	Middlesbrough	Stoke City
20 Lester, Jack W.	Grimsby Town	Doncaster Rovers
9 Marshall, Andrew J.	Norwich City	AFC Bournemouth
6 Mautone, Steve	West Ham United	Crewe Alexandra
6 McElhatton, Michael	AFC Bournemouth	Scarborough
2 McGleish, Scott	Peterborough United	Cambridge United
20 McGoldrick, Eddie J.	Arsenal	Manchester City
13 Moore, Ian R.	Tranmere Rovers	Bradford City

23 Morris, Mark J.	AFC Bournemouth	Gillingham
27 Neal, Ashley J.	Liverpool	Brighton & Hove Albion
13 Nixon, Eric W.	Tranmere Rovers	Bradford City
30 Omoyinmi, Emmanuel	West Ham United	AFC Bournemouth
19 Otto, Ricky	Birmingham City	Charlton Athletic
6 Palmer, Lee J.	Cambridge United	Woking
30 Regis, David	Barnsley	Peterborough United
8 Rigby, Malcolm R.	Nottingham Forest	Ilkeston Town
21 Scott, Andrew M.	Cardiff City	Merthyr Tydfil
13 Smart, Allan A.C.	Preston North End	Northampton Town
2 Sutton, Wayne F.	Derby County	Hereford United
27 Taylor, John P.	Luton Town	Lincoln City
20 Taylor, Martin J.	Derby County	Crewe Alexandra
6 Walker, John	Grimsby Town	Mansfield Town
11 Wassall, Darren P.	Derby County	Manchester City
23 Woodsford, Jamie M.	Luton Town	Kettering Town

OCTOBER 1996

23 Abrahams, Paul	Brentford	Colchester United
4 Baker, David P.	Torquay United	Scunthorpe United
18 Butters, Guy	Portsmouth	Gillingham
2 Crichton, Paul A.	Grimsby Town	West Bromwich Albion
18 Cureton, Jamie	Norwich City	Bristol Rovers
8 Druce, Mark A.	Oxford United	Rotherham United
14 Farrell, Sean P.	Peterborough United	Notts County
31 Finnan, Stephen J.	Birmingham City	Notts County
11 Griemink, Bart	Birmingham City	Peterborough United
11 Hendrie, John G.	Middlesbrough	Barnsley
8 Holdsworth, David G.	Watford	Sheffield United
31 Holland, Christopher J.	Newcastle United	Birmingham City
11 Kavanagh, Graham A.	Middlesbrough	Stoke City
11 Law, Nicholas	Chesterfield	Hereford United
14 Malkin, Christopher G.	Millwall	Blackpool
23 McElhatton, Michael T.	AFC Bournemouth	Scarborough
24 McGoldrick, Eddie J.P.	Arsenal	Manchester City
12 McGrath, Paul	Aston Villa	Derby County
31 Morris, Mark J.	AFC Bournemouth	Brighton & Hove Albion
2 Pennock, Adrian B.	AFC Bournemouth	Gillingham
9 Reeves, David	Carlisle United	Preston North End
25 Saville, Andrew V.	Preston North End	Wigan Athletic
11 Shipperley, Neil J.	Southampton	Crystal Palace
9 Smart, Allan A.C.	Preston North End	Carlisle United
24 Whitbread, Adrian R.	West Ham United	Portsmouth
18 Williams, Darren	York City	Sunderland

TEMPORARY TRANSFERS

23 Abbey, Nathanael	Luton Town	Worcester City
18 Armstrong, Steven C.	Nottingham Forest	Gillingham
11 Bass, Jonathan D.M.	Birmingham City	Carlisle United
28 Bennett, Frank	Southampton	Shrewsbury Town
28 Bent, Junior A.	Bristol City	Shrewsbury Town
25 Creaney, Gerard	Manchester City	Ipswich Town
14 Cundy, Jason V.	Tottenham Hotspur	Ipswich Town
29 Davies, Simon I.	Manchester United	Huddersfield Town
25 Davis, Neil	Aston Villa	Wycombe Wanderers
9 Davison, Aidan J.	Bolton Wanderers	Ipswich Town
14 Donowa, Brian L.	Birmingham City	Walsall
18 Duerden, Ian	Burnley	Glentoran
11 Fitzgerald, Scott B.	Wimbledon	Millwall
12 Gabbiadini, Marco	Derby County	Birmingham City
17 Gibson, Paul R.	Manchester United	Halifax Town
28 Gould, Jonathan A.	Bradford City	Gillingham
14 Grant, Anthony	Preston North End	Glenavon
14 Grazioli, Giuliano	Peterborough United	Woking
3 Griffiths, Carl B.	Peterborough United	Leyton Orient
11 Hay, Darren A.	Woking	Cambridge United
11 Helliwell, Ian	Burnley	Chester City

17 Hodgson, Douglas J.	Sheffield United	Burnley
16 Hulme, Kevin	Macclesfield Town	Halifax Town
4 Huxford, Richard	Bradford City	Peterborough United
4 Iga, Andrew	Millwall	Sittingbourne
18 Ireland, Simon P.	Mansfield Town	Doncaster Rovers
31 Jackson, Matthew A.	Everton	Birmingham City
1 Kelly, Anthony O.N.	Leyton Orient	Colchester United
4 Lock, Anthony	Colchester United	Chelmsford City
3 Lucas, David A.	Preston North End	Darlington
18 Ludlum, Craig	Sheffield Wednesday	Notts County
8 Martin, Jae A.	Birmingham City	Lincoln City
4 Mike, Adrian R.	Stockport County	Hartlepool United
4 Morgan, Philip J.	Stoke City	Chesterfield
4 Morrison, David E.	Peterborough United	Rushden & Diamonds
4 Neil, James	Grimsby Town	Grantham Town
5 Notley, Jay	Charlton Athletic	Dagenham & Redbridge
25 O'Kane, John A.	Manchester United	Bury
4 Pack, Lenny J.	Cambridge United	Baldock Town
10 Painter, Peter R.	Darlington	Rochdale
14 Patterson, Darren J.	Luton Town	Preston North End
4 Payne, Grant	Wimbledon	Woking
28 Rodger, Simon L.	Crystal Palace	Manchester City
24 Rowbotham, Darren	Shrewsbury Town	Exeter City
11 Rowbotham, Jason	Wycombe Wanderers	Plymouth Argyle
28 Rush, Matthew J.	Norwich City	Northampton Town
18 Scott, Andrew	Sheffield United	Chesterfield
25 Shirtliff, Peter A.	Barnsley	Carlisle United
4 Simpson, Michael	Notts County	Plymouth Argyle
11 Trollope, Paul J.	Derby County	Crystal Palace
14 Turner, Robert P.	Cambridge United	Hull City
3 Turpin, Simon A.	Crewe Alexandra	Ashton United
7 Van der Laan, Robertus P.	Derby County	Wolverhampton Wanderers
11 Warren, Christer	Southampton	Brighton & Hove Albion
11 Wells, David P.	AFC Bournemouth	Salisbury City
25 Williams, Lee	Leyton Orient	Purfleet
18 Williams, Michael A.	Sheffield Wednesday	Huddersfield Town
10 Williamson, David F.	Cambridge United	Coleraine
10 Woods, Billy	Tranmere Rovers	Blackpool
4 Wright, Thomas J.	Nottingham Forest	Reading

NOVEMBER 1996

22 Angell, Brett A.	Sunderland	Stockport County
8 Ashcroft, Lee	West Bromwich Albion	Preston North End
2 Barmby, Nicholas J.	Middlesbrough	Everton
29 Bennett, Frank	Southampton	Bristol Rovers
19 Bochenski, Simon	Barnsley	Scarborough
18 Carruthers, Martin G.	Stoke City	Peterborough United
26 Cundy, Jason V.	Tottenham Hotspur	Ipswich Town
7 Dreyer, John B.	Stoke City	Bradford City
29 Edwards, Andrew D.	Birmingham City	Peterborough United
1 Finnan, Stephen	Birmingham City	Notts County
29 Gregan, Sean M.	Darlington	Preston North End
27 Heaney, Neil A.	Southampton	Manchester City
7 Hemmings, Anthony G.	Macclesfield Town	Hednesford Town
4 Hillier, David	Arsenal	Portsmouth
1 Holcroft, Peter I.	Everton	Swindon Town
23 Huckerby, Darren	Newcastle United	Coventry City
29 Kavanagh, Jason C.	Derby County	Wycombe Wanderers
29 Little, Glen	Glentoran	Burnley
8 Martin, Jae A.	Birmingham City	Lincoln City
22 McGleish, Scott	Peterborough United	Leyton Orient
11 Mean, Scott	AFC Bournemouth	West Ham United
27 Norris, Richard	Marine	Crewe Alexandra
29 O'Connor, Martin J.	Peterborough United	Birmingham City
13 Poole, Gary J.	Birmingham City	Charlton Athletic
7 Rowbotham, Darren	Shrewsbury Town	Exeter City
29 Sealey, Leslie J.	Leyton Orient	West Ham United

131

15 Sharp, Raymond	Preston North End	Dunfermline Athletic
22 Spencer, John	Chelsea	Queens Park Rangers
8 Walker, John	Grimsby Town	Mansfield Town
8 Welsh, Steven G.	Peterborough United	Dunfermline Athletic
6 Wordsworth, Dean	Bromley	Crystal Palace

TEMPORARY TRANSFERS

29 Bimson, Stuart J.	Bury	Lincoln City
1 Blackmore, Clayton G.	Middlesbrough	Bristol City
18 Christie, Iyseden	Coventry City	AFC Bournemouth
6 Conlon, Paul R.	Sunderland	Gateshead
29 Cooke, Terence J.	Manchester United	Birmingham City
29 Davison, Aidan J.	Bolton Wanderers	Hull City
1 Eastwood, Philip	Burnley	Leek Town
8 Ferdinand, Rio G.	West Ham United	AFC Bournemouth
22 Gregory, Neil R.	Ipswich Town	Torquay United
8 Harper, Stephen	Newcastle United	Gateshead
22 Harris, Jason A.	Crystal Palace	Bristol Rovers
5 Hooks, John R.	Blackpool	Glentoran
29 Hurst, Glynn	Barnsley	Mansfield Town
29 Jardine, Jamie	Tranmere Rovers	Altrincham
1 Kavanagh, Jason C.	Derby County	Wycombe Wanderers
27 Kerslake, David	Tottenham Hotspur	Swindon Town
15 Le Bihan, Neil E.	Peterborough United	Bishops Stortford
19 Markey, Brendan	Millwall	Dundalk
21 Marshall, Andrew J.	Norwich City	Gillingham
6 Mildenhall, Stephen J.	Swindon Town	Gloucester City
29 Morgan, Alan M.	Tranmere Rovers	Altrincham
2 Morgan, Philip	Stoke City	Macclesfield Town
29 O'Halloran, Keith J.	Middlesbrough	Cardiff City
22 O'Toole, Gavin F.	Coventry City	Hereford United
1 Omoyinmi, Emmanuel	West Ham United	AFC Bournemouth
22 Peacock, Gavin K.	Chelsea	Queens Park Rangers
25 Reid, Shaun	Bury	Chester City
8 Richardson, Neil T.	Rotherham United	Exeter City
22 Sansome, Paul E.	Southend United	Gravesend & Northfleet
30 Scargill, Jonathan M.	Sheffield Wednesday	Matlock Town
13 Sheridan, John J.	Sheffield Wednesday	Bolton Wanderers
22 Stant, Philip R.	Bury	Northampton Town
22 Stein, Mark E.S.	Chelsea	Stoke City
8 Taylor, John P.	Luton Town	Colchester United
1 Thomson, Peter	Bury	Witton Albion
15 Tisdale, Paul R.	Southampton	Huddersfield Town
15 Tyler, Mark R.	Peterborough United	Yeovil Town
15 Wales, Danny P.	Crystal Palace	Worthing

DECEMBER 1996

13 Ashbee, Ian	Derby County	Cambridge United
30 Bimson, Stuart J.	Bury	Lincoln City
6 Charnock, Philip A.	Liverpool	Crewe Alexandra
6 Cornforth, John M.	Birmingham City	Wycombe Wanderers
4 Dykstra, Sieb	Queens Park Rangers	Dundee United
6 Forsyth, Michael E.	Notts County	Wycombe Wanderers
13 Halle, Gunnar	Oldham Athletic	Leeds United
10 Hamill, Rory	Fulham	Glentoran
24 Jackson, Matthew A.	Everton	Norwich City
31 Murphy, Shaun P.	Notts County	West Bromwich Albion
13 Neal, Ashley J.	Liverpool	Huddersfield Town
10 Nwadike, Chukwuemeka I.	Wolverhampton Wanderers	Shrewsbury Town
24 Peacock, Gavin K.	Chelsea	Queens Park Rangers
12 Randall, Adrian J.	York City	Bury
24 Samuels, Dean	Boreham Wood	Barnet
11 Scales, John R.	Liverpool	Tottenham Hotspur
27 Sheridan, John J.	Sheffield Wednesday	Bolton Wanderers
26 Stant, Philip R.	Bury	Lincoln City
20 Sutherland, Colin	Clydebank	Scarborough
31 Taylor, Maik S.	Barnet	Southampton
24 Williams, Lee	Leyton Orient	Purfleet

TEMPORARY TRANSFERS

13 Abbey, Nathanael	Luton Town	Basingstoke Town
19 Ayorinde, Samuel T.	Leyton Orient	Rushden & Diamonds
6 Boswell, Matthew H.	Port Vale	Redditch United
13 Bright, Mark A.	Sheffield Wednesday	Millwall
12 Brightwell, David J.	Bradford City	Blackpool
20 Brodie, Stephen E.	Sunderland	Scarborough
27 Brown, Kenneth J.	West Ham United	Birmingham City
12 Brown, Michael A.	Preston North End	Shrewsbury Town
24 Burton, Deon J.	Portsmouth	Cardiff City
2 Charnock, Philip A.	Liverpool	Crewe Alexandra
2 Clarke, Adrian J.	Arsenal	Rotherham United
21 Clough, Nigel H.	Manchester City	Nottingham Forest
6 Coady, Lewis	Wrexham	Sligo Rovers
20 Cook, Andrew C.	Swansea City	Portsmouth
2 Cross, Jonathan N.	Wrexham	Hereford United
1 Donowa, Brian L.	Birmingham City	Peterborough United
24 Fitzgerald, Scott B.	Wimbledon	Millwall
6 Futcher, Stephen A.	Wrexham	Sligo Rovers
6 Hanlon, Ritchie K.	Southend United	Dover Athletic
24 Inman, Niall E.	Peterborough United	Cambridge City
6 Kenworthy, Jonathan R.	Tranmere Rovers	Southport
24 Lancaster, David	Rochdale	Bamber Bridge
23 Lucas, David A.	Preston North End	Scunthorpe United
30 McGregor, Marc	Oxford United	Ards
20 McKeown, Gary J.	Dundee	Exeter City
27 Martin, Dean S.	Rochdale	Halifax Town
12 Moilanen, Teuvo	Preston North End	Scarborough
9 Myall, Stuart T.	Brentford	Hastings Town
21 Newell, Michael C.	Birmingham City	West Ham United
10 O'Reilly, Justin M.	Port Vale	Macclesfield Town
24 Phillips, Steven J.	Bristol City	Gloucester City
21 Riches, Steven A.	Leyton Orient	Billericay Town
24 Roberts, Neil	Wrexham	Bangor City
24 Rodosthenous, Michael	West Bromwich Albion	Telford United
13 Rogers, Paul A.	Notts County	Wigan Athletic
9 Rush, Matthew J.	Norwich City	Northampton Town
30 Scott, Andrew M.	Cardiff City	Bath City
20 Scott, Kevin W.	Tottenham Hotspur	Charlton Athletic
4 Selley, Ian	Arsenal	Southend United
12 Shearer, Lee	Leyton Orient	Hastings Town
5 Simpson, Michael	Notts County	Wycombe Wanderers
6 Simpson, Paul D.	Derby County	Sheffield United
20 Woodsford, Jamie	Luton Town	Hitchin Town

JANUARY 1997

13 Akinbiyi, Adeola P.	Norwich City	Gillingham
31 Breen, Gary	Birmingham City	Coventry City
27 Brown, Kenneth J.	West Ham United	Birmingham City
10 Brown, Michael A.	Preston North End	Shrewsbury Town
18 Elliott, Matthew S.	Oxford United	Leicester City
31 Fjortoft, Jan-Aage	Middlesbrough	Sheffield United
25 Forinton, Howard L.	Oxford City	Yeovil Town
31 Forster, Nicholas M.	Brentford	Birmingham City
16 Grant, Anthony	Preston North End	Glenavon
31 Horlock, Kevin	Swindon Town	Manchester City
14 Humphrey, John	Gillingham	Brighton & Hove Albion
28 Ireland, Simon P.	Mansfield Town	Doncaster Rovers
20 Limpar, Anders	Everton	Birmingham City
27 Linighan, Andrew	Arsenal	Crystal Palace
10 McFarlane, Andrew A.	Scunthorpe United	Torquay United
17 Minett, Jason	Lincoln City	Exeter City
1 Phelan, Terrence M.	Chelsea	Everton
17 Read, Paul	Arsenal	Wycombe Wanderers
27 Reid, Shaun	Bury	Chester City
31 Rush, David	Oxford United	York City

27 Simpson, Michael	Notts County	Wycombe Wanderers
31 Sinclair, David	Millwall	Dundee United
29 Stoker, Gareth	Hereford United	Cardiff City
18 Thomsen, Claus	Ipswich Town	Everton
17 Watson, Gordon W.	Southampton	Bradford City

TEMPORARY TRANSFERS

17 Appleton, Michael A.	Manchester United	Grimsby Town
24 Armstrong, Steven C.	Nottingham Forest	Watford
23 Beeston, Carl F.	Stoke City	Hereford United
27 Brady, Matthew	Barnet	Sligo Rovers
30 Brayson, Paul	Newcastle United	Swansea City
24 Broomes, Marlon C.	Blackburn Rovers	Swindon Town
29 Clapham, James R.	Tottenham Hotspur	Leyton Orient
24 Currie, David N.	Carlisle United	Scarborough
22 Foran, Mark J.	Peterborough United	Lincoln City
24 Frain, John W.	Birmingham City	Northampton Town
31 Gabbiadini, Marco	Derby County	Oxford United
30 Hills, John D.	Everton	Swansea City
17 Hope, Richard P.	Blackburn Rovers	Darlington
17 Howe, Stephen R.	Nottingham Forest	Ipswich Town
23 Innes, Gary J.	Darlington	Waterford United
1 Jones, Philip L.	Liverpool	Wrexham
27 Kenworthy, Jonathan	Tranmere Rovers	Portadown
24 Keown, Darren P.	Millwall	Harrow Borough
24 Landon, Richard J.	Stockport County	Macclesfield Town
10 McMahon, Sam K.	Leicester City	Kettering Town
8 Miller, Alan J.	Middlesbrough	Huddersfield Town
8 Miller, Alan J.	Middlesbrough	Grimsby Town
17 Moilanen, Teuvo J.	Preston North End	Darlington
8 Moore, Neil	Everton	Norwich City
27 Morgan, Alan M.	Tranmere Rovers	Portadown
16 O'Kane, John A.	Manchester United	Bury
6 Patterson, Gary	Wycombe Wanderers	Barnet
10 Pemberton, Martin	Oldham Athletic	Ards
23 Pilkington, Kevin W.	Manchester United	Rotherham United
1 Rees, Jason M.	Portsmouth	Exeter City
9 Rocastle, David C.	Chelsea	Norwich City
21 Scott, Kevin W.	Tottenham Hotspur	Norwich City
24 Street, Kevin	Crewe Alexandra	St Patricks Athletic
20 Turley, William L.	Northampton Town	Kettering Town
17 Wright, Thomas J.	Nottingham Forest	Manchester City

FEBRUARY 1997

14 Alsop, Julian M.	Halesowen Town	Bristol Rovers
4 Arkins, Vincent T.	Notts County	Portadown
6 Baddeley, Lee M.	Cardiff City	Exeter City
7 Beesley, Paul	Leeds United	Manchester City
28 Bennett, Gary M.	Preston North End	Wrexham
14 Blamey, Nathan	Southampton	Shrewsbury Town
21 Bowman, Robert A.	Leeds United	Rotherham United
14 Brodie, Stephen E.	Sunderland	Scarborough
18 Browning, Marcus T.	Bristol Rovers	Huddersfield Town
24 Bullock, Darren J.	Huddersfield Town	Swindon Town
6 Clarkson, Philip I.	Scunthorpe United	Blackpool
27 Cook, Andrew C.	Swansea City	Portsmouth
10 Donowa, Brian L.	Birmingham City	Peterborough United
28 Dunn, Iain G.W.	Huddersfield Town	Chesterfield
10 Gayle, John	Stoke City	Northampton Town
28 Guppy, Stephen A.	Port Vale	Leicester City
14 Hartson, John	Arsenal	West Ham United
24 Hendon, Ian M.	Leyton Orient	Notts County
28 Henry, Nicholas I.	Oldham Athletic	Sheffield United
28 Hodgson, Douglas J.H.	Sheffield United	Oldham Athletic
17 Hope, Richard P.	Blackburn Rovers	Darlington
14 Jones, Stephen G.	West Ham United	Charlton Athletic
10 Kitson, Paul	Newcastle United	West Ham United

	1995-96	1994-95	1993-94	1992-93	1991-92	1990-91	1989-90	1988-89	1987-88	1986-87	1985-86	1984-85	1983-84
Stockport Co	9	11	4	6	5	–	–	–	–	–	–	–	–
Stoke C	–	–	–	1	4	14	–	–	–	–	–	–	–
Sunderland	–	–	–	–	–	–	–	–	1	–	–	–	–
Swansea C	22	10	13	5	19	20	17	12	–	–	24	20	–
Swindon T	1	–	–	–	–	–	–	–	3	–	–	–	–
Torquay U	–	–	–	–	23	–	–	–	–	–	–	–	–
Tranmere R	–	–	–	–	–	5	4	–	–	–	–	–	–
Walsall	11	–	–	5	–	–	24	–	3	8	6	11	6
Watford	–	–	–	–	–	–	–	–	–	–	–	–	–
WBA	–	–	–	4	7	–	–	–	–	–	–	–	–
Wigan Ath	–	–	–	23	15	10	18	17	7	4	4	16	15
Wimbledon	–	–	–	–	–	–	–	–	–	–	–	–	2
Wolv'hampton W	–	–	–	–	–	–	–	1	–	–	23	–	–
Wrexham	8	13	12	–	–	–	–	–	–	–	–	–	–
Wycombe W	12	6	–	–	–	–	–	–	–	–	–	–	–
York C	20	9	5	–	–	–	–	–	23	20	7	8	–

	1995-96	1994-95	1993-94	1992-93	1991-92	1990-91	1989-90	1988-89	1987-88	1986-87	1985-86	1984-85	1983-84
Aldershot	–	–	–	–	*	23	22	–	–	6	16	13	5
Barnet	9	11	–	3	7	–	–	–	–	–	–	–	–
Barnsley	–	–	–	–	–	–	–	–	–	–	–	–	–
Barrow	–	–	–	–	–	–	–	–	–	–	–	–	–
Blackpool	–	–	–	–	4	5	–	–	–	–	–	2	6
Bolton W	–	–	–	–	–	–	–	–	3	–	–	–	–
Bournemouth	–	–	–	–	–	–	–	–	–	–	–	–	–
Bradford C	–	–	–	–	–	–	–	–	–	–	–	–	–
Brentford	–	–	–	–	–	–	–	–	–	–	–	–	–
Bristol C	–	–	–	–	–	–	–	–	–	–	–	–	4
Burnley	–	–	–	1	6	16	16	10	22	14	–	–	–
Bury	3	4	13	7	–	–	–	–	–	–	–	4	15
Cambridge U	16	–	–	–	–	–	6	8	15	11	22	–	–
Cardiff C	22	–	–	1	9	13	–	–	2	13	–	–	–
Carlisle U	–	1	7	18	22	20	8	12	23	–	–	–	–
Chester C	8	–	2	–	–	–	–	–	–	–	2	16	24
Chesterfield	–	3	8	12	13	18	7	–	–	–	–	1	13

*Record expunged

1982-83	1981-82	1980-81	1979-80	1978-79	1977-78	1976-77	1975-76	1974-75	1973-74	1972-73	1971-72	
–	1	8	–	–	–	–	–	–	–	–	–	Burnley
–	–	21	19	15	7	13	14	–	–	–	–	Bury
–	–	–	–	–	2	–	–	–	21	–	–	Cambridge U
2	–	–	–	–	–	–	2	–	–	–	–	Cardiff C
–	2	19	6	6	13	–	–	–	–	–	–	Carlisle U
–	–	3	–	–	–	–	–	3	14	11	–	Charlton Ath
–	24	18	9	16	5	13	17	–	–	–	–	Chester C
24	11	5	4	20	9	18	15	15	5	16	13	Chesterfield
–	–	22	5	7	8	–	22	11	–	–	–	Colchester U
–	–	–	–	–	–	–	–	–	–	–	–	Crewe Alex
–	–	–	–	–	3	5	5	–	–	–	–	Crystal Palace
–	–	–	–	–	–	–	–	–	–	–	–	Darlington
–	–	–	–	–	–	–	–	–	–	–	–	Derby C
23	19	–	–	–	–	–	–	–	–	–	–	Doncaster R
19	18	11	8	9	17	–	–	–	–	–	–	Exeter C
–	3	13	–	–	–	–	–	–	–	–	–	Fulham
13	6	15	16	4	7	12	14	10	–	–	–	Gillingham
–	–	–	1	–	–	23	18	16	6	9	–	Grimsby T
–	–	–	–	–	–	24	17	9	20	17	–	Halifax T
–	–	–	–	–	–	–	–	–	–	–	–	Hartlepool U
–	–	–	–	23	–	1	12	18	–	–	–	Hereford U
3	17	4	–	–	–	–	–	24	10	–	–	Huddersfield T
–	–	24	20	8	–	–	–	–	–	–	–	Hull C
20	–	–	–	–	–	–	–	–	–	–	–	Leyton Orient
4	–	–	24	16	9	–	–	–	–	–	–	Lincoln C
–	–	–	–	–	–	–	–	–	–	–	–	Luton T
–	–	23	18	–	1	11	–	–	–	–	21	Mansfield T
–	–	–	–	–	–	–	3	–	–	–	–	Middlesbrough
17	9	16	14	–	–	–	–	–	–	–	–	Millwall
4	16	12	–	–	–	–	–	–	–	–	–	Newport Co
–	–	–	–	–	22	–	–	–	–	–	–	Northampton T
–	–	–	–	–	–	–	–	–	–	2	4	Notts Co
–	–	–	–	–	–	–	–	–	1	4	11	Oldham Ath
5	5	14	17	11	18	17	–	–	–	–	–	Oxford U
–	–	–	21	4	16	10	7	–	–	–	–	Peterborough U
8	10	7	15	15	19	–	2	17	8	8	–	Plymouth Arg
1	13	6	–	–	24	20	–	–	–	–	–	Portsmouth
–	–	–	21	19	12	6	20	6	15	–	–	Port Vale
16	14	–	–	3	6	8	9	–	–	–	–	Preston NE
21	12	10	7	–	21	–	–	–	–	–	–	Reading
–	–	–	–	–	–	–	–	–	24	13	18	Rochdale
–	–	1	13	17	20	4	16	–	–	21	5	Rotherham U
–	–	–	–	–	–	–	–	–	24	–	–	Scunthorpe U
11	–	21	12	–	–	–	–	–	–	–	–	Sheffield U
–	–	–	3	14	14	8	20	–	–	–	–	Sheffield W
–	–	–	–	1	11	10	9	–	22	15	12	Shrewsbury T
15	7	–	22	13	–	23	18	12	14	–	–	Southend U
–	–	–	–	–	–	–	–	–	23	–	–	Southport

	First	Pts	Second	Pts	Third	Pts
1898–99d	Aston Villa	45	Liverpool	43	Burnley	39
1899–1900d	Aston Villa	50	Sheffield U	48	Sunderland	41
1900–01d	Liverpool	45	Sunderland	43	Notts Co	40
1901–02d	Sunderland	44	Everton	41	Newcastle U	37
1902–03d	The Wednesday	42	Aston Villa*	41	Sunderland	41
1903–04d	The Wednesday	47	Manchester C	44	Everton	43
1904–05d	Newcastle U	48	Everton	47	Manchester C	46
1905–06e	Liverpool	51	Preston NE	47	The Wednesday	44
1906–07e	Newcastle U	51	Bristol C	48	Everton*	45
1907–08e	Manchester U	52	Aston Villa*	43	Manchester C	43
1908–09e	Newcastle U	53	Everton	46	Sunderland	44
1909–10e	Aston Villa	53	Liverpool	48	Blackburn R*	45
1910–11e	Manchester U	52	Aston Villa	51	Sunderland*	45
1911–12e	Blackburn R	49	Everton	46	Newcastle U	44
1912–13e	Sunderland	54	Aston Villa	50	Sheffield W	49
1913–14e	Blackburn R	51	Aston Villa	44	Middlesbrough*	43
1914–15e	Everton	46	Oldham Ath	45	Blackburn R*	43
1919–20f	WBA	60	Burnley	51	Chelsea	49
1920–21f	Burnley	59	Manchester C	54	Bolton W	52
1921–22f	Liverpool	57	Tottenham H	51	Burnley	49
1922–23f	Liverpool	60	Sunderland	54	Huddersfield T	53
1923–24f	Huddersfield T*	57	Cardiff C	57	Sunderland	53
1924–25f	Huddersfield T	58	WBA	56	Bolton W	55
1925–26f	Huddersfield T	57	Arsenal	52	Sunderland	48
1926–27f	Newcastle U	56	Huddersfield T	51	Sunderland	49
1927–28f	Everton	53	Huddersfield T	51	Leicester C	48
1928–29f	Sheffield W	52	Leicester C	51	Aston Villa	50
1929–30f	Sheffield W	60	Derby Co	50	Manchester C*	47
1930–31f	Arsenal	66	Aston Villa	59	Sheffield W	52
1931–32f	Everton	56	Arsenal	54	Sheffield W	50
1932–33f	Arsenal	58	Aston Villa	54	Sheffield W	51
1933–34f	Arsenal	59	Huddersfield T	56	Tottenham H	49
1934–35f	Arsenal	58	Sunderland	54	Sheffield W	49
1935–36f	Sunderland	56	Derby Co*	48	Huddersfield T	48
1936–37f	Manchester C	57	Charlton Ath	54	Arsenal	52
1937–38f	Arsenal	52	Wolverhampton W	51	Preston NE	49
1938–39f	Everton	59	Wolverhampton W	55	Charlton Ath	50
1946–47f	Liverpool	57	Manchester U*	56	Wolverhampton W	56
1947–48f	Arsenal	59	Manchester U*	52	Burnley	52
1948–49f	Portsmouth	58	Manchester U*	53	Derby Co	53
1949–50f	Portsmouth*	53	Wolverhampton W	53	Sunderland	52
1950–51f	Tottenham H	60	Manchester U	56	Blackpool	50
1951–52f	Manchester U	57	Tottenham H*	53	Arsenal	53
1952–53f	Arsenal*	54	Preston NE	54	Wolverhampton W	51
1953–54f	Wolverhampton W	57	WBA	53	Huddersfield T	51
1954–55f	Chelsea	52	Wolverhampton W*	48	Portsmouth*	48
1955–56f	Manchester U	60	Blackpool*	49	Wolverhampton W	49
1956–57f	Manchester U	64	Tottenham H*	56	Preston NE	56
1957–58f	Wolverhampton W	64	Preston NE	59	Tottenham H	51
1958–59f	Wolverhampton W	61	Manchester U	55	Arsenal*	50
1959–60f	Burnley	55	Wolverhampton W	54	Tottenham H	53
1960–61f	Tottenham H	66	Sheffield W	58	Wolverhampton W	57
1961–62f	Ipswich T	56	Burnley	53	Tottenham H	52
1962–63f	Everton	61	Tottenham H	55	Burnley	54
1963–64f	Liverpool	57	Manchester U	53	Everton	52
1964–65f	Manchester U*	61	Leeds U	61	Chelsea	56

* Won or placed on goal average/goal difference.

	First	Pts	Second	Pts	Third	Pts
1965–66f	Liverpool	61	Leeds U*	55	Burnley	55
1966–67f	Manchester U	60	Nottingham F*	56	Tottenham H	56
1967–68f	Manchester C	58	Manchester U	56	Liverpool	55
1968–69f	Leeds U	67	Liverpool	61	Everton	57
1969–70f	Everton	66	Leeds U	57	Chelsea	55
1970–71f	Arsenal	65	Leeds U	64	Tottenham H*	52
1971–72f	Derby Co	58	Leeds U*	57	Liverpool*	57
1972–73f	Liverpool	60	Arsenal	57	Leeds U	53
1973–74f	Leeds U	62	Liverpool	57	Derby Co	48
1974–75f	Derby Co	53	Liverpool*	51	Ipswich T	51
1975–76f	Liverpool	60	QPR	59	Manchester U	56
1976–77f	Liverpool	57	Manchester C	56	Ipswich T	52
1977–78f	Nottingham F	64	Liverpool	57	Everton	55
1978–79f	Liverpool	68	Nottingham F	60	WBA	59
1979–80f	Liverpool	60	Manchester U	58	Ipswich T	53
1980–81f	Aston Villa	60	Ipswich T	56	Arsenal	53
1981–82g	Liverpool	87	Ipswich T	83	Manchester U	78
1982–83g	Liverpool	82	Watford	71	Manchester U	70
1983–84g	Liverpool	80	Southampton	77	Nottingham F*	74
1984–85g	Everton	90	Liverpool*	77	Tottenham H	77
1985–86g	Liverpool	88	Everton	86	West Ham U	84
1986–87g	Everton	86	Liverpool	77	Tottenham H	71
1987–88h	Liverpool	90	Manchester U	81	Nottingham F	73
1988–89k	Arsenal*	76	Liverpool	76	Nottingham F	64
1989–90k	Liverpool	79	Aston Villa	70	Tottenham H	63
1990–91k	Arsenal†	83	Liverpool	76	Crystal Palace	69
1991–92g	Leeds U	82	Manchester U	78	Sheffield W	53

No official competition during 1915–19 and 1939–46; Regional Leagues operating.
† 2 pts deducted

DIVISION 2 to 1991–92

Maximum points: a 44; b 56; c 60; d 68; e 76; f 84; g 126; h 132; k 138.

	First	Pts	Second	Pts	Third	Pts
1892–93a	Small Heath	36	Sheffield U	35	Darwen	30
1893–94b	Liverpool	50	Small Heath	42	Notts Co	39
1894–95c	Bury	48	Notts Co	39	Newton Heath*	38
1895–96c	Liverpool*	46	Manchester C	46	Grimsby T*	42
1896–97c	Notts Co	42	Newton Heath	39	Grimsby T	38
1897–98c	Burnley	48	Newcastle U	45	Manchester C	39
1898–99d	Manchester C	52	Glossop NE	46	Leicester Fosse	45
1899–1900d	The Wednesday	54	Bolton W	52	Small Heath	46
1900–01d	Grimsby T	49	Small Heath	48	Burnley	44
1901–02d	WBA	55	Middlesbrough	51	Preston NE*	42
1902–03d	Manchester C	54	Small Heath	51	Woolwich A	48
1903–04d	Preston NE	50	Woolwich A	49	Manchester U	48
1904–05d	Liverpool	58	Bolton W	56	Manchester U	53
1905–06e	Bristol C	66	Manchester U	62	Chelsea	53
1906–07e	Nottingham F	60	Chelsea	57	Leicester Fosse	48
1907–08e	Bradford C	54	Leicester Fosse	52	Oldham Ath	50
1908–09e	Bolton W	52	Tottenham H*	51	WBA	51
1909–10e	Manchester C	54	Oldham Ath*	53	Hull C*	53
1910–11e	WBA	53	Bolton W	51	Chelsea	49
1911–12e	Derby Co*	54	Chelsea	54	Burnley	52
1912–13e	Preston NE	53	Burnley	50	Birmingham	46
1913–14e	Notts Co	53	Bradford PA*	49	Woolwich A	49

116

7 Lawrence, Matthew J.	Wycombe Wanderers	Fulham
14 Partridge, Scott M.	Bristol City	Cardiff City
28 Pepper, Colin N.	York City	Bradford City
14 Potter, Graham S.	Southampton	West Bromwich Albion
13 Reinelt, Robert S.	Colchester United	Brighton & Hove Albion
21 Ritchie, Andrew T.	Scarborough	Oldham Athletic
19 Rowe, Rodney C.	Huddersfield Town	York City
26 Schwarzer, Mark	Bradford City	Middlesbrough
25 Scott, Kevin W.	Tottenham Hotspur	Norwich City

TEMPORARY TRANSFERS

21 Aiston, Sam J.	Sunderland	Chester City
14 Barclay, Dominic	Bristol City	Slough Town
26 Bartram, Vincent L.	Arsenal	Wolverhampton Wanderers
21 Bos, Gijsbert	Lincoln City	Gateshead
14 Bradley, Russell	Scunthorpe United	Hartlepool United
7 Brown, Stephen R.	Lincoln City	Dover Athletic
3 Castle, Stephen C.	Birmingham City	Leyton Orient
7 Christie, Iyseden	Coventry City	Mansfield Town
21 Clarke, Timothy J.	York City	Scunthorpe United
3 Cort, Carl E.R.	Wimbledon	Lincoln City
21 Crossley, Matthew	Wycombe Wanderers	Rushden & Diamonds
21 Crowe, Glen M.	Wolverhampton Wanderers	Exeter City
21 Davies, Gareth M.	Crystal Palace	Cardiff City
18 Davis, Kelvin G.	Luton Town	Doncaster Rovers
10 Duerden, Ian C.	Burnley	Bamber Bridge
28 Elliott, Stuart T.	Newcastle United	Hull City
28 Fleming, Hayden V.	Cardiff City	Inter Cable-Tel
21 Ford, Jonathan S.	Gillingham	Barnet
21 Gayle, Mark S.R.	Crewe Alexandra	Birmingham City
21 Gibson, Lee	Lincoln City	Lincoln United
28 Hardyman, Paul G.T.	Barnet	Slough Town
5 Hartfield, Charles J.	Sheffield United	Fulham
28 Hodges, Lee L.	West Ham United	Leyton Orient
21 Jones, Gary	Notts County	Scunthorpe United
19 Jones, Paul N.	Tranmere Rovers	Blackpool
5 Lee, Jason B.	Nottingham Forest	Charlton Athletic
14 Martin, Dean S.	Rochdale	Halifax Town
7 Martindale, Gary	Notts County	Mansfield Town
17 Mautone, Steve	West Ham United	Reading
5 McGargle, Stephen	Middlesbrough	Blyth Spartans
14 Mike, Adrian R.	Stockport County	Doncaster Rovers
28 Miller, Alan J.	Middlesbrough	West Bromwich Albion
14 Nogan, Lee M.	Reading	Notts County
6 Otto, Ricky	Birmingham City	Peterborough United
7 Palmer, Lee J.	Cambridge United	Dover Athletic
7 Patterson, Gary	Wycombe Wanderers	Chesterfield
7 Poric, Adem	Sheffield Wednesday	Southend United
14 Price, Christopher	Everton	Oxford United
19 Prudhoe, Mark	Stoke City	York City
10 Ramage, Craig D.	Watford	Peterborough United
21 Reed, Adam M.	Blackburn Rovers	Darlington
14 Reed, Ian	Shrewsbury Town	Stafford Rangers
7 Regis, David	Barnsley	Notts County
21 Rigby, Anthony A.	Bury	Scarborough
14 Robinson, Ian B.	Mansfield Town	Ilkeston Town
7 Rodger, Simon L.	Crystal Palace	Stoke City
7 Scargill, Jonathan M.	Sheffield Wednesday	Boston United
7 Scott, Keith	Norwich City	Watford
27 Scully, Anthony D.T.	Crystal Palace	Portadown
21 Sheffield, Jonathan	Peterborough United	Watford
21 Slade, Steven A.	Queens Park Rangers	Brentford
14 Stallard, Mark	Bradford City	Preston North End
14 Stevens, Mark	Oxford United	Ards
6 Teale, Shaun	Tranmere Rovers	Preston North End
20 Thorp, Michael S.	Reading	Fareham Town
7 Townsend, Quentin	Hereford United	Worcester City

3	Vaughan, John	Lincoln City	Colchester United
14	Weaver, Simon D.	Sheffield Wednesday	Doncaster Rovers
10	Wilkes, Timothy C.	Notts County	Grantham Town
17	Wrack, Darren	Grimsby Town	Shrewsbury Town

MARCH 1997

28	Agana, Patrick A.O.	Notts County	Hereford United
26	Anthony, Graham J.	Sheffield United	Swindon Town
24	Anthrobus, Stephen A.	Shrewsbury Town	Crewe Alexandra
27	Baker, David P.	Scunthorpe United	Hartlepool United
27	Beresford, David	Oldham Athletic	Huddersfield Town
27	Birch, Paul	Doncaster Rovers	Exeter City
27	Blake, Robert J.	Darlington	Bradford City
14	Brannan, Gerard D.	Tranmere Rovers	Manchester City
27	Charlery, Kenneth L.	Peterborough United	Stockport County
26	Clarke, Timothy J.	York City	Scunthorpe United
6	Collins, Simon	Huddersfield Town	Plymouth Argyle
24	Cowans, Gordon S.	Bradford City	Stockport County
27	Cunnington, Shaun G.	West Bromwich Albion	Notts County
14	Davison, Aidan J.	Bolton Wanderers	Bradford City
27	Desouza, Juan M.I.	Wycombe Wanderers	Peterborough United
11	Dibble, Andrew G.	Manchester City	Rangers
7	Duxbury, Lee E.	Bradford City	Oldham Athletic
27	Ebbrell, John K.	Everton	Sheffield United
1	Ebdon, Marcus	Peterborough United	Chesterfield
3	Edmondson, Darren S.	Carlisle United	Huddersfield Town
4	Evans, Michael J.	Plymouth Argyle	Southampton
17	Forbes, Steven D.	Millwall	Colchester United
27	Ford, Jonathan S.	Gillingham	Barnet
21	Forrester, Jamie M.	Grimsby Town	Scunthorpe United
27	Frain, John W.	Birmingham City	Northampton Town
27	Gilkes, Michael E.	Reading	Wolverhampton Wanderers
21	Granville, Daniel P.	Cambridge United	Chelsea
7	Griffiths, Carl B.	Peterborough United	Leyton Orient
27	Hamilton, Derrik V.	Bradford City	Newcastle United
14	Hateley, Mark	Queens Park Rangers	Rangers
12	Hughes, Bryan	Wrexham	Birmingham City
26	Jackson, Michael J.	Bury	Preston North End
4	Kearn, Stewart	AFC Bournemouth	Bashley
26	King, Philip G.	Aston Villa	Swindon Town
27	Linton, Desmond M.	Luton Town	Peterborough United
27	Marshall, Lee	Enfield	Norwich City
27	Mason, Andrew J.	Hull City	Chesterfield
27	McAuley, Sean	Hartlepool United	Scunthorpe United
27	McDermott, Andrew	Queens Park Rangers	West Bromwich Albion
27	McGorry, Brian P.	Wycombe Wanderers	Hereford United
27	McNally, Mark	Southend United	Stoke City
27	Miller, Alan J.	Middlesbrough	West Bromwich Albion
15	Moore, Ian R.	Tranmere Rovers	Nottingham Forest
21	Morrison, David E.	Peterborough United	Leyton Orient
13	Nogan, Kurt	Burnley	Preston North End
20	Pemberton, Martin C.	Oldham Athletic	Doncaster Rovers
27	Reid, Paul R.	Huddersfield Town	Oldham Athletic
7	Rogers, Paul A.	Notts County	Wigan Athletic
27	Rush, Matthew J.	Norwich City	Oldham Athletic
10	Sale, Mark D.	Mansfield Town	Colchester United
27	Shutt, Carl S.	Bradford City	Darlington
7	Stallard, Mark	Bradford City	Wycombe Wanderers
27	Stamps, Scott	Torquay United	Colchester United
26	Tiler, Carl	Aston Villa	Sheffield United
27	Tinkler, Mark R.	Leeds United	York City
20	Waddle, Christopher R.	Bradford City	Sunderland
14	White, Devon W.	Watford	Notts County
27	Wilder, Christopher J.	Notts County	Bradford City
14	Wilkes, Timothy C.	Notts County	Kettering Town
4	Wright, Thomas J.	Nottingham Forest	Manchester City

TEMPORARY TRANSFERS

14 Adams, Kieran C.	Barnet	St Albans City
18 Andrews, Ian E.	AFC Bournemouth	Leicester City
14 Armstrong, Steven C.	Nottingham Forest	Watford
21 Atkin, Paul A.	York City	Leyton Orient
27 Ayorinde, Samuel T.	Leyton Orient	Altrincham
21 Bankole, Ademola	Crewe Alexandra	Hyde United
3 Battersby, Anthony	Notts County	Bury
27 Bennett, Troy	Barnsley	Scarborough
27 Blatherwick, Steven S.	Nottingham Forest	Reading
14 Bracey, Lee M.I.	Bury	Ipswich Town
27 Brown, Michael R.	Manchester City	Hartlepool United
18 Carr-Lawton, Colin	Burnley	Leek Town
27 Chandler, Dean A.R.	Charlton Athletic	Torquay United
23 Clapham, James R.	Tottenham Hotspur	Bristol Rovers
7 Clarke, Adrian J.	Arsenal	Southend United
7 Clyde, Darron E.J.	Barnsley	Boston United
24 Cooper, Kevin L.	Derby County	Stockport County
25 Coughlan, Graham	Blackburn Rovers	Swindon Town
27 Cresswell, Richard P.W.	York City	Mansfield Town
27 Cutler, Neil A.	Crewe Alexandra	Leek Town
27 Duerden, Ian C.	Burnley	Southport
21 Dunwell, Richard K.	Barnet	Cheltenham Town
3 Evans, Paul A.	Leeds United	Bradford City
27 Evans, Thomas R.	Crystal Palace	Coventry City
27 Farrell, Sean P.	Notts County	Torquay United
27 Flynn, Sean M.	Derby County	Stoke City
3 Foran, Mark J.	Peterborough United	Oldham Athletic
26 Forrest, Craig L.	Ipswich Town	Chelsea
27 Fortune-West, Leo O.	Gillingham	Leyton Orient
26 Foster, Colin J.	Watford	Cambridge United
7 Freeman, Nathan	Manchester City	Fulham
3 Freestone, Christopher M.	Middlesbrough	Carlisle United
7 French, Jonathan C.F.	Bristol Rovers	Bath City
27 Galloway, Michael A.	Notts County	Gillingham
27 Gayle, Brian W.	Rotherham United	Bristol Rovers
27 Gilbert, David J.	West Bromwich Albion	York City
3 Glover, Edward L.	Rotherham United	Huddersfield Town
21 Gudmundsson, Niklas	Blackburn Rovers	Ipswich Town
27 Guinan, Stephen	Nottingham Forest	Burnley
10 Hanson, David P.	Leyton Orient	Chesterfield
27 Harper, Stephen A.	Newcastle United	Stockport County
27 Harris, Samuel R.	Manchester City	Altrincham
27 Harte, Stuart G.	Bristol Rovers	Bath City
3 Hinshelwood, Danny M.	Portsmouth	Torquay United
10 Howes, Shaun	Leyton Orient	Billericay Town
27 Janney, Mark	Tottenham Hotspur	Brentford
27 Jones, Philip L.	Liverpool	Tranmere Rovers
14 Jones, Stephen G.	Bury	Hyde United
7 Keown, Darren P.	Millwall	Ashford Town
27 Kiwomya, Andrew D.	Bradford City	Luton Town
5 Lancaster, David	Rochdale	Bamber Bridge
1 Landon, Richard J.	Stockport County	Rotherham United
27 Lee, Jason B.	Nottingham Forest	Grimsby Town
6 Lumsden, Todd M.	Oxford United	Ards
14 Mahorn, Paul G.	Tottenham Hotspur	Brentford
27 Martin, David	Northampton Town	Brighton & Hove Albion
3 McGibbon, Patrick C.	Manchester United	Wigan Athletic
27 McGowan, Gavin D.	Arsenal	Luton Town
7 McNiven, David J.	Oldham Athletic	Linfield
14 Midgley, Craig S.	Bradford City	Scarborough
27 Mildenhall, Stephen J.	Swindon Town	Salisbury City
27 Miles, Benjamin D.	Swansea City	Slough Town
27 Mison, Michael	Fulham	Stevenage Borough
27 Morrow, Stephen J.	Arsenal	Queens Park Rangers
17 Newell, Michael C.	Birmingham City	Bradford City
27 Patterson, Mark A.	Sheffield United	Southend United

17 Powell, Paul	Oxford United	Ards
31 Puttnam, David P.	Gillingham	Yeovil Town
24 Rattray, Kevin	Barnet	Welling United
28 Richardson, Dominic K.	Plymouth Argyle	Weston-Super-Mare
27 Ryan, Tim J.	Doncaster Rovers	Altrincham
25 Samways, Mark	Scunthorpe United	York City
21 Scott, Andrew	Sheffield United	Bury
27 Scott, Keith	Norwich City	Wycombe Wanderers
27 Sheffield, Jonathan	Peterborough United	Oldham Athletic
26 Tallon, Gerrit T.	Kilmarnock	Chester City
27 Taylor, Martin J.	Derby County	Wycombe Wanderers
27 Tindall, Jason	Charlton Athletic	Dulwich Hamlet
27 Turley, William L.	Northampton Town	Kettering Town
26 Walker, Justin	Nottingham Forest	Scunthorpe United
7 Warren, Christer	Southampton	Fulham
26 Wassall, Darren P.	Derby County	Birmingham City
19 Weaver, Luke D.S.	Leyton Orient	West Ham United
13 Westhead, Mark	Bolton Wanderers	Stalybridge Celtic
27 Williams, Michael A.	Sheffield Wednesday	Peterborough United
3 Williams, Steven D.	Cardiff City	Newport County
27 Wilson, Paul A.	Scunthorpe United	Cambridge United

APRIL 1997

16 Carroll, Roy E.	Hull City	Wigan Athletic
2 Gilkes, Earl G.M.	Reading	Wolverhampton Wanderers
1 Lomas, Stephen M.	Manchester City	West Ham United
3 Masters, Neil B.	Wolverhampton Wanderers	Gillingham
11 Mautone, Steve	West Ham United	Reading
9 Morrow, Stephen J.	Arsenal	Queens Park Rangers
1 Russell, Keith D.	Hednesford Town	Blackpool
30 Taylor, Craig	Dorchester Town	Swindon Town

MAY 1997

22 Battersby, Anthony	Notts County	Bury
14 Bilic, Slaven	West Ham	Everton
16 Collymore, Stanley V.	Liverpool	Aston Villa
27 Cox, Neil J.	Middlesbrough	Bolton Wanderers
14 Davies, Kevin C.	Chesterfield	Southampton
23 Foster, Stephen	Woking	Bristol Rovers
19 Hughes, Lee	Kidderminster Harriers	West Bromwich Albion
23 Hunt, Jonathan R.	Birmingham City	Derby County
23 Mendonca, Clive P.	Grimsby Town	Charlton Athletic
23 Murdoch, Colin J.	Manchester United	Preston North End
30 Parkinson, Gary	Burnley	Preston North End
20 Rose, Matthew	Arsenal	Queens Park Rangers
13 Stevens, Ian D.	Shrewsbury Town	Carlisle United
14 Upson, Matthew J.	Luton Town	Arsenal
14 Walker, Justin	Nottingham Forest	Scunthorpe United
17 Wassall, Darren P.	Derby County	Birmingham City

FA CUP REVIEW 1996–97

Middlesbrough's FA Cup Final game plan lasted all of 43 seconds before Roberto Di Matteo careered almost unchallenged into opposing territory before unleashing a searing drive which flew over Ben Roberts' head and into the roof of the net to give Chelsea the lead.

The gamble by Middlesbrough manager Bryan Robson of starting the match with Fabrizio Ravanelli and Robbie Mustoe, both of whom had been struggling with injuries before the match, then failed on both fronts. Ravanelli limped off after 24 minutes, Mustoe followed four minutes later.

Though Chelsea seemed content to rest on their single goal lead, deciding that at least two men keeping a watchful eye on Juninho would frustrate Boro's attempts to get back into the game, they might have been vulnerable to a more cohesive outfit. Alas, Middlesbrough looked the part of a team recently relegated.

When Eddie Newton added a second goal for Chelsea in the 83rd minute, what most Middlesbrough supporters feared had happened: relegation and a kind of double – being beaten in both major cup competition finals.

The first round had begun gently enough with non-League giant-killers Woking holding Millwall 2-2 on a Friday evening. The following day, Carlisle took six goals off Shepshed and though there were drawn games for Farnborough with Barnet, Cheltenham with Peterborough, Colwyn Bay with Wrexham and Sudbury with Brighton, there were no immediate fireworks. They came later. On the following day, Whitby drew with Hull, without a goal being scored.

The replays presented a slightly different picture. Out went crisis club Brighton on penalties and Millwall on their own ground. Whitby led Hull 4-3 after fifty minutes but incredibly lost 8-4 in extra time with Duane Darby scoring a rare double hat-trick.

Round two had more shocks. Hednesford Town won 1-0 at Blackpool, Woking 2-0 at Cambridge United and Stevenage Borough 2-1 at Leyton Orient.

Thus when the Third Round dawned, only Carlisle and Chester from Division Three remained representing the lowest division. It was the smallest contingent from this source since 1958 and even the Vauxhall Conference had three representatives.

So much for Chester, beaten 6-0 at Middlesbrough, though Sheffield Wednesday proved the highest scorers with seven goals without reply from Grimsby. Wrexham held West Ham 1-1 but the weather accounted for many other ties on a day when there was one Premiership casualty, Southampton losing 3-1 at Reading.

In the rearranged fixtures, Hednesford beat York 1-0 and Crewe held Wimbledon before losing the replay as the Third Round merged with Round Four on the same day.

A last-minute goal enabled Woking to draw at Coventry, an injury-time effort finished off West Ham, Bradford won 3-2 at Everton and Hednesford frightened Middlesbrough before themselves losing 3-2.

Then again, Liverpool appeared to be showing their Sunday best against Chelsea, leading 2-0 at half-time when the home team had scarcely had a worthwhile kick. Not so the second half, truly one of two such. Chelsea in rampant mood destroyed the opposition to win 4-2. Woking's run ended in the Coventry replay.

But plucky Chesterfield beat Nottingham Forest 1-0 in Round Five, Portsmouth won 3-2 at Leeds and Chelsea for once surrendered a 2-0 lead of their own to be held at Leicester before winning the replay.

Middlesbrough won 2-0 at Derby in the Sixth Round, Chesterfield edged out Wrexham 1-0 and Chelsea put Portsmouth to flight 4-1. Wimbledon completed the semi-finalists with a 2-0 success at Sheffield Wednesday.

Chesterfield stunned Middlesbrough by leading 2-0 at one time, then forcing a draw in the extra period, but Chelsea comfortably beat Wimbledon 3-0. Middlesbrough had less of a problem thereafter winning their replay 3-0.

The odds on Middlesbrough winning the Final were long indeed. Three times previously a team had reached the final in the same season they were relegated. All had lost: Manchester City in 1926, Leicester 1969 and Brighton 1983. Boro made it four.

FA CUP 1996–97 – sponsored by Littlewood Pools

FIRST ROUND

Woking	(1) 2	Millwall	(2) 2
Ashford T	(1) 2	Dagenham & Redbridge	(1) 2
Blackpool	(1) 1	Wigan Ath	(0) 0
Boreham Wood	(1) 1	Rushden & Diamonds	(1) 1
Boston U	(1) 3	Morecambe	(0) 0
Brentford	(1) 2	Bournemouth	(0) 0
Bristol R	(0) 1	Exeter C	(0) 2
Bromley	(1) 1	Enfield	(2) 3
Burnley	(1) 2	Lincoln C	(0) 1
Cambridge U	(3) 3	Welling U	(0) 0
Cardiff C	(1) 2	Hendon	(0) 0
Carlisle U	(3) 6	Shepshed Dynamo	(0) 0
Chester C	(0) 3	Stalybridge C	(0) 0
Chesterfield	(1) 1	Bury	(0) 0
Colchester U	(0) 1	Wycombe W	(1) 2
Colwyn Bay	(0) 1	Wrexham	(0) 1
Crewe Alex	(2) 4	Kidderminster H	(0) 0
Farnborough T	(2) 2	Barnet	(0) 2
Gillingham	(1) 1	Hereford U	(0) 0
Hartlepool U	(0) 0	York C	(0) 0
Hednesford T	(1) 2	Southport	(0) 1
Leyton Orient	(0) 2	Merthyr Tydfil	(0) 1
Macclesfield T	(0) 0	Rochdale	(2) 2
Mansfield T	(3) 4	Consett	(0) 0
Northwich V	(1) 2	Walsall	(0) 2
Peterborough U	(0) 0	Cheltenham T	(0) 0
Plymouth Arg	(1) 5	Fulham	(0) 0
Preston NE	(3) 4	Altrincham	(0) 1
Runcorn	(1) 1	Darlington	(2) 4
Scunthorpe U	(2) 4	Rotherham U	(1) 1
Shrewsbury T	(1) 1	Scarborough	(0) 1
Stevenage B	(1) 2	Hayes	(2) 2
Stockport Co	(0) 2	Doncaster R	(0) 1
Sudbury T	(0) 0	Brighton & HA	(0) 0
Swansea C	(0) 1	Bristol C	(1) 1
Torquay U	(0) 0	Luton T	(1) 1
Wisbech T	(0) 1	St Albans C	(0) 2
Newcastle T	(0) 0	Notts Co	(0) 2
(at Stoke.)			
Northampton T	(0) 0	Watford	(0) 1
Whitby T	(0) 0	Hull C	(0) 0

FIRST ROUND REPLAY

Dagenham & Redbridge	(1) 1	Ashford T	(0) 1
(aet; Ashford T won 4-3 on penalties)			
Barnet	(0) 1	Farnborough T	(0) 0
Brighton & HA	(1) 1	Sudbury T	(1) 1
(aet; Sudbury T won 4-3 on penalties)			
Bristol C	(1) 1	Swansea C	(0) 0
Hayes	(0) 0	Stevenage B	(1) 2
Hull C	(3) 8	Whitby T	(2) 4
Millwall	(0) 0	Woking	(1) 1
Rushden & D	(1) 2	Boreham Wood	(1) 3

Scarborough	(0) 1	Shrewsbury T	(0) 0
Walsall	(2) 3	Northwich V	(0) 1
Wrexham	(1) 2	Colwyn Bay	(0) 0
York C	(2) 3	Hartlepool U	(0) 0
Cheltenham T	(0) 1	Peterborough U	(0) 3

SECOND ROUND

Plymouth Arg	(2) 4	Exeter C	(1) 1
Barnet	(2) 3	Wycombe W	(0) 3
Blackpool	(0) 0	Hednesford T	(0) 1
Bristol C	(5) 9	St Albans C	(0) 2
Cambridge U	(0) 0	Woking	(0) 2
Cardiff C	(0) 0	Gillingham	(1) 2
Carlisle U	(0) 1	Darlington	(0) 0
Chester C	(1) 1	Boston U	(0) 0
Chesterfield	(1) 2	Scarborough	(0) 0
Enfield	(1) 1	Peterborough U	(0) 1
Hull C	(1) 1	Crewe Alex	(1) 5
Leyton Orient	(1) 1	Stevenage B	(2) 2
Luton T	(0) 2	Boreham Wood	(0) 0
Mansfield T	(0) 0	Stockport Co	(1) 3
Notts Co	(1) 3	Rochdale	(0) 1
Preston NE	(0) 2	York C	(2) 3
Sudbury T	(1) 1	Brentford	(0) 3
(at Colchester U)			
Walsall	(0) 1	Burnley	(0) 1
Watford	(0) 5	Ashford T	(0) 0
Wrexham	(1) 2	Scunthorpe U	(1) 2

SECOND ROUND REPLAY

Burnley	(0) 0	Walsall	(1) 1
(Match abandoned at half-time; floodlight failure.)			
Peterborough U	(3) 4	Enfield	(1) 1
Scunthorpe U	(1) 2	Wrexham	(0) 3
(aet)			
Wycombe W	(1) 3	Barnet	(1) 2
Burnley	(0) 1	Walsall	(0) 1
(aet; Burnley won 4-2 on penalties)			

THIRD ROUND

Arsenal	(1) 1	Sunderland	(1) 1
Blackburn R	(0) 1	Port Vale	(0) 0
Chelsea	(1) 3	WBA	(0) 0
Liverpool	(1) 1	Burnley	(0) 0
Middlesbrough	(3) 6	Chester C	(0) 0
Norwich C	(1) 1	Sheffield U	(0) 0
Nottingham F	(2) 3	Ipswich T	(0) 0
Plymouth Arg	(0) 0	Peterborough U	(0) 1
QPR	(0) 1	Huddersfield T	(0) 1
Reading	(1) 3	Southampton	(0) 1
Sheffield W	(3) 7	Grimsby T	(0) 1
Stevenage B	(0) 0	Birmingham C	(1) 2
(at Birmingham C)			
Wolverhampton W	(0) 1	Portsmouth	(0) 2
Wrexham	(1) 1	West Ham U	(1) 1
Charlton Ath	(0) 1	Newcastle U	(1) 1
Everton	(2) 3	Swindon T	(0) 0
Manchester U	(0) 2	Tottenham H	(0) 0

Wycombe W	(0) 0	Bradford C	(2) 2
Hednesford T	(1) 1	York C	(0) 0
Barnsley	(2) 2	Oldham Ath	(0) 0
Carlisle U	(1) 1	Tranmere R	(0) 0
Chesterfield	(0) 2	Bristol C	(0) 0
Crewe Alex	(1) 1	Wimbledon	(1) 1
Crystal Palace	(1) 2	Leeds U	(2) 2
Gillingham	(0) 0	Derby Co	(0) 0
(Abandoned after 66 minutes; frozen pitch.)		
Notts Co	(0) 0	Aston Villa	(0) 0
Leicester C	(1) 2	Southend U	(0) 0
Stoke C	(0) 0	Stockport Co	(1) 2
Gillingham	(0) 0	Derby Co	(0) 2
Luton T	(0) 1	Bolton W	(1) 1
Watford	(0) 2	Oxford U	(0) 0
Brentford	(0) 0	Manchester City	(0) 1
Coventry C	(0) 1	Woking	(0) 1

THIRD ROUND REPLAY

Huddersfield T	(1) 1	QPR	(1) 2
Newcastle U	(1) 2	Charlton Ath	(0) 1
Sunderland	(0) 0	Arsenal	(0) 2
Wimbledon	(1) 2	Crewe Alex	(0) 0
Aston Villa	(1) 3	Notts Co	(0) 0
Bolton W	(1) 6	Luton T	(2) 2
Leeds U	(1) 1	Crystal Palace	(0) 0
West Ham U	(0) 0	Wrexham	(0) 1
Woking	(1) 1	Coventry C	(1) 2

FOURTH ROUND

Birmingham C	(1) 3	Stockport Co	(0) 1
Carlisle U	(0) 0	Sheffield W	(1) 2
Derby Co	(2) 3	Aston Villa	(0) 3
Everton	(0) 2	Bradford C	(0) 3
Hednesford T	(1) 2	Middlesbrough	(1) 3
(at Middlesbrough.)		
Leicester C	(1) 2	Norwich C	(1) 1
Manchester U	(0) 1	Wimbledon	(0) 1
Portsmouth	(0) 3	Reading	(0) 0
QPR	(2) 3	Barnsley	(1) 2
Chelsea	(0) 4	Liverpool	(2) 2
Newcastle U	(0) 1	Nottingham F	(0) 2
Arsenal	(0) 0	Leeds U	(1) 1
Bolton W	(1) 2	Chesterfield	(1) 3
Peterborough U	(1) 2	Wrexham	(1) 4
Manchester C	(1) 3	Watford	(0) 1
Blackburn R	(1) 1	Coventry C	(2) 2

FOURTH ROUND REPLAY

Wimbledon	(0) 1	Manchester U	(0) 0

FIFTH ROUND

Birmingham C	(1) 1	Wrexham	(0) 3
Chesterfield	(0) 1	Nottingham F	(0) 0
Leeds U	(0) 2	Portsmouth	(1) 3
Manchester C	(0) 0	Middlesbrough	(0) 1
Wimbledon	(1) 2	QPR	(1) 1
Bradford C	(0) 0	Sheffield W	(0) 1
Leicester C	(0) 2	Chelsea	(2) 2

| Derby Co | (2) 3 | Coventry C | (2) 2 |

FIFTH ROUND REPLAY

| Chelsea | (0) 1 | Leicester C | (0) 0 |

SIXTH ROUND

Derby Co	(0) 0	Middlesbrough	(1) 2
Chesterfield	(0) 1	Wrexham	(0) 0
Portsmouth	(0) 1	Chelsea	(2) 4
Sheffield W	(0) 0	Wimbledon	(0) 2

SEMI FINALS

| Middlesbrough | (0) 3 | Chesterfield | (0) 3 |
| Wimbledon | (0) 0 | Chelsea | (1) 3 |

SEMI FINAL REPLAY

| Middlesbrough | (0) 3 | Chesterfield | (0) 1 |

FINAL at Wembley

17 MAY

Chelsea (1) 2 *(Di Matteo 1, Newton 82)*

Middlesbrough (0) 0   79,160

Chelsea: Grodas; Petrescu, Minto, Sinclair, Leboeuf, Clarke, Zola (Vialli 88), Di Matteo, Newton, Hughes M, Wise.
Middlesbrough: Roberts; Blackmore, Fleming, Stamp, Pearson, Festa, Emerson, Mustoe (Vickers 28), Ravanelli (Beck 23), Juninho, Hignett (Kinder 74).
Di Matteo's 43 seconds goal was the fastest in Wembley Cup Final history.

PAST FA CUP FINALS

Details of one goalscorer is not available in 1878.

1872	The Wanderers ....1 *Betts*	Royal Engineers 0	
1873	The Wanderers ....2 *Kinnaird, Wollaston*	Oxford University 0	
1874	Oxford University............2 *Mackarness, Patton*	Royal Engineers 0	
1875	Royal Engineers ....1 *Renny-Tailyour*	Old Etonians ....1* *Bonsor*	
Replay	Royal Engineers ....2 *Renny-Tailyour, Stafford*	Old Etonians 0	
1876	The Wanderers ....1 *Edwards*	Old Etonians ....1* *Bonsor*	
Replay	The Wanderers ....3 *Wollaston, Hughes 2*	Old Etonians 0	
1877	The Wanderers ....2 *Kenrick, Heron*	Oxford University ....1* *Kinnaird (og)*	
1878	The Wanderers ....3 *Kenrick 2, Kinnaird*	Royal Engineers ....1 *Unknown*	
1879	Old Etonians ....1 *Clerke*	Clapham Rovers 0	
1880	Clapham Rovers ....1 *Lloyd-Jones*	Oxford University 0	
1881	Old Carthusians ....3 *Wyngard, Parry, Todd*	Old Etonians 0	
1882	Old Etonians ....1 *Anderson*	Blackburn Rovers......................0	
1883	Blackburn Olympic ....2 *Costley, Matthews*	Old Etonians ....1* *Goodhart*	
1884	Blackburn Rovers.............2 *Brown, Forrest*	Queen's Park, Glasgow ....1 *Christie*	
1885	Blackburn Rovers.............2 *Forrest, Brown*	Queen's Park, Glasgow 0	
1886	Blackburn Rovers.............0	West Bromwich Albion 0	
Replay	Blackburn Rovers.............2 *Brown, Sowerbutts*	West Bromwich Albion 0	
1887	Aston Villa ....2 *Hunter, Hodgetts*	West Bromwich Albion 0	
1888	West Bromwich Albion ......2 *Woodhall, Bayliss*	Preston NE ....1 *Goodall*	
1889	Preston NE ....3 *Dewhurst, Ross, Thompson*	Wolverhampton W 0	
1890	Blackburn Rovers.............6 *Dewar, John Southworth, Lofthouse, Townley 3*	Sheffield W ....1 *Bennett*	

144

Year	Winners	Score	Runners-up	Score
1891	Blackburn Rovers *Dewar, John Southworth, Townley*	3	Notts Co *Oswald*	1
1892	West Browmwich Albion *Geddes, Nicholls, Reynolds*	3	Aston Villa	0
1893	Wolverhampton W *Allen*	1	Everton	0
1894	Notts Co *Watson, Logan 3*	4	Bolton W *Cassidy*	1
1895	Aston Villa *Devey*	1	West Bromwich Albion	0
1896	Sheffield W *Spiksley 2*	2	Wolverhampton W *Black*	1
1897	Aston Villa *Campbell, Wheldon, Crabtree*	3	Everton *Boyle, Bell*	2
1898	Nottingham F *Cape 2, McPherson*	3	Derby Co *Bloomer*	1
1899	Sheffield U *Bennett, Beers, Almond, Priest*	4	Derby Co *Boag*	1
1900	Bury *McLuckie 2, Wood, Plant*	4	Southampton	0
1901	Tottenham H *Brown 2*	2	Sheffield U *Bennett, Priest*	2
Replay	Tottenham H *Cameron, Smith, Brown*	3	Sheffield U *Priest*	1
1902	Sheffield U *Common*	1	Southampton *Wood*	1
Replay	Sheffield U *Hedley, Barnes*	2	Southampton *Brown*	1
1903	Bury *Ross, Sagar, Leeming 2, Wood, Plant*	6	Derby Co	0
1904	Manchester C *Meredith*	1	Bolton W	0
1905	Aston Villa *Hampton 2*	2	Newcastle U	0
1906	Everton *Young*	1	Newcastle U	0
1907	Sheffield W *Stewart, Simpson*	2	Everton *Sharp*	1
1908	Wolverhampton W *Hunt, Hedley, Harrison*	3	Newcastle U *Howie*	1
1909	Manchester U *A. Turnbull*	1	Bristol C	0
1910	Newcastle U *Rutherford*	1	Barnsley *Tuffnell*	1
Replay	Newcastle U *Shepherd 2 (1 pen)*	2	Barnsley	0

145

1911	Bradford C	0	Newcastle U	0
Replay	Bradford C	1	Newcastle U	0
	Spiers			
1912	Barnsley	0	West Bromwich Albion	0
Replay	Barnsley	1	West Bromwich Albion	0*
	Tuffnell			
1913	Aston Villa	1	Sunderland	0
	Barber			
1914	Burnley	1	Liverpool	0
	Freeman			
1915	Sheffield U	3	Chelsea	0
	Simmons, Fazackerley, Kitchen			
1920	Aston Villa	1	Huddersfield T	0*
	Kirton			
1921	Tottenham H	1	Wolverhampton W	0
	Dimmock			
1922	Huddersfield T	1	Preston NE	0
	Smith (pen)			
1923	Bolton W	2	West Ham U	0
	Jack, J.R. Smith			
1924	Newcastle U	2	Aston Villa	0
	Harris, Seymour			
1925	Sheffield U	1	Cardiff C	0
	Tunstall			
1926	Bolton W	1	Manchester C	0
	Jack			
1927	Cardiff C	1	Arsenal	0
	Ferguson			
1928	Blackburn Rovers	3	Huddersfield T	1
	Roscamp 2, McLean		*A. Jackson*	
1929	Bolton W	2	Portsmouth	0
	Butler, Blackmore			
1930	Arsenal	2	Huddersfield T	0
	James, Lambert			
1931	West Bromwich Albion	2	Birmingham	1
	W.G. Richardson 2		*Bradford*	
1932	Newcastle U	2	Arsenal	1
	Allen 2		*John*	
1933	Everton	3	Manchester C	0
	Stein, Dean, Dunn			
1934	Manchester C	2	Portsmouth	1
	Tilson 2		*Rutherford*	
1935	Sheffield W	4	West Bromwich Albion	2
	Rimmer 2, Palethorpe, Hooper		*Boyes, Sandford*	
1936	Arsenal	1	Sheffield U	0
	Drake			
1937	Sunderland	3	Preston NE	1
	Gurney, Carter, Burbanks		*F. O'Donnell*	

Year				
1938	Preston NE ....1 *Mutch (pen)*	Huddersfield T 0*		
1939	Portsmouth ....4 *Parker 2, Barlow,* *Anderson*	Wolverhampton W ....1 *Dorsett*		
1946	Derby Co ....4 *H. Turner (og), Doherty,* *Stamps 2*	Charlton Ath ....1* *H. Turner*		
1947	Charlton Ath ....1 *Duffy*	Burnley 0*		
1948	Manchester U ....4 *Rowley 2, Pearson,* *Anderson*	Blackpool ....2 *Shimwell (pen), Mortensen*		
1949	Wolverhampton W ....3 *Pye 2, Smyth,*	Leicester C ....1 *Griffiths*		
1950	Arsenal..................................2 *Lewis 2*	Liverpool 2		
1951	Newcastle U ....2 *Milburn 2*	Blackpool 0		
1952	Newcastle U ....1 *G. Robledo*	Arsenal 0		
1953	Blackpool...............................4 *Mortensen 3, Perry*	Bolton W ....3 *Lofthouse, Moir, Bell*		
1954	West Bromwich Albion ....3 *Allen 2 (1 pen), Griffin*	Preston NE ....2 *Morrison, Wayman*		
1955	Newcastle U ....3 *Milburn, Mitchell,* *Hannah*	Manchester C ....1 *Johnstone*		
1956	Manchester C ....3 *Hayes, Dyson, Johnstone*	Birmingham C ....1 *Kinsey*		
1957	Aston Villa ....2 *McParland 2*	Manchester U ....1 *T. Taylor*		
1958	Bolton W ....2 *Lofthouse 2*	Manchester U 0		
1959	Nottingham F ....2 *Dwight, Wilson*	Luton T ....1 *Pacey*		
1960	Wolverhampton W ....3 *McGrath (og), Deeley 2*	Blackburn Rovers.............................0		
1961	Tottenham H ....2 *Smith, Dyson*	Leicester C 0		
1962	Tottenham H ....3 *Greaves, Smith,* *Blanchflower (pen)*	Burnley ....1 *Robson*		
1963	Manchester U ....3 *Herd 2, Law*	Leicester C ....1 *Keyworth*		
1964	West Ham U ....3 *Sissons, Hurst, Boyce*	Preston NE ....2 *Holden, Dawson*		
1965	Liverpool ....2 *Hunt, St John*	Leeds U ....1* *Bremner*		

Year	Winner	Score	Runner-up	Score
1966	Everton	3	Sheffield W	2
	Trebilcock 2, Temple		*McCalliog, Ford*	
1967	Tottenham H	2	Chelsea	1
	Robertson, Saul		*Tambling*	
1968	West Browmwich Albion	1	Everton	0*
	Astle			
1969	Manchester C	1	Leicester C	0
	Young			
1970	Chelsea	2	Leeds U	2*
	Houseman, Hutchinson		*Charlton, Jones*	
Replay	Chelsea	2	Leeds U	1*
	Osgood, Webb		*Jones*	
1971	Arsenal	2	Liverpool	1*
	Kelly, George		*Heighway*	
1972	Leeds U	1	Arsenal	0
	Clarke			
1973	Sunderland	1	Leeds U	0
	Porterfield			
1974	Liverpool	3	Newcastle	0
	Keegan 2, Heighway			
1975	West Ham U	2	Fulham	0
	A. Taylor 2			
1976	Southampton	1	Manchester U	0
	Stokes			
1977	Manchester U	2	Liverpool	1
	Pearson, J. Greenhoff		*Case*	
1978	Ipswich T	1	Arsenal	0
	Osborne			
1979	Arsenal	3	Manchester U	2
	Talbot, Stapleton, Sunderland		*McQueen, McIlroy*	
1980	West Ham U	1	Arsenal	0
	Brooking			
1981	Tottenham H	1	Manchester C	1*
	Hutchison (og)		*Hutchison*	
Replay	Tottenham H	3	Manchester C	2
	Villa 2, Crooks		*Mackenzie, Reeves (pen)*	
1982	Tottenham H	1	QPR	1*
	Hoddle		*Fenwick*	
Replay	Tottenham H	1	QPR	0
	Hoddle (pen)			
1983	Manchester U	2	Brighton & HA	2*
	Stapleton, Wilkins		*Smith, Stevens*	
Replay	Manchester U	4	Brighton & HA	0
	Robson 2, Whiteside, Muhren (pen)			
1984	Everton	2	Watford	0
	Sharp, Gray			
1985	Manchester U	1	Everton	0*
	Whiteside			

1986	Liverpool 3	Everton 1
	Rush 2, Johnston	*Lineker*
1987	Coventry C 3	Tottenham H.............2*
	Bennett, Houchen,	*C. Allen, Kilcline (og)*
	Mabbutt (og)	
1988	Wimbledon 1	Liverpool 0
	Sanchez	
1989	Liverpool 3	Everton 2*
	Aldridge, Rush 2	*McCall 2*
1990	Manchester U.............3	Crystal Palace 3*
	Robson, Hughes 2	*O'Reilly, Wright 2*
Replay	Manchester U.............1	Crystal Palace 0
	Martin	
1991	Tottenham H...............2	Nottingham F.............1*
	Stewart, Walker (og)	*Pearce*
1992	Liverpool 2	Sunderland 0
	Thomas, Rush	
1993	Arsenal......................1	Sheffield W................1*
	Wright	*Hirst*
Replay	Arsenal......................2	Sheffield W................1*
	Wright, Linighan	*Waddle*
1994	Manchester U.............4	Chelsea 0
	Cantona 2 (2 pens),	
	Kanchelskis, McClair	
1995	Everton 1	Manchester U 0
	Rideout	
1996	Manchester U.............1	Liverpool 0
	Cantona	

*After extra time

SUMMARY OF FA CUP WINNERS SINCE 1871

Manchester United	9
Tottenham Hotspur	8
Aston Villa	7
Blackburn Rovers	6
Newcastle United	6
Arsenal	6
Everton	5
Liverpool	5
The Wanderers	5
West Bromwich Albion	5
Bolton Wanderers	4
Manchester City	4
Sheffield United	4
Wolverhampton Wanderers	4
Sheffield Wednesday	3
West Ham United	3
Bury	2
Chelsea	2
Nottingham Forest	2
Old Etonians	2
Preston North End	2
Sunderland	2
Barnsley	1
Blackburn Olympic	1
Blackpool	1
Bradford City	1
Burnley	1
Cardiff City	1
Charlton Athletic	1
Clapham Rovers	1
Coventry City	1
Derby County	1
Huddersfield Town	1
Ipswich Town	1
Leeds United	1
Notts County	1
Old Carthusians	1
Oxford University	1
Portsmouth	1
Royal Engineers	1
Southampton	1
Wimbledon	1

APPEARANCES IN FA CUP FINAL

Manchester United	14
Arsenal	12
Everton	12
Liverpool	11
Newcastle United	11
West Bromwich Albion	10
Aston Villa	9
Tottenham Hotspur	9
Blackburn Rovers	8
Manchester City	8
Wolverhampton Wanderers	8
Bolton Wanderers	7
Preston North End	7
Old Etonians	6
Sheffield United	6
Sheffield Wednesday	6
Chelsea	5
Huddersfield Town	5
The Wanderers	5
Derby County	4
Leeds United	4
Leicester City	4
Oxford University	4
Royal Engineers	4
Sunderland	4
West Ham United	4
Blackpool	3
Burnley	3
Nottingham Forest	3
Portsmouth	3
Southampton	3
Barnsley	2
Birmingham City	2
Bury	2
Cardiff City	2
Charlton Athletic	2
Clapham Rovers	2
Notts County	2
Queen's Park (Glasgow)	2
Blackburn Olympic	1
Bradford City	1
Brighton & Hove Albion	1
Bristol City	1
Coventry City	1
Crystal Palace	1
Fulham	1
Ipswich Town	1
Luton Town	1
Middlesbrough	1
Old Carthusians	1
Queen's Park Rangers	1
Watford	1
Wimbledon	1

COCA-COLA CUP REVIEW 1996–97

Cup Final appearances for Leicester City at Wembley were hugely disappointing before 1997. Four times they had suffered defeat in the FA Cup and only a 118th minute equaliser against Middlesbrough prevented a fifth such reverse in the Coca-Cola Cup. They left it late again in the replay at Hillsbrough but Steve Claridge's 100th minute effort was enough to disperse the ghosts of Wembley.

The one effective tactical plan of the tie was City manager Martin O'Neill's decision to detail Swedish International Pontus Kamark to man-mark Juninho. It worked almost perfectly until Middlesbrough scored through Fabrizio Ravanelli five minutes into extra time. Leicester had then to claw their way back into the match which they did with Emile Heskey's City saver.

Leicester had had a quieter start to the campaign beating Scarborough 4-1 over two legs at the stage when three Premier League teams were beaten by lower opposition: Sheffield Wednesday losing to Oxford, Derby County to Luton Town and Everton to York City, who had put out Manchester United the previous season. No such problems for Middlesbrough who cut through Hereford in cavalier fashion with their Latin trio of Ravanelli, Juninho and Emerson contributing to a 7-0 first leg success from a 10-0 on aggregate. Ravanelli scored four in the first match including a penalty.

The Football League had granted the five European entries: Arsenal, Aston Villa, Liverpool, Manchester United and Newcastle United a bye into the Third Round.

This quintet survived, but others were not as fortunate. Chelsea lost 2-1 at Bolton, Blackburn Rovers were beaten at home by an own goal against Stockport County and Coventry City failed in a replay on their own ground to Gillingham. But Leicester defeated York 2-0 while Middlesbrough were carving up Huddersfield Town 5-1.

Yet the biggest shock concerned attendances which plummeted as a result of the absence from the Second Round of the five European clubs. After 142 matches in the competition, crowds were down 115,000 compared with 1995–96.

The fourth round provided further surprises, the biggest of them being Tottenham Hotspur's 6-1 defeat at Bolton. Stockport edged out West Ham in a replay. And though it was not as eyebrow-raising in view of the team Manchester United selected to play against Leicester, United lost 2-0. Meanwhile Middlesbrough had a convincing 3-1 win over Newcastle.

The quarter-finals still had one senior casualty in store in a fragmented round. Southampton lost at The Dell in a replay with Stockport, but Leicester came through at Ipswich 1-0, Bolton's dreams faded 2-0 at home to Wimbledon while Middlesbrough gave another fine performance in beating Liverpool 2-1.

Wimbledon seemed to have accomplished enough at Leicester in the first leg of their semi-final when they returned with a goalless draw and Middlesbrough made light of Stockport's giant-killing stance by winning 2-0 at Edgeley Park.

But return games were not as clear cut. Leicester held on to draw 1-1 at Selhurst Park to reach the final by courtesy of the away goal, while Middlesbrough struggled at home to Stockport, going behind in the sixth minute and surviving 2-1 on aggregate against ten men, as County had a player sent off in the last quarter of an hour.

The final provided Leicester with their second League Cup Trophy, as they had previously won in 1964 when the competition was still decided on a two-legged basis. The following year, City were runners-up. For Middlesbrough, a semi-final place in 1976 had been their best previous performance. But after some inspired performances earlier in the competition, Middlesbrough's relegation worries seemed to have handicapped their later performances in the Cup.

PAST LEAGUE CUP FINALS

Played as two legs up to 1966

1961	Rotherham U 2	Aston Villa 0	
	Webster, Kirkman		
	Aston Villa 3	Rotherham U 0*	
	O'Neill, Burrows, McParland		
1962	Rochdale 0	Norwich C 3	
		Lythgoe 2, Punton	
	Norwich C 1	Rochdale 0	
	Hill		
1963	Birmingham C 3	Aston Villa 1	
	Leek 2, Bloomfield	*Thomson*	
	Aston Villa 0	Birmingham C 0	
1964	Stoke C 1	Leicester C 1	
	Bebbington	*Gibson*	
	Leicester C 3	Stoke C 2	
	Stringfellow, Gibson, Riley	*Viollet, Kinnell*	
1965	Chelsea 3	Leicester C 2	
	Tambling, Venables (pen), McCreadie	*Appleton, Goodfellow*	
	Leicester C 0	Chelsea 0	
1966	West Ham U 2	WBA 1	
	Moore, Byrne	*Astle*	
	WBA 4	West Ham U 1	
	Kaye, Brown, Clark, Williams	*Peters*	
1967	QPR 3	WBA 2	
	Morgan R, Marsh, Lazarus	*Clark C 2*	
1968	Leeds U 1	Arsenal 0	
	Cooper		
1969	Swindon T 3	Arsenal 1*	
	Smart, Rogers 2	*Gould*	
1970	Manchester C 2	WBA 1*	
	Doyle, Pardoe	*Astle*	
1971	Tottenham H 2	Aston Villa 0	
	Chivers 2		
1972	Chelsea 1	Stoke C 2	
	Osgood	*Conroy, Eastham*	
1973	Tottenham H 1	Norwich C 0	
	Coates		
1974	Wolverhampton W 2	Manchester C 1	
	Hibbitt, Richards	*Bell*	
1975	Aston Villa 1	Norwich C 0	
	Graydon		
1976	Manchester C 2	Newcastle U 1	
	Barnes, Tueart	*Gowling*	
1977	Aston Villa 0	Everton 0	
Replay	Aston Villa 1	Everton 1*	
	Kenyon (og)	*Latchford*	

Replay	Aston Villa 3	Everton 2*	
	Little 2, Nicholl	*Latchford, Lyons*	
1978	Nottingham F 0	Liverpool 0*	
Replay	Nottingham F 1	Liverpool 0	
	Robertson (pen)		
1979	Nottingham F 3	Southampton 2	
	Birtles 2, Woodcock	*Peach, Holmes*	
1980	Wolverhampton W 1	Nottingham F 0	
	Gray		
1981	Liverpool 1	West Ham U.................................1*	
	Kennedy A	*Stewart (pen)*	
Replay	Liverpool 2	West Ham U.................................1	
	Dalglish, Hansen	*Goddard*	
1982	Liverpool 3	Tottenham H.................................1*	
	Whelan 2, Rush	*Archibald*	
1983	Liverpool 2	Manchester U.................................1*	
	Kennedy, Whelan	*Whiteside*	
1984	Liverpool 0	Everton 0*	
Replay	Liverpool 1	Everton 0	
	Souness		
1985	Norwich C.................................1	Sunderland 0	
	Chisholm (og)		
1986	Oxford U.................................3	QPR.................................0	
	Hebberd, Houghton, Charles		
1987	Arsenal.................................2	Liverpool 1	
	Nicholas 2	*Rush*	
1988	Luton T.................................3	Arsenal.................................2	
	Stein B 2, Wilson	*Hayes, Smith*	
1989	Nottingham F.................................3	Luton T.................................1	
	Clough 2, Webb	*Harford*	
1990	Nottingham F.................................1	Oldham Ath 0	
	Jemson		
1991	Sheffield W.................................1	Manchester U.................................0	
	Sheridan		
1992	Manchester U.................................1	Nottingham F.................................0	
	McClair		
1993	Arsenal.................................2	Sheffield W.................................1	
	Merson, Morrow	*Harkes*	
1994	Aston Villa 3	Manchester U.................................1	
	Atkinson, Saunders 2 (1 pen)	*Hughes*	
1995	Liverpool 2	Bolton W.................................1	
	McManaman 2	*Thompson*	
1996	Aston Villa 3	Leeds U.................................0	
	Milosevic, Taylor, Yorke		

*After extra time

COCA COLA CUP 1996–97

FIRST ROUND, FIRST LEG

Brentford	(0) 1	Plymouth Arg	(0) 0
Cardiff C	(0) 1	Northampton T	(0) 0
Carlisle U	(1) 1	Chester C	(0) 0
Colchester U	(1) 2	WBA	(1) 3
Darlington	(1) 1	Rotherham U	(0) 0
Doncaster R	(1) 1	York C	(1) 1
Exeter C	(0) 0	Barnet	(3) 4
Hartlepool U	(0) 2	Lincoln C	(1) 2
Hereford U	(0) 3	Cambridge U	(0) 0
Huddersfield T	(2) 3	Wrexham	(0) 0
Hull C	(1) 2	Scarborough	(1) 2
Ipswich T	(1) 2	Bournemouth	(0) 1
Luton T	(1) 3	Bristol R	(0) 0
Mansfield T	(0) 0	Burnley	(1) 3
Notts Co	(0) 1	Bury	(0) 1
Oldham Ath	(0) 0	Grimsby T	(1) 1
Oxford U	(1) 1	Norwich C	(1) 1
Port Vale	(0) 1	Crewe Alex	(0) 0
Portsmouth	(1) 2	Leyton Orient	(0) 0
Reading	(0) 1	Wycombe W	(0) 1
Rochdale	(0) 2	Barnsley	(1) 1
Scunthorpe U	(2) 2	Blackpool	(1) 1
Sheffield U	(1) 3	Bradford C	(0) 0
Southend U	(0) 0	Fulham	(1) 2
Stockport Co	(1) 2	Chesterfield	(0) 1
Swansea C	(0) 0	Gillingham	(0) 1
Swindon T	(1) 2	Wolverhampton W	(0) 0
Torquay U	(1) 3	Bristol C	(0) 3
Walsall	(0) 1	Watford	(0) 0
Wigan Ath	(1) 2	Preston NE	(3) 3
Brighton & HA	(0) 0	Birmingham C	(0) 1
Millwall	(1) 1	Peterborough U	(0) 0
Shrewsbury T	(0) 0	Tranmere R	(1) 2

FIRST ROUND, SECOND LEG

Barnet	(2) 2	Exeter C	(0) 0
Barnsley	(1) 2	Rochdale	(0) 0
Blackpool	(1) 2	Scunthorpe U	(0) 0
Bournemouth	(0) 0	Ipswich T	(1) 3
Bradford C	(0) 1	Sheffield U	(0) 2
Bristol C	(0) 1	Torquay U	(0) 0
Burnley	(2) 2	Mansfield T	(0) 0
Bury	(1) 1	Notts Co	(0) 0
Cambridge U	(0) 1	Hereford U	(0) 1
Chester C	(0) 1	Carlisle U	(1) 3
Chesterfield	(0) 1	Stockport Co	(0) 2
Crewe Alex	(1) 1	Port Vale	(2) 5
Fulham	(0) 1	Southend U	(2) 2
Gillingham	(1) 2	Swansea C	(0) 0
Grimsby T	(0) 0	Oldham Ath	* (0) 1
(aet; Oldham Ath won 5-4 on penalties)			
Lincoln C	(2) 3	Hartlepool U	(0) 2

154

Northampton T	(0) 2	Cardiff C	(0) 0
Peterborough U	* (1) 2	Millwall	(0) 0
Plymouth Arg	(0) 0	Brentford	(0) 0
Preston NE	* (2) 4	Wigan Ath	(1) 4
Rotherham U	(0) 0	Darlington	(0) 1
Scarborough	(2) 3	Hull C	(0) 2
Tranmere R	(0) 1	Shrewsbury T	(0) 0
WBA	(0) 1	Colchester U	(1) 3
Watford	(1) 2	Walsall	(0) 0
Wrexham	(0) 1	Huddersfield T	(1) 2
Wycombe W	(0) 2	Reading	(0) 0
York C	(1) 2	Doncaster R	(0) 0
Birmingham C	(1) 2	Brighton & HA	(0) 0
Bristol R	(2) 2	Luton T	(0) 1
Leyton Orient	(0) 1	Portsmouth	(0) 0
Norwich C	(1) 2	Oxford U	* (0) 3
Wolverhampton W	(1) 1	Swindon T	(0) 0

SECOND ROUND, FIRST LEG

Barnsley	(0) 1	Gillingham	(0) 1
Brentford	(1) 1	Blackburn R	(2) 2
Bury	(1) 1	Crystal Palace	(2) 3
Charlton Ath	(3) 4	Burnley	(1) 1
Fulham	(1) 1	Ipswich T	(0) 1
Huddersfield T	(1) 1	Colchester U	(0) 1
Lincoln C	(2) 4	Manchester C	(1) 1
Luton T	(1) 1	Derby Co	(0) 0
Oldham Ath	(1) 2	Tranmere R	(2) 2
Port Vale	(0) 1	Carlisle U	(0) 0
Preston NE	(0) 1	Tottenham H	(1) 1
Scarborough	(0) 0	Leicester C	(1) 2
Stockport Co	(2) 2	Sheffield U	(0) 1
Watford	(0) 0	Sunderland	(2) 2
Barnet	(1) 1	West Ham U	(0) 1
Blackpool	(1) 1	Chelsea	(1) 4
Bristol C	(0) 0	Bolton W	(1) 1
Coventry C	(0) 1	Birmingham C	(1) 1
Everton	(0) 1	York C	(0) 1
Leeds U	(1) 2	Darlington	(1) 2
Middlesbrough	(3) 7	Hereford U	(0) 0
Nottingham F	(0) 1	Wycombe W	(0) 0
Sheffield W	(1) 1	Oxford U	(0) 1
Southampton	(1) 2	Peterborough U	(0) 1
Stoke C	(0) 1	Northampton T	(0) 0
Swindon T	(0) 1	QPR	(0) 2
Wimbledon	(0) 1	Portsmouth	(0) 0

SECOND ROUND, SECOND LEG

Birmingham C	(0) 0	Coventry C	(0) 1
Blackburn R	(1) 2	Brentford	(0) 0
Bolton W	(0) 3	Bristol C	(0) 1
Burnley	(1) 1	Charlton Ath	(1) 2
Carlisle U	(1) 2	Port Vale	(1) 2
Colchester U	(0) 0	Huddersfield T	(0) 2
Crystal Palace	(3) 4	Bury	(0) 0
Darlington	(0) 0	Leeds U	(2) 2
Gillingham	(0) 1	Barnsley	(0) 0

Hereford U	(0) 0	Middlesbrough	(1) 3
Ipswich T	(1) 4	Fulham	(1) 2
Manchester C	(0) 0	Lincoln C	(1) 1
Northampton T	(0) 1	Stoke C	(0) 2
Oxford U	(0) 1	Sheffield W	(0) 0
Sheffield U	(1) 2	Stockport Co	(3) 5
Sunderland	(1) 1	Watford	(0) 0
Tranmere R	(0) 0	Oldham Ath	(0) 1
Wycombe W	(1) 1	Nottingham F	(0) 1
York C	(1) 3	Everton	(1) 2
Chelsea	(0) 1	Blackpool	(1) 3
Derby Co	(2) 2	Luton T	(1) 2
Leicester C	(1) 2	Scarborough	(0) 0
Peterborough U	(0) 1	Southampton	(2) 4
Portsmouth	(1) 1	Wimbledon	(0) 1
QPR	(0) 1	Swindon T	(1) 3
Tottenham H	(1) 3	Preston NE	(0) 0
West Ham U	(0) 1	Barnet	(0) 0

THIRD ROUND

Blackburn R	(0) 0	Stockport Co	(1) 1
Bolton W	(2) 2	Chelsea	(1) 1
Gillingham	(0) 2	Coventry C	(2) 2
Ipswich T	(2) 4	Crystal Palace	(1) 1
Port Vale	(0) 0	Oxford U	(0) 0
Wimbledon	(1) 1	Luton T	(1) 1
York C	(0) 0	Leicester C	(0) 2
Charlton Ath	(1) 1	Liverpool	(1) 1
Leeds U	(0) 1	Aston Villa	(0) 2
Manchester U	(1) 2	Swindon T	(0) 1
Middlesbrough	(2) 5	Huddersfield T	(0) 1
Newcastle U	(1) 1	Oldham Ath	(0) 0
Southampton	(0) 2	Lincoln C	(1) 2
Stoke C	(1) 1	Arsenal	(1) 1
Tottenham H	(0) 2	Sunderland	(1) 1
West Ham U	(1) 4	Nottingham F	(1) 1

THIRD ROUND REPLAYS

Oxford U	(2) 2	Port Vale	(0) 0
Lincoln C	(1) 1	Southampton	(0) 3
Luton T	(1) 1	Wimbledon	(0) 2
Arsenal	(1) 5	Stoke C	(1) 2
Coventry C	(0) 0	Gillingham	(0) 1
Liverpool	(2) 4	Charlton Ath	(1) 1

FOURTH ROUND

Ipswich T	(0) 1	Gillingham	(0) 0
Oxford U	(0) 1	Southampton	(1) 1
Wimbledon	(1) 1	Aston Villa	(1) 1
Bolton W	(2) 6	Tottenham H	(1) 1
Leicester C	(1) 2	Manchester U	(1) 1
Liverpool	(2) 4	Arsenal	(1) 2
Middlesbrough	(1) 3	Newcastle U	(1) 1
West Ham U	(1) 1	Stockport Co	(0) 1

FOURTH ROUND REPLAYS

Southampton	(1) 3	Oxford U	(1) 2
Stockport Co	(2) 2	West Ham U	(1) 1

FIFTH ROUND

Bolton W	(0) 0	Wimbledon	(2) 2
Middlesbrough	(2) 2	Liverpool	(0) 1
Ipswich T	(0) 0	Leicester C	(1) 1
Stockport Co	(2) 2	Southampton	(1) 2

FIFTH ROUND REPLAY

Southampton	(1) 1	Stockport Co	(0) 2

SEMI-FINAL FIRST LEG

Leicester C	(0) 0	Wimbledon	(0) 0
Stockport Co	(0) 0	Middlesbrough	(0) 2

SEMI-FINAL SECOND LEG

Wimbledon	* (1) 1	Leicester C	(0) 1
Middlesbrough	(0) 0	Stockport Co	(1) 1

FINAL at Wembley
6 APRIL

Leicester C (0) 1 *(Heskey 118)*

Middlesbrough (0) 1 *(Ravanelli 95)*   76,757

Leicester C: Keller; Grayson, Whitlow (Robins), Kamark, Walsh, Prior, Lennon, Parker, Claridge, Izzet (Taylor), Heskey.
Middlesbrough: Schwarzer; Cox, Fleming, Mustoe, Pearson, Festa, Emerson, Hignett, Beck, Juninho, Ravanelli.

FINAL REPLAY at Hillsborough
16 APRIL

Leicester C (0) 1 *(Claridge 100)*

Middlesbrough (0) 0   39,428

Leicester C: Keller; Grayson, Whitlow (Lawrence), Kamark, Walsh, Prior, Lennon, Parker, Claridge (Robins), Izzet, Heskey.
Middlesbrough: Roberts; Cox (Moore), Kinder, Festa (Vickers), Pearson, Blackmore, Emerson, Mustoe, Ravanelli, Juninho, Hignett (Beck).
Referee: M. Bodenham (East Looe).

* after extra time

AUTO WINDSCREENS SHIELD 1996–97

SOUTHERN SECTION FIRST ROUND

Hereford U	(0) 0	Millwall	(2) 4
Bristol R	(0) 1	Brentford	(1) 2
Cambridge U	(0) 0	Colchester U	(0) 1
Gillingham	(0) 1	Cardiff C	(0) 2

(aet; Cardiff C won on sudden death.)

Luton T	(0) 2	Leyton Orient	(1) 1
Plymouth Arg	(1) 2	Bournemouth	(0) 0
Brighton & HA	(1) 3	Fulham	(1) 2

(aet; Brighton & HA won on sudden death.)

Swansea C	(0) 1	Wycombe W	(0) 1

(aet; Swansea C won 6-5 on penalties.)

NORTHERN SECTION FIRST ROUND

Chesterfield	(0) 0	Preston NE	(0) 2
Bury	(1) 3	Darlington	(1) 1
Carlisle U	(0) 2	Rochdale	(0) 0
Doncaster R	(1) 1	Stockport Co	(0) 2
Hartlepool U	(0) 0	Burnley	(1) 2
Hull C	(2) 3	Chester C	(1) 1
Rotherham U	(0) 0	Blackpool	(0) 1
Scarborough	(0) 0	Notts Co	(1) 1

SOUTHERN SECTION SECOND ROUND

Brentford	(1) 2	Barnet	(0) 1

(aet; Brentford won on sudden death.)

Millwall	(1) 2	Colchester U	(0) 3

(aet; Colchester U won on sudden death.)

Watford	(1) 2	Torquay U	(0) 1
Cardiff C	(0) 1	Exeter C	(0) 1

(aet; Exeter C won 4-2 on penalties.)

Plymouth Arg	(1) 1	Brighton & HA	(0) 0
Peterborough U	(0) 2	Walsall	(0) 0
Swansea C	(0) 0	Bristol C	(1) 1

NORTHERN SECTION SECOND ROUND

Bury	(1) 6	Mansfield T	(0) 0
Blackpool	(2) 4	Lincoln C	(0) 0
Shrewsbury T	(2) 3	Wigan Ath	(0) 2

(aet; Shrewsbury won on sudden death.)

York C	(0) 1	Preston NE	(0) 0
Carlisle U	(2) 4	Hull C	(0) 0
Scunthorpe U	(0) 0	Notts Co	(0) 1

(aet; Scunthorpe U won 4-2 on penalties.)

Wrexham	(0) 0	Crewe Alex	(0) 1
Burnley	(0) 0	Stockport Co	(1) 1
Northampton T	(0) 1	Luton T	(0) 0

SOUTHERN SECTION QUARTER FINALS

Brentford	(0) 0	Colchester U	(1) 1
Exeter C	(0) 0	Peterborough U	(0) 1
Plymouth Arg	(0) 0	Northampton T	(1) 2
Watford	(1) 2	Bristol C	(1) 1

NORTHERN SECTION QUARTER FINALS

Crewe Alex	(1) 1	Blackpool	(0) 0
York C	(0) 0	Carlisle U	(2) 2
Bury	(1) 1	Stockport Co	(1) 2

(aet; Stockport Co won on sudden death.)

Shrewsbury T	(1) 2	Scunthorpe U	(0) 1

(aet; Shrewsbury T won on sudden death.)

SOUTHERN SECTION SEMI FINALS

Colchester U	(0) 2	Northampton T	(0) 1
Watford	(0) 0	Peterborough U	(0) 1

NORTHERN SECTION SEMI FINALS

Shrewsbury T	(0) 1	Carlisle U	(0) 2
Crewe Alex	(1) 1	Stockport Co	(1) 1

(aet; Stockport Co won 5-3 on penalties.)

SOUTHERN FINAL FIRST LEG

Peterborough U	(2) 2	Colchester U	(0) 0

SOUTHERN FINAL SECOND LEG

Colchester U	(1) 3	Peterborough U	(0) 0

(aet; Colchester U won on sudden death.)

NORTHERN FINAL FIRST LEG

Carlisle U	(0) 2	Stockport Co	(0) 0

NORTHERN FINAL SECOND LEG

Stockport Co	(0) 0	Carlisle U	(0) 0

FINAL (at Wembley)
20 APRIL

Carlisle U	(0) 0	Colchester U	(0) 0

(aet; Carlisle U won 4-3 on penalties.)

FA CHARITY SHIELD WINNERS 1908–96

1908	Manchester U v QPR	
	4-0 after 1-1 draw	
1909	Newcastle U v Northampton T	2-0
1910	Brighton v Aston Villa	1-0
1911	Manchester U v Swindon T	8-4
1912	Blackburn R v QPR	2-1
1913	Professionals v Amateurs	7-2
1920	Tottenham H v Burnley	2-0
1921	Huddersfield T v Liverpool	1-0
1922	Not played	
1923	Professionals v Amateurs	2-0
1924	Professionals v Amateurs	3-1
1925	Amateurs v Professionals	6-1
1926	Amateurs v Professionals	6-3
1927	Cardiff C v Corinthians	2-1
1928	Everton v Blackburn R	2-1
1929	Professionals v Amateurs	3-0
1930	Arsenal v Sheffield W	2-1
1931	Arsenal v WBA	1-0
1932	Everton v Newcastle U	5-3
1933	Arsenal v Everton	3-0
1934	Arsenal v Manchester C	4-0
1935	Sheffield W v Arsenal	1-0
1936	Sunderland v Arsenal	2-1
1937	Manchester C v Sunderland	2-0
1938	Arsenal v Preston NE	2-1
1948	Arsenal v Manchester U	4-3
1949	Portsmouth v Wolverhampton W	1-1*
1950	World Cup Team v	4-2
	Canadian Touring Team	
1951	Tottenham H v Newcastle U	2-1
1952	Manchester U v Newcastle U	4-2
1953	Arsenal v Blackpool	3-1
1954	Wolverhampton W v WBA	4-4*
1955	Chelsea v Newcastle U	3-0
1956	Manchester U v Manchester C	1-0
1957	Manchester U v Aston Villa	4-0
1958	Bolton W v Wolverhampton W	4-1

1959	Wolverhampton W v	3-1
	Nottingham F	
1960	Burnley v Wolverhampton W	2-2*
1961	Tottenham H v FA XI	3-2
1962	Tottenham H v Ipswich T	5-1
1963	Everton v Manchester U	4-0
1964	Liverpool v West Ham U	2-2*
1965	Manchester U v Liverpool	2-2*
1966	Liverpool v Everton	1-0
1967	Manchester U v Tottenham H	3-3*
1968	Manchester C v WBA	6-1
1969	Leeds U v Manchester C	2-1
1970	Everton v Chelsea	2-1
1971	Leicester C v Liverpool	1-0
1972	Manchester C v Aston Villa	1-0
1973	Burnley v Manchester C	1-0
1974	Liverpool v Leeds U	1-1
1975	Derby Co v West Ham U	2-0
1976	Liverpool v Southampton	1-0
1977	Liverpool v Manchester U	0-0*
1978	Nottingham F v Ipswich T	5-0
1979	Liverpool v Arsenal	3-1
1980	Liverpool v West Ham U	1-0
1981	Aston Villa v Tottenham H	2-2*
1982	Liverpool v Tottenham H	1-0
1983	Manchester U v Liverpool	2-0
1984	Everton v Liverpool	1-0
1985	Everton v Manchester U	2-0
1986	Everton v Liverpool	1-1*
1987	Everton v Coventry C	1-0
1988	Liverpool v Wimbledon	2-1
1989	Liverpool v Arsenal	1-0
1990	Liverpool v Manchester U	1-1*
1991	Arsenal v Tottenham H	0-0*
1992	Leeds U v Liverpool	4-3
1993	Manchester U† v Arsenal	1-1
1994	Manchester U v Blackburn R	2-0
1995	Everton v Blackburn R	1-0

*Each club retained shield for six months. †Won on penalties.

FA CHARITY SHIELD 1996

Manchester U (2) 4, Newcastle U (0) 0

At Wembley, 11 August 1996, attendance 73,214

Manchester U: Schmeichel; Irwin (Neville G), Neville P, May, Keane, Pallister, Cantona, Beckham, Scholes (Cruyff), Butt (Poborsky), Giggs.

Scorers: Cantona 25, Butt 30, Beckham 86, Keane 88.

Newcastle U: Srnicek; Watson, Beresford, Batty, Peacock, Albert, Lee, Beardsley (Asprilla), Shearer, Ferdinand, Ginola (Gillespie).

SCOTTISH LEAGUE REVIEW 1996–97

Rangers duly completed their ninth successive League title to equal the achievement of Celtic between 1966 and 1974. Though the final margin was only five points, Rangers always seemed to be able to recover from the odd setback whereas Celtic often failed to take advantage of the occasions when Rangers were below their best.

At the end of September, Rangers held a five-point lead over their rivals. Celtic reduced this to two points until 2 November when Rangers were held to a 2-2 draw away to Raith while Celtic were beating Aberdeen 1-0. This put Celtic on top on goal difference. But two weeks later, Rangers restored their position by beating Celtic 1-0 at Parkhead. The lead increased dramatically early in December when Rangers took an eight point lead. Because of postponements, this lead increased to 14 points before the holiday period, though Celtic had three matches in hand.

Arguably, Celtic's last hope of catching Rangers disappeared on 2 January when Celtic equalised at 1-1 against Rangers and then had a perfectly good goal disallowed before going on to lose 3-1. By the time Celtic had caught up on matches, they were still seven points behind.

Since Celtic ended the season 15 points ahead of third placed Dundee United, the continuing problem seems to be one of the table which has only two teams capable of winning the Championship and even one of these is finding it difficult to break Rangers monopoly.

It was a totally different story in Europe, where Rangers had a miserable time winning only one of their six Champions League fixtures and finishing bottom of their four team group. This, after successfully negotiating the qualifying round. Hearts, in the Cup-Winners' Cup, Celtic and Aberdeen in the UEFA Cup had varying experiences without reaching beyond the second round.

While Raith Rovers were automatically relegated to the First Division, Hibernian succeeded in retaining their position in a play-off with Airdrieonians. Taking a slender one goal lead from their first match, albeit from an own goal, Hibs were rocked in the first minute of the second leg when Airdrie equalised. But with the help of two penalties and Airdrie losing a player, sent off later in the match, they won 5-2 on aggregate.

St Johnstone were clear winners of the First Division finishing 20 points ahead of Airdrieonians, but at the foot of the table East Fife had a poor record indeed. They managed only two wins, one of them their first away on the last day of the season at fellow relegated Clydebank by 4-0.

Up from the Second Division come Ayr United and Hamilton Academical. These two finished well clear of the opposition, though earlier in the season, it had seemed likely that Livingston would be the ultimate winners, their move from Meadowbank seemingly a most successful transplant. Dumbarton and Berwick Rangers went down from the Second Division to be replaced by Inverness Caledonian Thistle and Forfar Athletic, who had an incredible late run to pip Ross County for second place when it seemed likely that the two former Highland League clubs would be promoted.

In the Cup competitions, Kilmarnock defeated Falkirk 1-0 in the Scottish Cup, their first success in this competition since 1929, while in the Scottish Coca-Cola Cup Final Rangers were given a run for their money before they overcame Hearts 4-3.

There was a surprise in the final of the Scottish Challenge Cup when Stranraer beat St Johnstone 1-0. It was the West Coast club's first major trophy and their only noteworthy achievement during the season in which they were almost relegated.

Scottish football continues to attract leading foreign players. Last season, Rangers included Jorg Albertz, a German, Erik Bo Andersen a Dane like Brian Laudrup, Joachim Bjorklund (Sweden), Peter Van Vossen and Theo Snelders, both Dutch, Sebastian Rozental (Chilean), Craig Moore (Australian) and Gordan Petric (Yugoslavian) among their first team players.

Celtic also had the Portuguese Jorge Cadete and Paolo Di Canio an Italian, among several foreign players of their own. But these imports were not exclusive to Scotland's top two clubs, as most other Premier Division sides either had their own players from abroad or were looking to add them to their staff.

SCOTTISH LEAGUE TABLES 1996–97

Premier Division

		Home			Goals		Away			Goals			
	P	W	D	L	F	A	W	D	L	F	A	Pt	GD
Rangers	36	13	2	3	44	16	12	3	3	41	17	80	+52
Celtic	36	14	2	2	48	9	9	4	5	30	23	75	+46
Dundee U	36	10	4	4	21	10	7	5	6	25	23	60	+13
Hearts	36	8	6	4	27	20	6	4	8	19	23	52	+3
Dunfermline Ath	36	8	4	6	32	30	4	5	9	20	35	45	–13
Aberdeen	36	6	8	4	25	19	4	6	8	20	35	44	–9
Kilmarnock	36	8	4	6	28	26	3	2	13	13	35	39	–20
Motherwell	36	5	5	8	24	25	4	6	8	20	30	38	–11
Hibernian	36	6	4	8	18	25	3	7	8	20	30	38	–17
Raith R	36	3	5	10	18	39	3	2	13	11	34	25	–44

First Division

		Home			Goals		Away			Goals			
	P	W	D	L	F	A	W	D	L	F	A	Pt	GD
St Johnstone	36	12	5	1	37	10	12	3	3	37	13	80	+51
Airdrieonians	36	6	7	5	26	19	9	8	1	30	15	60	+22
Dundee	36	10	3	5	26	14	5	10	3	21	19	58	+14
St Mirren	36	12	0	6	28	21	5	7	6	20	20	58	+7
Falkirk	36	8	7	3	28	20	7	2	9	14	19	54	+3
Partick T	36	6	8	4	24	21	6	4	8	25	27	48	+1
Stirling Albion	36	8	3	7	27	25	4	7	7	27	36	46	–7
Greenock Morton	36	6	7	5	20	19	6	2	10	22	22	45	+1
Clydebank	36	6	4	8	19	24	1	3	14	12	35	28	–28
East Fife	36	1	5	12	15	48	1	3	14	13	44	14	–64

Second Division

		Home			Goals		Away			Goals			
	P	W	D	L	F	A	W	D	L	F	A	Pt	GD
Ayr U	36	12	3	3	32	16	11	5	2	29	17	77	+28
Hamilton A	36	11	5	2	47	17	11	4	3	28	11	74	+47
Livingston	36	11	3	4	32	18	7	7	4	24	20	64	+18
Clyde	36	8	4	6	21	18	6	6	6	21	21	52	+3
Queen of the S	36	8	3	7	27	27	4	5	8	28	30	47	–2
Stenhousemuir	36	4	6	8	19	23	7	5	6	30	20	44	+6
Brechin C	36	5	7	6	18	22	5	4	9	18	27	41	–13
Stranraer	36	6	5	7	17	18	4	4	11	12	33	36	–22
Dumbarton	36	2	7	9	21	35	7	1	10	31	35	35	–22
Berwick R	36	4	4	10	15	36	0	7	11	17	39	23	–43

Third Division

		Home			Goals		Away			Goals			
	P	W	D	L	F	A	W	D	L	F	A	Pt	GD
Inverness CT	36	13	3	2	37	19	10	4	4	33	18	76	+33
Forfar Ath	36	10	5	3	35	19	9	5	4	39	26	67	+29
Ross Co	36	10	4	4	33	22	10	3	5	25	19	67	+17
Alloa	36	9	4	5	24	21	5	8	26	26	55	+3
Albion R	36	8	4	6	27	22	5	6	7	23	25	49	+3
Montrose	36	6	5	7	19	27	6	2	10	27	35	43	–16
Cowdenbeath	36	6	6	6	22	23	4	3	11	16	28	39	–13
Queen's Park	36	7	3	8	27	29	2	6	10	19	30	36	–13
East Stirlingshire	36	6	4	8	21	29	2	5	11	15	29	33	–22
Arbroath	36	4	6	8	18	25	2	7	9	13	27	31	–21

PLAY-OFF: Hibernian (9th place, Premier Division) v Airdrieonians (runners-up, First Division) Hibernian 1 Airdrieonians 0; Airdrieonians 2 Hibernian 4.

BELL'S SCOTTISH LEAGUE—PREMIER DIVISION RESULTS 1996–97

	Aberdeen	Celtic	Dundee United	Dunfermline Athletic	Hearts	Hibernian	Kilmarnock	Motherwell	Raith Rovers	Rangers
Aberdeen	—	2-2	3-3	3-0	4-0	0-2	3-0	0-0	1-0	0-3
Celtic	1-2	—	1-1	0-2	0-0	1-1	2-1	0-0	2-0	2-2
Dundee United	1-0	1-1	—	5-1	2-2	5-0	6-0	1-0	4-1	0-1
Dunfermline Athletic	2-3	1-3	2-0	—	2-0	0-0	0-0	5-0	2-0	0-1
Hearts	0-0	2-2	2-3	2-1	—	1-0	2-0	1-1	3-2	1-0
Hibernian	0-1	0-4	1-0	1-1	1-3	—	1-2	2-0	2-0	2-5
Kilmarnock	3-0	1-3	2-1	2-2	0-4	2-4	—	3-1	0-0	0-3
Motherwell	2-2	0-1	1-3	2-3	0-2	1-1	1-0	—	3-2	1-4
Raith Rovers	1-4	1-0	0-1	0-1	1-1	0-1	0-1	1-5	—	3-1
Rangers	4-0	3-1	0-2	4-0	0-0	3-1	1-2	0-2	4-0	—

BELL'S SCOTTISH LEAGUE—DIVISION ONE RESULTS 1996–97

	Airdrieonians	Clydebank	Dundee	East Fife	Falkirk	Greenock Morton	Partick Thistle	St Johnstone	St Mirren	Stirling Albion
Airdrieonians	—	3-1	0-0	0-0	0-1	1-2	4-4	0-1	2-2	3-1
Clydebank	1-4	—	2-0	1-1	2-0	1-0	1-1	0-1	1-1	1-2
Dundee	1-1	4-1	—	2-0	0-1	2-1	1-3	2-1	0-1	1-0
East Fife	0-1	2-1	0-0	—	1-2	0-1	4-1	1-1	1-2	1-2
Falkirk	0-4	1-0	1-7	0-4	—	2-1	0-2	0-0	0-1	1-1
Greenock Morton	1-1	1-1	1-1	6-0	0-2	—	1-1	1-4	0-4	4-2
Partick Thistle	0-3	1-2	2-1	0-0	3-1	1-0	—	2-2	0-3	2-2
St Johnstone	1-1	2-0	0-1	2-0	0-2	0-3	1-3	—	1-0	1-3
St Mirren	0-0	0-1	1-0	6-0	1-0	1-4	1-3	2-0	—	5-2
Stirling Albion	1-1	1-1	3-2	3-1	0-2	3-0	0-2	1-4	1-1	—

BELL'S SCOTTISH LEAGUE—DIVISION TWO RESULTS 1996–97

	Ayr United	Berwick Rangers	Brechin City	Clyde	Dumbarton	Hamilton Academicals	Livingston	Queen of the South	Stenhousemuir	Stranraer
Ayr United	—	6-0 2-0	1-0 2-0	2-4 3-1	1-4 1-1	1-1 1-1	1-0 1-0	1-0 2-2	1-2 2-1	2-0 2-0
Berwick Rangers	1-2 0-2	—	0-0 1-0	1-5 0-2	3-1 0-3	0-2 0-5	1-2 0-0	2-2 1-1	0-6 0-0	1-2 2-0
Brechin City	1-1 1-1	3-2 3-1	—	1-2 2-1	2-1 0-3	0-1 1-1	1-0 2-0	3-3 0-1	1-1 0-4	0-2 0-0
Clyde	2-3 1-1	0-0 1-0	1-0 1-1	—	0-1 2-1	1-3 0-3	0-1 2-4	0-2 2-1	3-0 1-1	1-0 3-0
Dumbarton	1-3 1-1	2-2 4-2	1-2 4-0	2-2 2-0	—	2-0 4-0	2-3 3-3	1-2 0-3	0-2 2-1	1-1 2-2
Hamilton Academicals	1-2 1-0	4-1 2-2	2-3 1-5	5-1 2-0	2-0 4-0	—	1-0 1-2	2-2 4-1	1-1 1-3	4-0 2-1
Livingston	2-1 1-2	2-1 1-1	0-0 3-1	4-0 0-0	5-0 1-2	1-0 1-2	—	3-1 2-1	1-0 2-3	2-0 3-2
Queen of the South	1-3 1-2	1-1 1-1	0-1 0-1	0-2 0-0	4-0 0-1	1-1 0-1	2-2 1-2	—	2-1 0-3	1-1 4-0
Stenhousemuir	1-2 0-1			1-1 1-0	1-4 2-0	3-1 0-1	0-0 1-3	2-1 0-3	—	2-2 2-1
Stranraer	0-1				1-0		1-2 1-1	2-1 3-1	2-2 2-1	—

BELL'S SCOTTISH LEAGUE—DIVISION THREE RESULTS 1996–97

	Albion Rovers	Alloa	Arbroath	Cowdenbeath	East Stirling	Forfar Athletic	Inverness CT	Montrose	Queen's Park	Ross County
Albion Rovers	—	1-1	1-0	2-0	4-3	2-0	0-0	1-2	1-1	0-2
Alloa	3-0	—	1-2	4-0	1-1	1-3	0-3	2-1	2-1	1-2
Arbroath	2-0	0-2	—	1-1	1-1	3-4	0-2	3-1	2-1	1-3
Cowdenbeath	1-3	2-1	2-2	—	0-0	0-3	1-4	1-0	1-0	1-1
East Stirling	1-1	2-2	1-1	2-5	—	1-2	0-3	1-3	1-0	3-1
Forfar Athletic	0-0	0-3	3-0	3-0	3-0	—	3-1	4-2	2-2	2-1
Inverness CT	3-1	1-1	1-1	1-3	1-0	1-1	—	5-3	4-0	0-1
Montrose	1-1	1-0	4-1	2-1	2-0	0-4	2-2	—	2-2	1-1
Queen's Park	0-4	2-3	1-0	0-0	0-2	1-4	0-2	0-2	—	1-2
Ross County	3-2	3-1	4-0	1-0	1-1	1-1	0-3	3-1	2-0	—

ABERDEEN   PREM. DIV.

Ground: Pittodrie Stadium, Aberdeen AB2 1QH (01224) 632328
Ground capacity: 21,634. **Colours:** All red with white trim.
Manager: Roy Aitken.
League Appearances: Anderson R 14; Bernard P 13(1); Booth S 8(11); Buchan J 9(5); Craig M 2(3); Dodds W 31; Glass S 20(4); Grant B 2; Inglis J 15; Ingolfsson H 1(5); Irvine B 24(1); Kiriakov I 26(1); Kombouare A 30; Kpedekpo M (5); McKimmie S 14; Miller J 26(4); Rowson D 30(4); Shearer D 2(19); Stillie D 8; Tzvetanov T 27; Walker N 19; Watt M 9; Windass D 29; Woodthorpe C 14(5); Wyness D 1(6); Young D 22(4)
Goals–League (45): Dodds 15, Windass 10 (1 pen), Miller 4, Shearer 4, Kombouare 3, Rowson 2, Craig 1, Glass 1, Irvine 1, Kiriakov 1, Young 1, own goals 2.
Scottish Cup (2): Booth 1, Dodds 1.
Coca Cola Cup (10): Windass 5, Dodds 4, Glass 1.

AIRDRIEONIANS   DIV. 1

Ground: Broadwood Stadium, Cumbernauld G68 9NE (01236) 762067
Ground capacity: 6300. **Colours:** White shirts with red diamond, white shorts.
Manager: Alex MacDonald.
League Appearances: Black K 26(2); Boyle J 19(7); Connelly G 1(3); Connelly P 24(11); Cooper S 18(5); Davies J 31; Eadie K 9(6); Hetherston P 5; Jack P 30; Johnston F 15(6); Lawrence A 10(17); Mackay G 8; Martin A (1); Martin J 27; McIntyre T 5(2); McPhee B 24(4); Rhodes A 9; Sandison J 36; Smith A 21(7); Stewart A 31; Sweeney S 26; Wilson M 21(8)
Goals–League (56): Connolly P 8, Cooper 8 (2 pens), McPhee 8, Eadie 7 (1 pen), Davies 6, Black 4 (2 pens), Lawrence 3, Stewart 3, Smith 2, Jack 1, Johnston 1, Mackay 1, Sandison 1, Sweeney 1, Wilson 1, own goal 1.
Scottish Cup (1): Sandison 1.
Coca Cola Cup (3): Cooper 1, Eadie 1, Hetherston 1.
League Challenge Cup (0).

ALBION ROVERS   DIV. 3

Ground: Cliftonhill Stadium, Main Street, Coatbridge ML5 3RB (01236) 606334
Ground capacity: 1238. **Colours:** Yellow shirts with black trim, black shorts.
Manager: Vinnie Moore.
League Appearances: Angus I 8; Boal B 8(6); Brown M 6; Byrne D 29; Clark M 14(3); Cody S 8(1); Davidson A 1; Dickson J 17(4); Duncan C 10; Gallagher J 7(1); Gardner L 16; Harty I 4(5); Kelly G 4(1); Kennedy A 1; Leonard M 1(2); MacFarlane C 10(2); Martin P 25; McGowan N 16(1); McGuinness E 1; McGuire D 8(8); McInally A 13(3); McInnes I 9(3); McKenna A 1; McKenzie D 17(15); McKilligan N 28(2); Mitchell A 1; Mitchell C 11(2); Moore V 27; Pickering M 13; Reilly R 4(10); Robertson S 1; Ross S 24; Russell R (1); Shepherd A 5; Tannock R 4; Walker T 20(4); Watters W 23(1); Webster D 2(1)
Goals–League (50): Watters 11, McKenzie 7, Walker 6, Gardner 5, Moore 5, Dickson 4, McGuire 3 (1 pen), Clark 2, Boal 1, Cody 1, Kelly 1, McKilligan 1, Martin 1, Shepherd 1, own goal 1.

Scottish Cup (0).
Coca Cola Cup (7): McGuire 3, McKenzie 2, MacFarlane 1, McInally 1.
League Challenge Cup (1): McKenzie 1.

ALLOA ATHLETIC   DIV. 3

Ground: Recreation Park, Alloa FK10 1RR (01259) 722695
Ground capacity: 4111. **Colours:** Gold shirts with black trim, black shorts.
Manager: Tom Hendrie.
League Appearances: Balfour R 15; Cadden S (1); Cameron J 1; Cowan M 30; Dick
A (1); Dwyer P 14(1); Gilmour J 14(16); Irvine W 33; Johnston N (2); Kane K 27(1);
Lamont W 1; Little T 10(10); Mackay S 10(3); Mathieson M 3; McAnenay M 10(15);
McAneny P 30(2); McAvoy N 4(2); McCormack J 25; McCulloch K 11(4); Moffat B
12(3); Monaghan M 19; Nelson M 21(3); Pew D 20(1); Piggott J 5(9); Simpson P 8(3);
Tennant S 2; Valentine C 35; Wilson M 14(2); Wilson S 22; Wylie R (2)
Goals-League (50): Irvine 12, Dwyer 11, Cowan 3, McAneny P 3, Moffat 3, Pew 3,
Piggott 3, Simpson 3, Gilmour 2, McCormack 2, Kane 1, McAnenay M 1,
Mackay 1, Nelson 1, Wilson S 1.
Scottish Cup (4): Dwyer 1, Irvine 1, McAneny P 1, Mackay 1.
Coca Cola Cup (4): Dwyer 1, Irvine 1, McAneny P 1, McAvoy 1.
League Challenge Cup (3): Irvine 3.

ARBROATH   DIV. 3

Ground: Gayfield Park, Arbroath DD11 1QB (01241) 872157
Ground capacity: 6488. **Colours:** Maroon shirts with sky blue trim, white shorts.
Manager: David Baikie.
League Appearances: Arthur G 9; Balfour G 10; Bilsland B 6; Clark P 3(1);
Crawford J 26; Dunn G (1); Florence S 20(7); Gallagher J 24(1); Gardner L 10;
Grant B 15(2); Hinchcliffe C 27; Hope D 10; Kerr J 1; Longmuir K 2(3); Mackie B 3;
McAulay J 36; McCarron J 19(5); McCormick S 2(2); McVicar D 20(1); McWalter M
23(1); Moonlight P 1(1); Morrison P 8(2); Murray I (1); Orr J 6(1); Peters S 17; Pew
D 13; Phinn J 2; Reynolds C 9; Roberts P 7(7); Scott S 11(16); Tennant S 2;
Valentine S 1; Ward J 14(1); Waters M 7; Watters W 10; Welsh B 1(7); Wylie R 21
Goals-League (31): Grant 5, McAulay 4, Watters W 4, McCarron 3, McWalter 3,
McVicar 2 (2 pens), Pew 2, Scott 2, Gallagher 1, Hope 1, McCormick 1, Reynolds
1, Wylie 1, own goal 1.
Scottish Cup (5): McCormick 2, Grant 1, McCarron 1, Wylie 1.
Coca Cola Cup (0).
League Challenge Cup (2): Peters 1, Welsh 1.

AYR UNITED   DIV. 1

Ground: Somerset Park, Ayr KA8 9NB (01292) 263435
Ground capacity: 12,128. **Colours:** White shirts with black sleeves, white shorts.
Manager: Gordon Dalziel.
League Appearances: Bell R 5(1); Biggart K (3); Castilla D 1; Clark J (1); Connor
R 18; Coyle R 29(1); Dalziel G (1); English I 17; George D 17(3); Henderson D

19(10); Hood G 20(1); Horace A 21(1); Humphries M 22; Jamieson W 26; Kerrigan S 22(5); Kinnaird P 13(14); Law R 10(6); McStay J 6(4); Mercer J 1(12); Scott R 17(1); Smith C (1); Smith H 35; Smith P 27(6); Smith T 19(2); Traynor J 30(4); Ward M 1; Watson P 20(6)

Goals-League (61): Kerrigan 14, Smith P 9 (1 pen), English 7, Scott 6, Horace 5, Smith T 4 (1 pen), Jamieson 3, George 2, Kinnaird 2, Mercer 2, Traynor 2, Biggart 1, Connor 1, Henderson 1, Hood 1, own goal 1.

Scottish Cup (0).

Coca Cola Cup (7): English 2, Kerrigan 2, Connor 1, Henderson 1, Hood 1.

League Challenge Cup (4): Smith P 2, English 1, Jamieson 1.

BERWICK RANGERS   DIV. 3

Ground: Shielfield Park, Berwick-on-Tweed TD15 2EF (01289) 307424
Ground capacity: 4131. **Colours:** Black with gold diamonds, black shorts.
Manager: Jimmy Thomson.
League Appearances: Burgess M 9; Clegg N 11(3); Coates S 3; Collier D 16; Craig K 18(8); Finlayson D 19; Forrester P 24(6); Fraser G 33; Garrity J 1(1); Graham T 27(3); Grant D 18(4); Irvine N 24(1); Laidler M 15; Lamont W 3; Little G 6(7); Ludlow L 3(3); Manson C 8(3); McGlynn D 7(5); McParland I 8(1); Miller G 2(5); Neil M 21(1); Paxton G (3); Reid A 28(3); Robinson D 14(2); Smith I (1); Smith S 3; Stewart G 24(2); Walton K 31(4); Ward B 1(1); Watkins D 4; Wilson M 4; Young N 8

Goals-League (32): Forrester 6, Neil 4 (1 pen), Robinson 4 (2 pens), Clegg 3, Craig 2, Little 2 (1 pen), McGlynn 2 (1 pen), Manson 2, Walton 2, Fraser 1, Grant 1, McParland 1, Miller 1, Reid 1.

Scottish Cup (4): McParland 2, Neil 1, Walton 1.

Coca Cola Cup (0).

League Challenge Cup (0).

BRECHIN CITY   DIV. 2

Ground: Glebe Park, Brechin DD9 6BJ (01356) 622856
Ground capacity: 3980. **Colours:** Red with white trim.
Manager: John Young.
League Appearances: Allan R 12; Baillie R 7(1); Black R 1(2); Brand R 20(8); Brown R 34; Buick G 18(2); Cairney H 31; Christie G 27(2); Conway F 35; Dailly M 3; Farnan C 35; Ferguson S 17(3); Feroz C 16(15); Garden S 24(1); Heddle I 11(5); Kerrigan S 25(4); McKellar J 19(12); McNeill W 1(9); Ross A (2); Scott D 30; Smith G 8(1); Sorbie S 22(6)

Goals-League (36): Kerrigan 7, Brand 6, Feroz 4, McKellar 4, Sorbie 4, Brown 3, Christie 2, Conway 2, Ferguson 2, Buick 1, Farnan 1.

Scottish Cup (6): Brand 2, Sorbie 2, Brown 1, Kerrigan 1.

Coca Cola Cup (3): Feroz 2, Kerrigan 1.

League Challenge Cup (0).

CELTIC   PREM. DIV.

Ground: Celtic Park, Glasgow G40 3RE (0141) 556 2611
Ground capacity: 47,500. **Colours:** Green and white hooped shirts, white shorts.
Head Coach: Wim Jensen.
League Appearances: Annoni E 3; Anthony M (2); Boyd T 31; Cadete J 30(1); Di
Canio P 25(1); Donnelly S 20(9); Elliot B (1); Grant P 21(2); Gray S 7(4); Hannah
D 14(4); Hay C 4(10); Hughes J 5(1); Johnson T 3(1); Kelly P 1; Kerr S 25(1);
Mackay M 18(2); Marshall G 11; McBride J (2); McKinlay T 24(3); McLaughlin B
8(12); McNamara J 30; McStay P 14(1); O'Donnell P 19; O'Neil B 15(1); Stubbs A
20; Thom A 18(5); Van Hooijdonk P 19(2); Wieghorst M 11(6)
Goals-League (78): Cadete 25, Van Hooijdonk 14, Di Canio 12 (1 pen), Thom 7,
Donnelly 4, Hay 4, O'Donnell 2, O'Neil 2, Wieghorst 2, Johnson 1, Mackay 1,
McLaughlin 1, McNamara 1, McStay 1, own goal 1.
Scottish Cup (11): Di Canio 3, Cadete 2, Mackay 2, O'Donnell 2, Johnson 1, Van
Hooijdonk 1.
Coca Cola Cup (8): Cadete 5, Thom 2, Van Hooijdonk 1.

CLYDE   DIV. 2

Ground: Broadwood Stadium, Cumbernauld G68 9NE (01236) 451511
Ground capacity: 8200. **Colours:** White shirts with red and black trim, black shorts.
Manager: Gardner Spiers.
League Appearances: Annand E 29; Balfour R 7; Brown J 25(1); Brownlie P 30(3);
Campbell P 16(8); Carrigan B 5(9); Coleman S (1); Ferguson G 20(1); Gibson A
33(2); Gibson L (2); Gillies K 24(2); Harrison T 3(5); Knox K 36; Mathieson M
19(8); McCheyne G 4(4); McConnell I 8(2); McEwan C 31(3); McInulty S 28(3);
McLay J (1); McLean M 29; McPhee G (1); O'Neill Mart 21(8); O'Neill Mich
12(10); Parks G (2); Prunty J 15(2); Robertson G 1
Goals-League (42): Annand 21 (1 pen), Brownlie 5, Mathieson 4, Martin O'Neill 4,
Gibson A 2, Knox 2, McCheyne 2, Carrigan 1, Prunty 1.
Scottish Cup (9): Annand 2, A Gibson 2, Brownlie 1, McEwan 1, McInulty 1,
Mathieson 1, Michael O'Neill 1.
Coca Cola Cup (2): Annand 1, Brown 1.
League Challenge Cup (4): Mathieson 2, Annand 1, Knox 1.

CLYDEBANK   DIV. 2

Ground: Burnbrae, Milngavie, Glasgow G62 6HX (0141) 9559048
Ground capacity: 5503. **Colours:** Red and white stripes, black shorts.
Coach:
League Appearances: Adamson C 1; Agnew P 25(3); Barnes D 6; Bowman G 22;
Brannigan K 35; Brown J 12(1); Connaghan D 1; Connell G 25(3); Currie T 24(4);

Grady J 36; Hardie D (1); Irons D 35; Lovering P 25(1); Matthews G 11; McFarlane I 16; McKelvie D (1); McKinstry J 2(4); McMahon S 12(8); Melvin W 1(2); Miller S 11(13); Murdoch S 13(2); Nicholls D 33(1); Robertson J 6(19); Robertson S 2; Sutherland C 9; Teale G 32(1); Templeton R 1

Goals-League (31): Grady 8, Teale 6, Agnew 5 (2 pens), McMahon 3, Brown 2, Connell 2, Nicholls 2, Brannigan 1, Miller 1, own goal 1.

Scottish Cup (0).

Coca Cola Cup (0).

League Challenge Cup (0).

COWDENBEATH   DIV. 3

Ground: Central Park, Cowdenbeath KY4 9EY (01383) 610166
Ground capacity: 5268. **Colours:** Royal blue stripes with red trim, white shorts.
Manager: Samuel Conn.
League Appearances: Baillie R 15(2); Bowmaker K 15(5); Brough G 5(7); Conn S 28; Coulston D 12(14); Fairley S (1); Godfrey R 4; Hamilton A 12(5); Houston A (1); Humphreys M 22(3); Lockhart D (1); Malloy B 3(5); Manson S 1(1); McKinnon M (2); McMahon B 13; Meldrum G 33; Millar P 2(1); Miller G 2(1); Moffat J 2; Munro K 32; Nolan T 6; Petrie E 15(2); Ritchie A 24(7); Russell N 30; Scott M 14(3); Sinclair C 30; Stewart W 22(8); Winter C 31(1); Wood G 23
Goals-League (38): Wood 6, Coulston 5, Stewart 5, Sinclair 4, McMahon 3, Winter 3, Bowmaker 2, Conn 2, Nolan 2, Petrie 2, Scott 2, Malloy 1, Ritchie 1.
Scottish Cup (1): Scott 1.
Coca Cola Cup (1): Sinclair 1.
League Challenge Cup (0).

DUMBARTON   DIV. 3

Ground: Boghead Park, Dumbarton G82 2JA (01389) 762569
Ground capacity: 5503. **Colours:** White with yellow trim, white shorts.
Manager: Ian Wallace.
League Appearances: Barnes D 11; Bruce J 9; Dallas S 15(1); Davidson W 12(4); Dennison P 2; Glancy M 24(8); Goldie J 1(3); Gow S 21(3); Granger A 2(4); Hringsson H 3; King T 27; MacFarlane I 9; Marsland J 30(1); McCabe G 4; McCuaig R (1); McGall J (6); McGarvey M 7(5); McGivern S 1(1); McKenzie G 4(1); McKinnon C 34; Meechan J 36; Meechan K 14; Mellis A 1; Melvin M 23; Mooney M 18(4); Parks G 4; Reid D (1); Reilly R 2(6); Scott J (1); Sharp L 35; Ward H 26(9); Wilson W 21
Goals-League (44): Ward 7, Glancy 6, Meechan J 6, Sharp 5, McKinnon 4, Wilson 4, Hringsson 3, Dallas 2, King 2, Granger 1 (pen), McGivern 1, Mooney 1, Reilly 1, own goal 1.
Scottish Cup (0).
Coca Cola Cup (1): Dallas 1.
League Challenge Cup (0).

DUNDEE

Ground: Dens Park, Dundee DD3 7JY (01382) 826104
Ground capacity: 14,177. **Colours:** Dark blue shirts with red and white trim, white shorts.
Manager: John McCormack.
League Appearances: Adamczuk D 30; Anderson I 28(7); Annand E 5; Bain K 12; Bayne G (2); Cargill A (2); Charnley J 15; Croce L 1; Duffy J 2; Elliot J 1(3); Farningham R 3(5); Ferguson I 5(9); Hamilton J 12; Magee K 10(15); McGlynn D 11; McKeown G 16(3); McQueen T 16(1); O'Driscoll J 18(2); Power L 9(1); Rae G 11(8); Raeside R 34; Robertson H 15; Shaw G 18(3); Skonnard O 1(3); Smith B 36; Thomson W 25; Tosh P 19(5); Tully C 16(5); Ward M 1; Winnie D 26
Goals-League (47): O'Driscoll 10, Anderson 5, Shaw 5, Power 4, Raeside 4, Tosh 4, Charnley 3, Annand 2, Rae 2, Adamczuk 1, Ferguson 1, Hamilton 1, McKeown 1, Robertson 1, Winnie 1, own goals 2.
Scottish Cup (5): Anderson 2, Power 2, O'Driscoll 1.
Coca Cola Cup (7): Hamilton 5, Raeside 1, Tosh 1.
League Challenge Cup (6): Tosh 2, Farningham 1, Hamilton 1, Magee 1, Shaw 1.

DUNDEE UNITED

Ground: Tannadice Park, Dundee DD3 7JW (01382) 833166
Ground capacity: 12,616. **Colours:** Tangerine shirts with black trim, black shorts.
Manager: Thomas McLean.
League Appearances: Benneker A 6(1); Black P (1); Bowman D 26(2); Coyle O 6(4); Dijkstra S 22; Dolan J 11(2); Duffy C 6(7); Easton C 1(1); Hannah D 9(3); Johnson G 2(5); Key L 4; Malpas M 26; Maxwell A 10; McInally J 12(4); McKimmie S 6; McKinnon R 17(9); McLaren A 29(5); McQuilken J 6(3); McSwegan G 15(16); Olofsson K 22(3); Pedersen J 25; Perry M 33(2); Pressley S 36; Robertson A 1(3); Shannon R 7(2); Sinclair D 3(3); Thompson S (1); Walker P 2(1); Winters R 27(9); Wirmola J 1(2); Zetterlund L 25
Goals-League (46): Olofsson 12, Winters 8, McSwegan 7, McKinnon 6, McLaren 4 (1 pen), Pressley 2, Duffy 1, Hannah 1, McInally 1, Malpas 1, Zetterlund 1, own goals 2.
Scottish Cup (8): Winters 3, McLaren 2, McSwegan 1, Olofsson 1, own goal 1.
Coca Cola Cup (4): Coyle 2, McSwegan 1, Winters 1.

DUNFERMLINE ATHLETIC

Ground: East End Park, Dunfermline KY12 7RB (01383) 724295
Ground capacity: Under reconstruction. **Colours:** Black and white striped shirts, black shorts.
Manager: Bert Paton.
League Appearances: Bingham D 5(12); Britton G 27(6); Clark J 8; Curran H 18(2); Den Bieman I 21(7); Fleming D 23(3); Fraser J 2; French H 34(1); Ireland C

7(2); Lemajic Z 8; McCulloch M 4(5); Millar M 19(4); Miller C 19(3); Moore A 13(13); Petrie S 24(4); Rice B 4(4); Robertson C 31; Sharp R 14(1); Shaw G (3); Smith A 30(5); Tod A 35; Welsh S 20; Westwater I 28(1); Young S 2
Goals–League (52): Britton 13, Smith 10, Millar M 6 (1 pen), Tod 4, French 3, Moore 3, Petrie 3, Fleming 2, Bingham 1, Clark 1, Curran 1, Den Bieman 1, Ireland 1, Welsh 1, Young 1, own goal 1.
Scottish Cup (5): Smith 2, Curran 1, French 1, Petrie 1.
Coca Cola Cup (8): Bingham 2, Britton 2, French 2, Moore 2.

EAST FIFE   DIV. 2

Ground: Bayview Park, Methil, Fife KY8 3AG (moving 1998–99) (01333) 426323
Ground capacity: 5385. **Colours:** Amber shirts with black trim, amber shorts.
Manager: James Bone.
League Appearances: Allan G 30(2); Andrew B 27(4); Archibald S 5; Bailey L 5(5); Beaton D 5; Bogie G 5(3); Cameron R 13(2); Carmichael D (1); Christie K 9; Cusick J 25(5); Demmin C 1(5); Dixon A 26(2); Donaghy M 23; Dwarika A 12(6); Dyer M 9(2); Fennell K 1; Gartshore P 15(8); Gibb R 30; Hamilton L 30; Hope D 5(5); Hutcheon S 18(6); Johnston G 16; Kinnell A (1); Lewis G 6(10); MacFarlane C 9(2); Mair I (1); McPherson G 1(3); McStay J 9; Moffat B 7(1); Nicol G 1(4); Ritchie I 13; Robertson D 5(2); Ronald P 8; Rushford C 1; Scott R 15; Stiggson O 3; Sweeney C (1); Winiarski S 6(9); Yates D 2
Goals–League (28): Dyer 4, Ronald 4, Allan 2, Hutcheon 2, MacFarlane 2, Scott 2, Andrew 1, Baillie 1, Beaton 1, Cameron 1, Christie 1, Cusick 1, Donaghy 1, Moffat 1, Winiarski 1, own goals 3.
Scottish Cup (3): Christie 2, Baillie 1.
Coca Cola Cup (1): Dwarika 1.
League Challenge Cup (2): Archibald 1, Scott 1.

EAST STIRLINGSHIRE   DIV. 3

Ground: Firs Park, Falkirk FK2 7AY (01324) 623583
Ground capacity: 1880. **Colours:** Black and white stripes, black shorts.
Manager: John Brownlie.
League Appearances: Abercromby M 15(4); Campbell C 22; Cochrane M 7(10); Conway V 2(1); Devine W 1; Farquhar A 2(4); Hamilton G 20(1); Hringsson H 1; Hughes J 1; Hunter M 14(9); Inglis G 25(3); Jack A (1); Kerr R 3; Lamont W 3; MacNamee P 1(2); McBride M 31; McDougall G 22; McKenzie C 1; McStay R 1; Muirhead D 12(11); Murray N 3(3); Neill A 36; Nisbett I 1; Paterson P 7(7); Ramsay S 20(5); Ronald P 21(3); Ross B 13(1); Russell G 30; Scott M (8); Sneddon S 26(1); Stirling A 19(4); Watt D 25; Wilson E 10; Wilson S 1
Goals–League (36): Inglis 9, McBride 5, Watt 5, Neill 3 (1 pen), Sneddon 3, Muirhead 2, Ramsay 2, Abercromby 1, Hringsson 1, Hunter 1, McKenzie 1, Ronald 1, own goals 2.
Scottish Cup (4): Stirling 2, Abercromby 1, Inglis 1.
Coca Cola Cup (1): Ramsay.
League Challenge Cup (1): Ronald 1.

FALKIRK   DIV. 1

Ground: Brockville Park, Falkirk FK1 5AX (01324) 624121
Ground capacity: 9706. **Colours:** Navy blue shirts with white trim, white shorts.
Manager: Alex Totten.
League Appearances: Berry N 9; Corrigan M 8(9); Crabbe S 10(2); Craig A 10(3); Crawford G (2); De Massis S (1); Elliot D 8(9); Fellner G 4(3); Ferguson D 13(1); Foster W 10(4); Graham A 5(2); Gray A 13(5); Hagen D 31(3); Hamilton B 18(1); Huttunen T 2; James K 17(1); Kaijasilta P (1); Kelly T (1); Kidd W 1; Lawrie A 7(5); Mathers P 16; McAllister K 14(1); McGowan J 29; McGraw M 20(9); McGrillen P 24(7); McKenzie S 26(2); Mitchell G 17(3); Nelson C 20; Oliver N 14(1); Olson J (1); Seaton A 26(3); Tortolano J 11(1); Waddle C 4; Ward K 9(1); Whiteside G (1)
Goals-League (42): McGraw 8, McGrillen 7, Fellner 4, Ferguson 3, James 3, McAllister 3, Craig 2, McGowan 2, Elliot 1, Foster 1, Gray 1, Hagen 1, Hamilton 1, McKenzie 1, Mitchell 1, Oliver 1, Waddle 1, Ward 1.
Scottish Cup (9): Craig 2, Hagen 2, James 2, McAllister 1, McGraw 1, McGrillen 1.
Coca Cola Cup (2): Craig 2.
League Challenge Cup (2): Hagen 1, McGraw 1.

FORFAR ATHLETIC   DIV. 2

Ground: Station Park, Forfar, Angus (01307) 463576
Ground capacity: 8732. **Colours:** Sky blue and navy shirts, navy shorts.
Manager: Ian McPhee.
League Appearances: Allison J 34(1); Arthur G 6; Bowes M 30(2); Cargill A 15(1); Craig D 33; Donegan J 24(1); Farquharson S (1); Glennie S 18(2); Gray A 1; Hamilton J 31(1); Hannigan P 24(10); Higgins G 8(1); Honeyman B 29(6); Inglis G 1; Lee I 31(2); Loney J 23(9); Mann R 31(1); McPhee I 6(3); Morgan A 36; Nairn J (1); Orr J (2); Roberts P 7(11); Robertson D 6; Sexton B 2(1)
Goals-League (74): Honeyman 17, Morgan 15 (2 pens), Hannigan 7, Mann 7 (2 pens), Roberts 6, Loney 4, Cargill 3, Higgins 3, Lee 3, Allison 2, Craig 2, Bowes 1, Glennie 1, McPhee1, own goals 2.
Scottish Cup (4): Allison 1, Honeyman 1, Lee 1, Morgan 1.
Coca Cola Cup (2): Higgins 1, Inglis 1.
League Challenge Cup (0).

GREENOCK MORTON   DIV. 1

Ground: Cappielow Park, Greenock (01475) 723571
Ground capacity: 14,267. **Colours:** Royal blue and white shirts, royal blue shorts.
Manager: Allan McGraw.
League Appearances: Aitken S 10(3); Anderson J 31; Blaikie A 4(1); Blair P 11(5); Collins D 35; Cormack P 25; Flannery P 6(14); Hawke W 25(7); Hunter J 3; Johnstone D 11(2); Lilley D 25; Lindberg J 24; Mahood A 27; Mason B 2(2); Matheson R 8(13); McArthur S 24(3); McCahill S 22; McPherson C 17(12); Rajamaki M 23(10); Reid B 26; Slavin B 1; Willoughby J (1); Wylie D 32
Goals-League (42): Lilley 15 (1 pen), Hawke 7, Anderson 4, Rajamaki 4, Flannery 3, Mahood 3, Lindberg 2, Blair 1, Cormack 1, McPherson 1, Reid 1.

174

Scottish Cup (11): Hawke 3, Lilley 2 (1 pen), Mahood 2, Blair 1, Cormack 1, Mason 1, own goal 1.
Coca Cola Cup (4): Lilley 2, Anderson 1, Cormack 1.
League Challenge Cup (8): Lilley 3, Flannery 2, Anderson 1, Matheson 1, Rajamaki 1.

HAMILTON ACADEMICAL   DIV. 1

Ground: Cliftonville Stadium, Main St, Coatbridge ML5 3RB (01236) 606334 (match days only)
Ground capacity: 1238. **Colours:** Red and white hooped shirts, white shorts.
Manager: Sandy Clark.
League Appearances: Baptie C 11(4); Clark G 15(17); Cunnington E 8; Davidson W 5(7); Ferguson A 27; Fotheringham K 6(8); Geraghty M (1); Hillcoat C 36; Hillcoat J 2; Lorimer D (3); McBride J 2(1); McCormick S 16(3); McCulloch S 19(5); McEntegart S 23(2); McFarlane D 10(10); McGill D 8; McIntosh M 33; McKenzie P 12(7); McQuade J (4); Paris S 2; Quitongo J 31(3); Renicks S 33; Ritchie P 36; Scott C 5; Sherry J 24; Thomson S 32(3)
Goals-League (75): Ritchie 31, McCormick 7, McIntosh 7 (2 pens), McFarlane 6, Sherry 6, McGill 4, Quitongo 3, Clark 2, Fotheringham 2, McEntegart 2, Thomson 2, Davidson 1, Hillcoat C 1, McCulloch 1.
Scottish Cup (6): Ritchie 3, Clark 2, McEntegart 1.
Coca Cola Cup (1): Sherry 1.
League Challenge Cup (3): Quitongo 3.

HEART OF MIDLOTHIAN   PREM. DIV.

Ground: Tynecastle Park, Gorgie Road, Edinburgh EH11 2NL (0131) 337 6132
Ground capacity: 18,300. **Colours:** Maroon shirts, white shorts.
Manager: Jim Jefferies.
League Appearances: Beckford D 6(2); Bruno P 11(2); Burns J (2); Callaghan S 4; Cameron C 36; Colquhoun J 4(7); Frail S 4(5); Fulton S 25(4); Goss J 7(3); Hamilton J 12(6); Holmes D 1; Horn R 1; Locke G 11; Mackay G 20(7); McCann N 25(5); McKenzie R 3; McManus A 15(0); McPherson D 26; Murie D 6(1); Murray G 2(2); Naysmith G 10; Paille S 11(7); Pointon N 24(1); Ritchie P 27(1); Robertson J 26(2); Rousset G 33; Salvatori S 12(2); Thomas K 4(9); Thorn A 1; Weir D 34
Goals-League (46): Robertson 14 (2 pens), Cameron 8, Weir 6, Hamilton 5, McCann 5, Ritchie 3, Paille 2, Fulton 1, Mackay 1, McPherson 1.
Scottish Cup (6): Robertson 2, Cameron 1, Hamilton 1, Pointon 1, Weir 1.
Coca Cola Cup (11): Robertson 3, Beckford 2, Cameron 2 (1 pen), Fulton 1, McCann 1, Paille 1, Weir 1.

HIBERNIAN PREM. DIV.

Ground: Easter Road Stadium, Edinburgh EH7 5QG (0131) 661 2159
Ground capacity: 16,218. **Colours:** Green shirts with white sleeves and collar, white shorts.
Manager: Jim Duffy.
League Appearances: Cameron I 9(8); Charnley J 9; Dennis S 4; Dods D 17(3); Donald G 8(3); Dow A 17(5); Elliot D 5(2); Grant B 9(3); Harper K 23(3); Hughes J 4; Hunter G 16(1); Jackson C 15(4); Jackson D 30; Lavety B 6(4); Leighton J 35; Love G 6(1); McAllister K 10(9); McGinlay P 29; McLaughlin J 9; McQuilken J 9; Millen A 16(3); Miller G 3(3); Miller W 31; Power L 6; Reid C 1; Renwick M 6(3); Riipa J 1; Riley P (1); Schmugge T 1; Shannon R 5; Tosh P 6; Weir M 1(7); Welsh B 17; Wilkins R 15(1); Wright K 17(9)
Goals-League (38): Jackson D 11 (2 pens), McGinlay 6, Harper 5, Wright 4, Dow 2, Charnley 1, Dennis 1, Donald 1, McAllister 1, Weir 1, own goals 3.
Scottish Cup (3): Jackson D 1 (pen), McGinlay 1, Miller G 1.
Coca Cola Cup (4): Dow 1, Lavety 1, McGinlay 1, Wright 1.

INVERNESS CALEDONIAN THISTLE DIV. 2

Ground: Caledonian Stadium, East Longman, Inverness (01463) 222880
Ground capacity: 5600. **Colours:** Blue shirts with white trim, blue shorts.
Manager: S.W.Paterson.
League Appearances: Addicoat W 6(8); Bennett G 3(6); Calder J 35; Cherry P 31; Christie C 30(3); De Barros M 4(17); Hastings R 34; Hercher A 10(3); MacArthur I 34; MacMillan N 1; McLean S 17(3); Noble M 34; Ross D 26(5); Sinclair N (3); Stewart I 34(2); Teasdale M 36; Thomson B 21(2); Tokely R 13(11); Wilson B 27(2)
Goals-League (70): Stewart 27, Thomson 10 (3 pens), McLean 8, Wilson 5, Hercher 4, Ross 4, Christie 3, Noble 2, Teasdale 2, Tokely 2, Addicoat 1, Cherry 1, De Barros 1.
Scottish Cup (2): McLean 1, Stewart 1.
Coca Cola Cup (0).
League Challenge Cup (3): Cherry 1, Stewart 1, Thomson 1.

KILMARNOCK PREM. DIV.

Ground: Rugby Park, Kilmarnock KA1 2DP (01563) 525184
Ground capacity: 18,128. **Colours:** Blue and white striped shirts, blue shorts.
Manager: Bobby Williamson.
League Appearances: Anderson D 16(1); Bagen D 16(1); Brown T 7(17); Burke A 14(3); Findlay W 15(5); Hamilton S 6; Henry J 18(4); Holt G 10(2); Kerr A 2(2); Kerr D 27; Lauchlan J 7(3); Lekovic D 30; MacPherson A 33; McGowne K 30(1); McIntyre J 29(2); McKee C 14(11); Meldrum C 6; Mitchell A 23(7); Montgomerie R 19(2); Prytz R 1(2); Reilly M 31(2); Roberts M 2(8); Tallon G 4; Whitworth N 7; Wright P 29(2)
Goals-League (41): Wright 15 (1 pen), McIntyre 6, Burke 3, Henry 2, McKee 2, Mitchell 2, Reilly 2, Roberts 2, Brown 1, Findlay 1, Holt 1, Lauchlan 1, Montgomerie 1, own goals 2.
Scottish Cup (10): Henry 3, Wright 3 (1 pen), McIntyre 2, Brown 1, McGowne 1.
Coca Cola Cup (0).

LIVINGSTON   DIV. 2

Ground: Almondvale Stadium, Livingston EH54 7DN (01506) 417 000
Ground capacity: 6100. **Colours:** Black with yellow trim, black shorts.
Manager: Jim Leishman.
League Appearances: Alleyne D 14(9); Bailey L 13(10); Callaghan T 32; Callaghan W 7(13); Campbell S 30; Davidson G 20(1); Douglas R 36; Duthie M 32(1); Forrest G 5; Graham T 15; Harvey G 27(2); Laidlaw S 4(9); McLeod G 19; McMartin G 33(1); Sinclair C 4(8); Smart C 10(6); Tierney G 22; Watson G 20(3); Williamson S 32; Young J 21(13)
Goals-League (56): Harvey 15 (2 pens), Bailey 8, Duthie 7, McLeod 5, Young 5, Campbell 3, McMartin 3, Callaghan T 2, Laidlaw 2, Alleyne 1, Callaghan W 1, Forrest 1, Graham 1, Tierney 1, Williamson 1.
Scottish Cup (1): Bailey 1.
Coca Cola Cup (2): Callaghan T 1, Young 1.
League Challenge Cup (1): Young 1.

MONTROSE   DIV. 3

Ground: Links Park, Montrose DD10 8QD (01674) 673200
Ground capacity: 4338. **Colours:** Royal blue with white sleeves, white shorts.
Manager: Tommy Campbell.
League Appearances: Bird J 24(3); Butter J 12; Cassioe S (1); Cooper C 19(2); Craib M 26; Dorward R 2; Fisher D 20(2); Glass S 11(5); Haro M 30; Ingram N 20(9); Larter D 24; MacDonald I 24(2); Mailer C 31(1); Masson C 8; Masson P 14(9); McGlashan C 30; Purves S 13(4); Slythe M (1); Smith S 9(4); Stephen L 3(10); Taylor S 26(5); Thomson N 7(3); Tindal K 31; Tosh J 2(4); Winiarski S 10
Goals-League (46): McGlashan 11, Taylor 9, Ingram 4, Tindal 4 (1 pen), Smith 3, Bird 2, Haro 2, Masson C 2, Masson P 2, Cooper 1, Craib 1, Fisher 1, MacDonald 1, Mailer 1, Winiarski 1, own goal 1.
Scottish Cup (0).
Coca Cola Cup (0).
League Challenge Cup (9): McGlashan 4 (1 pen), Glass 1, Ingram 1, Masson P 1, Smith 1, Taylor 1.

MOTHERWELL   PREM. DIV.

Ground: Fir Park, Motherwell ML1 2QN (01698) 333333
Ground capacity: 13,742. **Colours:** Amber shirts with claret trim, claret shorts.
Manager: Alex McLeish.
League Appearances: Arnott D 11(4); Burns A 16(14); Christie K 3(1); Coyle O 15; Coyne T 24(3); Davies W 20(5); Denham G 5(4); Dolan J 18; Essandoh R (1); Falconer W 21; Hendry J 5(1); Howie S 30; Lehtonen J 4(2); Martin B 34; May E 34; McCart C 16(3); McCulloch L 1(14); McMillan S 13(3); McSkimming S 23; Philliben J 11(6); Roddie A 8(4); Ross I 21(9); Valakari S 11; Van Der Gaag M 26; Weir M 5; Wishart F 15(3); Woods S 6
Goals-League (44): Coyne 11 (1 pen), Coyle 7 (1 pen), Van Der Gaag 6, McSkimming 4 (1 pen), Arnott 3, Falconer 2, May 2, Ross 2, Weir 2, Burns 1, Davies 1, Philliben 1, own goals 2.
Scottish Cup (6): Coyle 3, Davies 1, McSkimming 1, Van Der Gaag 1.
Coca Cola Cup (0).

PARTICK THISTLE DIV. 1

Ground: Firhill Park, Glasgow G20 7BA (0141) 945 4811
Ground capacity: 20,876. **Colours:** Red and yellow striped shirts, black shorts.
Head Coach: John McVeigh. **Assistant Head Coach:** Gordon Chisholm.
League Appearances: Adams C 26(4); Apiliga R 1; Archibald A 2(3); Ayton S 3;
Cairns M 10; Dinnie A 13(1); Docherty S 8(14); Evans G 29; Farrell D 31;
Henderson N 12(4); Hillcoat J 26; Hringsson H 1(2); Lyons A 29(6); Macdonald W
11(5); Maskrey S 29(2); McCall I 1(6); McKenzie J 2(2); McWilliams D 18(4); Milne
C 22(3); Moss D 31; Ritchie J (1); Slavin J 17(1); Smith T (1); Stirling J 34; Te Jero
J (1); Turner T 7(4); Watson G 35
Goals-League (49): Moss 11, Evans 9, Adams 8, Stirling 7 (3 pens), Lyons 3,
Farrell 2, Henderson 2, McWilliams 2 (1 pen), Maskrey 2, Dinnie 1, Docherty 1,
Macdonald 1.
Scottish Cup (0).
Coca Cola Cup (4): Evans 3, Stirling 1.
League Challenge Cup (6): Stirling 2, Evans 1, Henderson 1, McWilliams 1,
Maskrey 1 (pen).

QUEEN OF THE SOUTH DIV. 2

Ground: Palmerston Park, Dumfries DG2 9BA (01387) 254853
Ground capacity: 8352. **Colours:** Royal blue shirts, white shorts.
Co-Managers: Rowan Alexander and Mark Shanks.
League Appearances: Aitken A 14; Alexander R 5(6); Brown J 15; Bryce T 34(1);
Brydson E (4); Cleeland M (1); Cochrane G 7(2); Doig C 2(2); Flannigan C 26(2);
Herriot S (3); Hughes J 2(2); Irving C (1); Kennedy D 20(1); Laing D 5(4);
Lancaster I 3(3); Lee P (1); Leslie S 17(3); Lilley D 20(2); MacLean J 2(5); Mallan
S 28(6); Mathieson D 36; McAllister J 4(2); McFarlane A 6; McKeown B 26;
McKeown D 27(2); Nesovic A 26(4); Rowe G 25(1); Thomson J 16; Townsley D
29(2); Wilson S 1
Goals-League (55): Mallan 13, Bryce 12, Flannigan 11 (2 pens), Nesovic 5, Rowe 5,
Alexander 2, Townsley 2, Leslie 1 (pen), Lilley 1, McFarlane 1, McKeown B 1,
Thomson 1.
Scottish Cup (4): Brown 1, Leslie 1, Mallan 1, Nesovic 1.
Coca Cola Cup (0).
League Challenge Cup (4): Flannigan 2, Mallan 1 (pen), Nesovic 1.

QUEEN'S PARK DIV. 3

Ground: Hampden Park, Glasgow G42 9BA (0141) 632 1275
Ground capacity: 9222 (during re-constructrion). **Colours:** Black and white hooped
shirts, white shorts.
Coach: Graeme J. Elder.
League Appearances: Arbuckle D 31; Bruce G 31; Callan D 1(1); Cameron C (3);
Caven R 27(2); Edgar S 16; Elder G 24; Falconer M 8(14); Ferguson P 9; Ferry D
21(11); Fitzpatrick I 14(2); Fraser R 7(1); Graham D 29; Hardie M 14(9); Kennedy
K 19(9); King D 9(3); Maxwell J 33; McGoldrick K 31; McLauchlan M 21(8); Orr
G 9(1); Reilly R (1); Smith D (8); Smith J 7(2); Smith M 12(6); Starr S 5; Wilson D
18(6)

Goals-League (46): Ferry 7, Kennedy 6, McGoldrick 5, McLauchlan 5, Maxwell 5, Hardie 4, Edgar 3, Graham 3, Caven 2, Falconer 2, Orr 2, Arbuckle 1, Fitzpatrick 1.
Scottish Cup (3): Caven 1, Falconer 1, own goal 1.
Coca Cola Cup (3): Falconer 1, McGoldrick 1, Maxwell 1.
League Challenge Cup (1): Falconer 1.

RAITH ROVERS   DIV. 1

Ground: Stark's Park, Pratt Street, Kirkcaldy KY1 1SA (01592) 263514
Ground capacity: 10,271. **Colours:** Navy blue shirts, white shorts.
Manager: Jimmy Nicholl.
League Appearances: Andersen S 7; Andersen V 18(1); Bergersen K 6; Bonar P 9(7); Browne P 4; Craig D 28; Dargo C 1(4); Dennis S 16; Duffield P 23(10); Geddes R 3; Hallum C 6; Harvey P 10(8); Kirk S 18(7); Kirkwood D 13(4); Krivokapic M 6; Lennon D 35; Lorimer D 1(2); Makela J 8; McCulloch G 3(3); McGill D 3(6); McInally J 4; Millar J 25(2); Millen A 13; Mitchell G 20; Rougier A 27(3); Scott C 5; Skonhoff O 1; Stein J (2); Taylor A 14(4); Thomson SM 18(4); Thomson SY 28; Twaddle K 23(5)
Goals-League (29): Duffield 5, Lennon 5, Twaddle 4, Andersen S 3, Craig 2, Taylor 2, Thomson SM 2, Bergersen 1, Bonar 1, Kirk 1, Kirkwood 1, Makela 1, Rougier 1.
Scottish Cup (6): Andersen S 2, Craig 1, Kirk 1, Kirkwood 1, Rougier 1.
Coca Cola Cup (2): Rougier 2.

RANGERS   PREM. DIV.

Ground: Ibrox Stadium, Glasgow G51 2XD (0141) 427 8500
Ground capacity: 50,500. **Colours:** Royal blue shirts, red and blue panels, white shorts.
Manager: Walter Smith, OBE. **Assistant Manager:** Archie Knox.
League Appearances: Albertz J 31(1); Andersen E 6(11); Bjorklund J 28; Boyack S (1); Cleland A 32; Dibble A 7; Durie G 14(2); Durrant I 4(4); Ferguson I 18(6); Fitzgerald D (1); Gascoigne P 23(3); Goram A 25; Gough R 27; Hateley M 4; Laudrup B 33; McCall S 7; McCoist A 13(12); McInnes D 10(11); McLaren A 17(1); Miller C 7(6); Moore C 23; Petric G 23(3); Robertson D 21(1); Rozental S (1); Shields G 6; Snelders T 4; Steven T 5(3); Van Vossen P 6(8); Wilson S 1; Wright S 1
Goals-League (85): Laudrup 16, Gascoigne 13 (1 pen), Albertz 10, McCoist 10 (1 pen), Andersen 9, Durie 5, Gough 5, Van Vossen 5, Robertson 4, Petric 2, Ferguson 1, Hateley 1, McInnes 1, Miller 1, Moore 1, Steven 1.
Scottish Cup (5): Andersen 1, McCoist 1, Robertson 1, Rozental 1, Steven 1.
Coca Cola Cup (20): Van Vossen 4, Albertz 3, Gascoigne 3, McCoist 3, Andersen 2, Laudrup 2, McInnes 2, Durie 1.

ROSS COUNTY   DIV. 3

Ground: Victoria Park, Dingwall IV15 9QW (01349) 862253
Ground capacity: 5400. **Colours:** Dark blue shirts, white shorts.
Manager: Neale Cooper.
League Appearances: Adams D 31(3); Bellshaw J 27(3); Bradshaw P 1(2); Broddle J 27(2); Clark J 1; Connelly G 13(5); Cooper N 4; Cormack D 4; Farrell G 22(1); Ferguson S 13(3); Ferries K 27(9); Fotheringham K 4(3); Furphy W 16(3); Gilbert K 13; Golabek S 9(7); Grant B 1(4); Hart R (4); Herd W 28(2); Hewitt J 2(5); Hutchison S 25; MacLeod Alex 1; MacLeod Andy 16(8); Mackay D 24; Matheson D 2; McBain R 26(1); Milne C (2); Morgan K 7; Ross A 22; Somerville C 7(1); Watt W 1; Williamson R 16(3); Wood G 6(1)
Goals-League (58): Adams 22 (3 pens), Ross 9, MacLeod 6, McBain 4, Ferguson 3, Golabek 3, Farrell 2, Ferries 2, Clark 1, Connelly 1, Gilbert 1, Hart 1, Herd 1, Hewitt 1, Wood 1.
Scottish Cup (3): Ross 3.
Coca Cola Cup (1): Adams 1.
League Challenge Cup (0).

ST JOHNSTONE   PREM. DIV.

Ground: McDiarmid Park, Crieff Road, Perth PH1 2SJ (01738) 626961
Ground capacity: 10,673. **Colours:** Royal blue shirts with white trim, white shorts.
Manager: Paul Sturrock.
League Appearances: Bowman G 4; Brown G (1); Colquhoun J 6; Dasovic N 14; Davidson C 18(2); Donaldson E 3(1); Farquhar G 3(2); Ferguson I 3(5); Fyhr P 3(1); Grant R 31(2); Griffin D 26(3); Jenkinson L 22(3); King C 2(2); Main A 34; McAnespie K 1(8); McCluskey S 7(3); McGowne K 2; McQuillan J 32; O'Boyle G 23(2); O'Halloran K 4(1); O'Neil J 25(4); Preston A 23(9); Robertson S 2; Scott P 24(5); Sekerlioglu A 22(2); Tosh S 22(3); Weir J 32; Whiteford A 8(3)
Goals-League (74): Grant 19 (2 pens), O'Boyle 12 (1 pen), Scott 12, Jenkinson 6, Sekerlioglu 6, O'Neil 3, Tosh 3, Weir 3, Davidson 2, Ferguson 2, McAnespie 2, Colquhoun 1, Griffin 1, McCluskey 1, Preston 1.
Scottish Cup (0).
Coca Cola Cup (6): Grant 2, O'Boyle 2, Scott 1. Tosh 1.
League Challenge Cup (15): Grant 5 (1 pen), Farquhar 2, O'Boyle 2 (1 pen), O'Neil 1, Preston 1, Scott 1, Sekerlioglu 1, Whiteford 1, own goal 1.

ST MIRREN   DIV. 1

Ground: St Mirren Park, Paisley PA3 2EJ (0141) 889 2558, 840 1337
Ground capacity: 15,410. **Colours:** Black and white striped shirts, black shorts.
Manager: Tony Fitzpatrick.
League Appearances: Archdeacon P 1(5); Baker M 31; Combe A 36; Dick J 24(1); Fallon W (2); Fenwick P 27; Foster W 8; Galloway G 1(1); Gillies R 29; Hetherston B 20(2); Iwelumo C 2(12); McGarry S 5(6); McGuire J (3); McLaren I (1); McLaughlin B 27(1); McWhirter N 26(1); Mendes J 32(4); Munro S 25(1); Murray H (1); Smith B 20(5); Taylor S 11(1); Turner T 17; Watson S 26; Yardley M 28(2)
Goals-League (48): Yardley 15, Fenwick 6, Gillies 6, Watson 4, Dick 3, Hetherston 3 (2 pens), Mendes 3, Foster 2, Turner 2, McGarry 1, Munro 1, Taylor 1, own goal 1.
Scottish Cup (1): Gillies 1.
Coca Cola Cup (5): Gillies 1, Hetherston 1, Iwelumo 1, Taylor 1, Yardley 1.
League Challenge Cup (1): Hetherston 1.

STENHOUSEMUIR   DIV. 2

Ground: Ochilview Park, Stenhousemuir FK5 5QL (01324) 562992
Ground capacity: 3520. **Colours:** Maroon shirts with silver trim, white shorts.
Manager: Terry Christie.
League Appearances: Alexander N 12; Armstrong G 34; Banks A 16(2); Brown S 3; Campbell M 7(5); Christie M 7(1); Ellison S 24; Fisher J 31; Haddow L 27(1); Henderson J 35(1); Hume A 5(18); Hunter P 29(1); Hutchison G 29(1); Innes C 23(1); Little I 35; Logan P 1(4); McGeachie G 20(5); McKee K 13; Roseburgh D 8(14); Sprott A 23(7); Stewart I 2(2); Thomson J 12(1); Whiteford S (1)
Goals-League (49): Little 14, Haddow 10 (2 pens), Hunter 7, Henderson 4, Hutchison 4, Hume 3, Fisher 2, Roseburgh 2, Innes 1, Sprott 1, Stewart 1.
Scottish Cup (1): Hume 1.
Coca Cola Cup (1): Sprott 1.
League Challenge Cup (0).

STIRLING ALBION   DIV. 1

Ground: Forthbank Stadium, Springkerse Industrial Estate, Stirling FK7 7UJ (01786) 450399
Ground capacity: 3808. **Colours:** Red and white halves.
Manager: Kevin Drinkell.
League Appearances: Bennett N 26(7); Bone A 34; Carberry G 10(1); Deas P 32; Forrest E 1; Gibson J 28(8); Hjartarsson G 20(1); Jack S 7(8); McCormick S 29(2); McGeown M 36; McGrotty G (12); McLaren S 8(15); McLeod J 5(1); McQuilter R 31; Mitchell C 13(1); Mortimer P (1); Paterson A 34; Paterson G 33; Taggart C 22(3); Tait T 22(4); Watson P (1); Wood D 5(8)
Goals-League (54): Bone 9 (1 pen), McCormick 8, Tait 6, Bennett 5 (2 pens), Hjartarsson 5, McLaren 5, Paterson G 4, McQuilter 2, Paterson A 2, Taggart 2, Deas 1, Gibson 1, Wood 1, own goals 3.
Scottish Cup (0).
Coca Cola Cup (1): Gibson 1.
League Challenge Cup (4): Bone 3, Gibson 1.

STRANRAER   DIV. 2

Ground: Stair Park, Stranraer DG9 8BS (01776) 703271
Ground capacity: 6100. **Colours:** Royal blue shirts with red quarters, white shorts.
Manager: Campbell Money.
League Appearances: Black T 26; Campbell M 1; Crawford D 14(6); Docherty R 25(6); Duffy B 27; Duffy J (1); Duncan G 9(6); Friels G 1(5); Gallacher I 14(4); Gallagher A 13; Hay G 9; Higgins G 17(4); Howard N 2(1); Hughes J 22(5); Jack A (1); Lansdowne A 30; Matthews G 9; McAulay I 25(1); McCaffrey J 25; McCrindle S (3); McIntyre P 28; McLaren J (1); McMillan J 9(17); McStay R (1); Millar G 20; Robertson J 20(11); Sloan T 26(5); Young G 24(6)
Goals-League (29): McIntyre 7, Young 5, Docherty 3, Sloan 3, Crawford 2, Higgins 2, McCaffrey 2, Black 1, Lansdowne 1, McAulay 1, McMillan 1, own goal 1.
Scottish Cup (1): Young 1.
Coca Cola Cup (3): Docherty 1, Sloan 1, Young 1.
League Challenge Cup (9): Sloan 4, Docherty 1 (pen), McAulay 1, McCaffrey 1, McIntyre 1, McMillan 1.

SCOTTISH LEAGUE HONOURS

*On goal average/difference. †Held jointly after indecisive play-off.
‡Won on deciding match. ††Held jointly. ¶Two points deducted for
fielding ineligible player. Competition suspended 1940–45 during war;
Regional Leagues operating.
‡‡Two points deducted for registration irregularities.

PREMIER DIVISION

Maximum points: 72

	First	Pts	Second	Pts	Third	Pts
1975–76	Rangers	54	Celtic	48	Hibernian	43
1976–77	Celtic	55	Rangers	46	Aberdeen	43
1977–78	Rangers	55	Aberdeen	53	Dundee U	40
1978–79	Celtic	48	Rangers	45	Dundee U	44
1979–80	Aberdeen	48	Celtic	47	St Mirren	42
1980–81	Celtic	56	Aberdeen	49	Rangers*	44
1981–82	Celtic	55	Aberdeen	53	Rangers	43
1982–83	Dundee U	56	Celtic*	55	Aberdeen	55
1983–84	Aberdeen	57	Celtic	50	Dundee U	47
1984–85	Aberdeen	59	Celtic	52	Dundee U	47
1985–86	Celtic*	50	Hearts	50	Dundee U	47

Maximum points: 88

	First	Pts	Second	Pts	Third	Pts
1986–87	Rangers	69	Celtic	63	Dundee U	60
1987–88	Celtic	72	Hearts	62	Rangers	60

Maximum points: 72

	First	Pts	Second	Pts	Third	Pts
1988–89	Rangers	56	Aberdeen	50	Celtic	46
1989–90	Rangers	51	Aberdeen*	44	Hearts	44
1990–91	Rangers	55	Aberdeen	53	Celtic*	41

Maximum points: 88

	First	Pts	Second	Pts	Third	Pts
1991–92	Rangers	72	Hearts	63	Celtic	62
1992–93	Rangers	73	Aberdeen	64	Celtic	60
1993–94	Rangers	58	Aberdeen	55	Motherwell	54

Maximum points: 108

	First	Pts	Second	Pts	Third	Pts
1994–95	Rangers	69	Motherwell	54	Hibernian	53
1995–96	Rangers	87	Celtic	83	Aberdeen*	55
1996–97	Rangers	80	Celtic	75	Dundee U	60

DIVISION 1

Maximum points: 52

	First	Pts	Second	Pts	Third	Pts
1975–76	Partick T	41	Kilmarnock	35	Montrose	30

Maximum points: 78

	First	Pts	Second	Pts	Third	Pts
1976–77	St Mirren	62	Clydebank	58	Dundee	51
1977–78	Morton*	58	Hearts	58	Dundee	57
1978–79	Dundee	55	Kilmarnock*	54	Clydebank	54
1979–80	Hearts	53	Airdrieonians	51	Ayr U*	44
1980–81	Hibernian	57	Dundee	52	St Johnstone	51
1981–82	Motherwell	61	Kilmarnock	51	Hearts	50
1982–83	St Johnstone	55	Hearts	54	Clydebank	50
1983–84	Morton	54	Dumbarton	51	Partick T	46
1984–85	Motherwell	50	Clydebank	48	Falkirk	45
1985–86	Hamilton A	56	Falkirk	45	Kilmarnock	44

			Maximum points: 88			
1986–87	Morton	57	Dunfermline Ath	56	Dumbarton	53
1987–88	Hamilton A	56	Meadowbank T	52	Clydebank	49
			Maximum points: 78			
1988–89	Dunfermline Ath	54	Falkirk	52	Clydebank	48
1989–90	St Johnstone	58	Airdrieonians	54	Clydebank	44
1990–91	Falkirk	54	Airdrieonians	53	Dundee	52
			Maximum points: 88			
1991–92	Dundee	58	Partick T*	57	Hamilton A	57
1992–93	Raith R	65	Kilmarnock	54	Dunfermline Ath	52
1993–94	Falkirk	66	Dunfermline Ath	65	Airdrieonians	54
			Maximum points: 108			
1994–95	Raith R	69	Dunfermline Ath*	68	Dundee	68
1995–96	Dunfermline Ath	71	Dundee U*	67	Morton	67
1996–97	St Johnstone	80	Airdrieonians	60	Dundee*	58

DIVISION 2

			Maximum points: 52			
1975–76	Clydebank*	40	Raith R	40	Alloa	35
			Maximum points: 78			
1976–77	Stirling A	55	Alloa	51	Dunfermline Ath	50
1977–78	Clyde*	53	Raith R	53	Dunfermline Ath	48
1978–79	Berwick R	54	Dunfermline Ath	52	Falkirk	50
1979–80	Falkirk	50	East Stirling	49	Forfar Ath	46
1980–81	Queen's Park	50	Queen of the S	46	Cowdenbeath	45
1981–82	Clyde	59	Alloa*	50	Arbroath	50
1982–83	Brechin C	55	Meadowbank T	54	Arbroath	49
1983–84	Forfar Ath	63	East Fife	47	Berwick R	43
1984–85	Montrose	53	Alloa	50	Dunfermline Ath	49
1985–86	Dunfermline Ath	57	Queen of the S	55	Meadowbank T	49
1986–87	Meadowbank T	55	Raith R*	52	Stirling A*	52
1987–88	Ayr U	61	St Johnstone	59	Queen's Park	51
1988–89	Albion R	50	Alloa	45	Brechin C	43
1989–90	Brechin C	49	Kilmarnock	48	Stirling A	47
1990–91	Stirling A	54	Montrose	46	Cowdenbeath	45
1991–92	Dumbarton	52	Cowdenbeath	51	Alloa	50
1992–93	Clyde	54	Brechin C*	53	Stranraer	53
1993–94	Stranraer	56	Berwick R	48	Stenhousemuir*	47
			Maximum points: 108			
1994–95	Morton	64	Dumbarton	60	Stirling A	58
1995–96	Stirling A	81	East Fife	67	Berwick R	60
1996–97	Ayr U	77	Hamilton A	74	Livingston	64

DIVISION 3

			Maximum points: 108			
1994–95	Forfar Ath	80	Montrose	67	Ross Co	60
1995–96	Livingston	72	Brechin C	63	Caledonian T	57
1996–97	Inverness CT	76	Forfar Ath*	67	Ross Co	67

DIVISION 1 to 1974–75

Maximum points: a 36; b 44; c 40; d 52; e 60; f 68; g 76; h 84.

	First	Pts	Second	Pts	Third	Pts
1890–91a	Dumbarton††	29	Rangers††	29	Celtic	21
1891–92b	Dumbarton	37	Celtic	35	Hearts	34

1892–93a	Celtic	29	Rangers	28	St Mirren	20		
1893–94a	Celtic	29	Hearts	26	St Bernard's	23		
1894–95a	Hearts	31	Celtic	26	Rangers	22		
1895–96a	Celtic	30	Rangers	26	Hibernian	24		
1896–97a	Hearts	28	Hibernian	26	Rangers	25		
1897–98a	Celtic	33	Rangers	29	Hibernian	22		
1898–99a	Rangers	36	Hearts	26	Celtic	24		
1899–								
1900a	Rangers	32	Celtic	25	Hibernian	24		
1900–01c	Rangers	35	Celtic	29	Hibernian	25		
1901–02a	Rangers	28	Celtic	26	Hearts	22		
1902–03b	Hibernian	37	Dundee	31	Rangers	29		
1903–04d	Third Lanark	43	Hearts	39	Celtic*	38		
1904–05d	Celtic‡	41	Rangers	41	Third Lanark	35		
1905–06e	Celtic	49	Hearts	43	Airdrieonians	38		
1906–07f	Celtic	55	Dundee	48	Rangers	45		
1907–08f	Celtic	55	Falkirk	51	Rangers	50		
1908–09f	Celtic	51	Dundee	50	Clyde	48		
1909–10f	Celtic	54	Falkirk	52	Rangers	46		
1910–11f	Rangers	52	Aberdeen	48	Falkirk	44		
1911–12f	Rangers	51	Celtic	45	Clyde	42		
1912–13f	Rangers	53	Celtic	49	Hearts*	41		
1913–14g	Celtic	65	Rangers	59	Hearts*	54		
1914–15g	Celtic	65	Hearts	61	Rangers	50		
1915–16g	Celtic	67	Rangers	56	Morton	51		
1916–17g	Celtic	64	Morton	54	Rangers	53		
1917–18f	Rangers	56	Celtic	55	Kilmarnock*	43		
1918–19f	Celtic	58	Rangers	57	Morton	47		
1919–20h	Rangers	71	Celtic	68	Motherwell	57		
1920–21h	Rangers	76	Celtic	66	Hearts	50		
1921–22h	Celtic	67	Rangers	66	Raith R	51		
1922–23g	Rangers	55	Airdrieonians	50	Celtic	46		
1923–24g	Rangers	59	Airdrieonians	50	Celtic	46		
1924–25g	Rangers	60	Airdrieonians	57	Hibernian	52		
1925–26g	Celtic	58	Airdrieonians*	50	Hearts	50		
1926–27g	Rangers	56	Motherwell	51	Celtic	49		
1927–28g	Rangers	60	Celtic*	55	Motherwell	55		
1928–29g	Rangers	67	Celtic	51	Motherwell	50		
1929–30g	Rangers	60	Motherwell	55	Aberdeen	53		
1930–31g	Rangers	60	Celtic	58	Motherwell	56		
1931–32g	Motherwell	66	Rangers	61	Celtic	48		
1932–33g	Rangers	62	Motherwell	59	Hearts	50		
1933–34g	Rangers	66	Motherwell	62	Celtic	47		
1934–35g	Rangers	55	Celtic	52	Hearts	50		
1935–36g	Celtic	66	Rangers*	61	Aberdeen	61		
1936–37g	Rangers	61	Aberdeen	54	Celtic	52		
1937–38g	Celtic	61	Hearts	58	Rangers	49		
1938–39g	Rangers	59	Celtic	48	Aberdeen	46		
1946–47e	Rangers	46	Hibernian	44	Aberdeen	39		
1947–48e	Hibernian	48	Rangers	46	Partick T	36		
1948–49e	Rangers	46	Dundee	45	Hibernian	39		
1949–50e	Rangers	50	Hibernian	49	Hearts	43		
1950–51e	Hibernian	48	Rangers*	38	Dundee	38		

184

1951–52e	Hibernian	45	Rangers	41	East Fife	37
1952–53e	Rangers*	43	Hibernian	43	East Fife	39
1953–54e	Celtic	43	Hearts	38	Partick T	35
1954–55e	Aberdeen	49	Celtic	46	Rangers	41
1955–56f	Rangers	52	Aberdeen	46	Hearts*	45
1956–57f	Rangers	55	Hearts	53	Kilmarnock	42
1957–58f	Hearts	62	Rangers	49	Celtic	46
1958–59f	Rangers	50	Hearts	48	Motherwell	44
1959–60f	Hearts	54	Kilmarnock	50	Rangers*	42
1960–61f	Rangers	51	Kilmarnock	50	Third Lanark	42
1961–62f	Dundee	54	Rangers	51	Celtic	46
1962–63f	Rangers	57	Kilmarnock	48	Partick T	46
1963–64f	Rangers	55	Kilmarnock	49	Celtic*	47
1964–65f	Kilmarnock*	50	Hearts	50	Dunfermline Ath	49
1965–66f	Celtic	57	Rangers	55	Kilmarnock	45
1966–67f	Celtic	58	Rangers	55	Clyde	46
1967–68f	Celtic	63	Rangers	61	Hibernian	45
1968–69f	Celtic	54	Rangers	49	DunfermlineAth	45
1969–70f	Celtic	57	Rangers	45	Hibernian	44
1970–71f	Celtic	56	Aberdeen	54	St Johnstone	44
1971–72f	Celtic	60	Aberdeen	50	Rangers	44
1972–73f	Celtic	57	Rangers	56	Hibernian	45
1973–74f	Celtic	53	Hibernian	49	Rangers	48
1974–75f	Rangers	56	Hibernian	49	Celtic	45

DIVISION 2 to 1974–75

Maximum points: a 76; b 72; c 68; d 52; e 60; f 36; g 44.

1893–94f	Hibernian	29	Cowlairs	27	Clyde	24
1894–95f	Hibernian	30	Motherwell	22	Port Glasgow	20
1895–96f	Abercorn	27	Leith Ath	23	Renton	21
1896–97f	Partick T	31	Leith Ath	27	Kilmarnock*	21
1897–98f	Kilmarnock	29	Port Glasgow	25	Morton	22
1898–99f	Kilmarnock	32	Leith Ath	27	Port Glasgow	25
1899–					
1900f	Partick T	29	Morton	28	Port Glasgow	20
1900–01f	St Bernard's	25	Airdrieonians	23	Abercorn	21
1901–02g	Port Glasgow	32	Partick T	31	Motherwell	26
1902–03g	Airdrieonians	35	Motherwell	28	Ayr U*	27
1903–04g	Hamilton A	37	Clyde	29	Hamilton A	28
1904–05g	Clyde	32	Falkirk	28	Hamilton A	27
1905–06g	Leith Ath	34	Clyde	31	Albion R	27
1906–07g	St Bernard's	32	Vale of Leven*	27	Arthurlie	27
1907–08g	Raith R	30	Dumbarton	‡‡27	Ayr U	28
1908–09g	Abercorn	31	Raith R*	28	Vale of Leven	28
1909–10g	Leith Ath‡	33	Raith R	33	St Bernard's	27
1910–11g	Dumbarton	31	Ayr U	27	Albion R	25
1911–12g	Ayr U	35	Abercorn	30	Dumbarton	27
1912–13d	Ayr U	34	Dunfermline Ath	33	East Stirling	32
1913–14g	Cowdenbeath	31	Albion R	27	Dunfermline Ath*	27
1914–15d	Cowdenbeath*	37	St Bernard's*	37	Leith Ath	37
1921–22a	Alloa	60	Cowdenbeath	47	Armadale	45
1922–23a	Queen's Park	57	Clydebank ¶		St Johnstone ¶	45

1923–24a	St Johnstone	56	Cowdenbeath	55	Bathgate	44
1924–25a	Dundee U	50	Clydebank	48	Clyde	47
1925–26a	Dunfermline Ath	59	Clyde	53	Ayr U	52
1926–27a	Bo'ness	56	Raith R	49	Clydebank	45
1927–28a	Ayr U	54	Third Lanark	45	King's Park	44
1928–29b	Dundee U	51	Morton	50	Arbroath	47
1929–30a	Leith Ath*	57	East Fife	57	Albion R	54
1930–31a	Third Lanark	61	Dundee U	50	Dunfermline Ath	47
1931–32a	East Stirling*	55	St Johnstone	55	Raith R*	46
1932–33c	Hibernian	54	Queen of the S	49	Dunfermline Ath	47
1933–34c	Albion R	45	Dunfermline Ath*	44	Arbroath	44
1934–35c	Third Lanark	52	Arbroath	50	St Bernard's	47
1935–36c	Falkirk	59	St Mirren	52	Morton	48
1936–37c	Ayr U	54	Morton	51	St Bernard's	48
1937–38c	Raith R	59	Albion R	48	Airdrieonians	47
1938–39c	Cowdenbeath	60	Alloa*	48	East Fife	48
1946–47d	Dundee	45	Airdrieonians	42	East Fife	31
1947–48e	East Fife	53	Albion R	42	Hamilton A	40
1948–49e	Raith R*	42	Stirling A	42	Airdrieonians*	41
1949–50e	Morton	47	Airdrieonians	44	Dunfermline Ath*	36
1950–51e	Queen of the S*	45	Stirling A	45	Ayr U*	36
1951–52e	Clyde	44	Falkirk	43	Ayr U	39
1952–53e	Stirling A	44	Hamilton A	43	Queen's Park	37
1953–54e	Motherwell	45	Kilmarnock	42	Third Lanark*	36
1954–55e	Airdrieonians	46	Dunfermline Ath	42	Hamilton A	39
1955–56b	Queen's Park	54	Ayr U	51	St Johnstone	49
1956–57b	Clyde	64	Third Lanark	51	Cowdenbeath	45
1957–58b	Stirling A	55	Dunfermline Ath	53	Arbroath	47
1958–59b	Ayr U	60	Arbroath	51	Stenhousemuir	46
1959–60b	St Johnstone	53	Dundee U	50	Queen of the S	49
1960–61b	Stirling A	55	Falkirk	54	Stenhousemuir	50
1961–62b	Clyde	54	Queen of the S	53	Morton	44
1962–63b	St Johnstone	55	East Stirling	49	Morton	48
1963–64b	Morton	67	Clyde	53	Arbroath	46
1964–65b	Stirling A	59	Hamilton A	50	Queen of the S	45
1965–66b	Ayr U	53	Airdrieonians	50	Queen of the S	47
1966–67a	Morton	69	Raith R	58	Arbroath	57
1967–68b	St Mirren	62	Arbroath	53	East Fife	49
1968–69b	Motherwell	64	Ayr U	53	East Fife*	48
1969–70b	Falkirk	56	Cowdenbeath	55	Queen of the S	50
1970–71b	Partick T	56	East Fife	51	Arbroath	46
1971–72b	Dumbarton*	52	Arbroath	52	Stirling A	50
1972–73b	Clyde	56	Dumfermline Ath	52	Raith R*	47
1973–74b	Airdrieonians	60	Kilmarnock	58	Hamilton A	55
1974–75a	Falkirk	54	Queen of the S*	53	Montrose	53

Elected to Division 1: 1894 Clyde; 1895 Hibernian; 1896 Abercorn; 1897 Partick T; 1899 Kilmarnock; 1900 Morton and Partick T; 1902 Port Glasgow and Partick T; 1903 Airdrieonians and Motherwell; 1905 Falkirk and Aberdeen; 1906 Clyde and Hamilton A; 1910 Raith R; 1913 Ayr U and Dumbarton.

RELEGATED CLUBS

From Premier Division

1974–75 *No relegation due to League reorganisation*
1975–76 Dundee, St Johnstone
1976–77 Hearts, Kilmarnock
1977–78 Ayr U, Clydebank
1978–79 Hearts, Motherwell
1979–80 Dundee, Hibernian
1980–81 Kilmarnock, Hearts
1981–82 Partick T, Airdrieonians
1982–83 Morton, Kilmarnock
1983–84 St Johnstone, Motherwell
1984–85 Dumbarton, Morton
1985–86 *No relegation due to League reorganization*
1986–87 Clydebank, Hamilton A
1987–88 Falkirk, Dunfermline Ath, Morton
1988–89 Hamilton A
1989–90 Dundee
1990–91 None
1991–92 St Mirren, Dunfermline Ath
1992–93 Falkirk, Airdrieonians
1993–94 *See footnote*
1994–95 Dundee U
1995–96 Partick T, Falkirk
1996–97 Raith R

Relegated from Division 2

1994–95 Meadowbank T, Brechin C
1995–96 Forfar Ath, Montrose
1996–97 Dumbarton, Berwick R

From Division 1

1974–75 *No relegation due to League reorganisation*
1975–76 Dunfermline Ath, Clyde
1976–77 Raith R, Falkirk
1977–78 Alloa Ath, East Fife
1978–79 Montrose, Queen of the S
1979–80 Arbroath, Clyde
1980–81 Stirling A, Berwick R
1981–82 East Stirling, Queen of the S
1982–83 Dunfermline Ath, Queen's Park
1983–84 Raith R, Alloa
1984–85 Meadowbank T, St Johnstone
1985–86 Ayr U, Alloa

1986–87 Brechin C, Montrose
1987–88 East Fife, Dumbarton

1988–89 Kilmarnock, Queen of the S
1989–90 Albion R, Alloa
1990–91 Clyde, Brechin C
1991–92 Montrose, Forfar Ath
1992–93 Meadowbank T, Cowdenbeath
1993–94 *See footnote*
1994–95 Ayr U, Stranraer
1995–96 Hamilton A, Dumbarton
1996–97 Clydebank, East Fife

Relegated from Division 1 1973–74

1921–22 *Queen's Park, Dumbarton, Clydebank
1922–23 Albion R, Alloa Ath
1923–24 Clyde, Clydebank
1924–25 Third Lanark, Ayr U
1925–26 Raith R, Clydebank
1926–27 Morton, Dundee U
1927–28 Dunfermline Ath, Bo'ness
1928–29 Third Lanark, Raith R
1929–30 St Johnstone, Dundee U
1930–31 Hibernian, East Fife
1931–32 Dundee U, Leith Ath
1932–33 Morton, East Stirling
1933–34 Third Lanark, Cowdenbeath

1934–35 St Mirren, Falkirk
1935–36 Airdrieonians, Ayr U
1936–37 Dunfermline Ath, Albion R
1937–38 Dundee, Morton
1938–39 Queen's Park, Raith R
1946–47 Kilmarnock, Hamilton A
1947–48 Airdrieonians, Queen's Park
1948–49 Morton, Albion R
1949–50 Queen of the S, Stirling A
1950–51 Clyde, Falkirk
1951–52 Morton, Stirling A
1952–53 Motherwell, Third Lanark
1953–54 Airdrieonians, Hamilton A
1954–55 *No clubs relegated*

1955–56 Stirling A, Clyde
1956–57 Dunfermline Ath, Ayr U
1957–58 East Fife, Queen's Park
1958–59 Queen of the S, Falkirk
1959–60 Arbroath, Stirling A
1960–61 Ayr U, Clyde
1961–62 St Johnstone, Stirling A
1962–63 Clyde, Raith R
1963–64 Queen of the S, East Stirling
1964–65 Airdrieonians, Third Lanark

1965–66 Morton, Hamilton A
1966–67 St Mirren, Ayr U
1967–68 Motherwell, Stirling A
1968–69 Falkirk, Arbroath
1969–70 Raith R, Partick T
1970–71 St Mirren, Cowdenbeath
1971–72 Clyde, Dunfermline Ath
1972–73 Kilmarnock, Airdrieonians
1973–74 East Fife, Falkirk

*Season 1921–22 – only 1 club promoted, 3 clubs relegated.

Scottish League championship wins: Rangers 47, Celtic 35, Aberdeen 4, Hearts 4, Hibernian 4, Dumbarton 2, Dundee 1, Dundee U 1, Kilmarnock 1, Motherwell 1, Third Lanark 1.

The Scottish Football League was reconstructed into three divisions at the end of the 1974–75 season, so the usual relegation statistics do not apply. Further reorganization took place at the end of the 1985–86 season. From 1986–87, the Premier and First Division had 12 teams each. The Second Division remained at 14. From 1988–89, the Premier Division reverted to 10 teams, and the First Division to 14 teams but in 1991–92 the Premier and First Division reverted to 12.

PAST SCOTTISH LEAGUE CUP FINALS

1946–47	Rangers	4	Aberdeen	0
1947–48	East Fife	0 4	Falkirk	0* 1
1948–49	Rangers	2	Raith Rovers	0
1949–50	East Fife	3	Dunfermline	0
1950–51	Motherwell	3	Hibernian	0
1951–52	Dundee	3	Rangers	2
1952–53	Dundee	2	Kilmarnock	0
1953–54	East Fife	3	Partick Thistle	2
1954–55	Hearts	4	Motherwell	2
1955–56	Aberdeen	2	St Mirren	1
1956–57	Celtic	0 3	Partick Thistle	0 0
1957–58	Celtic	7	Rangers	1
1958–59	Hearts	5	Partick Thistle	1
1959–60	Hearts	2	Third Lanark	1
1960–61	Rangers	2	Kilmarnock	0
1961–62	Rangers	1 3	Hearts	1 1
1962–63	Hearts	1	Kilmarnock	0
1963–64	Rangers	5	Morton	0
1964–65	Rangers	2	Celtic	1
1965–66	Celtic	2	Rangers	1
1966–67	Celtic	1	Rangers	0
1967–68	Celtic	5	Dundee	3
1968–69	Celtic	6	Hibernian	2
1969–70	Celtic	1	St Johnstone	0
1970–71	Rangers	1	Celtic	0
1971–72	Partick Thistle	4	Celtic	1
1972–73	Hibernian	2	Celtic	1
1973–74	Dundee	1	Celtic	0
1974–75	Celtic	6	Hibernian	3
1975–76	Rangers	1	Celtic	0
1976–77	Aberdeen	2	Celtic	1
1977–78	Rangers	2	Celtic	1*
1978–79	Rangers	2	Aberdeen	1
1979–80	Aberdeen	0 0	Dundee U	0* 3
1980–81	Dundee	0	Dundee U	3
1981–82	Rangers	2	Dundee U	1
1982–83	Celtic	2	Rangers	1
1983–84	Rangers	3	Celtic	2
1984–85	Rangers	1	Dundee U	0
1985–86	Aberdeen	3	Hibernian	0
1986–87	Rangers	2	Celtic	1
1987–88	Rangers†	3	Aberdeen	3*
1988–89	Aberdeen	2	Rangers	3*
1989–90	Aberdeen	2	Rangers	1
1990–91	Rangers	2	Celtic	1
1991–92	Rangers	2	Aberdeen	1
1992–93	Rangers	2	Aberdeen	1*
1993–94	Rangers	2	Hibernian	1
1994–95	Raith R†	2	Celtic	2*
1995–96	Aberdeen	2	Dundee	0

†Won on penalties *After extra time

SCOTTISH COCA-COLA CUP 1996–97

FIRST ROUND

Albion R	(1) 4	Arbroath	(0) 0
Ayr U	(1) 5	Livingston	(1) 2
Brechin C	(3) 3	Montrose	(0) 0
Clyde	(0) 1	Inverness CT	(0) 0
(aet)			
Cowdenbeath	(0) 1	Forfar Ath	(1) 2
(aet)			
East Stirling	(1) 1	Alloa	(1) 3
(aet)			
Queen's Park	(0) 3	Ross Co	(0) 1
(aet)			
Stranraer	(1) 2	Queen of the S	(0) 0

SECOND ROUND

Airdrieonians	(1) 3	Raith R	(1) 2
(aet)			
Brechin C	(0) 0	Hibernian	(1) 2
Clydebank	(0) 0	Rangers	(2) 3
Clyde	(0) 1	Celtic	(1) 3
Dundee	(0) 2	Dumbarton	(1) 1
East Fife	(1) 1	St Johnstone	(3) 5
Falkirk	(1) 2	Albion R	(2) 3
Greenock Morton	(1) 1	Hamilton A	(1) 1
(aet; Greenock Morton won 4-3 on penalties)			
Hearts	(0) 1	Stenhousemuir	(1) 1
(aet; Hearts won 5-4 on penalties)			
Kilmarnock	(0) 0	Ayr U	(1) 1
Motherwell	(0) 0	Alloa	(0) 0
(aet; Alloa won 4-2 on penalties)			
Partick T	(0) 3	Forfar Ath	(0) 0
Queen's Park	(0) 0	Aberdeen	(1) 2
Stirling Albion	(1) 1	Dundee U	(1) 2
St Mirren	(1) 4	Berwick R	(0) 0
Stranraer	(0) 1	Dunfermline Ath	(2) 2

THIRD ROUND

Albion R	(0) 0	Hibernian	(1) 2
Alloa	(0) 1	Celtic	(1) 5
Dundee U	(1) 2	Dundee	(1) 2
(aet; Dundee won 4-2 on penalties)			
Dunfermline Ath	(1) 3	St Mirren	(1) 1
Greenock Morton	(0) 3	Aberdeen	(2) 7
(aet)			
Partick T	(1) 1	Airdrieonians	(0) 0
Rangers	(0) 3	Ayr U	(0) 1
St Johnstone	(0) 1	Hearts	(1) 3
(aet)			

QUARTER-FINALS

Dundee	(1) 2	Aberdeen	(0) 1
Dunfermline Ath	(0) 2	Partick T	(0) 0
Hearts	(0) 1	Celtic	(0) 0
(aet)			
Rangers	(1) 4	Hibernian	(0) 0

SEMI-FINALS

Dunfermline Ath	(0) 1	Rangers	(1) 6
Hearts	(2) 3	Dundee	(0) 1

FINAL

Rangers	(2) 4	Hearts	(1) 3

SCOTTISH LEAGUE CHALLENGE CUP 1996–97

FIRST ROUND

Albion R	(0) 1	St Johnstone	(0) 2
(aet)			
Alloa	(0) 3	Clyde	(3) 3
(aet; Clyde won 5-4 on penalties)			
Arbroath	(0) 2	Queen of the S	(0) 3
(aet)			
Berwick R	(0) 0	Stranraer	(2) 2
Brechin C	(0) 0	Stirling Albion	(0) 0
(aet; Stirling Albion won 3-0 on penalties)			
Clydebank	(0) 0	East Stirling	(0) 0
(aet; East Stirling won 3-2 on penalties)			
Cowdenbeath	(0) 0	Falkirk	(0) 2
(aet)			
Dundee	(1) 3	Stenhousemuir	(0) 0
Forfar Ath	(0) 0	Greenock Morton	(2) 4
Hamilton A	(1) 2	St Mirren	(0) 1
Livingston	(0) 1	Inverness C T	(1) 2
Montrose	(1) 2	Dumbarton	(0) 0
Partick T	(0) 3	Queen's Park	(0) 1
(aet)			
Ross Co	(0) 0	Ayr U	(1) 4

SECOND ROUND

Ayr U	(0) 0	St Johnstone	(1) 4
Airdrieonians	(0) 0	Dundee	(1) 2
East Fife	(1) 2	Falkirk	(0) 0
Greenock Morton	(1) 2	Queen of the S	(0) 1
Montrose	(1) 2	East Stirling	(1) 1
Partick T	(0) 2	Hamilton A	(0) 1
Stirling Albion	(0) 3	Inverness C T	(0) 1
Stranraer	(0) 2	Clyde	(1) 1

QUARTER-FINALS

Dundee	(0) 1	St Johnstone	(4) 5
East Fife	(0) 0	Stranraer	(0) 1
Greenock Morton	(2) 2	Partick T	(1) 1
Stirling Albion	(0) 1	Montrose	(1) 3

SEMI FINALS

St Johnstone	(1) 4	Montrose	(1) 2
Stranraer	(2) 3	Greenock Morton	(0) 0

FINAL

Stranraer	(1) 1	St Johnstone	(0) 0

TENNENT'S SCOTTISH CUP 1996–97

FIRST ROUND

Albion R	(0) 0	Forfar Ath	(0) 0
Alloa	(1) 3	Hawick Royal Albert	(1) 1
Elgin C	(0) 0	Whitehill Welfare	(3) 3
Huntly	(1) 1	Clyde	(0) 1

FIRST ROUND REPLAY

Clyde	(1) 3	Huntly	(1) 2
(aet)			
Forfar Ath	(1) 4	Albion R	(0) 0

SECOND ROUND

Berwick R	(0) 2	Peterhead	(1) 1
Brechin C	(2) 2	Livingston	(0) 1
Cowdenbeath	(0) 1	Dumbarton	(0) 0
East Stirling	(2) 4	Brora R	(1) 3
Forfar Ath	(0) 0	Alloa	(0) 1
Queen's Park	(0) 2	Gala Fairydean	(1) 1
Ross Co	(2) 3	Montrose	(0) 0
Spartans	(0) 0	Arbroath	(0) 0
Stenhousemuir	(0) 1	Hamilton A	(0) 2
Stranraer	(0) 1	Inverness CT	(0) 1
Whitehill Welfare	(1) 2	Queen of the S	(1) 3

SECOND ROUND REPLAY

Arbroath	(1) 3	Spartans	(0) 0
Inverness CT	(0) 0	Stranraer	(0) 0
(aet; Inverness CT won 4-3 on penalties)			

THIRD ROUND

Airdrieonians	(1) 1	Raith R	(0) 4
Arbroath	(2) 2	Greenock Morton	(1) 2
Brechin C	(2) 3	Alloa	(0) 0
Clydebank	(0) 0	Celtic	(3) 5
Clyde	(1) 3	St Mirren	(0) 1
Dundee	(1) 3	Queen of the S	(1) 1
Dunfermline Ath	(3) 4	Ross Co	(0) 0
Falkirk	(0) 1	Berwick R	(1) 1
Hearts	(3) 5	Cowdenbeath	(0) 0
Hibernian	(0) 2	Aberdeen	(0) 2
Inverness CT	(1) 1	Hamilton A	(1) 3
Kilmarnock	(1) 2	East Stirling	(0) 0
Partick T	(0) 0	Motherwell	(0) 2
Queen's Park	(0) 1	East Fife	(1) 3
Rangers	(2) 2	St Johnstone	(0) 0
Stirling Albion	(0) 0	Dundee U	(0) 2

THIRD ROUND REPLAYS

Aberdeen	(0) 0	Hibernian	(0) 0
(aet; Hibernian won 5-3 on penalties)			
Berwick R	(1) 1	Falkirk	(1) 2
Greenock Morton	(0) 4	Arbroath	(0) 0

FOURTH ROUND

Brechin C	(1) 1	Raith R	(0) 2
Clyde	(0) 0	Kilmarnock	(0) 1
Falkirk	(1) 2	Dunfermline Ath	(1) 1
Greenock Morton	(1) 2	Dundee	(0) 2
Hearts	(0) 1	Dundee U	(0) 1
Hibernian	(0) 1	Celtic	(1) 1
Motherwell	(1) 1	Hamilton A	(0) 1
Rangers	(3) 3	East Fife	(0) 0

FOURTH ROUND REPLAYS

Dundee U	(1) 1	Hearts	(0) 0
Dundee	(0) 0	Greenock Morton	(0) 1
(aet)			
Celtic	(1) 2	Hibernian	(0) 0
Hamilton A	(0) 0	Motherwell	(1) 2

QUARTER-FINALS

Celtic	(2) 2	Rangers	(0) 0
Dundee U	(0) 4	Motherwell	(0) 1
Falkirk	(1) 2	Raith R	(0) 0
Greenock Morton	(0) 2	Kilmarnock	(3) 5

SEMI-FINALS

Celtic	(0) 1	Falkirk	(0) 1
Kilmarnock	(0) 0	Dundee U	(0) 0

SEMI-FINALS REPLAYS

Dundee U	(0) 0	Kilmarnock	(0) 1
Falkirk	(1) 1	Celtic	(0) 0

FINAL

Kilmarnock	(1) 1	Falkirk	(0) 0

Year	Home	Score	Away	Score
1874	Queen's Park	2	Clydesdale	0
1875	Queen's Park	3	Renton	0
1876	Queen's Park	1 2	Third Lanark	1 0
1877	Vale of Leven	0 1 3	Rangers	0 1 2
1878	Vale of Leven	1	Third Lanark	0
1879	Vale of Leven	1	Rangers	1
	Vale of Leven awarded cup, Rangers did not appear for replay			
1880	Queen's Park	3	Thornlibank	0
1881	Queen's Park	2 3	Dumbarton	1 1
	Replayed because of protest			
1882	Queen's Park	2 4	Dumbarton	2 1
1883	Dumbarton	2 2	Vale of Leven	2 1
1884	*Queen's Park awarded cup when Vale of Leven did not appear for the final*			
1885	Renton	0 3	Vale of Leven	0 1
1886	Queen's Park	3	Renton	1
1887	Hibernian	2	Dumbarton	1
1888	Renton	6	Cambuslang	1
1889	Third Lanark	3 2	Celtic	0 1
	Replayed because of protest			
1890	Queen's Park	1 2	Vale of Leven	1 1
1891	Hearts	1	Dumbarton	0
1892	Celtic	1 5	Queen's Park	0 1
	Replayed because of protest			
1893	Queen's Park	2	Celtic	1
1894	Rangers	3	Celtic	1
1895	St Bernards	3	Renton	1
1896	Hearts	3	Hibernian	1
1897	Rangers	5	Dumbarton	1
1898	Rangers	2	Kilmarnock	0
1899	Celtic	2	Rangers	0
1900	Celtic	4	Queen's Park	3
1901	Hearts	4	Celtic	3
1902	Hibernian	1	Celtic	0
1903	Rangers	1 0 2	Hearts	1 0 0
1904	Celtic	3	Rangers	2
1905	Third Lanark	0 3	Rangers	0 1
1906	Hearts	1	Third Lanark	0
1907	Celtic	3	Hearts	0
1908	Celtic	5	St Mirren	1
1909	*After two drawn games between Celtic and Rangers, 2.2, 1.1, there was a riot and the cup was withheld*			
1910	Dundee	2 0 2	Clyde	2 0 1
1911	Celtic	0 2	Hamilton Acad	0 0
1912	Celtic	2	Clyde	0
1913	Falkirk	2	Raith R	0
1914	Celtic	0 4	Hibernian	0 1
1920	Kilmarnock	3	Albion R	2
1921	Partick Th	1	Rangers	0
1922	Morton	1	Rangers	0
1923	Celtic	1	Hibernian	0
1924	Airdrieonians	2	Hibernian	0
1925	Celtic	2	Dundee	1
1926	St Mirren	2	Celtic	0
1927	Celtic	3	East Fife	1
1928	Rangers	4	Celtic	0
1929	Kilmarnock	2	Rangers	0
1930	Rangers	0 2	Partick Th	0 1
1931	Celtic	2 4	Motherwell	2 2

1932	Rangers	1 3	Kilmarnock	1 0
1933	Celtic	1	Motherwell	0
1934	Rangers	5	St Mirren	0
1935	Rangers	2	Hamilton Acad	1
1936	Rangers	1	Third Lanark	0
1937	Celtic	2	Aberdeen	1
1938	East Fife	1 4	Kilmarnock	1 2
1939	Clyde	4	Motherwell	0
1947	Aberdeen	2	Hibernian	1
1948	Rangers	1 1	Morton	1 0
1949	Rangers	4	Clyde	1
1950	Rangers	3	East Fife	0
1951	Celtic	1	Motherwell	0
1952	Motherwell	4	Dundee	0
1953	Rangers	1 1	Aberdeen	1 0
1954	Celtic	2	Aberdeen	1
1955	Clyde	1 1	Celtic	1 0
1956	Hearts	3	Celtic	1
1957	Falkirk	1 2	Kilmarnock	1 1
1958	Clyde	1	Hibernian	0
1959	St Mirren	3	Aberdeen	1
1960	Rangers	2	Kilmarnock	0
1961	Dunfermline Ath	0 2	Celtic	0 0
1962	Rangers	2	St Mirren	0
1963	Rangers	1 3	Celtic	1 0
1964	Rangers	3	Dundee	1
1965	Celtic	3	Dunfermline Ath	2
1966	Rangers	0 1	Celtic	0 0
1967	Celtic	2	Aberdeen	0
1968	Dunfermline Ath	3	Hearts	1
1969	Celtic	4	Rangers	0
1970	Aberdeen	3	Celtic	1
1971	Celtic	1 2	Rangers	1 1
1972	Celtic	6	Hibernian	1
1973	Rangers	3	Celtic	2
1974	Celtic	3	Dundee U	0
1975	Celtic	3	Airdrieonians	1
1976	Rangers	3	Hearts	1
1977	Celtic	1	Rangers	0
1978	Rangers	2	Aberdeen	1
1979	Rangers	0 0 3	Hibernian	0 0 2
1980	Celtic	1	Rangers	0
1981	Rangers	0 4	Dundee U	0 1
1982	Aberdeen	4	Rangers	1 (aet)
1983	Aberdeen	1	Rangers	0 (aet)
1984	Aberdeen	2	Celtic	1 (aet)
1985	Celtic	2	Dundee U	1
1986	Aberdeen	3	Hearts	0
1987	St Mirren	1	Dundee U	0 (aet)
1988	Celtic	2	Dundee U	1
1989	Celtic	1	Rangers	0
1990	Aberdeen†	0	Celtic	0
1991	Motherwell	4	Dundee U	3 (aet)
1992	Rangers	2	Airdrieonians	1
1993	Rangers	2	Aberdeen	1
1994	Dundee U	1	Rangers	0
1995	Celtic	1	Airdrieonians	0
1996	Rangers	5	Hearts	1

†won on penalties

WELSH FOOTBALL 1996–97

LEAGUE OF WALES

		Home			Goals		Away			Goals		
	P	W	D	L	F	A	W	D	L	F	A	Pts
Barry Town	40	18	2	0	78	15	15	4	1	51	11	105
Inter Cable-Tel	40	15	3	2	46	14	11	3	6	34	18	84
Ebbw Vale	40	13	4	3	50	14	10	5	5	37	26	78
Caernarfon Town	40	12	4	4	39	26	11	5	4	42	32	78
Newtown	40	10	5	5	32	22	12	0	8	42	27	71
Llansantffraid	40	11	4	6	40	30	9	8	3	38	24	69
Conwy United	40	11	5	4	33	13	9	3	8	33	31	68
Bangor City	40	12	3	5	41	22	8	2	10	41	40	65
Cwmbran Town	40	9	4	7	39	24	10	4	6	32	27	65
Porthmadog	40	10	4	6	38	27	8	4	8	26	33	62
Connah's Quay Nomads	40	9	3	8	35	34	7	6	7	27	30	57
Cemaes Bay	40	5	5	10	26	33	8	5	7	36	39	49
Aberystwyth Town	40	8	2	10	41	35	5	6	9	26	47	47
Caersws	40	6	4	10	23	39	5	5	10	30	38	42
Flint Town United	40	5	3	12	26	43	6	5	9	22	33	41
Carmarthen Town	40	5	3	12	19	41	6	4	10	22	38	40
Welshpool	40	4	7	9	27	37	6	2	12	23	43	39
Ton Pentre	40	7	3	10	33	45	5	0	15	26	54	39
Rhyl	40	6	5	9	24	23	4	3	13	27	48	38
Holywell Town	40	4	4	12	30	43	3	4	13	22	38	29
Briton Ferry Athletic	40	4	1	15	26	60	1	0	19	13	69	16

Only two clubs relegated because Ton Pentre decided to withdraw from the League. As a result, only Holywell and Briton Ferry Athletic went down.

NORTHERN IRISH FOOTBALL 1996–97

SMIRNOFF IRISH LEAGUE

Premier Division

	P	W	D	L	F	A	Pts
Crusaders	28	12	10	6	39	26	46
Coleraine	28	10	13	5	37	31	43
Glentoran	28	10	11	7	36	30	41
Portadown	28	10	8	10	36	32	38
Linfield	28	10	8	10	35	33	38
Glenavon	28	8	11	9	35	34	35
Cliftonville	28	7	9	12	23	38	30
Ards	28	5	10	13	33	50	25

Relegation play-off: First leg: Bangor (third placed in first division) 0 Ards 1; second leg: Ards 1 Bangor 0.

LEAGUE OF WALES—RESULTS 1996–97

	Aberystwyth T	Bangor City	Barry Town	Briton Ferry Ath	Caernarfon T	Caersws	Carmarthen Town	Cemaes Bay	Connah's Quay	Conwy United	Cwmbran Town	Ebbw Vale	Flint Town United	Holywell Town	Inter Cable-Tel	Llansantffraid	Newtown	Porthmadog	Rhyl	Ton Pentre	Welshpool
Aberystwyth Town	—	1-2	1-4	3-1	4-5	1-2	2-0	6-2	3-3	0-1	4-1	2-3	2-0	1-2	0-1	1-2	1-0	3-0	2-1	2-3	2-2
Bangor City	5-1	—	0-0	1-0	0-2	4-0	6-0	4-3	1-1	5-0	4-2	4-2	3-1	2-1	3-0	3-3	3-1	1-0	3-0	8-1	2-2
Barry Town	8-1	0-0	—	4-0	5-2	4-0	6-0	4-0	4-3	5-0	6-0	0-2	1-0	1-0	3-0	3-3	3-1	1-0	6-1	7-1	4-0
Briton Ferry Athletic	1-3	3-2	0-4	—	1-3	2-2	0-2	2-2	3-1	2-4	3-1	0-2	0-0	4-3	1-4	1-8	2-5	2-1	0-3	0-2	1-2
Caernarfon Town	2-2	0-4	0-2	6-2	—	2-5	1-1	2-1	3-2	2-2	1-3	2-3	0-1	1-1	0-0	2-5	1-0	1-0	1-0	1-0	1-2
Caersws	0-1	2-2	0-4	1-3	3-2	—	3-2	1-1	2-1	3-1	2-1	0-1	1-5	2-1	2-1	1-1	1-1	2-2	2-0	0-3	2-0
Carmarthen Town	0-4	2-0	1-0	2-0	1-4	3-1	—	0-2	1-0	2-6	1-2	0-5	0-1	0-0	1-1	0-0	0-3	0-2	2-0	0-4	2-0
Cemaes Bay	1-1	2-1	0-5	2-3	1-1	1-1	1-4	—	1-2	1-2	1-0	2-1	1-2	3-3	1-0	3-3	2-2	0-3	0-4	0-4	2-3
Connah's Quay Nomads	4-1	2-4	2-3	4-2	1-3	3-1	2-2	3-1	—	0-3	1-0	2-3	0-1	0-0	0-1	0-1	1-0	0-3	4-1	5-1	2-0
Conwy United	4-0	1-3	0-3	6-0	2-2	3-1	1-0	1-1	0-1	—	3-1	1-0	1-2	0-3	0-3	0-0	0-3	4-0	3-2	1-0	1-0
Cwmbran Town	6-0	1-3	1-2	2-3	3-1	2-1	3-3	3-0	3-0	3-1	—	2-2	1-2	1-2	1-0	1-3	1-3	2-1	4-4	4-1	3-0
Ebbw Vale	4-0	1-2	2-2	0-1	3-3	2-2	2-1	4-1	1-3	0-1	1-2	—	0-1	5-0	0-1	2-1	1-3	2-1	3-1	3-1	2-0
Flint Town United	0-1	1-3	0-1	3-1	1-4	1-1	2-1	1-3	3-4	0-1	0-1	0-1	—	2-1	2-1	0-1	1-3	2-3	4-1	3-0	2-1
Holywell Town	3-3	0-4	0-2	1-4	3-2	3-1	3-1	1-2	2-2	1-4	1-1	2-1	0-1	—	0-3	1-3	1-3	1-0	3-0	3-2	1-1
Inter Cable-Tel	1-0	4-1	0-1	7-0	3-0	3-0	1-2	1-2	2-2	2-0	2-0	3-1	0-1	2-1	—	1-1	1-3	0-2	3-2	2-3	2-3
Llansantffraid	3-2	1-0	0-4	2-3	2-3	2-3	2-1	6-2	0-0	0-0	0-0	2-1	0-1	2-2	1-1	—	1-3	1-1	2-1	1-0	3-4
Newtown	2-1	2-0	0-4	3-3	2-0	0-1	2-1	2-4	2-1	2-1	1-3	1-2	4-1	1-3	1-3	0-4	—	3-0	1-3	1-7	1-0
Porthmadog	2-2	2-0	0-1	3-0	2-3	1-3	2-0	2-1	2-2	3-0	1-3	2-3	3-0	0-2	0-2	0-1	3-0	—	6-0	3-4	0-1
Rhyl	0-2	1-2	1-0	0-0	3-0	2-3	3-1	2-0	4-3	2-1	4-4	3-2	3-0	3-2	3-2	1-2	3-2	0-1	—	2-1	1-2
Ton Pentre	1-1	4-3	0-1	2-3	2-3	1-2	0-1	2-1	3-2	0-2	4-1	0-2	1-0	1-0	3-1	1-1	1-7	3-4	2-1	—	4-3
Welshpool	0-0	3-2	4-0	4-0	4-0	3-2	0-2	2-1	1-1	0-1	2-2	0-2	2-2	1-1	1-4	1-1	1-3	1-1	2-1	4-3	—

EUROPEAN REVIEW 1996–97

Italian teams having dominated European finals in recent years, it was not expected that Borussia Dortmund would upset hotter-than-hot favourites Juventus in the Champions Cup any more than Schalke would cause Internazionale much of a problem in the UEFA Cup. Squeezed in between, Paris St Germain might have considered themselves likely to hold on to their Cup-Winners' Cup title against Bobby Robson's Barcelona.

In the end, all three were roundly upset. Dortmund gained ample revenge for their 1993 UEFA Cup Final reverse against Juventus by winning 3-1 not only against the odds, but frequently against the run of play. For Juventus, it was their 99th Champion Clubs match, while Dortmund were appearing in their 96th European match.

Juventus had also met Borussia Dortmund in the 1993–94 UEFA Cup semi-finals and in the group matches of the 1995–96 Champions League, to hold a psychological advantage of four wins and a draw against one solitary victory by the Germans.

But history now records a tenth appearance and fifth triumph for a German club in the Champion Clubs Cup Final. Borussia, unusually, called upon the services of no fewer than 24 players during their Champions Cup run. They twice beat Manchester United 1-0, even though they were deprived of the services of six of their international players, this after Manchester United had pulled off one of the best performances by the club in recent European matches by beating Porto 4-0.

In the Cup-Winners' Cup Final, a penalty by Ronaldo was enough to give Barcelona their first win in the competition since 1989, though they lost in the final to Manchester United two years later.

A slender 1-0 lead from the first leg of the UEFA Cup Final did not appear enough for Schalke to survive in the return with Internazionale. But they held on to force extra time and in the resultant penalty shoot-out, they won 4-1.

On the purely domestic front, eternal favourites Bayern Munich were the German champions, though there was a shock in the German Cup Final when Energie Cottbus from the former GDR reached the final. Now plying their trade in the equivalent of the Third Division, they surprised everyone in the competition except Stuttgart who beat them 2-0.

In Bulgaria, double winners CSKA Sofia made a come-back following a few poor seasons by winning their 28th League title. Bottom of this League came Rakovski almost with the worst record in Europe, just one point and 29 defeats including one 9-0 against the champions. Yet the poorest came from Andorra where Spordany Juvenil lost all 22.

Hungarian League leaders MTK Budapest lost only one match in 34. Pyunik Erevan in Armenia and Principat in Andorra one in 22, Anorthosis one in 26 in Cyprus, Dynamo Tbilisi one in 30 in Georgia. In the smaller, less competitive Luxembourg League, Jeunesse Esch were unbeaten in 22 matches.

To Barry Town in Wales went the honour of the highest individual goal scorer in Europe with Tony Bird scoring 45 goals. The club lost just one of 40 matches and achieved a double by beating Cwmbran 2-1 in the Welsh Cup Final. Another European team to lose just once in the League was Partizan Belgrade in Yugoslavia, edging out rivals Red Star by six points in the Championship. In Italy, Juventus captured their 24th title, Real Madrid their 27th in Spain, while Monaco were the French champions for only the sixth time.

With the Inter-Toto competition now running through most of the summer months and the three major European Cup tournaments starting earlier, European football has become an all-year round sport, with increasing calls on players at leading clubs to perform at domestic and European level. Small wonder that there are moves to investigate the increasing number of injuries suffered by top players.

However, for the 1997–98 season, there will be 188 clubs representing 48 of UEFA's 51 member associations taking part. Only Albania, Bosnia and San Marino will be absent. There will be no less than 439 matches comprising 147 in the Champion Clubs Cup, 91 in the Cup-Winners' Cup and 201 in the UEFA Cup.

The group stage of the Champions League will involve 24 clubs divided into six groups. For the first time, the UEFA Cup competition will see a final staged in one match and at a neutral venue rather than a two-legged final.

EUROPEAN CUP 1996–97

Qualifying Round, First Leg

FC Brügge	(1) 2	Steaua	(1) 2
IFK Gothenburg	(1) 3	Ferencvaros	(0) 0
Grasshoppers	(2) 5	Slavia Prague	(0) 0
Maccabi Tel Aviv	(0) 0	Fenerbahce	(1) 1
Panathinaikos	(1) 1	Rosenborg	(0) 0
Rangers	(0) 3	Alania Vladikavkaz	(1) 1
Rapid Vienna	(1) 2	Dynamo Kiev	(0) 0
Widzew Lodz	(1) 2	Brondby	(0) 1

Qualifying Round, Second Leg

Alania Vladikavkaz	(2) 2	Rangers	(4) 7
Brondby	(2) 3	Widzew Lodz	(0) 2
Dynamo Kiev	(1) 2	Rapid Vienna	(3) 4
Fenerbahce	(1) 1	Maccabi Tel Aviv	(0) 1
Ferencvaros	(1) 1	IFK Gothenburg	(0) 1
Rosenborg	(0) 3	Panathinaikos	(0) 0
Slavia Prague	(0) 0	Grasshoppers	(0) 1
Steaua	(2) 3	FC Brügge	(0) 0

CHAMPIONS LEAGUE

Group A

Auxerre	(0) 0	Ajax	(1) 1
Grasshoppers	(2) 3	Rangers	(0) 0
Ajax	(0) 0	Grasshoppers	(0) 1
Rangers	(0) 1	Auxerre	(0) 2
Ajax	(2) 4	Rangers	(0) 1
Auxerre	(1) 1	Grasshoppers	(0) 0
Grasshoppers	(2) 3	Auxerre	(0) 1
Rangers	(0) 0	Ajax	(1) 1
Ajax	(1) 1	Auxerre	(1) 2
Rangers	(0) 2	Grasshoppers	(0) 1
Auxerre	(2) 2	Rangers	(1) 1
Grasshoppers	(0) 0	Ajax	(1) 1

Final table	P	W	D	L	F	A	Pts
Auxerre	6	4	0	2	8	7	12
Ajax	6	4	0	2	8	4	12
Grasshoppers	6	3	0	3	8	5	9
Rangers	6	1	0	5	5	13	3

Group B

Atletico Madrid	(2) 4	Steaua Bucharest	(0) 0
Borussia Dortmund	(1) 2	Widzew Lodz	(0) 1
Steaua Bucharest	(0) 0	Borussia Dortmund	(2) 3
Widzew Lodz	(1) 1	Atletico Madrid	(2) 4
Atletico Madrid	(0) 0	Borussia Dortmund	(0) 1
Steaua Bucharest	(0) 1	Widzew Lodz	(0) 0
Borussia Dortmund	(1) 1	Atletico Madrid	(2) 2
Widzew Lodz	(1) 2	Steaua Bucharest	(0) 0
Steaua Bucharest	(0) 1	Atletico Madrid	(1) 1
Widzew Lodz	(2) 2	Borussia Dortmund	(1) 2
Atletico Madrid	(0) 1	Widzew Lodz	(0) 0
Borussia Dortmund	(3) 5	Steaua Bucharest	(1) 3

Final table	P	W	D	L	F	A	Pts
Atletico Madrid	6	4	1	1	12	4	13
Borussia Dortmund	6	4	1	1	14	8	13
Widzew Lodz	6	1	1	4	6	10	4
Steaua Bucharest	6	1	1	4	5	15	4

Group C

Juventus	(1) 1	Manchester U	(0) 0
Rapid Vienna	(0) 1	Fenerbahce	(1) 1
Fenerbahce	(0) 0	Juventus	(1) 1
Manchester U	(2) 2	Rapid Vienna	(0) 0
Fenerbahce	(0) 0	Manchester U	(0) 2
Rapid Vienna	(1) 1	Juventus	(1) 1
Juventus	(3) 5	Rapid Vienna	(0) 0
Manchester U	(0) 0	Fenerbahce	(0) 1
Fenerbahce	(0) 1	Rapid Vienna	(0) 0
Manchester U	(0) 0	Juventus	(1) 1
Juventus	(1) 2	Fenerbahce	(0) 0
Rapid Vienna	(0) 0	Manchester U	(1) 2

Final table	P	W	D	L	F	A	Pts
Juventus	6	5	1	0	11	1	16
Manchester U	6	3	0	3	6	3	9
Fenerbahce	6	2	1	3	3	6	7
Rapid Vienna	6	0	2	4	2	12	2

Group D

IFK Gothenburg	(1) 2	Rosenborg	(1) 3
AC Milan	(1) 2	Porto	(0) 3
Porto	(1) 2	IFK Gothenburg	(0) 1
Rosenborg	(1) 1	AC Milan	(3) 4
IFK Gothenburg	(0) 2	AC Milan	(0) 1
Rosenborg	(0) 1	Porto	(0) 1
AC Milan	(3) 4	IFK Gothenburg	(2) 2
Porto	(2) 3	Rosenborg	(0) 0
Porto	(0) 1	AC Milan	(0) 1
Rosenborg	(0) 1	IFK Gothenburg	(0) 0
IFK Gothenburg	(0) 0	Porto	(0) 2
AC Milan	(1) 1	Rosenborg	(1) 2

Final table	P	W	D	L	F	A	Pts
Porto	6	5	1	0	12	4	16
Rosenborg	6	3	0	3	7	11	9
AC Milan	6	2	1	3	13	11	7
IFK Gothenburg	6	1	0	5	7	13	3

Quarter-Finals, First Leg

Ajax	(0) 1	Atletico Madrid	(1) 1
Borussia Dortmund	(1) 3	Auxerre	(0) 1
Manchester U	(2) 4	Porto	(0) 0
Rosenborg	(0) 1	Juventus	(0) 1

Quarter-Finals, Second Leg

Atletico Madrid	(1) 2	Ajax	(0) 3
Auxerre	(0) 0	Borussia Dortmund	(0) 1
Juventus	(1) 2	Rosenborg	(0) 0
Porto	(0) 0	Manchester U	(0) 1

Semi-Finals, First Leg

Ajax	(0) 1	Juventus	(2) 2
Borussia Dortmund	(0) 1	Manchester U	(0) 0

Semi-Finals, Second Leg

Juventus	(2) 4	Ajax	(0) 1
Manchester U	(0) 0	Borussia Dortmund	(1) 1

EUROPEAN CUP FINAL
Borussia Dortmund (2) 3, Juventus (0) 1

(in Munich, 28 May 1997, 59,000)

Borussia Dortmund: Klos; Kohler, Sammer, Kree, Reuter, Lambert, Paulo Sousa, Heinrich, Moller (Zorc 88), Chapuisat (Ricken 70), Riedle (Herrlich 67).
Scorers: Riedle 29, 34, Ricken 71.
Juventus: Peruzzi; Porrini (Del Piero 46), Ferrara, Montero, Juliano, Di Livio, Deschamps, Jugovic, Zidane, Vieri (Amoruso 70), Boksic.
Scorer: Del Piero 64.

EUROPEAN CUP WINNERS' CUP 1996–97

Qualifying Round, First Leg

Chemlon Humenne	(0) 1	Flamurtari	(0) 0
Constructorul	(1) 1	Hapoel Ironi Rishon	(0) 0
Dynamo Batumi	(3) 6	HB	(0) 0
Glentoran	(0) 1	Sparta Prague	(0) 2
Karabach	(0) 0	MyPa	(0) 1
Kispest Honved	(1) 1	Sloga	(0) 0
Kotaik	(0) 1	AEK Larnaca	(0) 0
Llansantffraid	(0) 1	Ruch Chorzow	(1) 1
MPKC	(0) 2	KR Reykjavik	(0) 2
Olimpija Ljubljana	(0) 1	Levski Sofia	(0) 0
Red Star Belgrade	(0) 0	Hearts	(0) 0
Sadam Tallinn	(1) 2	Niva Vinnitsa	(0) 1
Shelbourne	(1) 1	Brann	(2) 3
Sion	(3) 4	Kareda	(0) 2
Universitate	(0) 1	Vaduz	(1) 1
Valletta	(0) 1	Gloria	(0) 2
Varteks	(1) 2	Union Luxembourg	(0) 1

Qualifying Round, Second Leg

AEK Larnaca	(2) 5	Kotaik	(0) 0
Brann	(1) 2	Shelbourne	(1) 1
Flamurtari	(0) 0	Chemlon Humenne	(0) 2
Gloria	(1) 2	Valletta	(1) 1
Hapoel Ironi Rishon	(2) 3	Constructorul	(1) 2
HB	(0) 0	Dynamo Batumi	(2) 3
Hearts	(1) 1	Red Star Belgrade	(0) 1
Kareda	(0) 0	Sion	(0) 0
KR Reykjavik	(0) 1	MPKC	(0) 0
Levski Sofia	(0) 1	OlimpijaLjubljana	(0) 0
MyPa	(0) 1	Karabach	(1) 1
Niva Vannitsa	(0) 1	Sadam Tallinn	(0) 0
Ruch Chorzow	(1) 5	Llansantffraid	(0) 0
Sloga	(0) 0	Kispest Honved	(0) 1
Sparta Prague	(4) 8	Glentoran	(0) 0
Union Luxembourg	(0) 0	Varteks	(0) 3
Vaduz	(0) 1	Universitate	(0) 1

First Round, First Leg

Aarhus	(1) 1	Olimpija Ljubljana	(0) 1
AEK Athens	(1) 1	Chemlon Humenne	(0) 0
Barcelona	(1) 2	AEK Larnaca	(0) 0
Benfica	(3) 5	Ruch Chorzow	(0) 1
CS Brugge	(3) 3	Brann	(1) 2
Constructorul	(0) 0	Galatasaray	(0) 1
Dynamo Batumi	(1) 1	PSV Eindhoven	(1) 1
Gloria	(1) 1	Fiorentina	(0) 1
Kaiserslautern	(1) 1	Red Star Belgrade	(0) 0
Lokomotiv Moscow	(1) 1	Varteks	(0) 0
MyPa	(0) 0	Liverpool	(0) 1
Nimes	(0) 3	Kispest Honved	(0) 1
KR Reykjavik	(0) 0	AIK Stockholm	(0) 1
Sion	(0) 2	Niva Vinnitsa	(0) 0
Sturm Graz	(1) 2	Sparta Prague	(1) 2
Vaduz	(0) 0	Paris St Germain	(3) 4

First Round, Second Leg

AIK Stockholm	(0) 1	KR Reykjavik	(0) 1
AEK Larnaca	(0) 0	Barcelona	(0) 0
Brann	(1) 4	CS Brugge	(0) 0
Chemlon Humenne	(1) 1	AEK Athens	(2) 2
Fiorentina	(1) 1	Gloria	(0) 0

Galatasaray	(0) 4	Constructorul	(0) 0
Kispest Honved	(0) 1	Nimes	(2) 2
Liverpool	(1) 3	MyPa	(0) 1
Niva Vinnitsa	(0) 0	Sion	(2) 4
Olympija Ljubljana	(0) 0	Aarhus	(0) 0
Paris St Germain	(2) 3	Vaduz	(0) 0
PSV Eindhoven	(1) 3	Dynamo Batumi	(0) 0
Red Star Belgrade	(0) 4	Kaiserslautern	(0) 0
Ruch Chorzow	(0) 0	Benfica	(0) 0
Sparta Prague	(0) 1	Sturm Graz	(0) 1
Varteks	(0) 2	Lokomotiv Moscow	(1) 1

Second Round, First Leg

Barcelona	(2) 3	Red Star Belgrade	(1) 1
Benfica	(1) 1	Lokomotiv Moscow	(0) 0
Brann	(2) 2	PSV Eindhoven	(0) 1
Fiorentina	(1) 2	Sparta Prague	(0) 1
Galatasaray	(3) 4	Paris St Germain	(2) 2
Nimes	(0) 1	AIK Stockholm	(2) 3
Olimpija Ljubljana	(0) 0	AEK Athens	(1) 2
Sion	(1) 1	Liverpool	(1) 2

Second Round, Second Leg

AEK Athens	(2) 4	Olimpija Ljubljana	(0) 0
AIK Stockholm	(0) 0	Nimes	(0) 1
Liverpool	(1) 6	Sion	(2) 3
Lokomotiv Moscow	(1) 2	Benfica	(0) 3
Paris St Germain	(2) 4	Galatasaray	(0) 0
PSV Eindhoven	(0) 2	Brann	(1) 2
Red Star Belgrade	(0) 1	Barcelona	(0) 1
Sparta Prague	(1) 1	Fiorentina	(0) 1

Quarter Finals, First Leg

Barcelona	(1) 3	AIK Stockholm	(1) 1
Benfica	(0) 0	Fiorentina	(1) 2
Brann	(0) 1	Liverpool	(1) 1
Paris St Germain	(0) 0	AEK Athens	(0) 0

Quarter Finals, Second Leg

AEK Athens	(0) 0	Paris St Germain	(2) 3
AIK Stockholm	(0) 1	Barcelona	(1) 1
Fiorentina	(0) 0	Benfica	(1) 1
Liverpool	(1) 3	Brann	(0) 0

Semi Finals, First Leg

Barcelona	(1) 1	Fiorentina	(0) 1
Paris St Germain	(2) 3	Liverpool	(0) 0

Semi Finals, Second Leg

Fiorentina	(0) 0	Barcelona	(2) 2
Liverpool	(1) 2	Paris St Germain	(0) 0

Final

Barcelona (1) 1, Paris St Germain (0) 0

(in Rotterdam, 14 May 1997, 45,000)

Barcelona: Vitor Baia; Ferrer, Abelardo, Fernando Couto, Sergi, Figo, Popescu (Amor 46), Guardiola, De la Pena (Stoichkov 84), Luis Enrique (Pizzi 89), Ronaldo.
Scorer: Ronaldo 38 (pen).
Paris St Germain: Lama; Domi, Le Guen (Dely Vales 68), N'Gotty, Fournier (Algerino 57), Leroy, Guerin, Rai, Cauet, Leonardo, Loko (Pouget 78).
Referee: Merk (Germany).

UEFA CUP 1996–97

Preliminary Round, First Leg

Akranes	(1) 2	Sileks	(0) 0
Anorthosis	(0) 4	Shirak	(0) 0
B36	(1) 1	Apoel	(4) 5
Barry Town	(0) 0	Dinaburg	(0) 0
Becej	(0) 0	Mura	(0) 0
Beitar Jerusalem	(3) 3	Floriana	(0) 1
Bohemians	(1) 1	Dynamo Minsk	(0) 1
Croatia Zagreb	(2) 4	SK Tirana	(0) 0
Dynamo 93 Minsk	(3) 3	Tiligul	(0) 1
Dynamo Tbilisi	(1) 4	Grevenmacher	(0) 0
Haka	(0) 2	Flora Tallinn	(1) 2
HIT Gorica	(0) 0	Vardar	(1) 1
Hutnik	(2) 9	Khazri	(0) 0
Jazz Pori	(1) 3	GI Gotu	(0) 1
Jeunesse Esch	(2) 2	Legia Warsaw	(3) 4
Lantana	(0) 2	IBV	(0) 1
Maccabi Haifa	(0) 0	Partizan Belgrade	(1) 1
Neftchi Baku	(0) 2	Lokomotiv Sofia	(1) 1
Newtown	(0) 1	Vojvodina	(1) 1
Portadown	(0) 0	HJK Helsinki	(1) 1
Pyunik	(1) 3	Slovan Bratislava	(3) 4
St Patrick's Ath	(1) 3	Inkaras	(2) 3
Slavia Sofia	(2) 4	Margveti	(1) 3
Silema Wanderers	(0) 1	Kosice	(0) 4
Teuta	(1) 1	Crusaders	(0) 0
Zalgiris	(0) 2	Hajduk Split	(2) 4
Zimbru Chisinau	(0) 0		

Preliminary Round, Second Leg

Apoel	(1) 4	B36	(2) 2
Crusaders	(0) 2	Zalgiris	(1) 1
Dinaburg	(0) 1	Barry Town	(1) 2
Dynamo Minsk	(0) 0	Bohemians	(0) 0
Flora Tallinn	(0) 0	Haka	(1) 1
Floriana	(0) 1	Beitar Jerusalem	(3) 5
GI Gotu	(0) 0	Jazz Pori	(0) 1
Grevenmacher	(1) 2	Dynamo Tbilisi	(0) 2
Hajduk Split	(0) 2	Zimbru Chisinau	(0) 1
HJK Helsinki	(1) 5	Pyunik	(1) 2
IBV	(0) 0	Lantana	(0) 0
Inkaras	(1) 1	Slavia Sofia	(0) 1
Khazri	(2) 2	Hutnik	(1) 2
Kosice	(0) 2	Teuta	(0) 1
Legia Warsaw	(1) 3	Jeunesse Esch	(0) 0
Lokomotiv Sofia	(3) 6	Neftchi Baku	(0) 0
Margveti	(0) 0	Silma Wanderers	(1) 3
Mura	(1) 2	Becej	(0) 0
Partizan Belgrade	(1) 3	Maccabi Haifa	(1) 1
Shirak	(1) 2	Anorthosis	(1) 2
Sileks	(1) 1	Akranes	(0) 0
Skonto Riga	(1) 3	Newtown	(0) 0
Slovan Bratislava	(0) 1	St Patrick's Ath	(0) 0
Tiligul	(0) 1	Dynamo 93 Minsk	(1) 1
SK Tirana	(2) 2	Croatia Zagreb	(3) 6
Vardar	(1) 2	HIT Gorica	(1) 1
Vojvodina	(2) 4	Portadown	(0) 1

Qualifying Round, First Leg

Akranes	(0) 0	CSKA Moscow	(2) 2
Anorthosis	(1) 1	Neuchatel Xamax	(1) 2

Aarau	(1) 4	Lantana	(0) 0
Beitar Jerusalem	(0) 1	Bodo Glimt	(2) 5
BVSC	(2) 3	Barry Town	(1) 1
Croatia Zagreb	(1) 3	Spartak Moscow	(1) 1
Dynamo Minsk	(0) 2	Besiktas	(0) 1
Dynamo Moscow	(0) 1	Jazz Pori	(1) 1
Dynamo Tbilisi	(2) 2	Molde	(0) 1
Graz	(0) 2	Vojvodina	(0) 0
Hajduk Split	(0) 1	Torpedo Moscow	(0) 0
Halmstad	(0) 0	Vardar	(0) 0
Helsingborg	(1) 1	Dynamo 93 Minsk	(0) 1
HJK Helsinki	(0) 2	Odessa	(2) 2
Iraklis	(0) 0	Apoel	(0) 1
Kosice	(1) 0	Celtic	(0) 0
Legia Warsaw	(2) 3	Haka	(0) 0
Lyngby	(0) 0	Mura	(0) 0
Partizan Belgrade	(0) 0	National	(0) 0
Rapid Bucharest	(0) 1	Lokomotiv Sofia	(0) 0
Sigma Olomouc	(0) 1	Hutnik	(0) 0

Played behind closed doors.

Skonto Riga	(0) 0	Malmo	(1) 3
Slavia Sofia	(0) 1	Tirol	(1) 1
Silema Wanderers	(0) 0	Odense	(0) 2
Slovan Bratislava	(1) 2	Trabzonspor	(1) 1
Zalgiris	(0) 1	Aberdeen	(1) 4

Qualifying Round, Second Leg

Aberdeen	(0) 1	Zalgiris	(0) 3
Apoel	(1) 2	Iraklis	(0) 1
Barry Town	(1) 3	BVSC	(0) 1

aet; Barry Town won 4-2 on penalties.

Besiktas	(0) 2	Dynamo Minsk	(0) 0
Bodo Glimt	(1) 2	Beitar Jerusalem	(0) 1
Celtic	(0) 1	Kosice	(0) 0
CSKA Moscow	(2) 4	Akranes	(0) 1
Dynamo 93 Minsk	(0) 0	Helsingborg	(2) 3
Haka	(0) 1	Legia Warsaw	(1) 1
Hutnik	(2) 3	Sigma Olomouc	(1) 1
Jazz Pori	(1) 1	Dynamo Moscow	(0) 3
Lantana	(0) 2	Aarau	(0) 0
Lokomotiv Sofia	(0) 0	Rapid Bucharest	(0) 0
Malmo	(0) 1	Skonto Riga	(0) 1
Molde	(0) 0	Dynamo Tbilisi	(0) 0
Mura	(0) 0	Lyngby	(1) 2
National	(1) 1	Partizan Belgrade	(0) 0
Neuchatel Xamax	(4) 4	Anorthosis	(0) 0
Odense	(4) 7	Sliema Wanderers	(1) 1
Odessa	(0) 1	HJK Helsinki	(0) 0
Spartak Moscow	(1) 2	Croatia Zagreb	(0) 1
Tirol	(3) 4	Slavia Sofia	(0) 1
Torpedo Moscow	(1) 2	Hajduk Split	(0) 0
Trabzonspor	(2) 4	Slovan Bratislava	(0) 1
Vardar	(0) 0	Halmstad	(0) 1
Vojvodina	(0) 1	Graz	(2) 5

First Round, First Leg

Aberdeen	(1) 3	Barry Town	(1) 1
Alania Vladikavkaz	(1) 2	Anderlecht	(1) 1
Apoel	(1) 2	Espanyol	(2) 2
Arsenal	(0) 2	Moenchengladbach	(1) 3
Aston Villa	(1) 1	Helsingborg	(0) 0
Bodo Glimt	(1) 1	Trabzonspor	(1) 2
Brondby	(2) 5	Aarau	(0) 0
FC Brugge	(1) 1	Lyngby	(1) 1

204

Celtic	(0) 0	Hamburg	(1) 2
CSKA Moscow	(0) 0	Feyenoord	(0) 1
Dynamo Kiev	(0) 0	Neuchatel Xamax	(0) 0
Ekeren	(0) 3	Graz	(1) 1
Ferencvaros	(2) 3	Olympiakos	(1) 1
Guingamp	(0) 0	Internazionale	(1) 3
Hutnik	(0) 0	Monaco	(0) 1
Lens	(0) 0	Lazio	(0) 1
Malmo	(0) 1	Slavia Prague	(0) 2
Montpellier	(1) 1	Sporting Lisbon	(0) 1
Newcastle U	(2) 4	Halmstad	(0) 0
Odense	(2) 2	Boavista	(0) 3
Odessa	(0) 0	National	(0) 0
Panathiniakos	(3) 4	Legia Warsaw	(2) 2
Parma	(1) 2	Guimaraes	(0) 1
Rapid Bucharest	(0) 1	Karlsruhe	(0) 0
Roma	(3) 3	Dynamo Moscow	(0) 0
RWD Molenbeek	(0) 0	Besiktas	(0) 0
Schalke	(2) 3	Roda	(0) 0
Spartak Moscow	(3) 3	Silkeborg	(0) 2
Tenerife	(0) 3	Maccabi Tel Aviv	(0) 2
Tirol	(0) 0	Metz	(0) 0
Torpedo Moscow	(0) 0	Dynamo Tbilisi	(1) 1
Valencia	(2) 3	Bayern Munich	(0) 0

First Round, Second Leg

Aarau	(0) 0	Brondby	(1) 2
Anderlecht	(2) 4	Alania Vladikavkaz	(0) 0
Barry Town	(1) 3	Aberdeen	(2) 3
Bayern Munich	(1) 1	Valencia	(0) 0
Besiktas	(1) 3	RWD Molenbeek	(0) 0
Boavista	(1) 1	Odense	(0) 2
Dynamo Moscow	(1) 1	Roma	(1) 3
Dynamo Tbilisi	(0) 1	Torpedo Moscow	(0) 0
Espanyol	(0) 1	Apoel	(0) 0
Feyenoord	(0) 1	CSKA Moscow	(0) 1
Graz	(0) 2	Ekeren	(0) 0
Guimaraes	(1) 2	Parma	(0) 0
Halmstad	(0) 2	Newcastle U	(1) 1
Hamburg	(1) 2	Celtic	(0) 0
Helsingborg	(0) 0	Aston Villa	(0) 0
Internazionale	(1) 1	Guingamp	(0) 1
Karlsruhe	(0) 4	Rapid Bucharest	(0) 1
Lazio	(1) 1	Lens	(0) 1
Legia Warsaw	(0) 2	Panathinaikos	(0) 0
Lyngby	(0) 0	FC Brugge	(0) 2
Maccabi Tel Aviv	(0) 1	Tenerife	(1) 1
Metz	(1) 1	Tirol	(0) 0
Moenchengladbach	(1) 3	Arsenal	(1) 2
Monaco	(1) 3	Hutnik	(0) 1
National	(0) 2	Odessa	(0) 0
Neuchatel Xamax	(1) 2	Dynamo Kiev	(0) 1
Olympiakos	(1) 2	Ferencvaros	(1) 2
Roda	(1) 2	Schalke	(1) 2
Silkeborg	(1) 1	Spartak Moscow	(1) 2
Slavia Prague	(2) 3	Malmo	(0) 1
Sporting Lisbon	(0) 1	Montpellier	(0) 0
Trabzonspor	(3) 3	Bodo Glimt	(0) 1

Second Round, First Leg

Aberdeen	(0) 0	Brondby	(1) 2
FC Brugge	(2) 2	National	(0) 0
Dynamo Tbilisi	(1) 1	Boavista	(0) 0
Espanyol	(0) 0	Feyenoord	(1) 3

Ferencvaros	(2) 3	Newcastle U	(2) 2
Guimaraes	(1) 1	Anderlecht	(0) 1
Hamburg	(2) 3	Spartak Moscow	(0) 0
Helsingborg	(1) 2	Neuchatel Xamax	(0) 0
Internazionale	(0) 1	Graz	(0) 0
Karlsruhe	(1) 3	Roma	(0) 0
Lazio	(0) 1	Tenerife	(0) 0
Legia Warsaw	(0) 1	Besiktas	(0) 1
Metz	(2) 2	Sporting Lisbon	(0) 0
Moenchengladbach	(0) 2	Monaco	(1) 4
Schalke	(0) 1	Trabzonspor	(0) 0
Slavia Prague	(0) 0	Valencia	(0) 1

Second Round, Second Leg

Anderlecht	(0) 0	Guimaraes	(0) 0
Besiktas	(1) 2	Legia Warsaw	(1) 1
Boavista	(2) 5	Dynamo Tbilisi	(0) 0
Brondby	(0) 0	Aberdeen	(0) 0
Feyenoord	(0) 0	Espanyol	(1) 1
Graz	(1) 1	Internazionale	(0) 0

Internazionale won 5-3 on penalties.

Monaco	(0) 0	Moenchengladbach	(0) 1
Newcastle U	(1) 4	Ferencvaros	(0) 0
National	(0) 1	FC Brugge	(0) 1
Neuchatel Xamax	(0) 1	Helsingborg	(1) 1
Roma	(2) 2	Karlsruhe	(0) 1
Spartak Moscow	(2) 2	Hamburg	(1) 2
Sporting Lisbon	(0) 2	Metz	(1) 1
Tenerife	(3) 5	Lazio	(2) 3
Trabzonspor	(0) 3	Schalke	(2) 3
Valencia	(0) 0	Slavia Prague	(0) 0

Third Round, First Leg

Brondby	(0) 1	Karlsruhe	(2) 3
FC Brugge	(0) 2	Schalke	(0) 1
Helsingborg	(0) 0	Anderlecht	(0) 0
Internazionale	(3) 5	Boavista	(0) 1
Metz	(0) 1	Newcastle U	(1) 1
Monaco	(1) 3	Hamburg	(0) 0
Tenerife	(0) 0	Feyenoord	(0) 0
Valencia	(2) 3	Besiktas	(0) 1

Third Round, Second Leg

Anderlecht	(0) 1	Helsingborg	(0) 0
Besiktas	(2) 2	Valencia	(2) 2
Boavista	(0) 0	Internazionale	(1) 2
Feyenoord	(0) 2	Tenerife	(2) 4
Hamburg	(0) 0	Monaco	(0) 2
Karlsruhe	(0) 0	Brondby	(2) 5
Newcastle U	(0) 2	Metz	(0) 0
Schalke	(1) 2	FC Brugge	(0) 0

Quarter-Finals, First Leg

Anderlecht	(1) 1	Internazionale	(0) 1
Newcastle U	(0) 0	Monaco	(0) 1
Schalke	(1) 2	Valencia	(0) 0
Tenerife	(0) 0	Brondby	(1) 1

Quarter-Finals, Second Leg

Brondby	(0) 0	Tenerife	(0) 2
Internazionale	(1) 2	Anderlecht	(1) 1
Monaco	(1) 3	Newcastle U	(0) 0
Valencia	(1) 1	Schalke	(1) 1

Semi-Finals, First Leg

Internazionale	(3) 3	Monaco	(0) 1

| Tenerife | (1) 1 | Schalke | (0) 0 |

Semi-Finals, Second Leg

| Monaco | (0) 1 | Internazionale | (0) 0 |
| Schalke | (0) 2 | Tenerife | (0) 0 |

FINAL First Leg

Schalke (0) 1, Internazionale (0) 0

(in Gelsenkirchen, 7 May 1997, 56,824)

Schalke: Lehmann; De Kock, Thon, Linke, Eigenrauch, Muller, Anderbrugge, Nemec, Buskens (Max 67), Latal, Wilmots.
Scorer: Wilmots 71.
Internazionale: Pagliuca; Bergomi, Paganin M, Galante, Pistone, Zanetti, Sforza, Fresi (Berti 61), Winter, Zamorano.
Referee: Batta (France).

FINAL Second Leg

Internazionale (0) 1, Schalke (0) 0

(in Milan, 21 May 1997, 81,670)

Internazionale: Pagliuca; Bergomi (Angloma 70), Paganin M, Fresi, Pistone, Zanetti (Berti 120), Ince, Sforza (Winter 81), Djorkaeff, Ganz, Zamorano.
Scorer: Zamorano 84.
Schalke: Lehmann; Latal (Held 111), De Kock, Thon, Linke, Buskens, Eigenrauch, Nemec, Muller (Anderbrugge 97), Max, Wilmots.
(aet; Schalke won 4-1 on penalties).
Referee: Aranda (Spain).

PAST EUROPEAN CUP FINALS

Year	Winner		Runner-up	
1956	Real Madrid	4	Stade de Rheims	3
1957	Real Madrid	2	Fiorentina	0
1958	Real Madrid	3	AC Milan	2*
1959	Real Madrid	2	Stade de Rheims	0
1960	Real Madrid	7	Eintracht Frankfurt	3
1961	Benfica	3	Barcelona	2
1962	Benfica	5	Real Madrid	3
1963	AC Milan	2	Benfica	1
1964	Internazionale	3	Real Madrid	1
1965	Internazionale	1	SL Benfica	0
1966	Real Madrid	2	Partizan Belgrade	1
1967	Celtic	2	Internazionale	1
1968	Manchester U	4	Benfica	1*
1969	AC Milan	4	Ajax	1
1970	Feyenoord	2	Celtic	1*
1971	Ajax	2	Panathinaikos	0
1972	Ajax	2	Internazionale	0
1973	Ajax	1	Juventus	0
1974	Bayern Munich	1 4	Atletico Madrid	1 0
1975	Bayern Munich	2	Leeds U	0
1976	Bayern Munich	1	St Etienne	0
1977	Liverpool	3	Borussia Moenchengladbach	1
1978	Liverpool	1	FC Brugge	0
1979	Nottingham F	1	Malmö	0
1980	Nottingham F	1	Hamburg	0
1981	Liverpool	1	Real Madrid	0
1982	Aston Villa	1	Bayern Munich	0
1983	Hamburg	1	Juventus	0
1984	Liverpool†	1	Roma	1
1985	Juventus	1	Liverpool	0
1986	Steaua Bucharest†	0	Barcelona	0
1987	Porto	2	Bayern Munich	1
1988	PSV Eindhoven†	0	Benfica	0
1989	AC Milan	4	Steaua Bucharest	0
1990	AC Milan	1	Benfica	0
1991	Red Star Belgrade†	0	Marseille	0
1992	Barcelona	1	Sampdoria	0
1993	Marseille	1	AC Milan	0

(Marseille subsequently stripped of title)

Year	Winner		Runner-up	
1994	AC Milan	4	Barcelona	0
1995	Ajax	1	AC Milan	0
1996	Juventus†	1	Ajax	1

PAST EUROPEAN CUP-WINNERS FINALS

Year	Winner		Runner-up	
1961	Fiorentina	4	Rangers	1‡
1962	Atletico Madrid	1 3	Fiorentina	1 0
1963	Tottenham H	5	Atletico Madrid	1
1964	Sporting Lisbon	3 1	MTK Budapest	3* 0
1965	West Ham U	2	Munich 1860	0
1966	Borussia Dortmund	2	Liverpool	1*
1967	Bayern Munich	1	Rangers	0*
1968	AC Milan	2	Hamburg	0
1969	Slovan Bratislava	3	Barcelona	2

Year	Winner	Score	Runner-up	Score
1970	Manchester C	2	Gornik Zabrze	1
1971	Chelsea	1 2	Real Madrid	1* 1*
1972	Rangers	3	Dynamo Moscow	2
1973	AC Milan	1	Leeds U	0
1974	Magdeburg	2	AC Milan	0
1975	Dynamo Kiev	3	Ferencvaros	0
1976	Anderlecht	4	West Ham U	2
1977	Hamburg	2	Anderlecht	0
1978	Anderlecht	4	Austria Vienna	0
1979	Barcelona	4	Fortuna Dusseldorf	3*
1980	Valencia†	0	Arsenal	0
1981	Dynamo Tbilisi	2	Carl Zeiss Jena	1
1982	Barcelona	2	Standard Liege	1
1983	Aberdeen	2	Real Madrid	1*
1984	Juventus	2	Porto	1
1985	Everton	3	Rapid Vienna	1
1986	Dynamo Kiev	3	Atletico Madrid	0
1987	Ajax	1	Lokomotiv Leipzig	0
1988	Mechelen	1	Ajax	0
1989	Barcelona	2	Sampdoria	0
1990	Sampdoria	2	Anderlecht	0
1991	Manchester U	2	Barcelona	1
1992	Werder Bremen	2	Monaco	0
1993	Parma	3	Antwerp	1
1994	Arsenal	1	Parma	0
1995	Real Zaragoza	2	Arsenal	1*
1996	Paris St Germain	1	Rapid Vienna	0

PAST FAIRS CUP FINALS

Year	Winner	Score	Runner-up	Score
1958	Barcelona	8	London	2‡
1960	Barcelona	4	Birmingham C	1‡
1961	Roma	4	Birmingham C	2‡
1962	Valencia	7	Barcelona	3‡
1963	Valencia	4	Dynamo Zagreb	1‡
1964	Real Zaragoza	2	Valencia	1
1965	Ferencvaros	1	Juventus	0
1966	Barcelona	4	Real Zaragoza	3‡
1967	Dynamo Zagreb	2	Leeds U	0‡
1968	Leeds U	1	Ferencvaros	0‡
1969	Newcastle U	6	Ujpest Dozsa	2‡
1970	Arsenal	4	Anderlecht	3‡
1971	Leeds U	3**	Juventus	3‡

PAST UEFA CUP FINALS

Year	Winner	Score	Runner-up	Score
1972	Tottenham H	2 1	Wolverhampton W	1 1
1973	Liverpool	3 0	Borussia Moenchengladbach	0 2
1974	Feyenoord	2 2	Tottenham H	2 0
1975	Borussia Moenchengladbach	0 5	Twente Enschede	0 1
1976	Liverpool	3 1	FC Brugge	2 1
1977	Juventus**	1 1	Athletic Bilbao	0 2
1978	PSV Eindhoven	0 3	SEC Bastia	0 0
1979	Borussia Moenchengladbach	1 1	Red Star Belgrade	1 0
1980	Borussia Moenchengladbach	3 0	Eintracht Frankfurt**	2 1
1981	Ipswich T	3 2	AZ 67 Alkmaar	0 4

1982	IFK Gothenburg	1 3	SV Hamburg	0 0
1983	Anderlecht	1 1	Benfica	0 1
1984	Tottenham H†	1 1	RSC Anderlecht	1 1
1985	Real Madrid	3 0	Videoton	0 1
1986	Real Madrid	5 0	Cologne	1 2
1987	IFK Gothenburg	1 1	Dundee U	0 1
1988	Bayer Leverkusen†	0 3	Espanol	0 3
1989	Napoli	2 3	Stuttgart	1 3
1990	Juventus	3 0	Fiorentina	1 0
1991	Internazionale	2 0	AS Roma	0 1
1992	Ajax**	0 2	Torino	0 2
1993	Juventus	3 3	Borussia Dortmund	1 0
1994	Internazionale	1 1	Salzburg	0 0
1995	Parma	1 1	Juventus	0 1
1996	Bayern Munich	2 3	Bordeaux	0 1

*After extra time ** Won on away goals † Won on penalties ‡ Aggregate score*

EUROPEAN CUP DRAWS 1997–98

EUROPEAN CUP
First Qualifying Round (British and Irish clubs only):
Derry City v Branik Maribor (Slovenia); Crusaders v Dynamo Tbilisi (Georgia); GI Gotu (Faeroes) v Rangers; Dynamo Kiev (Ukraine) v Barry Town.
Second Qualifying Round:
Besiktas (Turkey) v Derry City or Branik Maribor; IFK Gothenburg (Sweden) v GI Gotu or Rangers; Brondby (Denmark) v Dynamo Kiev or Barry Town; Newcastle U v Partizan Belgrade (Yugoslavia) or Croatia Zagreb (Croatia); Bayer Leverkusen (Germany) v Crusaders or Dynamo Tbilisi.

EUROPEAN CUP-WINNERS' CUP
First Qualifying Round (British and Irish clubs only):
Legia Warsaw (Poland) v Glenavon; Cwmbran v Nacional (Romania); Kilmarnock v Shelbourne.

UEFA CUP
First Qualifying Round (British and Irish clubs only):
Inter-Cable Tel v Celtic; Grasshoppers (Switzerland) v Coleraine; Bohemians v Ferencvaros (Hungary); Principat (Andorra) v Dundee U.

PAST EUROPEAN CHAMPIONSHIP FINALS

Paris, 10 July 1960
USSR 2, YUGOSLAVIA 1*
USSR: Yachin; Tchekeli, Kroutikov, Voinov, Maslenkin, Netto, Metreveli, Ivanov, Ponedelnik, Bubukin, Meshki. **Scorers:** Metreveli, Ponedelnik.
Yugoslavia: Vidinic; Durkovic, Jusufi, Zanetic, Miladinovic, Perusic, Sekularac, Jerkovic, Galic, Matus, Kostic. **Scorer:** Netto (og).

Madrid, 21 June 1964
SPAIN 2, USSR 1
Spain: Iribar; Rivilla, Calleja, Fuste, Olivella, Zoco, Amancio, Pereda, Marcellino, Suarez, Lapetra. **Scorers:** Pereda, Marcellino.
USSR: Yachin; Chustikov, Mudrik, Voronin, Shesternjev, Anitchkin, Chislenko, Ivanov, Ponedelnik, Kornaev, Khusainov. **Scorer:** Khusainov.

Rome, 8 June 1968
ITALY 1, YUGOSLAVIA 1
Italy: Zoff; Burgnich, Facchetti, Ferrini, Guarneri, Castano, Domenghini, Juliano, Anastasi, Lodetti, Prati. **Scorer:** Domenghini.
Yugoslavia: Pandelic; Fazlagic, Damjanovic, Pavlovic, Paunovic, Holcer, Petkovic, Acimovic, Musemic, Trivic, Dzajic. **Scorer:** Dzajic.

Replay: Rome, 10 June 1968
ITALY 2, YUGOSLAVIA 0
Italy: Zoff; Burgnich, Facchetti, Rosato, Guarneri, Salvadore, Domenghini, Mazzola, Anastasi, De Sista, Riva. **Scorers:** Riva, Anastasi.
Yugoslavia: Pantelic; Fazlagic, Damjanovic, Pavlovic, Paunovic, Holcer, Hosic, Acimovic, Musemic, Trivic, Dzajic.

Brussels, 18 June 1972
WEST GERMANY 3, USSR 0
West Germany: Maier; Hottges, Schwarzenbeck, Beckenbauer, Breitner, Hoeness, Wimmer, Netzer, Heynckes, Müller, Kremers. **Scorers:** Müller 2, Wimmer.
USSR: Rudakov; Dzodzuashvili, Khurtsilava, Kaplichny, Istomin, Troshkin, Kolotov, Baidachni, Konkov (Dolmatov), Banishevski (Konzinkievits), Onishenko.

Belgrade, 20 June 1976
CZECHOSLOVAKIA 2, WEST GERMANY 2*
Czechoslovakia: Viktor; Dobias (Vesely F), Pivarnik, Ondrus, Capkovic, Gogh, Moder, Panenka, Svehlik (Jurkemik), Masny, Nehoda. **Scorers:** Svehlik, Dobias.
West Germany: Maier; Vogts, Beckenbauer, Schwarzenbeck, Dietz, Bonhof, Wimmer (Flohe), Müller D, Beer (Bongartz), Hoeness, Holzenbein. **Scorers:** Müller, Holzenbein.
Czechoslovakia won 5-3 on penalties.

Rome, 22 June 1980
WEST GERMANY 2, BELGIUM 1
West Germany: Schumacher; Briegel, Forster K, Dietz, Schuster, Rummenigge, Hrubesch, Müller, Allofs, Stielike, Kalz. **Scorers:** Hrubesch 2.
Belgium: Pfaff; Gerets, Millecamps, Meeuws, Renquin, Cools, Van der Eycken, Van Moer, Mommens, Van der Elst, Ceulemans. **Scorer:** Van der Eycken.

Paris, 27 June 1984
FRANCE 2, SPAIN 0
France: Bats; Battiston (Amoros), Le Roux, Bossis, Domergue, Giresse, Platini, Tigana, Fernandez, Lacombe (Genghini), Bellone. **Scorers:** Platini, Bellone.
Spain: Arconada; Urquiaga, Salva (Roberto), Gallego, Camacho, Francisco, Julio Alberto (Sarabia), Senor, Victor, Carrasco, Santilana.

Munich, 25 June 1988
HOLLAND 2, USSR 0
Holland: Van Breukelen; Van Aerle, Van Tiggelen, Wouters, Koeman R, Rijkaard, Vanenburg, Gullit, Van Basten, Muhren, Koeman E. **Scorers:** Gullit, Van Basten.
USSR: Dassayev; Khidiatulin, Aleinikov, Mikhailichenko, Litovchenko, Demianenko, Belanov, Gotsmanov (Baltacha), Protasov (Pasulko), Zavarov, Rats.

Gothenburg, 26 June 1992
DENMARK 2, GERMANY 0
Denmark: Schmeichel; Sivebaek (Christiansen), Nielsen K, Olsen L, Christofte, Jensen, Povlsen, Laudrup, Piechnik, Larsen, Vilfort. **Scorers:** Jensen, Vilfort.
Germany: Illgner; Reuter, Brehme, Kohler, Buchwald, Hässler, Riedle, Helmer, Sammer (Doll), Effenberg (Thon), Klinsmann.

Wembley, 30 June 1996
GERMANY 2, CZECH REPUBLIC 1†
Germany: Kopke; Helmer, Sammer, Scholl (Bierhoff), Hassler, Kuntz, Babbel, Ziege, Klinsmann, Strunz, Eilts (Bode). **Scorer:** Bierhoff 2.
Czech Republic: Kouba; Suchoparek, Nedved, Kadlec, Nemec, Poborsky (Smicer), Kuka, Bejbl, Berger, Hornak, Rada. **Scorer:** Berger (pen).

* *After extra time*
† *Won on sudden death*

PAST WORLD CUP FINALS

Uruguay 1930
URUGUAY 4, ARGENTINA 2 (1-2) *Montevideo*
Uruguay: Ballesteros; Nasazzi (capt), Mascheroni, Andrade, Fernandez, Gestido, Dorado, Scarone, Castro, Cea, Iriarte. **Scorers:** Dorado, Cea, Iriarte, Castro.
Argentina: Botasso; Della, Torre, Paternoster, Evaristo, J., Monti, Suarez, Peucelle, Varallo, Stabile, Ferreira (capt), Evaristo, M. **Scorers:** Peucelle, Stabile.
Leading scorer: Stabile (Argentina) 8.

Italy 1934
ITALY 2, CZECHOSLOVAKIA 1 (0-0) (1-1)* *Rome*
Italy: Combi (capt); Monseglio, Allemandi, Ferraris IV, Monti, Bertolini, Guaita, Meazza, Schiavio, Ferrari, Orsi. **Scorers:** Orsi, Schiavio.
Czechoslovakia: Planicka (capt); Zenisek, Ctyroky, Kostalek, Cambal, Krcil, Junek, Svoboda, Sobotka, Nejedly, Puc. **Scorer:** Puc.
Leading scorers: Schiavio (Italy), Nejedly (Czechoslovakia), Conen (Germany) each 4.

France 1938
ITALY 4, HUNGARY 2 (3-1) *Paris*
Italy: Olivieri; Foni, Rava, Serantoni, Andreolo, Locatelli, Biaveti, Meazza (capt), Piola, Ferrari, Colaussi. **Scorer:** Colaussi 2, Piola 2.
Hungary: Szabo; Polgar, Biro, Szalay, Szucs, Lazar, Vincze, Sarosi (capt), Szengeller, Titkos. **Scorers:** Titkos, Sarosi.
Leading scorer: Leonidas (Brazil) 8.

Brazil 1950
Final pool (replaced knock-out system)
Uruguay 2, Spain 2   Brazil 6, Spain 1
Brazil 7, Sweden 1   Sweden 3, Spain 1
Uruguay 3, Sweden 2   Uruguay 2, Brazil 1

Final positions	P	W	D	L	F	A	Pts
Uruguay	3	2	1	0	7	5	5
Brazil	3	2	0	1	14	4	4
Sweden	3	1	0	2	6	11	2
Spain	3	0	1	2	4	11	1

Leading scorers: Ademir (Brazil) 7, Schiaffino (Uruguay), Basora (Spain) 5.

Switzerland 1954
WEST GERMANY 3, HUNGARY 2 (2-2) *Berne*
West Germany: Turek; Posipal, Kohlmeyer, Eckel, Liebrich, Rahn, Morlock, Walter, O., Walter, F. (capt), Schaefer. **Scorers:** Morlock, Rahn 2.
Hungary: Grosics; Buzansky, Lantos, Bozsik, Lorant, Zakarias, Czibor, Kocsis, Hidegkuti, Puskas (capt), Toth, J. **Scorers:** Puskas, Czibor.
Leading scorer: Kocsis (Hungary) 11.

Sweden 1958
BRAZIL 5, SWEDEN 2 (2-1) *Stockholm*
Brazil: Gilmar; Santos, D., Santos, N., Zito, Bellini, Orlando, Garrincha, Didi, Vavà, Pelé, Zagalo. **Scorers:** Vavà 2, Pelé 2, Zagalo.
Sweden: Svensson; Bergmark, Axbom, Boerjesson, Gustavsson, Parling, Hamrin, Gren, Simonsson, Liedholm, Skoglund. **Scorers:** Liedholm, Simonsson.
Leading scorer: Fontaine (France) 13 (present record total).

Chile 1962
BRAZIL 3, CZECHOSLOVAKIA 1 (1-1) *Santiago*
Brazil: Gilmar; Santos, D., Mauro, Zozimo, Santos, N., Zito, Didi, Garrincha, Vavà, Amarildo, Zagalo. **Scorers:** Amarildo, Zito, Vavà.
Czechoslovakia: Schroiff; Tichy, Novak, Pluskal, Popluhar, Masopust, Pospichal, Scherer, Kvasniak, Kadraba, Jelinek. **Scorer:** Masopust.
Leading scorer: Jerkovic (Yugoslavia) 5.

England 1966
ENGLAND 4, WEST GERMANY 2 (1-1) (2-2)* *Wembley*
England: Banks; Cohen, Wilson, Stiles, Charlton, J., Moore, Ball, Hurst, Hunt, Charlton, R., Peters. **Scorers:** Hurst 3, Peters.
West Germany: Tilkowski; Hottges, Schulz, Weber, Schnellinger, Haller, Beckenbauer, Overath, Seeler, Held, Emmerich. **Scorers:** Haller, Weber.
Leading scorer: Eusebio (Portugal) 9.

Mexico 1970
BRAZIL 4, ITALY 1 (1-1) *Mexico City*
Brazil: Felix; Carlos Alberto, Piazza, Everaldo, Gerson, Clodoaldo, Jairzinho, Pelé, Tostão, Rivelino. **Scorers:** Pelé, Gerson, Jairzinho, Carlos Alberto.
Italy: Albertosi; Burgnich, Cera, Rosato, Fachetti, Bertini (Juliano), Riva, Domenghini, Mazzola, De Sista, Boninsegna (Rivera). **Scorer:** Boninsegna.
Leading scorer: Müller (West Germany) 10.

West Germany 1974
WEST GERMANY 2, HOLLAND 1 (2-1) *Munich*
West Germany: Maier; Vogts, Schwarzenbeck, Beckenbauer, Breitner, Bonhof, Hoeness, Overath, Grabowski, Müller, Holzenbein. **Scorers:** Breitner (pen), Müller.
Holland: Jongbloed; Suurbier, Rijsbergen (De Jong), Haan, Krol, Jansen, Van Hanegem, Neeskens, Rep (Nanninga), Cruyff, Rensenbrink (Van der Kerkhof, R.)
Scorer: Neeskens (pen).
Leading scorer: Lato (Poland) 7.

Argentina 1978
ARGENTINA 3, HOLLAND 1 (1-1)* *Buenos Aires*
Argentina: Fillol; Olguin, Passarella, Galvan, Tarantini, Ardiles (Larrosa), Gallego, Ortiz (Houseman), Bertoni, Luque, Kempes. **Scorers:** Kempes 2, Bertoni.
Holland: Jongbloed; Poortvliet, Brandts, Krol, Jansen (Suurbier), Neeskens, Van der Kerkhof, W., Van der Kerkhof, R., Haan, Rep (Nanninga), Rensenbrink.
Scorer: Nanninga.
Leading scorer: Kempes (Argentina) 6.

Spain 1982
ITALY 3, WEST GERMANY 1 (0-0) *Madrid*
Italy: Zoff; Bergomi, Cabrini, Collovati, Scirea, Gentile, Oriali, Tardelli, Conti, Graziani (Altobelli), Rossi (Causio). **Scorers:** Rossi, Tardelli, Altobelli.
West Germany: Schumacher; Kaltz, Forster, K-H., Stielike, Forster, B., Breitner, Dremmler (Hrubesch), Littbarski, Briegel, Fischer, Rummenigge (Müller). **Scorer:** Breitner.
Leading scorer: Rossi (Italy) 6.

Mexico 1986
ARGENTINA 3, WEST GERMANY 2 (1-0) *Mexico City*
Argentina: Pumpido; Cuciuffo, Olarticoechea, Ruggeri, Brown, Giusti, Burruchaga (Trobbiani), Batista, Valdano, Maradona, Enrique. **Scorers:** Brown, Valdano, Burruchaga.
West Germany: Schumacher; Berthold, Briegel, Jacobs, Forster, Eder, Brehme, Matthäus, Allofs (Völler), Magath (Hoeness), Rummenigge. **Scorers:** Rummenigge, Völler.
Leading scorer: Lineker (England) 6.

Italy 1990

WEST GERMANY 1, ARGENTINA 0 (0-0) *Rome*

West Germany: Ilgner; Berthold (Reuter), Kohler, Augenthaler, Buchwald, Brehme, Littbaski, Hässler, Matthäus, Völler, Klinsmann. **Scorer:** Brehme (pen).

Argentina: Goycochea; Lorenzo, Serrizeula, Sensini, Ruggeri (Monzon), Simon, Basualdo, Burruchago (Calderon), Maradona, Troglio, Dezotti.

Referee: Codesal (Mexico). Monzon and Dezotti sent off.

Leading scorer: Schillaci (Italy) 6.

USA 1994

BRAZIL 0, ITALY 0* *Los Angeles*

Brazil: Taffarel; Jorginho (Cafu 21), Marcio Santos, Aldair, Branco, Mazinho, Mauro Silva, Dunga, Zinho (Viola 109), Bebeto, Romario.

Italy: Pagliuca; Mussi (Apolloni 34), Maldini, Baresi, Benarrivo, Donadoni, Albertini, Dino Baggio (Evani 101), Berti, Roberto Baggio, Massaro.

Brazil won 3-2 on penalties

Referee: Puhl (Hungary).

Penalty sequence: Baresi (shot over); Marcio Santos (saved); Albertini (scored); Romario (scored off upright); Evani (scored); Branco (scored); Massaro (saved); Dunga (scored); Roberto Baggio (shot over).

Leading scorers: Salenko (Russia) 6, Stoichkov (Bulgaria) 6.

* *After extra time*

WORLD CUP 1998

Qualifying draw for France 1998

OCEANIA (Members 10, Entries 10)
Either one or no team qualifies

First Round (League System + 1 play-off match)
Melanesian Group: Papua New Guinea 1, Soloman Islands 1; Soloman Islands 1, Vanuatu 1; Papua New Guinea 0, Vanuatu 1.
Polynesian Group: Tonga 2, Cook Islands 0; Western Samoa 2, Cook Islands 1; Tonga 1, Western Samoa 0.
Play-off: Tonga 0, Soloman Islands 4; Soloman Islands 9, Tonga 0.

Second Round (League System)
Group 1: Australia 13, Soloman Islands 0; Australia 5, Tahiti 0; Soloman Islands 4, Tahiti 1; Soloman Islands 2, Australia 6; Tahiti 0, Australia 2; Tahiti 1, Soloman Islands 1.
Group 2: Papua New Guinea 1, New Zealand 0; Fiji 0, New Zealand 1; New Zealand 7, Papua New Guinea 0; Fiji 3, Papua New Guinea 1; New Zealand 5, Fiji 0; Papua New Guinea 0, Fiji 1.

Third Round (Cup System)
Winner of group 1 v winner of group 2
Third Round Winner plays team finishing fourth in Asia.
New Zealand 0, Australia 3; Australia 2, New Zealand 0.

ASIA (Members 41 +1, Entries 36)
Three or four teams qualify

First Round (League System)
Group 1: Taiwan 0, Saudi Arabia 2; Malaysia 2, Bangladesh 0; Bangaldesh 1, Taiwan 3; Malaysia 0, Saudi Arabia 0; Bangladesh 1, Saudi Arabia 4; Malaysia 2, Taiwan 0; Taiwan 0, Malaysia 0; Saudi Arabia 3, Bangladesh 0; Taiwan 1, Bangladesh 2; Saudi Arabia 3, Malaysia 0; Bangladesh 0, Malaysia 1; Saudi Arabia 6, Taiwan 0.
Group 2: Maldives 0, Iran 17; Syria 12, Maldives 0; Kyrgyzstan 0, Iran 7; Syria 0, Iran 1; Kyrgyzstan 3, Maldives 0; Iran 3, Kyrgyzstan 1; Maldives 0, Syria 12; Iran 9, Maldives 0; Kyrgyzstan 2, Syria 1; Iran 2, Syria 2; Maldives 0, Kyrgyzstan 6.
Group 3: Jordan 0, United Arab Emirates 0; Bahrain 1, United Arab Emirates 2; Bahrain 1, Jordan 0; Jordan 4, Bahrain 1; United Arab Emirates 3, Bahrain 2; United Arab Emirates 2, Jordan 0.
Group 4: Nepal 1, Macao 1; Oman 0, Japan 1; Macao 0, Japan 10; Oman 1, Nepal 0; Japan 6; Oman 4, Macao 0; Japan 10, Macao 0; Nepal 0, Oman 6; Japan 3, Nepal 0; Macao 0, Oman 2; Japan 1, Oman 1; Macao 2, Nepal 1.
Group 5: Indonesia 8, Cambodia 0; Indonesia 0, Yemen 0; Cambodia 0, Yemen 1, Cambodia 1, Indonesia 1; Yemen 0, Uzbekistan 5; Yemen 7, Cambodia 0; Uzbekistan 6, Cambodia 0; Indonesia 1, Uzbekistan 1; Yemen 1, Indonesia 1; Uzbekistan 3, Indonesia 0; Cambodia 1, Uzbekistan 4.
Group 6: Hong Kong 0, Korea Republic 2; Thailand 1, Korea Republic 3; Thailand 2, Hong Kong 0; Hong Kong 2, Thailand 2; Korea Republic 4, Hong Kong 0; Korea Republic 0, Thailand 0.
Group 7: Lebanon 1, Singapore 1; Singapore 0, Kuwait 1; Kuwait 2, Lebanon 0; Singapore 1, Lebanon 2; Kuwait 4, Singapore 0; Lebanon 1, Kuwait 3.
Group 8: Tajikistan 4, Vietnam 0; Turkmenistan 1, China 4, Tajikistan 0, China 1; Turkmenistan 2, Vietnam 1; Vietnam 1, China 3; Turkmenistan 1, Tajikistan 2; China 1, Turkmenistan 0; Vietnam 0, Tajikistan 4; China 3, Tajikistan 0; Vietnam 0, Turkmenistan 4; China 4, Vietnam 0; Tajikistan 5, Turkmenistan 0.
Group 9: Kazakhstan 3, Pakistan 0; Pakistan 2, Iraq 6; Iraq 1, Kazakhstan 2; Pakistan 0, Kazakhstan 7; Iraq 6, Pakistan 1; Kazakhstan 3, Iraq 1.
Group 10: Qatar 3, Sri Lanka 0; India 2, Philippines 0; Qatar 5, Philippines 0; Sri Lanka 1, India 1; Philippines 0, Sri Lanka 3; Qatar 6, India 0.

Second Round (League System)
Two groups of five teams

Third Round (Cup System)
Group winners and runners-up qualify for the semi-finals. The winners qualify for the finals, the losers compete in a play-off , the winner qualifiying for the finals, the losing team meets the winners of the Oceania zone.

CONCACAF (Members 30, Entries 30, including 2 late entries Bermuda and Cuba)
Three teams qualify

First Round (Cup System – Caribbean zone)
Dominican Republic 3, Aruba 2; Aruba 1, Dominican Republic 3; Bahamas withdrew v St Kitts & Nevis w.o.; Guyana 1, Grenada 2; Grenada 6, Guyana 0; Dominica 3, Antigua 3; Antigua 1, Dominica 3.

Second Round (Cup System – Caribbean zone)
Bermuda withdrew v Trinidad & Tobago w.o.; Puerto Rico 1, St Vincent & the Grenadines 2; St Vincent & the Grenadines 7, Puerto Rico 0; Cuba 1, Cayman Islands 0; Cayman Islands 0, Cuba 5;
St Kitts & Nevis 5, St Lucia 1; St Lucia 0, St Kitts & Nevis 1; Haiti 6, Grenada 1; Grenada 0, Haiti 1; Syrinam 0, Jamaica 1; Jamaica 1, Syrinam 0; Dominica 0, Barbados 1; Barbados 1, Dominica 0; Dominican Republic 2, Netherlands Antilles 1; Netherlands Antilles 0, Dominican Republic 0.

Third Round (Cup System – Caribbean zone)
Cuba 5, Haiti 1; Haiti 1, Cuba 1; Dominican Republic 1, Trinidad & Tobago 4; Barbados 0, Jamaica 1; Jamaica 2, Barbados 0; St Kitts & Nevis 2, St Vincent 2; St Vincent 0, St Kitts & Nevis 0.

First Round (Cup System – Central American zone)
Nicaragua 0, Guatemala 1; Guatemala 2, Nicaragua 1; Belize 1, Panama 2; Panama 4, Belize 1.

Semi-final Round (League System)
Group 1: Trinidad & Tobago 0, Costa Rica 1; Trinidad & Tobago 1, Guatemala 1; USA 2, Guatemala 0; USA 2, Trinidad & Tobago 0; Costa Rica 3, Guatemala 0; Guatemala 1, Costa Rica 0; Trinidad & Tobago 0, USA 1; Costa Rica 2, USA 1; Guatemala 2, Trinidad & Tobago 1; USA 2, Costa Rica 1; Costa Rica 2, Trinidad & Tobago 1; Guatemala 1, USA 2.
Group 2: Canada 3, Panama 1; Cuba 0, El Salvador 5; Cuba 3, Panama 1, El Salvador 1; Canada 2, Cuba 0; Cuba 0, Canada 2; Panama 1, Canada 0; Canada 1, El Salvador 0; El Salvador 3, Panama 2; El Salvador 3, Cuba 0; Panama 3, Cuba 1; El Salvador 0, Canada 2.
Group 3: Jamaica 3, Honduras 0; St Vincent & the Genadines 0, Mexico 3; Honduras 2, Mexico 1; St Vincent & the Grenadines 1, Jamaica 2; St Vincent & the Grenadines 1, Honduras 4; Mexico 2, Jamaica 1; Honduras 0, Jamaica 0; Mexico 5, St Vincent & the Grenadines 1; Mexico 3, Honduras 1; Jamaica 5, St Vincent & the Grenadines 0; Honduras 11, St Vincent & the Grenadines 3; Jamaica 1, Mexico 0.

Final Round (League System)
Jamaica 0, USA 0; Mexico 4, Canada 0; Costa Rica 0, Mexico 0; USA 3, Canada 0; Costa Rica 3, USA 2; Canada 0, El Salvador 0; Mexico 6, Jamaica 0; USA 2, Mexico 2; Canada 0, Jamaica 0; El Salvador 2, Costa Rica 1; Costa Rica 3, Jamaica 1; Jamaica 1, El Salvador 0; Canada 1, Costa Rica 0; El Salvador 0, Mexico 1; El Salvador 1, USA 1.

AFRICA (Members 51, Entries 38, Withdrawals 2)
Five teams qualify

First Round (Cup System)
Sudan 2, Zambia 0; Namibia 2, Mozambique 0; Tanzania 0, Ghana 0; Swaziland 0, Gabon 1; Uganda 0, Angola 2; Mauritius 1, Zaire 5; Malawi 0, South Africa 1; Madagascar 1, Zimbabwe 2; Guinea-Bissau 3, Guinea 2; Rwanda 1,Tunisia 1; Congo 2, Ivory Coast 0; Kenya 3, Algeria 1; Burundi 1, Sierra Leone 0; Mauritania 0, Burkina Faso 0; Togo 2, Senegal 1; Gambia 2, Liberia 1; Algeria 1, Kenya 0; Senegal 1, Togo 1; South Africa 3, Malawi 0; Sierra Leone 0, Burundi 1; Angola 3, Uganda 1; Gabon 2, Swaziland 0; Guinea 3, Guinea-Bissau 1; Ivory Coast 1, Congo

217

1; Mozambique 1, Namibia 1; Tunisia 2, Rwanda 0; Burkina Faso 2, Mauritania 0; Zaire 2, Mauritius 0; Zambia 3, Sudan 0; Zimbabwe 2, Madagascar 2; Ghana 2, Tanzania 1; Liberia 4, Gambia 0.

Second Round (League System)
Group 1: Nigeria 2, Burkina Faso 0; Guinea 3, Kenya 1; Kenya 1, Nigeria 1; Burkina Faso 0, Guinea 2; Nigeria 2, Guinea 1; Kenya 4, Burkina Faso 3; Kenya 1, Guinea 0; Burkina Faso 1, Nigeria 2; Nigeria 3, Kenya 0; Guinea 3, Burkina Faso 1.

Nigeria qualify for finals.
Group 2: Egypt 7, Namibia 1; Liberia 0, Tunisia 1; Namibia 0, Liberia 0; Tunisia 1, Egypt 0; Liberia 1, Egypt 0; Namibia 1, Tunisia 2; Namibia 2, Egypt 3; Tunisia 1, Liberia 0; Egypt 0, Tunisia 0; Liberia 1, Namibia 2.

Tunisia qualify for finals.
Group 3: South Africa 1, Zaire 0; Congo 1, Zambia 0; Zambia 0, South Africa 0; Zaire 1, Congo 1; Congo 2, South Africa 0; Zaire 2, Zambia 2; Zaire 1, South Africa 2; Zambia 3, Congo 0; Congo 1, Zaire 0; South Africa 3, Zambia 0.
Group 4: Angola 2, Zimbabwe 1; Togo 2, Cameroon 4; Cameroon 0, Angola 0; Zimbabwe 1, Togo 0; Angola 1, Togo 1; Cameroon 1, Zimbabwe 0; Cameroon 2, Togo 0; Zimbabwe 0, Angola 1; Cameroon 1, Togo 2; Zimbabwe 2, Togo 2, Zimbabwe 1.
Group 5: Morocco 4, Sierra Leone 1; Gabon 1, Ghana 1; Sierra Leone 1, Gabon 0; Ghana 2, Morocco 2; Sierra Leone 1, Ghana 1; Gabon 0, Morocco 4; Sierra Leone 0, Morocco 1; Ghana 3, Gabon 0; Morocco 1, Ghana 0.
Morocco qualify for finals.

EUROPE (Members 49 + 1, Entries 50)
Fifteen teams qualify including France as the host nation.
The nine group winners and the best runner-up qualify. The eight other runners-up will be drawn in pairs, the four winners also qualifying for the final.

GROUP 1
Greece 2 Slovenia 0, Greece 3 Bosnia 0, Slovenia 0 Denmark 2, Bosnia 1 Croatia 4, Denmark 2 Greece 1, Croatia 1 Greece 1, Slovenia 1 Bosnia 2, Croatia 1 Denmark 1, Bosnia 0 Greece 1, Croatia 3 Slovenia 3, Denmark 4 Slovenia 0, Greece 0 Croatia 1, Denmark 2 Bosnia 0

Group 1	P	W	D	L	F	A	Pts
Denmark	5	4	1	0	11	2	13
Greece	6	3	1	2	8	4	10
Croatia	5	2	3	0	10	6	9
Bosnia	5	1	0	4	3	11	3
Slovenia	5	0	1	4	4	13	1

GROUP 2

Chisinau, 1 September 1996, 15,000

Moldova (0) 0

England (2) 3 *(Barmby 23, Gascoigne 24, Shearer 61)*
Moldova: Romanenco; Secu, Nani, Testimitanu, Gaidamasciuc, Belous (Siscin 58), Epureanu, Curtianu, Clescenco, Miterev (Rebeja 61), Popovici.
England: Seaman; Neville G, Pearce, Southgate, Pallister, Hinchcliffe, Barmby (Le Tissier 81), Ince, Shearer, Gascoigne (Batty 81), Beckham.
Referee: Koho (Finland).

Wembley, 9 October 1996, 74,663

England (2) 2 *(Shearer 24, 38)*
Poland (1) 1 *(Citko 7)*
England: Seaman; Neville G, Pearce, Southgate (Pallister 51), Ince, Hinchcliffe, McManaman, Gascoigne, Shearer, Ferdinand, Beckham.
Poland: Wozniak; Waldoch, Zielinski, Juskowiak, Hajto, Michalski, Baluszynski, Wojtala, Nowak, Citko, Warzycha (Sagamowski 75).
Referee: Krug (Germany).

Tbilisi, 9 November 1996, 48,000
Georgia (0) 0
England (2) 2 *(Sheringham 15, Ferdinand 37)*
Georgia: Zoidze; Lobjanidze, Tskhadadze, Shelia, Gogichaishvili (Gudushauri 60), Nemsadze, Kinkladze, Jamarauli, Kobiashvili, Ketsbaia, Aveladze S (Gogrichiani 52).
England: Seaman; Campbell, Hinchcliffe, Batty, Southgate, Adams, Beckham, Gascoigne, Ferdinand (Wright 81), Sheringham, Ince.
Referee: Monteiro (Portugal).

Wembley, 12 February 1997, 75,055
England (0) 0
Italy (1) 1 *(Zola 18)*
England: Walker; Neville G, Pearce, Ince, Campbell, Batty (Wright 88), McManaman (Merson 76), Le Tissier (Ferdinand 60), Shearer, Beckham, Le Saux.
Italy: Peruzzi; Ferrara, Costacurta, Cannavaro, Di Livio, Dino Baggio, Albertini, Di Matteo, Maldini, Zola (Fuser 90), Casiraghi (Ravanelli 76).
Referee: Puhl (Hungary).

Wembley, 30 April 1997, 71,206
England (1) 2 *(Sheringham 42, Shearer 90)*
Georgia (0) 0
England: Seaman; Neville G, Le Saux, Batty, Campbell, Adams (Southgate 87), Lee, Ince (Redknapp 77), Shearer, Sheringham, Beckham.
Georgia: Zoidze; Chikhradze, Sheqiladze, Tskhadadze, Shelia, Machavariani (Gogrichiani 30) (Arveladze A 76), Nemsadze, Jamarauli, Ketsbaia, Kinkladze (Gakhokidze 61), Arveladze S.
Referee: Harrel (France).

Katowice, 31 May 1997, 35,000
Poland (0) 0
England (1) 2 *(Shearer 6, Sheringham 90)*
Poland: Wozniak; Jozwiak, Zielinski, Kaluzny, Ledwon, Bukalski (Swierczewski P 46), Nowak (Kucharski 57), Majak, Waldoch, Juskowiak (Adamczyk 51), Dembinski.
England: Seaman; Neville G, Le Saux, Southgate, Campbell, Ince, Lee, Gascoigne (Batty 16), Shearer, Sheringham, Beckham (Neville P 88).
Referee: Meier (Switzerland).

Moldova 1 Italy 3, Italy 1 Georgia 0, Poland 2 Moldova 1, Italy 3 Moldova 0, Poland 0 Italy 0, Italy 3 Poland 0, Georgia 2 Moldova 0, Poland 4 Georgia 1.

Group 2	P	W	D	L	F	A	Pts
Italy	6	5	1	0	11	1	16
England	6	5	0	1	11	2	15
Poland	6	2	1	3	7	9	7
Georgia	5	1	0	4	3	9	3
Moldova	5	0	0	5	2	13	0

GROUP 3
Norway 5 Azerbaijan 0, Azerbaijan 1 Switzerland 0, Hungary 1 Finland 0, Finland 2 Switzerland 3, Norway 3 Hungary 0, Azerbaijan 0 Hungary 3, Switzerland 0 Norway 1, Azerbaijan 1 Finland 2, Norway 1 Finland 1, Switzerland 1 Hungary 0, Finland 3 Azerbaijan 0, Hungary 1 Norway 1.

Group 3	P	W	D	L	F	A	Pts
Norway	5	3	2	0	11	2	11
Finland	5	2	1	2	8	6	7
Hungary	5	2	1	2	5	5	7
Switzerland	4	2	0	2	4	4	6
Azerbaijan	5	1	0	4	2	13	3

GROUP 4

Vienna, 31 August 1996, 29,500
Austria (0) 0
Scotland (0) 0
Austria: Konsel; Schopp, Schottel, Pfeffer, Feiersinger, Marasek, Ramusch (Ogris 76), Kuhbauer, Polster (Sabitzer 68), Herzog, Heraf.
Scotland: Goram; Burley, McKinlay T, Calderwood, Hendry, Boyd, McCall, Ferguson, McCoist (Durie 75), McAllister, Collins.
Referee: Piraux (Belgium).

Riga, 5 October 1996, 9500
Latvia (0) 0
Scotland (1) 2 *(Collins 18, Jackson 78)*
Latvia: Karavayev; Troitsky, Astafyev, Zemlinsky, Shevlyakov, Stepanov, Ivanov, Bleidelis, Rimkus (Boulders 78), Babichev (Shtolcers 46), Pakhar.
Scotland: Goram; Burley, Boyd, McKinlay T (McNamara 65), Calderwood, Whyte, Spencer (Dodds 59), McCall (Lambert 46), Jackson, McAllister, Collins.
Referee: Ulrich (Czech Republic).

Tallinn, 9 October 1996
Estonia (0) 0
Scotland (0) 0
Game abandoned.

Hampden Park, 10 November 1996, 50,000
Scotland (1) 1 *(McGinlay 8)*
Sweden (0) 0
Scotland: Leighton; McNamara (Lambert 46), Boyd, Calderwood, Hendry, McKinlay T, Burley, McKinlay W, Jackson (Gallacher 78), McGinlay (McCoist 84), Collins.
Sweden: Ravelli; Nilsson R, Andersson P, Bjorklund, Sundgren, Alexandersson (Larsson 68), Thern, Zetterberg (Andersson A 76), Schwarz, Blomqvist, Dahlin (Andersson K 16).
Referee: Aranda (Spain).

Monaco, 11 February 1997, 4000
Estonia (0) 0
Scotland (0) 0
Estonia: Poom; Kirs, Hohlov-Simson, Lemsalu, Rooba U, Reim, Leetma (Oper 75), Rooba M (Pari 67), Alonen, Kristal, Zelinski.
Scotland: Goram; McNamara (McKinlay T 75), Boyd, McStay (Ferguson I 63), Hendry, Calderwood, Gallacher, McAllister, Ferguson D, McGinlay (McCoist 72), Collins.
Referee: Radoman (Yugoslavia).

Kilmarnock, 29 March 1997, 17,996
Scotland (1) 2 *(Boyd 25, Meet 52 (og))*
Estonia (0) 0
Scotland: Leighton; Burley, McKinlay T, Calderwood, Hendry (McKinlay W 65), Boyd, Gemmill, Jackson (McGinlay 83), Gallacher, McAllister, McStay.
Estonia: Poom; Kirs, Hohlov-Simson, Lemsalu, Meet, Reim, Viikmae (Leetma 72), Zelinski (Arbeiter 81), Pari (Rooba M 54), Kristal, Oper.
Referee: Heynemann (Germany).

Celtic Park, 2 April 1997, 43,295
Scotland (1) 2 *(Gallacher 24, 77)*
Austria (0) 0
Scotland: Leighton; Burley, Boyd, Lambert, Hendry, Calderwood, McKinlay T, Gallacher (McCoist 85), Jackson (McGinlay 75), McAllister (McStay 89), Collins.
Austria: Konsel; Schottel (Kogler W 46), Feiersinger, Pfeffer, Schopp, Heraf, Aigner (Ogris 81), Wetl, Stoger (Vastic 67), Herzog, Polster.
Referee: Levnikov (Russia).

Gothenburg, 30 April 1997, 40,000
Sweden (1) 2 *(Andersson K 44, 64)*
Scotland (0) 1 *(Gallacher 84)*
Sweden: Ravelli; Sundgren, Andersson P, Bjorklund, Kamark, Thern, Zetterberg, Schwarz (Mild 12), Andersson A, Andersson K, Dahlin.
Scotland: Leighton; Burley, Boyd, Lambert, Hendry, Calderwood, McKinlay T (Gemmill 67), Gallacher, Jackson (Durie 66), McAllister, Collins.
Referee: Collina (Italy).

Minsk, 8 June 1997, 12,000
Belarus (0) 0
Scotland (0) 1 *(McAllister G 49 (pen))*
Belarus: Satsunkhevich; Lavrik, Ostrovski, Yakhimovich, Gurenko, Dovnar (Belkevich 53), Romashchenko, Shtanyuk, Orlovski (Balachov 66), Khlebossolov (Makovski 61), Gerasimets.
Scotland: Leighton; Burley, Boyd, Lambert, Dailly, Hopkin (Gemmill 68), McKinlay T (McAllister B 79), Gallacher, Jackson (Dodds 87), McAllister G, Durie.
Referee: Cakar (Turkey).

Sweden 5 Belarus 1, Belarus 1 Estonia 0, Latvia 1 Sweden 2, Estonia 1 Belarus 0, Belarus 1 Latvia 1, Sweden 0 Austria 1, Austria 2 Latvia 1, Austria 2 Estonia 0, Latvia 2 Belarus 0, Estonia 1 Latvia 3, Estonia 2 Sweden 3, Latvia 1 Austria 3.

Group 4	P	W	D	L	F	A	Pts
Scotland	8	5	2	1	9	2	17
Austria	6	4	1	1	8	4	13
Sweden	6	4	0	2	12	7	12
Latvia	7	2	1	4	9	11	7
Belarus	6	1	1	4	3	10	4
Estonia	7	1	1	5	4	11	4

GROUP 5
Israel 2 Bulgaria 1, Russia 4 Cyprus 0, Luxembourg 1 Bulgaria 2, Israel 1 Russia 1, Cyprus 2 Israel 0, Luxembourg 0 Russia 4, Cyprus 1 Bulgaria 3, Israel 1 Luxembourg 0, Cyprus 1 Russia 1, Luxembourg 0 Israel 3, Bulgaria 4 Cyprus 1, Israel 2 Cyprus 0, Russia 3 Luxembourg 0, Bulgaria 4 Luxembourg 0, Russia 2 Israel 0.

Group 5	P	W	D	L	F	A	Pts
Russia	6	4	2	0	15	2	14
Israel	7	4	1	2	9	6	13
Bulgaria	5	4	0	1	14	5	12
Cyprus	6	1	1	4	5	14	4
Luxembourg	6	0	0	6	1	17	0

GROUP 6
Yugoslavia 3 Faeroes 1, Yugoslavia 6 Malta 0, Faeroes 1 Slovakia 2, Faeroes 2 Spain 6, Czech Republic 6 Malta 0, Slovakia 6 Malta 0, Faeroes 1 Yugoslavia 8, Czech Republic 0 Spain 0, Slovakia 3 Faeroes 0, Yugoslavia 1 Czech Republic 0, Spain 4 Slovakia 1, Spain 2 Yugoslavia 0, Malta 0 Spain 3, Spain 4 Malta 0, Malta 0 Slovakia 2, Czech Republic 1 Yugoslavia 2, Malta 1 Faeroes 2, Yugoslavia 1 Spain 1, Faeroes 2 Malta 1, Spain 1 Czech Republic 0, Yugoslavia 2 Slovakia 0.

Group 6	P	W	D	L	F	A	Pts
Spain	8	6	2	0	21	4	20
Yugoslavia	8	6	1	1	23	6	19
Slovakia	6	4	0	2	14	7	12
Faeroes	7	2	0	5	9	24	6
Czech Republic	5	1	1	3	7	4	4
Malta	8	0	0	8	2	31	0

GROUP 7

Serravalle, 2 June 1996, 1613

San Marino (0) 0

Wales (3) 5 *(Melville 20, Hughes M 32, 43, Giggs 50, Pembridge 85)*
San Marino: Muccioli S; Gasperoni L, Valentini M, Guerra, Gobbi, Manzaroli, Pasolini (Muccioli R 69), Mazza, Casadei (Peverani 74), Mularoni M (Valentini V 46), Montagna.
Wales: Southall; Bowen, Melville, Coleman, Pembridge, Browning (Goss 74), Horne (Savage 81), Robinson (Legg 80), Hughes M, Saunders, Giggs.
Referee: Lubos (Slovakia).

Cardiff, 31 August 1996, 15,150

Wales (4) 6 *(Saunders 2, 75, Hughes M 24, 54, Melville 34, Robinson 45)*

San Marino (0) 0
Wales: Southall (Roberts 72); Bowen, Melville, Coleman (Taylor 81), Pembridge, Robinson (Speed 78), Browning, Horne, Saunders, Hughes M, Giggs.
San Marino: Muccioli S; Gasperoni L (Matteoni 67), Guerra, Gobbi, Valentini V, Mazza (Pasolini 80), Gennari, Bacciocchi (Francini 44), Gasperoni B, Manzaroli, Montagna.
Referee: Hamer (Luxembourg).

Cardiff, 5 October 1996, 37,000

Wales (1) 1 *(Saunders 17)*

Holland (0) 3 *(Van Hooijdonk 72, 75, Ronald de Boer 80)*
Wales: Southall; Bowen, Pembridge (Legg 65), Browning (Jenkins 83), Symons, Melville, Robinson, Horne, Saunders, Hughes M, Speed.
Holland: Van der Sar; Vierklau (Van Hooijdonk 71), Frank de Boer, Valckx, Bogarde, Winter, Jonk, Seedorf, Cocu, Cruyff (Makaay 46), Ronald de Boer (Van Bronckhorst 90).
Referee: Nieto (Spain).

Eindhoven, 9 November 1996, 25,000

Holland (4) 7 *(Bergkamp 22, 72, 78, Jonk 34, Ronald de Boer 33, Frank de Boer 45, Cocu 61)*

Wales (1) 1 *(Saunders 40)*
Holland: Van der Sar; Stam, Frank de Boer, Numan, Reiziger, Winter, Jonk (Van Bronckhorst 82), Cocu, Seedorf (Van Hooijdonk 69), Bergkamp, Ronald de Boer (Overmars 58).
Wales: Southall; Bowen M, Nielson, Symons, Melville, Jones, Bowen J (Robinson 58), Hartson (Taylor 67), Saunders, Pembridge, Speed.
Referee: Pereira (Portugal).

Cardiff, 14 December 1996, 14,200

Wales (0) 0

Turkey (0) 0
Wales: Southall; Page, Jenkins, Jones, Melville, Pembridge, Speed, Horne, Saunders (Hartson 81), Hughes M, Giggs.
Turkey: Engin; Recep, Alpay, Ogun, Bulent K, Ilker (Tolunay 88), Kemalettin (Saffet 88), Tugay, Abdullah, Arif (Oktay 70), Hakan Sukur.
Referee: Huzu (Romania).

Cardiff, 29 March 1997, 15,000

Wales (0) 1 *(Speed 67)*

Belgium (2) 2 *(Crasson 24, Staelens 44)*
Wales: Southall; Blackmore, Page, Symons, Pembridge, Jones, Horne, Hughes M, Saunders (Hartson 64), Speed, Giggs.
Belgium: De Wilde; De Roover, Van Meir, Smidts, Crasson, Van der Elst F, Staelens, Lemoine, Van Kerckhoven, Mpenza L (Mpenza M 64), Oliveira (Scifo 79).
Referee: Fallstrom (Sweden).

Belgium 2 Turkey 1, San Marino 0 Belgium 3, Turkey 7 San Marino 0, Belgium 0 Holland 1, Holland 4 San Marino 0, Turkey 1 Holland 0, San Marino 0 Holland 6, Turkey 1 Belgium 3, Belgium 6 San Marino 0.

Group 7	P	W	D	L	F	A	Pts
Holland	6	5	0	1	23	3	15
Belgium	6	5	0	1	16	6	15
Turkey	5	2	1	2	10	5	7
Wales	6	2	1	3	14	12	7
San Marino	7	0	0	7	0	37	0

GROUP 8

Eschen, 31 August 1996, 4000
Liechtenstein (0) 0
Republic of Ireland (4) 5 *(Townsend 5, O'Neill 9, Quinn 12, 61, Harte 20)*
Liechtenstein: Heeb; Hefti, Hasler, Stocklasa, Quaderer, Hilti, Hanselmann (Telser D 82), Zech H (Bicker 65), Schadler F (Klaunzer 78), Frick M, Schadler H.
Republic of Ireland: Given; Irwin, Kenna, McLoughlin, Breen, Staunton, Houghton, Townsend (Cascarino 83), Quinn, O'Neill (Moore 73), Harte.
Referee: Shmolik (Belarus).

Dublin, 9 October 1996, 31,671
Republic of Ireland (1) 3 *(McAteer 8, Cascarino 46, 70)*
Macedonia (0) 0
Republic of Ireland: Kelly A; Kenna, Irwin, McAteer, Breen, Staunton, Townsend, McLoughlin (O'Brien 85), Cascarino, Harte (Moore 83), O'Neill (Aldridge 81).
Macedonia: Celeski; Sedloski, Nikolovski, Jovanovski, Milosavov, Gosev, Beganovic (Saciri 73), Micevski T, Ciric, Milosevski (Zaharievski 57), Hristov.
Referee: Fisker (Denmark).

Dublin, 10 November 1996, 33,869
Republic of Ireland (0) 0
Iceland (0) 0
Republic of Ireland: Kelly A; Kenna (Cunningham 65), Irwin (Harte 65), Keane, Breen, Babb, McLoughlin, McAteer, Kelly D (Moore 80), Cascarino, Townsend.
Iceland: Kristinsson B; Adolfsson, Jonsson S, Sigurdsson L, Birgisson, Gudjonsson H (Thordarson O 86), Kristinsson R (Gretarsson A 71), Sverrisson, Gylfason, Thordur Gudjonsson, Sigurdsson H.
Referee: Ormandjiev (Bulgaria).

Skopje, 2 April 1997, 8000
Macedonia (2) 3 *(Stojkovski 28 (pen), 44 (pen), Hristov 59)*
Republic of Ireland (1) 2 *(McLoughlin 8, Kelly D 78)*
Macedonia: Celeski; Sedloski, Nikolovski, Markovski, Gosev, Milosavov, Sainovski (Georgioski 82), Stojkovski, Saciri, Hristov (Beganovic 78), Glavevski (Micevski V 87).
Republic of Ireland: Kelly A; McAteer, Irwin, McLoughlin, Breen, Staunton, Townsend, Keane, Cascarino (O'Neill 46) (Kelly D 76), Goodman, Phelan (Harte 57).
Referee: Trentalange (Italy).

Bucharest, 30 April 1997, 21,500
Romania (1) 1 *(Ilie A 32)*
Republic of Ireland (0) 0
Romania: Stelea; Petrescu, Dobos, Prodan, Hagi (Craioveanu 87), Filipescu, Georghe Popescu (Rotariu 72), Munteanu, Selymes, Moldovan, Ilie A (Gabriel Popescu 83).
Republic of Ireland: Kelly A; Kelly G, Irwin (Kenna 46) Cunningham, Staunton, Harte (Cascarino 75), Townsend, Keane, Connolly (Goodman 75), Houghton, Kennedy.
Referee: Van den Ende (Holland).

Dublin, 21 May 1997, 28,575
Republic of Ireland (3) 5 *(Connolly 29, 34, 40, Cascarino 60, 77)*
Liechtenstein (0) 0
Republic of Ireland: Given; Kenna, Cunningham, Keane, Harte, Staunton, Houghton (Cascarino 53), Kelly G, Connolly (Goodman 77), Townsend, Kennedy (Fleming 63).
Liechtenstein: Heeb; Telser D (Verling 58), Stocklasa, Hefti, Hanselmann (Ackermann 80), Frick C, Hasler D, Schadler, Frick M (Ospelt 46), Klaunzer, Frick D.
Referee: Boutenko (Russia).

Macedonia 3 Liechtenstein 0, Iceland 1 Macedonia 1, Romania 3 Lithuania 0, Lithuania 2 Iceland 0, Iceland 0 Romania 4, Lithuania 2 Liechtenstein 0, Liechtenstein 1 Macedonia 11, Macedonia 0 Romania 3, Romania 8 Liechtenstein 0, Lithuania 0 Romania 1, Liechtenstein 0 Lithuania 2, Macedonia 1 Iceland 0, Iceland 0 Lithuania 0.

Group 8	P	W	D	L	F	A	Pts
Romania	6	6	0	0	20	0	18
Macedonia	7	4	1	2	19	10	13
Republic of Ireland	6	3	1	2	15	4	10
Lithuania	6	3	1	2	6	5	10
Iceland	6	0	3	3	1	8	3
Liechtenstein	7	0	0	7	2	36	0

GROUP 9

Belfast, 31 August 1996, 9358
Northern Ireland (0) 0
Ukraine (0) 1 *(Rebrov 79)*
Northern Ireland: Fettis; Griffin (O'Neill 52), Rowland (Magilton 84), Lomas, Morrow, Hill, Gillespie, Lennon, Dowie, Gray, Hughes.
Ukraine: Shovkovskyi; Luzhnyi (Parfenov 70), Skrypnyk, Golovko, Bezhenar, Popov, Orbu, Kalitvintsev (Kriventsov 74), Luchkeyvich (Rebrov 46), Maximov, Leonenko.
Referee: Sars (France).

Belfast, 5 October 1996, 8357
Northern Ireland (1) 1 *(Lennon 29)*
Armenia (1) 1 *(Assadourian 7)*
Northern Ireland: Fettis; Nolan, Rowland, Lomas, Hunter, Hill, Gillespie (O'Neill 80), Lennon (Magilton 60), Dowie, Gray P (McMahon 65), Hughes.
Armenia: Berezovski; Soukiassian, Kachatrian V, Hovsepian, Hovhaffifyaf, Vardanian, Art Petrossian (Avetissian A 82), Tonoyan (Minassian 56), Mikhitarian H, Assadourian, Mikayelian (Ter Petrossian 70).
Referee: Danilovski (Macedonia).

Nuremburg, 9 November 1996, 40,700
Germany (1) 1 *(Moller 41)*
Northern Ireland (1) 1 *(Taggart 39)*
Germany: Kopke; Strunz, Reuter, Kohler, Babbel, Tarnat, Hassler, Eilts (Passlack 62), Moller, Klinsmann, Bobic (Bierhoff 70).
Northern Ireland: Wright; Hill, Nolan, Hunter, Taggart, Horlock, Morrow, Lomas, Dowie (Gray 78), Lennon (Rogan 85), Hughes.
Referee: Cakar (Turkey).

Belfast, 14 December 1996, 7935
Northern Ireland (2) 2 *(Dowie 12, 21)*
Albania (0) 0
Northern Ireland: Wright; Nolan, Horlock, Hunter, Hill, Taggart, Lomas, Lennon, Dowie (Quinn 89), Morrow (McMahon 72), Hughes.
Albania: Nallbani; Dede (Tole 35), Vata R, Malko, Shulku, Vata F, Fakaj, Kola, Haxhi (Fraholli 38), Rraklli, Paco.
Referee: Georgiou (Cyprus).

Belfast, 29 March 1997, 9392
Northern Ireland (0) 0
Portugal (0) 0
Northern Ireland: Wright; Gillespie, Hill, Morrow, Taggart, Nolan, Lennon, Lomas, Quinn (McMahon 68), Dowie, Magilton.
Portugal: Vitor Baia; Paulinho Santos, Fernando Couto, Jorge Costa, Dimas (Cadete 63), Conceicao, Paulo Sousa, Rui Costa, Oceano (Martins 63), Figo, Joao Pinto II.
Referee: Cesari (Italy).

Kiev, 2 April 1997, 70,000
Ukraine (1) 2 *(Kossovski V 2, Shevchenko 70)*
Northern Ireland (1) 1 *(Dowie 14 (pen))*
Ukraine: Kossovski O; Luzhni, Bezhenar, Golovko, Skrypnyk, Mikhailenko, Kardash, Kalitvintsev (Kriventsov 88), Kossovski V (Orbu 77), Shevchenko, Rebrov.
Northern Ireland: Wright; Gillespie (McMahon 82), Nolan, Hill, Taggart, Morrow, Lennon (Quinn 75), Lomas, Dowie, Horlock, Hughes.
Referee: Krondl (Czech Republic).

Erevan, 30 April 1997, 10,000
Armenia (0) 0
Northern Ireland (0) 0
Armenia: Berezovski; Soukiassian, Khachatrian V, Hovsepian, Ter-Zakarian, Art Petrossian (Khodgoyan 84), Mikhitarian H, Yepiskoposyan (Minassian 86), Avalian (Avetissian A 76), Mikaelian, Assadourian.
Northern Ireland: Fettis; Jenkins, Morrow, Hill, Taggart, Lomas, McCarthy (Mulryne 71), Lennon, Quinn (McMahon 59), Dowie, Horlock.
Referee: Nielsen (Sweden).

Armenia 0 Portugal 0, Ukraine 2 Portugal 1, Albania 0 Portugal 3, Armenia 0 Germany 5, Albania 1 Armenia 1, Portugal 1 Ukraine 0, Portugal 0 Germany 0, Albania 0 Ukraine 1, Albania 2 Germany 3, Germany 2 Ukraine 0, Ukraine 1 Armenia 1, Portugal 2 Albania 0, Ukraine 0 Germany 0.

Group 9	—	P	W	D	L	F	A	Pts
Ukraine		8	4	2	2	7	6	14
Germany		6	3	3	0	11	4	12
Portugal		7	3	3	1	7	2	12
Northern Ireland		7	1	4	2	5	5	7
Armenia		6	0	5	1	4	8	5
Albania		6	0	1	5	3	12	1

SOUTH AMERICA (Members 10, Entries 10)
Five teams qualify including Brazil as champions
The nine competing teams play each other twice, the first four qualifying for the finals.

Argentina 3 Bolivia 1, Colombia 1 Paraguay 0, Ecuador 4 Peru 1, Venezuela 0 Uruguay 2, Ecuador 2 Argentina 0, Peru 1 Colombia 1, Uruguay 0 Paraguay 2, Venezuela 1 Chile 1, Chile 4 Ecuador 1, Bolivia 6 Venezuela 1, Colombia 3 Uruguay 1, Peru 0 Argentina 0, Argentina 1 Paraguay 1, Bolivia 0 Peru 0, Colombia 4 Chile 1, Ecuador 1 Venezuela 0, Uruguay 1 Bolivia 0, Ecuador 0 Colombia 1, Paraguay 2 Chile 1, Venezuela 2 Argentina 5, Bolivia 2 Colombia 2, Paraguay 1 Ecuador 0, Peru 4 Venezuela 1, Chile 1 Uruguay 0, Argentina 1 Chile 1, Bolivia 0 Paraguay 0, Uruguay 2 Peru 0, Venezuela 0 Colombia 2, Bolivia 2 Ecuador 0, Peru 2 Chile 1, Uruguay 0 Argentina 0, Venezuela 0 Paraguay 2, Bolivia 1 Chile 1, Colombia 1 Argentina 1, Ecuador 4 Uruguay 0, Paraguay 2 Peru 1, Bolivia 2 Argentina 1, Colombia 1 Paraguay 2, Peru 1 Ecuador 1, Uruguay 3 Venezuela 1, Chile 6 Venezuela 0, Argentina 2 Ecuador 1, Colombia 0 Peru 1, Paraguay 3 Argentina 2 Peru 0, Ecuador 1 Chile 1, Uruguay 1 Colombia 1, Venezuela 1 Bolivia 1. Chile 4 Colombia 1, Paraguay 1 Argentina 2, Venezuela 1 Ecuador 1, Peru 2 Bolivia 2.

1998 FIFA WORLD CUP – REMAINING FIXTURES

EUROPE

Group 1

20.08.97	Bosnia-Herzegovina v Denmark
06.09.97	Croatia v Bosnia-Herzegovina
06.09.97	Slovenia v Greece
10.09.97	Denmark v Croatia
10.09.97	Bosnia-Herzegovina v Slovenia
11.10.97	Greece v Denmark
11.10.97	Slovenia v Croatia

Group 2

10.09.97	England v Moldova
10.09.97	Georgia v Italy
24.09.97	Moldova v Georgia
07.10.97	Moldova v Poland
11.10.97	Italy v England
11.10.97	Georgia v Poland

Group 3

20.08.97	Finland v Norway
20.08.97	Hungary v Switzerland
06.09.97	Switzerland v Finland
06.09.97	Azerbaijan v Norway
10.09.97	Hungary v Azerbaijan
10.09.97	Norway v Switzerland
11.10.97	Finland v Hungary
11.10.97	Switzerland v Azerbaijan

Group 4

20.08.97	Estonia v Austria
20.08.97	Belarus v Sweden
06.09.97	Austria v Sweden
06.09.97	Scotland v Belarus
06.09.97	Latvia v Estonia
10.09.97	Sweden v Latvia
10.09.97	Belarus v Austria
11.10.97	Austria v Belarus
11.10.97	Scotland v Latvia
11.10.97	Sweden v Estonia

Group 5

20.08.97	Bulgaria v Israel
07.09.97	Luxembourg v Cyprus
10.09.97	Bulgaria v Russia
11.10.97	Cyprus v Luxembourg
11.10.97	Russia v Bulgaria

Group 6

20.08.97	Czech Republic v Faeroes
24.08.97	Slovakia v Czech Republic
06.09.97	Faeroes v Czech Republic
10.09.97	Slovakia v Yugoslavia
24.09.97	Malta v Czech Republic
24.09.97	Slovakia v Spain
11.10.97	Malta v Yugoslavia
11.10.97	Czech Republic v Slovakia
11.10.97	Spain v Faeroes

Group 7

20.08.97	Turkey v Wales
06.09.97	Netherlands v Belgium
10.09.97	San Marino v Turkey
11.10.97	Belgium v Wales
11.10.97	Netherlands v Turkey

Group 8

20.08.97	Liechtenstein v Iceland
20.08.97	Republic of Ireland v Lithuania
20.08.97	Romania v Macedonia
06.09.97	Iceland v Republic of Ireland
06.09.97	Liechtenstein v Romania
06.09.97	Lithuania v Macedonia
10.09.97	Romania v Iceland
10.09.97	Lithuania v Republic of Ireland
11.10.97	Iceland v Liechtenstein
11.10.97	Republic of Ireland v Romania
11.10.97	Macedonia v Lithuania

Group 9

20.08.97	Northern Ireland v Germany
20.08.97	Portugal v Armenia
20.08.97	Ukraine v Albania
06.09.97	Germany v Portugal
06.09.97	Armenia v Albania
10.09.97	Albania v Northern Ireland
10.09.97	Germany v Armenia
11.10.97	Germany v Albania
11.10.97	Portugal v Northern Ireland
11.10.97	Armenia v Ukraine

SOUTH AMERICA

20.07.97	Argentina v Venezuela
20.07.97	Bolivia v Uruguay
20.07.97	Colombia v Ecuador
20.07.97	Chile v Paraguay.
20.08.97	Uruguay v Chile
20.08.97	Colombia v Bolivia
20.08.97	Ecuador v Paraguay
20.08.97	Venezuela v Peru.
10.09.97	Chile v Argentina
10.09.97	Peru v Uruguay
10.09.97	Colombia v Venezuela
10.09.97	Paraguay v Bolivia.
12.10.97	Argentina v Uruguay
12.10.97	Chile v Peru
12.10.97	Paraguay v Venezuela
12.10.97	Ecuador v Bolivia.
16.11.97	Argentina v Colombia
16.11.97	Uruguay v Ecuador
16.11.97	Peru v Paraguay
16.11.97	Chile v Bolivia.

WORLD CLUB CHAMPIONSHIP

Played annually up to 1974 and intermittently since then between the winners of the European Cup and the winners of the South American Champions Cup — known as the Copa Libertadores. In 1980 the winners were decided by one match arranged in Tokyo in February 1981 and the venue has been the same since. AC Milan replaced Marseille who had been stripped of their European Cup title in 1993.

1960   Real Madrid beat Penarol 0-0, 5-1
1961   Penarol beat Benfica 0-1, 5-0, 2-1
1962   Santos beat Benfica 3-2, 5-2
1963   Santos beat AC Milan 2-4, 4-2, 1-0
1964   Inter-Milan beat Independiente 0-1, 2-0, 1-0
1965   Inter-Milan beat Independiente 3-0, 0-0
1966   Penarol beat Real Madrid 2-0, 2-0
1967   Racing Club beat Celtic 0-1, 2-1, 1-0
1968   Estudiantes beat Manchester United 1-0, 1-1
1969   AC Milan beat Estudiantes 3-0, 1-2
1970   Feyenoord beat Estudiantes 2-2, 1-0
1971   Nacional beat Panathinaikos* 1-1, 2-1
1972   Ajax beat Independiente 1-1, 3-0
1973   Independiente beat Juventus* 1-0
1974   Atlético Madrid* beat Independiente 0-1, 2-0
1975   Independiente and Bayern Munich could not agree dates; no matches.
1976   Bayern Munich beat Cruzeiro 2-0, 0-0
1977   Boca Juniors beat Borussia Moenchengladbach* 2-2, 3-0
1978   Not contested
1979   Olimpia beat Malmö* 1-0, 2-1
1980   Nacional beat Nottingham Forest 1-0
1981   Flamengo beat Liverpool 3-0
1982   Penarol beat Aston Villa 2-0
1983   Gremio Porto Alegre beat SV Hamburg 2-1
1984   Independiente beat Liverpool 1-0
1985   Juventus beat Argentinos Juniors 4-2 on penalties after a 2-2 draw
1986   River Plate beat Steaua Bucharest 1-0
1987   FC Porto beat Penarol 2-1 after extra time
1988   Nacional (Uru) beat PSV Eindhoven 7-6 on penalties after 1-1 draw
1989   AC Milan beat Atletico Nacional (Col) 1-0 after extra time
1990   AC Milan beat Olimpia 3-0
1991   Red Star Belgrade beat Colo Colo 3-0
1992   Sao Paulo beat Barcelona 2-1
1993   Sao Paulo beat AC Milan 3-2
1994   Velez Sarsfield beat AC Milan 2-0
1995   Ajax beat Gremio Porto Alegre 4-3 on penalties after 0-0 draw

*European Cup runners-up; winners declined to take part.

1996

26 November in Tokyo

Juventus (0) 1

River Plate (0) 0   55,000

Juventus: Peruzzi; Ferrara, Porrini, Torricelli, Montero, Di Livio, Deschamps, Jugovic, Zidane (Tacchinardi 86), Del Piero, Boksic.
Scorer: Del Piero 82.
River Plate: Bonano; Diaz, Berizzo, Ayala, Sorin, Astrada, Montserrat, Berti (Gancedo 75), Ortega, Francescoli, Cruz (Salas 84).
Referee: De Freitas (Brazil).

EUROPEAN SUPER CUP

Played annually between the winners of the European Champions' Cup and the European Cup-Winners' Cup. AC Milan replaced Marseille in 1993–94.

Previous Matches

1972	Ajax beat Rangers 3-1, 3-2
1973	Ajax beat AC Milan 0-1, 6-0
1974	Not contested
1975	Dynamo Kiev beat Bayern Munich 1-0, 2-0
1976	Anderlecht beat Bayern Munich 4-1, 1-2
1977	Liverpool beat Hamburg 1-1, 6-0
1978	Anderlecht beat Liverpool 3-1, 1-2
1979	Nottingham F beat Barcelona 1-0, 1-1
1980	Valencia beat Nottingham F 1-0, 1-2
1981	Not contested
1982	Aston Villa beat Barcelona 0-1, 3-0
1983	Aberdeen beat Hamburg 0-0, 2-0
1984	Juventus beat Liverpool 2-0
1985	Juventus v Everton not contested due to UEFA ban on English clubs
1986	Steaua Bucharest beat Dynamo Kiev 1-0
1987	FC Porto beat Ajax 1-0, 1-0
1988	KV Mechelen beat PSV Eindhoven 3-0, 0-1
1989	AC Milan beat Barcelona 1-1, 1-0
1990	AC Milan beat Sampdoria 1-1, 2-0
1991	Manchester U beat Red Star Belgrade 1-0
1992	Barcelona beat Werder Bremen 1-1, 2-1
1993	Parma beat AC Milan 0-1, 2-0
1994	AC Milan beat Arsenal 0-0, 2-0
1995	Ajax beat Zaragoza 1-1, 4-0

1996–97

First Leg, 15 January 1997, Paris

Paris St Germain 0 (1) *(Rai 53 (pen))*   29,519

Juventus (4) 6 *(Porrini 5, Padovano 22, 40, Ferrara 36, Lombardo 83, Amoruso 89)*

Paris St Germain: Lama; Domi (Leonardo 55), Le Guen, N'Gotty, Algerino (Kenedy 34), Fournier, Guerin, Leroy, Rai, Loko, Dely Valdes (Pouget 61).
Juventus: Peruzzi; Torricelli, Ferrara (Iuliano 73), Porrini, Pessotto, Deschamps, Di Livio, Zidane, Tacchinardi (Lombardo 67), Padovano (Amoruso 73), Del Piero.
Referee: Levnikov (Russia).

Second Leg, 5 February 1997, Palermo

Juventus (1) 3 *(Del Piero 36, 70, Vieri 90)*

Paris St Germain (0) 1 *(Rai 64 (pen))*   35,100

Juventus: Peruzzi; Torricelli (Porrini 72), Ferrara, Montero, Pessotto, Di Livio, Tacchinardi (Lombardo 67), Zidane, Jugovic, Del Piero, Padovano (Vieri 67).
Paris St Germain: Lama; Kenedy, Le Guen, Domi, Algerino, Cauet, Leonardo (Allou 80), Guerin (Leroy 75), Rai, Dely Valdes, Loko (Calenda 90).
Referee: Muhmenthaler (Switzerland).

SOUTH AMERICAN CHAMPIONSHIP

(Copa America)

1916	Uruguay	1937	Argentina	1959	Uruguay
1917	Uruguay	1939	Peru	1963	Bolivia
1919	Brazil	1941	Argentina	1967	Uruguay
1920	Uruguay	1942	Uruguay	1975	Peru
1921	Argentina	1945	Argentina	1979	Paraguay
1922	Brazil	1946	Argentina	1983	Uruguay
1923	Uruguay	1947	Argentina	1987	Uruguay
1924	Uruguay	1949	Brazil	1989	Brazil
1925	Argentina	1953	Paraguay	1991	Argentina
1926	Uruguay	1955	Argentina	1993	Argentina
1927	Argentina	1956	Uruguay	1995	Uruguay
1929	Argentina	1957	Argentina	1997	Brazil
1935	Uruguay	1959	Argentina		

SOUTH AMERICAN CUP

(Copa Libertadores)

1960	Penarol (Uruguay)	1979	Olimpia (Paraguay)
1961	Penarol	1980	Nacional
1962	Santos (Brazil)	1981	Flamengo (Brazil)
1963	Santos	1982	Penarol
1964	Independiente (Argentina)	1983	Gremio Porto Alegre (Brazil)
1965	Independiente	1984	Independiente
1966	Penarol	1985	Argentinos Juniors (Argentina)
1967	Racing Club (Argentina)	1986	River Plate (Argentina)
1968	Estudiantes (Argentina)	1987	Penarol
1969	Estudiantes	1988	Nacional (Uruguay)
1970	Estudiantes	1989	Nacional (Colombia)
1971	Nacional (Uruguay)	1990	Olimpia
1972	Independiente	1991	Colo Colo (Chile)
1973	Independiente	1992	São Paulo (Brazil)
1974	Independiente	1993	São Paulo
1975	Independiente	1994	Velez Sarsfield (Argentina)
1976	Cruzeiro (Brazil)	1995	Gremio Porto Alegre
1977	Boca Juniors (Argentina)	1996	River Plate
1978	Boca Juniors	1997	*Not finished yet*

OTHER BRITISH AND IRISH INTERNATIONAL MATCHES 1996–97

FRIENDLIES

Palermo, 22 January 1997, 30,866

Italy (1) 2 *(Zola 8, Del Piero 88)*

Northern Ireland (0) 0

Italy: Peruzzi; Ferrara, Costacurta (Cannavaro 71), Maldini, Di Livio (Iranio 79), Dino Baggio, Albertini, Di Matteo (Fuser 57), Carboni, Zola (Del Piero 61), Casiraghi (Ravanelli 57).
Northern Ireland: Wright; Griffin, Worthington, Taggart, Hunter, Lomas, McCarthy (Dennison 83), Morrow, Quinn (O'Boyle 60), Horlock, Hughes (Rowland 69).
Referee: Frohlich (Germany).

Belfast, 11 February 1997, 7126

Northern Ireland (1) 3 *(Quinn 14, Magilton 62 (pen), Mulryne 88)*

Belgium (0) 0

Northern Ireland: Wright; Gillespie, Horlock (Whitley 85), Lomas, Taggart, Hunter (Griffin 46), Lennon (Worthington 68), Magilton, Quinn (O'Boyle 57), Morrow, McMahon (Mulryne 46).
Belgium: De Wilde; Medved, De Roover, Staelens, Albert, Van der Elst F, Verheyen (Pierre 71), Scifo (Lemoine 77), Kerckhoven (Schepens 85), Wilmots (Jbari 80), Nilis (Mpenza L 46).
Referee: Rowbotham (Scotland).

Cardiff Arms Park, 11 February 1997, 7000

Wales (0) 0

Republic of Ireland (0) 0

Wales: Crossley; Pembridge, Legg, Jones (Hughes C 74), Symons, Ready, Robinson (Bowen M 63), Horne, Hartson (Taylor 69), Hughes M (Savage 88), Speed.
Republic of Ireland: Branagan; McAteer, Phelan, Cunningham, McGrath, Harte, McLoughlin (Kelly G 53), Keane (Kelly D 75), Goodman, Cascarino, Staunton.
Referee: Young (Scotland).

Wembley, 29 March 1997, 48,076

England (1) 2 *(Sheringham 20 (pen), Fowler 55)*

Mexico (0) 0

England: James; Keown, Pearce, Batty (Redknapp 62), Southgate, Le Saux, Lee, Ince, Fowler, Sheringham (Wright I 38), McManaman (Butt 68).
Mexico: Rios (Sanchez 60); Pardo, Suarez, Davino, Ramirez R, Alfaro, Coyote (Ramirez N 67), Galindo (Bernal 56), Garcia Aspe, Hermosillo (Pelaez 46), Roberto Alvez (Hernandez 46).
Referee: Pereira (Portugal).

Old Trafford, 24 May 1997, 52,676

England (1) 2 *(Lee 20, Wright 76)*

South Africa (1) 1 *(Masinga 43)*

England: Martyn; Neville P, Pearce, Keown, Southgate, Le Saux (Beckham 68), Redknapp (Batty 56), Gascoigne, Wright, Sheringham (Scholes 64), Lee (Butt 80).
South Africa: Arendse; Fish, Tovey, Radebe, Moutaung, Tinkler, Moeti, Khumalo (Mkhalele 76), Moshoeu, Masinga (Buthelezi 85), Augustine (Sikhosana 55).
Referee: Frisk (Sweden).

Kilmarnock, 27 May 1997, 8000

Scotland (0) 0

Wales (0) 1 *(Hartson 46)*

Scotland: Sullivan (Leighton 80); Weir, Boyd, McAllister B, Dailly (McNamara 75), McKinlay T, Gallacher (Donnelly 80), Gemmill, Dodds, McAllister G, Jackson (Spencer 46).
Wales: Marriott (Jones P 46); Jenkins, Pembridge, Page, Symons, Trollope, Robinson (Browning 88), Savage, Saunders (Jones L 88), Hartson (Haworth 71), Speed.
Referee: Snoddy (Northern Ireland).

Valletta, 1 June 1997, 3500

Malta (1) 2 *(Suda 17, Sultana 57)*

Scotland (2) 3 *(Dailly 4, Jackson 44, 81)*

Malta: Muscat; Attard (Turner 66), Brincat, Debono, Chetcuti, Carabott, Vella (Giglio 75), Zammit, Saliba, Suda (Sultana 46), Agius.
Scotland: Leighton; Burley, Boyd, McAllister B (Weir 46), Dailly, McKinlay T, Hopkin (Gemmill 60), Gallacher (Durie 60), Jackson, McAllister G, Collins.
Referee: Braschi (Italy).

TOYOTA INVITATION

Bangkok, 21 May 1997, 15,000

Thailand (0) 0

Northern Ireland (0) 0

Thailand: Kampian; Tinnakorn, Krisada, Jirasirachote, Promrut, Chalermsan, Kijmongkolsak, Jaturapattarapong, Damkong-Ongtrakul, Daorung, Pivapong.
Northern Ireland: Davison (Carroll 46); Jenkins (Whitley 46), Hill, McGibbon, Griffin, McCarthy (McMahon 46), Lomas, Lennon, Horlock, Mulryne (Quinn 46), Dowie (Robinson 63).
Referee: Hanlumyaung (Thailand).

TOURNOI DE FRANCE

Lyon, 3 June 1997, 28,193

France (0) 1 *(Keller 59)*

Brazil (1) 1 *(Roberto Carlos 21)*

France: Barthez; Candela, Blanc, Desailly (Thuram 66), Karembeu (Viera 14), Ba, Zidane, Deschamps, Lizarazu, Maurice, Pires (Keller 59).
Brazil: Taffarel; Cafu, Celio Silva, Aldair (Goncalves 87), Mauro Silva, Giovanni (Djalminha 72), Dunga, Leonardo, Roberto Carlos, Ronaldo, Romario (Paolo Nunes 79).
Referee: Nielsen (Denmark).

Nantes, 4 June 1997, 25,000

Italy (0) 0

England (2) 2 *(Wright 26, Scholes 43)*

Italy: Peruzzi; Ferrara (Nesta 46), Cannavaro, Di Livio (Maini 46), Costacurta, Albertini, Dino Baggio, Di Matteo (Fuser 17), Casiraghi, Benarrivo, Zola.
England: Flowers; Neville P, Pearce, Keown, Southgate, Le Saux (Neville G 46), Scholes, Ince, Wright (Cole 76), Sheringham (Gascoigne 79), Beckham.
Referee: Renko (Austria).

Montpellier, 7 June 1997, 25,000

France (0) 0

England (0) 1 *(Shearer 86)*

France: Barthez; Thuram, Blanc, N'Gotty, Laigle (Lizarazu 81), Deschamps, Viera, Keller, Djorkaeff, Dugarry (Zidane 73), Ouedec (Loko 62).
England: Seaman; Neville G, Neville P, Batty (Ince 46), Southgate, Campbell, Beckham (Lee 73), Gascoigne, Shearer, Wright (Sheringham 78), Le Saux.
Referee: Belqola (Morocco).

Lyon, 8 June 1997, 30,000

Brazil (1) 3 *(Lombardo 35 (og), Ronaldo 71, Romario 85)*

Italy (2) 3 *(Del Piero 7, 62 (pen), Aldair 23 (og))*

Brazil: Taffarel; Cafu, Aldair, Celio Silva, Denilson, Mauro Silva (Flavio Conceicao 63), Dunga, Ronaldo, Romario, Leonardo, Roberto Carlos.
Italy: Pagliuca; Panucci, Maldini (Di Livio 90), Cannavaro, Costacurta, Albertini, Dino Baggio (Fuser 46), Di Matteo, Vieri (Inzaghi 60), Del Piero, Lombardo.
Referee: Muhmenthaler (Switzerland).

Paris, 10 June 1997, 50,000

England (0) 0

Brazil (0) 1 *(Romario 61)*

England: Seaman; Neville P, Le Saux, Keown (Neville G 19), Southgate, Campbell, Scholes (Lee 78), Gascoigne, Shearer, Sheringham (Wright 78), Ince.
Brazil: Taffarel; Cafu, Roberto Carlos, Celio Silva, Dunga, Aldair, Flavio, Denilson (Djalminha 21), Ronaldo, Leonardo (Ze Roberto 82), Romario.
Referee: Rendon (Colombia).

Paris, 11 June 1997, 30,000

France (1) 2 *(Zidane 12, Djorkaeff 73)*

Italy (0) 2 *(Casiraghi 61, Del Piero 90 (pen))*

France: Charbonnier; Thuram, Leboeuf, Desailly (N'Gotty 85), Lizarazu, Ba, Deschamps, Karembeu (Vieira 66), Zidane, Dugarry, Maurice (Djorkaeff 63).
Italy: Pagliuca; Cannavaro, Maldini, Di Livio, Costacurta (Torrisi 46), Nesta, Lombardo, Di Matteo, Casiraghi (Vieri 78), Del Piero, Zola (Panucci 56).
Referee: Nieto (Spain).

ENGLAND UNDER-21 TEAMS 1996–97

ENGLAND UNDER-21 INTERNATIONALS

31 Aug
Moldova (0) 0
England (1) 2 *(Dyer 39, Eadie 53)*   850
England: Day; Scimeca, Thatcher, Duberry, Potter, Newton, Ford, Holland, Dyer, Eadie (Moore 70), Bowyer.

8 Oct
England (0) 0
Poland (0) 0   3183
England: Marshall; Scimeca, Thatcher, Duberry, Hall, Holland (Morris 72), Butt, Scowcroft, Humphreys (Thompson 46), Newton, Heskey (Branch 72).

8 Nov
Georgia (0) 0
England (0) 1 *(Duberry 81)*   4000
England: Day; Scimeca, Neville P, Duberry, Carbon, Thompson, Butt, Scowcroft, Dyer, Newton (Rose 69), Eadie (Humphreys 87).

12 Feb
England (0) 1 *(Eadie 50)*
Italy (0) 0   13,850
England: Marshall; Scimeca, Hall, Rose, Rufus, Carbon, Murray, Hughes, Heskey (Scowcroft 89), Eadie (Huckerby 60), Bowyer (Carragher 16).

1 Apr
England (0) 0
Switzerland (0) 0   10,167
England: Day (Roberts 62); Broomes, Hall, Ferdinand (Morris 55), Carbon (Briscoe 46), Holland, Carragher, Hughes, Huckerby (Moore 84), Humphreys (Bridges 67), Bowyer.

29 Apr
England (0) 0
Georgia (0) 0   12,714
England: Wright; Oakley, Hall, Broomes (Granville 46), Ferdinand, Carragher, Scowcroft, Hughes, Heskey (Huckerby 46), Eadie (Morris 68), Bowyer.

30 May
Poland (0) 1 *(Dubicki 66)*
England (1) 1 *(Heskey 35)*   2000
England: Wright; Hamilton, Granville, Moses, Hall, Carragher, Murray, Quashie, Heskey (Huckerby 67), Hughes, Bradbury.

POST-WAR INTERNATIONAL APPEARANCES
As at July 1997

ENGLAND
A'Court, A. (5) (Liverpool) 1957/8, 1958/9.
Adams, T.A. (47) (Arsenal) 1986/7, 1987/8, 1988/9, 1990/91, 1992/93, 1993/94, 1994/95, 1995/96, 1996/97.
Allen, C. (5) (QPR) 1983/4, 1986/7 (Tottenham Hotspur) 1987/8.
Allen, R. (5) (West Bromwich Albion) 1951/2, 1953/4, 1954/5.
Allen, T. (3) (Stoke City) 1959/60.
Anderson, S. (2) (Sunderland) 1961/2.
Anderson, V. (30) (Nottingham Forest) 1978/9, 1979/80, 1980/1, 1981/2, 1983/84, (Arsenal) 1984/5, 1985/6, 1986/7, (Manchester United).
Anderton, D.R. (16) (Tottenham Hotspur) 1993/94, 1994/95, 1995/96.
Angus, J. (1) (Burnley) 1960/1.
Armfield, J. (43) (Blackpool) 1958/9, 1959/60, 1960/1, 1961/2, 1962/3, 1963/4, 1965/6.
Armstrong, D. (3) (Middlesbrough) 1979/80, (Southampton) 1982/3, 1983/4.
Armstrong, K. (1) (Chelsea) 1954/5.
Astall, G. (2) (Birmingham) 1955/6.
Astle, J. (5) (West Bromwich Albion) 1968/9, 1969/70.
Aston, J. (17) (Manchester United) 1948/9, 1949/50, 1950/1.
Atyeo, J. (6) (Bristol City) 1955/6, 1956/7.

Bailey, G.R. (2) Manchester United) 1984/5.
Bailey, M. (2) (Charlton) 1963/4, 1964/5.
Baily, E. (9) (Tottenham Hotspur) 1949/50, 1950/1, 1951/2, 1952/3.
Baker, J. (8) (Hibernian) 1959/60, 1965/6, (Arsenal).
Ball, A. (72) (Blackpool) 1964/5, 1965/6, 1966/7, (Everton) 1967/8, 1968/9, 1969/70, 1970/1, 1971/2 (Arsenal) 1972/3, 1973/4, 1974/5.
Banks, G. (73) (Leicester) 1962/3, 1963/4, 1964/5, 1965/6, 1966/7, 1967/8, (Stoke City) 1968/9, 1969/70, 1970/1, 1971/2.
Banks, T. (6) (Bolton Wanderers) 1957/8, 1958/9.
Bardsley, D. (2) (QPR) 1992/93.
Barham, M. (2) (Norwich City) 1982/3.
Barlow, R. (1) (West Bromwich Albion) 1954/5.
Barmby, N.J. (10) (Tottenham Hotspur) 1994/95, (Middlesbrough) 1995/96, 1996/97 (Everton).
Barnes, J. (79) (Watford) 1982/3, 1983/4, 1984/5, 1985/6, 1986/7, (Liverpool) 1987/8, 1988/9, 1989/90, 1990/91, 1991/2, 1992/93, 1994/95, 1995/96.
Barnes, P. (22) (Manchester City) 1977/8, 1978/9, 1979/80 (West Bromwich Albion) 1980/1, 1981/2 (Leeds United).
Barrass, M. (3) (Bolton Wanderers) 1951/2, 1952/3.
Barrett, E.D. (3) (Oldham Athletic) 1990/91 (Aston Villa) 1992/93.
Barton, W.D. (3) (Wimbledon) (Blackburn Rovers) 1994/95.
Batty, D. (25) (Leeds United) 1990/91, 1991/2, 1992/93, (Blackburn Rovers) 1993/94, 1994/95, (Newcastle United) 1996/97.
Baynham, R. (3) (Luton Town) 1955/6.
Beardsley, P.A. (59) (Newcastle United) 1985/6, 1986/7 (Liverpool) 1987/8, 1988/9, 1989/90, 1990/1, (Newcastle United) 1993/94, 1994/95, 1995/96.
Beasant, D.J. (2) (Chelsea), 1989/90.
Beattie, T.K. (9) (Ipswich Town) 1974/5, 1975/6, 1976/7, 1977/8.
Beckham, D.R.J. (9) (Manchester United) 1996/97.
Bell, C. (48) (Manchester City) 1967/8, 1968/9, 1969/70, 1971/2, 1972/3, 1973/4, 1974/5, 1975/6.

Bentley, R. (12) (Chelsea) 1948/9, 1949/50, 1952/3, 1954/5.
Berry, J. (4) (Manchester United) 1952/3, 1955/6.
Birtles, G. (3) (Nottingham Forest) 1979/80, 1980/1 (Manchester United).
Blissett, L. (14) (Watford) 1982/3, 1983/4 (AC Milan).
Blockley, J. (1) (Arsenal) 1972/3.
Blunstone, F. (5) (Chelsea) 1954/5, 1956/7.
Bonetti, P. (7) (Chelsea) 1965/6, 1966/7, 1967/8, 1969/70.
Bould, S.A. (2) (Arsenal) 1993/94.
Bowles, S. (5) (QPR) 1973/4, 1976/7.
Boyer, P. (1) (Norwich City) 1975/6.
Brabrook, P. (3) (Chelsea) 1957/8, 1959/60.
Bracewell, P.W. (3) (Everton) 1984/5, 1985/6.
Bradford, G. (1) (Bristol Rovers) 1955/6.
Bradley, W. (3) (Manchester United) 1958/9.
Bridges, B. (4) (Chelsea) 1964/5, 1965/6.
Broadbent, P. (7) (Wolverhampton Wanderers) 1957/8, 1958/9, 1959/60.
Broadis, I. (14) (Manchester City) 1951/2, 1952/3 (Newcastle United) 1953/4.
Brooking, T. (47) (West Ham United) 1973/4, 1974/5, 1975/6, 1976/7, 1977/8, 1978/9, 1979/80, 1980/1, 1981/2.
Brooks, J. (3) (Tottenham Hotspur) 1956/7.
Brown, A. (1) (West Bromwich Albion) 1970/1.
Brown, K. (1) (West Ham United) 1959/60.
Bull, S.G. (13) (Wolverhampton Wanderers) 1988/9, 1989/90, 1990/1
Butcher, T. (77) (Ipswich Town) 1979/80, 1980/1, 1981/2, 1982/3, 1983/4, 1984/5, 1985/6, 1986/7 (Rangers) 1987/8, 1988/9, 1989/90.
Butt, N. (2) (Manchester United) 1996/97.
Byrne, G. (2) (Liverpool) 1962/3, 1965/6.
Byrne, J. (11) (Crystal Palace) 1961/2, 1962/3, (West Ham United) 1963/4, 1964/5.
Byrne, R. (33) (Manchester United) 1953/4, 1954/5, 1955/6, 1956/7, 1957/8.

Callaghan, I. (4) (Liverpool) 1965/6, 1977/8.
Campbell, S. (8) (Tottenham Hotspur) 1995/96, 1996/97.
Carter, H. (7) (Derby County) 1946/7.
Chamberlain, M. (8) (Stoke City) 1982/3, 1983/4, 1984/5.
Channon, M. (46) (Southampton) 1972/3, 1973/4, 1974/5, 1975/6, 1976/7, (Manchester City) 1977/8.
Charles, G.A. (2) (Nottingham Forest) 1990/1.
Charlton, J. (35) (Leeds United) 1964/5, 1965/6, 1966/7, 1967/8, 1968/9, 1969/70.
Charlton, R. (106) (Manchester United) 1957/8, 1958/9, 1959/60, 1960/1, 1961/2, 1962/3, 1963/4, 1964/5, 1965/6, 1966/7, 1967/8, 1968/9, 1969/70.
Charnley, R. (1) (Blackpool) 1961/2.
Cherry, T. (27) (Leeds United) 1975/6, 1976/7, 1977/8, 1978/9, 1979/80.
Chilton, A. (2) (Manchester United) 1950/1, 1951/2.
Chivers, M. (24) (Tottenham Hotspur) 1970/1, 1971/2, 1972/3, 1973/4.
Clamp, E. (4) (Wolverhampton Wanderers) 1957/8.
Clapton, D. (1) (Arsenal) 1958/9.
Clarke, A. (19) (Leeds United) 1969/70, 1970/1, 1972/3, 1973/4, 1974/5, 1975/6.
Clarke, H. (1) (Tottenham Hotspur) 1953/4.
Clayton, R. (35) (Blackburn Rovers) 1955/6, 1956/7, 1957/8, 1958/9, 1959/60.
Clemence, R (61) (Liverpool) 1972/3, 1973/4, 1974/5, 1975/6, 1976/7, 1977/8, 1978/9, 1979/80, 1980/1, 1981/2, (Tottenham Hotspur) 1982/3, 1983/4.
Clement, D. (5) (QPR) 1975/6, 1976/7.
Clough, B. (2) (Middlesbrough) 1959/60.
Clough, N.H. (14) (Nottingham Forest) 1988/9, 1990/91, 1991/2, 1992/93.
Coates, R. (4) (Burnley) 1969/70, 1970/1, (Tottenham Hotspur).
Cockburn, H. (13) (Manchester United) 1946/7, 1947/8, 1948/9, 1950/1, 1951/2.
Cohen, G. (37) (Fulham) 1963/4, 1964/5, 1965/6, 1966/7, 1967/8.

Cole, A. (2) (Manchester United) 1994/95, 1996/97.
Collymore, S. V. (2) (Nottingham Forest) 1994/95.
Compton, L. (2) (Arsenal) 1950/1.
Connelly, J. (20) (Burnley) 1959/60, 1961/2, 1962/3, 1964/5 (Manchester United) 1965/6.
Cooper, C. T. (2) (Nottingham Forest) 1994/95.
Cooper, T. (20) (Leeds United) 1968/9, 1969/70, 1970/1, 1971/2, 1974/5.
Coppell, S. (42) (Manchester United) 1977/8, 1978/9, 1979/80, 1980/1, 1981/2, 1982/3.
Corrigan, J. (9) (Manchester City) 1975/6, 1977/8, 1978/9, 1979/80, 1980/1, 1981/2.
Cottee, A. R. (7) (West Ham United) 1986/7, 1987/8, (Everton) 1988/9.
Cowans, G. (10) (Aston Villa) 1982/3, 1985/6 (Bari) 1990/1 (Aston Villa).
Crawford, R. (2) (Ipswich Town) 1961/2.
Crowe, C. (1) (Wolverhampton Wanderers) 1962/3.
Cunningham, L. (6) (West Bromwich Albion) 1978/9 (Real Madrid) 1979/80, 1980/1.
Curle, K. (3) (Manchester City) 1991/2.
Currie, A. (17) (Sheffield United) 1971/2, 1972/3, 1973/4, 1975/6 (Leeds United) 1977/8, 1978/9.

Daley, A. M. (7) (Aston Villa) 1991/2.
Davenport, P. (1) (Nottingham Forest) 1984/5.
Deane, B. C. (3) (Sheffield United) 1990/91, 1992/93.
Deeley, N. (2) (Wolverhampton Wanderers) 1958/9.
Devonshire, A. (8) (West Ham United) 1979/80, 1981/2, 1982/3, 1983/4
Dickinson, J. (48) (Portsmouth) 1948/9, 1949/50, 1950/1, 1951/2, 1952/3, 1953/4, 1954/5, 1955/6, 1956/7.
Ditchburn, E. (6) (Tottenham Hotspur) 1948/9, 1952/3, 1956/7.
Dixon, K. M. (8) (Chelsea) 1984/5, 1985/6, 1986/7.
Dixon, L. M. (21) (Arsenal) 1989/90, 1990/1, 1991/2, 1992/93, 1993/94.
Dobson, M. (5) (Burnley) 1973/4, 1974/5 (Everton).
Dorigo, A. R. (15) (Chelsea) 1989/90, 1990/1, (Leeds United) 1991/2, 1992/93, 1993/94.
Douglas, B. (36) (Blackburn Rovers) 1957/8, 1958/9, 1959/60, 1960/1, 1961/2, 1962/3.
Doyle, M. (5) (Manchester City) 1975/6, 1976/7
Duxbury, M. (10) (Manchester United) 1983/4, 1984/5.

Eastham, G. (19) (Arsenal) 1962/3, 1963/4, 1964/5, 1965/6.
Eckersley, W. (17) (Blackburn Rovers) 1949/50, 1950/1, 1951/2, 1952/3, 1953/4.
Edwards, D. (18) (Manchester United) 1954/5, 1955/6, 1956/7, 1957/8.
Ehiogu, U. (1) (Aston Villa) 1995/96.
Ellerington, W. (2) (Southampton) 1948/9.
Elliott, W. H. (5) (Burnley) 1951/2, 1952/3.

Fantham, J. (1) (Sheffield Wednesday) 1961/2.
Fashanu, J. (2) (Wimbledon) 1988/9.
Fenwick, T. (20) (QPR) 1983/4, 1984/5, 1985/6 (Tottenham Hotspur) 1987/8.
Ferdinand, L. (13) (QPR) 1992/93, 1993/94, 1994/95 (Newcastle United) 1995/96, 1996/97.
Finney, T. (76) (Preston North End) 1946/7, 1947/8, 1948/9, 1949/50, 1950/1, 1951/2, 1952/3, 1953/4, 1954/5, 1955/6, 1956/7, 1957/8, 1958/9.
Flowers, R. (49) (Wolverhampton Wanderers) 1954/5, 1958/9, 1959/60, 1960/1, 1961/2, 1962/3, 1963/4, 1964/5, 1965/6.
Flowers, T. (9) (Southampton) 1992/93, (Blackburn Rovers) 1993/94, 1994/95, 1995/96, 1996/97.
Foster, S. (3) (Brighton) 1981/2.

Foulkes, W. (1) (Manchester United) 1954/5.
Fowler, R. B. (6) (Liverpool) 1995/96, 1996/97.
Francis, G. (12) (QPR) 1974/5, 1975/6.
Francis, T. (52) (Birmingham City) 1976/7, 1977/8 (Nottingham Forest) 1978/9, 1979/80, 1980/1, 1981/2 (Manchester City) 1982/3, (Sampdoria) 1983/4, 1984/5, 1985/6.
Franklin, N. (27) (Stoke City) 1946/7, 1947/8, 1948/9, 1949/50.
Froggatt, J. (13) (Portsmouth) 1949/50, 1950/1, 1951/2, 1952/3.
Froggatt, R. (4) (Sheffield Wednesday) 1952/3.

Garrett, T. (3) (Blackpool) 1951/2, 1953/4.
Gascoigne, P. J. (51) (Tottenham Hotspur) 1988/9, 1989/90, 1990/1 (Lazio) 1992/93, 1993/94, 1994/95 (Rangers) 1995/96, 1996/97.
Gates, E. (2) (Ipswich Town) 1980/1.
George, F. C. (1) (Derby County) 1976/7.
Gidman, J. (1) (Aston Villa) 1976/7.
Gillard, I. (3) (QPR) 1974/5, 1975/6.
Goddard, P. (1) (West Ham United) 1981/2.
Grainger, C. (7) (Sheffield United) 1955/6, 1956/7 (Sunderland).
Gray, A. A. (1) (Crystal Palace) 1991/2.
Greaves, J. (57) (Chelsea) 1958/9, 1959/60, 1960/1, 1961/2 (Tottenham Hotspur) 1962/3, 1963/4, 1964/5, 1965/6, 1966/7.
Greenhoff, B. (18) (Manchester United) 1975/6, 1976/7, 1977/8, 1979/80.
Gregory, J. (6) (QPR) 1982/3, 1983/4.

Hagan, J. (1) (Sheffield United) 1948/9.
Haines, J. (1) (West Bromwich Albion) 1948/9.
Hall, J. (17) (Birmingham City) 1955/6, 1956/7.
Hancocks, J. (3) (Wolverhampton Wanderers) 1948/9, 1949/50, 1950/1.
Hardwick, G. (13) (Middlesbrough) 1946/7, 1947/8.
Harford, M. G. (2) (Luton Town) 1987/8, 1988/9.
Harris, G. (1) (Burnley) 1965/6.
Harris, P. (2) (Portsmouth) 1949/50, 1953/4.
Harvey, C. (1) (Everton) 1970/1.
Hassall, H. (5) (Huddersfield Town) 1950/1, 1951/2 (Bolton Wanderers) 1953/4.
Hateley, M. (32) (Portsmouth) 1983/4, 1984/5, (AC Milan) 1985/6, 1986/7, (Monaco) 1987/8, (Rangers) 1991/2.
Haynes, J. (56) (Fulham) 1954/5, 1955/6, 1956/7, 1957/8, 1958/9, 1959/60, 1960/1, 1961/2.
Hector, K. (2) (Derby County) 1973/4.
Hellawell, M. (2) (Birmingham City) 1962/3.
Henry, R. (1) (Tottenham Hotspur) 1962/3.
Hill, F. (2) (Bolton Wanderers) 1962/3.
Hill, G. (6) (Manchester United) 1975/6, 1976/7, 1977/8.
Hill, R. (3) (Luton Town) 1982/3, 1985/6.
Hinchcliffe, A. G. (3) (Everton) 1996/97.
Hinton A. (3) (Wolverhampton Wanderers) 1962/3, 1964/5 (Nottingham Forest).
Hirst, D. E. (3) (Sheffield Wednesday) 1990/91, 1991/2.
Hitchens, G. (7) (Aston Villa) 1960/1, (Inter Milan) 1961/2.
Hoddle, G. (53) (Tottenham Hotspur) 1979/80, 1980/1, 1981/2, 1982/3, 1983/4, 1984/5, 1985/6, 1986/7 (Monaco) 1987/8.
Hodge, S. B. (24) (Aston Villa) 1985/6, 1986/7, (Tottenham Hotspur), (Nottingham Forest) 1988/9, 1989/90, 1990/1.
Hodgkinson, A. (5) (Sheffield United) 1956/7, 1960/1.
Holden, D. (5) (Bolton Wanderers) 1958/9.
Holliday, E. (3) (Middlesbrough) 1959/60.
Hollins, J. (1) (Chelsea) 1966/7.

Hopkinson, E. (14) (Bolton Wanderers) 1957/8, 1958/9, 1959/60.
Howe, D. (23) (West Bromwich Albion) 1957/8, 1958/9, 1959/60.
Howe, J. (3) (Derby County) 1947/8, 1948/9.
Howey, S. N. (4) (Newcastle United) 1994/95, 1995/96.
Hudson, A. (2) (Stoke City) 1974/5.
Hughes, E. (62) (Liverpool) 1969/70, 1970/1, 1971/2, 1972/3, 1973/4, 1974/5, 1976/7, 1977/8, 1978/9 (Wolverhampton Wanderers) 1979/80.
Hughes, L. (3) (Liverpool) 1949/50.
Hunt, R. (34) (Liverpool) 1961/2, 1962/3, 1963/4, 1964/5, 1965/6, 1966/7, 1967/8, 1968/9.
Hunt, S. (2) (West Bromwich Albion) 1983/4.
Hunter, N. (28) (Leeds United) 1965/6, 1966/7, 1967/8, 1968/9, 1969/70, 1970/1, 1971/2, 1972/3, 1973/4, 1974/5.
Hurst, G. (49) (West Ham United) 1965/6, 1966/7, 1967/8, 1968/9, 1969/70, 1970/1, 1971/2.

Ince, P. (33) (Manchester United) 1992/93, 1993/94, 1994/95, (Internazionale) 1995/96, 1996/97.

James, D. B. (1) (Liverpool) 1996/97.
Jezzard, B. (2) (Fulham) 1953/4, 1955/6.
Johnson, D. (8) (Ipswich Town) 1974/5, 1975/6, (Liverpool) 1979/80.
Johnston, H. (10) (Blackpool) 1946/7, 1950/1, 1952/3, 1953/4.
Jones, M. (3) (Sheffield United) 1964/5 (Leeds United) 1969/70.
Jones, R. (8) (Liverpool) 1991/2, 1993/94, 1994/95.
Jones, W. H. (2) (Liverpool) 1949/50.

Kay, A. (1) (Everton) 1962/3.
Keegan, K. (63) (Liverpool) 1972/3, 1973/4, 1974/5, 1975/6, 1976/7 (SV Hamburg) 1977/8, 1978/9, 1979/80 (Southampton) 1980/1, 1981/2.
Kennedy, A. (2) (Liverpool) 1983/4.
Kennedy, R. (17) (Liverpool) 1975/6, 1977/8, 1979/80.
Keown, M. R. (15) (Everton) 1991/2 (Arsenal) 1992/93, 1996/97.
Kevan, D. (14) (West Bromwich Albion) 1956/7, 1957/8, 1958/9, 1960/1.
Kidd, B. (2) (Manchester United) 1969/70.
Knowles, C. (4) (Tottenham Hotspur) 1967/8.

Labone, B. (26) (Everton) 1962/3, 1966/7, 1967/8, 1968/9, 1969/70.
Lampard, F. (2) (West Ham United) 1972/3, 1979/80.
Langley, J. (3) (Fulham) 1957/8.
Langton, R. (11) (Blackburn Rovers) 1946/7, 1947/8, 1948/9, (Preston North End) 1949/50, (Bolton Wanderers) 1950/1.
Latchford, R. (12) (Everton) 1977/8, 1978/9.
Lawler, C. (4) (Liverpool) 1970/1, 1971/2.
Lawton, T. (15) (Chelsea) 1946/7, 1947/8, (Notts County) 1948/9.
Lee, F. (27) (Manchester City) 1968/9, 1969/70, 1970/1, 1971/2.
Lee, J. (1) (Derby County) 1950/1.
Lee, R. M. (13) (Newcastle United) 1994/95, 1995/96, 1996/97.
Lee, S. (14) (Liverpool) 1982/3, 1983/4.
Le Saux, G. P. (20) (Blackburn Rovers) 1993/94, 1994/95, 1995/96, 1996/97.
Le Tissier, M. P. (8) (Southampton) 1993/94, 1994/95, 1996/97.
Lindsay, A. (4) (Liverpool) 1973/4.
Lineker, G. (80) (Leicester City) 1983/4, 1984/5 (Everton) 1985/6, 1986/7, (Barcelona) 1987/8, 1988/9 (Tottenham H) 1989/90, 1990/1, 1991/2.
Little, B. (1) (Aston Villa) 1974/5.
Lloyd, L. (4) (Liverpool) 1970/1, 1971/2, (Nottingham Forest) 1979/80.

Lofthouse, N. (33) (Bolton Wanderers) 1950/1, 1951/2, 1952/3, 1953/4, 1954/5, 1955/6, 1958/9.

Lowe, E. (3) (Aston Villa) 1946/7.

Mabbutt, G. (16) (Tottenham Hotspur) 1982/3, 1983/4, 1986/7, 1987/8, 1991/2.

Macdonald, M. (14) (Newcastle United) 1971/2, 1972/3, 1973/4, 1974/5, (Arsenal) 1975/6.

Madeley, P. (24) (Leeds United) 1970/1, 1971/2, 1972/3, 1973/4, 1974/5, 1975/6, 1976/7.

Mannion, W. (26) (Middlesbrough) 1946/7, 1947/8, 1948/9, 1949/50, 1950/1, 1951/2.

Mariner, P. (35) (Ipswich Town) 1976/7, 1977/8, 1979/80, 1980/1, 1981/2, 1982/3, 1983/4, 1984/5 (Arsenal)

Marsh, R. (9) (QPR) 1971/2 (Manchester City) 1972/3.

Martin, A. (17) (West Ham United) 1980/1, 1981/2, 1982/3, 1983/4, 1984/5, 1985/6, 1986/7.

Marwood, B. (1) (Arsenal) 1988/9.

Matthews, R. (5) (Coventry City) 1955/6, 1956/7.

Matthews, S. (37) (Stoke City) 1946/7, (Blackpool) 1947/8, 1948/9, 1949/50, 1950/1, 1953/4, 1954/5, 1955/6, 1956/7.

McDermott, T. (25) (Liverpool) 1977/8, 1978/9, 1979/80, 1980/1, 1981/2.

McDonald, C. (8) (Burnley) 1957/8, 1958/9.

McFarland, R. (28) (Derby County) 1970/1, 1971/2, 1972/3, 1973/4, 1975/6, 1976/7.

McGarry, W. (4) (Huddersfield Town) 1953/4, 1955/6.

McGuinness, W. (2) (Manchester United) 1958/9.

McMahon, S. (17) (Liverpool) 1987/8, 1988/9, 1989/90, 1990/1.

McManaman, S. (18) (Liverpool) 1994/95, 1995/96, 1996/97.

McNab, R. (4) (Arsenal) 1968/9.

McNeil, M. (9) (Middlesbrough) 1960/1, 1961/2.

Martyn, A.N. (4) (Crystal Palace) 1991/2, 1992/93 (Leeds United) 1996/97..

Meadows, J. (1) (Manchester City) 1954/5.

Medley, L. (Tottenham Hotspur) 1950/1, 1951/2.

Melia, J. (2) (Liverpool) 1962/3.

Merrick, G. (23) (Birmingham City) 1951/2, 1952/3, 1953/4.

Merson, P. C. (15) (Arsenal) 1991/2, 1992/93, 1993/94, 1996/97.

Metcalfe, V. (2) (Huddersfield Town) 1950/1.

Milburn, J. (13) (Newcastle United) 1948/9, 1949/50, 1950/1, 1951/2, 1955/6.

Miller, B. (1) (Burnley) 1960/1.

Mills, M. (42) (Ipswich Town) 1972/3, 1975/6, 1976/7, 1977/8, 1978/9, 1979/80, 1980/1, 1981/2.

Milne, G. (14) (Liverpool) 1962/3, 1963/4, 1964/5.

Milton, C. A. (1) (Arsenal) 1951/2.

Moore, R. (108) (West Ham United) 1961/2, 1962/3, 1963/4, 1964/5, 1965/6, 1966/7, 1967/8, 1968/9, 1969/70, 1970/1, 1971/2, 1972/3, 1973/4.

Morley, A. (6) (Aston Villa) 1981/2, 1982/3.

Morris, J. (3) (Derby County) 1948/9, 1949/50.

Mortensen, S. (25) (Blackpool) 1946/7, 1947/8, 1948/9, 1949/50, 1950/1, 1953/4.

Mozley, B. (3) (Derby County) 1949/50.

Mullen, J. (12) (Wolverhampton Wanderers) 1946/7, 1948/9, 1949/50, 1953/4.

Mullery, A. (35) (Tottenham Hotspur) 1964/5, 1966/7, 1967/8, 1968/9, 1969/70, 1970/1, 1971/2.

Neal, P. (50) (Liverpool) 1975/6, 1976/7, 1977/8, 1978/9, 1979/80, 1980/1, 1981/2, 1982/3, 1983/4.

Neville, G. A. (22) (Manchester United) 1994/95, 1995/96, 1996/97.

Neville, P. J. (6) (Manchester United) 1995/96, 1996/97.

Newton, K. (27) (Blackburn Rovers) 1965/6, 1966/7, 1967/8, 1968/9, 1969/70, (Everton).

Nicholls, J. (2) (West Bromwich Albion) 1953/4.
Nicholson, W. (1) (Tottenham Hotspur) 1950/1.
Nish, D. (5) (Derby County) 1972/3, 1973/4.
Norman, M. (23) (Tottenham Hotspur) 1961/2, 1962/3, 1963/4, 1964/5.

O'Grady, M. (2) (Huddersfield Town) 1962/3, 1968/9 (Leeds United).
Osgood, P. (4) (Chelsea) 1969/70, 1973/4.
Osman, R. (11) (Ipswich Town) 1979/80, 1980/1, 1981/2, 1982/3, 1983/4.
Owen, S. (3) (Luton Town) 1953/4.

Paine, T. (19) (Southampton) 1962/3, 1963/4, 1964/5, 1965/6.
Pallister, G. (22) (Middlesbrough) 1987/8, 1990/91 (Manchester United), 1991/2, 1992/93, 1993/94, 1994/95, 1995/96, 1996/97.
Palmer, C. L. (18) (Sheffield Wednesday) 1991/2, 1992/93, 1993/94.
Parker, P. A. (19) (QPR) 1988/9, 1989/90, 1990/1, (Manchester United) 1991/2, 1993/94.
Parkes, P. (1) (QPR) 1973/4.
Parry, R. (2) (Bolton Wanderers) 1959/60.
Peacock, A. (6) (Middlesbrough) 1961/2, 1962/3, 1965/6 (Leeds United).
Pearce, S. (76) (Nottingham Forest) 1986/7, 1987/8, 1988/9, 1989/90, 1990/1, 1991/2, 1992/93, 1993/94, 1994/95, 1995/96, 1996/97.
Person, Stan (8) (Manchester United) 1947/8, 1948/9, 1949/50, 1950/1, 1951/2.
Pearson, Stuart (15) (Manchester United) 1975/6, 1976/7, 1977/8.
Pegg, D. (1) (Manchester United) 1956/7.
Pejic, M. (4) (Stoke City) 1973/4.
Perry, W. (3) (Blackpool) 1955/6.
Perryman, S. (1) (Tottenham Hotspur) 1981/2.
Peters, M. (67) (West Ham United) 1965/6, 1966/7, 1967/8, 1968/9, 1969/70, (Tottenham Hotspur) 1970/1, 1971/2, 1972/3, 1973/4.
Phelan, M. C. (1) (Manchester United) 1989/90.
Phillips, L. (3) (Portsmouth) 1951/2, 1954/5.
Pickering, F. (3) (Everton) 1963/4, 1964/5.
Pickering, N. (1) (Sunderland) 1982/3.
Pilkington, B. (1) (Burnley) 1954/5.
Platt, D. (62) (Aston Villa) 1989/90, 1990/1, (Bari) 1991/2 (Juventus), 1992/93 (Sampdoria) 1993/94, 1994/95, (Arsenal) 1995/96.
Pointer, R. (3) (Burnley) 1961/2.
Pye, J. (1) (Wolverhampton Wanderers) 1949/50.

Quixall, A. (5) (Sheffield Wednesday) 1953/4, 1954/5.

Radford, J. (2) (Arsenal) 1968/9, 1971/2.
Ramsey, A. (32) (Southampton) 1948/9, 1949/50, (Tottenham Hotspur) 1950/1, 1951/2, 1952/3, 1953/4.
Reaney, P. (3) (Leeds United) 1968/9, 1969/70, 1970/1.
Redknapp, J. F. (8) (Liverpool) 1995/96, 1996/97.
Reeves, K. (2) (Norwich City) 1979/80.
Regis, C. (5) (West Bromwich Albion) 1981/2, 1982/3, (Coventry City).
Reid, P. (13) (Everton) 1984/5, 1985/6, 1986/7.
Revie, D. (6) (Manchester City) 1954/5, 1955/6, 1956/7.
Richards, J. (1) (Wolverhampton Wanderers) 1972/3.
Richardson, K. (1) (Aston Villa) 1993/94.
Rickaby, S. (1) (West Bromwich Albion) 1953/4.
Rimmer, J. (1) (Arsenal) 1975/6.
Ripley, S. E. (1) (Blackburn Rovers) 1993/94.
Rix, G. (17) (Arsenal) 1980/1, 1981/2, 1982/3, 1983/4.
Robb, G. (1) (Tottenham Hotspur) 1953/4.

Roberts, G. (6) (Tottenham Hotspur) 1982/3, 1983/4.
Robson, B.(90) (West Bromwich Albion) 1979/80, 1980/1, 1981/2, (Manchester United) 1982/3, 1983/4, 1984/5, 1985/6, 1986/7, 1987/8, 1988/9, 1989/90, 1990/1, 1991/2.
Robson, R. (20) (West Bromwich Albion) 1957/8, 1959/60, 1960/1, 1961/2.
Rocastle, D. (14) (Arsenal) 1988/9, 1989/90, 1991/2.
Rowley, J. (6) (Manchester United) 1948/9, 1949/50, 1951/2.
Royle, J. (6) (Everton) 1970/1, 1972/3, (Manchester City) 1975/6, 1976/7.
Ruddock, N. (1) (Liverpool) 1994/95.

Sadler, D. (4) (Manchester United) 1967/8, 1969/70, 1970/1.
Salako, J. A. (5) (Crystal Palace) 1990/91, 1991/2.
Sansom, K. (86) (Crystal Palace) 1978/9, 1979/80, 1980/1, (Arsenal) 1981/2, 1982/3, 1983/4, 1984/5, 1985/6, 1986/7, 1987/8.
Scales, J. R. (3) (Liverpool) 1994/95.
Scholes, P. (3) (Manchester United) 1996/97.
Scott, L. (17) (Arsenal) 1946/7, 1947/8. 1948/9.
Seaman, D. A. (36) (QPR) 1988/9, 1989/90, 1990/1 (Arsenal), 1991/2, 1993/94, 1994/95, 1995/96, 1996/97.
Sewell, J. (6) (Sheffield Wednesday) 1951/2, 1952/3, 1953/4.
Shackleton, L. (5) (Sunderland) 1948/9, 1949/50, 1954/5.
Sharpe, L. S. (8) (Manchester United) 1990/1, 1992/93, 1993/94.
Shaw, G. (5) (Sheffield United) 1958/9, 1962/3.
Shearer, A. (35) (Southampton) 1991/2 (Blackburn Rovers), 1992/93, 1993/94, 1994/95, 1995/96 (Newcastle United) 1996/97.
Shellito, K. (1) (Chelsea) 1962/3.
Sheringham, E. (28) (Tottenham Hotspur) 1992/93, 1994/95, 1995/96, 1996/97.
Shilton, P. (125) (Leicester City) 1970/1, 1971/2, 1972/3, 1973/4, 1974/5, (Stoke City) 1976/7, (Nottingham Forest) 1977/8, 1978/9, 1979/80, 1980/1, 1981/2, (Southampton) 1982/3, 1983/4, 1984/5, 1985/6, 1986/7, (Derby County) 1987/8, 1988/9, 1989/90.
Shimwell, E. (1) (Blackpool) 1948/9.
Sillett, P. (3) (Chelsea) 1954/5.
Sinton, A. (12) (QPR) 1991/2, 1992/93 (Sheffield Wednesday) 1993/94.
Slater, W. (12) (Wolverhampton Wanderers) 1954/5, 1957/8, 1958/9, 1959/60.
Smith, A. M. (13) (Arsenal) 1988/9, 1990/1, 1991/2.
Smith, L. (6) (Arsenal) 1950/1, 1951/2, 1952/3.
Smith, R. (15) (Tottenham Hotspur) 1960/1, 1961/2, 1962/3, 1963/4.
Smith, Tom (1) (Liverpool) 1970/1.
Smith, Trevor (2) (Birmingham City) 1959/60.
Southgate, G. (19) (Aston Villa) 1995/96, 1996/97.
Spink, N. (1) (Aston Villa) 1982/3.
Springett, R. (33) (Sheffield Wednesday) 1959/60, 1960/1, 1961/2, 1962/3, 1965/6.
Staniforth, R. (8) (Huddersfield Town) 1953/4, 1954/5.
Statham, D. (3) (West Bromwich Albion) 1982/3.
Stein, B. (1) (Luton Town) 1983/4.
Stepney, A. (1) (Manchester United) 1967/8.
Sterland, M. (1) (Sheffield Wednesday) 1988/9.
Steven, T. M. (36) (Everton) 1984/5, 1985/6, 1986/7, 1987/8, 1988/9 (Glasgow Rangers) 1989/90, 1990/1, (Marseille) 1991/2.
Stevens, G. A. (7) (Tottenham Hotspur) 1984/5, 1985/6.
Stevens, M. G. (46) (Everton) 1984/5, 1985/6, 1986/7, 1987/8 (Rangers) 1988/9, 1989/90, 1990/1, 1991/2.
Stewart, P. A. (3) (Tottenham Hotspur) 1991/2.
Stiles, N. (28) (Manchester United) 1964/5, 1965/6, 1966/7, 1967/8, 1968/9, 1969/70.
Stone, S. B. (9) (Nottingham Forest) 1995/96.
Storey-Moore, I. (1) (Nottingham Forest) 1969/70.

Storey, P. (19) (Arsenal) 1970/1, 1971/2, 1972/3.
Streten, B. (1) (Luton Town) 1949/50.
Summerbee, M. (8) (Manchester City) 1967/8, 1971/2, 1972/3.
Sunderland, A. (1) (Arsenal) 1979/80.
Swan, P. (19) (Sheffield Wednesday) 1959/60, 1960/1, 1961/2.
Swift, F. (19) (Manchester City) 1946/7, 1947/8, 1948/9.

Talbot, B. (6) (Ipswich Town) 1976/7, 1979/80.
Tambling, R. (3) (Chelsea) 1962/3, 1965/6.
Taylor, E. (1) (Blackpool) 1953/4.
Taylor, J. (2) (Fulham) 1950/1.
Taylor, P. H. (5) (Liverpool) 1947/8.
Taylor, P. J. (4) (Crystal Palace) 1975/6.
Taylor, T. (19) (Manchester United) 1952/3, 1953/4, 1955/6, 1956/7, 1958/9.
Temple, D. (1) (Everton) 1964/5.
Thomas, Danny (2) (Coventry City) 1982/3.
Thomas, Dave (8) (QPR) 1974/5, 1975/6.
Thomas, G. R. (9) (Crystal Palace) 1990/1, 1991/2.
Thomas, M. L. (2) (Arsenal) 1988/9, 1989/90.
Thompson, P. (16) (Liverpool) 1963/4, 1964/5, 1965/6, 1967/8, 1969/70.
Thompson, P. B. (42) (Liverpool) 1975/6, 1976/7, 1978/9, 1979/80, 1980/1, 1981/2, 1982/3.
Thompson, T. (2) (Aston Villa) 1951/2, (Preston North End) 1956/7.
Thomson, R. (8) (Wolverhampton Wanderers) 1963/4, 1964/5.
Todd, C. (27) (Derby County) 1971/2, 1973/4, 1974/5, 1975/6, 1976/7.
Towers, T. (3) (Sunderland) 1975/6.
Tueart, D. (6) (Manchester City) 1974/5, 1976/7.

Ufton, D. (1) (Charlton Athletic) 1953/4.
Unsworth, D. G. (1) (Everton) 1994/95.

Venables, T. (2) (Chelsea) 1964/5.
Venison, B. (2) (Newcastle United) 1994/95.
Viljoen, C. (2) (Ipswich Town) 1974/5.
Viollet, D. (2) (Manchester United) 1959/60, 1961/2.

Waddle, C. R. (62) (Newcastle United) 1984/5, (Tottenham Hotspur) 1985/6, 1986/7, 1987/8, 1988/9, (Marseille) 1989/90, 1990/1, 1991/2.
Waiters, A. (5) (Blackpool) 1963/4, 1964/5.
Walker, D. S. (59) (Nottingham Forest) 1988/9, 1989/90, 1990/1, 1991/2 (Sampdoria) 1992/93, (Sheffield Wednesday) 1993/94.
Walker, I. M. (3) (Tottenham Hotspur) 1995/96, 1996/97.
Wallace, D. L. (1) (Southampton) 1985/6.
Walsh, P. (5) (Luton Town) 1982/3, 1983/4.
Walters, K. M. (1) (Rangers) 1990/91.
Ward, P. (1) (Brighton) 1979/80.
Ward, T. (2) (Derby County) 1947/8, 1948/9.
Watson, D. (12) (Norwich City) 1983/4, 1984/5, 1985/6, 1986/7 (Everton) 1987/8.
Watson D.V. (65) (Sunderland) 1973/4, 1974/5, 1975/6 (Manchester City) 1976/7, 1977/8, (Southampton) 1978/9 (Werder Bremen), 1979/80, (Southampton) 1980/1, 1981/2, (Stoke City).
Watson, W. (4) (Sunderland) 1949/50, 1950/1.
Webb, N. (26) (Nottingham Forest) 1987/8, 1988/9 (Manchester United) 1989/90, 1991/2.
Weller, K. (4) (Leicester City) 1973/4.
West, G. (3) (Everton) 1968/9.
Wheeler, J. (1) (Bolton Wanderers) 1954/5.

White, D. (1) (Manchester City) 1992/93.
Whitworth, S. (7) (Leicester City) 1974/5, 1975/6.
Whymark, T. (1) (Ipswich Town) 1977/8.
Wignall, F. (2) (Nottingham Forest) 1964/5.
Wilcox, J. M. (1) (Blackburn Rovers) 1995/96.
Wilkins, R. (84) (Chelsea) 1975/6, 1976/7, 1977/8, 1978/9, (Manchester United) 1979/80, 1980/1, 1981/2, 1982/3, 1983/4, 1984/5, (AC Milan) 1985/6, 1986/7.
Williams, B. (24) (Wolverhampton Wanderers) 1948/9, 1949/50, 1950/1, 1951/2, 1954/5, 1955/6.
Williams, S. (6) (Southampton) 1982/3, 1983/4, 1984/5.
Willis, A. (1) (Tottenham Hotspur) 1951/2.
Wilshaw, D. (12) (Wolverhampton Wanderers) 1953/4, 1954/5, 1955/6, 1956/7.
Wilson, R. (63) (Huddersfield Town) 1959/60, 1961/2, 1962/3, 1963/4, 1964/5, (Everton) 1965/6, 1966/7, 1967/8.
Winterburn, N. (2) (Arsenal) 1989/90, 1992/93.
Wise, D. F. (12) (Chelsea) 1990/91, 1993/94, 1994/95, 1995/96.
Withe, P. (11) (Aston Villa) 1980/1, 1981/2, 1982/3, 1983/4, 1984/5.
Wood, R. (3) (Manchester United) 1954/5, 1955/6.
Woodcock, A. (42) (Nottingham Forest) 1977/8, 1978/9, 1979/80 (FC Cologne) 1980/1, 1981/2, (Arsenal) 1982/3, 1983/4, 1984/5, 1985/6.
Woods, C.C.E. (43) (Norwich City) 1984/5, 1985/6, 1986/7, (Rangers) 1987/8, 1988/9, 1989/90, 1990/1, (Sheffield Wednesday) 1991/2, 1992/93.
Worthington, F. (8) (Leicester City) 1973/4, 1974/5.
Wright, I. E. (27) (Crystal Palace) 1990/1, 1991/2 (Arsenal) 1992/93, 1993/94, 1994/95, 1996/97.
Wright M. (45) (Southampton) 1983/4, 1984/5, 1985/6, 1986/7, (Derby County) 1987/8, 1988/9, 1989/90, 1990/1, (Liverpool) 1991/2, 1992/93, 1995/96.
Wright, T. (11) (Everton) 1967/8, 1968/9, 1969/70.
Wright, W. (105) (Wolverhampton Wanderers) 1946/7, 1947/8, 1948/9, 1949/50, 1950/1, 1951/2, 1952/3, 1953/4, 1954/5, 1955/6, 1956/7, 1957/8, 1958/9.
Young, G. (1) (Sheffield Wednesday) 1964/5.

NORTHERN IRELAND
Aherne, T. (4) (Belfast Celtic) 1946/7, 1947/8, 1948/9, 1949/50 (Luton Town).
Anderson, T. (22) (Manchester United) 1972/3, 1973/4, 1974/5, (Swindon Town) 1975/6, 1976/7, 1977/8, (Peterborough United) 1978/9.
Armstrong, G. (63) (Tottenham Hotspur) 1976/7, 1977/8, 1978/9, 1979/80, 1980/1, (Watford) 1981/2, 1982/3, (Real Mallorca) 1983/4, 1984/5, (West Bromwich Albion) 1985/6 (Chesterfield).

Barr, H. (3) (Linfield) 1961/2, 1962/3, (Coventry City).
Best, G. (37) (Manchester United) 1963/4, 1964/5, 1965/6, 1966/7, 1967/8, 1968/9, 1969/70, 1970/1, 1971/2, 1972/3, 1973/4 (Fulham) 1976/7, 1977/8.
Bingham, W. (56) (Sunderland) 1950/1, 1951/2, 1952/3, 1953/4, 1954/5, 1955/6, 1956/7, 1957/8, 1958/9 (Luton Town) 1959/60, 1960/1 (Everton) 1961/2, 1962/3, 1963/4 (Port Vale).
Black, K. (30) (Luton Town) 1987/8, 1988/9, 1989/90, 1990/1, (Nottingham Forest) 1991/2, 1992/93, 1993/94.
Blair, R. (5) (Oldham Athletic) 1974/5, 1975/6.
Blanchflower, D. (54) (Barnsley) 1949/50, 1950/1 (Aston Villa) 1951/2, 1952/3, 1953/4, 1954/5, (Tottenham Hotspur) 1955/6, 1956/7, 1957/8, 1958/9, 1959/60, 1960/1, 1961/2, 1962/3.
Blanchflower, J. (12) (Manchester United) 1953/4, 1954/5, 1955/6, 1956/7, 1957/8.
Bowler, G. (3) (Hull City) 1949/50.
Braithwaite, R. (10) (Linfield) 1961/2, 1962/3 (Middlesbrough) 1963/4, 1964/5.

243

Brennan, R. (5) (Luton Town) 1948/9, 1949/50 (Birmingham City) (Fulham), 1950/1.

Briggs, R. (2) (Manchester United) 1961/2, 1964/5 (Swansea).

Brotherston, N. (27) (Blackburn Rovers) 1979/80, 1980/1, 1981/2, 1982/3, 1983/4, 1984/5.

Bruce, W. (2) (Glentoran) 1960/1, 1966/7.

Campbell, A. (2) (Crusaders) 1962/3, 1964/5.

Campbell, D. A. (10) (Nottingham Forest) 1985/6, 1986/7, 1987/8 (Charlton Athletic).

Campbell, J. (2) (Fulham) 1950/1.

Campbell, R. M. (2) (Bradford City) 1981/2.

Campbell, W. (6) (Dundee) 1967/8, 1968/9, 1969/70.

Carey, J. (7) (Manchester United) 1946/7, 1947/8, 1948/9.

Carroll, R. E. (1) (Wigan Ath) 1996/97.

Casey, T. (12) (Newcastle United) 1954/5, 1955/6, 1956/7, 1957/8, 1958/9, (Portsmouth).

Caskey, A. (7) (Derby County) 1978/9, 1979/80, 1981/2 (Tulsa Roughnecks).

Cassidy, T. (24) (Newcastle United) 1970/1, 1971/2, 1973/4, 1974/5, 1975/6, 1976/7, 1979/80 (Burnley) 1980/1, 1981/2.

Caughey, M. (2) (Linfield) 1985/6.

Clarke, C. J. (38) (Bournemouth) 1985/6, 1986/7 (Southampton) 1987/8, 1988/9, 1989/90, 1990/1 (Portsmouth), 1991/2, 1992/93.

Cleary, J. (5) (Glentoran) 1981/2, 1982/3, 1983/4, 1984/5.

Clements, D. (48) (Coventry City) 1964/5, 1965/6, 1966/7, 1967/8, 1968/9, 1969/70, 1970/1, 1971/2 (Sheffield Wednesday) 1972/3 (Everton) 1973/4, 1974/5, 1975/6 (New York Cosmos).

Cochrane, D. (10) (Leeds United) 1946/7, 1947/8, 1948/9, 1949/50.

Cochrane, T. (26) (Coleraine) 1975/6, (Burnley) 1977/8, 1978/9, (Middlesbrough) 1979/80, 1980/1, 1981/2, (Gillingham) 1983/4.

Cowan, J. (1) (Newcastle United) 1969/70.

Coyle, F. (4) (Coleraine) 1955/6, 1956/7, 1957/8 (Nottingham Forest).

Coyle, L. (1) (Derry C) 1988/9.

Coyle, R. (5) (Sheffield Wednesday) 1972/3, 1973/4.

Craig, D. (25) (Newcastle United) 1966/7, 1967/8, 1968/9, 1969/70, 1970/1, 1971/2, 1972/3, 1973/4, 1974/5.

Crossan, E. (3) (Blackburn Rovers) 1949/50, 1950/1, 1954/5.

Crossan, J. (23) (Rotterdam Sparta) 1959/60, 1962/3 (Sunderland), 1963/4, 1964/5, (Manchester City) 1965/6, 1966/7, 1967/8 (Middlesbrough).

Cunningham, W. (30) (St Mirren) 1950/1, 1952/3, 1953/4, 1954/5, 1955/6, 1956/7, (Leicester City) 1957/8, 1958/9, 1959/60, 1960/1 (Dunfermline Athletic) 1961/2.

Cush, W. (26) (Glentoran) 1950/1, 1953/4, 1956/7, 1957/8 (Leeds United) 1958/9, 1959/60, 1960/1 (Portadown) 1961/2.

D'Arcy, S. (5) (Chelsea) 1951/2, 1952/3 (Brentford).

Davison, A. J. (2) (Bolton Wanderers) 1995/96 (Bradford City) 1996/97.

Dennison, R. (18) (Wolverhampton Wanderers) 1987/8, 1988/9, 1989/90, 1990/1, 1991/2, 1992/93, 1993/94, 1996/97.

Devine, J. (1) (Glentoran) 1989/90.

Dickson, D. (4) (Coleraine) 1969/70, 1972/3.

Dickson, T. (1) (Linfield) 1956/7.

Dickson, W. (12) (Chelsea) 1950/1, 1951/2, 1952/3 (Arsenal) 1953/4, 1954/5.

Doherty, L. (2) (Linfield) 1984/5, 1987/8.

Doherty, P. (6) (Derby County) 1946/7, (Huddersfield Town) 1947/8, 1948/9, (Doncaster Rovers) 1950/1.

Donaghy, M. (91) (Luton Town) 1979/80, 1980/1, 1981/2, 1982/3, 1983/4, 1984/5, 1985/6, 1986/7, 1987/8, (Manchester United) 1988/9, 1989/90, 1990/1, 1991/2 (Chelsea) 1992/93, 1993/94.

Dougan, D. (43) (Portsmouth) 1957/8, 1959/60, (Blackburn Rovers), 1960/1, 1962/3 (Aston Villa) 1965/6 (Leicester City), 1966/7 (Wolverhampton Wanderers) 1967/8, 1968/9, 1969/70, 1970/1, 1971/2, 1972/3.

Douglas, J. P. (1) (Belfast Celtic) 1946/7.

Dowd, H. (3) (Glentoran) 1972/3, 1974/5 (Sheffield Wednesday).

Dowie, I. (44) (Luton Town) 1989/90, 1990/1, (Southampton) 1991/2, 1992/93, 1993/94, 1994/95 (Crystal Palace) 1995/96 (West Ham), 1996/97.

Dunlop, G. (4) (Linfield) 1984/5, 1986/7.

Eglington, T. (6) (Everton) 1946/7, 1947/8, 1948/9.

Elder, A. (40) (Burnley) 1959/60, 1960/1, 1961/2, 1962/3, 1963/4, 1964/5, 1965/6, 1966/7, (Stoke City) 1967/8, 1968/9, 1969/70.

Farrell, P. (7) (Everton) 1946/7, 1947/8, 1948/9.

Feeney, J. (2) (Linfield) 1946/7 (Swansea City) 1949/50.

Feeney, W. (1) (Glentoran) 1975/6.

Ferguson, W. (2) (Linfield) 1965/6, 1966/7.

Ferris, R. (3) (Birmingham City) 1949/50, 1950/1, 1951/2.

Fettis, A. (18) (Hull City) 1991/2, 1992/93, 1993/94, 1994/95, (Nottingham Forest) 1995/96, 1996/97.

Finney, T. (14) (Sunderland) 1974/5, 1975/6 (Cambridge United), 1979/80.

Fleming, J. G. (31) (Nottingham Forest) 1986/7, 1987/8, 1988/9 (Manchester City) 1989/90, 1990/1 (Barnsley), 1991/2, 1992/93, 1993/94, 1994/95.

Forde, T. (4) (Ards) 1958/9, 1960/1.

Gallogly, C. (2) (Huddersfield Town) 1950/1.

Garton, R. (1) (Oxford United) 1968/9.

Gillespie, K. R. (17) (Manchester United) 1994/95 (Newcastle United) 1995/96, 1996/97.

Gorman, W. (4) (Brentford) 1946/7, 1947/8.

Graham, W. (14) (Doncaster Rovers) 1950/1, 1951/2, 1952/3, 1953/4, 1954/5, 1955/6, 1958/9.

Gray, P. (20) (Luton Town) 1992/93, (Sunderland) 1993/94, 1994/95, 1995/96 (Nancy) 1996/97.

Gregg, H. (25) (Doncaster Rovers) 1953/4, 1956/7, 1957/8, (Manchester United) 1958/9, 1959/60, 1960/1, 1961/2, 1963/4.

Griffin, D. J. (5) (St Johnstone) 1995/96, 1996/97.

Hamilton, B. (50) (Linfield) 1968/9, 1970/1, 1971/2 (Ipswich Town), 1972/3, 1973/4, 1974/5, 1975/6 (Everton) 1976/7, 1977/8, (Millwall), 1978/9 (Swindon Town).

Hamilton, W. (41) (QPR) 1977/8, 1979/80 (Burnley) 1980/1, 1981/2, 1982/3, 1983/4, 1984/5, (Oxford United) 1985/6.

Harkin, T. (5) (Southport) 1967/8, 1968/9 (Shrewsbury Town), 1969/70, 1970/1.

Harvey, M. (34) (Sunderland) 1960/1, 1961/2, 1962/3, 1963/4, 1964/5, 1965/6, 1966/7, 1967/8, 1968/9, 1969/70, 1970/1.

Hatton, S. (2) (Linfield) 1962/3.

Healy, F. (4) (Coleraine) 1981/2 (Glentoran) 1982/3.

Hegan, D. (7) (West Bromwich Albion) 1969/70, 1971/2 (Wolverhampton Wanderers) 1972/3.

Hill, C. F. (22) (Sheffield United), 1989/90, 1990/1, 1991/2, 1994/95 (Leicester City) 1995/96, 1996/97.

Hill, J. (7) (Norwich City) 1958/9, 1959/60, 1960/1, (Everton) 1961/2, 1963/4.

Hinton, E. (7) (Fulham) 1946/7, 1947/8 (Millwall) 1950/1.

Horlock, K. (9) (Swindon Town), 1994/95 (Manchester City) 1996/97.

Hughes, M. E. (37) (Manchester City) 1991/2 (Strasbourg) 1992/93, 1993/94, 1994/95, 1995/96 (West Ham United) 1996/97.
Hughes, P. (3) (Bury) 1986/7.
Hughes, W. (1) (Bolton Wanderers) 1950/1.
Humphries, W. (14) (Ards) 1961/2 (Coventry City) 1962/3, 1963/4, 1964/5 (Swansea Town).
Hunter, A. (53) (Blackburn Rovers) 1969/70, 1970/1, 1971/2 (Ipswich Town) 1972/3, 1973/4, 1974/5, 1975/6, 1976/7, 1977/8, 1978/9, 1979/80.
Hunter, B. V. (11) (Wrexham) 1994/95, 1995/96 (Reading) 1996/97.

Irvine, R. (8) (Linfield) 1961/2, 1962/3 (Stoke City) 1964/5.
Irvine, W. (23) (Burnley) 1962/3, 1964/5, 1965/6, 1966/7, 1967/8, 1968/9 (Preston North End) (Brighton & Hove Albion) 1971/2.

Jackson, T. (35) (Everton) 1968/9, 1969/70, 1970/1 (Nottingham Forest) 1971/2, 1972/3, 1973/4, 1974/5 (Manchester United) 1975/6, 1976/7.
Jamison, A. (1) (Glentoran) 1975/6.
Jenkins, I. (2) (Chester City) 1996/97.
Jennings, P. (119) (Watford) 1963/4, 1964/5, (Tottenham Hotspur) 1965/6, 1966/7, 1967/8, 1968/9, 1969/70, 1970/1, 1971/2, 1972/3, 1973/4, 1974/5, 1975/6, 1976/7, (Arsenal) 1977/8, 1978/9, 1979/80, 1980/1, 1981/2, 1982/3, 1983/4, 1984/5, (Tottenham Hotspur) 1985/6.
Johnston, W. (1) (Glentoran) 1961/2, (Oldham Athletic) 1965/6.
Jones, J. (3) (Glenavon) 1955/6, 1956/7.

Keane, T. (1) (Swansea Town) 1948/9.
Kee, P. V. (9) (Oxford United) 1989/90, 1990/91, (Ards) 1994/95.
Keith, R. (23) (Newcastle United) 1957/8, 1958/9, 1959/60, 1960/1, 1961/2.
Kelly, H. (4) (Fulham) 1949/50 (Southampton) 1950/1.
Kelly, P. (1) (Barnsley) 1949/50.

Lawther, I. (4) (Sunderland) 1959/60, 1960/1, 1961/2 (Blackburn Rovers).
Lockhart, N. (8) (Linfield) 1946/7, 1949/50, (Coventry City) 1950/1, 1951/2, 1953/4, (Aston Villa) 1954/5, 1955/6.
Lennon, N. F. (15) (Crewe Alexandra) 1993/94, 1994/95, (Leicester City) 1995/96, 1996/97.
Lomas, S. M. (22) (Manchester City) 1993/94, 1994/95, 1995/96 (West Ham United) 1996/97.
Lutton, B. (6) (Wolverhampton Wanderers) 1969/70, 1972/3 (West Ham United) 1973/4.

Magill, E. (26) (Arsenal) 1961/2, 1962/3, 1963/4, 1964/5, 1965/6 (Brighton & Hove Albion).
Magilton, J. (36) (Oxford United) 1990/1, 1991/2, 1992/93, (Southampton) 1993/94, 1994/95, 1995/96, 1996/97.
Martin, C. (6) (Glentoran) 1946/7, 1947/8 (Leeds United) 1948/9 (Aston Villa) 1949/50.
McAdams, W. (15) (Manchester City) 1953/4, 1954/5, 1956/7, 1957/8, 1960/1 (Bolton Wanderers) 1961/2 (Leeds United).
McAlinden, J. (2) (Portsmouth) 1946/7, 1948/9, (Southend United).
McBride, S. (4) (Glenavon) 1990/1, 1991/2.
McCabe, J. (6) (Leeds United) 1948/9, 1949/50, 1950/1, 1952/3, 1953/4.
McCarthy, J. D. (4) (Port Vale) 1995/96, 1996/97.
McCavana, T. (3) (Coleraine) 1954/5, 1955/6.
McCleary, J. W. (1) (Cliftonville) 1954/5.
McClelland, J. (6) (Arsenal) 1960/1, 1965/6 (Fulham).

McClelland, J. (53) (Mansfield Town) 1979/80, 1980/1, 1981/2 (Rangers) 1982/3, 1983/4, 1984/5 (Watford) 1985/6, 1986/7, 1987/8, 1988/9 (Leeds U) 1989/90.

McCourt, F. (6) (Manchester City) 1951/2, 1952/3.

McCoy, R. (1) (Coleraine) 1986/7.

McCreery, D. (67) (Manchester United) 1975/6, 1976/7, 1977/8, 1978/9, 1979/80 (QPR) 1980/1 (Tulsa Roughnecks) 1981/2, 1982/3 (Newcastle United), 1983/4, 1984/5, 1985/6, 1986/7, 1987/8, 1988/9 (Hearts) 1989/90.

McCrory, S. (1) (Southend United) 1957/8.

McCullough, W. (10) (Arsenal) 1960/1, 1962/3, 1963/4, 1964/5, 1966/7, (Millwall).

McCurdy, C. (1) (Linfield) 1979/80.

McDonald, A. (52) (QPR) 1985/6, 1986/7, 1987/8, 1988/9, 1990/1, 1991/2, 1992/93, 1993/94, 1994/95, 1995/96.

McElhinney, G. (6) (Bolton Wanderers) 1983/4, 1984/5.

McFaul, I. (6) (Linfield) 1966/7, 1969/70 (Newcastle United) 1970/1, 1971/2, 1972/3, 1973/4.

McGarry, J. K. (3) (Cliftonville) 1950/1.

McGaughey, M. (1) (Linfield) 1984/5.

McGibbon, P.C.G. (5) (Manchester United) 1994/95, 1995/96, 1996/97.

McGrath, R. (21) (Tottenham Hotspur) 1973/4, 1974/5, 1975/6 (Manchester United) 1976/7, 1977/8, 1978/9.

McIlroy, J. (55) (Burnley) 1951/2, 1952/3, 1953/4, 1954/5, 1955/6, 1956/7, 1957/8, 1958/9, 1959/60, 1960/1, 1961/2, 1962/3, 1965/6 (Stoke City).

McIlroy, S. B. (88) (Manchester United) 1971/2, 1973/4, 1974/5, 1975/6, 1976/7, 1977/8, 1978/9, 1979/80, 1980/1, 1981/2, (Stoke City), 1982/3, 1983/4, 1984/5 (Manchester City) 1985/6, 1986/7.

McKeag, W. (2) (Glentoran) 1967/8.

McKenna, J. (7) (Huddersfield Town) 1949/50, 1950/1, 1951/2.

McKenzie, R. (1) (Airdrieonians) 1966/7.

McKinney, W. (1) (Falkirk) 1965/6.

McKnight, A. (10) (Celtic) 1987/8, (West Ham United) 1988/9.

McLaughlin, J. (12) (Shrewsbury Town) 1961/2, 1962/3 (Swansea City), 1963/4, 1964/5, 1965/6.

McMahon, G. J. (14) (Tottenham Hotspur) 1994/95, 1995/96 (Stoke City) 1996/97.

McMichael, A. (39) (Newcastle United) 1949/50, 1950/1, 1951/2, 1952/3, 1953/4, 1954/5, 1955/6, 1956/7, 1957/8, 1958/9, 1959/60.

McMillan, S. (2) (Manchester United) 1962/3.

McMordie, E. (21) (Middlesbrough) 1968/9, 1969/70, 1970/1, 1971/2, 1972/3.

McMorran, E. (15) (Belfast Celtic) 1946/7 (Barnsley) 1950/1, 1951/2, 1952/3, (Doncaster Rovers) 1953/4, 1955/6, 1956/7.

McNally, B. A. (5) (Shrewsbury Town) 1985/6, 1986/7, 1987/8.

McParland, P. (34) (Aston Villa) 1953/4, 1954/5, 1955/6, 1956/7, 1957/8, 1958/9, 1959/60, 1960/1, 1961/2 (Wolverhampton Wanderers).

Montgomery, F. J. (1) (Coleraine) 1954/5.

Moore, C. (1) (Glentoran) 1948/9.

Moreland, V. (6) (Derby County) 1978/9, 1979/80.

Morgan, S. (18) (Port Vale) 1971/2, 1972/3, 1973/4 (Aston Villa), 1974/5, 1975/6 (Brighton & Hove Albion) (Sparta Rotterdam) 1978/9.

Morrow, S. J. (27) (Arsenal) 1989/90, 1990/1, 1991/2, 1992/93, 1993/94, 1994/95, 1995/96 (Queens Park Rangers) 1996/97.

Mullan, G. (4) (Glentoran) 1982/3.

Mulryne, P. P. (3) (Manchester United) 1996/97.

Napier, R. (1) (Bolton Wanderers) 1965/6.

Neill, T. (59) (Arsenal) 1960/1, 1961/2, 1962/3, 1963/4, 1964/5, 1965/6, 1966/7, 1967/8, 1968/9, 1969/70 (Hull City) 1970/1, 1971/2, 1972/3.

Nelson, S. (51) (Arsenal) 1969/70, 1970/1, 1971/2, 1972/3, 1973/4, 1974/5, 1975/6, 1976/7, 1977/8, 1978/9, 1979/80, 1980/1, 1981/2 (Brighton & Hove Albion).

Nicholl, C. (51) (Aston Villa) 1974/5, 1975/6, 1976/7 (Southampton) 1977/8, 1978/9, 1979/80, 1980/1, 1981/2, 1982/3 (Grimsby Town) 1983/4.

Nicholl, J. M. (73) (Manchester United) 1975/6, 1976/7, 1977/8, 1978/9, 1979/80, 1980/1, 1981/2 (Toronto Blizzard) 1982/3 (Sunderland) (Toronto Blizzard) (Rangers) 1983/4 (Toronto Blizzard) 1984/5 (West Bromwich Albion) 1985/6.

Nicholson, J. (41) (Manchester United) 1960/1, 1961/2, 1962/3, 1964/5, (Huddersfield Town) 1965/6, 1966/7, 1967/8, 1968/9, 1969/70, 1970/1, 1971/2.

Nolan, I. R. (5) (Sheffield Wednesday) 1996/97.

O'Boyle, G. (10) (Dunfermline Athletic) 1993/94 (St Johnstone) 1994/95, 1995/96, 1996/97.

O'Doherty, A. (2) (Coleraine) 1969/70.

O'Driscoll, J. (3) (Swansea City) 1948/9.

O'Kane, L. (20) (Nottingham Forest) 1969/70, 1970/1, 1971/2, 1972/3, 1973/4, 1974/5.

O'Neill, C. (3) (Motherwell) 1988/9, 1989/90, 1990/91.

O'Neill, H. M. (64) (Distillery) 1971/2 (Nottingham Forest) 1972/3, 1973/4, 1974/5, 1975/6, 1976/7, 1977/8, 1978/9, 1979/80, 1980/1 (Norwich City) 1981/2 (Manchester City) (Norwich City) 1982/3 (Notts County) 1983/4, 1984/5.

O'Neill, J. (1) (Sunderland) 1961/2.

O'Neill, J. (39) (Leicester City) 1979/80, 1980/1, 1981/2, 1982/3, 1983/4, 1984/5, 1985/6.

O'Neill, M. A. (31) (Newcastle United) 1987/8, 1988/9 (Dundee United) 1989/90, 1990/1, 1991/2, 1992/93, (Hibernian) 1993/94, 1994/95, 1995/96 (Coventry City) 1996/97.

Parke, J. (13) (Linfield) 1963/4 (Hibernian), 1964/5 (Sunderland), 1965/6, 1966/7, 1967/8.

Patterson, D. J. (10) (Crystal Palace) 1993/94, 1994/95, (Luton Town) 1995/96.

Peacock, R. (31) (Celtic) 1951/2, 1952/3, 1953/4, 1954/5, 1955/6, 1956/7, 1957/8, 1958/9, 1959/60, 1960/1 (Coleraine) 1961/2.

Penney, S. (17) (Brighton & Hove Albion) 1984/5, 1985/6, 1986/7, 1987/8, 1988/9.

Platt, J. A. (23) (Middlesbrough) 1975/6, 1977/8, 1979/80, 1980/1, 1981/2, 1982/3, (Ballymena United) 1983/4 (Coleraine) 1985/6.

Quinn, J. M. (46) (Blackburn Rovers) 1984/5, 1985/6, 1986/7, 1987/8 (Leicester) 1988/9 (Bradford City) 1989/90 (West Ham United), 1990/1, (Bournemouth) 1991/2 (Reading) 1992/93, 1993/94, 1994/95, 1995/96.

Quinn, S. J. (8) (Blackpool) 1995/96, 1996/97.

Rafferty, P. (1) (Linfield) 1979/80.

Ramsey, P. (14) (Leicester City) 1983/4, 1984/5, 1985/6, 1986/7, 1987/8, 1988/9.

Rice, P. (49) (Arsenal) 1968/9, 1969/70, 1970/1, 1971/2, 1972/3, 1973/4, 1974/5, 1975/6, 1976/7, 1977/8, 1978/9, 1979/80.

Robinson, S. (1) (AFC Bournemouth) 1996/97.

Rogan, A. (18) (Celtic) 1987/8, 1988/9, 1989/90, 1990/1 (Sunderland) 1991/2 (Millwall) 1996/97.

Ross, E. (1) (Newcastle United) 1968/9.

Rowland, K. (11) (West Ham United) 1994/95, 1995/96, 1996/97.

Russell, A. (1) (Linfield) 1946/7.

Ryan, R. (1) (West Bromwich Albion) 1949/50.

Sanchez, L. P. (3) (Wimbledon) 1986/7, 1988/9.

Scott, J. (2) (Grimsby Town) 1957/8.

Scott, P. (10) (Everton) 1974/5, 1975/6, (York City) 1977/8, (Aldershot) 1978/9.

Sharkey, P. (1) (Ipswich Town) 1975/6.
Shields, J. (1) (Southampton) 1956/7.
Simpson, W. (12) (Rangers) 1950/1, 1953/4, 1954/5, 1956/7, 1957/8, 1958/9.
Sloan, D. (2) (Oxford) 1968/9, 1970/1.
Sloan, T. (3) (Manchester United) 1978/9.
Sloan, W. (1) (Arsenal) 1946/7.
Smyth, S. (9) (Wolverhampton Wanderers) 1947/8, 1948/9, 1949/50 (Stoke City) 1951/2.
Smyth, W. (4) (Distillery) 1948/9, 1953/4.
Spence, D. (29) (Bury) 1974/5, 1975/6, (Blackpool) 1976/7, 1978/9, 1979/80, (Southend United) 1980/1, 1981/2.
Stevenson, A. (3) (Everton) 1946/7, 1947/8.
Stewart, A. (7) (Glentoran) 1966/7, 1967/8 (Derby) 1968/9.
Stewart, D. (1) (Hull City) 1977/8.
Stewart, I. (31) (QPR) 1981/2, 1982/3, 1983/4, 1984/5, (Newcastle United) 1985/6, 1986/7.
Stewart, T. (1) (Linfield) 1960/1.

Taggart, G. P. (42) (Barnsley) 1989/90, 1990/1, 1991/2, 1992/93, 1993/94, 1994/95 (Bolton Wanderers) 1996/97.
Todd, S. (11) (Burnley) 1965/6, 1966/7, 1967/8, 1968/9, 1969/70 (Sheffield Wednesday) 1970/1.
Trainor, D. (1) (Crusaders) 1966/7.
Tully, C. (10) (Celtic) 1948/9, 1949/50, 1951/2, 1952/3, 1953/4, 1955/6, 1958/9.

Uprichard, N. (18) (Swindon Town) 1951/2, 1952/3 (Portsmouth) 1954/5, 1955/6, 1957/8, 1958/9.

Vernon, J. (17) (Belfast Celtic) 1946/7 (West Bromwich Albion) 1947/8, 1948/9, 1949/50, 1950/1 , 1951/2.

Walker, J. (1) (Doncaster Rovers) 1954/5.
Walsh, D. (9) (West Bromwich Albion) 1946/7, 1947/8, 1948/9, 1949/50.
Walsh, W. (5) (Manchester City) 1947/8, 1948/9.
Watson, P. (1) (Distillery) 1970/1.
Welsh, S. (4) (Carlisle United) 1965/6, 1966/7.
Whiteside, N. (38) (Manchester United) 1981/2, 1982/3, 1983/4, 1984/5, 1985/6, 1986/7, 1987/8, (Everton) 1989/90.
Whitley, J. (2) (Manchester City) 1996/97.
Williams, P. (1) (WBA) 1990/1.
Wilson, D. J. (24) (Brighton & Hove Albion) 1986/7 (Luton) 1987/8, 1988/9, 1989/90, 1990/1, (Sheffield Wednesday) 1991/2.
Wilson, K. J. (42) (Ipswich Town) 1986/7 (Chelsea) 1987/8, 1988/9, 1989/90, 1990/1, 1991/2 (Notts County) 1992/93, 1993/94 (Walsall) 1994/95.
Wilson, S. (12) (Glenavon) 1961/2, 1963/4, (Falkirk) 1964/5 (Dundee) 1965/6, 1966/7, 1967/8.
Wood, T. J. (1) (Walsall) 1995/96.
Worthington, N. (66) (Sheffield Wednesday) 1983/4, 1984/5, 1985/6, 1986/7, 1987/8, 1988/9, 1989/90, 1990/1, 1991/2, 1992/93, 1993/94 (Leeds United) 1994/95, 1995/96 (Stoke City) 1996/97.
Wright, T. J. (28) (Newcastle United) 1988/9, 1989/90, 1991/2, 1992/93 (Nottingham Forest) 1993/94 (Manchester City) 1996/97.

SCOTLAND
Aird, J. (4) (Burnley) 1953/4.
Aitken, G. G. (8) (East Fife) 1948/9, 1949/50, 1952/3 (Sunderland) 1953/4.

Aitken, R. (57) (Celtic) 1979/80, 1982/3, 1983/4, 1984/5, 1985/6, 1986/7, 1987/8, (Newcastle United) 1989/90, (St Mirren) 1991/2.
Albiston, A. (14) (Manchester United) 1981/2, 1983/4, 1984/5, 1985/6.
Allan, T. (2) (Dundee) 1973/4.
Anderson, J. (1) (Leicester City) 1953/4.
Archibald, S. (27) (Aberdeen) 1979/80 (Tottenham Hotspur) 1980/1, 1981/2, 1982/3, 1983/4, 1984/5, (Barcelona) 1985/6.
Auld, B. (3) (Celtic) 1958/9, 1959/60.

Baird, H. (1) (Airdrieonians) 1955/6.
Baird, S. (7) (Rangers) 1956/7, 1957/8.
Bannon, E. (11) (Dundee United) 1979/80, 1982/3, 1983/4, 1985/6.
Bauld, W. (3) (Heart of Midlothian) 1949/50.
Baxter, J. (34) (Rangers) 1960/1, 1961/2, 1962/3, 1963/4, 1964/5 (Sunderland) 1965/6, 1966/7, 1967/8.
Bell, W. (2) (Leeds United) 1965/6.
Bernard, P. R. (2) (Oldham Athletic) 1994/95.
Bett, J. (25) (Rangers) 1981/2, 1982/3 (Lokeren) 1983/4, 1984/5 (Aberdeen) 1985/6, 1986/7, 1987/8, 1988/9, 1989/90.
Black, E. (2) (Metz) 1987/8.
Black, I. (1) (Southampton) 1947/8.
Blacklaw, A. (3) (Burnley) 1962/3, 1965/6.
Blackley, J. (7) (Hibernian) 1973/4, 1975/6, 1976/7.
Blair, J. (1) (Blackpool) 1946/7.
Blyth, J. (2) (Coventry City) 1977/8.
Bone, J. (2) (Norwich City) 1971/2, 1972/3.
Booth, S. (13) (Aberdeen) 1992/93, 1993/94, 1994/95, 1995/96.
Bowman, D. (6) (Dundee United) 1991/2, 1992/93, 1993/94.
Boyd, T. (48) (Motherwell) 1990/1 (Chelsea) 1991/2 (Celtic) 1992/93, 1993/94, 1994/95, 1995/96, 1996/97.
Brand, R. (8) (Rangers) 1960/1, 1961/2.
Brazil, A. (13) (Ipswich Town) 1979/80, 1981/2, 1982/3 (Tottenham Hotspur).
Bremner, D. (1) (Hibernian) 1975/6.
Bremner, W. (54) (Leeds United) 1964/5, 1965/6, 1966/7, 1967/8, 1968/9, 1969/70, 1970/1, 1971/2, 1972/3, 1973/4, 1974/5, 1975/6.
Brennan, F. (7) (Newcastle United) 1946/7, 1952/3, 1963/4.
Brogan, J. (4) (Celtic) 1970/1.
Brown, A. (14) (East Fife) 1949/50 (Blackpool) 1951/2, 1952/3, 1953/4.
Brown, H. (3) (Partick Thistle) 1946/7.
Brown, J. (1) (Sheffield United) 1974/5.
Brown, R. (3) (Rangers) 1946/7, 1948/9, 1951/2.
Brown, W. (28) (Dundee) 1957/8, 1958/9, 1959/60 (Tottenham Hotspur) 1961/2, 1962/3, 1963/4, 1964/5, 1965/6.
Brownlie, J. (7) (Hibernian) 1970/1, 1971/2, 1972/3, 1975/6.
Buchan, M. (34) (Aberdeen) 1971/2 (Manchester United) 1972/3, 1973/4, 1974/5, 1975/6, 1976/7, 1977/8, 1978/9.
Buckley, P. (3) (Aberdeen) 1953/4, 1954/5.
Burley, C. W. (20) (Chelsea) 1994/95, 1995/96, 1996/97.
Burley, G. (11) (Ipswich Town) 1978/9, 1979/80, 1981/2.
Burns, F. (1) (Manchester United) 1969/70.
Burns, K. (20) (Birmingham City) 1973/4, 1974/5, 1976/7 (Nottingham Forest) 1977/8, 1978/9, 1979/80, 1980/1.
Burns, T. (8) (Celtic) 1980/1, 1981/2, 1982/3, 1987/8.

Calderwood, C. (21) (Tottenham Hotspur) 1994/95, 1995/96, 1996/97.
Caldow, E. (40) (Rangers) 1956/7, 1957/8, 1958/9, 1959/60, 1960/1, 1961/2, 1962/3.
Callaghan, W. (2) (Dunfermline) 1969/70.

Campbell, R. (5) (Falkirk) 1946/7 (Chelsea) 1949/50.
Campbell, W. (5) (Morton) 1946/7, 1947/8.
Carr, W. (6) (Coventry City) 1969/70, 1970/1, 1971/2, 1972/3.
Chalmers, S. (5) (Celtic) 1964/5, 1965/6, 1966/7.
Clark, J. (4) (Celtic) 1965/6, 1966/7.
Clark, R. (17) (Aberdeen) 1967/8, 1969/70, 1970/1, 1971/2, 1972/3.
Clarke, S. (6) (Chelsea) 1987/8, 1993/94.
Collins, J. (43) (Hibernian) 1987/8, 1989/90, 1990/1 (Celtic) 1991/2, 1992/93, 1993/94, 1994/95, 1995/96 (Monaco) 1996/97.
Collins, R. (31) (Celtic) 1950/1, 1954/5, 1955/6, 1956/7, 1957/8, 1958/9, (Everton) 1964/5, (Leeds United).
Colquhoun, E. (9) (Sheffield United) 1971/2, 1972/3.
Colquhoun, J. (1) (Hearts) 1987/8.
Combe, R. (3) (Hibernian) 1947/8.
Conn, A. (1) (Heart of Midlothian) 1955/6.
Conn, A. (2) (Tottenham Hotspur) 1974/5.
Connachan, E. (2) (Dunfermline Athletic) 1961/2.
Connelly, G. (2) (Celtic) 1973/4.
Connolly, J. (1) (Everton) 1972/3.
Connor, R. (4) (Dundee) 1985/6 (Aberdeen) 1987/8, 1988/9, 1990/91.
Cooke, C. (16) (Dundee) 1965/6 (Chelsea) 1967/8, 1968/9, 1969/70, 1970/1, 1974/5.
Cooper, D. (22) (Rangers) 1979/80, 1983/4, 1984/5, 1985/6, 1986/7 (Motherwell) 1989/90.
Cormack, P. (9) (Hibernian) 1965/6, 1969/70 (Nottingham Forest) 1970/1, 1971/2.
Cowan, J. (25) (Morton) 1947/8, 1948/9, 1949/50, 1950/1, 1951/2 (Motherwell).
Cowie, D. (20) (Dundee) 1952/3, 1953/4, 1954/5, 1955/6, 1956/7, 1957/8.
Cox, C. (1) (Hearts) 1947/8.
Cox, S. (24) (Rangers) 1947/8, 1948/9, 1949/50, 1950/1, 1951/2, 1952/3, 1953/4.
Craig, J. (1) (Celtic) 1976/7.
Craig, J. P. (1) (Celtic) 1967/8.
Craig, T. (1) (Newcastle United) 1975/6.
Crawford, S. (1) (Raith Rovers) 1994/95.
Crerand, P. (16) (Celtic) 1960/1, 1961/2, 1962/3 (Manchester United) 1963/4, 1964/5, 1965/6.
Cropley, A. (2) (Hibernian) 1971/2.
Cruickshank, J. (6) (Heart of Midlothian) 1963/4, 1969/70, 1970/1, 1975/6.
Cullen, M. (1) (Luton Town) 1955/6.
Cumming, J. (9) (Heart of Midlothian) 1954/5, 1959/60.
Cunningham, W. (8) (Preston North End) 1953/4, 1954/5.
Curran, H. (5) (Wolverhampton Wanderers) 1969/70, 1970/1.

Dailly, C. (3) (Derby County) 1996/97.
Dalglish, K. (102) (Celtic) 1971/2, 1972/3, 1973/4, 1974/5, 1975/6, 1976/7, (Liverpool) 1977/8, 1978/9, 1979/80, 1980/1, 1981/2, 1982/3, 1983/4, 1984/5, 1985/6, 1986/7.
Davidson, J. (8) (Partick Thistle) 1953/4, 1954/5.
Dawson, A. (5) (Rangers) 1979/80, 1982/3.
Deans, D. (2) (Celtic) 1974/5.
Delaney, J. (4) (Manchester United) 1946/7, 1947/8.
Dick, J. (1) (West Ham United) 1958/9.
Dickson, W. (5) (Kilmarnock) 1969/70, 1970/1.
Docherty, T. (25) (Preston North End) 1951/2, 1952/3, 1953/4, 1954/5, 1956/7, 1957/8, 1958/9 (Arsenal).
Dodds, D. (2) (Dundee United) 1983/4.
Dodds, W. (3) (Aberdeen) 1996/97.
Donachie, W. (35) (Manchester City) 1971/2, 1972/3, 1973/4, 1975/6, 1976/7, 1977/8, 1978/9.

Donnelly, S. (1) (Celtic) 1996/97.
Dougall, C. (1) (Birmingham City) 1946/7.
Dougan, R. (1) (Heart of Midlothian) 1949/50.
Doyle, J. (1) (Ayr United) 1975/6.
Duncan, A. (6) (Hibernian) 1974/5, 1975/6.
Duncan, D. (3) (East Fife) 1947/8.
Duncanson, J. (1) (Rangers) 1946/7.
Durie, G. S. (35) (Chelsea) 1987/8, 1988/9, 1989/90, 1990/1, (Tottenham Hotspur) 1991/2, 1992/93, (Rangers) 1993/94, 1995/96, 1996/97.
Durrant, I. (11) (Rangers) 1987/8, 1988/9, 1992/93, 1993/94.

Evans, A. (4) (Aston Villa) 1981/2.
Evans, R. (48) (Celtic) 1948/9, 1949/50, 1950/1, 1951/2, 1952/3, 1953/4, 1954/5, 1955/6, 1956/7, 1957/8, 1958/9, 1959/60 (Chelsea).
Ewing, T. (2) (Partick Thistle) 1957/8.

Farm, G. (10) (Blackpool) 1952/3, 1953/4, 1958/9.
Ferguson, D. (2) (Rangers) 1987/8.
Ferguson, D. (7) (Dundee United) 1991/2, 1992/93 (Everton) 1994/95, 1996/97.
Ferguson, I. (9) (Rangers) 1988/9, 1992/93, 1993/94, 1996/97.
Ferguson, R. (7) (Kilmarnock) 1965/6, 1966/7.
Fernie, W. (12) (Celtic) 1953/4, 1954/5, 1956/7, 1957/8.
Flavell, R. (2) (Airdrieonians) 1946/7.
Fleck, R. (4) (Norwich City) 1989/90, 1990/1.
Fleming, C. (1) (East Fife) 1953/4.
Forbes, A. (14) (Sheffield United) 1946/7, 1947/8 (Arsenal) 1949/50, 1950/1, 1951/2.
Ford, D. (3) (Heart of Midlothian) 1973/4.
Forrest, J. (1) (Motherwell) 1957/8.
Forrest, J. (5) (Rangers) 1965/6 (Aberdeen) 1970/1.
Forsyth, A. (10) (Partick Thistle) 1971/2, 1972/3 (Manchester United) 1974/5, 1975/6.
Forsyth, C. (4) (Kilmarnock) 1963/4, 1964/5.
Forsyth, T. (22) (Motherwell) 1970/1 (Rangers) 1973/4, 1975/6, 1976/7, 1977/8.
Fraser, D. (2) (West Bromwich Albion) 1967/8, 1968/9.
Fraser, W. (2) (Sunderland) 1954/5.

Gabriel, J. (2) (Everton) 1960/1, 1961/2.
Gallacher, K. W. (31) (Dundee United) 1987/8, 1988/9, 1990/91 (Coventry City), 1991/2 (Blackburn Rovers) 1992/93, 1993/94, 1995/96, 1996/97.
Galloway, M. (1) (Celtic) 1991/2.
Gardiner, W. (1) (Motherwell) 1957/8.
Gemmell, T. (2) (St Mirren) 1954/5.
Gemmell, T. (18) (Celtic) 1965/6, 1966/7, 1967/8, 1968/9, 1969/70, 1970/1.
Gemmill, A. (43) (Derby County) 1970/1, 1971/2, 1975/6, 1976/7, 1977/8 (Nottingham Forest) 1978/9 (Birmingham City) 1979/80, 1980/1.
Gemmill, S. (11) (Nottingham Forest) 1994/95, 1995/96, 1996/97.
Gibson, D. (7) (Leicester City) 1962/3, 1963/4, 1964/5.
Gillespie, G.T. (13) (Liverpool) 1987/8, 1988/9, 1989/90, (Celtic) 1990/91.
Gilzean, A. (22) (Dundee) 1963/4, 1964/5 Tottenham Hotspur) 1965/6, 1967/8, 1968/9, 1969/70, 1970/1.
Glavin, R. (1) (Celtic) 1976/7.
Glen, A. (2) (Aberdeen) 1955/6.
Goram, A. L. (42) (Oldham Athletic) 1985/6, 1986/7, (Hibernian) 1988/9, 1989/90, 1990/1, (Rangers) 1991/2, 1992/93, 1993/94, 1994/95, 1995/96, 1996/97.
Gough, C. R. (61) (Dundee United) 1982/3, 1983/4, 1984/5, 1985/6, 1986/7 (Tottenham Hotspur) 1987/8 (Rangers) 1988/9, 1989/90, 1990/1, 1991/2, 1992/93.
Govan, J. (6) (Hibernian) 1947/8, 1948/9.

252

Graham, A. (10) (Leeds United) 1977/8, 1978/9, 1979/80, 1980/1.
Graham, G. (12) (Arsenal) 1971/2, 1972/3 (Manchester United).
Grant, J. (2) (Hibernian) 1958/9.
Grant, P. (2) (Celtic) 1988/9.
Gray, A. (20) (Aston Villa) 1975/6, 1976/7, 1978/9 (Wolverhampton Wanderers) 1979/80, 1980/1, 1981/2, 1982/3, 1984/5 (Everton).
Gray, E. (12) (Leeds United) 1968/9, 1969/70, 1970/71, 1971/2, 1975/6, 1976/7.
Gray F. (32) (Leeds United) 1975/6, 1978/9, 1979/80 (Nottingham Forest) 1980/1, (Leeds United) 1981/2, 1982/3.
Green, A. (6) (Blackpool) 1970/1 (Newcastle United) 1971/2.
Greig, J. (44) (Rangers) 1963/4, 1964/5, 1965/6, 1966/7, 1967/8, 1968/9, 1969/70, 1970/1, 1975/6.
Gunn, B. (6) (Norwich C) 1989/90, 1992/93, 1993/94.

Haddock, H. (6) (Clyde) 1954/5, 1957/8.
Haffey, F. (2) (Celtic) 1959/60, 1960/1.
Hamilton, A. (24) (Dundee) 1961/2, 1962/3, 1963/4, 1964/5, 1965/6.
Hamilton, G. (5) (Aberdeen) 1946/7, 1950/1, 1953/4.
Hamilton, W. (1) (Hibernian) 1964/5.
Hansen, A. (26) (Liverpool) 1978/9, 1979/80, 1980/1, 1981/2, 1982/3, 1984/5, 1985/6, 1986/7.
Hansen J. (2) (Partick Thistle) 1971/2.
Harper, J. (4) (Aberdeen) 1972/3, 1975/6, 1978/9.
Hartford, A. (50) (West Bromwich Albion) 1971/2, 1975/6 (Manchester City) 1976/7, 1977/8, 1978/9, 1979/80 (Everton) 1980/1, 1981/2 (Manchester City).
Harvey, D. (16) (Leeds United) 1972/3, 1973/4, 1974/5, 1975/6, 1976/7.
Haughney, M. (1) (Celtic) 1953/4.
Hay, D. (27) (Celtic) 1969/70, 1970/1, 1971/2, 1972/3, 1973/4.
Hegarty, P. (8) (Dundee United) 1978/9, 1979/80, 1982/3.
Henderson, J. (7) (Portsmouth) 1952/3, 1953/4, 1955/6, 1958/9 (Arsenal).
Henderson, W. (29) (Rangers) 1962/3, 1963/4, 1964/5, 1965/6, 1966/7, 1967/8, 1968/9, 1969/70.
Hendry, E.C.J. (27) (Blackburn Rovers) 1992/93, 1993/94, 1994/95, 1995/96, 1996/97.
Herd, D. (5) (Arsenal) 1958/9, 1960/1.
Herd, G. (5) (Clyde) 1957/8, 1959/60, 1960/1.
Herriot, J. (8) (Birmingham City) 1968/9, 1969/70.
Hewie, J. (19) (Charlton Athletic) 1955/6, 1956/7, 1957/8, 1958/9, 1959/60.
Holt, D. (5) (Heart of Midlothian) 1962/3, 1963/4.
Holton, J. (15) (Manchester United) 1972/3, 1973/4, 1974/5.
Hope, R. (2) (West Bromwich Albion) 1967/8, 1968/9.
Hopkin, D. (2) (Crystal Palace) 1996/97.
Houliston, W. (3) (Queen of the South) 1948/9.
Houston, S. (1) (Manchester United) 1975/6.
Howie, H. (1) (Hibernian) 1948/9.
Hughes, J. (8) (Celtic) 1964/5, 1965/6, 1967/8, 1968/9, 1969/70.
Hughes, W. (1) (Sunderland) 1974/5.
Humphries, W. (1) (Motherwell) 1951/2.
Hunter, A. (4) (Kilmarnock) 1971/2, 1972/3, (Celtic) 1973/4.
Hunter, W. (3) (Motherwell) 1959/60, 1960/1.
Husband, J. (1) (Partick Thistle) 1946/7.
Hutchison, T. (17) (Coventry City) 1973/4, 1974/5, 1975/6.

Imlach, S. (4) (Nottingham Forest) 1957/8.
Irvine, B. (9) (Aberdeen) 1990/1, 1992/93, 1993/94.

Jackson, C. (8) (Rangers) 1974/5, 1975/6.

Jackson, D. (20) (Hibernian) 1994/95, 1995/96, 1996/97.

Jardine, A. (38) (Rangers) 1970/1, 1971/2, 1972/3, 1973/4, 1974/5, 1976/7, 1977/8, 1978/9, 1979/80.

Jarvie, A. (3) (Airdrieonians) 1970/1.

Jess, E. (13) (Aberdeen) 1992/93, 1993/94, 1994/95, 1995/96.

Johnston, M. (38) (Watford) 1983/4, 1984/5 (Celtic) 1985/6, 1986/7, (Nantes) 1987/8, 1988/9 (Rangers) 1989/90, 1991/2.

Johnston, W. (22) (Rangers) 1965/6, 1967/8, 1968/9, 1969/70, 1970/1. (West Bromwich Albion) 1976/7, 1977/8.

Johnstone, D. (14) (Rangers) 1972/3, 1974/5, 1975/6, 1977/8, 1979/80.

Johnstone, J. (23) (Celtic) 1964/5, 1965/6, 1966/7, 1967/8, 1968/9, 1969/70, 1970/1, 1971/2, 1973/4, 1974/5.

Johnstone, L. (2) (Clyde) 1947/8.

Johnstone, R. (17) (Hibernian) 1950/1, 1951/2, 1952/3, 1953/4, 1954/5, (Manchester City) 1955/6.

Jordan, J. (52) (Leeds United) 1972/3, 1973/4, 1974/5, 1975/6, 1976/7, 1977/8, (Manchester United) 1978/9, 1979/80, 1980/1, 1981/2 (AC Milan).

Kelly, H. (1) (Blackpool) 1951/2.

Kelly, J. (2) (Barnsley) 1948/9.

Kennedy, J. (6) (Celtic) 1963/4, 1964/5.

Kennedy, S. (8) (Aberdeen) 1977/8, 1978/9, 1981/2.

Kennedy, S. (5) (Rangers) 1974/5.

Kerr, A. (2) (Partick Thistle) 1954/5.

Lambert, P. (7) (Motherwell) 1994/95 (Borussia Dortmund) 1996/97.

Law, D. (55) (Huddersfield Town) 1958/9, 1959/60 (Manchester City) 1960/1, 1961/2 (Torino) 1962/3 (Manchester United) 1963/4, 1964/5, 1965/6, 1966/7, 1967/8, 1968/9, 1971/2, 1973/4 (Manchester City).

Lawrence, T. (3) (Liverpool) 1962/3, 1968/9.

Leggat, G. (18) (Aberdeen) 1955/6, 1956/7, 1957/8, 1958/9 (Fulham) 1959/60.

Leighton, J. (81) (Aberdeen) 1982/3, 1983/4, 1984/5, 1985/6, 1986/7, 1987/8, (Manchester United) 1988/9, 1989/90 (Hibernian) 1993/94, 1994/95, 1995/96, 1996/97.

Lennox, R. (10) (Celtic) 1966/7, 1967/8, 1968/9.

Leslie, L. (5) (Airdrieonians) 1960/1.

Levein, C. (16) (Hearts) 1989/90, 1991/2, 1992/93, 1993/94, 1994/95.

Liddell, W. (28) (Liverpool) 1946/7, 1947/8, 1949/50, 1950/1, 195/2, 1952/3, 1953/4, 1954/5, 1955/6.

Linwood, A. (1) (Clyde) 1949/50.

Little, A. (1) (Rangers) 1952/3.

Logie, J. (1) (Arsenal) 1952/3.

Long, H. (1) (Clyde) 1946/7.

Lorimer, P. (21) (Leeds United) 1969/70, 1970/1, 1971/2, 1972/3, 1973/4, 1974/5, 1975/6.

Macari, L. (24) (Celtic) 1971/2, 1972/3 (Manchester United) 1974/5, 1976/7, 1977/8, 1978/9.

Macaulay, A. (7) (Brentford) 1946/7 (Arsenal) 1947/8.

MacDougall, E. (7) (Norwich City) 1974/5, 1975/6.

Mackay, D. (22) (Heart of Midlothian) 1956/7, 1957/8, 1958/9 (Tottenham Hotspur) 1959/60, 1960/1, 1962/3, 1963/4, 1965/6.

Mackay, G. (4) (Heart of Midlothian) 1987/8.

Malpas, M. (55) (Dundee United) 1983/4, 1984/5, 1985/6, 1986/7, 1987/8, 1988/9, 1989/90, 1990/1, 1991/2, 1992/93.

Marshall, G. (1) (Celtic) 1991/2.

Martin, B. (2) (Motherwell) 1994/95.

Martin, F. (6) (Aberdeen) 1953/4, 1954/5.

Martin, N. (3) (Hibernian) 1964/5, 1965/6 (Sunderland).

Martis, J. (1) (Motherwell) 1960/1.

Mason, J. (7) (Third Lanark) 1948/9, 1949/50, 1950/1.

Masson, D. (17) (QPR) 1975/6, 1976/7, 1977/8 (Derby County) 1978/9.

Mathers, D. (1) (Partick Thistle) 1953/4.

McAllister, B. (3) (Wimbledon) 1996/97.

McAllister, G. (53) (Leicester City) 1989/90, 1990/1 (Leeds United), 1991/2, 1992/93, 1993/94, 1994/95, 1995/96 (Coventry City) 1996/97.

McAvennie, F. (5) (West Ham United) 1985/6 (Celtic) 1987/8.

McBride, J. (2) (Celtic) 1966/7.

McCall, S. M. (39) (Everton) 1989/90, 1990/1, (Rangers) 1991/2, 1992/93, 1993/94, 1994/95, 1995/96, 1996/97.

McCalliog, J. (5) (Sheffield Wednesday) 1966/7, 1967/8, 1968/9 1970/1 (Wolverhampton Wanderers).

McCann, R. (5) (Motherwell) 1958/9, 1959/60, 1960/1.

McClair, B. (30) (Celtic) 1986/7 (Manchester United) 1987/8, 1988/9, 1989/90, 1990/1, 1991/2, 1992/93.

McCloy, P. (4) (Rangers) 1972/3.

McCoist, A. (58) (Rangers) 1985/6, 1986/7, 1987/8, 1988/9, 1989/90, 1990/1, 1991/2, 1992/93, 1995/96, 1996/97.

McColl, I. (14) (Rangers) 1949/50, 1950/1, 1956/7, 1957/8.

McCreadie, E. (23) (Chelsea) 1964/5, 1965/6, 1966/7, 1967/8, 1968/9.

MacDonald, A. (1) (Rangers) 1975/6.

MacDonald, J. (2) (Sunderland) 1955/6.

McFarlane, W. (1) (Heart of Midlothian) 1946/7.

McGarr, E. (2) (Aberdeen) 1969/70.

McGarvey, F. (7) (Liverpool) 1978/9 (Celtic) 1983/4.

McGhee, M. (4) (Aberdeen) 1982/3, 1983/4.

McGinlay, J. (13) (Bolton Wanderers) 1993/94, 1994/95, 1995/96, 1996/97.

McGrain, D. (62) (Celtic) 1972/3, 1973/4, 1974/5, 1975/6, 1976/7, 1977/8, 1979/80, 1980/1, 1981/2.

McGrory, J. (3) (Kilmarnock) 1964/5, 1965/6.

McInally, A. (8) (Aston Villa) 1988/9 (Bayern Munich) 1989/90.

McInally, J. (10) (Dundee United) 1986/7, 1987/8, 1990/1, 1991/2, 1992/93.

McKay, D. (14) (Celtic) 1958/9, 1959/60, 1960/1, 1961/2.

McKean, R. (1) (Rangers) 1975/6.

McKenzie, J. (9) (Partick Thistle) 1953/4, 1954/5, 1955/6.

McKimmie, S. (40) (Aberdeen) 1988/9, 1989/90, 1990/1, 1991/2, 1992/93, 1993/94, 1994/95, 1995/96.

McKinlay, T. (16) (Celtic) 1995/96, 1996/97.

McKinlay, W. (20) (Dundee United) 1993/94, 1994/95, 1995/96 (Blackburn Rovers) 1996/97.

McKinnon, R. (28) (Rangers) 1965/6, 1966/7, 1967/8, 1968/9, 1969/70, 1970/1.

McKinnon, R. (3) (Motherwell) 1993/94, 1994/95.

McLaren, A. (4) (Preston North End) 1946/7, 1947/8.

McLaren, A. (24) (Heart of Midlothian) 1991/2, 1992/93, 1993/94, 1994/95 (Rangers), 1995/96.

McLean, G. (1) (Dundee) 1967/8.

McLean, T. (6) (Kilmarnock) 1968/9, 1969/70, 1970/1.

McLeish, A. (77) (Aberdeen) 1979/80, 1980/1, 1981/2, 1982/3, 1983/4, 1984/5, 1985/6, 1986/7, 1987/8, 1988/9, 1989/90, 1990/1, 1992/93.

McLeod, J. (4) (Hibernian) 1960/1.

MacLeod, M. (20) (Celtic) 1984/5, 1986/7 (Borussia Dortmund) 1987/8, 1988/9, 1989/90, 1990/1 (Hibernian).

McLintock, F. (9) (Leicester City) 1962/3, 1964/5 (Arsenal) 1966/7, 1969/70, 1970/1.

McMillan, I. (6) (Airdrieonians) 1951/2, 1954/5, 1955/6 (Rangers) 1960/1.

McNamara, J. (4) (Celtic) 1996/97.

McNaught, W. (5) (Raith Rovers) 1950/1, 1951/2, 1954/5.
McNeill, W. (29) (Celtic) 1960/1, 1961/2, 1962/3, 1963/4, 1964/5, 1965/6, 1966/7, 1967/8, 1968/9, 1969/70, 1971/2.
McPhail, J. (5) (Celtic) 1949/50, 1950/1, 1953/4.
McPherson, D. (27) (Hearts) 1988/9, 1989/90, 1990/1, 1991/2 (Rangers) 1992/93.
McQueen, G. (30) (Leeds United) 1973/4, 1974/5, 1975/6, 1976/7, 1977/8, (Manchester United) 1978/9, 1979/80, 1980/1.
McStay, P. (76) (Celtic) 1983/4, 1984/5, 1985/6, 1986/7, 1987/8, 1988/9, 1989/90, 1990/1, 1991/2, 1992/93, 1993/94, 1994/95, 1995/96, 1996/97.
Millar, J. (2) (Rangers) 1962/3.
Miller, W. (6) (Celtic) 1946/7, 1947/8.
Miller, W. (65) (Aberdeen) 1974/5, 1977/8, 1979/80, 1980/1, 1981/2, 1982/3, 1983/4, 1984/5, 1985/6, 1986/7, 1987/8, 1988/9, 1989/90.
Mitchell, R. (2) (Newcastle United) 1950/1.
Mochan, N. (3) (Celtic) 1953/4.
Moir, W. (1) (Bolton Wanderers) 1949/50.
Moncur, R. (16) (Newcastle United) 1967/8, 1969/70, 1970/1, 1971/2.
Morgan, W. (21) (Burnley) 1967/8 (Manchester United) 1971/2, 1972/3, 1973/4.
Morris, H. (1) (East Fife) 1949/50.
Mudie, J. (17) (Blackpool) 1956/7, 1957/8.
Mulhall, G. (3) (Aberdeen) 1959/60, 1962/3 (Sunderland) 1963/4.
Munro, F. (9) (Wolverhampton Wanderers) 1970/1, 1974/5.
Munro, I. (7) (St Mirren) 1978/9, 1979/80.
Murdoch, R. (12) (Celtic) 1965/6, 1966/7, 1967/8, 1968/9, 1969/70.
Murray, J. (5) (Heart of Midlothian) 1957/8.
Murray, S. (1) (Aberdeen) 1971/2.

Narey, D. (35) (Dundee United) 1976/7, 1978/9, 1979/80, 1980/1, 1981/2, 1982/3, 1985/6, 1986/7, 1988/9.
Nevin, P.K.F. (28) (Chelsea) 1985/6, 1986/7, 1987/8 (Everton) 1988/9, 1990/1, 1991/2 (Tranmere Rovers) 1992/93, 1993/94, 1994/95, 1995/96.
Nicholas, C. (20) (Celtic) 1982/3, (Arsenal) 1983/4, 1984/5, 1985/6, 1986/7, (Aberdeen) 1988/9.
Nicol, S. (27) (Liverpool) 1984/5, 1985/6, 1987/8, 1988/9, 1989/90, 1990/1, 1991/2.

O'Donnell, P. (1) (Motherwell) 1993/94.
O'Hare, J. (13) (Derby County) 1969/70, 1970/1, 1971/2.
O'Neil, B. (1) (Celtic) 1995/96.
Ormond, W. (6) (Hibernian) 1953/4, 1958/9.
Orr, T. (2) (Morton) 1951/2.

Parker, A. (15) (Falkirk) 1954/5, 1955/6, 1956/7, 1957/8.
Parlane, D. (12) (Rangers) 1972/3, 1974/5, 1975/6, 1976/7.
Paton, A. (2) (Motherwell) 1951/2.
Pearson, T. (2) (Newcastle United) 1946/7.
Penman, A. (1) (Dundee) 1965/6.
Pettigrew, W. (5) (Motherwell) 1975/6, 1976/7.
Plenderleith, J. (1) (Manchester City) 1960/1.
Provan, D. (5) (Rangers) 1963/4, 1965/6.
Provan, D. (10) (Celtic) 1979/80, 1980/1, 1981/2.

Quinn, P. (4) (Motherwell) 1960/1, 1961/2.

Redpath, W. (9) (Motherwell) 1948/9, 1950/1, 1951/2.
Reilly, L. (38) (Hibernian) 1948/9, 1949/50, 1950/1, 1951/2, 1952/3, 1953/4, 1954/5, 1955/6, 1956/7.
Ring, T. (12) (Clydebank) 1952/3, 1954/5, 1956/7, 1957/8.

Rioch, B. (24) (Derby County) 1974/5, 1975/6, 1976/7, (Everton) 1977/8, (Derby County) 1978/9.

Robb, D. (5) (Aberdeen) 1970/1.

Robertson, A. (5) (Clyde) 1954/5, 1957/8.

Robertson, D. (3) (Rangers) 1991/2, 1993/94.

Robertson, H. (1) (Dundee) 1961/2.

Robertson, J. (1) (Tottenham Hotspur) 1964/5.

Robertson, J. (16) (Heart of Midlothian) 1990/1, 1991/2, 1992/93, 1994/95, 1995/96.

Robertson, J. N. (28) (Nottingham Forest) 1977/8, 1978/9, 1979/80, 1980/1, 1981/2, 1982/3 (Derby County) 1983/4.

Robinson, B. (4) (Dundee) 1973/4, 1974/5.

Rough, A. (53) (Partick Thistle) 1975/6, 1976/7, 1977/8, 1978/9, 1979/80, 1980/1, 1981/2, (Hibernian) 1985/6.

Rougvie, D. (1) (Aberdeen) 1983/4.

Rutherford, E. (1) (Rangers) 1947/8.

St John, I. (21) (Motherwell) 1958/9, 1959/60, 1960/1, 1961/2 (Liverpool) 1962/3, 1963/4, 1964/5.

Schaedler, E. (1) (Hibernian) 1973/4.

Scott, A. (16) (Rangers) 1956/7, 1957/8, 1958/9, 1961/2 (Everton) 1963/4, 1964/5, 1965/6.

Scott, J. (1) (Hibernian) 1965/6.

Scott, J. (2) (Dundee) 1970/1.

Scoular, J. (9) (Portsmouth) 1950/1, 1951/2, 1952/3.

Sharp, G. M. (12) (Everton) 1984/5, 1985/6, 1986/7, 1987/8.

Shaw, D. (8) (Hibernian) 1946/7, 1947/8, 1948/9.

Shaw, J. (4) (Rangers) 1946/7, 1947/8.

Shearer, D. (7) (Aberdeen) 1993/94, 1994/95, 1995/96.

Shearer, R. (4) (Rangers) 1960/1.

Simpson, N. (4) (Aberdeen) 1982/3, 1983/4, 1986/7, 1987/8.

Simpson, R. (5) (Celtic) 1966/7, 1967/8, 1968/9.

Sinclair, J. (1) (Leicester City) 1965/6.

Smith, D. (2) (Aberdeen) 1965/6, 1967/8 (Rangers).

Smith, E. (2) (Celtic) 1958/9.

Smith, G. (18) (Hibernian) 1946/7, 1947/8, 1951/2, 1954/5, 1955/6, 1956/7.

Smith, H. G. (3) (Heart of Midlothian) 1987/8, 1991/2.

Smith, J. (4) (Aberdeen) 1967/8, 1973/4 (Newcastle United).

Souness, G. (54) (Middlesbrough) 1974/5 (Liverpool) 1977/8, 1978/9, 1979/80, 1980/1, 1981/2, 1982/3, 1983/4, (Sampdoria) 1984/5, 1985/6.

Speedie, D. R. (10) (Chelsea) 1984/5, 1985/6, (Coventry City) 1988/9.

Spencer, J. (14) (Chelsea) 1994/95, 1995/96 (Queens Park Rangers) 1996/97.

Stanton, P. (16) (Hibernian) 1965/6, 1968/9, 1969/70, 1970/1, 1971/2, 1972/3, 1973/4.

Steel, W. (30) (Morton) 1946/7, 1947/8 (Derby County) 1948/9, 1949/50, (Dundee) 1950/1, 1951/2, 1952/3.

Stein, C. (21) (Rangers) 1968/9, 1969/70, 1970/1, 1971/2 (Coventry City).

Stephen, J. (2) (Bradford City) 1946/7, 1947/8.

Stewart, D. (1) (Leeds United) 1977/8.

Stewart, J. (2) (Kilmarnock) 1976/7 (Middlesbrough) 1978/9.

Stewart, R. (10) (West Ham United) 1980/1, 1981/2, 1983/4, 1986/7.

Strachan, G. (50) (Aberdeen) 1979/80, 1980/1, 1981/2, 1982/3, 1983/4 (Manchester United) 1984/5, 1985/6, 1986/7, 1987/8, 1988/9 (Leeds United) 1989/90, 1990/1, 1991/2.

Sturrock, P. (20) (Dundee United) 1980/1, 1981/2, 1982/3, 1983/4, 1984/5, 1985/6, 1986/7.

Sullivan, N. (1) (Wimbledon) 1996/97.

Telfer, W. (1) (St Mirren) 1953/4.

Thomson, W. (7) (St Mirren) 1979/80, 1980/1, 1981/2, 1982/3, 1983/4.
Thornton, W. (7) (Rangers) 1946/7, 1947/8, 1948/9, 1951/2.
Toner, W. (2) (Kilmarnock) 1958/9.
Turnbull, E. (8) (Hibernian) 1947/8, 1950/1, 1957/8.

Ure, I. (11) (Dundee) 1961/2, 1962/3 (Arsenal) 1963/4, 1967/8.

Waddell, W. (17) (Rangers) 1946/7, 1948/9, 1949/50, 1950/1, 1951/2, 1953/4, 1954/5.
Walker, A. (3) (Celtic) 1987/8, 1994/95.
Walker, J. N. (2) (Heart of Midlothian) 1992/93 (Partick Thistle) 1995/96.
Wallace, L. A. (3) (Coventry City) 1977/8, 1978/9.
Wallace, W.S.B. (7) (Heart of Midlothian) 1964/5, 1965/6, 1966/7 (Celtic) 1967/8, 1968/9.
Wardhaugh, J. (2) (Heart of Midlothian) 1954/5, 1956/7.
Wark, J. (29) (Ipswich Town) 1978/9, 1979/80, 1980/1, 1981/2, 1982/3, 1983/4 (Liverpool) 1984/5.
Watson, J. (2) (Motherwell) 1947/8 (Huddersfield Town) 1953/4.
Watson, R. (1) (Motherwell) 1970/1.
Weir, A. (6) (Motherwell) 1958/9, 1959/60.
Weir, D. G. (2) (Heart of Midlothian) 1996/97.
Weir, P. (6) (St Mirren) 1979/80, 1982/3, (Aberdeen) 1983/4.
White, J. (22) (Falkirk) 1958/9, 1959/60 (Tottenham Hotspur) 1960/1, 1961/2, 1962/3, 1963/4.
Whyte, D. (10) (Celtic) 1987/8, 1988/9, 1991/2 (Middlesbrough) 1992/93, 1994/95, 1995/96, 1996/97.
Wilson, A. (1) (Portsmouth) 1953/4.
Wilson, D. (22) (Rangers) 1960/1, 1961/2, 1962/3, 1963/4, 1964/5.
Wilson, I. A. (5) (Leicester City) 1986/7, (Everton) 1987/8.
Wilson, P. (1) (Celtic) 1974/5.
Wilson, R. (2) (Arsenal) 1971/2.
Wood, G. (4) (Everton) 1978/9, 1981/2 (Arsenal).
Woodburn, W. (24) (Rangers) 1946/7, 1947/8, 1948/9, 1949/50, 1950/1, 1951/2.
Wright, K. (1) (Hibernian) 1991/2.
Wright, S. (2) (Aberdeen) 1992/93.
Wright, T. (3) (Sunderland) 1952/3.

Yeats, R. (2) (Liverpool) 1964/5, 1965/6.
Yorston, H. (1) (Aberdeen) 1954/5.
Young, A. (9) (Heart of Midlothian) 1959/60. 1960/1 (Everton) 1965/6.
Young, G. (53) (Rangers) 1946/7, 1947/8, 1948/9, 1949/50, 1950/1, 1951/2, 1952/3, 1953/4, 1954/5, 1955/6, 1956/7.
Younger, T. (24) (Hibernian) 1954/5, 1955/6, 1956/7 (Liverpool) 1957/8.

WALES
Aizlewood, M. (39) (Charlton Athletic) 1985/6, 1986/7 (Leeds United) 1987/8, 1988/9 (Bradford City) 1989/90, 1990/1 (Bristol City), 1991/2, 1992/93, 1993/94 (Cardiff City) 1994/95.
Allchurch, I. (68) (Swansea Town) 1950/1, 1951/2, 1952/3, 1953/4, 1954/5, 1955/6, 1956/7, 1957/8, 1958/9 (Newcastle United) 1959/60, 1960/1, 1961/2, 1962/3 (Cardiff City) 1963/4, 1964/5, 1965/6 (Swansea Town).
Allchurch, L. (11) (Swansea Town) 1954/5, 1955/6, 1957/8, 1958/9, 1961/2, (Sheffield United) 1963/4.
Allen, B. (2) (Coventry City) 1950/1.
Allen, M. (14) (Watford) 1985/6, (Norwich City) 1988/9 (Millwall) 1989/90, 1990/1, 1991/2, 1992/93 (Newcastle United) 1993/94.

258

Baker, C. (7) (Cardiff City) 1957/8, 1959/60. 1960/1, 1961/2.
Baker, W. (1) (Cardiff City) 1947/8.
Barnes, W. (22) (Arsenal) 1947/8, 1948/9, 1949/50, 1950/1, 1951/2, 1953/4, 1954/5.
Berry, G. (5) (Wolverhampton Wanderers) 1978/9, 1979/80, 1982/3 (Stoke City).
Blackmore, C. G. (39) (Manchester United) 1984/5, 1985/6, 1986/7, 1987/8, 1988/9, 1989/90, 1990/1, 1991/2, 1992/93, 1993/94 (Middlesbrough) 1996/97.
Blake, N. (6) (Sheffield United) 1993/94, 1994/95, 1995/96 (Bolton Wanderers).
Bodin, P.J. (23) (Swindon Town) 1989/90, 1990/1 (Crystal Palace), 1991/2 (Swindon Town) 1992/93, 1993/94, 1994/95.
Bowen, D. (19) (Arsenal) 1954/5, 1956/7, 1957/8, 1958/9.
Bowen, J. P. (2) (Swansea City) 1993/94 (Birmingham City) 1996/97.
Bowen, M. R. (41) (Tottenham Hotspur) 1985/6 (Norwich City) 1987/8, 1988/9, 1989/90, 1991/2, 1992/93, 1993/94, 1994/95, 1995/96 (West Ham United) 1996/97.
Boyle, T. (2) (Crystal Palace) 1980/1.
Browning, M. T. (5) (Bristol Rovers) 1995/96 (Huddersfield Town) 1996/97.
Burgess, R. (32) (Tottenham Hotspur) 1946/7, 1947/8, 1948/9, 1949/50, 1950/1, 1951/2, 1952/3, 1953/4.
Burton, O. (9) (Norwich City) 1962/3 (Newcastle United) 1963/4, 1968/9, 1971/2.

Cartwright, L. (7) (Coventry City) 1973/4, 1975/6, 1976/7 (Wrexham) 1977/8, 1978/9.
Charles, J. (38) (Leeds United) 1949/50, 1950/1, 1952/3, 1953/4, 1954/5, 1955/6, 1956/7 (Juventus) 1957/8, 1959/60, 1961/2, 1962/3, (Leeds United) (Cardiff City) 1963/4, 1964/5.
Charles, J. M. (19) (Swansea Town) 1980/1, 1981/2, 1982/3, 1983/4 (QPR), (Oxford United) 1984/5, 1985/6, 1986/7.
Charles, M. (31) (Swansea Town) 1954/5, 1955/6, 1956/7, 1957/8, 1958/9 (Arsenal) 1960/1, 1961/2 (Cardiff City) 1962/3.
Clarke, R. (22) (Manchester City) 1948/9, 1949/50, 1950/1, 1951/2, 952/3, 1953/4, 1954/5, 1955/6.
Coleman, C. (15) (Crystal Palace) 1991/2, 1992/93, 1993/94, 1994/95, 1995/96 (Blackburn Rovers) 1996/97.
Cornforth, J. M. (2) (Swansea City) 1994/95.
Coyne, D. (1) (Tranmere Rovers) 1995/96.
Crossley, M. G. (1) (Nottingham Forest) 1996/97.
Crowe, V. (16) (Aston Villa) 1958/9, 1959/60, 1960/1, 1961/2, 1962/3.
Curtis, A. (35) (Swansea City) 1975/6, 1976/7, 1977/8, 1978/9, 1979/80, 1981/2, 1982/3, 1983/4 (Southampton) 1984/5, 1985/6, 1986/7 (Cardiff City).

Daniel, R. (21) (Arsenal) 1950/1, 1951/2, 1952/3, 1953/4 (Sunderland) 1954/5, 1956/7.
Davies, A. (13) (Manchester United) 1982/3, 1983/4, 1984/5, (Newcastle United) 1985/6 (Swansea City) 1987/8, 1988/9 Bradford City) 1989/90.
Davies, D. (52) (Everton) 1974/5, 1975/6, 1976/7, 1977/8, (Wrexham) 1978/9, 1979/80, 1980/1 (Swansea City) 1981/2, 1982/3.
Davies, G. (16) (Fulham) 1979/80, 1981/2, 1982/3, 1983/4, 1984/5 (Chelsea), (Manchester City) 1985/6.
Davies, R. Wyn (34) (Bolton Wanderers) 1963/4, 1964/5, 1965/6, 1966/7 (Newcastle United) 1967/8, 1968/9, 1969/70, 1970/1, 1971/2 (Manchester City), (Blackpool) 1972/3 (Manchester United) 1973/4.
Davies, Reg (6) (Newcastle United) 1952/3, 1953/4, 1957/8.
Davies, Ron (29) (Norwich City) 1963/4, 1964/5, 1965/6, 1966/7, (Southampton) 1967/8, 1968/9, 1969/70, 1970/1, 1971/2, 1973/4 (Portsmouth).
Davies, S. I. (1) (Manchester United) 1995/96.
Davis, C. (1) (Charlton Athletic) 1971/2.
Davis, G. (4) (Wrexham) 1977/8.
Deacy, N. (11) (PSV Eindhoven) 1976/7, 1977/8 (Beringen) 1978/9.

259

Derrett, S. (4) (Cardiff City) 1968/9, 1969/70, 1970/1.
Dibble, A. (3) (Luton Town) 1985/6, (Manchester City) 1988/9.
Durban, A. (27) (Derby County) 1965/6, 1966/7, 1967/8, 1968/9, 1969/70, 1970/1, 1971/2.
Dwyer, P. (10) (Cardiff City) 1977/8, 1978/9, 1979/80.

Edwards. C.N.H. (1) (Swansea City) 1995/96.
Edwards, I. (4) (Chester) 1977/8, 1978/9, 1979/80.
Edwards, G. (12) (Birmingham City) 1946/7, 1947/8 (Cardiff City) 1948/9, 1949/50.
Edwards, T. (2) (Charlton Athletic) 1956/7.
Emanuel, J. (2) (Bristol City) 1972/3.
England, M. (44) (Blackburn Rovers) 1961/2, 1962/3, 1963/4, 1964/5, 1965/6, 1966/7 (Tottenham Hotspur) 1967/8, 1968/9, 1969/70, 1970/1, 1971/2, 1972/3, 1973/4, 1974/5.
Evans, B. (7) (Swansea City) 1971/2, 1972/3 (Hereford United) 1973/4.
Evans, I. (13) (Crystal Palace) 1975/6, 1976/7, 1977/8.
Evans, R. (1) (Swansea Town) 1963/4.

Felgate, D. (1) (Lincoln City) 1983/4.
Flynn, B. (66) (Burnley) 1974/5, 1975/6, 1976/7, 1977/8 (Leeds United) 1978/9, 1979/80, 1980/1, 1981/2, 1982/3 (Burnley) 1983/4.
Ford, T. (38) (Swansea City) 1946/7 (Aston Villa) 1947/8, 1948/9, 1949/50, 1950/1 (Sunderland) 1951/2, 1952/3 (Cardiff City) 1953/4, 1954/5, 1955/6, 1956/7.
Foulkes, W. (11) (Newcastle United) 1951/2, 1952/3, 1953/4.

Giggs, R. J. (19) (Manchester United) 1991/2, 1992/93, 1993/94, 1994/95, 1995/96, 1996/97.
Giles, D. (12) (Swansea City) 1979/80, 1980/1, 1981/2 (Crystal Palace) 1982/3.
Godfrey, B. (3) (Preston North End) 1963/4, 1964/5.
Goss, J. (9) (Norwich City) 1990/1, 1991/2, 1993/94, 1994/95, 1995/96.
Green, C. (15) (Birmingham City) 1964/5, 1965/6, 1966/7, 1967/8, 1968/9
Griffiths, A. (17) (Wrexham) 1970/1, 1974/5, 1975/6, 1976/7.
Griffiths, H. (1) (Swansea Town) 1952/3.
Griffiths, M. (11) (Leicester City) 1946/7, 1948/9, 1949/50, 1950/1, 1953/4.

Hall, G. D. (9) (Chelsea) 1987/8, 1988/9, 1990/91, 1991/2.
Harrington, A. (11) (Cardiff City) 1955/6, 1956/7, 1957/8, 1960/1, 1961/2.
Harris, C. (24) (Leeds United) 1975/6, 1977/8, 1978/9, 1979/80, 1980/1, 1981/2.
Harris, W. (6) (Middlesbrough) 1953/4, 1956/7, 1957/8.
Hartson, J. (10) (Arsenal) 1994/95, 1995/96 (West Ham United) 1996/97.
Haworth, S. O. (1) (Cardiff City) 1996/97.
Hennessey, T. (39) (Birmingham City) 1961/2, 1962/3, 1963/4, 1964/5, 1965/6, (Nottingham Forest) 1966/7, 1967/8, 1968/9, 1969/70 (Derby County) 1971/2, 1972/3.
Hewitt, R. (5) (Cardiff City) 1957/8.
Hill, M. (2) (Ipswich Town) 1971/2.
Hockey, T. (9) (Sheffield United) 1971/2, 1972/3 (Norwich City) 1973/4, (Aston Villa).
Hodges, G. (18) (Wimbledon) 1983/4, 1986/7 (Newcastle United) 1987/8, (Watford) 1989/90, (Sheffield United) 1991/2, 1995/96.
Holden, A. (1) (Chester City) 1983/4.
Hole, B. (30) (Cardiff City) 1962/3, 1963/4, 1964/5, 1965/6, 1966/7, (Blackburn Rovers) 1967/8, 1968/9 (Aston Villa) 1969/70 (Swansea Town) 1970/71.
Hollins, D. (11) (Newcastle United) 1961/2, 1962/3, 1963/4, 1964/5, 1965/6.
Hopkins, J. (16) (Fulham) 1982/3, 1983/4, 1984/5 (Crystal P) 1989/90.
Hopkins, M. (34) (Tottenham Hotspur) 1955/6, 1956/7, 1957/8, 1958/9, 1959/60, 1960/1, 1961/2, 1962/3.

Horne, B. (59) (Portsmouth) 1987/8, (Southampton) 1988/9, 1989/90, 1990/1, 1991/2 (Everton) 1992/93, 1993/94, 1994/95, 1995/96 (Birmingham City) 1996/97.
Howells, R. (2) (Cardiff City) 1953/4.
Hughes, C. M. (6) (Luton Town) 1991/2, 1993/94, 1995/96, 1996/97.
Hughes, I. (4) (Luton Town) 1950/1.
Hughes, L. M. (65) (Manchester United) 1983/4, 1984/5, 1985/6, 1986/7 (Barcelona) 1987/8, 1988/9 (Manchester United) 1989/90, 1990/1, 1991/2, 1992/93, 1993/94, 1994/95 (Chelsea) 1995/96, 1996/97.
Hughes, W. (3) (Birmingham City) 1946/7.
Hughes, W. A. (5) (Blackburn Rovers) 1948/9.
Humphreys, J. (1) (Everton) 1946/7.

Jackett, K. (31) (Watford) 1982/3, 1983/4, 1984/5, 1985/6, 1986/7, 1987/8.
James, G. (9) (Blackpool) 1965/6, 1966/7, 1967/8, 1970/1.
James, L. (54) (Burnley) 1971/2, 1972/3, 1973/4, 1974/5, 1975/6 (Derby County) 1976/7, 1977/8 (QPR) (Burnley) 1978/9, 1979/80 (Swansea City) 1980/1, 1981/2 (Sunderland) 1982/3.
James, R. M. (47) (Swansea City) 1978/9, 1979/80, 1981/2, 1982/3 (Stoke City) 1983/4, 1984/5 (QPR) 1985/6, 1986/7 (Leicester City) 1987/8 (Swansea City).
Jarvis, A. (3) (Hull City) 1946/7.
Jenkins, S. R. (6) (Swansea City) 1995/96 (Huddersfield Town) 1996/97.
Johnson, M. (1) (Swansea City) 1963/4.
Jones, A. (6) (Port Vale) 1946/7, 1987/8 (Charlton Athletic) 1989/90.
Jones, Barrie (15) (Swansea Town) 1962/3, 1963/4, 1964/5 (Plymouth Argyle) 1968/9 (Cardiff City).
Jones, Bryn. (4) (Arsenal) 1946/7, 1947/8, 1948/9.
Jones, C. (59) (Swansea Town) 1953/4, 1955/6, 1956/7, 1957/8 (Tottenham Hotspur) 1958/9, 1959/60, 1960/1, 1961/2, 1962/3, 1963/4, 1964/5, 1966/7, 1967/8, 1968/9 (Fulham) 1969/70.
Jones, D. (8) (Norwich City) 1975/6, 1977/8, 1979/80.
Jones, E. (4) (Swansea Town) 1947/8 (Tottenham Hotspur) 1948/9.
Jones, J. (72) (Liverpool) 1975/6, 1976/7, 1977/8 (Wrexham) 1978/9, 1979/80, 1980/1, 1981/2, 1982/3 (Chelsea) 1983/4, 1984/5 (Huddersfield Town) 1985/6.
Jones, K. (1) (Aston Villa) 1949/50.
Jones, P. L. (1) (Liverpool) 1996/97.
Jones, P. S. (1) (Stockport County) 1996/97.
Jones, R. (1) (Sheffield Wednesday) 1993/94.
Jones, T. G. (13) (Everton) 1946/7, 1947/8, 1948/9, 1949/50.
Jones, V.P. (9) (Wimbledon) 1994/95, 1995/96, 1996/97.
Jones, W. (1) (Bristol City) 1970/1.

Kelsey, J. (41) (Arsenal) 1953/4, 1954/5, 1955/6, 1956/7, 1957/8, 1958/9, 1959/60, 1960/1, 1961/2.
King, J. (1) (Swansea Town) 1954/5.
Kinsey, N. (7) (Norwich City) 1950/1, 1951/2, 1953/4 (Birmingham City) 1955/6.
Knill, A. R. (1) (Swansea City) 1988/9.
Krzywicki, R. (West Bromwich Albion) 1969/70 (Huddersfield Town) 1970/1, 1971/2.

Lambert, R. (5) (Liverpool) 1946/7, 1947/8, 1948/9.
Law, B. J. (1) (QPR) 1989/90.
Lea, C. (2) (Ipswich Town) 1964/5.
Leek, K. (13) (Leicester City) 1960/1, 1961/2 (Newcastle United) (Birmingham City) 1962/3, 1964/5.
Legg, A. (4) (Birmingham City) 1995/96, 1996/97.
Lever, A. (1) (Leicester City) 1952/3.
Lewis, D. (1) (Swansea City) 1982/3.

Lloyd, B. (3) (Wrexham) 1975/6.
Lovell, S. (6) (Crystal Palace) 1981/2 (Millwall) 1984/5, 1985/6.
Lowndes, S. (10) (Newport County) 1982/3 (Millwall) 1984/5, 1985/6, 1986/7, (Barnsley) 1987/8.
Lowrie, G. (4) (Coventry City) 1947/8, 1948/9 (Newcastle United).
Lucas, M. (4) (Leyton Orient) 1961/2, 1962/3.
Lucas, W. (7) (Swansea Town) 1948/9, 1949/50, 1950/1.

Maguire, G. T. (7) (Portsmouth) 1989/90, 1991/2.
Mahoney, J. (51) (Stoke City) 1967/8, 1968/9 1970/1, 1972/3, 1973/4, 1974/5, 1975/6, 1976/7 (Middlesbrough) 1977/8, 1978/9 (Swansea City) 1979/80, 1981/2, 1982/3.
Mardon, P. J. (1) (West Bromwich Albion) 1995/96.
Marriott, A. (2) (Wrexham) 1995/96, 1996/97.
Marustik, C. (6) (Swansea City) 1981/2, 1982/3.
Medwin, T. (30) (Swansea Town) 1952/3, 1956/7 (Tottenham Hotspur) 1957/8, 1958/9, 1959/60, 1960/1, 1962/3.
Melville, A. K. (31) (Swansea C), 1989/90, 1990/1 (Oxford United), 1991/2, 1992/93 (Sunderland) 1993/94, 1994/95, 1995/96, 1996/97.
Mielczarek, R. (1) (Rotherham United) 1970/1.
Millington, A. (21) (West Bromwich Albion) 1962/3, 1964/5 (Crystal Palace) 1965/6 (Peterborough United) 1966/7, 1967/8, 1968/9, 1969/70 (Swansea City) 1970/1, 1971/2.
Moore, G. (21) (Cardiff City) 1959/60, 1960/1, 1961/2 (Chelsea) 1962/3, (Manchester United) 1963/4 (Northampton Town) 1965/6, 1968/9 (Charlton Athletic) 1969/70, 1970/1.
Morris, W. (5) (Burnley) 1946/7, 1948/9, 1951/2.

Nardiello, D. (2) (Coventry City) 1977/8.
Neilson, A. B. (5) (Newcastle United) 1991/2, 1993/94, 1994/95 (Southampton) 1996/97.
Nicholas, P. (73) (Crystal Palace) 1978/9, 1979/80, 1980/1 (Arsenal) 1981/2, 1982/3, 1983/4 (Crystal Palace) 1984/5, (Luton Town) 1985/6, 1986/7, 1987/8 (Aberdeen), (Chelsea) 1988/9, 1989/90, 1990/1 (Watford), 1991/2.
Niedzwiecki, E. A. (2) (Chelsea) 1984/5, 1987/8.
Nogan, L. M. (2) (Watford) 1991/2 (Reading) 1995/96.
Nurse, E. A. (2) (Chelsea) 1984/5, 1987/8.
Norman, A. J. (5) (Hull City) 1985/6, 1987/8.
Nurse, M. (12) (Swansea Town) 1959/60, 1960/1, 1962/3 (Middlesbrough) 1963/4.

O'Sullivan, P. (3) (Brighton & Hove Albion) 1972/3, 1975/6, 1978/9.

Page, M. (28) (Birmingham City) 1970/1, 1971/2, 1972/3, 1973/4, 1974/5, 1975/6, 1976/7, 1977/8, 1978/9.
Page, R. J. (3) (Watford) 1996/97.
Palmer, D. (3) (Swansea Town) 1956/7, 1957/8.
Parry, J. (1) (Swansea Town) 1950/1.
Pascoe, C. (10) (Swansea Town) 1983/4, (Sunderland) 1988/9, 1989/90 1990/91, 1991/2.
Paul, R. (33) (Swansea Town) 1948/9, 1949/50 (Manchester City) 1950/1, 1951/2, 1952/3, 1953/4, 1954/5, 1955/6.
Pembridge, M. A. (23) (Luton Town) 1991/2 (Derby County) 1992/93, 1993/94, 1994/95 (Sheffield Wednesday) 1995/96, 1996/97.
Perry, J. (1) (Cardiff City) 1993/94.
Phillips, D. (62) (Plymouth Argyle) 1983/4 (Manchester City) 1984/5, 1985/6, 1986/7 (Coventry City) 1987/8, 1988/9 (Norwich City) 1989/90, 1990/1, 1991/2, 1992/93 (Nottingham Forest) 1993/94, 1994/95, 1995/96.
Phillips, J. (4) (Chelsea) 1972/3, 1973/4, 1974/5, 1977/8.

Phillips, L. (58) (Cardiff City) 1970/1, 1971/2, 1972/3, 1973/4, 1974/5, (Aston Villa) 1975/6, 1976/7, 1977/8, 1978/9 (Swansea City) 1979/80, 1980/1, 1981/2 (Charlton Athletic).
Pontin, K. (2) (Cardiff City) 1979/80.
Powell, A. (8) (Leeds United) 1946/7, 1947/8, 1948/9 (Everton) 1949/50, 1950/1 (Birmingham City).
Powell, D. (11) (Wrexham) 1967/8, 1968/9 (Sheffield United) 1969/70, 1970/1.
Powell, I. (8) (QPR) 1946/7, 1947/8, 1948/9 (Aston Villa) 1949/50, 1950/1.
Price, P. (25) (Luton Town) 1979/80, 1980/1, 1981/2 (Tottenham Hotspur) 1982/3, 1983/4.
Pring, K. (3) (Rotherham United) 1965/6, 1966/7.
Pritchard, H. K. (1) (Bristol City) 1984/5.

Rankmore, F. (l (Peterborough United) 1965/6.
Ratcliffe, K. (59) (Everton) 1980/1, 1981/2, 1982/3, 1983/4, 1984/5, 1985/6, 1986/7, 1987/8, 1988/9, 1989/90, 1990/1, 1991/2 (Cardiff City) 1992/93.
Ready, K. (1) (Queens Park Rangers) 1996/97.
Reece, G. (29) (Sheffield United) 1965/6, 1966/7, 1969/70, 1970/1, 1971/2, (Cardiff City) 1972/3, 1973/4, 1974/5.
Reed, W. (2) (Ipswich Town) 1954/5.
Rees, A. (1) (Birmingham City) 1983/4.
Rees, J. M. (1) (Luton Town) 1991/2.
Rees, R. (39) (Coventry City) 1964/5, 1965/6, 1966/7, 1967/8 (West Bromwich Albion) 1968/9 (Nottingham Forest) 1969/70, 1970/1, 1971/2.
Rees, W. (4) (Cardiff City) 1948/9 (Tottenham Hotspur) 1949/50.
Richards, S. (1) (Cardiff City) 1946/7.
Roberts, A. M. (2) (Queens Park Rangers) 1992/93, 1996/97.
Roberts, D. (17) (Oxford United) 1972/3, 1973/4, 1974/5 (Hull City) 1975/6, 1976/7, 1977/8.
Roberts, I. W. (7) (Watford) 1989/90, (Huddersfield Town) 1991/2, (Leicester City) 1993/94, 1994/95.
Roberts, J. G. (22) (Arsenal) 1970/1, 1971/2, 1972/3, (Birmingham City) 1973/4, 1974/5, 1975/6..
Roberts, J. H. (1) (Bolton Wanderers) 1948/9.
Roberts, P. (4) (Portsmouth) 1973/4, 1974/5.
Robinson, J.R.C. (8) (Charlton Athletic) 1995/96, 1996/97.
Rodrigues, P. (40) (Cardiff City) 1964/5, 1965/6 (Leicester City) 1966/7, 1967/8, 1968/9, 1969/70 (Sheffield Wednesday) 1970/1, 1971/2, 1972/3, 1973/4.
Rouse, V. (1) (Crystal Palace) 1958/9.
Rowley, T. (1) (Tranmere Rovers) 1958/9.
Rush, I. (73) (Liverpool) 1979/80, 1980/1, 1981/2, 1982/3, 1983/4, 1984/5, 1985/6, 1986/7 (Juventus) 1987/8, (Liverpool) 1988/9, 1989/90, 1990/1, 1991/2, 1992/93, 1993/94, 1994/95, 1995/96.

Saunders, D. (58) (Brighton & Hove Albion) 1985/6, 1986/7 (Oxford United) 1987/8, (Derby County) 1988/9, 1989/90, 1990/91, (Liverpool) 1991/2 (Aston Villa) 1992/93, 1993/94, 1994/95 (Galatasaray) 1995/96 (Nottingham Forest) 1996/97.
Savage, R. W. (5) (Crewe Alexandra) 1995/96, 1996/97.
Sayer, P. (7) (Cardiff City) 1976/7, 1977/8.
Scrine, F. (2) (Swansea Town) 1949/50.
Sear, C. (1) (Manchester City) 1962/3.
Sherwood, A. (41) (Cardiff City) 1946/7, 1947/8, 1948/9, 1949/50, 1950/1, 1951/2, 1952/3, 1953/4, 1954/5, 1955/6, 1956/7 (Newport County).
Shortt, W. (12) (Plymouth Argyle) 1946/7, 1949/50, 1951/2, 1952/3.
Showers, D. (2) (Cardiff City) 1974/5.
Sidlow, C. (7) (Liverpool) 1946/7, 1947/8, 1948/9, 1949/50.

Slatter, N. (22) (Bristol Rovers) 1982/3, 1983/4, 1984/5 (Oxford United) 1985/6, 1986/7, 1987/8, 1988/9.

Smallman, D. (7 (Wrexham) 1973/4 (Everton) 1974/5, 1975/6.

Southall, N. (91) (Everton) 1981/2, 1982/3, 1983/4, 1984/5, 1985/6, 1986/7, 1987/8, 1988/9, 1989/90, 1990/1, 1991/2, 1992/93, 1993/94, 1994/95, 1995/96, 1996/97.

Speed, G. A. (42) (Leeds United), 1989/90, 1990/91, 1991/2, 1992/93, 1993/94, 1994/95, 1995/96 (Everton) 1996/97.

Sprake, G. (37) (Leeds United) 1963/4, 1964/5, 1965/6, 1966/7, 1967/8, 1968/9, 1969/70, 1970/1, 1971/2, 1972/3, 1973/4 (Birmingham City) 1974/5.

Stansfield, F. (1) (Cardiff City) 1948/9.

Stevenson, B. (15) (Leeds United) 1977/8, 1978/9, 1979/80, 1981/2 (Birmingham City).

Stevenson, N. (4) (Swansea City) 1981/2, 1982/3.

Stitfall, R. (2) (Cardiff City) 1952/3, 1956/7.

Sullivan, D. (17) (Cardiff City) 1952/3, 1953/4, 1954/5, 1956/7, 1957/8, 1958/9, 1959/60.

Symons, C. J. (27) (Portsmouth) 1991/2, 1992/93, 1993/94, 1994/95 (Manchester City) 1995/96, 1996/97.

Tapscott, D. (14) (Arsenal) 1953/4, 1954/5, 1955/6, 1956/7, 1958/9 (Cardiff City).

Taylor, G. K. (6) (Crystal Palace) 1995/96 (Sheffield United) 1996/97.

Thomas, D. (2) (Swansea Town) 1956/7, 1957/8.

Thomas, M. (51) (Wrexham) 1976/7, 1977/8, 1978/9 (Manchester United) 1979/80, 1980/1, 1981/2 (Everton) (Brighton) 1982/3 (Stoke City) 1983/4, (Chelsea) 1984/5, 1985/6 (West Bromwich Albion).

Thomas, M. R. (1) (Newcastle United) 1986/7.

Thomas, R. (50) (Swindon Town) 1966/7, 1967/8, 1968/9, 1969/70, 1970/1, 1971/2, 1972/3, 1973/4 (Derby County) 1974/5, 1975/6, 1976/7, 1977/8 (Cardiff City).

Thomas, S. (4) (Fulham) 1947/8, 1948/9.

Toshack, J. (40) (Cardiff City) 1968/9, 1969/70 (Liverpool) 1970/1, 1971/2, 1972/3, 1974/5, 1975/6, 1976/7, 1977/8 (Swansea City) 1978/9, 1979/80.

Trollope, P. J. (1) (Derby County) 1996/97.

Van Den Hauwe, P.W.R. (13) (Everton) 1984/5, 1985/6, 1986/7, 1987/8, 1988/9.

Vaughan, N. (10) (Newport County) 1982/3, 1983/4 (Cardiff City) 1984/5.

Vearncombe, G. (2) (Cardiff City) 1957/8, 1960/1.

Vernon, R. (32) (Blackburn Rovers) 1956/7, 1957/8, 1958/9, 1959/60 (Everton) 1960/1, 1961/2, 1962/3, 1963/4, 1964/5 (Stoke City) 1965/6, 1966/7, 1967/8.

Villars, A. (3) (Cardiff City) 1973/4.

Walley, T. (1) (Watford) 1970/1.

Walsh, I. (18) (Crystal Palace) 1979/80, 1980/1, 1981/2 (Swansea City).

Ward, D. (2) (Bristol Rovers) 1958/9, 1961/2 (Cardiff City).

Webster, C. (4) (Manchester United) 1956/7, 1957/8.

Williams, A. (7) (Reading) 1993/94, 1994/95, 1995/96.

Williams, D. G. (13) 1987/8 (Derby County) 1988/9, 1989/90 (Ipswich Town) 1992/93, 1995/96.

Williams, D. M. (5) (Norwich City) 1985/6, 1986/7.

Williams, G. (1) (Cardiff City) 1950/1.

Williams, G. E. (26) (West Bromwich Albion) 1959/60, 1960/1, 1962/3, 1963/4, 1964/5, 1965/6, 1966/7, 1967/8, 1968/9.

Williams, G.G. (5) (Swansea Town) 1960/1, 1961/2.

Williams, H. (4) (Newport County) 1948/9 (Leeds United) 1949/50, 1950/1.

Williams, Herbert (3) (Swansea Town) 1964/5, 1970/1.

Williams, S. (43) (West Bromwich Albion) 1953/4, 1954/5, 1955/6, 1957/8, 1958/9, 1959/60, 1960/1, 1961/2, 1962/3 (Southampton) 1963/4, 1964/5, 1965/6.

Witcomb, D. (3) (West Bromwich Albion) 1946/7 (Sheffield Wednesday).

Woosnam, P. (17) (Leyton Orient) 1958/9 (West Ham United) 1959/60, 1960/1, 1961/2, 1962/3 (Aston Villa).

Yorath, T. (59) (Leeds United) 1969/70, 1970/1, 1971/2, 1972/3, 1973/4, 1974/5, 1975/6 (Coventry City) 1976/7, 1977/8, 1978/9 (Tottenham Hotspur) 1979/80, 1980/1.

Young, E. (21) (Wimbledon) 1989/90, 1990/1 (Crystal Palace), 1991/2, 1992/93, 1993/94, (Wolverhampton Wanderers) 1995/96.

EIRE

Aherne, T. (16) (Belfast Celtic) 1945/6 (Luton Town) 1949/50, 1950/1, 1951/2, 1952/3, 1953/4.

Aldridge, J. W. (69) (Oxford United) 1985/6, 1986/7 (Liverpool) 1987/8, 1988/9 (Real Sociedad) 1989/90, 1990/1, (Tranmere Rovers) 1991/2, 1992/93, 1993/94, 1994/95, 1995/96, 1996/97.

Ambrose, P. (5) (Shamrock Rovers) 1954/5, 1963/4.

Anderson, J. (16) (Preston North End) 1979/80, 1981/2 (Newcastle United) 1983/4, 1985/6, 1986/7, 1987/8, 1988/9.

Babb, P. (21) (Coventry City) 1993/94 (Liverpool) 1994/95, 1995/96, 1996/97.

Bailham, E. (1) (Shamrock Rovers) 1963/4.

Barber, E. (2) (Shelbourne) 1965/6 (Birmingham City) 1965/6.

Beglin, J. (15) (Liverpool) 1983/4, 1984/5, 1985/6, 1986/7.

Bonner, P. (80) (Celtic) 1980/1, 1981/2, 1983/4, 1984/5, 1985/6, 1986/7, 1987/8, 1988/9, 1989/90, 1990/1, 1991/2, 1992/93, 1993/94, 1994/95, 1995/96.

Braddish, S. (1) (Dundalk) 1977/8.

Brady, T.R. (6) (QPR) 1963/4.

Brady, W. L. (72) (Arsenal) 1974/5, 1975/6, 1976/7, 1977/8, 1978/9, 1979/80 (Juventus) 1980/1, 1981/2 (Sampdoria) 1982/3, 1983/4 (Internazionale) 1984/5, 1985/6 (Ascoli) 1986/7 (West Ham United) 1987/8, 1988/9, 1989/90.

Branagan, K. G. (1) (Bolton Wanderers) 1996/97.

Breen, G. (10) (Birmingham City) 1995/96 (Coventry City) 1996/97.

Breen, T. (3) (Shamrock Rovers) 1946/7.

Brennan, F. (1) (Drumcondra) 1964/5.

Brennan, S. A. (19) (Manchester United) 1964/5, 1965/6, 1966/7, 1968/9, 1969/70 (Waterford) 1970/1.

Browne, W. (3) (Bohemians) 1963/4.

Buckley, L. (2) (Shamrock Rovers) 1983/4 (Waregem) 1984/5.

Burke, F. (1) (Cork Athletic) 1951/2.

Byrne, A. B. (14) (Southampton) 1969/70, 1970/1, 1972/3, 1973/4.

Byrne, J. (23) (QPR) 1984/5, 1986/7, 1987/8 (Le Havre) 1989/90, 1990/1 (Brighton & Hove Albion), 1991/2 (Sunderland) 1992/93 (Millwall).

Byrne, P. (8) (Shamrock Rovers) 1983/4, 1984/5, 1985/6.

Campbell, A. (3) (Santander) 1984/5.

Campbell, N. (11) (St Patrick's Athletic) 1970/1 (Fortuna Cologne) 1971/2, 1972/3, 1974/5, 1975/6.

Cantwell, N. (36) (West Ham United) 1953/4, 1955/6, 1956/7, 1957/8, 1958/9, 1959/60, 1960/1 (Manchester United) 1960/1, 1961/2, 1962/3, 1963/4, 1964/5, 1965/6, 1966/7.

Carey, B. P. (3) (Manchester United) 1991/2, 1992/93 (Leicester City) 1993/94.

Carey, J. J. (21) (Manchester United) 1945/6, 1946/7, 1947/8, 1948/9, 1949/50, 1950/1, 1952/3.

Carolan, J. (2) (Manchester United) 1959/60.

Carroll, B. (2) (Shelbourne) 1948/9, 1949/50.

Carroll, T. R. (17) (Ipswich Town) 1967/8, 1968/9, 1969/70, 1970/1 (Birmingham City) 1971/2, 1972/3.

Cascarino, A. G. (70) (Gillingham) 1985/6 (Millwall) 1987/8, 1988/9, 1989/90 (Aston Villa), 1990/9 (Celtic) 1991/2 (Chelsea) 1992/93, 1993/94 (Marseille) 1994/95, 1995/96 (Nancy) 1996/97.

Chandler, J. (2) (Leeds United) 1979/80.

Clarke, J. (1) (Drogheda United) 1977/8.

Clarke, K. (2) (Drumcondra) 1947/8.

Clarke, M. (1) (Shamrock Rovers) 1949/50.

Clinton, T. J. (3) (Everton) 1950/1, 1953/4.

Coad, P. (11) (Shamrock Rovers) 1946/7, 1947/8, 1948/9, 1950/1, 1951/2.

Coffey, T. (1) (Drumcondra) 1949/50.

Colfer, M. D. (2) (Shelbourne) 1949/50, 1950/1.

Conmy, O. M. (5) (Peterborough United) 1964/5, 1966/7, 1967/8, 1969/70.

Connolly, D. J. (6) (Watford) 1995/96, 1996/97.

Conroy, G. A. (27) (Stoke City) 1969/70, 1970/1, 1972/3, 1973/4, 1974/5, 1975/6, 1976/7.

Conway, J. P. (20) (Fulham) 1966/7, 1967/8, 1968/9, 1969/70, 1970/1, 1973/4, 1974/5, 1975/6 (Manchester City) 1976/7.

Corr, P. J. (4) (Everton) 1948/9.

Courtney, E. (1) (Cork United) 1945/6.

Coyle, O. (1) (Bolton Wanderers) 1993/94.

Coyne, T. (21) (Celtic) 1991/2, (Tranmere Rovers) 1992/93, (Motherwell) 1993/94, 1994/95, 1995/96.

Cummins, G. P. (19) (Luton Town) 1953/4, 1954/5, 1955/6, 1957/8, 1958/9, 1959/60, 1960/1.

Cuneen, T. (1) (Limerick) 1950/1.

Cunningham, K. (10) (Wimbledon) 1995/96, 1996/97.

Curtis, D. P. (17) (Shelbourne) 1956/7 (Bristol City) 1956/7, 1957/8, (Ipswich Town) 1958/9, 1959/60, 1960/1, 1961/2, 1962/3 (Exeter City) 1963/4.

Cusack, S. (1) (Limerick) 1952/3.

Daish, L. S. (5) (Cambridge United) 1991/2, (Coventry City) 1995/96.

Daly, G. A. (48) (Manchester United) 1972/3, 1973/4, 1974/5, 1976/7 (Derby County) 1977/8, 1978/9, 1979/80 (Coventry City) 1980/1, 1981/2, 1982/3, 1983/4 (Birmingham City) 1984/5, 1985/6 (Shrewsbury Town) 1986/7.

Daly, M. (2) (Wolverhampton Wanderers) 1977/8.

Daly, P. (1) (Shamrock Rovers) 1949/50.

De Mange, K.J.P.P. (2) (Liverpool) 1986/7, (Hull City) 1988/9.

Deacy, E. (4) (Aston Villa) 1981/2.

Dempsey, J. T. (19) (Fulham) 1966/7, 1967/8, 1968/9 (Chelsea) 1968/9, 1969/70, 1970/1, 1971/2.

Dennehy, J. (11) (Cork Hibernian) 1971/2 (Nottingham Forest) 1972/3, 1973/4, 1974/5 (Walsall) 1975/6, 1976/7.

Desmond, P. (4) (Middlesbrough) 1949/50.

Devine, J. (12) (Arsenal) 1979/80, 1980/1, 1981/2, 1982/3 (Norwich City) 1983/4, 1984/5.

Donovan, D. C. (5) (Everton) 1954/5, 1956/7.

Donovan, T. (1) (Aston Villa) 1979/80.

Doyle, C. (1) (Shelbourne) 1958/9.

Duffy, B. (1) (Shamrock Rovers) 1949/50.

Dunne, A. P. (33) (Manchester United) 1961/2, 1962/3, 1963/4, 1964/5, 1965/6, 1966/7, 1968/9, 1969/70, 1970/1 (Bolton Wanderers) 1973/4, 1974/5, 1975/6.

Dunne, J. C. (1) (Fulham) 1970/1.

Dunne, P.A.J. (5) (Manchester United) 1964/5, 1965/6, 1966/7.

Dunne, S. (15) (Luton Town) 1952/3, 1953/4, 1955/6, 1956/7, 1957/8, 1958/9, 1959/60.

Dunne, T. (3) (St Patrick's Athletic) 1955/6, 1956/7.
Dunning, P. (2) (Shelbourne) 1970/1.
Dunphy, E. M. (23) (York City) 1965/6 (Millwall) 1965/6, 1966/7, 1967/8, 1968/9, 1969/70, 1970/1.
Dwyer, N. M. (14) (West Ham United) 1959/60 (Swansea Town) 1960/1, 1961/2, 1963/4, 1964/5.

Eccles, P. (1) (Shamrock Rovers) 1985/6.
Eglington, T. J. (24) (Shamrock Rovers) 1945/6 (Everton) 1946/7, 1947/8, 1948/9, 1950/1, 1951/2, 1952/3, 1953/4, 1954/5, 1955/6.

Fagan, E. (1) (Shamrock Rovers) 1972/3.
Fagan, F. (8) (Manchester City) 1954/5, 1959/60 (Derby County) 1959/60, 1960/1.
Fairclough, M. (2) (Dundalk) 1981/2.
Fallon, S. (8) (Celtic) 1950/1, 1951/2, 1952/3, 1954/5.
Farrell, P. D. (28) (Shamrock Rovers) 1945/6 (Everton) 1946/7, 1947/8, 1948/9, 1949/50, 1950/1, 1951/2, 1952/3, 1953/4, 1954/5, 1955/6, 1956/7.
Farrelly, G. (3) (Aston Villa) 1995/96.
Finucane, A. (11) (Limerick) 1966/7, 1968/9, 1969/70, 1970/1, 1971/2.
Fitzgerald, F. J. (2) (Waterford) 1954/5, 1955/6.
Fitzgerald, P. J. (5) (Leeds United) 1960/1 (Chester) 1961/2.
Fitzpatrick, K. (1) (Limerick) 1969/70.
Fitzsimons, A. G. (26) (Middlesbrough) 1949/50, 1951/2, 1952/3, 1953/4, 1954/5, 1955/6, 1956/7, 1957/8, 1958/9 (Lincoln City) 1958/9.
Fleming, C. (8) (Middlesbrough) 1995/96, 1996/97.
Fogarty, A. (11) (Sunderland) 1959/60, 1960/1, 1961/2, 1962/3, 1963/4, (Hartlepool United) 1963/4.
Foley, T. C. (9) (Northampton Town) 1963/4, 1964/5, 1965/6, 1966/7.
Fullam, J. (Preston North End) 1960/1 (Shamrock Rovers) 1963/4, 1965/6, 1967/8, 1968/9, 1969/70.

Gallagher, C. (2) (Celtic) 1966/7.
Gallagher, M. (1) (Hibernian) 1953/4.
Galvin, A. (29) (Tottenham Hotspur) 1982/3, 1983/4, 1984/5, 1985/6, 1986/7 (Sheffield Wednesday) 1987/8, 1988/9, 1989/90.
Gannon, E. (14) (Notts County) 1948/9 (Sheffield Wednesday) 1948/9, 1949/50, 1950/1, 1951/2, 1953/4, 1954/5 (Shelbourne K) 1954/5.
Gannon, M. (1) (Shelbourne) 1971/2.
Gavin, J.T. (7) (Norwich City) 1949/50, 1952/3, 1953/4 (Tottenham Hotspur) 1954/5 (Norwich City) 1956/7.
Gibbons, A. (4) (St Patrick's Athletic) 1951/2, 1953/4, 1955/6.
Gilbert, R. (1) (Shamrock Rovers) 1965/6.
Giles, C. (1) (Doncaster Rovers) 1950/1.
Giles, M. J. (59) (Manchester United) 1959/60, 1960/1, 1961/2, 1962/3 (Leeds United) 1963/4, 1964/5, 1965/6, 1966/7, 1968/9, 1969/70, 1970/1, 1972/3, 1973/4, 1974/5 (West Bromwich Albion) 1975/6, 1976/7 (Shamrock Rovers) 1977/8, 1978/9.
Given, S.J.J. (9) (Blackburn Rovers) 1995/96, 1996/97.
Givens, D. J. (56) (Manchester United) 1968/9, 1969/70 (Luton Town) 1969/70, 1970/1, 1971/2 (QPR) 1972/3, 1973/4, 1974/5, 1975/6, 1976/7, 1977/8 (Birmingham City) 1978/9, 1979/80, 1980/1 (Neuchatel Xamax) 1981/2.
Glynn, D. (2) (Drumcondra) 1951/2, 1954/5.
Godwin, T. F. (13) (Shamrock Rovers) 1948/9, 1949/50 (Leicester City) 1949/50, 1950/1 (Bournemouth) 1955/6, 1956/7, 1957/8.
Goodman, J. (4) (Wimbledon) 1996/97.
Gorman, W. C. (2) (Brentford) 1946/7.

Grealish, A. (44) (Orient) 1975/6, 1978/9 (Luton Town) 1979/80, 1980/1, (Brighton & Hove Albion) 1981/2, 1982/3, 1983/4 (West Bromwich Albion) 1984/5, 1985/6.

Gregg, E. (8) (Bohemians) 1977/8, 1978/9, 1979/80.

Grimes, A. A. (17) (Manchester United) 1977/8, 1979/80, 1980/1, 1981/2, 1982/3 (Coventry City) 1983/4 (Luton Town) 1987/8.

Hale, A. (13) (Aston Villa) 1961/2 (Doncaster Rovers) 1962/3, 1963/4, (Waterford) 1966/7, 1967/8, 1968/9, 1969/70, 1970/1, 1971/2.

Hamilton, T. (2) (Shamrock Rovers) 1958/9.

Hand, E. K. (20) (Portsmouth) 1968/9, 1969/70, 1970/1, 1972/3, 1973/4, 1974/5, 1975/6.

Harte, I. P. (11) (Leeds United) 1995/96, 1996/97.

Hartnett, J. B. (2) (Middlesbrough) 1948/9, 1953/4.

Haverty, J. (32) (Arsenal) 1955/6, 1956/7, 1957/8, 1958/9, 1959/60, 1960/1, (Blackburn Rovers) 1961/2 (Millwall) 1962/3, 1963/4 (Celtic) 1964/5, (Bristol Rovers) 1964/5 (Shelbourne) 1965/6, 1966/7.

Hayes, A.W.P. (1) (Southampton) 1978/9.

Hayes, W. E. (2) (Huddersfield Town) 1946/7.

Hayes, W. J. (1) (Limerick) 1948/9.

Healey, R. (2) (Cardiff City) 1976/7, 1979/80.

Heighway, S .D. (34) (Liverpool) 1970/1, 1972/3, 1974/5, 1975/6, 1976/7, 1977/8, 1978/9, 1979/80, 1980/1 (Minnesota Kicks) 1981/2.

Henderson, B. (2) (Drumcondra) 1947/8.

Hennessy, J. (5) (Shelbourne) 1955/6, 1965/6 (St Patrick's Athletic) 1968/9.

Herrick, J. (3) (Cork Hibernians) 1971/2 (Shamrock Rovers) 1972/3.

Higgins, J. (1) (Birmingham City) 1950/1.

Holmes, J. (Coventry City) 1970/1, 1972/3, 1973/4, 1974/5, 1975/6, 1976/7 (Tottenham Hotspur) 1977/8, 1978/9, 1980/1 (Vancouver Whitecaps) 1980/1.

Houghton, R. J. (69) (Oxford United) 1985/6, 1986/7, 1987/8 (Liverpool) 1987/8, 1988/9, 1989/90, 1990/1, 1991/2 (Aston Villa) 1992/93, 1993/94 (Crystal Palace) 1994/95, 1995/96, 1996/97.

Howlett, G. (1) (Brighton & Hove Albion) 1983/4.

Hughton, C. (53) (Tottenham Hotspur) 1979/80, 1980/1, 1981/2, 1982/3, 1983/4, 1984/5, 1985/6, 1986/7, 1987/8, 1988/9, 1989/90, 1990/1 (West Ham United), 1991/2.

Hurley, C. J. (40) (Millwall) 1956/7, 1957/8 (Sunderland) 1958/9, 1959/60, 1960/1, 1961/2, 1962/3, 1963/4, 1964/5, 1965/6, 1966/7, 1967/8 (Bolton Wanderers) 1968/9.

Irwin, D. J. (45) (Manchester United) 1990/1, 1991/2, 1992/93, 1993/94, 1994/95, 1995/96, 1996/97.

Keane, R. M. (35) (Nottingham Forest) 1990/1, 1991/2, 1992/93, (Manchester United) 1993/94, 1994/95, 1995/96, 1996/97.

Keane, T. R. (4) (Swansea Town) 1948/9.

Kearin, M. (1) (Shamrock Rovers) 1971/2.

Kearns, F. T. (1) (West Ham United) 1953/4.

Kearns, M. (18) (Oxford United) 1969/70 (Walsall) 1973/4, 1975/6, 1976/7, 1977/8, 1978/9 (Wolverhampton Wanderers) 1979/80.

Kelly, A. T. (18) (Sheffield United) 1992/93, 1993/94, 1994/95, 1995/96, 1996/97.

Kelly, D. T. (23) (Walsall) 1987/8 (West Ham) 1988/9 (Leicester City) 1989/90, 1990/1 (Newcastle United) 1991/2, 1992/93 (Wolverhampton Wanderers) 1993/94, 1994/95 (Sunderland) 1995/96, 1996/97.

Kelly, G. (21) (Leeds United) 1993/94, 1994/95, 1995/96, 1996/97.

Kelly J. A. (48) (Drumcondra) 1956/7 (Preston North End) 1961/2, 1962/3, 1963/4, 1964/5, 1965/6, 1966/7, 1967/8, 1969/70, 1970/1, 1971/2, 1972/3.

Kelly, J.P.V. (5) (Wolverhampton Wanderers) 1960/1, 1961/2.

Kelly, M. J. (4) (Portsmouth) 1987/8, 1988/9, 1990/1.

Kelly, N. (1) (Nottingham Forest) 1953/4.
Kenna, J. J. (17) (Blackburn Rovers) 1994/95, 1995/96, 1996/97.
Kennedy, M. (12) (Liverpool) 1995/96, 1996/97.
Kennedy, M. F. (2) (Portsmouth) 1985/6.
Keogh, J. (1) (Shamrock Rovers) 1965/6.
Keogh, S. (1) (Shamrock Rovers) 1958/9.
Kernaghan, A. N. (22) (Middlesbrough) 1992/93 (Manchester City) 1993/94, 1994/95, 1995/96.
Kiernan, F. W. (5) (Shamrock Rovers) 1950/1 (Southampton) 1951/2.
Kinnear, J. P. (26) (Tottenham Hotspur) 1966/7, 1967/8, 1968/9, 1969/70, 1970/1, 1971/2, 1972/3, 1973/4, 1974/5 (Brighton & Hove Albion) 1975/6.

Langan, D. (25) (Derby County) 1977/8, 1979/80 (Birmingham City) 1980/1, 1981/2 (Oxford United) 1984/5, 1985/6, 1986/7, 1987/8.
Lawler, J. F. (8) (Fulham) 1952/3, 1953/4, 1954/5, 1955/6.
Lawlor, J. C. (3) (Drumcondra) 1948/9 (Doncaster Rovers) 1950/1.
Lawlor, M. (5) (Shamrock Rovers) 1970/1, 1972/3.
Lawrenson, M. (38) (Preston North End) 1976/7 (Brighton & Hove Albion) 1977/8, 1978/9, 1979/80, 1980/1 (Liverpool) 1981/2, 1982/3, 1983/4, 1984/5, 1985/6, 1986/7, 1987/8.
Leech, M. (8) (Shamrock Rovers) 1968/9, 1971/2, 1972/3.
Lowry, D. (1) (St Patrick's Athletic) 1961/2.

McAlinden, J. (2) (Portsmouth) 1945/6.
McAteer, J. W. (22) (Bolton Wanderers) 1993/94, 1994/95 (Liverpool) 1995/96, 1996/97.
McCann, J. (1) (Shamrock Rovers) 1956/7.
McCarthy, M. (57) (Manchester City) 1983/4, 1984/5, 1985/6, 1986/7 (Celtic) 1987/8, 1988/9 (Lyon) 1989/90, 1990/1 (Millwall), 1991/2.
McConville, T. (6) (Dundalk) 1971/2 (Waterford) 1972/3.
McDonagh, J. (24) (Everton) 1980/1 (Bolton Wanderers) 1981/2, 1982/3, (Notts County) 1983/4, 1984/5, 1985/6.
McDonagh, Joe (3) (Shamrock Rovers) 1983/4, 1984/5.
McEvoy, M. A. (17) (Blackburn Rovers) 1960/1, 1962/3, 1963/4, 1964/5, 1965/6, 1966/7.
McGee, P. (15) (QPR) 1977/8, 1978/9, 1979/80 (Preston North End) 1980/1.
McGoldrick, E. J. (15) (Crystal Palace) 1991/2, 1992/93, (Arsenal) 1993/94, 1994/95.
McGowan, D. (3) (West Ham United) 1948/9.
McGowan, J. (1) (Cork United) 1946/7.
McGrath, M. (22) (Blackburn Rovers) 1957/8, 1958/9, 1959/60, 1960/1, 1961/2, 1962/3, 1963/4, 1964/5, 1965/6 (Bradford Park Avenue) 1965/6, 1966/7.
McGrath, P. (83) (Manchester United) 1984/5, 1985/6, 1986/7, 1987/8, 1988/9 (Aston Villa) 1989/90, 1990/1, 1991/2, 1992/93, 1993/94, 1994/95, 1995/96 (Derby County) 1996/97.
Macken, A. (1) (Derby County) 1976/7.
Mackey, G. (3) (Shamrock Rovers) 1956/7.
McLoughlin, A. F. (28) (Swindon T) 1989/90, 1990/1 (Southampton) 1991/2 (Portsmouth) 1992/93, 1993/94, 1994/95, 1995/96, 1996/97.
McMillan, W. (2) (Belfast Celtic) 1945/6.
McNally, J. B. (3) (Luton Town) 1958/9, 1960/1, 1962/3.
Malone, G. (1) (Shelbourne) 1948/9.
Mancini, T. J. (5) (QPR) 1973/4 (Arsenal) 1974/5.
Martin, C. J. (30) (Glentoran) 1945/6, 1946/7 (Leeds United) 1946/7, 1947/8, (Aston Villa) 1948/9, 1949/50 1950/1, 1951/2, 1953/4, 1954/5, 1955/6.

Martin, M. P. (51) (Bohemians) 1971/2, 1972/3 (Manchester United) 1972/3, 1973/4, 1974/5 (West Bromwich Albion) 1975/6, 1976/7 (Newcastle United) 1978/9, 1979/80, 1981/2, 1982/3.

Meagan, M. K. (17) (Everton) 1960/1, 1961/2, 1962/3, 1963/4 (Huddersfield Town) 1964/5, 1965/6, 1966/7, 1967/8 (Drogheda) 1969/70.

Milligan, M. J. (1) (Oldham Athletic) 1991/2.

Mooney, J. (2) (Shamrock Rovers) 1964/5.

Moore, A. (8) (Middlesbrough) 1995/96, 1996/97.

Moran, K. (70) (Manchester United) 1979/80, 1980/1, 1981/2, 1982/3, 1983/4, 1984/5, 1985/6, 1986/7, 1987/8 (Sporting Gijon) 1988/9 (Blackburn Rovers) 1989/90, 1990/1, 1991/2, 1992/93, 1993/94.

Moroney, T. (12) (West Ham United) 1947/8, 1948/9, 1949/50, 1950/1, 1951/2, 1953/4.

Morris, C. B. (35) (Celtic) 1987/8, 1988/9, 1989/90, 1990/1, 1991/2 (Middlesbrough) 1992/93.

Moulson, G. B. (3) (Lincoln City) 1947/8, 1948/9.

Mucklan, C. (1) (Drogheda) 1977/8.

Mulligan, P. M. (50) (Shamrock Rovers) 1968/9, 1969/70 (Chelsea) 1969/70, 1970/1, 1971/2 (Crystal Palace) 1972/3, 1973/4, 1974/5 (West Bromwich Albion) 1975/6, 1976/7, 1977/8, 1978/9 (Shamrock Rovers) 1979/80.

Munroe, L. (1) (Shamrock Rovers) 1953/4.

Murphy, A. (1) (Clyde) 1955/6.

Murphy, B. (1) (Bohemians) 1985/6.

Murphy, J. (1) (Crystal Palace) 1979/80.

Murray, T. (1) (Dundalk) 1949/50.

Newman, W. (1) (Shelbourne) 1968/9.

Nolan, R. (10) (Shamrock Rovers) 1956/7, 1957/8, 1959/60, 1961/2, 1962/3.

O'Brien, F. (4) (Philadelphia Fury) 1979/80.

O'Brien, L. (16) (Shamrock Rovers) 1985/6 (Manchester United) 1986/7, 1987/8 (Newcastle United) 1988/9, 1991/2, 1992/93 (Tranmere Rovers) 1993/94, 1995/96, 1996/97.

O'Brien, R. (4) (Notts County) 1975/6, 1976/7.

O'Byrne, L.B. (1) (Shamrock Rovers) 1948/9.

O'Callaghan, B. R. (6) (Stoke City) 1978/9, 1979/80, 1980/1, 1981/2.

O'Callaghan, K. (20) (Ipswich Town) 1980/1, 1981/2, 1982/3, 1983/4, 1984/5, (Portsmouth) 1985/6, 1986/7.

O'Connell, A. (2) (Dundalk) 1966/7 (Bohemians) 1970/1.

O'Connor, T. (4) (Shamrock Rovers) 1949/50.

O'Connor, T. (7) (Fulham) 1967/8 (Dundalk) 1971/2 (Bohemians) 1972/3.

O'Driscoll, J. F. (3) (Swansea Town) 1948/9.

O'Driscoll, S. (3) (Fulham) 1981/2.

O'Farrell, F. (9) (West Ham United) 1951/2, 1952/3, 1953/4, 1954/5, 1955/6 (Preston North End) 1957/8, 1958/9.

O'Flanagan, K. P. (3) (Arsenal) 1946/7.

O'Flanagan, M. (1) (Bohemians) 1946/7.

O'Hanlon, K. G. (1) (Rotherham United) 1987/8.

O'Keefe, E. (5) (Everton) 1980/1 (Port Vale) 1983/4.

O'Leary, D. (67) (Arsenal) 1976/7, 1977/8, 1978/9, 1979/80, 1980/1, 1981/2, 1982/3, 1983/4, 1984/5, 1985/6, 1988/9, 1989/90, 1990/1, 1991/2, 1992/93.

O'Leary, P. (7) (Shamrock Rovers) 1979/80, 1980/1.

O'Neill, F. S. (20) (Shamrock Rovers) 1961/2, 1964/5, 1965/6, 1966/7, 1968/9, 1971/2.

O'Neill, J. (17) (Everton) 1951/2, 1952/3, 1953/4, 1954/5, 1955/6, 1956/7, 1957/8, 1958/9.

O'Neill, J. (1) (Preston North End) 1960/1.

O'Neill, K. P. (9) (Norwich City) 1995/96, 1996/97.
O'Regan, K. (4) (Brighton & Hove Albion) 1983/4, 1984/5.
O'Reilly, J. (2) (Cork United) 1945/6.

Peyton, G. (33) (Fulham) 1976/7, 1977/8, 1978/9, 1979/80, 1980/1, 1981/2, 1984/5, 1985/6 (Bournemouth) 1987/8, 1988/9, 1989/90, 1990/1 (Everton) 1991/2.
Peyton, N. (6) (Shamrock Rovers) 1956/7 (Leeds United) 1959/60, 1960/1, 1962/3.
Phelan, T. (37) (Wimbledon) 1991/2 (Manchester City) 1992/93, 1993/94, 1994/95, 1995/96 (Chelsea) (Everton) 1996/97.

Quinn, N. J. (61) (Arsenal) 1985/6, 1986/7, 1987/8, 1988/9 (Manchester City) 1989/90, 1990/1, 1991/2, 1992/93, 1993/94, 1994/95, 1995/96 (Sunderland) 1996/97.

Richardson, D. J. (3) (Shamrock Rovers) 1971/2 (Gillingham) 1972/3, 1979/80.
Ringstead, A. (20) (Sheffield United) 1950/1, 1951/2, 1952/3, 1953/4, 1954/5, 1955/6, 1956/7, 1957/8, 1958/9.
Robinson, M. (23) (Brighton & Hove Albion) 1980/1, 1981/2, 1982/3, (Liverpool) 1983/4, 1984/5 (QPR) 1985/6.
Roche, P. J. (8) (Shelbourne) 1971/2 (Manchester United) 1974/5, 1975/6.
Rogers, E. (19) (Blackburn Rovers) 1967/8, 1968/9, 1969/70, 1970/1, (Charlton Athletic) 1971/2, 1972/3.
Ryan, G. (16) (Derby County) 1977/8 (Brighton & Hove Albion) 1978/9, 1979/80, 1980/1, 1981/2, 1983/4, 1984/5.
Ryan, R. A. (16) (West Bromwich Albion) 1949/50, 1950/1, 1951/2, 1952/3, 1953/4, 1954/5 (Derby County) 1955/6.

Savage, D.P.T. (5) (Millwall) 1995/96.
Saward, P. (18) (Millwall) 1953/4 (Aston Villa) 1956/7, 1957/8, 1958/9, 1959/60, 1960/1 (Huddersfield Town) 1960/1, 1961/2, 1962/3.
Scannell, T. (1) (Southend United) 1953/4.
Scully, P. J. (1) (Arsenal) 1988/9.
Sheedy, K. (45) (Everton) 1983/4, 1984/5, 1985/6, 1986/7, 1987/8, 1988/9, 1989/90, 1990/1 (Newcastle United) 1991/2, 1992/93.
Sheridan, J. J. (34) (Leeds United) 1987/8, 1988/9 (Sheffield Wednesday) 1989/90, 1990/1, 1991/2, 1992/93, 1993/94, 1994/95, 1995/96.
Slaven, B. (7) (Middlesbrough) 1989/90, 1990/91, 1992/93.
Sloan, J. W. (2) (Arsenal) 1945/6.
Smyth, M. (1) (Shamrock Rovers) 1968/9.
Stapleton, F. (70) (Arsenal) 1976/7, 1977/8, 1978/9, 1979/80, 1980/1 (Manchester United) 1981/2, 1982/3, 1983/4, 1984/5, 1985/6, 1986/7 (Ajax) 1987/8 (Derby County) 1987/8 (Le Havre) 1988/9 (Blackburn Rovers) 1989/90.
Staunton, S. (68) (Liverpool) 1988/9, 1989/90, 1990/1 (Aston Villa) 1991/2, 1992/93, 1993/94, 1994/95, 1995/96, 1996/97.

Stevenson, A. E. (6) (Everton) 1946/7, 1947/8, 1948/9.
Strahan, F. (5) (Shelbourne) 1963/4, 1964/5, 1965/6.
Swan, M.M.G. (1) (Drumcondra) 1959/60.
Synott, N. (3) (Shamrock Rovers) 1977/8, 1978/9.

Thomas, P. (2) (Waterford) 1973/4.
Townsend, A. D. (66) (Norwich City) 1988/9, 1989/90, 1990/1 (Chelsea) 1991/2, 1992/93 (Aston Villa) 1993/94, 1994/95, 1995/96, 1996/97.
Traynor, T. J. (8) (Southampton) 1953/4, 1961/2, 1962/3, 1963/4.
Treacy, R.C.P. (42) (West Bromwich Albion) 1965/6, 1966/7, 1967/8 (Charlton Athletic) 1967/8, 1968/9, 1969/70, 1970/1 (Swindon Town) 1971/2, 1972/3, 1973/4 (Preston North End) 1973/4, 1974/5, 1975/6 (West Bromwich Albion) 1976/7, 1977/8 (Shamrock Rovers) 1979/80.

Tuohy, L. (8) (Shamrock Rovers) 1955/6, 1958/9 (Newcastle United) 1961/2, 1962/3 (Shamrock Rovers) 1963/4, 1964/5.
Turner, P. (2) (Celtic) 1962/3, 1963/4.

Vernon, J. (2) (Belfast Celtic) 1945/6.

Waddock, G. (20) (QPR) 1979/80, 1980/1, 1981/2, 1982/3, 1983/4, 1984/5, 1985/6 (Millwall) 1989/90.
Walsh, D. J. (20) (West Bromwich Albion) 1945/6, 1946/7, 1947/8, 1948/9, 1949/50, 1950/1 (Aston Villa) 1951/2, 1952/3, 1953/4.
Walsh, J. (1) (Limerick) 1981/2.
Walsh, M. (21) (Blackpool) 1975/6, 1976/7 (Everton) 1978/9 (QPR) 1978/9 (Porto) 1980/1, 1981/2, 1982/3, 1983/4, 1984/5.
Walsh, M. (4) (Everton) 1981/2, 1982/3 (Norwich City) 1982/3.
Walsh, W. (9) (Manchester City) 1946/7, 1947/8, 1948/9, 1949/50.
Waters, J. (2) (Grimsby Town) 1976/7, 1979/80.
Whelan, R. (2) (St Patrick's Athletic) 1963/4.
Whelan, R. (53) (Liverpool) 1980/1, 1981/2, 1982/3, 1983/4, 1984/5, 1985/6, 1986/7, 1987/8, 1988/9, 1989/90, 1990/1, 1991/2, 1992/93, 1993/94 (Southend United) 1994/95.
Whelan, W. (4) (Manchester United) 1955/6, 1956/7.
Whittaker, R. (1) (Chelsea) 1958/9.

BRITISH ISLES INTERNATIONAL GOALSCORERS SINCE 1946

ENGLAND

Name	Goals
A'Court, A.	1
Adams, T.A.	4
Allen, R.	2
Anderson, V.	2
Anderton, D.R.	5
Astall, G.	1
Atyeo, P.J.W.	5
Baily, E.F.	5
Baker, J.H.	3
Ball, A.J.	8
Barnes, J.	11
Barnes, P.S.	4
Barmby, N.J.	3
Beardsley, P.A.	9
Beattie, I.K.	1
Bell, C.	9
Bentley, R.T.F.	9
Blissett, L.	3
Bowles, S.	1
Bradford, G.R.W.	1
Bradley, W.	2
Bridges, B.J.	1
Broadbent, P.F.	2
Broadis, I.A.	8
Brooking, T.D.	5
Brooks, J.	2
Bull, S.G.	4
Butcher, T.	3
Byrne, J.J.	8
Carter, H.S.	7
(inc. 2 scored pre-war)	
Chamberlain, M.	1
Channon, M.R.	21
Charlton, J.	6
Charlton, R.	49
Chivers, M.	13
Clarke, A.J.	10
Connelly, J.M.	7
Coppell, S.J.	7
Cowans, G.	2
Crawford, R.	1
Currie, A.W.	3
Dixon, L.M.	1
Dixon, K.M.	4
Douglas, B.	11
Eastham, G.	2
Edwards, D.	5
Elliott, W.H.	3
Ferdinand, L.	5
Finney, T.	30
Flowers, R.	10
Fowler, R.B.	1
Francis, G.C.J.	3
Francis, T.	12
Froggatt, J.	2
Froggatt, R.	2
Gascoigne, P.J.	9
Goddard, P.	1
Grainger, C.	3
Greaves, J.	44
Haines, J.T.W.	2
Hancocks, J.	2
Hassall, H.W.	4
Hateley, M.	9
Haynes, J.N.	18
Hirst, D.E.	1
Hitchens, G.A.	5
Hoddle, G.	8
Hughes, E.W.	1
Hunt, R.	18
Hunter, N.	2
Hurst, G.C.	24
Johnson, D.E.	6
Kay, A.H.	1
Keegan, J.K.	21
Kennedy, R.	3
Keown, M.R.	1
Kevan, D.T.	8
Kidd, B.	1
Langton, R.	1
Latchford, R.D.	5
Lawler, C.	1
Lawton, T.	22
(inc. 6 scored pre-war)	
Lee, F.	10
Lee, J.	1
Lee, R.M.	2
Lee, S.	2
Le Saux, G.P.	1
Lineker, G.	48
Lofthouse, N.	30
Mabbutt, G.	1
McDermott, T.	3
Macdonald, M.	6
Mannion, W.J.	11
Mariner, P.	13
Marsh, R.W.	1
Matthews, S.	11
(inc. 8 scored pre-war)	
Medley, L.D.	1
Melia, J.	1
Merson, P.C.	1
Milburn, J.E.T.	10
Moore, R.F.	2
Morris, J.	3
Mortensen, S.H.	23
Mullen, J.	6
Mullery, A.P.	1
Neal, P.G.	5
Nicholls, J.	1
Nicholson, W.E.	1
O'Grady, M.	3
Own goals	23
Paine, T.L.	7
Palmer, C.L.	1
Parry, R.A.	1
Peacock, A.	3
Pearce, S.	4
Pearson, J.S.	5
Pearson, S.C.	5
Perry, W.	2
Peters, M.	20
Pickering, F.	5
Platt, D.	27
Pointer, R.	2
Ramsay, A.E.	3
Revie, D.G.	4
Robson, B.	26
Robson, R.	4
Rowley, J.F.	6
Royle, J.	2

Sansom, K.	1	Bremner, W.J.	3	Hewie, J.D.	2
Scholes, P.		Brown, A.D.	6	Holton, J.A.	2
Sewell, J.	3	Buckley, P.	1	Houliston, W.	2
Shackleton, L.F.	1	Burns, K.	1	Howie, H.	1
Shearer, A.	16			Hughes, J.	1
Sheringham, E.P.	8	Calderwood, C.	1	Hunter, W.	1
Smith, A.M.		Caldow, E.	4	Hutchison, T.	1
Smith, R.	13	Campbell, R.	1		
Steven, T.M.	4	Chalmers, S.	3		
Stiles, N.P.	13	Collins, J.	9	Jackson, C.	1
Stone, S.B.	2	Collins, R.V.	10	Jackson, D.	3
Summerbee, M.G.	1	Combe, J.R.	1	Jardine, A.	1
		Conn, A.	1	Jess, E.	1
Tambling, R.V.	1	Cooper, D.	6	Johnston, L.H.	1
Taylor, P.J.	2	Craig, J.	1	Johnston, M.	14
Taylor, T.	16	Crawford, S.	1	Johnstone, D.	2
Thompson, P.B.	1	Curran, H.P.	1	Johnstone, J.	4
Tueart, D.	2			Johnstone, R.	9
		Dailly, C.	1	Jordan, J.	11
Viollet, D.S.	1	Dalglish, K.	30		
		Davidson, J.A.	1		
Waddle, C.R.	6	Docherty, T.H.	1	Law, D.	30
Wallace, D.L.	1	Dodds, D.	1	Leggat, G.	8
Walsh, P.	1	Duncan, D.M.	1	Lennox, R.	3
Watson, D.V.	4	Durie, G.S.	5	Liddell, W.	6
Webb, N.	4			Linwood, A.B.	1
Weller, K.	1	Fernie, W.	1	Lorimer, P.	4
Wignall, F.	2	Flavell, R.	2		
Wilkins, R.G.	3	Fleming, C.	2	Macari, L.	5
Wilshaw, D.J.	10			McAllister, G.	5
Wise, D.F.	1	Gallacher, K.W.	5	MacDougall, E.J.	3
Withe, P.	1	Gemmell, T.K		MacKay, D.C.	4
Woodcock, T.	16	(St Mirren)	1	Mackay, G.	1
Worthington, F.S.	2	Gemmell, T.K		MacKenzie, J.A.	1
Wright, I.E.	7	(Celtic)	1	MacLeod, M.	1
Wright, M.	1	Gemmill, A.	8	McAvennie, F.	1
Wright, W.A.	3	Gibson, D.W.	3	McCall, S.M.	1
		Gilzean, A.J.	12	McCalliog, J.	1
SCOTLAND		Gough, C.R.	6	McClair, B.	2
Aitken, R.	1	Graham, A.	2	McCoist, A.	19
Archibald, S.	4	Graham, G.	3	McGhee, M.	2
		Gray, A.	7	McGinlay, J.	3
Baird, S.	2	Gray, E.		McInally, A.	3
Bannon, E.	1	Gray, F.	1	McKimmie, S.I.	1
Bauld, W.	2	Greig, J.	3	McKinlay, W.	4
Baxter, J.C.	3			McKinnon, R.	
Bett, J.	1	Hamilton, G.	4	McLaren, A.	4
Bone, J.	1	Harper, J.M.	2	McLean, T.	1
Booth, S.	5	Hartford, R.A.	4	McLintock, F.	1
Boyd, T.	1	Henderson, J.G.	1	McMillan, I.L.	2
Brand, R.	8	Henderson, W.	5	McNeill, W.	3
Brazil, A.	1	Hendry, E.C.J.	1	McPhail, J.	3
		Herd, D.G.	4	McQueen, G.	5

NORTHERN IRELAND

Anderson, T. 4
Armstrong, G. 12

Barr, H.H. 1
Best, G. 9
Bingham, W.L. 10
Black, K. 1
Blanchflower, D. 2
Blanchflower, J. 1
Brennan, R.A. 1
Brotherston, N. 3

Campbell, W.G. 1
Casey, T. 2
Caskey, W. 1
Cassidy, T. 1
Clarke, C.J. 13
Clements, D. 2
Cochrane, T. 1
Crossan, E. 1
Crossan, J.A. 10
Cush, W.W. 5

D'Arcy, S.D. 1
Doherty, I. 1
Doherty, P.D. 3
(inc. 1 scored pre-war)
Dougan, A.D. 8
Dowie, I. 11

Elder, A.R. 1

Ferguson, W. 1
Ferris, R.O. 1
Finney, T. 2

Gillespie, K.R. 1
Gray, P. 5

Hamilton, B. 4
Hamilton, W. 5
Harkin, J.T. 2
Harvey, M. 3
Hill, C.F. 1
Humphries, W. 1
Hughes, M.E. 2
Hunter, A. 1
Hunter, B.V. 1
Irvine, W.J. 8

Johnston, W.C. 1
Jones, J. 1

Lennon, N.F. 1
Lockhart, N. 3
Lomas, S.M. 1

Magilton, J. 5
McAdams, W.J. 7
McClelland, J. 1
McCrory, S. 1
McCurdy, C. 1
McDonald, A. 3
McGarry, J.K. 1
McGrath, R.C. 4
McIlroy, J. 10
McIlroy, S.B. 5
McLaughlin, J.C. 6
McMahon, G.J. 2
McMordie, A.S. 3
McMorran, E.J. 4
McParland, P.J. 10
Moreland, V. 1
Morgan, S. 3
Morrow, S.J. 1
Mulryne, P.P. 1

Neill, W.J.T. 2
Nelson, S. 1
Nicholl, C.J. 3
Nicholl, J.M. 1
Nicholson, J.J. 6

O'Boyle, G. 1
O'Kane, W.J. 1
O'Neill, J. 1
O'Neill, M.A. 4
O'Neill, M.H. 8
Own goals 4

Peacock, R. 2
Penney, S. 2

Quinn, J.M. 12
Quinn, S.J. 1

Simpson, W.J. 5
Smyth, S. 1
Spence, D.W. 3
Stewart, I. 2

Taggart, G.P. 6
Tully, C.P. 3

Walker, J. 1
Walsh, D.J. 5
Welsh, E. 1
Whiteside, N. 9
Wilson, D.J. 1
Wilson, K.J. 6
Wilson, S.J. 7

EIRE

Aldridge, J. 19
Ambrose, P. 1
Anderson, J. 1

Bermingham, P. 1
Bradshaw, P. 4
Brady, L. 9
Breen, G. 1
Brown, D. 1
Byrne, J. (Bray) 1
Byrne, J. (QPR) 4

Cantwell, J. 14
Carey, J. 3
Carroll, T. 1
Cascarino, A. 16
Coad, P. 3
Connolly, D.J. 5
Conroy, T. 2
Conway, J. 3
Coyne, T. 6
Cummings, G. 5
Curtis, D. 8

Daly, G. 13
Davis, T. 4
Dempsey, J. 1
Dennehy, M. 2
Donnelly, J. 3
Donnelly, T. 1
Duffy, B. 1
Duggan, H. 1
Dunne, J. 12
Dunne, L. 1

Eglinton, T. 2
Ellis, P. 1

Fagan, F. 5
Fallon, S. 2
Fallon, W. 2
Farrell, P. 3
Fitzgerald, J. 1

UEFA UNDER-21 CHAMPIONSHIP 1996–8

Group 1
Greece 0, Slovenia 2
Greece 3, Bosnia 3
Slovenia 0, Denmark 3
Denmark 1, Greece 3
Slovenia 2, Bosnia 0
Bosnia 3, Croatia 1
Croatia 0, Greece 1
Croatia 2, Denmark 0
Bosnia 0, Greece 0
Croatia 2, Slovenia 0
Denmark 2, Slovenia 1
Greece 2, Croatia 0
Denmark 5, Bosnia 0

Group 2
Moldova 0, England 2
Moldova 0, Italy 3
England 0, Poland 0
Georgia 0, England 1
Italy 6, Georgia 0
Poland 1, Moldova 0
England 1, Italy 0
Italy 6, Moldova 0
Poland 1, Italy 1
England 0, Georgia 0
Italy 1, Poland 1
Poland 1, England 1
Georgia 1, Moldova 0
Poland 2, Georgia 2

Group 3
France 1, Switzerland 0
Finland 1, Switzerland 1
France 2, Hungary 0
Switzerland 3, Norway 7
Norway 4, Hungary 1
Norway 1, France 1
Hungary 0, Finland 1
Norway 3, Finland 0
Switzerland 4, Hungary 1
France 2, Finland 1
Finland 1, France 1
Hungary 2, Norway 0

Group 4
Austria 4, Scotland 0
Estonia 1, Belarus 1
Latvia 0, Scotland 0
Belarus 2, Latvia 0
Sweden 1, Belarus 3
Belarus 3, Estonia 1
Sweden 4, Austria 1
Estonia 0, Scotland 1
Latvia 0, Sweden 2
Austria 0, Latvia 0
Scotland 1, Sweden 4

Scotland 4, Estonia 0
Scotland 1, Austria 2
Austria 7, Estonia 1
Sweden 2, Scotland 1
Latvia 0, Belarus 3
Estonia 0, Sweden 2
Latvia 1, Austria 3
Belarus 1, Scotland 0
Estonia 0, Latvia 1

Group 5
Israel 2, Bulgaria 0
Russia 2, Cyprus 1
Cyprus 1, Israel 1
Israel 2, Bulgaria 0
Luxembourg 0, Bulgaria 4
Israel 1, Russia 0
Luxembourg 1, Russia 7
Cyprus 3, Bulgaria 0
Israel 2, Luxembourg 1
Cyprus 0, Russia 4
Luxembourg 0, Israel 5
Bulgaria 3, Cyprus 1
Russia 8, Luxembourg 0
Israel 4, Cyprus 3
Bulgaria 3, Luxembourg 0
Russia 1, Israel 1

Group 6
Czech Repblic 4, Malta 0
Yugoslavia 1, Malta 0
Slovakia 3, Malta 0
Czech Republic 1, Spain 2
Yugoslavia 3, Czech Republic 0
Spain 1, Slovakia 1
Spain 1, Yugoslavia 0
Malta 0, Spain 3
Spain 1, Malta 0
Malta 0, Slovakia 6
Czech Republic 0, Yugoslavia 1
Yugoslavia 1, Spain 2
Spain 4, Czech Republic 0
Yugoslavia 1, Slovakia 0

Group 7
Wales 4, San Marino 0
Wales 0, Holland 2
San Marino 0, Wales 3
Belgium 1, Turkey 2
San Marino 1, Belgium 5
Turkey 3, San Marino 0
Holland 0, Wales 1
Wales 1, Belgium 0
Turkey 0, Holland 1
Holland 6, San Marino 0
Wales 0, Turkey 3
Belgium 2, Holland 2

Wales 1, Belgium 0
Turkey 1, Belgium 2
San Marino 0, Holland 7
Belgium 3, San Marino 0

Group 8
Republic of Ireland 0, Iceland 1
Lithuania 0, Iceland 3
Iceland 2, Macedonia 0
Romania 2, Lithuania 1
Republic of Ireland 4, Macedonia 0
Iceland 2, Romania 3
Macedonia 0, Romania 1
Lithuania 1, Romania 2
Macedonia 0, Republic of Ireland 4
Romania 1, Republic of Ireland 0
Macedonia 1, Iceland 1

Iceland 0, Lithuania 2

Group 9
Albania 3, Armenia 2
Ukraine 1, Portugal 0
Armenia 3, Portugal 4
Portugal 1, Ukraine 0
Albania 2, Portugal 4
Armenia 0, Germany 1
Portugal 1, Germany 2
Albania 0, Ukraine 3
Albania 0, Germany 4
Ukraine 7, Armenia 0
Germany 2, Ukraine 0
Portugal 2, Albania 1
Ukraine 1, Germany 1

OLYMPIC FOOTBALL

Previous winners

1896	Athens*	1.	Denmark	1960	Rome	1.	Yugoslavia
		2.	Greece			2.	Denmark
1900	Paris*	1.	England			3.	Hungary
		2.	France	1964	Tokyo	1.	Hungary
1904	St Louis**	1.	Canada			2.	Czechoslovakia
		2.	USA			3.	East Germany
1908	London	1.	England	1968	Mexico City	1.	Hungary
		2.	Denmark			2.	Bulgaria
		3.	Holland			3.	Japan
1912	Stockholm	1.	England	1972	Munich	1.	Poland
		2.	Denmark			2.	Hungary
		3.	Holland			3.	East Germany/
1920	Antwerp	1.	Belgium				USSR joint bronze
		2.	Spain	1976	Montreal	1.	East Germany
		3.	Holland			2.	Poland
1924	Paris	1.	Uruguay			3.	USSR
		2.	Switzerland	1980	Moscow	1.	Czechoslovakia
		3.	Sweden			2.	East Germany
1928	Amsterdam	1.	Uruguay			3.	USSR
		2.	Argentina	1984	Los Angeles	1.	France
		3.	Italy			2.	Brazil
1932	Los Angeles no competition					3.	Yugoslavia
1936	Berlin	1.	Italy	1988	Seoul	1.	USSR
		2.	Austria			2.	Brazil
		3.	Norway			3.	West Germany
1948	London	1.	Sweden	1992	Barcelona	1.	Spain
		2.	Yugoslavia			2.	Poland
		3.	Denmark			3.	Ghana
1952	Helsinki	1.	Hungary				
		2.	Yugoslavia				
		3.	Sweden				
1956	Melbourne	1.	USSR				
		2.	Yugoslavia				
		3.	Bulgaria				

*No official tournament
**No official tournament but gold medal later awarded by IOC

WORLD YOUTH UNDER-20 CHAMPIONSHIP

UEFA (As Under 18's)

Group A
Belgium 2, Portugal 2
Hungary 1, France 2
Belgium 2, Hungary 1
Portugal 0, France 1
France 1, Belgium 1
Portugal 0, Hungary 3

Group B
England 0, Spain 0
Italy 1, Republic of Ireland 1
Republic of Ireland 0, Spain 0
Italy 1, England 1
Republic of Ireland 0, England 1
Spain 3, Italy 0

3rd/4th Place
Belgium 2, England 2
(England won on sudden death).

Final
France 1, Spain 0

AFRICA

Group A
Morocco 0, Egypt 0
Sudan 0, Ghana 4
Egypt 0, Ghana 1
Morocco 2, Sudan 0
Egypt 2, Sudan 1
Ghana 1, Morocco 0

Group B
Mali 2, Zambia 2
South Africa 0, Ivory Coast 1
Mali 1, South Africa 2
Zambia 1, Ivory Coast 1
Ivory Coast 4, Mali 1
South Africa 2, Zambia 1

Semi-Finals
Ghana 1, South Africa 1
(South Africa won 4-3 on penalties).
Ivory Coast 1, Morocco 2

3rd/4th Place
Ghana 0, Ivory Coast 2

FINAL
Morocco 1, South Africa 0

SOUTH AMERICA

Group A
Chile 3, Peru 1
Venezuela 2, Brazil 10
Chile 3, Venezuela 4
Ecuador 1, Brazil 2
Brazil 2, Peru 0
Venezuela 1, Ecuador 0
Chile 1, Ecuador 0
Peru 2, Venezuela 2
Chile 1, Brazil 3
Peru 0, Ecuador 0

Group B
Argentina 5, Paraguay 2
Bolivia 3, Colombia 4
Argentina 1, Colombia 1
Uruguay 3, Paraguay 1
Argentina 2, Bolivia 1
Uruguay 1, Colombia 1
Colombia 0, Paraguay 3
Uruguay 2, Bolivia 1
Argentina 0, Uruguay 1
Paraguay 2, Bolivia 0

FINAL
Brazil 3, Paraguay 0
Uruguay 2, Chile 2
Venezuela 0, Argentina 3
Brazil 2, Chile 2
Uruguay 1, Argentina 1
Venezuela 1, Paraguay 2
Brazil 0, Argentina 2
Chile 0, Paraguay 0
Uruguay 3, Venezuela 0
Argentina 3, Chile 0
Brazil 2, Venezuela 2
Uruguay 1, Paraguay 2
Argentina 1, Paraguay 1
Brazil 0, Uruguay 0
Venezuela 4, Chile 1

ASIA

Group A
Bangladesh 1, UAE 6
Korea Republic 4, Thailand 0
Iran 0, Thailand 0
Korea Republic 3, UAE 0
Iran 0, Bangladesh 0
Thailand 2, UAE 3
Iran 0, UAE 0
Korea Republic 5, Bangladesh 2
Iran 1, Korea Republic 2
Thailand 1, Bangladesh 0

Group B
India 1, Qatar 1
Syria 1, Japan 3
China 2, Japan 1
Syria 2, Qatar 0
China 2, India 1
Japan 4, Qatar 0
China 5, Qatar 2
Syria 1, India 0
China 1, Syria 1
Japan 2, India 0

Semi-Finals
Korea Republic 1, Japan 0
China 5, UAE 1

3rd/4th Place
Japan 2, UAE 2
(UAE won 4-3 on penalty kicks).

FINAL
Korea Republic 3, China 0

OCEANIA
Australia 10, Fiji 0
Tahiti 0, New Zealand 5
Australia 3, New Zealand 0
Tahiti 2, Fiji 4
New Zealand 3, Fiji 1
Tahiti 0, Australia 10

3rd/4th Place
Tahiti 1, Fiji 1
(Fiji won 5-4 on penalties).

FINAL
Australia 2, New Zealand 1

CONCACAF

Group 1
Mexico 4, Netherlands Antilles 0
El Salvador 2, Guatemala 3
Mexico 1, Guatemala 0
Netherlands Antilles 1, El Salvador 1
Guatemala 0, Netherlands Antilles 0
Mexico 2, El Salvador 0

Group 2
Honduras 3, Martinique 0
USA 4, Jamaica 1
Jamaica 1, Honduras 0
Martinique 0, USA 2
USA 0, Honduras 0
Martinique 0, Jamaica 3

Group 3
Costa Rica 3, Nicaragua 0
Trinidad & Tobago 0, Canada 1
Costa Rica 5, Trinidad & Tobago 0
Nicaragua 0, Canada 3
Canada 2, Costa Rica 0
Trinidad & Tobago 6, Nicaragua 1

Championship Round
Mexico 2, Canada 1
USA 0, Canada 2
Mexico 2, USA 1

Qualification Round
Guatemala 1, Costa Rica 2
Jamaica 1, Costa Rica 2
Guatemala 0, Jamaica 0

FIFA UNDER-20 CHAMPIONSHIP

GROUP A
Malaysia 1, Morocco 3
Uruguay 3, Belgium 0
Malaysia 1, Uruguay 3
Morocco 1, Belgium 1
Malaysia 0, Belgium 3
Morocco 0, Uruguay 0

GROUP B
Korea Republic 0, South Africa 0
Brazil 3, France 0
France 4, Korea Republic 2
Brazil 2, South Africa 0
Brazil 10, Korea Republic 3
France 4, South Africa 2

GROUP C
Ghana 2, Republic of Ireland 1
USA 1, China 0
Ghana 1, USA 0
Republic of Ireland 2, USA 1
Ghana 1, USA 0
Republic of Ireland 1, China 1

GROUP D
Spain 2, Japan 1
Costa Rica 1, Paraguay 1
Japan 6, Costa Rica 2
Spain 2, Paraguay 1
Japan 3, Paraguay 3
Spain 4, Costa Rica 0

GROUP E
Argentina 3, Hungary 0
Australia 0, Canada 0
Australia 1, Hungary 0
Argentina 2, Canada 1
Canada 2, Hungary 1
Australia 4, Argentina 3

GROUP F
Mexico 5, UAE 0
England 2, Ivory Coast 1
Mexico 1, Ivory Coast 1
England 5, UAE 0
England 1, Mexico 0
UAE 2, Ivory Coast 0

SECOND ROUND
Uruguay 3, USA 0
Republic of Ireland 2, Morocco 1
Brazil 10, Belgium 0
France 1, Mexico 0
Ghana 3, UAE 0
Spain 2, Canada 0
Japan 1, Australia 0
Argentina 2, England 1

QUARTER-FINALS
Uruguay 1, France 1
(Uruguay won 7-6 on penalties)
Republic of Ireland 1, Spain 0
Argentina 2, Brazil 0
Ghana 2, Japan 1

SEMI-FINALS
Uruguay 2, Ghana 2
(Uruguay won on sudden death)
Argentina 1, Republic of Ireland 0

THIRD PLACE
Republic of Ireland 2, Ghana 1

FINAL
Argentina 2, Uruguay 1

15th UEFA UNDER-16 CHAMPIONSHIP

(in Germany)

Group A
Germany 3, Israel 0
Switzerland 2, Northern Ireland 1
Germany 2, Switzerland 0
Israel 1, Northern Ireland 2
Germany 1, Northern Ireland 0
Israel 2, Switzerland 3

Group B
Poland 0, Austria 4
Spain 6, Ukraine 1
Poland 1, Spain 2
Austria 0, Ukraine 2
Ukraine 2, Poland 3
Austria 0, Spain 2

Group C
Hungary 6, Georgia 3
Belgium 1, Italy 0
Hungary 0, Belgium 1
Georgia 3, Italy 5
Italy 1, Hungary 2
Georgia 1, Belgium 5

Group D
Turkey 2, Slovenia 0

Slovakia 1, Iceland 0
Turkey 1, Slovakia 0
Slovenia 0, Iceland 2
Iceland 1, Turkey 4
Slovenia 2, Slovakia 2

Quarter Finals
Germany 3, Hungary 1
Belgium 0, Switzerland 0
(Switzerland won 5-4 on penalties).
Spain 3, Slovakia 1
Turkey 0, Austria 3

Semi Finals
Germany 1, Spain 2
Switzerland 0, Austria 0
(Austria won 6-5 on penalties).

3rd/4th Place
Germany 3, Switzerland 1

FINAL
Spain 0, Austria 0
(Spain won 5-4 on penalties)

7th WORLD UNDER-17 CHAMPIONSHIP

SOUTH AMERICA

Final Round
Argentina 3, Chile 0
Brazil 5, Paraguay 0
Argentina 0, Paraguay 0
Brazil 5, Chile 3
Argentina 1, Brazil 2
Paraguay 1, Chile 2

OCEANIA

Semi-Finals
Australia 4, Solomon Islands 0
New Zealand 2, Fiji 0

3rd/4th Place
Fiji 0, Solomon Islands 3

Final
New Zealand 1, Australia 0

ASIA

Semi-Finals
Oman 1, Bahrain 0
Thailand 1, Japan 0

3rd/4th Place
Bahrain 0, Japan 0
(Bahrain won 4-1 on penalties).

Final
Oman 1, Thailand 0

CONCACAF

Final
Canada 1, Costa Rica 3
Mexico 3, USA 1
Costa Rica 0, Mexico 4
USA 2, Canada 0
Canada 0, Mexico 1
USA 1, Costa Rica 1

VAUXHALL CONFERENCE 1996–97

	Home						Goals	Away					Goals	
	P	W	D	L	F	A	W	D	L	F	A	Pts
Macclesfield Town	42	15	4	2	41	11	12	5	4	39	19	90
Kidderminster Harriers	42	14	4	3	48	18	12	3	6	36	24	85
Stevenage Borough	42	15	4	2	53	23	9	6	6	34	30	82
Morecambe	42	10	5	6	34	23	9	4	8	35	33	66
Woking	42	10	5	6	41	29	8	5	8	30	34	64
Northwich Victoria	42	11	5	5	31	20	6	7	8	30	34	63
Farnborough Town	42	9	6	6	35	29	7	7	7	23	24	61
Hednesford Town	42	10	7	4	28	17	6	5	10	24	33	60
Telford United	42	6	7	8	21	30	10	3	8	25	26	58
Gateshead	42	8	6	7	32	27	7	5	9	27	36	56
Southport	42	8	7	6	27	28	7	5	9	24	33	55
Rushden & Diamonds	42	8	8	5	30	25	6	3	12	31	38	53
Stalybridge Celtic	42	9	7	5	35	29	5	5	11	18	29	52
Kettering Town	42	9	4	8	30	28	5	5	11	23	34	51
Hayes	42	7	7	7	27	21	5	7	9	27	34	50
Slough Town	42	7	7	7	42	32	5	7	9	20	33	50
Dover Athletic	42	7	9	5	32	30	5	5	11	25	38	50
Welling United	42	9	2	10	24	26	4	7	10	26	34	48
Halifax Town	42	9	5	7	29	37	3	7	11	16	37	48
Bath City	42	9	5	7	27	28	3	6	12	26	52	47
Bromsgrove Rovers	42	8	4	9	29	30	4	1	16	12	37	41
Altrincham	42	6	3	12	25	34	3	9	9	24	39	39

Leading Goalscorers 1996–97

Conf.		FAC	SCC	FAT
30	Lee Hughes *(Kidderminster Harriers)* +	1	1	2
21	Lennie Dennis *(Welling United)* +	1	2	1
19	Andy Whittaker *(Southport)* +	6	–	2
18	Gary Abbott *(Slough Town)* +	–	–	–
17	Justin Jackson *(Woking)* +	4	–	2
16	Barry Hayles *(Stevenage Borough)* +	3	–	2
	David Leworthy *(Rushden & Diamonds)* +	4	–	–
	Lee Steele *(Northwich Victoria)* +	–	–	–
15	Joe O'Connor *(Hednesford Town)* +	9	–	–
	Paul Thompson *(Gateshead)* +	6	1	1
	Clive Walker *(Woking)* +	3	–	1
	Steve Wood *(Macclesfield Town)* +	–	1	–
14	Mike Davis *(Bath City)* +	7	–	–
	Neil Doherty *(Kidderminster Harriers)* +	1	–	1
	Niell Hardy *(Altrincham)* +	3	–	1
	Mick Norbury *(Halifax Town)* +	–	–	–
13	Carl Alford *(Rushden & Diamonds)* +	2	–	–
	Ian Arnold *(Stalybridge Celtic)* +	–	–	–
	Chris Boothe *(Farnborough Town)* +	9	3	–
	Martin Randall *(Hayes)* +	–	–	4
	Phil Wingfield *(Farnborough Town)* +	2	–	1

FAC: FA Cup; SCC: Spalding Challenge Cup; FAT: FA Trophy.

VAUXHALL CONFERENCE RESULTS 1996-97

Home \ Away	Altrincham	Bath City	Bromsgrove Rovers	Dover Athletic	Farnborough Town	Gateshead	Halifax Town	Hayes	Hednesford Town	Kettering Town	Kidderminster H.	Macclesfield Town	Morecambe	Northwich Victoria	Rushden & Diamonds	Slough Town	Southport	Stalybridge Celtic	Stevenage Borough	Telford United	Welling United	Woking
Altrincham	—	1-3	3-1	1-2	0-1	2-1	2-1	0-2	1-1	4-3	0-1	0-1	0-1	2-3	4-3	0-1	1-0	1-0	1-2	2-3	1-1	1-1
Bath City	1-2	—	2-0	2-1	1-1	4-5	0-1	2-2	3-0	1-0	6-0	1-2	2-0	3-1	3-2	5-2	0-1	1-0	1-1	2-3	1-1	1-1
Bromsgrove Rovers	4-0	2-1	—	3-1	2-1	1-0	3-0	2-2	2-0	1-0	1-2	2-3	0-5	2-3	4-1	4-1	3-0	2-2	1-1	1-4	1-0	0-3
Dover Athletic	2-1	2-0	1-1	—	2-3	1-2	3-0	2-2	3-0	1-2	0-5	2-3	2-1	0-5	3-2	2-1	3-0	0-1	1-4	3-0	1-0	0-3
Farnborough Town	1-1	4-1	2-1	2-3	—	3-0	0-1	2-2	0-3	1-2	0-0	3-0	2-2	2-2	1-1	2-1	3-3	0-1	3-1	0-2	2-1	5-1
Gateshead	1-1	4-5	1-0	1-2	1-0	—	0-1	2-2	5-1	1-0	1-0	1-0	0-3	1-1	2-2	2-1	2-0	1-1	4-2	0-2	2-1	1-2
Halifax Town	1-1	1-0	1-3	3-0	3-0	2-0	—	4-0	0-0	2-3	1-3	0-3	0-1	4-1	1-0	5-0	4-1	3-0	1-3	2-3	2-1	0-4
Hayes	2-2	0-1	3-0	2-0	0-0	0-0	0-1	—	4-0	2-1	0-2	0-2	1-2	1-3	2-0	0-0	2-1	4-1	1-2	1-1	0-3	3-2
Hednesford Town	3-1	1-0	2-0	0-1	0-1	4-1	1-0	2-1	—	0-0	0-2	2-3	2-3	3-0	1-0	0-0	2-1	2-1	1-3	2-3	0-0	0-4
Kettering Town	3-1	6-0	1-2	2-3	2-3	4-0	1-2	1-0	4-0	—	3-1	1-4	0-1	0-2	1-5	3-0	2-1	1-2	1-2	4-1	2-3	3-2
Kidderminster H.	1-1	1-2	4-0	1-0	1-0	1-0	1-0	2-4	0-1	5-2	—	3-1	0-2	0-1	2-0	3-2	1-1	2-0	1-0	1-0	3-2	5-0
Macclesfield Town	1-1	2-1	1-0	1-0	4-2	0-2	0-1	2-0	4-0	2-0	1-1	—	1-0	1-0	1-1	3-0	5-1	1-1	1-2	2-1	1-1	1-2
Morecambe	3-2	4-1	1-2	2-0	0-2	1-0	1-1	2-1	2-0	5-2	1-1	1-2	—	2-0	1-2	2-2	1-0	1-0	2-1	0-3	3-3	3-0
Northwich Victoria	0-1	5-2	2-0	0-1	1-0	1-2	0-1	1-3	0-2	1-0	1-1	0-0	3-4	—	2-0	5-0	4-1	4-6	0-1	0-0	2-1	4-1
Rushden & Diamonds	1-3	3-1	3-0	3-1	6-0	0-1	2-3	3-1	1-0	0-2	0-3	2-3	2-2	1-5	—	2-1	3-0	1-1	2-2	6-0	3-2	0-3
Slough Town	1-0	2-2	0-0	2-0	0-0	4-1	1-0	0-1	1-0	1-0	1-1	0-1	0-1	0-1	2-0	—	0-1	1-0	2-1	2-1	0-1	2-1
Southport	1-0	2-2	3-0	4-2	4-1	2-5	6-0	3-1	2-2	1-0	3-0	2-3	4-2	0-2	0-5	2-1	—	4-1	3-0	2-2	2-1	0-3
Stalybridge Celtic	0-0	1-1	1-1	3-1	3-0	4-1	0-1	0-0	1-1	1-0	2-0	0-3	2-2	2-0	0-5	1-1	3-0	—	0-3	1-1	2-1	1-1
Stevenage Borough	1-0	2-1	3-0	4-1	6-0	4-1	2-3	3-1	1-0	1-0	0-2	1-0	0-0	2-2	0-5	1-0	1-1	4-1	—	3-0	2-1	0-3
Telford United	0-0	1-1	1-1	3-1	1-1	2-2	0-1	0-0	1-4	1-0	0-1	2-2	3-1	1-1	1-2	0-2	0-0	1-1	2-1	—	2-1	0-3
Welling United	1-0	0-2	1-2	1-1	2-1	0-3	0-2	0-1	3-2	0-2	3-1	0-3	1-2	1-1	1-0	3-0	0-3	2-1	3-1	1-0	—	1-1
Woking	7-1	2-2	1-3	1-1	0-2	2-0	0-1	1-2	2-0	2-1	2-1	2-3	1-2	3-1	4-2	2-1	3-2	3-1	3-1	0-0	2-1	—

DR MARTENS LEAGUE 1996–97

Premier Division

	P	W	D	L	F	A	Pts
Gresley Rovers	42	25	10	7	75	40	85
Cheltenham Town	42	21	11	10	76	44	74
Gloucester City	42	21	10	11	81	56	73
Halesowen Town	42	21	10	11	77	54	73
King's Lynn	42	20	8	14	65	61	68
Burton Albion	42	18	12	12	70	53	66
Nuneaton Borough	42	19	9	14	61	52	66
Sittingbourne	42	19	7	16	76	65	64
Merthyr Tydfil	42	17	9	16	69	61	60
Worcester City	42	15	14	13	52	50	59
Atherstone United	42	15	13	14	46	47	58
Salisbury City	42	15	13	14	57	66	58
Sudbury Town	42	16	7	19	72	72	55
Gravesend & Northfleet	42	16	7	19	63	73	55
Dorchester Town	42	14	9	19	62	66	51
Hastings Town	42	12	15	15	49	60	51
Crawley Town	42	13	8	21	49	67	47
Cambridge City	42	11	13	18	57	65	46
Ashford Town	42	9	18	15	53	79	45
Baldock Town	42	11	8	23	52	90	41
Newport AFC	42	9	13	20	40	60	40
Chelmsford City	42	6	14	22	49	70	32

**Leading Goalscorers 1996–97
(League and Cup)**

Premier Division

R. Straw (Nuneaton Borough)	28
E. Wright (Halesowen Town)	28
O. Pickard (Dorchester Town)	26
I. Brown (Sudbury Town)	25
D. Watkins (Gloucester City)	25
D. Arter (Gravesend & Northfleet)	20
I. Stringfellow (King's Lynn)	19
D. Fenton (Baldock Town)	17
C. McLean (Sudbury Town)	17
S. Restarick (Crawley Town)	17
C. Summers (Merthyr Tydfil)	17
A. Walker (Sittingbourne)	17
M. Cotter (Burton Albion)	15
M. Nuttell (Burton Albion)	15
P. Evans (Merthyr Tydfil)	14
A. Garner (Gresley Rovers)	14
T. Marsden (Gresley Rovers)	14
B. McNamara (King's Lynn)	14
L. Webb (Salisbury Town)	14
S. Cuggy (Hastings Town)	13
M. Boyle (Cheltenham Town)	12
N. Dent (Ashford Town)	12
R. Harbut (Salisbury City)	12
A. Mings (Gloucester City)	12
A. Thomas (Worcester City)	12
D. Webb (Gloucester City)	12

DR MARTENS PREMIER LEAGUE RESULTS 1996–97

	Ashford Town	Atherstone United	Baldock Town	Burton Albion	Cambridge City	Chelmsford City	Cheltenham Town	Crawley Town	Dorchester Town	Gloucester City	Gravesend & Northfleet	Gresley Rovers	Halesowen Town	Hastings Town	King's Lynn	Merthyr Tydfil	Newport AFC	Nuneaton Borough	Salisbury City	Sittingbourne	Sudbury Town	Worcester City
Ashford Town	—	0-3	2-2	3-3	2-2	1-0	1-1	3-3	2-1	0-3	1-1	1-3	3-3	4-0	4-0	0-1	1-1	2-0	0-1	1-1	2-2	0-0
Atherstone United	1-1	—	1-1	1-3	0-3	1-0	1-0	3-0	2-0	1-0	0-2	1-2	6-0	1-1	4-2	2-0	2-0	2-1	2-0	3-2	1-1	0-0
Baldock Town	1-0	0-2	—	1-3	0-3	1-0	4-0	2-0	3-2	5-0	3-1	2-4	3-0	6-0	3-1	2-1	0-0	4-0	2-1	2-3	0-1	0-3
Burton Albion	1-0	1-3	1-0	—	0-3	1-0	3-3	0-0	5-0	0-2	1-1	2-0	1-1	2-1	3-1	0-0	2-0	5-1	0-0	2-3	1-1	0-1
Cambridge City	4-0	0-3	0-3	1-0	—	1-0	3-3	2-0	0-2	0-2	2-2	3-1	0-1	1-2	1-2	2-2	0-0	0-2	0-2	1-2	3-2	1-2
Chelmsford City	1-1	1-0	4-1	1-0	1-0	—	1-4	2-4	1-1	0-1	4-2	2-3	1-3	2-1	0-2	2-2	3-1	2-2	1-1	1-4	1-3	1-2
Cheltenham Town	6-0	1-0	1-0	3-3	3-3	1-4	—	2-0	2-0	2-2	2-2	0-0	0-3	0-2	1-2	1-0	1-3	1-0	4-2	1-0	2-0	2-0
Crawley Town	2-3	3-0	2-0	0-0	2-0	2-4	2-0	—	2-5	2-2	2-2	0-1	3-1	0-1	3-5	0-1	1-2	0-0	1-3	3-3	4-5	2-0
Dorchester Town	0-2	1-0	3-2	5-0	0-2	1-1	2-0	2-5	—	2-2	3-1	1-3	0-2	0-1	3-0	2-0	1-3	1-0	2-1	1-2	2-0	2-1
Gloucester City	6-1	1-0	5-0	0-2	0-2	0-1	2-2	2-2	2-2	—	3-1	2-2	0-1	3-0	1-0	6-3	1-3	4-0	1-3	3-0	3-1	1-0
Gravesend & Northfleet	1-3	0-2	3-1	1-1	2-2	4-2	2-2	2-2	3-1	3-1	—	2-1	3-0	1-2	1-0	0-2	0-0	5-1	3-2	1-3	4-2	3-0
Gresley Rovers	2-1	1-2	2-4	2-0	3-1	2-3	0-0	0-1	1-3	2-2	2-1	—	1-2	3-0	0-2	1-2	1-1	0-2	1-1	2-1	2-3	0-0
Halesowen Town	0-0	6-0	3-0	1-1	0-1	1-3	0-3	3-1	0-2	0-1	3-0	1-2	—	3-0	2-3	4-1	0-2	4-2	2-3	1-4	4-2	0-0
Hastings Town	2-2	1-1	6-0	2-1	1-2	2-1	0-2	0-1	0-1	3-0	1-2	3-0	3-0	—	1-4	1-2	0-0	4-1	2-3	3-0	3-0	0-1
King's Lynn	2-0	4-2	3-1	3-1	1-2	0-2	1-2	3-5	3-0	1-0	1-0	0-2	2-3	1-4	—	0-1	2-4	1-2	5-0	3-2	3-0	2-0
Merthyr Tydfil	3-0	2-0	2-1	0-0	2-2	2-2	1-0	0-1	2-0	6-3	0-2	1-2	4-1	1-2	0-1	—	1-0	2-1	1-3	3-1	3-1	2-1
Newport AFC	3-0	2-0	0-0	2-0	0-1	3-1	1-3	1-2	1-3	1-3	0-0	1-1	0-2	0-0	2-4	1-0	—	0-0	0-1	4-0	0-1	2-1
Nuneaton Borough	3-0	2-1	4-0	5-1	0-2	2-2	1-0	0-0	1-0	4-0	5-1	0-2	4-2	4-1	1-2	2-1	0-0	—	2-3	1-2	4-3	2-1
Salisbury City	4-1	2-0	2-1	0-0	2-3	1-1	4-2	1-3	2-1	1-3	3-2	1-1	2-3	2-3	5-0	1-3	0-1	2-3	—	2-1	3-1	1-1
Sittingbourne	2-2	3-2	2-3	2-3	1-4	1-4	1-0	3-3	1-2	3-0	1-3	2-1	1-4	3-0	3-2	3-1	4-0	1-2	2-1	—	0-1	1-1
Sudbury Town	2-2	1-1	0-1	1-1	3-2	1-3	2-0	4-5	2-0	3-1	4-2	2-3	4-2	3-0	3-0	3-1	0-1	4-3	5-1	0-1	—	3-2
Worcester City	2-2	2-3	0-3	0-1	1-2	1-2	2-0	2-0	2-1	1-0	3-0	0-0	0-0	0-1	2-0	2-1	2-1	2-1	1-1	1-1	3-2	—

UNIBOND LEAGUE 1996–97

Premier Division

	P	W	D	L	F	A	Pts
Leek Town	44	28	9	7	71	35	93
Bishop Auckland	44	23	14	7	88	43	83
Hyde United	44	22	16	6	93	46	82
Emley	44	23	12	9	89	54	81
Barrow	44	23	11	10	71	45	80
Boston United	44	22	13	9	74	47	79
Blyth Spartans	44	22	11	11	74	49	77
Marine	44	20	15	9	53	37	75
Guiseley	44	20	11	13	63	54	71
Gainsborough Trinity	44	18	12	14	65	46	66
Accrington Stanley	44	18	12	14	77	70	66
Runcorn	44	15	15	14	63	62	60
Chorley	44	16	9	19	69	66	57
Winsford United	44	13	14	17	50	56	53
Knowsley United*	44	12	14	18	58	79	49
Colwyn Bay	44	11	13	20	60	76	46
Lancaster City	44	12	9	23	48	75	45
Frickley Athletic	44	12	8	24	62	91	44
Spennymoor United	44	10	10	24	52	68	40
Bamber Bridge	44	11	7	26	59	99	40
Alfreton Town	44	8	13	23	45	83	37
Witton Albion	44	5	14	25	41	91	29
Buxton	44	5	12	27	33	86	27

*1pt deducted; breach of rule

Leading Goalscorers 1996–97

Lge	Cup	Tot	
28	12	40	Nick Peverill (Bishop Auckland)
22	4	26	Neil Morton (Barrow)
20	2	22	Steve Soley (Leek Town)
19	6	25	Neil Matthews (Guiseley)
18	11	29	Deiniol Graham (Emley)
18	5	23	Jock Russell (Winsford United)
17	7	24	Phil Brown (Boston United)
17	5	22	Tony Carroll (Hyde United)
17	5	22	Ged Kimmins (Hyde United)
16	4	20	Jason Maxwell (Gainsborough Trinity)
16	3	19	Damien Henderson (Blyth Spartans)
16	2	18	Brian Ross (Chorley)
15	13	28	Brett Ormerod (Accrington Stanley)
15	6	21	Dave Nolan (Hyde United)
15	5	20	Stuart Young (Blyth Spartans)
15	4	19	Joey Dunn (Runcorn)
15	-	15	Andy Green (Barrow)

UNIBOND LEAGUE—PREMIER DIVISION RESULTS 1996–97

	Accrington Stanley	Alfreton Town	Bamber Bridge	Barrow	Bishop Auckland	Blyth Spartans	Boston United	Buxton	Chorley	Colwyn Bay	Emley	Frickley Athletic	Gainsborough Trinity	Guiseley	Hyde United	Knowsley United	Lancaster City	Leek Town	Marine	Runcorn	Spennymoor United	Winsford United	Witton Albion
Accrington Stanley	—	4-2	4-1	1-2	1-4	2-3	3-1	5-3	0-3	3-1	1-1	4-0	0-4	1-2	3-2	1-1	2-1	1-2	1-0	2-2	2-0	0-0	4-1
Alfreton Town	1-3	—	2-1	2-3	1-0	2-1	0-2	2-2	0-1	1-0	3-0	5-1	1-1	1-0	1-4	6-0	1-0	1-0	1-1	2-2	1-3	1-1	4-2
Bamber Bridge	4-3	3-2	—	1-3	0-1	0-1	0-2	2-0	0-2	2-3	0-3	6-4	1-1	1-0	2-3	1-1	0-2	0-4	0-5	0-5	1-3	1-2	4-2
Barrow	1-1	2-0	1-3	—	0-1	2-1	1-0	2-2	1-0	1-0	1-3	5-1	1-1	6-1	1-0	1-1	3-0	0-4	2-1	0-5	1-3	1-2	2-0
Bishop Auckland	1-1	2-1	0-1	0-1	—	1-3	1-2	5-0	1-0	3-1	2-2	2-3	1-1	1-0	3-0	1-0	4-2	2-0	2-2	1-1	4-1	1-2	5-0
Blyth Spartans	3-1	2-1	1-0	3-5	1-1	—	3-0	3-0	0-1	3-2	4-1	6-3	1-1	1-1	1-0	6-0	3-1	1-1	2-2	3-2	1-1	2-1	2-1
Boston United	1-3	0-1	0-1	0-1	1-1	2-1	—	0-2	3-4	2-2	2-3	1-1	1-1	0-3	0-0	1-0	0-2	0-0	2-2	2-1	0-2	0-1	2-1
Buxton	3-1	1-3	1-2	1-1	1-1	1-1	0-2	—	1-5	4-0	1-3	1-3	3-4	0-3	3-3	2-4	0-2	3-1	4-0	2-0	2-0	1-2	6-1
Chorley	1-3	2-1	1-3	1-3	1-0	2-1	3-4	2-2	—	0-1	1-2	3-4	1-0	1-1	3-3	2-2	1-3	2-3	2-1	4-0	1-1	0-1	1-1
Colwyn Bay	3-1	4-0	1-2	2-0	2-1	3-0	1-5	3-4	4-0	—	3-2	2-1	3-4	4-0	0-3	2-4	2-2	2-3	0-2	4-0	1-1	2-0	1-2
Emley	0-1	1-2	1-2	1-2	1-2	2-1	2-0	3-1	1-1	0-1	—	0-2	2-2	2-0	2-4	2-0	2-3	3-2	0-2	3-3	0-2	0-1	1-1
Frickley Athletic	3-1	7-2	3-0	3-0	2-2	1-2	1-0	2-0	2-1	1-0	3-1	—	3-3	1-0	0-3	2-0	2-2	2-3	0-1	2-1	5-2	1-2	4-1
Gainsborough Trinity	2-2	3-0	0-2	3-0	0-1	2-0	1-2	2-0	4-0	2-0	1-0	1-0	—	1-0	2-0	4-1	1-1	1-1	4-1	5-2	2-1	3-2	1-2
Guiseley	1-0	1-1	5-0	1-3	1-3	2-1	1-2	2-0	1-4	1-1	1-1	1-0	1-0	—	2-3	2-0	1-1	1-0	2-0	4-0	2-1	1-1	3-0
Hyde United	7-2	5-0	2-2	0-3	1-1	1-0	4-1	0-1	1-1	3-0	2-3	5-1	2-2	2-1	—	4-0	3-1	3-2	2-0	0-0	2-2	1-1	3-1
Knowsley United	1-1	1-0	3-0	0-5	1-2	1-0	0-1	1-3	1-3	1-1	1-3	2-2	0-3	1-3	2-3	—	3-1	0-3	2-2	3-0	2-2	0-3	2-1
Lancaster City	1-2	2-3	1-0	2-1	1-1	2-3	1-0	0-1	1-0	0-1	0-2	0-2	0-2	1-2	0-4	3-1	—	0-3	5-1	3-2	1-0	0-3	2-1
Leek Town	2-1	4-0	4-1	2-1	2-3	1-0	1-0	2-3	1-0	1-0	2-0	3-1	3-1	1-0	0-2	1-0	1-1	—	2-1	0-3	0-1	2-0	1-1
Marine	2-1	1-0	1-1	2-1	1-1	2-3	1-1	1-0	2-3	0-0	1-3	3-1	0-3	1-3	0-3	2-0	5-1	2-1	—	1-1	1-0	3-4	2-1
Runcorn	1-3	1-0	1-2	2-1	1-0	0-3	1-1	3-0	5-0	5-0	1-3	1-1	2-0	1-0	1-1	4-0	3-2	2-0	0-0	—	1-0	6-0	4-0
Spennymoor United	0-0	3-2	1-2	1-2	0-2	1-0	1-3	1-1	0-2	5-0	1-1	0-0	3-1	2-0	0-1	5-0	1-0	4-1	2-2	0-1	—	1-0	1-1
Winsford United	1-1	2-1	4-2	1-2	2-1	0-2	1-1	1-0	1-3	3-0	2-2	0-3	1-1	2-1	0-1	1-1	0-1	0-3	1-0	4-3	2-0	—	1-3
Witton Albion	0-1	1-1	1-3	1-0	1-1	1-2	1-4	2-1	1-1	0-1	2-1	2-1	2-1	2-2	0-0	2-1	1-2	0-0	1-0	1-5	1-2	1-3	—

ICIS FOOTBALL LEAGUE 1996–97
Premier Division

		Home			Away			Total			Goals		
	P	W	D	L	W	D	L	W	D	L	F	A	Pts
Yeovil Town	42	17	3	1	14	5	2	31	8	3	83	34	101
Enfield	42	14	4	3	14	7	0	28	11	3	91	29	95
Sutton United	42	10	7	4	8	6	7	18	13	11	87	70	67
Dagenham & Redbridge	42	11	3	7	7	8	6	18	11	13	57	43	65
Yeading	42	10	6	5	8	5	8	18	11	13	58	47	65
St Albans City	42	7	7	7	11	4	6	18	11	13	65	55	65
Aylesbury United	42	11	5	5	7	6	8	18	11	13	64	54	65
Purfleet	42	8	9	4	9	2	10	17	11	14	67	63	62
Heybridge Swifts	42	9	7	5	7	7	7	16	14	12	62	62	62
Boreham Wood	42	9	7	5	6	6	9	15	13	14	56	52	58
Kingstonian	42	10	4	7	6	4	11	16	8	18	79	79	56
Dulwich Hamlet	42	9	4	8	6	5	10	15	9	18	57	57	54
Carshalton Athletic	42	10	5	6	4	6	11	14	11	17	51	56	53
Hitchin Town	42	10	3	8	5	4	12	15	7	20	67	73	52
Oxford City	42	8	5	8	6	5	10	14	10	18	67	83	52
Hendon	42	8	5	8	5	7	9	13	12	17	53	59	51
Harrow Borough	42	8	7	6	4	7	10	12	14	16	58	62	50
Bromley	42	10	5	6	3	4	14	13	9	20	67	72	48
Bishop's Stortford	42	7	7	7	3	6	12	10	13	19	43	64	43
Staines Town	42	6	6	9	4	2	15	10	8	24	46	71	38
Grays Athletic	42	3	6	12	5	3	13	8	9	25	43	78	33
Chertsey Town	42	4	5	12	4	2	15	8	7	27	40	98	31

Leading Goalscorers 1996–97

Premier Division

		Lge	GIC	FMC
38	Howard Forinton (Yeovil Town)	37	1	–
	(includes 14 league and 1 GIC goal for Oxford City)			
35	Paul Cobb (Purfleet)	29	5	1
27	Steve Clark (St Albans City)	21	6	–
26	Mark Hynes (Sutton United)	20	4	2
25	Eddie Akaumoah (Kingstonian)	20	4	1
24	Steve Darlington (Kingstonian)	22	1	1

Division One

		Lge	GIC	FMC
22	Neil Pearson (Whyteleafe)	22	–	–
21	Paul Coombs (Basingstoke Town)	21	–	–
20	Ansil Bushay (Walton & Hersham)	20	–	–
	John Lawford (Chesham United)	18	2	–
	Andy Jones (Canvey Island)	18	–	2
	Leon Gutzmore (Billericay Town)	17	3	–

Division Two

		Lge	GIC	AMT
44	Steve Lunn (Leatherhead)	41	1	2
37	Jason Reed (Bedford Town)	30	5	2
32	Simon Liddle (Banstead Athletic)	31	1	–
27	Nigel Webb (Leatherhead)	23	1	3

Division Three

		Lge	GIC	FMC
31	Wade Falana (Braintree Town)	29	2	–
25	Gary Bennett (Braintree Town)	14	8	3
23	Paul Halbert (Northwood)	22	–	1
22	Andy Boxhall (Epsom & Ewell)	21	1	–

Lge: ICIS League; GIC: Guardian Insurance Cup; FMC: Full Members Cup; AMT: Associate Members Trophy

ICIS FOOTBALL LEAGUE—PREMIER DIVISION RESULTS 1996–97

	Aylesbury United	Bishop's Stortford	Boreham Wood	Bromley	Carshalton Athletic	Chertsey Town	Dagenham & Redbridge	Dulwich Hamlet	Enfield	Grays Athletic	Harrow Borough	Hendon	Heybridge Swifts	Hitchin Town	Kingstonian	Oxford City	Purfleet	St Albans City	Staines Town	Sutton United	Yeading	Yeovil Town
Aylesbury United	—	2-2	1-1	1-1	2-1	3-1	1-0	0-2	2-0	0-0	2-0	2-0	1-2	2-1	6-1	2-1	2-3	2-1	1-0	3-3	0-1	0-1
Bishop's Stortford	2-0	—	4-1	4-3	2-1	3-1	0-3	2-0	0-1	2-4	1-0	2-1	0-0	4-0	2-5	2-2	2-3	1-1	1-0	2-5	1-1	0-1
Boreham Wood	1-1	4-1	—	2-2	3-0	1-2	2-1	0-0	2-1	2-4	0-1	2-1	0-0	3-2	0-0	3-2	0-1	0-1	1-2	3-3	1-1	0-3
Bromley	2-0	1-0	3-0	—	3-2	2-0	1-0	2-2	4-0	2-1	1-2	2-0	1-1	1-1	2-1	2-2	2-3	1-0	1-2	1-1	5-1	1-2
Carshalton Athletic	3-1	0-3	1-2	2-3	—	3-1	0-3	3-1	0-1	3-0	2-1	0-0	3-5	0-5	0-3	1-1	0-2	0-5	3-0	3-3	0-2	0-1
Chertsey Town	1-1	0-0	2-1	0-2	2-3	—	0-3	1-1	1-0	2-1	1-0	1-0	3-0	1-1	2-0	2-4	2-0	0-1	1-3	1-3	0-1	0-2
Dagenham & Redbridge	0-2	3-0	2-1	0-2	4-1	3-0	—	2-3	2-0	1-0	0-0	2-1	1-2	2-0	2-0	4-2	3-0	2-0	3-0	0-1	0-1	4-1
Dulwich Hamlet	1-1	2-0	0-1	0-1	2-1	1-1	1-1	—	5-0	0-3	1-0	0-0	1-2	0-5	1-0	0-0	2-1	1-0	4-0	0-1	1-2	3-0
Enfield	2-0	1-1	4-1	5-0	2-0	1-0	3-0	2-3	—	4-0	3-2	0-0	2-1	4-0	1-1	3-3	3-0	1-0	4-0	3-1	1-1	3-0
Grays Athletic	0-0	0-1	2-4	4-3	2-0	1-0	1-1	2-2	0-1	—	0-2	3-1	1-1	2-3	2-3	2-3	2-1	0-2	2-1	2-5	0-5	2-3
Harrow Borough	0-0	3-1	0-0	0-2	0-2	4-1	4-1	1-1	2-4	1-0	—	2-2	1-1	3-0	1-2	4-2	1-3	2-1	1-2	0-2	0-1	1-3
Hendon	1-3	0-0	2-1	4-3	3-2	2-0	2-3	1-1	1-0	2-1	0-1	—	1-1	3-1	4-1	2-0	2-3	1-0	1-2	1-2	3-0	2-3
Heybridge Swifts	0-1	1-0	0-0	5-1	3-2	2-1	0-2	4-2	0-2	2-4	0-2	1-2	—	1-1	1-2	4-1	1-3	2-3	3-1	2-5	0-1	1-3
Hitchin Town	2-1	4-1	2-1	2-0	1-1	2-0	0-0	2-2	0-3	2-0	2-0	0-0	1-0	—	3-1	3-2	2-1	3-1	0-5	2-5	1-1	0-1
Kingstonian	3-1	3-0	2-2	2-0	1-0	2-2	0-0	2-2	1-1	1-0	4-1	2-0	3-3	3-1	—	4-1	3-1	2-1	2-1	3-5	4-2	3-0
Oxford City	0-0	0-1	0-2	0-3	1-0	2-3	0-1	1-0	2-0	1-0	3-3	0-0	1-0	3-1	1-2	—	2-1	0-2	1-2	1-3	4-2	0-1
Purfleet	0-0	1-1	0-2	2-1	2-0	1-0	2-4	1-4	1-2	3-0	1-0	3-2	1-0	1-0	4-1	4-2	—	2-3	1-3	1-2	3-2	0-1
St Albans City	3-1	1-1	0-3	0-0	2-2	2-2	1-4	2-2	0-1	4-5	2-2	1-0	1-0	2-1	2-1	1-2	2-1	—	1-0	2-1	0-0	1-1
Staines Town	3-1	2-1	2-1	4-2	0-0	1-3	0-0	0-0	3-3	0-0	4-3	3-1	1-1	1-2	0-4	1-2	1-3	1-2	—	1-0	3-0	0-3
Sutton United	0-1	2-1	2-2	2-2	0-0	3-0	1-0	1-3	3-1	1-1	3-3	3-1	3-3	2-1	2-3	1-2	1-2	3-1	2-1	—	1-2	3-2
Yeading	3-3	2-1	1-1	1-0	4-2	0-0	1-1	3-0	5-1	1-0	0-2	3-1	0-2	4-3	5-2	1-2	0-3	2-3	1-0	3-0	—	0-0
Yeovil Town	3-2	1-0	0-0	3-0	3-0	4-0	2-2	6-1	2-3	1-0	2-0	2-0	1-0	1-0	2-3	4-1	4-3	3-1	3-1	3-2	2-0	—

PONTIN'S CENTRAL LEAGUE

Premier Division	P	W	D	L	F	A	Pts
Manchester United	24	15	6	3	55	24	51
Blackburn Rovers	24	13	4	7	28	23	43
Sheffield Wednesday	24	12	4	8	42	32	40
Stoke City	24	11	2	11	34	37	35
Leeds United	24	10	4	10	29	34	34
Derby County	24	9	6	9	41	32	33
Birmingham City	24	8	7	9	34	31	31
Nottingham Forest	24	9	4	11	33	45	31
Tranmere Rovers	24	9	3	12	48	48	30
Everton	24	8	6	10	31	42	30
Liverpool	24	8	5	11	32	39	29
Bolton Wanderers	24	7	5	12	31	38	26
Oldham Athletic	24	5	8	11	27	40	23

Division One	P	W	D	L	F	A	Pts
Preston North End	24	16	6	2	42	14	54
Aston Villa	24	16	4	4	62	25	52
Notts County	24	12	5	7	38	35	41
Middlesbrough	24	10	8	6	42	36	38
Wolverhampton W	24	11	5	8	37	32	38
Leicester City	24	11	3	10	37	42	36
Sunderland	24	9	8	7	47	37	35
Huddersfield Town	24	8	5	11	32	39	29
Port Vale	24	7	6	11	30	37	27
Coventry City	24	6	8	10	22	25	26
West Bromwich Albion	24	6	6	12	21	36	24
Sheffield United	24	7	3	14	26	44	24
Blackpool	24	1	5	18	12	46	8

Division Two	P	W	D	L	F	A	Pts
Grimsby Town	24	15	5	4	54	29	50
Manchester City	24	14	6	4	43	26	48
York City	24	13	6	5	41	30	45
Wrexham	24	13	5	6	51	30	44
Barnsley	24	12	5	7	53	39	41
Shrewsbury Town	24	10	5	9	42	38	35
Rotherham United	24	10	4	10	29	30	34
Burnley	24	9	5	10	46	41	32
Carlisle United	24	10	2	12	37	38	32
Stockport County	24	7	5	12	34	43	26
Bradford City	24	7	5	12	36	47	26
Hull City	24	7	4	13	27	45	25
Mansfield Town	24	0	1	23	29	86	1

Division Three	P	W	D	L	F	A	Pts
Rochdale	20	14	4	2	39	20	46
Lincoln City	20	11	7	2	35	20	40
Walsall	20	9	8	3	35	16	35
Doncaster Rovers	20	7	5	8	37	35	26
Bury	20	7	7	6	20	25	25
Chesterfield	20	7	4	9	25	31	25
Wigan Athletic	20	6	5	9	24	33	23
Chester City	20	6	4	10	26	30	22
Scunthorpe United	20	6	4	10	29	35	22
Darlington	20	4	7	9	25	37	19
Scarborough	20	5	3	12	22	35	18

AVON INSURANCE COMBINATION

Division One	P	W	D	L	F	A	Pts
Wimbledon	22	14	5	3	44	25	47
Portsmouth	22	14	2	6	40	23	44
Tottenham Hotspur	22	13	4	5	50	26	43
Ipswich Town	22	12	5	5	41	18	45
Crystal Palace	22	10	6	6	37	32	36
Arsenal	22	10	5	7	49	30	35
Brighton & Hove Albion	22	9	8	5	40	31	35
Luton Town	22	10	5	7	32	24	35
Swindon Town	22	9	5	8	37	35	32
Chelsea	22	9	5	8	31	35	32
Queens Park Rangers	22	9	4	9	37	37	31
Watford	22	7	8	7	28	32	29
Swansea City	22	7	7	8	24	33	28
Charlton Athletic	22	7	6	9	30	38	27
Southampton	22	7	5	10	34	40	26
AFC Bournemouth	22	7	5	10	34	43	26
Millwall	22	7	4	11	30	38	25
Bristol City	22	6	5	11	38	37	23
Oxford United	22	6	5	11	37	40	23
West Ham United	22	6	4	12	29	45	22
Bristol Rovers	22	6	4	12	22	42	22
Cardiff City	22	4	7	11	17	42	19
Norwich City	22	4	6	12	32	47	18

LEAGUE CUP

Group 1
QPR 3, Charlton Ath 0
Millwall 2, Watford 0
Watford 3, QPR 2
Millwall 1, Tottenham H 2
QPR 0, Millwall 0
Watford 1, Charlton Ath 1
Charlton Ath 8, Millwall 0
Tottenham H 1, Watford 2
Charlton Ath 2, Tottenham H 2
Tottenham H 1, QPR 0

Group 2
Wimbledon 1, Bournemouth 1
Brighton & HA 0, Portsmouth 1
Crystal Palace 2, Wimbledon 3
Bournemouth 0, Southampton 4
Brighton & HA 0, Bournemouth 0
Crystal Palace 0, Southampton 0
Bournemouth 4, Crystal Palace 3
Southampton 3, Portsmouth 1
Wimbledon 6, Brighton & HA 1
Crystal Palace 3, Brighton & HA 2
Southampton 0, Wimbledon 1
Wimbledon 1, Portsmouth 1
Southampton 4, Brighton & HA 3
Portsmouth 1, Bournemouth 2
Portsmouth v Crystal Palace not played.

Group 3
Ipswich T 0, Arsenal 2
Norwich C 1, Ipswich T 0

Norwich C 0, West Ham U 1
Luton T 3, Norwich C 0
Luton T 0, West Ham U 3
West Ham U 3, Ipswich T 1
Arsenal 0, Luton T 1
West Ham U 0, Arsenal 2
Arsenal 1, Norwich C 3
Ipswich T 2, Luton T 0

Group 4
Bristol R 6, Cardiff C 0
Oxford U 2, Swindon T 1
Oxford U 1, Cardiff C 0
Swindon T 0, Bristol R 0
Swansea C 1, Swindon T 2
Bristol C 2, Oxford U 2
Bristol C 3, Bristol R 1
Cardiff C 1, Swansea C 1
Bristol R 1, Swansea C 2
Swansea C 0, Bristol C 0
Swindon T 1, Cardiff C 0
Oxford U 2, Bristol R 0
Swansea C 1, Oxford U 1
Cardiff C 0, Bristol C 3
Bristol C 1, Swindon T 2

Semi-Finals
West Ham U 2, Tottenham H 5
Wimbledon 2, Oxford U 1

Final
Tottenham H 3, Wimbledon 2

SOUTH EAST COUNTIES LEAGUE

Divison One

	P	W	D	L	F	A	Pts
Norwich City	30	20	6	4	66	26	46
Chelsea	30	19	4	7	61	41	42
West Ham United	30	16	7	7	74	31	39
Arsenal	30	14	7	9	51	38	35
Tottenham Hotspur	30	14	6	10	46	31	34
Watford	30	16	2	12	60	50	34
Queens Park Rangers	30	14	5	11	53	44	33
Gillingham	30	12	9	9	50	47	33
Ipswich Town	30	11	8	11	57	62	30
Portsmouth	30	11	4	15	45	54	26
Millwall	30	10	6	14	47	64	26
Cambridge United	30	7	8	15	34	55	22
Charlton Athletic	30	6	9	15	46	66	21
Southend United	30	7	7	16	38	62	21
Fulham	30	8	5	17	36	65	21
Leyton Orient	30	3	11	16	35	63	17

Divison Two

	P	W	D	L	F	A	Pts
Luton Town	30	22	5	3	70	30	49
Crystal Palace	30	19	7	4	69	27	45
Southampton	30	20	2	8	59	25	42
Oxford United	30	14	11	5	54	37	39
Tottenham Hotspur	30	12	9	9	48	33	33
Colchester United	30	12	8	10	51	40	32
Swindon Town	30	12	8	10	54	46	32
Wimbledon	30	11	8	11	40	27	30
Brighton & Hove Albion	30	12	6	12	41	51	30
Wycombe Wanderers	30	11	7	12	32	33	29
AFC Bournemouth	30	10	7	13	44	59	27
Bristol City	30	9	7	14	46	63	25
Bristol Rovers	30	9	5	16	44	56	23
Brentford	30	5	7	18	37	65	17
Reading	30	7	3	20	35	86	17
Barnet	30	2	6	22	27	73	10

REPUBLIC OF IRELAND LEAGUE

	P	W	D	L	F	A	Pts
Derry City	33	19	10	4	58	27	67
Bohemians	33	16	9	8	43	32	57
Shelbourne	34	15	9	10	54	39	54
Cork City	33	15	9	9	38	24	54
St Patrick's Ath	33	13	14	6	45	33	53
Sligo Rovers	33	12	11	10	43	43	47
Shamrock Rovers	33	10	13	10	43	46	43
UCD	33	12	7	14	34	39	43
Finn Harps	34	11	9	14	44	45	42
Dundalk	33	9	9	15	32	50	36
Bray Wanderers	33	5	8	20	30	59	23
Home Farm	33	3	10	20	26	53	19

HIGHLAND LEAGUE

	P	W	D	L	F	A	Pts	GD
Huntly	30	23	4	3	86	26	73	+60
Keith	30	21	3	6	76	36	66	+40
Peterhead	30	17	7	6	77	30	58	+47
Lossiemouth	30	18	4	8	66	31	58	+35
Clachnacuddin	30	16	5	9	59	46	53	+13
Fraserburgh	30	15	7	8	56	38	52	+18
Cove Rangers	30	15	5	10	84	47	50	+37
Deveronvale	30	16	2	12	55	54	50	+1
Elgin City	30	13	4	13	64	66	43	-2
Wick Academy	30	9	8	13	41	46	35	-5
Rothes	30	9	8	13	44	52	35	-8
Forres Mechanics	30	8	5	17	40	60	29	-20
Buckie Thistle	30	8	4	18	41	55	28	-14
Brora Rangers	30	5	10	15	43	88	25	-45
Nairn County	30	4	3	23	21	93	15	-72
Fort William	30	2	3	25	31	116	9	-85

FA UMBRO TROPHY 1996–97

First Qualifying Round

Atherstone United v Whitley Bay 0-2
Atherton LR v Moor Green 1-1, 1-6
Stafford Rangers v Curzon Ashton 1-2
Droylsden v Leigh RMI 1-1, 3-1
Nuneaton Borough v Congleton Town
0-3
Alfreton Town v Bilston Town
4-4, 1-4
Warrington Town v Lancaster City
0-2
Bedworth United v Gretna 0-0, 4-1
Hinckley Town v Worksop Town 0-2
Harrogate Town v Knowsley United
2-3
Grantham Town v Leek Town 1-0
Racing Club Warwick v Frickley
Athletic 1-2
Tamworth v Great Harwood Town
2-2, 0-1
Paget Rangers v Eastwood Town 0-1
Buxton v VS Rugby 2-1
Matlock Town v Winsford United 1-4
Stocksbridge Park Steels v Sutton
Coldfield Town 1-0
Solihull Borough w.o. v Leicester
United withdrew
Witton Albion v Workington 3-3, 0-1
Netherfield v Farsley Celtic 2-3
Cirencester Town v Cambridge City
2-2, 5-6
Wokingham Town v Erith & Belvedere
1-0
Ashford Town v Hitchin Town 4-1
Tonbridge v Aylesbury United 0-2
Fareham Town v Weymouth 2-2, 0-7
Whyteleafe v Yeading
Baldock Town v Stourbridge 3-2
Margate v Aldershot Town 1-2
Buckingham Town v Forest Green
Rovers 0-1
Hendon v Thame United 1-1, 1-1, 3-0
Chesham United v Walton &
Hersham 1-1, 3-1
Bishops Stortford v Croydon 3-0
Hampton v Trowbridge Town 4-1
Raunds Town v Barton Rovers 4-1
Canvey Island v Heybridge Swifts 0-1
Gravesend & Northfleet v
St Leonards Stamcroft 2-2, 3-4
Yate Town v Kings Lynn 1-3
Sittingbourne v Fleet Town 3-2
Weston-Super-Mare v Worthing 2-0
Newport (IW) v Leyton Pennant
3-3, 1-3
Abingdon Town v Evesham United 0-2
Maidenhead United v Corby Town 4-2
Bromley v Uxbridge 1-0
Cinderford Town v Havant Town 2-3
Grays Athletic v Bashley 2-1

Billericay Town v Berkhamsted Town
3-0
Fisher v Molesey 2-2, 2-1
Marlow v Witney Town 1-1, 1-2
Dorchester Town v Waterlooville 1-0

Second Qualifying Round

Moor Green v Ilkeston Town 2-1
Workington v Redditch United 1-0
Farsley Celtic v Worksop Town
1-1, 1-2
Stocksbridge Park Steels v Shepshed
Dynamo 2-2, 1-0
Buxton v Eastwood Town 1-0
Congleton Town v Solihull Borough
1-3
Whitley Bay v Bradford (Park Avenue)
0-1
Bilston Town v Great Harwood Town
4-0
Lancaster City v Droylsden 2-0
Lincoln United v Frickley Athletic 3-4
Grantham Town v Winsford United
2-1
Curzon Ashton v Bedworth United
0-2
Knowsley United v Flixton 3-2
Heybridge Swifts v Grays Athletic 2-1
Oxford City v Basingstoke Town 1-6
Weymouth v Clevedon Town 4-1
Aylesbury United v Sittingbourne
1-1, 1-2
Salisbury City v Witney Town 1-0
Weston-Super-Mare v Raunds Town
1-3
Forest Green Rovers v Cambridge City
1-2
Maidenhead United v Bromley 1-3
Aldershot Town v Chesham United
3-0
Hendon v Sutton United 1-3
Hampton v St Leonards Stamcroft 0-1
Chertsey Town v Yeading 1-1, 1-3
Fisher Athletic v Havant Town 3-2
Dartford v Tooting & Mitcham United
1-1, 3-2
Wokingham Town v Leyton Pennant
2-0
Billericay Town v Dorcester Town 0-4
Staines Town v Kings Lynn 0-1
Ashford Town v Bishops Stortford 6-1
Baldock Town v Evesham Town 0-1

Third Qualifying Round

Bradford (Park Avenue) v Barrow
1-1, 1-0
Marine v Gainsborough Trinity 0-1
Buxton v Grantham Town 1-1, 1-2
Runcorn v Solihull Borough 2-1

Moor Green v Dudley Town 6-1
Ashton United v Burton Albion 1-0
Colwyn Bay v Frickley Athletic 1-0
Blyth Spartans v Bilston Town 7-3
Worksop Town v Lancaster City
    0-0, 2-4
Bishop Auckland v Stocksbridge Park
   Steels 2-1
Spennymoor United v Radcliffe
   Borough 1-0
Bedworth United v Accrington Stanley
   2-0
Rothwell Town v Workington 1-7
Knowsley United v Emley 2-2, 2-5
Dartford v Dulwich Hamlet 0-0, 1-3
Bromley v Worcester City 1-1, 0-2
Sutton United v Dorchester Town 0-2
Aldershot Town v Dagenham &
   Redbridge 1-3
Crawley Town v Chelmsford City 0-2
Yeovil Town v Evesham United 2-0
Carshalton Athletic v Heybridge Swifts
   0-3
St Leonards Stamcroft v Purfleet 6-0
Weymouth v Ashford Town 2-0
Raunds Town v Bognor Regis Town
   4-2
Harrow Borough v Salisbury City
   2-2, 1-2
Sudbury Town v Cheltenham Town
   2-3
Cambridge City v Newport AFC
   1-1, 1-4
Sittingbourne v Yeading 0-0, 1-3
Basingstoke Town v Hastings Town
   0-1
St Albans City v Kings Lynn 3-1
Gloucester City v Kingstonian 3-1
Fisher Athletic v Wokingham Town
   1-2

First Round

Gresley Rovers v Altrincham 3-3, 0-1
Morecambe v Chorley 3-1
Workington v Bamber Bridge 2-5
Colwyn Bay v Lancaster City 6-0
Gainsborough Trinity v Bradford (Park
   Avenue) 1-3
Emley v Boston United 2-1
Spennymoor United v
   Bishop Auckland 0-2
Northwich Victoria v
   Hednesford Town 0-1
Blyth Spartans v
   Grantham Town 1-1, 1-1, 1-3
Southport v Halesowen Town 0-0, 2-0
Hyde United v Bedworth United 4-2
Guiseley v Telford United 2-1
Kidderminster Harriers v
   Macclesfield Town 3-0
Gateshead v Runcorn 1-2
Ashton United v Moor Green 5-3

Stalybridge Celtic v Halifax Town 0-1
Bath City v Stevenage Borough
   1-1, 1-6
Slough Town v Dorchester Town
   2-2, 2-2, 1-2
Cheltenham Town v Dulwich Hamlet
   1-2
St Leonards Stamcroft v Newport AFC
   1-0
St Albans City v Weymouth 2-0
Rushden & Diamonds v Farnborough
   Town 1-2
Enfield v Boreham Wood 1-3
Hastings Town v Salisbury City 1-3
Wokingham Town v Woking 0-1
Kettering Town v Chelmsford City
   0-1
Raunds Town v Welling United 0-1
Yeovil Town v Hayes 2-2, 2-2, 1-2
Bromsgrove Rovers v Merthyr Tydfil
   2-1
Yeading v Gloucester City 0-3
Worcester City v Heybridge Swifts 1-2
Dover Athletic v Dagenham &
   Redbridge 0-2

Second Round

Bishop Auckland v Northwich Victoria
   3-2
Grantham Town v Heybridge Swifts
   0-1
Dagenham & Redbridge v
   Chelmsford City 2-1
St Albans City v Woking 1-1, 1-3
Gloucester City v Halifax Town 3-0
Ashton United v Bamber Bridge 3-1
Boreham Wood v Stevenage Borough
   0-1
Bradford (Park Avenue) v Morecambe
   0-1
Bromsgrove Rovers v Hyde United
   1-1, 2-2, 0-2
Welling United v Guiseley 1-1, 0-1
Farnborough Town v Altrincham 0-2
Colwyn Bay v Southport 2-0
Hayes v Runcorn 1-2
Kidderminster Harriers v Emley
   0-0, 5-1
Salisbury City v Dorchester Town
   1-1, 2-3
St Leonards Stamcroft v Dulwich
   Hamlet 2-1

Third Round

Colwyn Bay v St Leonards Stamcroft
   2-2, 0-0, 2-1
Ashton United v Hyde United 2-0
Stevenage Borough v Guiseley 1-0
Gloucester City v Runcorn 3-1
Dorchester Town v Woking 2-3
Altrincham v Bishop Auckland 0-1

Morecambe v Dagenham &
Redbridge   0-0, 1-2
Heybridge Swifts v Kidderminster
Harriers   3-0

Fourth Round

Dagenham & Redbridge v Ashton
United   1-0
Heybridge Swifts v Woking   0-1

FINAL AT WEMBLEY

18 MAY

Dagenham & Redbridge (0) 0

Woking (0) 1 *(Hay)*   24,376

Dagenham & Redbridge: Gothard; Culverhouse, Conner, Creaser, Jacques (Double),
Davidson, Pratt (Naylor), Parratt, Broom, Rogers, Stimson (John).
Woking: Batty; Brown, Howard, Foster, Taylor, Wye S, Thompson (Jones), Ellis,
Steele (Wye L), Walker, Jackson (Hay).
Referee: J. Winter (North Riding).

FA CARLSBERG VASE 1996–97

Second Round

Haslingden v Trafford	1-2
North Ferriby United v Hebburn	4-0
Blackpool (Wren) Rovers v South Shields	1-1, 1-3
Brandon United v Brigg Town	0-3
Chester-Le-Street Town v Dunston FB	1-3
Tow Law Town v Murton	5-2
Guisborough Town v Prudhoe Town	2-0
Whitby Town v Billingham Synthonia	1-0
Poulton Victoria v RTM Newcastle	3-1
Seaham Red Star v Ossett Albion	0-4
Mossley v Morpeth Town	2-1
Formby v Tetley Walker	0-5
Durham City v Easington Colliery	2-1
Cammell Laird v Bedlington Terriers	0-2
West Auckland Town v Holker Old Boys	2-3
Vauxhall GM v Clitheroe	3-1
Stewarts & Lloyds v Glapwell	3-2
Boldmere St Michaels v Belper Town	3-1
Dunkirk v Cogenhoe United	0-5
Hallam v Sandwell Borough	1-1, 1-3
Oadby Town v Arnold Town	3-1
Hinckley Athletic v Eastwood Hanley	2-0
Denaby United v Newcastle Town	2-4

Bridgnorth Town v Stapenhill	2-2, 2-1
Brackley Town v Hucknall Town	2-4
Gedling Town v Barwell	2-1
Thackley v Louth United	0-0, 1-2
Nantwich Town v St Andrews	2-1
Bury Town v Collier Row & Romford	1-2
Histon v Ware	3-2
Wivenhoe Town v Harlow Town	3-4
Woodbridge Town v Brentwood	2-0
Northwood v Chalfont St Peter	3-1
Wembley v Spalding United	0-1
Swaffham Town v Saffron Walden Town	1-1, 0-3
Feltham v Braintree Town	2-4
Boston Town v Barking	1-3
Eynesbury Rovers v Concord Rangers	1-2
Stamford AFC v Lowestoft Town	2-1
Diss Town v Potton United	2-1
Halstead Town v Gorleston	2-1
Tiptree United v Southend Manor	0-3
Aveley v Arlesey Town	2-2, 2-3
Brache Sparta v Wisbech Town	1-3
Ashford Town (Middlesex) v Burnham	0-1
Burgess Hill Town v North Leigh	3-0
Sheppey United v Metropolitan Police	0-1
Wick v Thatcham Town	2-4
Banstead Athletic v Bracknell Town	2-0

Abingdon United v Herne Bay 0-3
Reading Town v Chatham Town 2-1
Whitstable Town v Slade Green 1-0
Beckenham Town v Peacehaven & Telscombe 2-5
First Tower United v Hailsham Town 4-2
Whitehawk v Greenwich Borough 2-3
Gosport Borough v Saltash United 0-2
Chippenham Town v Amesbury Town 6-0
Tiverton Town v Bideford 3-0
Paulton Rovers v Taunton Town 0-0, 1-2
Odd Down v Bemerton Heath Harlequins 0-1
Falmouth Town v Truro City 1-2
Christchurch v Mangotsfield United 0-2
Bridgwater Town v Brockenhurst 2-1
Wimborne Town v Backwell United 1-2
(Abandoned after 71 minutes; floodlight failure) 5-1

Third Round

Brigg Town v Tow Law Town 1-3
South Shields v Bedlington Terriers 1-3
Louth United v Whitby Town 2-4
Dunston FB v Holker Old Boys 5-0
Tetley Walker v Trafford 1-0
Hallam v North Ferriby United 1-3
Guisborough Town v Poulton Victoria 4-3
Ossett Albion v Nantwich Town 0-1
Vauxhall GM v Mossley 1-3
Gedling Town v Durham City 0-1
Hucknall Town v Newcastle Town
(Abandoned after 33 minutes at 1-0 due to injury to a match official) 2-1
Woodbridge Town v Halstead Town 3-1
Hinckley Athletic v Stamford AFC 0-1
Oadby Town v Cogenhoe United 1-3
Spalding United v Bridgnorth Town 1-1, 2-1
Barking v Saffron Walden Town 1-1, 3-1
Northwood v Harlow Town 3-1
Histon v Metropolitan Police 2-1
Stewarts & Lloyds v Southend Manor 0-1
Collier Row & Romford v Braintree Town 2-2
(abandoned after 112 minutes: floodlight failure) 1-1, 3-1
Wisbech Town v Diss Town 3-0
Concord Rangers v Greenwich Borough 1-1, 3-1

Arlesey Town v Boldmere St Michaels 3-0
Burgess Hill Town v Bemerton Heath Harlequins 0-1
Bridgwater Town v Taunton Town 1-3
Mangotsfield United v Chippenham Town 2-1
Tiverton Town v Peacehaven & Telscombe 8-0
First Tower United v Reading Town 1-5
Burnham v Whitstable Town 1-2
Herne Bay v Saltash United 3-0
Banstead Athletic v Truro City 3-1
Thatcham Town v Wimborne Town 4-1

Fourth Round

Stamford AFC v North Ferriby United 1-1, 0-1
Guisborough Town v Tow Law Town 4-2
Mossley v Cogenhoe United 3-2
Bedlington Terriers v Dunston FB 4-1
Tetley Walker v Durham City 0-1
Hucknall Town v Spalding United 2-5
Whitby Town v Nantwich Town 3-1
Barking v Woodbridge Town 1-0
Arlesey Town v Herne Bay 2-3
Southend Manor v Wisbech Town 0-1
Mangotsfield United v Taunton Town 2-3
Thatcham Town v Tiverton Town 0-1
Concord Rangers v Whitstable Town 0-0, 1-2
Bemerton Heath Harlequins v Collier Row & Romford 0-2
Histon v Northwood 0-2
Reading Town v Banstead Athletic 0-2

Fifth Round

Guisborough Town v Wisbech Town 2-0
Taunton Town v Spalding United 3-0
North Ferriby United v Whitstable Town 1-0
Durham City v Northwood 0-2
Mossley v Barking 1-0
Whitby Town v Tiverton Town 1-0
Banstead Athletic v Herne Bay 2-0
Collier Row & Romford v Bedlington Terriers 2-2, 1-2

Sixth Round

Northwood v Banstead Athletic 0-1
Guisborough Town v Taunton Town 3-0
Whitby Town v Mossley 5-1
North Ferriby United v Bedlington Terriers 2-0

Semi-finals (two legs)

Guisborough Town v North Ferriby
   United   0-2, 1-1

Banstead Athletic v Whitby Town
                           0-1, 1-1

FINAL AT WEMBLEY

10 MAY

North Ferriby United (0) 0

Whitby Town (3) 1 *(Logan, Williams, Toman)*   11,098

North Ferriby United: Sharp; Deacey, Walmsley, Brentano, Smith A, Harrison (Horne), Smith M, Phillips (Milner), Tennison, France (Newman), Flounders.
Whitby Town: Campbell; Goodchild, Pearson, Cook, Williams, Hodgson, Goodrick (Borthwick), Toman (Pyle), Logan, Robinson, Pitman (Hall).
Referee: G. Poll (Herts).

FA YOUTH CHALLENGE CUP 1996–97

First Round

Rotherham United v Barnsley	3-1
Notts County v Bury	0-0, 0-2
Huddersfield Town v Leicester City	0-0, 1-0
Preston North End v Port Vale	0-1
Shrewsbury Town v Wrexham	0-5
Grimsby Town v Bradford City	5-0
Leeds United v Sheffield Wednesday	2-2, 4-0
Blackburn Rovers v Blackpool	3-1
Newcastle United v Burnley	1-2
Everton v Nuneaton Borough	3-0
Bolton Wanderers v Derby County	5-0
Walsall v Bromsgrove Rovers	3-0
Peterborough United v Stevenage Borough	2-1
Hereford United v Luton Town	1-3
Rushden & Diamonds v Hillingdon Borough	6-1
Welling United v Wolverhampton Wanderers	0-1
Enfield v Boreham Wood	0-0, 2-1
Leighton Town v Watford	0-3
Birmingham City v Boldmere St Michaels	3-0
Northampton Town v Chelsea	0-5
Charlton Athletic v Aveley	6-1
Cambridge United v Colchester United	2-4
Bognor Regis Town v Viking Sports	1-4
Reading v Dulwich Hamlet	2-1
Plymouth Argyle v Brighton & Hove Albion	3-0
Exeter City v Torquay United	0-7
Bristol Rovers v Woking	4-1
Oxford United v Cardiff City	2-1
Croydon Athletic v Gravesend & Northfleet	1-5
Wycombe Wanderers v Corinthian	5-0
Fulham v Gillingham	0-3
Yeovil Town v AFC Bournemouth	3-3, 0-4
Southampton v Sittingbourne	1-0
Wokingham Town v Swansea City	1-4

Second Round

Tranmere Rovers v Grimsby Town	2-0
Oldham Athletic v York City	3-0
Blackburn Rovers v Port Vale	2-0
Bury v Huddersfield Town	1-0
Bolton Wanderers v Sheffield United	1-1, 5-4
Coventry City v Aston Villa	2-1
Liverpool v Burnley	5-2
Manchester City v Walsall	2-2, 4-2
Manchester United v Wrexham	7-0
Rotherham United v Stoke City	2-1
Nottingham Forest v Middlesbrough	3-1
Leeds United v Crewe Alexandra	2-0
Sunderland v Birmingham City	1-0
West Bromwich Albion v Everton	1-2
Oxford United v Luton Town	1-1, 2-3
Enfield v Gravesend & Northfleet	1-1, 0-2
Ipswich Town v Arsenal	1-0
Chelsea v Crystal Palace	2-3
AFC Bournemouth v Portsmouth	2-1
Swansea City v Norwich City	0-6
Charlton Athletic v Brentford	2-1
Millwall v Gillingham	1-0
Viking Sports v Wimbledon	0-2
Wolverhampton Wanderers v Wycombe Wanderers	2-3

Leyton Orient v Bristol City 1-2
Colchester United v West Ham
United 1-3
Rushden & Diamonds v Southend
United 2-2, 0-4
Bristol Rovers v Queens Park
Rangers 0-0, 0-1
Southampton v Tottenham Hotspur
1-3
Torquay United v Swindon Town
1-1, 2-0
Plymouth Argyle v Peterborough
United 1-2
Watford v Reading 8-0

Third Round

Nottingham Forest v Rotherham United
1-0
Manchester City v Leeds United 1-2
Oldham Athletic v Sunderland 1-2
Bury v Blackburn Rovers 0-0, 2-3
Bolton Wanderers v Everton 1-2
Liverpool v Manchester United 1-2
Coventry City v Tranmere Rovers 0-1
Southend United v Watford 0-0
(Abandoned at half-time; frozen pitch)
2-3r
Norwich City v Wycombe Wanderers
5-1
Torquay United v Luton Town 0-2
Crystal Palace v West Ham United 2-1
Bristol City v AFC Bournemouth 2-3
Queens Park Rangers v Wimbledon
3-2

Tottenham Hotspur v Gravesend &
Northfleet 2-5
Peterborough United v Millwall 3-0
Charlton Athletic v Ipswich Town
5-4

Fourth Round

Leeds United v Queens Park
Rangers 2-0
Norwich City v Everton 1-1, 2-0
Nottingham Forest v Blackburn Rovers
0-3
Charlton Athletic v Tottenham Hotspur
0-2
Sunderland v Luton Town 2-5
Manchester United v Watford 1-1, 2-3
AFC Bournemouth v Tranmere Rovers
0-3
Peterborough United v Crystal Palace
1-3

Fifth Round

Luton Town v Watford 0-0, 1-1
(Luton Town won 5-3 on penalties.)
Leeds United v Tranmere Rovers
0-0, 1-0
Blackburn Rovers v Norwich City 2-1
Crystal Palace v Tottenham Hotspur
1-0

Semi-finals (two legs)

Luton Town v Leeds United 1-2, 0-1
Crystal Palace v Blackburn Rovers
2-1, 2-2

FINAL FIRST LEG

24 APR

Leeds United (2) 2 *(Boyle, Jones)*
Crystal Palace (0) 1 *(Harris)* 6649
Leeds United: Robinson; Maybury, Woodgate, Lynch, Kewell, Dixon, Knarvik, McPhail, Boyle, Jones, Matthews.
Crystal Palace: Ormshaw; Hibbert, Mullins, Woozley, Folan, Carlisle, Kennedy, Stevens, Graham, Martin, Morrison (Harris).
Referee: G. Barber (Warwick).

FINAL SECOND LEG

15 MAY

Crystal Palace (0) 0
Leeds United (0) 1 *(Matthews)* 4759
Crystal Palace: Ormshaw; Hibbert, Mullins, Woozley, Folan, Carlisle (Harris), Kennedy, Stevens, Graham, Martin, Morrison (Sears).
Leeds United: Robinson; Maybury, Woodgate, Lynch, Kewell, Dixon, Knarvik, McPhail, Boyle, Jones (Wright), Matthews.
Referee: G. Barber (Warwick).

BRITISH FOOTBALL RECORDS

Records during 1996–97

HIGHEST SCORES

Football League, Division 3
Colchester U 7, Lincoln C 1.
Wigan Ath 7, Scarborough 1.

HIGHEST AGGREGATE

FA Premier League
Southampton 6, Manchester U 3.
Football League, Division 2
Peterborough U 6, Wycombe W 3.

MOST GOALS IN A SEASON

Football League, Division 1
Bolton W 100 in 46 matches.

FEWEST GOALS IN A SEASON

FA Premier League
Leeds U 28 in 38 matches.

MOST GOALS AGAINST IN A SEASON

Scottish League, Division 1
East Fife 92 in 36 matches.

FEWEST GOALS AGAINST IN A SEASON

Scottish League, Division 1
St. Johnstone 23 in 36 matches.

MOST POINTS IN A SEASON

Football League, Division 1
Bolton W 98 in 46 matches.

FEWEST POINTS IN A SEASON

Scottish League, Division 1
East Fife, 14 in 36 matches.

MOST WINS IN A SEASON

Football League, Division 1
Bolton W 28 in 46 matches.

FEWEST WINS IN A SEASON

Scottish League, Division 1
East Fife 2 in 36 matches.

MOST DEFEATS IN A SEASON

Football League, Division 2
Rotherham U 25 in 46 matches.
Notts Co 25 in 46 matches.

FEWEST DEFEATS IN A SEASON

Football League, Division 1
Bolton W 4 in 46 matches.
Scottish League, Division 1
St Johnstone 4 in 36 matches.

MOST DRAWS IN A SEASON

Football League, Division 2
Watford 19 in 46 matches.

MOST INDIVIDUAL GOALS IN A SEASON

Football League, Division 3
Graeme Jones (Wigan Ath) 31.

OTHER AWARDS 1996–97

FOOTBALLER OF THE YEAR
The Football Writers' Association Award for the Footballer of the Year went to Gianfranco Zola of Chelsea and Italy.

Past Winners
1947–48 Stanley Matthews (Blackpool); 1948–49 Johnny Carey (Manchester U); 1949–50 Joe Mercer (Arsenal); 1950–51 Harry Johnston (Blackpool); 1951–52 Billy Wright (Wolverhampton W); 1952–53 Nat Lofthouse (Bolton W); 1953–54 Tom Finney (Preston NE); 1954–55 Don Revie (Manchester C); 1955–56 Bert Trautmann (Manchester C); 1956–57 Tom Finney (Preston NE); 1957–58 Danny Blanchflower (Tottenham H); 1958–59 Syd Owen (Luton T); 1959–60 Bill Slater (Wolverhampton W); 1960–61 Danny Blanchflower (Tottenham H); 1961–62 Jimmy Adamson (Burnley); 1962–63 Stanley Matthews (Stoke C); 1963–64 Bobby Moore (West Ham U); 1964–65 Bobby Collins (Leeds U); 1965–66 Bobby Charlton (Manchester U); 1966–67 Jackie Charlton (Leeds U); 1967–68 George Best (Manchester U); 1968–69 Dave Mackay (Derby Co) shared with Tony Book (Manchester C); 1969–70 Billy Bremner (Leeds U); 1970–71 Frank McLintock (Arsenal); 1971–72 Gordon Banks (Stoke C); 1972–73 Pat Jennings (Tottenham H); 1973–74 Ian Callaghan (Liverpool); 1974–75 Alan Mullery (Fulham); 1975–76 Kevin Keegan (Liverpool); 1976–77 Emlyn Hughes (Liverpool); 1977–78 Kenny Burns (Nottingham F); 1978–79 Kenny Dalglish (Liverpool); 1979–80 Terry McDermott (Liverpool); 1980–81 Frans Thijssen (Ipswich T); 1981–82 Steve Perryman (Tottenham H); 1982–83 Kenny Dalglish (Liverpool); 1983–84 Ian Rush (Liverpool); 1984–85 Neville Southall (Everton); 1985–86 Gary Lineker (Everton); 1986–87 Clive Allen (Tottenham H); 1987–88 John Barnes (Liverpool); 1988–89 Steve Nicol (Liverpool); 1989–90 John Barnes (Liverpool); 1990–91 Gordon Strachan (Leeds U); 1991–92 Gary Lineker (Tottenham H); 1992–93 Chris Waddle (Sheffield W); 1993–94 Alan Shearer (Blackburn R); 1994–95 Jurgen Klinsmann (Tottenham H); 1995–96 Eric Cantona (Manchester U).

THE PFA AWARDS 1997
Player of the Year: Alan Shearer (Newcastle U).
Previous Winners: 1974 Norman Hunter (Leeds U); 1975 Colin Todd (Derby Co); 1976 Pat Jennings (Tottenham H); 1977 Andy Gray (Aston Villa); 1978 Peter Shilton (Nottingham F); 1979 Liam Brady (Arsenal); 1980 Terry McDermott (Liverpool); 1981 John Wark (Ipswich T); 1982 Kevin Keegan (Southampton); 1983 Kenny Dalglish (Liverpool); 1984 Ian Rush (Liverpool); 1985 Peter Reid (Everton); 1986 Gary Lineker (Everton); 1987 Clive Allen (Tottenham H); 1988 John Barnes (Liverpool); 1989 Mark Hughes (Manchester U); 1990 David Platt (Aston Villa); 1991 Mark Hughes (Manchester U); 1992 Gary Pallister (Manchester U); 1993 Paul McGrath (Aston Villa); 1994 Eric Cantona (Manchester U); 1995 Alan Shearer (Blackburn R); 1996 Les Ferdinand (Newcastle U).
Young Player of the Year: David Beckham (Manchester U).
Previous Winners: 1974 Kevin Beattie (Ipswich T); 1975 Mervyn Day (West Ham U); 1976 Peter Barnes (Manchester C); 1977 Andy Gray (Aston Villa); 1978 Tony Woodcock (Nottingham F); 1979 Cyrille Regis (WBA); 1980 Glenn Hoddle (Tottenham H); 1981 Gary Shaw (Aston Villa); 1982 Steve Moran (Southampton); 1983 Ian Rush (Liverpool); 1984 Paul Walsh (Luton T); 1985 Mark Hughes (Manchester U); 1986 Tony Cottee (West Ham U); 1987 Tony Adams (Arsenal); 1988 Paul Gascoigne (Tottenham H); 1989 Paul Merson (Arsenal); 1990 Matthew Le Tissier (Southampton); 1991 Lee Sharpe (Manchester U); 1992 Ryan Giggs (Manchester U); 1993 Ryan Giggs (Manchester U); 1994 Andy Cole (Newcastle U); 1995 Robbie Fowler (Liverpool); 1996 Robbie Fowler (Liverpool).

Merit Award: Peter Beardsley (Newcastle U).
Previous Winners: 1974 Bobby Charlton CBE, Cliff Lloyd OBE; 1975 Denis Law; 1976 George Eastham OBE; 1977 Jack Taylor OBE; 1978 Bill Shankly OBE; 1979 Tom Finney OBE; 1980 Sir Matt Busby CBE; 1981 John Trollope MBE; 1982 Joe Mercer OBE; 1983 Bob Paisley OBE; 1984 Bill Nicholson; 1985 Ron Greenwood; 1986 The 1966 England World Cup team, Sir Alf Ramsey, Harold Shepherdson; 1987 Sir Stanley Matthews; 1988 Billy Bonds MBE; 1989 Nat Lofthouse; 1990 Peter Shilton; 1991 Tommy Hutchison; 1992 Brian Clough; 1993 the 1968 Manchester United team; 1994 Billy Bingham; 1995 Gordon Strachan; 1996 Pelé.

THE SCOTTISH PFA AWARDS 1997

Player of the Year: Paolo Di Canio (Celtic).
Previous Winners: 1978 Derek Johnstone (Rangers); 1979 Paul Hegarty (Dundee U); 1980 Davie Provan (Celtic); 1981 Sandy Clark (Airdrieonians); 1982 Mark McGhee (Aberdeen); 1983 Charlie Nicholas (Celtic); 1984 Willie Miller (Aberdeen); 1985 Jim Duffy (Morton); 1986 Richard Gough (Dundee U); 1987 Brian McClair (Celtic); 1988 Paul McStay (Celtic); 1989 Theo Snelders (Aberdeen); 1990 Jim Bett (Aberdeen); 1991 Paul Elliott (Celtic); 1993 Ally McCoist (Rangers); 1993 Andy Goram (Rangers); 1994 Mark Hateley (Rangers); 1995 Brian Laudrup (Rangers); 1996 Paul Gascoigne (Rangers).

Young Player of the Year: Alex Burke (Kilmarnock).
Previous Winners: 1978 Graeme Payne (Dundee U); 1979 Graham Stewart (Dundee U); 1980 John MacDonald (Rangers); 1981 Francis McAvennie (St Mirren); 1982 Charlie Nicholas (Celtic); 1983 Pat Nevin (Clyde); 1984 John Robertson (Hearts); 1985 Craig Levein (Hearts); 1986 Craig Levein (Hearts); 1987 Robert Fleck (Rangers); 1988 John Collins (Hibernian); 1989 Bill McKinlay (Dundee U); 1990 Scott Crabbe (Hearts); 1991 Eoin Jess (Aberdeen); 1992 Phil O'Donnell (Motherwell); 1993 Eoin Jess (Aberdeen); 1994 Phil O'Donnell (Motherwell); 1995 Charlie Miller (Rangers); 1996 Jackie McNamara (Celtic).

SCOTTISH FOOTBALL WRITERS' ASSOCIATION

Player of the Year 1997 – Brian Laudrup (Rangers)

1965 Billy McNeill (Celtic)	1981 Alan Rough (Partick Th)
1966 John Greig (Rangers)	1982 Paul Sturrock (Dundee U)
1967 Ronnie Simpson (Celtic)	1983 Charlie Nicholas (Celtic)
1968 Gordon Wallace (Raith R)	1984 Willie Miller (Aberdeen)
1969 Bobby Murdoch (Celtic)	1985 Hamish McAlpine (Dundee U)
1970 Pat Stanton (Hibernian)	1986 Sandy Jardine (Hearts)
1971 Martin Buchan (Aberdeen)	1987 Brian McClair (Celtic)
1972 Dave Smith (Rangers)	1988 Paul McStay (Celtic)
1973 George Connelly (Celtic)	1989 Richard Gough (Rangers)
1974 Scotland's World Cup Squad	1990 Alex McLeish (Aberdeen)
1975 Sandy Jardine (Rangers)	1991 Maurice Malpas (Dundee U)
1976 John Greig (Rangers)	1992 Ally McCoist (Rangers)
1977 Danny McGrain (Celtic)	1993 Andy Goram (Rangers)
1978 Derek Johnstone (Rangers)	1994 Mark Hateley (Rangers)
1979 Andy Ritchie (Morton)	1995 Brian Laudrup (Rangers)
1980 Gordon Strachan (Aberdeen)	1996 Paul Gascoigne (Rangers)

WORLD PLAYER OF THE YEAR

Ronaldo (Barcelona) the Brazilian international striker was overwhelmingly voted FIFA world player of the year for 1996 with 329 points. The runner-up was Liberian international **George Weah** (AC Milan) with 140, whilst Newcastle United's England international **Alan Shearer** came third with 123.

EUROPEAN FOOTBALLER OF THE YEAR 1996

Matthias Sammer (Borussia Dortmund), captain of the 1997 European Cup winners, was originally capped by the now non-existent East Germany, before being honoured at full level by Germany, whom he led to the 1996 European Championship.

Past winners

1956 **Stanley Matthews** (Blackpool)
1957 **Alfredo Di Stefano** (Real Madrid)
1958 **Raymond Kopa** (Real Madrid)
1959 **Alfredo Di Stefano** (Real Madrid)
1960 **Luis Suarez** (Barcelona)
1961 **Omar Sivori** (Juventus)
1962 **Josef Masopust** (Dukla Prague)
1963 **Lev Yashin** (Moscow Dynamo)
1964 **Denis Law** (Manchester United)
1965 **Eusebio** (Benfica)
1966 **Bobby Charlton** (Manchester United)
1967 **Florian Albert** (Ferencvaros)
1968 **George Best** (Manchester United)
1969 **Gianni Rivera** (AC Milan)
1970 **Gerd Muller** (Bayern Munich)
1971 **Johan Cruyff** (Ajax)
1972 **Franz Beckenbauer** (Bayern Munich)
1973 **Johan Cruyff** (Barcelona)
1974 **Johan Cruyff** (Barcelona)
1975 **Oleg Blokhin** (Dynamo Kiev)
1976 **Franz Beckenbauer** (Bayern Munich)
1977 **Allan Simonsen** (Borussia Moenchengladbach)
1978 **Kevin Keegan** (SV Hamburg)
1979 **Kevin Keegan** (SV Hamburg)
1980 **Karl-Heinz Rummenigge** (Bayern Munich)
1981 **Karl-Heinz Rummenigge** (Bayern Munich)
1982 **Paolo Rossi** (Juventus)
1983 **Michel Platini** (Juventus)
1984 **Michel Platini** (Juventus)
1985 **Michel Platini** (Juventus)
1986 **Igor Belanov** (Dynamo Kiev)
1987 **Ruud Gullit** (AC Milan)
1988 **Marco Van Basten** (AC Milan)
1989 **Marco Van Basten** (AC Milan)
1990 **Lothar Matthaus** (Inter-Milan)
1991 **Jean-Pierre Papin** (Marseille)
1992 **Marco Van Basten** (AC Milan)
1993 **Roberto Baggio** (Juventus)
1994 **Hristo Stoichkov** (Barcelona)
1995 **George Weah** (AC Milan)

Carling Manager of the Month

August	David Pleat	Sheffield Wednesday
September	Joe Kinnear	Wimbledon
October	Graeme Souness	Southampton
November	Jim Smith	Derby County
December	Gordon Strachan	Coventry City
January	Stuart Pearce	Nottingham Forest
February	Alex Ferguson	Manchester United
March	Bryan Robson	Middlesbrough
April	Graeme Souness	Southampton

Carling Manager of the Season   **Alex Ferguson**   **Manchester United**

Carling Player of the Month

August	David Beckham	Manchester United
September	Patrik Berger	Liverpool
October	Matt Le Tissier	Southampton
November	Ian Wright	Arsenal
December	Gianfranco Zola	Chelsea
January	Tim Flowers	Blackburn Rovers
February	Robbie Earle	Wimbledon
March	Juninho	Middlesbrough
April	Mickey Evans	Southampton

Carling Player of the Season   **Juninho**   **Middlesbrough**

Carling No. 1 Awards

Awarded for outstanding contributions to the national game.

Peter Shilton, for achieving a record of 1000 League appearances during his distinguished career.
John Motson, in recognition for his 25 years as a BBC TV commentator.
Tony Parkes, for his work as caretaker/manager of Blackburn Rovers.

NATIONAL LIST OF REFEREES FOR SEASON 1997–98

* Alcock, P.E. (Redhill, Surrey)
* Ashby, G.R. (Worcester)
  Bailey, M.C. (Impington, Cambridge)
  Baines, S.J. (Chesterfield)
* Barber, G.P. (Pyrford, Surrey)
* Barry, N.S. (Scunthorpe)
  Bates, A. (Stoke-on-Trent)
  Bennett, S.G. (Redhill, Surrey)
* Bodenham, M.J. (East Looe, Cornwall)
  Brandwood, M.J. (Lichfield, Staffs)
* Burge, K.W. (Tonypandy)
  Burns, W.C. (Scarborough)
  Butler, A.N. (Sutton-in-Ashfield)
  Cain, G. (Bootle)
  Coddington, B. (Sheffield)
– Crick, D.R. (Worcester Park, Surrey)
  Danson, P.S. (Leicester)
– Dean, M.L. (Eastham, Wirral)
– Dunn, S.W. (Bristol)
* Durkin, P.A. (Portland, Dorset)
  D'Urso, A.P. (Billericay, Essex)
* Elleray, D.R. (Harrow-on-the-Hill)
  Finch, C.T. (Bury St Edmunds)
  Fletcher, M. (Warley, West Midlands)
  Foy, C.J. (St Helens)
  Frankland, G.B. (Middlesbrough)
  Furnandiz, R.D. (Doncaster)
* Gallagher, D.J. (Banbury, Oxon)
– Hall, A.R. (Birmingham)
  Halsey, M.R. (Welwyn Garden City, Herts)
  Harris, R.J. (Oxford)
  Heilbron, T. (Newton Aycliffe)
– Jones, M.J. (Chester)
* Jones, P. (Loughborough)
  Jones, T. (Barrow-in-Furness)
  Kirkby, J.A. (Sheffield)

  Knight, B. (Orpington)
  Laws, D. (Whitley Bay)
  Laws, G. (Whitley Bay)
  Leach, K.A. (Wolverhampton)
  Leake, A.R. (Darwen, Lancashire)
* Lodge, S.J. (Barnsley)
  Lomas, E. (Manchester)
  Lynch, K.M. (Knaresborough)
  Mathieson, S.W. (Stockport)
– Messias, M.D. (York)
  Orr, D. (Iver, Bucks)
  Pearson, R. (Peterlee, Durham)
  Pierce, M.E. (Portsmouth)
– Pike, M.S. (Barrow-in-Furness)
  Poll, G. (Tring, Hertfordshire)
  Pugh, D. (Wirral)
* Reed, M.D. (Birmingham)
  Rejer, P. (Tipton, West Midlands)
  Rennie, U.D. (Sheffield)
  Richards, P.R. (Preston)
* Riley, M.A. (Leeds)
  Robinson, J.P. (Hull)
  Singh, G. (Wolverhampton)
  Stretton, F.G. (Nottingham)
  Styles, R. (Waterlooville, Hants)
  Taylor, P. (Cheshunt, Hertfordshire)
  Wiley, A.G. (Burntwood, Staffs)
  Wilkes, C.R. (Gloucester)
* Wilkie, A.B. (Chester-le-Street)
* Willard, G.S. (Worthing, W. Sussex)
* Winter, J.T. (Stockton-on-Tees)
  Wolstenholme, E.K. (Blackburn)

* Denotes Premiership Referee.
– Denotes promotion to list for first time.

VAUXHALL CONFERENCE FIXTURES 1997–98

	Cheltenham Town	Dover Athletic	Farnborough Town	Gateshead	Halifax Town	Hayes	Hednesford Town	Hereford United	Kettering Town	Kidderminster H.
Cheltenham Town	—	11.10	6.12	22.11	1.11	19.8	17.1	13.4	28.3	14.3
Dover Athletic	16.8	—	10.2	7.3	14.2	8.11	30.8	29.12	17.3	20.9
Farnborough Town	21.2	3.9	—	13.4	20.9	4.10	25.4	23.8	6.9	29.11
Gateshead	18.10	28.3	16.8	—	26.12	25.4	8.11	24.1	28.2	3.1
Halifax Town	25.4	3.1	28.2	1.1	—	21.2	20.12	22.11	4.10	8.11
Hayes	16.9	21.4	11.4	1.11	16.8	—	27.9	6.9	14.3	17.1
Hednesford Town	7.2	2.5	3.1	4.4	14.3	24.1	—	18.8	26.12	4.10
Hereford United	25.8	29.11	9.9	15.11	11.4	24.2	13.12	—	17.1	26.12
Kettering Town	30.8	15.11	24.1	7.2	29.12	18.10	1.1	20.9	—	25.4
Kidderminster H.	29.9	23.3	27.9	23.8	18.4	30.8	7.3	1.1	22.11	—
Leek Town	29.11	1.11	7.3	21.4	13.12	20.9	14.2	2.9	3.1	6.9
Morecambe	21.3	4.10	2.5	6.12	28.10	3.1	13.9	1.11	20.12	25.8
Northwich Victoria	24.1	6.9	8.11	29.9	20.4	4.4	11.10	7.3	23.8	13.4
Rushden & Diamonds	7.3	13.12	13.9	30.8	7.2	29.11	25.8	11.10	28.10	29.12
Slough Town	8.11	19.8	29.12	14.3	23.8	26.12	28.3	7.2	4.4	13.12
Southport	15.11	14.3	30.8	20.12	25.8	7.2	16.8	21.2	1.11	11.10
Stalybridge Celtic	20.9	7.2	18.4	28.10	7.3	13.9	29.11	4.4	2.5	16.8
Stevenage Borough	20.12	13.4	22.11	4.10	17.1	1.9	25.10	6.12	18.8	4.4
Telford United	4.4	23.8	18.10	6.9	2.9	7.3	21.3	4.10	13.4	7.2
Welling United	21.4	1.1	24.3	17.1	2.5	13.4	28.2	20.12	2.9	21.2
Woking	11.4	30.9	26.12	21.2	29.11	13.12	18.4	2.5	14.2	21.3
Yeovil Town	1.1	21.2	25.8	2.5	28.3	15.11	11.4	18.4	6.12	16.9

Leek Town	Morecambe	Northwich Victoria	Rushden & Diamonds	Slough Town	Southport	Stalybridge Celtic	Stevenage Borough	Telford United	Welling United	Woking	Yeovil Town
9.9	13.12	4.10	6.9	23.9	2.5	3.1	14.2	18.4	29.12	23.8	26.12
17.1	25.4	20.12	24.1	11.4	18.4	18.10	25.8	28.2	26.12	6.12	9.9
7.2	11.10	17.1	20.8	17.9	4.4	20.12	21.3	14.3	1.11	1.1	13.12
11.10	20.8	25.8	14.2	18.4	3.9	25.3	13.12	29.12	11.4	20.9	29.11
30.9	17.3	9.12	21.3	24.1	13.4	6.12	18.10	16.9	30.8	4.4	6.9
2.5	23.8	29.12	20.12	1.1	21.3	11.10	28.2	6.12	25.8	28.10	14.2
22.9	13.4	21.2	6.12	22.11	20.9	23.8	29.12	6.10	18.10	6.9	1.11
28.2	14.2	13.9	25.4	21.3	18.10	27.9	30.8	3.1	16.8	28.3	8.11
21.3	8.11	18.4	21.2	16.8	7.3	11.4	29.11	25.8	13.12	9.9	10.3
20.12	24.1	18.8	18.10	2.5	14.2	31.1	13.9	11.4	28.3	1.11	28.2
—	29.12	28.3	23.8	4.10	7.10	24.1	8.11	26.12	25.4	13.4	4.4
16.8	—	11.4	22.11	28.2	26.12	7.4	18.4	30.8	20.9	7.2	17.1
31.1	1.9	—	3.1	14.2	13.12	26.12	27.9	1.11	29.11	25.4	21.3
11.4	28.3	16.8	—	1.11	17.1	28.2	26.12	2.5	18.4	4.10	21.4
15.11	18.10	20.9	2.9	—	29.11	25.4	3.1	21.2	7.10	7.3	13.4
6.12	1.1	7.4	27.9	6.9	—	22.11	11.4	28.3	24.1	28.2	25.4
21.2	6.9	2.5	1.1	16.3	23.8	28.3	—	20.9	7.3	11.10	7.2
25.8	21.2	1.1	13.4	30.8	29.12	—	1.11	13.12	21.3	17.1	4.10
1.1	29.11	24.2	7.4	17.1	8.11	19.8	25.4	—	14.2	20.12	17.3
14.3	4.4	7.2	8.11	6.12	4.10	6.9	16.9	22.11	—	19.8	23.8
18.10	27.9	30.8	14.3	25.8	13.9	8.11	24.1	16.8	3.1	—	29.12
30.8	7.3	18.10	20.9	20.12	3.1	14.3	16.8	24.1	31.1	22.11	—

FA CARLING PREMIERSHIP FIXTURES 1997–98

	Arsenal	Aston Villa	Barnsley	Blackburn R	Bolton W	Chelsea	Coventry C	Crystal Palace
Arsenal	—	26.10	4.10	13.12	13.9	7.2	11.8	21.2
Aston Villa	10.5	—	14.2	13.8	25.4	1.11	6.12	14.3
Barnsley	25.4	13.9	—	1.11	27.8	24.8	20.10	17.1
Blackburn R	13.4	17.1	7.3	—	6.12	22.11	28.9	28.12
Bolton W	14.2	4.10	26.12	11.4	—	26.10	31.1	2.5
Chelsea	21.9	7.3	31.1	28.3	10.5	—	10.1	14.2
Coventry C	17.1	11.4	21.2	2.5	23.8	9.8	—	24.9
Crystal Palace	18.10	8.11	12.8	30.8	27.9	13.9	28.2	—
Derby Co	1.11	7.2	30.8	10.1	13.4	4.4	22.11	20.12
Everton	27.9	28.3	20.9	14.3	28.12	17.1	10.5	9.8
Leeds U	9.8	28.12	4.4	14.2	20.12	13.4	25.4	23.8
Leicester C	27.8	9.8	2.5	24.9	22.11	21.2	4.4	6.12
Liverpool	4.4	22.9	22.11	31.1	7.3	5.10	20.12	13.4
Manchester U	14.3	15.2	25.10	29.11	7.2	24.9	30.8	4.10
Newcastle U	6.12	23.8	13.4	25.10	17.1	2.5	14.3	4.4
Sheffield W	22.11	2.5	8.12	26.12	8.11	20.12	20.9	25.10
Southampton	23.8	18.4	8.11	21.2	9.8	29.12	14.2	27.8
Tottenham H	28.12	27.8	20.12	20.9	28.2	6.12	13.4	24.11
West Ham U	28.2	29.11	10.1	18.4	18.10	14.3	26.12	3.11
Wimbledon	22.12	21.2	23.9	4.10	4.4	27.8	1.11	20.9

Derby Co	Everton	Leeds U	Leicester C	Liverpool	Manchester U	Newcastle U	Sheffield W	Southampton	Tottenham H	West Ham U	Wimbledon
7.3	2.5	10.1	26.12	30.11	9.11	11.4	28.3	31.1	30.8	24.9	18.4
20.9	22.11	30.8	10.1	28.2	13.4	31.1	27.9	20.12	26.12	4.4	18.10
28.12	7.2	29.11	27.9	28.3	10.5	13.12	11.4	14.3	18.4	9.8	28.2
9.8	8.11	14.9	28.2	23.8	4.4	10.5	25.8	18.10	7.2	20.12	25.4
14.12	1.9	18.4	28.3	1.11	20.9	1.12	14.3	10.1	23.9	21.2	29.11
29.11	26.11	13.12	18.10	25.4	28.2	27.9	18.4	30.8	11.4	9.11	26.12
28.3	25.10	4.10	29.11	18.4	28.12	8.11	7.2	13.9	13.12	27.8	7.3
18.4	10.1	31.1	11.4	13.12	25.4	29.11	10.5	26.12	28.3	7.3	7.2
—	13.9	14.3	25.4	10.5	18.10	26.12	28.2	27.9	31.1	6.12	13.8
14.2	—	11.4	18.4	18.10	27.8	28.2	25.4	2.11	29.11	23.8	13.12
8.11	6.12	—	20.9	26.8	27.9	18.10	17.1	28.2	7.3	23.11	10.5
6.10	20.12	7.2	—	17.1	23.8	7.3	28.12	14.4	13.9	27.10	10.11
25.10	21.2	26.12	13.8	—	6.12	31.8	13.9	7.2	8.11	2.5	10.1
21.2	26.12	2.5	31.1	11.4	—	18.4	1.11	13.8	10.1	13.9	28.3
17.12	24.9	21.2	1.11	28.12	21.12	—	9.8	22.11	4.10	7.2	13.9
24.9	4.10	13.8	30.8	14.2	7.3	10.1	—	4.4	21.2	13.4	31.1
2.5	7.3	24.9	13.12	20.9	17.1	28.3	29.11	—	25.10	4.10	11.4
23.8	4.4	1.11	14.2	14.3	10.8	25.4	19.10	10.5	—	17.1	27.9
11.4	31.1	28.3	10.5	27.9	14.2	20.9	13.2	25.4	13.8	—	30.8
17.1	13.4	25.10	14.3	9.8	22.11	14.2	23.8	7.12	2.5	28.12	—

NATIONWIDE FOOTBALL LEAGUE FIXTURES 1997–98

DIVISION ONE

	Birmingham C	Bradford C	Bury	Charlton Ath	Crewe Alex	Huddersfield T	Ipswich T	Manchester C	Middlesbrough	Norwich C
Birmingham C	—	4.11	24.2	3.5	4.10	17.1	6.9	13.12	7.2	8.11
Bradford C	14.3	—	13.12	7.2	25.10	28.12	23.8	28.3	13.9	29.11
Bury	18.10	13.4	—	23.8	28.12	4.4	25.4	12.9	6.12	7.3
Charlton Ath	22.10	21.9	31.1	—	15.11	28.2	1.11	30.8	10.1	26.12
Crewe Alex	17.2	25.4	2.9	21.3	—	6.12	21.10	26.12	18.10	31.1
Huddersfield T	16.8	2.9	29.11	11.10	11.4	—	13.9	3.3	26.12	13.12
Ipswich T	26.12	31.1	25.10	7.3	3.5	14.2	—	4.10	17.8	21.2
Manchester C	13.4	22.11	14.2	28.1	6.9	7.11	18.2	—	20.12	20.9
Middlesbrough	20.9	14.2	11.4	9.8	25.2	9.9	17.1	18.4	—	21.3
Norwich C	4.3	4.4	1.11	6.9	23.8	13.4	26.9	7.2	15.11	—
Nottingham F	15.11	6.12	14.3	22.11	1.11	18.2	4.4	3.9	28.2	15.8
Oxford U	25.4	27.9	15.11	17.1	3.3	9.8	18.10	1.11	21.10	28.3
Port Vale	6.12	18.10	20.9	13.4	27.1	21.10	20.12	14.3	25.4	14.2
Portsmouth	4.4	21.10	3.3	20.12	13.9	25.4	13.4	10.1	14.3	2.9
QPR	1.11	20.12	3.5	4.10	7.2	22.11	9.8	26.10	4.3	11.10
Reading	31.1	30.8	10.1	6.12	11.10	21.3	22.11	24.2	13.4	3.5
Sheffield U	27.9	28.2	18.4	28.12	29.11	27.1	3.3	15.11	17.2	11.4
Stockport Co	29.8	10.1	16.8	21.2	28.3	20.9	14.3	29.11	2.9	24.2
Stoke C	10.1	16.1	4.10	25.2	13.12	7.3	7.2	3.5	31.1	18.4
Sunderland	14.2	26.12	28.3	4.11	18.4	18.10	28.2	16.8	28.9	30.8
Swindon T	20.12	8.11	11.10	4.4	9.8	23.8	28.12	21.2	22.11	25.10
Tranmere R	2.9	21.3	26.12	25.10	21.2	4.11	6.12	31.1	30.8	4.10
WBA	23.11	7.3	21.2	8.11	17.1	20.12	27.1	11.10	4.4	4.11
Wolverhampton W	28.2	18.2	30.8	13.9	14.3	27.9	15.11	11.4	1.11	10.1

Nottingham F	Oxford U	Port Vale	Portsmouth	QPR	Reading	Sheffield U	Stockport Co	Stoke C	Sunderland	Swindon T	Tranmere R	WBA	Wolverhampton W
21.3	25.10	11.4	29.11	7.3	23.8	21.2	27.1	9.8	14.9	18.4	28.12	28.3	12.10
11.4	21.2	24.2	3.5	18.4	27.1	11.10	9.8	15.8	5.9	3.3	15.11	1.11	4.10
4.11	21.3	7.2	8.11	21.10	9.8	20.12	17.1	17.2	22.11	28.2	6.9	27.9	27.1
28.3	16.8	13.12	18.4	17.2	11.4	2.9	27.9	19.10	14.3	28.11	25.4	3.3	14.2
7.3	8.11	31.8	14.2	20.9	28.2	4.4	22.11	13.4	20.12	10.1	27.9	16.8	4.11
3.10	10.1	3.5	25.10	28.3	15.11	30.8	7.2	1.11	24.2	31.1	14.3	18.4	21.2
29.11	24.2	18.4	13.12	10.1	28.3	9.11	4.11	20.9	11.10	2.9	11.4	30.8	21.3
28.12	7.3	4.11	9.8	25.4	18.10	21.3	4.4	22.10	17.1	27.9	22.8	28.2	6.12
11.10	3.5	25.10	5.11	8.11	13.12	5.10	28.12	23.8	21.2	28.3	28.1	29.11	7.3
17.1	22.11	13.9	30.12	28.2	22.10	6.12	18.10	20.12	28.1	25.4	18.2	14.3	9.8
—	31.1	10.1	20.9	30.8	25.4	14.2	20.12	27.9	4.3	26.12	18.10	22.10	13.4
23.8	—	29.11	27.1	12.12	14.2	20.9	28.2	14.3	28.12	11.4	18.4	17.2	7.9
9.8	4.4	—	17.1	27.9	1.11	22.11	6.9	1.3	23.8	17.2	3.3	15.11	28.12
7.2	30.8	16.8	—	26.12	27.9	31.1	17.2	6.12	15.11	31.10	28.2	18.10	22.11
28.1	14.4	21.2	6.9	—	28.12	25.2	23.8	15.11	6.12	14.3	17.1	13.9	4.4
24.10	13.9	7.3	21.2	2.9	—	4.11	8.11	4.4	4.10	16.8	7.2	26.12	20.12
13.9	7.2	28.3	23.8	18.10	14.3	—	21.10	6.9	10.8	13.12	1.11	25.4	17.1
18.4	11.10	26.12	4.10	31.1	3.3	3.5	—	14.2	1.11	15.11	13.12	11.4	25.10
21.2	5.11	12.10	11.4	21.3	29.11	26.12	13.9	—	25.10	30.8	28.3	3.9	8.11
8.11	2.9	31.1	21.3	11.4	17.2	10.1	7.3	25.4	—	21.10	29.11	13.12	20.9
6.9	6.12	4.10	7.3	5.11	17.1	13.4	21.3	28.1	3.5	—	13.9	7.2	25.2
24.2	20.12	8.11	11.10	16.8	20.9	7.3	13.4	22.11	4.4	14.2	—	10.1	3.5
3.5	4.10	21.3	24.2	14.2	6.9	25.10	6.12	28.12	13.4	20.9	9.8	—	24.8
14.12	26.12	3.9	28.3	29.11	18.4	16.8	25.4	4.3	7.2	18.10	22.10	31.1	

NATIONWIDE FOOTBALL LEAGUE FIXTURES 1997–98

DIVISION TWO

	Blackpool	AFC Bournemouth	Brentford	Bristol C	Bristol R	Burnley	Carlisle U	Chesterfield	Fulham	Gillingham
Blackpool	—	17.1	13.4	3.1	25.4	8.11	6.9	21.10	28.2	21.3
AFC Bournemouth	30.8	—	1.11	7.2	2.9	25.4	22.11	14.2	18.10	26.12
Brentford	13.12	7.3	—	8.11	21.10	27.9	4.11	16.8	11.4	2.9
Bristol C	16.8	20.9	3.3	—	14.3	2.12	4.4	20.12	2.9	14.2
Bristol R	25.10	28.12	2.5	4.11	—	17.1	23.8	7.2	8.11	13.9
Burnley	3.3	25.10	21.2	11.4	30.8	—	11.10	26.12	18.4	16.8
Carlisle U	26.12	28.3	14.3	29.11	24.1	28.2	—	18.11	13.12	27.9
Chesterfield	2.5	4.10	3.1	18.4	20.9	6.9	21.3	—	7.3	4.1
Fulham	11.10	24.2	2.12	28.12	3.3	20.12	13.4	1.11	—	21.11
Gillingham	18.11	6.9	28.12	4.10	31.1	3.1	21.2	14.3	28.3	—
Grimsby T	24.2	21.2	17.1	9.8	13.4	22.11	20.12	3.3	31.1	4.4
Luton T	10.1	31.1	25.10	21.2	20.12	4.11	2.5	14.4	24.1	2.12
Millwall	4.10	2.5	9.8	6.9	4.4	21.3	8.11	22.11	5.11	7.3
Northampton T	14.3	9.8	18.11	23.8	1.11	4.4	17.1	2.12	25.4	18.10
Oldham Ath	7.2	23.8	22.11	7.3	27.9	28.12	2.12	18.10	14.2	8.11
Plymouth Arg	11.4	8.11	13.9	21.3	10.1	21.10	7.2	30.8	26.12	25.4
Preston N E	18.4	11.10	4.10	2.5	18.11	7.2	24.2	24.1	29.11	10.1
Southend U	21.2	21.3	6.9	11.10	22.11	23.8	9.8	3.4	20.9	13.4
Walsall	29.11	13.12	24.2	25.10	26.12	7.3	4.10	10.1	16.8	24.1
Watford	1.11	18.4	23.8	13.12	28.2	9.8	3.1	13.9	21.10	7.2
Wigan Ath	13.9	3.1	20.12	17.1	2.12	13.4	28.12	28.2	27.9	21.10
Wrexham	2.9	4.11	4.4	13.9	14.2	18.10	7.3	27.9	10.1	20.12
Wycombe W	24.1	29.11	7.2	28.3	18.10	14.2	13.9	25.4	30.8	28.2
York C	28.3	11.4	11.10	24.2	16.8	13.9	25.10	2.9	21.3	30.8

Grimsby T	Luton T	Millwall	Northampton T	Oldham Ath	Plymouth Arg	Preston N E	Southend U	Walsall	Watford	Wigan Ath	Wrexham	Wycombe W	York C
18.10	9.8	14.2	4.11	20.9	2.12	20.12	27.9	4.4	7.3	31.1	28.12	23.8	22.11
27.9	13.9	21.10	10.1	24.1	3.3	28.2	18.11	14.4	20.12	16.8	14.3	4.4	2.12
30.8	25.4	10.1	21.3	28.3	31.1	14.2	26.12	18.10	24.1	18.4	29.11	19.9	28.2
10.1	27.9	26.12	24.1	1.11	18.11	21.10	28.2	25.4	13.4	30.8	31.1	22.11	17.10
12.12	18.4	29.11	7.3	21.2	9.8	21.3	27.3	6.9	11.10	11.4	4.10	24.2	3.1
28.3	14.3	18.11	29.11	2.9	2.5	20.9	24.1	1.11	10.1	13.12	24.2	4.10	31.1
18.4	21.10	3.3	30.8	11.4	20.9	17.10	10.1	14.2	16.8	2.9	1.11	31.1	25.4
8.11	13.12	28.3	11.4	24.2	17.1	23.8	29.11	9.8	31.1	11.10	21.2	25.10	28.12
13.9	23.8	14.3	25.10	4.10	6.9	4.4	7.2	3.1	2.5	21.2	9.8	17.1	18.11
29.11	11.4	1.11	24.2	3.3	25.10	9.8	13.12	23.8	20.9	2.5	18.4	11.10	17.1
—	18.11	20.9	11.10	2.5	3.1	28.12	1.11	14.3	25.10	4.10	23.8	2.12	6.9
21.3	—	2.9	26.12	30.8	11.10	8.11	18.8	22.11	4.10	24.2	20.9	7.3	4.4
7.2	28.12	—	21.2	11.10	13.4	3.1	13.9	3.12	25.2	25.10	17.1	20.12	23.8
28.2	6.9	27.9	—	31.1	20.12	13.4	14.2	28.12	22.11	20.9	3.3	3.1	21.10
21.10	17.1	28.2	13.9	—	4.4	6.9	25.4	19.12	21.3	4.11	3.1	13.4	9.8
16.8	28.2	13.12	18.4	29.11	—	7.3	18.10	27.9	2.9	24.1	28.3	4.11	14.2
2.9	3.3	16.8	13.12	26.12	1.11	—	11.4	13.9	30.8	28.3	25.10	21.2	14.3
7.3	3.1	31.1	4.10	25.10	24.2	2.12	—	17.1	4.11	8.11	2.5	28.12	19.12
4.11	28.3	11.4	2.9	18.4	21.2	31.1	30.8	—	8.11	21.3	11.10	2.5	20.9
25.4	14.2	18.10	28.3	18.11	28.12	17.1	14.3	3.3	—	29.11	11.4	6.9	27.9
14.2	18.10	25.4	7.2	14.3	23.8	22.11	3.3	18.11	4.4	—	8.9	9.8	1.11
24.1	7.2	30.9	8.11	16.8	22.11	25.4	21.10	28.2	2.12	26.12	—	21.3	13.4
10.4	1.11	18.4	16.8	13.12	14.3	27.9	2.9	21.10	26.12	10.1	18.11	—	3.3
26.12	29.11	24.1	2.5	10.1	4.10	4.11	18.4	7.2	21.2	7.3	13.12	8.11	—

NATIONWIDE FOOTBALL LEAGUE FIXTURES 1997–98

DIVISION THREE

	Barnet	Brighton & H A	Cambridge U	Cardiff C	Chester C	Colchester U	Darlington	Doncaster R	Exeter C	Hartlepool U
Barnet	—	14.3	31.1	14.2	30.8	24.1	29.11	8.11	16.8	28.3
Brighton & H A	5.11	—	21.3	22.11	28.2	26.12	13.9	14.2	18.10	7.3
Cambridge U	13.9	18.11	—	27.9	24.1	2.9	28.3	7.2	12.12	29.11
Cardiff C	4.10	28.3	21.2	—	16.8	11.4	2.5	14.3	26.12	25.10
Chester C	17.1	11.10	23.8	3.1	—	18.4	13.12	11.4	29.11	4.10
Colchester U	22.8	6.9	29.12	2.12	19.12	—	9.8	21.10	27.9	3.1
Darlington	4.4	31.1	22.11	21.10	13.4	10.1	—	18.10	24.1	21.9
Doncaster R	3.3	4.10	20.9	4.11	2.12	2.5	24.2	—	30.8	11.10
Exeter C	3.1	24.2	13.4	6.9	4.4	21.2	23.8	17.1	—	9.8
Hartlepool U	22.11	1.11	4.4	25.4	14.2	16.8	7.2	28.2	10.1	—
Hull C	24.2	25.10	2.5	21.3	26.12	13.12	7.3	29.11	4.11	11.4
Leyton O	2.12	17.1	6.9	9.8	8.11	25.10	21.3	28.12	13.9	24.2
Lincoln C	21.2	2.5	4.10	20.9	10.1	28.3	25.10	18.11	11.4	13.12
Macclesfield T	13.4	3.1	8.11	20.12	25.4	4.11	6.9	23.8	21.10	17.1
Mansfield T	25.10	13.12	11.10	23.8	20.9	4.10	21.2	6.9	21.3	18.4
Notts Co	7.3	11.4	25.10	17.1	4.11	21.3	4.10	13.12	8.11	28.12
Peterborough U	6.9	28.12	2.12	13.4	21.3	11.10	8.11	3.1	7.3	2.5
Rochdale	2.5	21.2	24.2	31.1	7.3	8.11	11.10	28.3	18.4	21.3
Rotherham U	9.8	3.3	3.1	18.10	27.9	29.11	17.1	18.4	7.2	23.8
Scarborough	19.12	22.8	9.8	3.4	21.10	31.1	28.12	1.11	14.2	6.9
Scunthorpe U	7.2	29.11	4.11	28.2	2.9	7.3	18.4	13.9	25.4	8.11
Shrewsbury T	11.10	18.4	17.1	28.12	31.1	24.2	11.4	9.8	28.3	21.2
Swansea C	28.12	9.8	20.12	7.3	22.11	20.9	3.1	25.4	28.2	4.11
Torquay U	21.3	20.9	7.3	3.3	18.10	30.8	4.11	27.9	2.9	31.1

Hull C	Leyton O	Lincoln C	Macclesfield T	Mansfield T	Notts Co	Peterborough U	Rochdale	Rotherham U	Scarborough	Scunthorpe U	Shrewsbury T	Swansea C	Torquay U
18.10	11.4	27.9	13.12	25.4	1.11	26.12	21.10	10.1	18.4	20.9	28.2	2.9	18.11
25.4	30.8	22.10	16.8	13.4	3.12	3.9	27.9	8.11	24.1	4.4	20.12	10.1	7.2
21.10	26.12	14.2	3.3	28.2	25.4	11.4	18.10	16.8	10.1	14.3	30.8	18.4	1.11
18.11	10.1	7.2	18.4	24.1	30.8	13.12	13.9	24.2	29.11	11.10	2.9	2.11	8.11
6.9	3.3	9.8	25.10	7.2	14.3	18.11	1.11	21.2	2.5	28.12	13.9	28.3	24.2
13.4	25.4	22.11	14.3	13.2	18.11	27.2	3.3	3.4	12.9	31.10	18.10	6.2	16.1
1.11	18.11	25.4	26.12	27.9	14.2	3.3	28.2	30.8	2.9	20.12	2.12	16.8	14.3
4.4	2.9	21.3	24.1	26.12	13.4	16.8	22.11	19.12	6.3	30.1	10.1	24.10	21.2
14.3	31.1	2.12	2.5	18.11	3.3	1.11	20.12	20.9	4.10	25.10	22.11	11.10	28.12
2.12	18.10	13.4	30.8	20.12	2.9	21.10	18.11	24.1	26.12	3.3	27.9	14.3	13.9
—	18.4	13.9	28.3	10.1	16.8	24.1	7.2	2.9	11.10	21.2	8.11	30.8	4.10
20.12	—	7.3	4.10	4.4	22.11	7.2	23.8	11.10	4.11	3.1	13.4	21.2	2.5
31.1	1.11	—	29.11	2.9	24.1	18.4	14.3	26.12	30.8	24.2	16.8	3.3	11.10
22.11	14.2	4.4	—	18.10	28.2	27.9	28.12	7.3	7.2	2.12	21.3	13.9	9.8
9.8	29.11	28.12	24.2	—	31.1	28.3	3.1	4.11	8.11	17.1	7.3	2.5	11.4
3.1	28.3	23.8	11.10	13.9	—	29.11	9.8	2.5	21.2	6.9	7.2	24.2	18.4
23.8	20.9	20.12	21.2	22.11	4.4	—	17.1	31.1	24.2	9.8	4.11	4.10	25.10
20.9	24.1	4.11	2.9	16.8	10.1	30.8	—	25.10	11.4	4.10	26.12	13.12	29.11
28.12	28.2	6.9	1.11	14.3	21.10	13.9	25.4	—	28.3	18.11	14.2	11.4	13.12
28.2	14.3	17.1	20.9	3.3	27.9	18.10	2.12	22.11	—	13.4	25.4	18.11	3.1
27.9	16.8	18.10	11.4	30.8	26.12	10.1	14.2	21.3	13.12	—	21.10	24.1	28.3
3.3	13.12	3.1	18.11	1.11	20.9	14.3	6.9	4.10	25.10	2.5	—	29.11	23.8
17.1	27.9	8.11	31.1	21.10	18.10	14.2	13.4	2.12	21.3	23.8	4.4	—	6.9
14.2	21.10	28.2	10.1	2.12	20.12	25.4	4.4	13.4	16.8	22.11	24.1	26.12	—

INTERNATIONAL FIXTURES – SEASON 1997–98

August

3 Sun Littlewoods FA Charity Shield

9 Sat Commencement of FA Premier League and Football League

13 Wed Euro Comps Prel (1)
FL Coca-Cola Cup 1 (1)

20 Wed Northern Ireland v Germany (WC)
Republic of Ireland v Lithuania (WC)
Turkey v Wales (WC)

27 Wed Euro Comps Prel (2)
FL Coca-Cola Cup 1 (2)

30 Sat FA Cup Sponsored by Littlewoods Prel Rd

September

6 Sat Iceland v Republic of Ireland
Scotland v Belarus
FA Carlsberg Vase 1st Qual Rd
FA Youth Cup Extra Prel Rd*

7 Sun UK Living FA Women's FA Cup Prel Rd

10 Wed Albania v Northern Ireland (WC)
England v Moldova (WC)
Lithuania v Republic of Ireland (WC)

13 Sat FA Cup Sponsored by Littlewoods 1st Qual Rd

17 Wed Euro Comps 1st Rd (1)
FA Coca-Cola Cup 2 (1)

20 Sat FA Youth Cup Prel Rd*

24 Wed FL Coca-Cola Cup 2 (2)

27 Sat FA Cup Sponsored by Littlewoods 2nd Qual Rd

28 Sun UK Living FA Women's Cup 1st Rd

October

1 Wed Euro Comps 1st Rd (2)

4 Sat FA Carlsberg Vase 2nd Rd Qual

11 Sat FA Cup Sponsored by Littlewoods 3rd Rd Qual
FA Cup 1st Rd Qual Rd*
FA County Youth Cup 1st Rd*
Belgium v Wales (WC)
Italy v England (WC)
Portugal v Northern Ireland (WC)
Republic of Ireland v Romania (WC)
Scotland v Latvia (WC)

15 Wed FL Coca-Cola Cup 3rd Rd

18 Sat FA Umbro Trophy 1st Rd Qual

22 Wed Euro Comps 2nd Rd (1)

25 Sat FA Cup Sponsored by Littlewoods 4th Rd Qual

26 Sun FA Sunday Cup 1st Rd

29 Wed FL Coca-Cola Cup 3rd Rd (Replays)
Possible World Cup Play Off

November

1 Sat FA Carlsberg Vase 1st Rd Proper
FA Youth Cup 2nd Rd Qual*

2 Sun UK Living Women's FA Cup 2nd Rd

5 Wed Euro Comps 2nd Rd (2)

8 Sat FA Umbro Trophy 2nd Rd Qual

15 Sat FA Cup Sponsored by Littlewoods 1st Rd Proper
Possible World Cup Play-Off

19 Wed INTERNATIONAL
FL Coca-Cola Cup 4th Rd

22 Sat FA Carlsberg Vase 2nd Rd Proper
FA Youth Cup 1st Rd Proper*
FA County Youth Cup 2nd Rd*

23 Sun FA Sunday Cup 2nd Rd

26 Wed FA Cup Sponsored by Littlewoods 1st Rd Proper Replays
Euro Comps 3rd Rd (1)

29 Sat FA Umbro Trophy 3rd Rd Qual

30 Sun UK Living Women's FA Cup 3rd Rd

December

3 Wed FL Coca-Cola Cup 4th Rd (Replay)

6 Sat FA Cup Sponsored by Littlewoods 2nd Rd Proper

10 Wed Euro Comps 3rd Rd (2)

13 Sat FA Carlsberg Vase 3rd Rd Proper
FA Youth Cup 2nd Rd Proper*

14 Sun FA Sunday Cup 3rd Rd

17 Wed FA Cup Sponsored by Littlewoods 2nd Rd Proper Replays
INTERNATIONAL

January 1998

3 Sat FA Cup Sponsored by Littlewoods 3rd Rd Proper

4 Sun UK Living Women's FA Cup 4th Rd

7 Wed FL Coca-Cola Cup 5th Rd
Auto Windscreens Shield (2)

10 Sat FA Umbro Trophy 1st Rd Proper
FA Youth Cup 3rd Rd Proper*
FA County Youth Cup 3rd Rd*

11 Sun FA Sunday Cup 4th Rd

14 Wed FA Cup Sponsored by Littlewoods 3rd Rd Proper Replays
INTERNATIONAL

17 Sat FA Carlsberg Vase 4th Rd Proper

21 Wed FL Coca-Cola Cup 5th Rd Replays

24 Sat FA Cup Sponsored by Littlewoods 4th Rd Proper

31 Sat FA Umbro Trophy 2nd Rd Proper

February

1 Sun UK Living Women's FA Cup 5th Rd
4 Wed FA Cup Sponsored by Littlewoods 4th Rd Proper Replays
7 Sat FA Carlsberg Vase 5th Rd Proper
8 Sun FA Sunday Cup 5th Rd
11 Wed INTERNATIONAL
14 Sat FA Cup Sponsored by Littlewoods 5th Rd Proper
       FA Youth Cup 4th Rd Proper*
       FA County Youth Cup 4th Rd*
18 Wed FL Coca-Cola Cup Semi-Finals (1)
21 Sat FA Umbro Trophy 3rd Rd
22 Sun FL Coca-Cola Cup Semi-Finals (2)
25 Wed FA Cup Sponsored by Littlewoods 5th Rd Proper Replays
28 Sat FA Carlsberg Vase 6th Rd Proper

March

1 Sun UK Living Women's FA Cup 6th Rd
4 Wed Euro Comps QF (1)
7 Sat FA Cup Sponsored by Littlewoods 6th Rd Proper
       FA Youth Cup 5th Rd Proper*
14 Sat FA Umbro Trophy 4th Rd Proper
       FA Carlsberg Vase Semi-Finals (1)
       FA County Youth Cup Semi-Finals*
15 Sun FA Sunday Cup Semi-Final
18 Wed Euro Comps QF (2)
       FA Cup Sponsored by Littlewoods 6th Rd Proper Replays
21 Sat FA Carlsberg Vase Semi-Finals (2)
25 Wed INTERNATIONAL
28 Sat FA Umbro Trophy Semi-Finals (1)
29 Sun UK Living Women's FA Cup Semi-Finals
       FL Coca-Cola Cup Final

April

1 Wed Euro Comps Semi-Finals (1)

4 Sat FA Umbro Trophy Semi-Finals (2)
       FA Youth Cup Semi-Finals*
5 Sun FA Cup Sponsored by Littlewoods Semi-Finals
8 Wed FA Cup Sponsored by Littlewoods Semi-Final Replay (prov)
15 Wed Euro Comps Semi-Finals (2)
       FA Cup Sponsored by Littlewoods Semi-Final Replay (prov)
19 Sun Auto Windscreens Shield Final
22 Wed INTERNATIONAL
25 Sat FA County Youth Final (fixed date)
16 Sun FA Sunday Cup Final
29 Wed UEFA Cup Final (1)

May

2 Sat Final matches in Football League
3 Sun UK Living Women's FA Cup Final
6 Wed UEFA Cup Winners Cup Final
9 Sat Final matches in FA Premier League
       FA Carlsberg Vase Final – Wembley Stadium
       FA Youth Cup Final*
10 Sun FA Umbro Trophy Final – Wembley Stadium
       FL Play off Semi-Finals (1)
13 Wed UEFA Cup Final (2)
       FL Play off Semi-Finals (2)
16 Sat FA Cup Sponsored by Littlewoods Final – Wembley Stadium
20 Wed UEFA Champions Cup Final
21 Thu FA Cup Sponsored by Littlewoods Final replay – Wembley Stadium
23 Sat FL Play off Final Division 3
24 Sun FL Play off Final Division 2
25 Mon FL Play off Final Division 1

June

10 Wed Commencement of World Cup Final

July

12 Sun World Cup Final

*closing date of rounds

USEFUL ADDRESSES

The Football Association: R. H. G. Kelly, F.C.I.S., 16 Lancaster Gate, London W2 3LW *0171-262 4542*

Scotland: J. Farry, 6 Park Gardens, Glasgow G3 7YE. *0141-332 6372*

Northern Ireland (Irish FA): D. I. Bowen, 20 Windsor Avenue, Belfast BT9 6EG. *01232-669458*

Wales: A. Evans, 3 Westgate Street, Cardiff, South Glamorgan CF1 1JF. *01222-372325*

Republic of Ireland (FA of Ireland): S. Connolly, 80 Merrion Square South, Dublin 2. *01001-766864*

International Federation (FIFA): S. Blatter, FIFA House, Hitzigweg 11, CH-8032 Zurich, Switzerland. *0041-384-9595. Fax: 0041-384-9696*

Union of European Football Associations: G. Aigner, Chemin de la Redoute 54, Case Postale 303 CH-1260 Nyon, Switzerland. *0041 22 994 4444. Fax: 0041 22 994 4488*

The Premier League: P. Leaver, 16 Lancaster Gate, London W2 3LW. *0171 262 4542*

The Football League: J. D. Dent, F.C.I.S., The Football League, Lytham St Annes, Lancs FY8 1JG. *01253-729421. Telex 67675*

The Scottish League: P. Donald, 188 West Regent Street, Glasgow G2 4RY. *0141-248 3844*

The Irish League: H. Wallace, 87 University Street, Belfast BT7 1HP. *01232-242888*

Football League of Ireland: E. Morris, 80 Merrion Square South, Dublin 2. *01001-765120*

Vauxhall Conference: J. A. Moules, Collingwood House, Schooner Court, Crossways, Dartford DA2 6QQ. *01322 303120*

Northern Premier: R. D. Bayley, 22 Woburn Drive, Hale, Altrincham, Cheshire. *0161-980 7007*

Isthmian League: N. Robinson, 226 Rye Lane, Peckham, SE15 4NL. *0181-409 1978*

English Schools FA: M. R. Berry, 1/2 Eastgate Street, Stafford ST16 2NN. *01785-51142*

Southern League: D.J. Studwick, 11 Welland Close, Durrington, Worthing, W. Sussex BN13 3NR. *01903-267788.*

National Federation of Football Supporters' Clubs: Chairman: Tony Kershaw, 87 Brookfield Avenue, Loughborough, Leicestershire LE11 3LN. *01509 267643 (and fax).* National Secretary: Mark Agate, "The Stadium", 14 Coombe Close, Lordswood, Chatham, Kent ME5 8NU. *01634 319461 (and fax)*

Professional Footballers' Association: G. Taylor, 2 Oxford Court, Bishopsgate, Off Lower Mosley Street, Manchester M2 3W2. *0161-236 0575*

Referees' Association: A. Smith, 1 Westhill Road, Coundon, Coventry CV6 2AD. *01203 601701*

Women's Football Alliance: Miss K. Simmons, 9 Wyllyotts Place, Potters Bar, Herts EN6 2JB. *01707 651840*

The Association of Football Statisticians: R. J. Spiller, P.O. Box 5828, Basildon, Essex SS15 5GQ. *01268-732041*

The Football Programme Directory: David Stacey, 'The Beeches', 66 Southend Road, Wickford, Essex SS11 8EN. *01268 732041.*

England Football Supporters Association: Publicity Officer, David Stacey, 66 Southend Road, Wickford, Essex SS11 8EN. *01268 732041*

The Football Trust: Second Floor, Walkden House, 10 Melton Street, London NW1 2EJ. *0171-388 4504*

The Football Supporters Association: PO Box 11, Liverpool L26 1XP. *0151-709-2594.*

SAVE £1.00 ON *PLAYFAIR FOOTBALL WHO'S WHO 1998*

PLAYFAIR launches its first Football Who's Who (rrp £6.99) with the most comprehensive A to Z listing of British footballers. The Who's Who will give career details which include date and place of birth, height, weight, international honours and a season-by-season breakdown of league appearances and goals.

This indispensable pocket guide is a must for all aficionados and excellent value for money.

And, as a special introductory offer to PLAYFAIR's 1998 edition of the Who's Who, you can obtain £1.00 off with the money-off voucher below.